To our parents
Bob and Ruth
Virgil and Lois
for their support and love

6-7, 6-12, 7-6, 7-9, 8-1, 8-7, 8-10, 8-11, A-4, A-11, A-14, A-17, A-19, A-22, 9-1, 9-2, 9-3, 9-4, B-14, B-16, 10-2, 10-3, 10-5, 11-5, 11-6, 11-7, pp. 2, 72, 200, 226, 436, International Business Machines Corporation; 9-12, International Data Corporation; 15-2, McGraw-Hill Book Company; A-3, A-23, NCR Corporation; A-20, Northern Telecom Systems Corporation; pp. 164, 248, 364, 456, Prime Computer, Inc.; 9-10, Radio Shack, A Division of Tandy Corporation; 15-5, *Computer Based Information Systems in Organizations* by Henry C. Lucas, Jr. © 1973, Science Research Associates, Inc.; 4-3, 17-3, pp. 16, 58, 266, 328, 384, Sperry Univac, A Division of Sperry Corporation; p. 346, Tektronix, Inc.; A-16, A-18, Texas Instruments Incorporated; A-13, Transcom Incorporated; D-1, *U.S. News & World Report;* 13-5, from *Data Processing* by Perry Edwards and Bruce Broadwell. © 1979 by Wadsworth Publishing Company, Inc., © 1980 by Wadsworth, Inc.; A-26, A-27, 9-6, App. A-1, Wang Laboratories, Inc.

Claudia S. Miller

PRINCIPLES OF
BUSINESS DATA PROCESSING
with MIS . . . including BASIC

Cover: Many of the electronic components in today's computers consist of a series of integrated circuits made from silicon. Each square contains a silicon chip connected to the other chips on the printed circuit board.

FOURTH EDITION

PRINCIPLES OF BUSINESS DATA PROCESSING with MIS . . . including BASIC

V. THOMAS DOCK ○ **EDWARD L. ESSICK**
University of Southern California   College of Marin

SCIENCE RESEARCH ASSOCIATES, INC.
Chicago, Palo Alto, Toronto, Henley-on-Thames, Sydney
A Subsidiary of IBM

Compositor *Interactive Composition Corporation*
Illustrator *House of Graphics*
Designer *Janet Bollow*
Cover Photographer *Tom Tracy*
Acquisition Editor *Terry Baransy*
Project Editor *Ron Lewton*
Special Editorial Assistance by Marilyn Bohl

Acknowledgments

The following illustrations are reproduced or adapted through the courtesy of the sources noted:

D-3, D-4, Apple Computer Inc.; A-12, AT&T; A-21, pp. 226, 278, Burroughs Corporation; D-2, *Changing Times Magazine*, Oct., 1975, © 1975 Kiplinger Washington Editors, Inc.; App. A-8, App. A-10, App. A-11, App. A-12, *Datamation*® magazine. © Copyright by Technical Publishing Co., A Dun & Bradstreet Company, 1979. All rights reserved; App. A-2, App. A-3, App. A-4, Datapoint Corporation; A-15, 9-8, Digital Equipment Corporation; pp. 100, 118, 314, Fireman's Fund, Inc.; A-2, First National Bank; A-24, 9-5, 17-2, App. A-9, pp. 44, 144, 414, Hewlett-Packard Company; 14-8, Inforex, Inc.; 9-7, 9-9, Intel Corporation; 4-1, 4-4, 4-5, 5-4, 6-5, 6-6,

(*Continued on facing page*)

Library of Congress Cataloging in Publication Data

Dock, V. Thomas
 Principles of business data processing with MIS ... including BASIC.

 Third ed. published in 1978 under title:
Principles of business data processing, with BASIC.
 Includes index.
 1. Business—Data processing. 2. Basic (Computer program language) 3. Management information systems. I. Essick, Edward L., joint author.
II. Title.
HF5548.2.D582 1981 651.8 80-22877
ISBN 0-574-21305-8

© 1981, 1978, 1974, 1970 Science Research Associates, Inc.
All rights reserved.

Printed in the United States of America.

10 9 8 7 6 5 4

CONTENTS

UNIT ONE
SOME FUNDAMENTALS OF DATA PROCESSING

Chapter 1   Introduction to Data Processing   3

THE PROCESSING OF DATA   4
Origination • Input • Manipulation • Output • Storage
HOW DATA PROCESSING AFFECTS THE OPERATIONS
  OF A BUSINESS   7
How Data Processing Affects the Cost of Running a Business •
How Data Processing Affects Customer Service • How Data Processing
Affects the Management of a Company

Chapter 2   Data Processing Applications   17

THE PURPOSE OF A DATA PROCESSING SYSTEM   18
DATA-RECORDING MEDIA FOR A DATA PROCESSING SYSTEM   21
The 80-Column Punched Card • The 96-Column Punched Card
THE USES OF A DATA PROCESSING SYSTEM   28
THE BASIC BUSINESS OPERATIONS   28
THE COMMON APPLICATIONS   29
Order Writing • Billing • Accounts Receivable • Inventory Control •
Sales Analysis
THE OTHER COMMON APPLICATIONS   39
HOW THE APPLICATIONS ARE RELATED   40

Chapter 3   System Analysis and Design   45

THE STEPS IN SYSTEM ANALYSIS AND DESIGN   46
SYSTEM FLOWCHARTING   47
ALTERNATE WAYS OF PROCESSING DATA   50
THE RELATIONSHIPS BETWEEN APPLICATIONS   51
EVALUATING ALTERNATIVES   53
Career Profile

CONTENTS

UNIT TWO
COMPUTER SYSTEMS

Chapter 4 Introduction to Computer Systems — 59

THE EVOLUTION OF THE COMPUTER — 60
Charles Babbage's Analytical Engine • The Mark I Computer • The ENIAC • The EDVAC
COMPUTER GENERATIONS — 63
AN OVERVIEW OF COMPUTER SYSTEMS — 67
A COMPARISON OF HUMAN AND COMPUTER CAPABILITIES — 67
Career Profile

Chapter 5 Computer Concepts — 73

THE CLASSIFICATION OF COMPUTERS — 74
Analog and Digital Computers • Hybrid Computers • Special-Purpose and General-Purpose Computers
THE COMPONENTS OF A COMPUTER SYSTEM — 76
Hardware • System Software • Application Software • Procedures • Data Processing Personnel
BINARY REPRESENTATION OF DATA — 82
Magnetic Cores • Semiconductors • Magnetic Bubbles • Binary Codes • Parity Bits
HEXADECIMAL REPRESENTATION — 95
THE EXECUTION OF PROGRAM STATEMENTS — 95

Chapter 6 Basic Input and Output Devices — 101

CARD INPUT AND OUTPUT — 102
CHECKING FOR ERRORS — 106
ADVANTAGES AND LIMITATIONS OF PUNCHED-CARD INPUT/OUTPUT — 108
PRINTER OUTPUT — 109
Impact Printers • Nonimpact Printers
ADVANTAGES AND LIMITATIONS OF PRINTER OUTPUT — 115

Chapter 7 Magnetic Tape Input and Output — 119

DATA REPRESENTATION ON TAPE — 120
THE TAPE DRIVE — 124
THE SPEED OF TAPE INPUT/OUTPUT OPERATIONS — 129
THE CAPACITY OF TAPE REELS — 131
ADVANTAGES AND LIMITATIONS OF TAPE AS AN INPUT/OUTPUT MEDIUM — 132
AN EXAMPLE OF MAGNETIC TAPE UTILIZATION — 133
DISCUSSION — 138
Career Profile

Chapter 8 Mass Storage Devices — **145**

THE DISK PACK — 146
DATA REPRESENTATION ON DISK — 150
THE SPEED OF DISK INPUT/OUTPUT OPERATIONS — 152
AN EXAMPLE OF MAGNETIC DISK UTILIZATION — 153
ADVANTAGES AND LIMITATIONS OF DISK INPUT/OUTPUT — 155
OTHER DIRECT ACCESS INPUT/OUTPUT DEVICES — 157
The Magnetic Drum • The Mass Storage Subsystem

Module A Special-Purpose Input and Output Devices — **165**

CHARACTER RECOGNITION INPUT DEVICES — 166
Magnetic Character Readers • Optical Character Readers
DATA COMMUNICATIONS — 176
TERMINALS — 177
Touch-Tone Devices • Audio-Response Units • Visual Display Devices • Hard-Copy Devices • Point-of-Sale Devices • Intelligent Terminals
KEY-ENTRY DEVICES — 185
Key-to-Tape Devices • Key-to-Disk Devices • Key-to-Diskette Devices
OTHER INPUT/OUTPUT DEVICES — 189
Paper Tape and Paper Tape Devices • Console Display-Keyboard • Plotters • Computer Output Microfilm • Word Processors • Floppy Disk Devices

Chapter 9 Computer Systems — **201**

MAINFRAME SYSTEMS — 203
Large Computers • Medium-Size Computers • Small Computers
MINICOMPUTER SYSTEMS — 210
MICROCOMPUTER SYSTEMS — 215
THE SIZE OF COMPUTERS AND SCOPE OF THE
   COMPUTER INDUSTRY: A RESTATEMENT AND COMPARISON — 220
Career Profile

UNIT THREE
COMPUTER PROGRAMMING AND DESIGN

Module B Program Flowcharting — **227**

PROGRAM FLOWCHARTS — 231
PROGRAM FLOWCHART SYMBOLS AND USAGE — 231
PROGRAM LOOPS — 236
USE OF CONNECTORS — 238
SPECIALIZED FLOWCHART SYMBOLS — 240
FLOWCHARTING AIDS — 243

Chapter 10 The Programming Cycle — 249

RECOGNIZING AND DEFINING THE PROBLEM — 250
The Problem Statement • Acquiring Data • Establishing Formats • The Structure of the Problem • Establishing Procedures
PLANNING THE SOLUTION TO THE PROBLEM — 255
SELECTING A PROGRAMMING LANGUAGE — 257
PROGRAM CODING — 257
PROGRAM DEBUGGING AND TESTING — 259
Debugging • Testing
PROGRAM DOCUMENTATION AND MAINTENANCE — 261

Module C Top-Down Program Design and Structured Programming — 267

TOP-DOWN PROGRAM DESIGN — 268
PSEUDOCODE — 271
STRUCTURED PROGRAMMING — 271
Sequence Structure • Selection Structure • Loop Structure
DISCUSSION — 274

Chapter 11 An Overview of Programming Languages — 279

MACHINE LANGUAGE — 280
MACHINE-ORIENTED ASSEMBLER (SYMBOLIC) LANGUAGE — 282
MACRO-INSTRUCTIONS — 285
HIGH-LEVEL PROGRAMMING LANGUAGES — 286
Procedure-Oriented and Problem-Oriented Languages •
FORTRAN • COBOL • BASIC • RPG
LANGUAGE SELECTION — 308
Career Profile

UNIT FOUR

AN OVERVIEW OF SYSTEMS

Chapter 12 Overlapped Systems — 315

OVERLAPPED PROCESSING — 317
TYPES OF OVERLAPPED PROCESSING — 321
Multiprogramming • Spooling

Chapter 13 Introduction to Operating Systems — 329

AN OPERATING SYSTEM AND STACKED-JOB PROCESSING — 330
AN OPERATING SYSTEM AND THE PROGRAMMER — 336
VIRTUAL STORAGE — 337
Sharing the Internal Storage Unit • Sharing the Computer
Career Profile

Chapter 14 Introduction to Data Communications — 347

ONLINE COMMUNICATION SYSTEMS — 349
ONLINE REALTIME COMMUNICATION SYSTEMS — 350
TIME-SHARING SYSTEMS — 353
DISTRIBUTED SYSTEMS — 357
Career Profile

UNIT FIVE
MANAGEMENT INFORMATION SYSTEMS

Chapter 15 Management Information Systems — 365

THE NEED FOR MANAGEMENT INFORMATION — 366
What Information Is Needed? • Desired Properties of Management Information
DISTINCTION BETWEEN DATA PROCESSING SYSTEM
  AND MANAGEMENT INFORMATION SYSTEM — 370
THE INFORMATION THAT AN MIS PROVIDES — 370
Information for Planning • Management Control Information
THE CONCEPT OF AN MIS — 372
MIS AS SEEN BY THE USER — 374
Functional Subsystems
DESIGN OF THE MIS — 376
Top-Down Design Approach • Bottom-Up Design Approach • Combination Design Approach
INSTALLATION OF THE MIS — 377
OPERATION AND CONTROL OF THE MIS — 377
THE BEHAVIORAL SIDE OF THE MIS — 379
EVALUATION OF THE MIS — 380

Chapter 16 Management Information Systems Applications — 385

ESSENTIAL PRINCIPLES OF INFORMATION
  SYSTEMS DEVELOPMENT — 386
Background • Technical and Developmental Factors • Behavioral and Organizational Factors • Conclusion
MARKETING INFORMATION SYSTEM — 397

AN INTEGRATED MERCHANDISING INFORMATION SYSTEM	398
AN MIS IN HIGHER EDUCATION	400

Objectives for Design • Conceptual Design • System Outputs; Key Data Elements • Information Flow • System Software • Data Classification Scheme • Information Systems • Planning Model • Implementation Plan • MIS Implementation Considerations • Conclusion

UNIT SIX
DATA PROCESSING MANAGEMENT AND THE COMPUTER INDUSTRY

Chapter 17 The Organization and the Data Processing Department — 415

THE APPLICATION OF COMPUTERS IN BUSINESS ORGANIZATIONS	416
THE SELECTION AND INSTALLATION OF A COMPUTER SYSTEM	416

The Cost of the System • The Time Required for Installation • General Practices

THE CONTROL OF A DATA PROCESSING SYSTEM	419

Top Management Control • Data Processing Department Management Control • Controls during the Processing of Data • The Evaluation of Error Controls

COMPUTER SYSTEM SECURITY	423

Fraud • Physical Security • Recovery Procedures

THE DATA PROCESSING DEPARTMENT	425

Job Descriptions • The Separation of Functions • The Location of the Data Processing Department within the Organization
Career Profile

Module D Social Implications of the Computer — 437

AUTOMATION	439
INDIVIDUALITY AND THE COMPUTER	442
PRIVACY AND THE COMPUTER	443
ELECTRONIC FUNDS TRANSFER	445
THE CONTROL OF COMPUTER SYSTEMS	446
MICROCOMPUTERS AND PERSONAL COMPUTING	448
SOCIETAL IMPACT	451
THE FUTURE	453

Chapter 18 The Computer Industry — 457

COMPUTER MANUFACTURERS	458
INDEPENDENT COMPUTER PERIPHERAL EQUIPMENT MANUFACTURERS	458

SOFTWARE COMPANIES	459
LEASING COMPANIES	460
COMPUTER SERVICES COMPANIES	461
Career Profile	

Appendix A Computer System Applications — 465

MANUFACTURING—Crown Auto Top Manufacturing Company	467
WHOLESALING—Catto & Putty, Inc.	471
RETAILING—Big 4 Rents, Inc.	477
CENTRALIZE? DECENTRALIZE? DISTRIBUTE?	484

Appendix B BASIC Programming — 499

TIME-SHARING OPERATING-SYSTEM AND EDITING COMMANDS	502
AN INTRODUCTORY PROGRAM	507
PROGRAM STATEMENT NUMBERS AND LENGTH	509
CONSTANTS AND VARIABLES	510
THE LET STATEMENT	513
THE PRINT STATEMENT	519
THE END STATEMENT	524
THE READ AND DATA STATEMENTS	524
THE RESTORE STATEMENT	529
THE INPUT STATEMENT	529
THE REM STATEMENT	531
THE STOP STATEMENT	532
CONTROL STATEMENTS	532
EXAMPLES OF BASIC PROGRAMS	543
ARRAYS	550
AN EXAMPLE OF A BASIC PROGRAM USING ARRAYS	557
THE MAT STATEMENTS	559
EXAMPLES OF MAT STATEMENTS	564
FUNCTIONS	568
THE RANDOMIZE STATEMENT	575
SUBROUTINES	575
AN EXAMPLE OF THE GOSUB AND RETURN STATEMENTS	578
A SUMMARY OF THE BASIC LANGUAGE	580

Appendix C BASIC Programming Problems — 584

INPUT/OUTPUT STATEMENTS	585
CONTROL STATEMENTS	586
ARRAYS	588
FUNCTIONS	588
SUBROUTINES	588

Glossary and Index — 589

PREFACE

New developments in computer data processing continue to appear at a rapid pace. Technological advances are making computers faster and smaller in size. They can do more work at a lower cost. In such a dynamic and diverse field, it is a challenge to keep a textbook current and yet limit the content to what is appropriate for the introductory data processing student. We feel that we have met this challenge. The purpose of this textbook is to meet the needs of students who want a basic understanding of data processing as well as of those who plan careers as business application programmers. All the features that made the third edition one of the top-selling introductory data processing texts have been retained. At the same time, we have carefully reviewed and edited each chapter to insure that both the text and the illustrations reflect the latest technology and equipment.

There are three versions of this text. Two versions include a discussion of management information systems and their impact on organizations. Several examples reinforce these concepts. One of those versions of the book also covers the BASIC language. Students learn to write BASIC programs to solve a variety of business problems. Those two versions are designed for the instructor who wants to maximize the coverage of management information systems and, if desired, the BASIC programming language.

The third version of the text includes a comprehensive discussion of punched-card data processing and punched-card machines and systems. In that version, Appendix B explains how to use a card punch.

Many of the improvements in this new edition are responses to a national survey of users and former users. The reading level and knowledge base of the students were primary considerations when making these changes. We wanted to insure that the material is appropriate for the students using the book. We also wanted to present it in a clear and concise manner. All new terms are defined as they are used and explained again in the glossary, conveniently combined with the index. Like the third edition, the fourth edition is not encyclopedic; it presents an up-to-date survey of business data processing.

Among the major changes in the fourth edition are:

1. An expanded discussion of computer systems is given in Chapter 9. The microprocessor and its applications in business data processing are discussed. Emphasis is placed on the microcomputer, the minicomputer, and small business systems.

2. Recently emerging methods of data entry and output such as word processors and plotters are covered in Module A.
3. An updated discussion of the social implications of the computer, including the effects of microcomputers and personal computing, is given in Module D.
4. Four computer system applications are described in Appendix A. Through these, students are exposed to the factors involved in evaluating, installing, and implementing computer systems for particular applications.
5. Review questions at the end of each chapter and module reinforce the student's learning of the main points discussed.
6. The instructor-support materials include an extended student study guide, instructor's guide, and transparency masters correlated to each chapter, and a computerized test bank also correlated to each chapter.

The following key aspects of the third edition have been retained:

1. The grouping of the chapters into logical units.
2. The inclusion of modules to present specific topics. Each module is placed at a strategic point to support the presentation of material in the chapters. The modules can be skipped by the student without disrupting the continuity of learning the essential principles and functions of business data processing. The module topics are: Special-Purpose Input and Output Devices, Flowcharting, Top-Down Program Design and Structured Programming, and Social Implications of the Computer.
3. A chapter outline at the beginning of each chapter.
4. A unique approach to the discussion of high-level programming languages (Chapter 11).
5. A discussion of the typical relationship between the business organization and the data processing department and of the structure of a data processing department (Chapter 17).
6. A discussion of the computer industry (Chapter 18).
7. A series of career profiles that acquaint students with the actual experiences of individuals who hold positions in data processing. In these profiles, the individuals relate the duties and responsibilities involved in their jobs and the education and training or other experiences that were most valuable to them in obtaining the positions they hold.

This edition has the same twofold objectives as the third edition: (a) to illustrate the use of various data processing systems for business applications, and (b) to familiarize the student with the functional and operational characteristics of data processing systems. Thus, the basic business applications of order writing, billing, accounts receivable, inventory control, and sales analysis are discussed. We note particularly how data within these systems can be machine-processed. Throughout the text, major emphasis is placed on the appropriate principles and functions of business data processing rather than on the specific details of equipment.

We would like to express our appreciation to the following individuals who reviewed the manuscript and provided us with many valuable comments and suggestions:

John C. Beers, *Rockland Community College*
Anthony M. Bonarti, *Tompkins-Cortland Community College*
John B. Cage, *Waukesha County Technical Institute*
Robert C. Cooper, *Monroe Community College*
Janet M. Cowger, *Central Missouri State University*
John DeLuca, *Middlesex Community College*
W. L. Dinsmore, *Kansas City Kansas Community College*
Richard D. Featheringham, *Central Michigan University*
David Harris, *College of the Redwoods*
R. C. Hopkins, *L.A. Pierce College*
James M. Hoyt, *University of Nevada, Reno*
Gary Klotz, *Milwaukee Area Technical College*
James G. Kriz, *Cuyahoga Community College–Western Campus*
Antonio M. Lopez, Jr., *Loyola University, New Orleans*
C. Gardner Mallonee II, *Essex Community College*
Mike Michaelson, *Palomar College*
B. L. Phifer, *Coleman College*
David Rosteck, *Henry Ford Community College*
Joe W. Shambley, *Sullivan County Community College*
Deanna W. Shelton, *Cheyney State College*
Dollie A. Tarrant, *Thomas Nelson Community College*
Thomas W. Voight, *Franklin University*
Susan P. White, *Catonsville Community College*
Stephen A. Wright, *Western Michigan University*

As was true in the previous editions, Marilyn Bohl, a colleague and friend, contributed to this project not just as a reviewer but also as an editor and consultant. Her comments and suggestions have given the text and ancillary materials a "perfectionist quality." We are indebted to her for her contributions, and wish to express our deepest appreciation.

UNIT ONE

SOME FUNDAMENTALS OF DATA PROCESSING

CHAPTER 1

INTRODUCTION TO DATA PROCESSING

THE PROCESSING OF DATA
Origination
Input
Manipulation
Output
Storage

HOW DATA PROCESSING AFFECTS
THE OPERATIONS OF A BUSINESS
How Data Processing Affects
the Cost of Running a Business
How Data Processing Affects Customer Service
How Data Processing Affects
the Management of a Company

Opposite: Wiring pattern of one of 23 layers for
an integrated circuit used in the IBM 4341 computer.

Every organization, whether business, government, or social, requires a certain amount of paperwork. This paperwork is called *data processing*. Any procedures, equipment, programs, and people by which this paperwork is accomplished make up the data processing system. Data processing systems are essential in handling the informational needs of an organization.

Today, data processing is generally assumed to be *computer* data processing. It is known as *electronic data processing*, or *EDP*. In the past, data processing consisted of manual procedures to do paperwork. With the advances in technology, electromechanical machines were introduced in many organizations to replace manual data processing systems. The term *automatic data processing*, or *ADP*, was used to describe the systems using these machines. ADP systems were used to reduce the amount of paperwork needed and the clerical functions associated with it. Computer systems were used initially in many organizations to perform essentially the same functions as ADP systems.

As organizations grow in size and complexity, they become more dependent on computers to process data and provide information for decision making. Recently, significant technological advances have reduced the cost and size of the computer to such an extent that organizations of almost any size can now benefit by using computer data processing. Through computer data processing, organizations of all sizes are attempting to meet the ever-increasing needs for information in a complex and ever-changing society.

Unorganized facts are *data*. Data processing, whether manual, electromechanical, or electronic, consists of the operations needed to capture and transform data into useful information and the transmission of this information to managers or other specific individuals or groups. Thus, data processing is a means to an end, not an end in itself. When the results from the capture and organization of data are used, they become *information.* Information, then, is the basis upon which efficient and effective decisions can be made. This is one of the major reasons why data processing is very important to the successful operation of any organization.

THE PROCESSING OF DATA

Data processing is usually divided into two major areas: business and scientific. The major function of business data processing is the establishment of files of data, the retention of this data, and the processing of it to produce meaningful information. Business data processing usually involves large volumes of data, few mathematical and/or logical operations performed on this data, and a large volume of results. For example, a public utility must maintain a record for each customer and, each month, present a bill to the customer for services used. This requires reading the customer record to determine name, address, and any past due amount. The customer bill involves a few simple calculations. Then it is printed. In this example, many thousands of records have to be read, updated, and printed; thus, the majority of processing time is spent manipulating data.

Scientific data processing usually involves a small volume of data. Many logical and/or mathematical operations are performed on the data, producing typically a small volume of results. For example, a weather satellite collects data for a period of time, then the data is analyzed by a computer to produce a weather forecast. Scientific data may be retained in files for future analysis, but the emphasis is on data analysis rather than on extensive file processing.

Whether the processing of data is business-oriented or scientific-oriented, it involves five basic functions—origination, input, manipulation, output, and storage.

Origination

The first function involved in the processing of data is the origination of the data to be processed. Specifically, the nature, type, and origin of the source documents must be determined. The **source documents** are records such as sales orders, purchase orders, or employee time cards, produced in the process of communicating within an organization, that contain data to be processed.

Input

The second function involved in the processing of data is the input of data stored on the source documents into the data processing system. The input of data into a data processing system occurs when the data stored on the source documents is recorded in some manner acceptable for entry into the data processing system. In some data processing systems, the source document itself is acceptable for input.

Manipulation

The third function involved in the processing of data is the manipulation of the data. This function centers around the performance of certain necessary operations on the data. The operations may include classifying, sorting, calculating, recording, and summarizing the data.

Classifying. The classifying of data involves the identification of like data according to one or more characteristics useful to management. For example, employee time cards may be grouped by department; each employee time card belongs in the group for the department in which the employee works.

Sorting. After data is classified, it is usually necessary to arrange or rearrange the data into some logical order to facilitate processing. This arranging or rearranging procedure is called *sorting*. For example, employee time cards classified by department may be sorted within each department by employee last name. This insures that the time cards in each department group are arranged alphabetically. The data to be sorted can be alphabetic, numeric, or special characters, or any combination of these characters. On EDP systems, the fastest sorting is usually accomplished when using only numeric data.

Calculating. The arithmetic and/or logical manipulation of data to create meaningful results is known as *calculating*. This process is usually the most significant part of the manipulation operation because the results are generally provided as part of the output. For instance, after employee time card data has been classified and sorted, the net pay for each employee can be calculated.

Recording. Generally, the processing of data involves the obtaining of intermediate results. These intermediate results must be recorded until further processing of them occurs. For instance, in the calculation of each employee's net pay, intermediate results such as the gross pay, retirement, and taxes of the employee must be retained temporarily for later use.

Summarizing. Finally, to be of value, large amounts of data are often reduced to a concise usable form. This process is called *summarizing*. The extent to which the data is summarized depends on who is to use the resulting information. For example, each employee's gross pay, retirement, and taxes accumulated since the beginning of the year can be summarized (totaled) for the payroll department. This same data might be summarized further to provide top management with a report of total wages paid to date.

Output

After the various operations on the data have been completed, the results (information) must be communicated in an intelligible form (to appropriate individuals and groups). For example, each employee would receive a report of gross pay earned and the amounts subtracted for various deductions; the payroll department would receive a report summarizing the same information for all employees.

Storage

Finally, the results of the processing of data must be retained for future use or reference. This function is called *storage*. The media used to store data depends on its intended future use. If large amounts of data must be stored for future processing, it is likely to be stored in machine-readable form. Information that is to be kept only for reference is usually stored as printed reports or on microfilm.

HOW DATA PROCESSING AFFECTS THE OPERATIONS OF A BUSINESS

The processing of data takes place in many parts of an organization. For instance, a manufacturing company requires data processing in its research, manufacturing, and financial departments. The research scientist records the data from experiments, makes calculations on the data, and then summarizes the data in various recommendations and reports. The manufacturing department requires summarized data to control the production of the company. The financial department processes data to keep track of profit and loss and the total worth of the business. Data processing takes place in many other departments of the company as well.

Any of several methods can be used to process data. The method chosen to process data should be based on the size of the organization, its information needs, and the cost of processing. Small organizations may find that manual data processing methods are satisfactory. Many organizations are using computer data processing systems, but the simplest systems require only paper and pencil. Between the pencil and paper and the computer is a range of equipment from typewriters to electronic calculators. Because computers that do not cost much more than a good electric typewriter are now available, it is likely they will be used to replace a variety of other data processing equipment.

Whatever the method used, data processing directly affects the success of the organization. Whether or not a company's data processing system is efficient and effective can, in part, determine whether or not the operations of the company are efficient and effective. A data processing system can greatly influence whether or not a company makes a profit.

UNIT ONE: SOME FUNDAMENTALS OF DATA PROCESSING

Although it is easy to say that data processing is important to an organization, it is not so easy to say exactly how it is important. For example, can you explain how data processing affects the operations of a company? Or can you understand why an executive may complain that the data processing system of a company has made it impossible to make a profit? One may well ask, "How can paper juggling be that important?"

If you analyze a business such as a manufacturing company, you can see that data processing, or paperwork, affects the business in several important ways. Among these are the following:

1. Data processing affects the cost of running the business.
2. Data processing affects customer service.
3. Data processing affects the management of the company.

How Data Processing Affects the Cost of Running a Business

Data processing affects the cost of running a business because it is one of the costs of running a business. In fact, it may be one of the major costs. As such, it must be controlled. Think, for example, of an insurance company. Its product is represented by a paper policy, and all phases of its operations involve paperwork. If the cost of its data processing operations can be reduced, an overall cost reduction for the company is likely. Thus, the efficiency of the data processing system is important.

Why be concerned about cost reduction? If the cost of doing something in a business is reduced without lowering the quality of the end result, this reduction has a direct effect on the profits of the company. To show a profit, a company tries to make the most sales at the least cost. At the end of the year, a company determines it total profits by subtracting total costs from total sales. Thus, if the cost of data processing can be decreased without decreasing its value, the profits of the company can be increased by the same amount. In this respect, then, one can say that data processing affects not only the cost of running a company but also the profits of the company.

How Data Processing Affects Customer Service

When a customer places an order with a company, he wants the order to be delivered to the right place at the right time. He wants the correct items delivered in the correct quantities. Later, when he is billed for the shipment, he wants to be billed for the correct items in the correct amounts. The quality of a company's service depends upon how well the company meets these and other customer requirements.

Data processing affects customer service because it is involved in fulfilling customer requirements. Consider, for example, whether or not a company delivers its orders promptly. One might think that the company's ability to do so is determined by how efficient its shipping department is in packaging goods for shipment. However, between the time an order is received and the time it reaches the shipping department, many data processing steps take place. The steps vary from company to company, but most, if not all, of the following processes may occur:

1. The order is received in the sales department. It is either mailed or phoned in by the customer, or taken in person by a salesclerk. In the sales department, the order is checked for accuracy. The customer's address, the item numbers, and the item descriptions are checked to make sure that the order has been taken correctly.
2. The original order is sent from the sales department to the credit department where a credit check is performed to make sure that the customer is able to pay for the items ordered.
3. The customer's order is typed so that it can be read accurately. (The original is often handwritten.) Several copies are made.
4. The typed order (now called the shipping order) is checked to make sure that it has been typed correctly. Then one or more copies are sent to the shipping department where the order is filled.

From this example of what may happen to an order, one can see how data processing can affect whether or not a company delivers its orders promptly. Before an order reaches the shipping department, much data processing must take place. If several days are required to complete this paperwork, shipments tend to arrive that much later.

Accuracy in processing data is also important for customer service. If mistakes are made in preparing a shipping order, the shipment may contain wrong items or wrong quantities, or it may be shipped to the wrong address. If mistakes are made in preparing a customer's bill, the customer may be charged too much or too little. Clearly, data processing affects many aspects of customer service.

Inventory control is another area in which data processing can affect customer service. One of the functions of inventory control is to insure that items are on hand when needed. To do this, inventory-control personnel rely on records and reports that are prepared by processing data. If the reports and records are accurate and up to date, inventory-control personnel can identify and reorder items that are running low. When a customer orders an item, it is in stock and can be shipped promptly. On the other hand, if the inventory records are not accurate and up to date, it is difficult to determine which items are running low. The shipping department may discover a stockout when a customer orders an item. If this happens, the customer does not get what was ordered (at least not when it is wanted); the lack of inventory control will have affected customer service unfavorably.

How Data Processing Affects the Management of a Company

So far, shipping orders and inventory records produced by a data processing system have been mentioned. Other routine outputs include payroll checks, monthly statements to customers, checks to suppliers, and purchase orders. Now consider the effect of data processing output on the management of a company.

There are one or more levels of management in a company. A large company, for example, is led by a board of directors and top-level management, followed by several levels of middle management and front-line management. Regardless of the level, however, the basic functions of management are the same: to plan, organize, staff, direct, and control the operations that take place in the company. To carry out these basic functions, management relies on data processing for necessary information.

Information, to be of the greatest value to management, should be accurate, complete, concise, timely, and relevant. Information that reflects the situation or status of the event that is being managed is considered to be *accurate*. A manager may receive information from a data processing system and believe it is accurate when in fact it is false. The individuals who provide the input data for data processing are responsible for its accuracy.

Information is *complete* when it provides a manager with all of the details that need to be considered about a specific situation. The cost of producing complete information may exceed its value to management and should be considered when determining how complete information should be.

Information is *concise* when it is summarized in the format desired by a particular manager. Information is *timely* if it is received when it is needed and is up to date. Information is *relevant* to managers when they need it to perform their jobs.

Take, for example, a sales manager. The major part of this job is to plan and control the efforts and expenses of the sales department. Suppose that one of the information reports the manager gets is the **Comparative Income Statement** in Illustration 1-1. The report shows sales and selling expenses for the current month and totals for the year to date.

In the "Increase or Decrease" column, the report compares the totals for the current year with the totals for the same period in the preceding year. How might the information in this report help the sales manager to control the expenses of the department?

CHAPTER 1: INTRODUCTION TO DATA PROCESSING

| ROUTING | ☐ PRESIDENT'S OFFICE
☐ TREASURER
☐ COMPTROLLER
☐ ACCOUNTING
☑ SALES MANAGER
☐ PLANT SUPERINTENDENT | COMPARATIVE INCOME STATEMENT | | | | PERIOD ENDING 05/31/81
PAGE 1 | |

ACCT. NUMBER	DESCRIPTION	CURRENT MONTH		YEAR-TO-DATE		INCREASE* OR DECREASE —	%* —
		THIS YEAR	LAST YEAR	THIS YEAR	LAST YEAR		
411	SALES						
411-100	GROSS SALES	$1,223,195.85	$1,283,474.02	$4,739,999.14	$4,915,174.67	$175,175.53 -	3.6 -
411-200	LESS RETURNS & ALLOWANCES	1,726.40	1,912.71	3,245.97	3,464.22	218.25 -	6.3 -
	NET SALES	$1,221,469.45	$1,281,561.31	$4,736,753.17	$4,911,710.45	$174,957.28 -	3.6 -
412-100	LESS COST OF GOODS SOLD	581,786.15	611,950.16	2,352,146.73	2,408,762.23	56,615.50 -	2.4 -
	GROSS PROFIT	$639,683.30	$669,611.15	$2,384,606.44	$2,502,948.22	$118,341.78 -	4.7 -
421	SELLING EXPENSES						
421-100	SALARIES & COMMISSION	$184,373.27	$189,264.48	$705,623.06	$725,579.46	$19,956.40 -	2.8 -
421-200	TRAVELING	14,425.15	13,790.80	53,726.92	48,968.21	4,758.71 ※	9.7 ※
421-300	DELIVERY	6,140.20	6,256.00	28,364.15	29,428.19	1,064.04 -	3.6 -
421-400	ADVERTISING	1,582.00	1,450.25	18,250.00	15,225.75	3,024.25 ※	19.9 ※
421-500	OFFICE SALARIES	27,684.35	25,829.15	94,342.18	85,415.14	8,927.04 ※	10.5 ※
421-600	STATIONERY & SUPPLIES	1,380.60	1,295.00	4,982.76	4,576.82	405.94 ※	8.9 ※
421-700	TELEPHONE	1,315.85	1,305.62	4,148.15	3,381.26	766.89 ※	22.7 ※
421-800	BUILDING	4,725.00	4,215.10	21,175.00	18,634.55	2,540.45 ※	13.6 ※
421-900	MISCELLANEOUS	1,460.38	1,460.38	4,965.48	3,519.47	1,446.01 ※	41.1 ※
	TOTAL SELLING EXPENSE	$243,086.80	$244,866.78	$935,577.70	$934,728.85	$848.85 ※	0.1 ※

ILLUSTRATION 1-1 Comparative Income Statement

By comparing expense items for the current year with those for the preceding year, the sales manager can identify expenses that have increased beyond reasonable limits. The manager can then try to find and eliminate the causes of the increases.

But, does the Comparative Income Statement give information that helps the sales manager to increase the company's sales?

From the report, one can tell that sales are decreasing, but one cannot tell the cause of the decrease. Has a salesperson stopped calling on certain customers with the result that they have given their business to someone else? Have salespersons failed to give enough attention to selling the high-profit items in the product line? These are the kinds of questions that a sales manager has to answer. The Comparative Income Statement will not help; the manager needs more information. The reports in Illustration 1-2 may give this information.

The first report in Illustration 1-2 is a *Sales-by-Customer Report*. It indicates which customers are buying less of the company's products than they did in the preceding year. This decrease may be the result of competition, or poor sales techniques, or a combination of causes. In any case, the report points out where sales have been lost. The same thing is true of the second report, the *Sales-by-Item Report*. This report indicates which products have increased or decreased in demand. The items that have dropped in sales may have been replaced by another product in the company's

UNIT ONE: SOME FUNDAMENTALS OF DATA PROCESSING

SALES-BY-CUSTOMER REPORT

DATE 04/30/81 PAGE 1

DESCRIPTION	ITEM CODE OR CUST. NO.	CURRENT SALES	GROSS PROFIT	SALES/YEAR-TO-DATE THIS YEAR	LAST YEAR	INCREASE DECR "CR"
BARRETT MACHINE	4	88.26	23.01	3,285.40	2,853.20	432.20
CHANEL WHOLESALE	20	651.30	153.00	1,752.20	5,271.20	3,519.00 CR
CHOLMAR FURNITURE	24	669.96	159.40	4,862.10	2,864.20	1,997.90
COLUMBIA MFG CO	35	938.38	223.62	3,110.00	2,172.30	937.70
EMPIRE EQUIPMENT CO						
GEN PORTABLE EQUIP						
INDUSTRIAL CART CO						
NEW MEXICO CO						
SANBORN INDUSTRIAL						

SALES-BY-ITEM REPORT

DATE 04/30/81 PAGE 19

DESCRIPTION	ITEM CODE OR CUST. NO.	CURRENT SALES	GROSS PROFIT	SALES/YEAR-TO-DATE THIS YEAR	LAST YEAR	INCREASE DECR "CR"
SQ SHANK SWIVEL	11202			2,788.53	2,696.02	92.51
CUSTOM BUILT	15102	483.00	119.70	5,063.68	4,832.24	231.44
SQ SOCKET RIGID	16102	30.60	6.10	32.90	53.72	20.82 CR
EXT SHANK WITH BRK	17203	380.70	75.20	4,981.42	4,616.85	364.57
SQ SHANK RIGID	21103			6,235.70	60.68	6,175.02
						8.19 CR
						479.44
						133.54
						305.38
						118.34 CR
						144.69 CR
						17.39 CR

SALES-BY-SALESPERSON REPORT

DATE 12/31/81 PAGE 3

SALESPERSON'S NAME	SALESPERSON NUMBER	SALES	RETURNS AND ALLOWANCES	NET SALES	COST OF SALES	GROSS PROFIT
MACY	67	7,621.43	525.75	7,095.68	5,381.85	1,713.83
NELSON	69	16,943.32	378.45	16,564.87	12,583.59	3,981.28
NEVINS	71	6,622.84		6,622.84	5,039.39	1,583.45
NORDEN	74	4,362.35		4,362.35	3,335.41	1,026.94
POTTER	76	6,112.01	188.72	5,923.29	4,556.09	1,367.20
REVERE	79	10,397.49	261.17	10,136.32	7,992.84	2,143.48
TANNER	81	9,357.31		9,357.31	7,106.69	2,250.62
WILSON	85	1,608.58		1,608.58	1,232.55	376.03

ILLUSTRATION 1-2 Three sales reports

AGED ACCOUNTS RECEIVABLE

DATE 04/30/81 PAGE 2

CUSTOMER	ACCOUNT NUMBER	BR	SALES-PERSON	BALANCE	CURRENT	OVER 30 DAYS	OVER 60 DAYS	OVER 90 DAYS
CRANDAL & COMMINS	46346	1	44	503.42	503.42			
CULVER CONSTRUCTION CO	58607	1	19	1,696.34	1,315.67	380.67		
CUMBERLAND DAIRY	32264	3	72	379.05	379.05			
CUTTERBILL INC	88211	1	68	2,791.22	1,136.00	1,256.20	321.12	77.90
CUYENSTAHL DIE WORKS	10910	1	43	4,537.29	4,131.29	406.00		
DADAROLA CONTRACTING	19777	1	11	55.80			55.80	
DADE & FORSTERMAN INC	20791	2	30	747.65	737.65			10.00
DAHL DAHL & YONKO	49382	2	19	2,492.10	2,492.10			
DARCHESTER PLATING CO	11071	1	84	146.43	146.43			
DEAN HARDWARE CO	52086	1	26	1,087.50	1,087.50			
DEULEVIN SUPPLY CO	14125	1	44	727.77	727.77			
DEVENY AND SONS	22767	1	11	54.83		54.83		

ILLUSTRATION 1-3 Aged Accounts Receivable

product line, or they may have been affected by an item in a competitor's product line. Once again, the sales manager is alerted to trouble spots. The last report in the illustration, a *Sales-by-Salesperson Report*, shows the gross profit made by each salesperson. By studying this report, a sales manager can determine which of the salespersons has sold the most and which one has made the most profit for the company. This report may indicate that some changes in the bonus plan for salespersons should be made—changes that will encourage them to sell the high-profit items in the product line.

One can see how information provided by a company's data processing system affects how well a company's management can manage. Without accurate information, managers do not know which operations are not going as planned. With dependable information, they know what the trouble areas are and can act accordingly.

Take a different example—a manager in charge of credit or collections. This manager's job is to keep the amount of money owed to the company as low as possible without offending customers. In other words, the credit manager tries to get customers to pay their bills on time without exerting undue pressure. Suppose that the amount of money owed to the company has been increasing. The credit manager must try to reduce the amount. Can information provided by a data processing system help?

The *Aged Accounts Receivable* report in Illustration 1-3 (opposite) may help the credit manager collect outstanding debts. It tells which customers owe money and how long they have owed it. The collection department, by using this report, can first contact customers who have owed money for more than ninety days, then customers who have owed money for more than sixty days, and so on. This reasonable approach to collecting is impossible without the information given in this report.

From these two examples, one can see that information intended to indicate problem areas or exceptional conditions must be provided in sufficient detail. Another characteristic of good information is that it must be up to date, or current. The Aged Accounts Receivable report in Illustration 1-3 gives the status of accounts as of April 30. Between April 30 and the date the report was available, some of the debts listed on the report may have been paid. If the report was prepared quickly—say, in one day— and the credit manager had access to it by May 2, chances are that all debts listed on the report were still owed. Such a report is up to date. On the other hand, if it takes three weeks to prepare such a report, many of the debts listed on the report will have been paid before the report is received. In this case, unless new records are checked, some customers who have paid their bills will receive notices that their payments are ninety days overdue. This leads to confusion and ill will and is one of the reasons why it is important to the credit manager that the Aged Accounts Receivable report be up to date.

UNIT ONE: SOME FUNDAMENTALS OF DATA PROCESSING

In the same way, all management information is most valuable when it is current. If information does not reflect the most recent conditions, it runs the risk of indicating trouble spots that have been corrected or that have corrected themselves. Similarly, if information that is delivered to management reflects conditions as they were a month ago, management may not find out about a problem until long after anything can be done about it.

When a computer data processing system is installed, managers may find that the computer produces more information than they can analyze for decision-making purposes. In order to provide only the information needed for decision making, selected items requiring management attention can be listed on exception reports. Only items requiring attention are indicated. For example, an exception report listing only customers who have overdue accounts rather than all customers, as in Illustration 1-3, could be prepared for the credit manager. Exception reports are the basis for a management technique called **management-by-exception**.

Another type of data processing system that is gaining popularity with management is called a **management information system**, or **MIS**. The objective of an MIS is to provide appropriate information to all levels of management when it is needed. This information may include exception reports, specialized reports required by managers, and reports that forecast possible outcomes of management decisions.

○ SUMMARY

1. Data processing is collecting, processing, and distributing facts and figures. It may be automated, but it need not be.

2. Data processing is divided into two basic types: scientific data processing, which deals with small amounts of data requiring extensive calculations, and business data processing, which involves large volumes of data but few calculations.

3. Data processing systems originate, input, manipulate, output, and store data. The series of steps involved in manipulating data include classifying, sorting, calculating, recording, and summarizing.

4. Data processing is important to business because it affects the success of a business in several ways. It represents one of the costs of running a business and can be a major cost. It can help or hinder the customer service that a company provides. It can affect how well the managers of a company are able to manage.

5. The cost of processing data is one of the costs of running a company. If the cost of the data processing system can be decreased without

decreasing its value, the profits of the company can be increased by the same amount.

6. Data processing can affect customer service in many ways. It can affect whether or not orders are shipped promptly, the accuracy of shipments, the accuracy of bills sent to customers, and whether items are available for shipment.

7. The management information provided by a data processing system should be accurate, complete, concise, timely, and relevant.

REVIEW QUESTIONS

1. How does data differ from information?
2. How does scientific data processing differ from business data processing?
3. What is the function of source documents in a data processing system?
4. Why is summarizing an important step in data processing?
5. How can data processing affect the customer service offered by a company?
6. How does data processing affect the costs of running a company?

CHAPTER 2

DATA PROCESSING APPLICATIONS

THE PURPOSE OF A
DATA PROCESSING SYSTEM

DATA-RECORDING MEDIA
FOR A DATA PROCESSING SYSTEM
The 80-Column Punched Card
The 96-Column Punched Card

THE USES OF A
DATA PROCESSING SYSTEM

THE BASIC BUSINESS OPERATIONS

THE COMMON APPLICATIONS
Order Writing
Billing
Accounts Receivable
Inventory Control
Sales Analysis

THE OTHER COMMON APPLICATIONS

HOW THE APPLICATIONS ARE RELATED

Opposite: One important kind of output from a data processing system is the reports used by management.

UNIT ONE: SOME FUNDAMENTALS OF DATA PROCESSING

To gain an understanding of data processing, there are four things one needs to know:

1. What a data processing system is used for—its function and objectives
2. How a data processing system is designed—its inputs and outputs, procedures, and criteria for judging its merits
3. What types of equipment are available for processing data
4. How the pieces of equipment are set up and used to do specific jobs

○ THE PURPOSE OF A DATA PROCESSING SYSTEM

Data processing systems are used to collect, manipulate, and store data for reporting and analyzing business activities and events. Data is organized into *files* to achieve these purposes.

A file can be defined as an organized group of associated **records** that relate to a particular area of a business. Each record generally contains data about a single unit in the file such as an inventory item, a customer, or an employee. Illustration 2-1 is an example of a payroll file. It contains a record for each employee, and each record contains *fields*. A field is a specified area reserved for data of a specific nature such as the employee's number, name, pay rate, or address. It is the smallest element of a file that is processed.

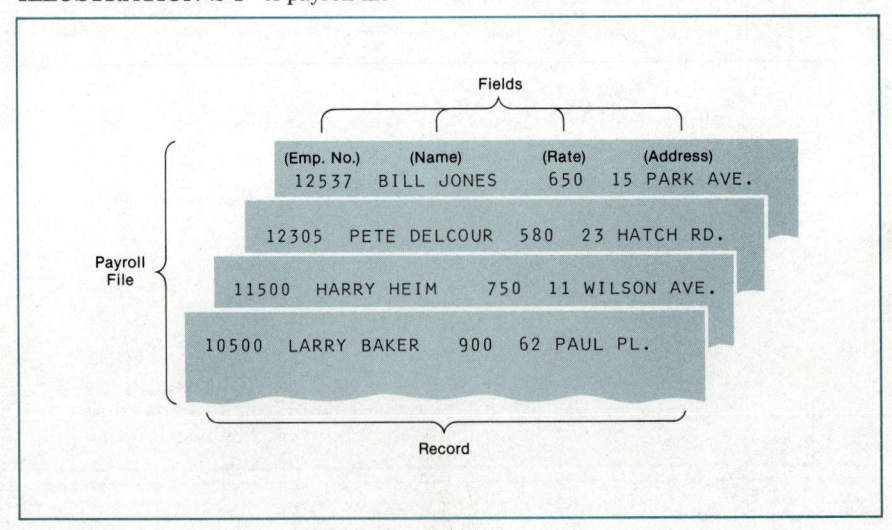

ILLUSTRATION 2-1   A payroll file

	(Emp. No.)	(Name)	(Rate)	(Address)
	12537	BILL JONES	650	15 PARK AVE.
	12305	PETE DELCOUR	580	23 HATCH RD.
	11500	HARRY HEIM	750	11 WILSON AVE.
	10500	LARRY BAKER	900	62 PAUL PL.

Payroll File — Fields — Record

A field is made up of a specified number of *characters*. A character is actually the smallest subdivision of a file. It can be alphabetic, numeric, or special. Generally, a single character within a field is not dealt with as an entity; rather, the entire field is manipulated during processing.

Files are usually divided into two classifications: master and transaction. *Master files* contain semipermanent data, as does the payroll file. *Transaction* (or *detail*) *files* contain data of a temporary nature; an example is a file of weekly employee time card data. Files may be established on a variety of media depending on the data processing system in use. In selecting the storage medium, one should consider whether the file is a master or transaction file, the frequency of use of each record, and how quickly a record must be made available for processing.

Most data processing involves file manipulation. When it is determined there is a need for information concerning some area of business, a file may be created to provide the data necessary to create the information (see Illustration 2-2). *File creation* involves building a master file for the first time. The master file is organized in some manner to simplify processing. The *file organization* can be based on some field that is contained in each record. For example, each employee record contains an employee-number field. The contents of that field can be used to sort the records in the payroll file according to employee number. The employee number is referred to as a *record key*. A file that is organized in a record key order is called a *sequential file*. A file containing records that need not be accessed in record key order may be called a *direct file*. Whether a file is organized as a sequential file or a direct file depends on the purpose of the file and the storage medium used.

The method used to read records from a file is referred to as *file access*. Files may be accessed sequentially or randomly. When records are read from a file using *sequential access*, each record in the file is read, starting with the first record in the file. Some file storage media require that records be retrieved sequentially. *Random access* involves reading only the records needed from a file. Random access provides the fastest possible retrieval of records because a desired record can be accessed without first reading all preceding records in the file. When processing a direct file, random access must be used, because the records are not arranged in the order needed for processing.

Once a file has been created, it is often necessary to add records to it. For example, when an employee is hired, a new record must be added to the payroll file. When a record is no longer useful, say, when an employee leaves a company, it is usually deleted from the file. It is sometimes necessary to change fields of a record, such as when an employee's pay rate or job classification is changed. In this case, a record is updated.

At times, if the purpose or nature of a sequential file is altered, it is necessary to change the order of the records in the file. For example, if

UNIT ONE: SOME FUNDAMENTALS OF DATA PROCESSING

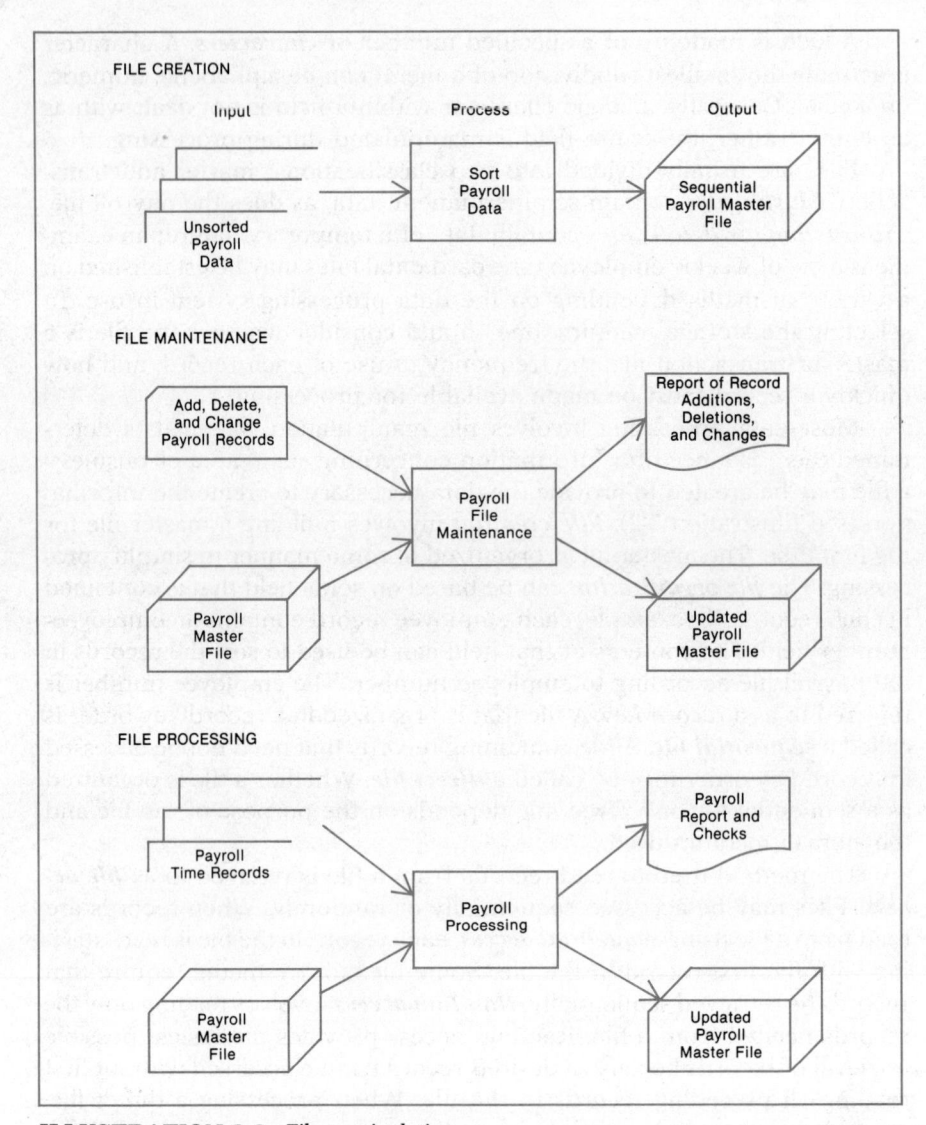

ILLUSTRATION 2-2 File manipulation

employee records in a payroll file are organized by department, but at a later date it is necessary to organize them by division, it is necessary to resequence the file.

The process of updating, adding, and deleting records in a file only when it is necessary to reflect record changes is referred to as *file maintenance*. The output from performing file maintenance on the payroll master file includes the updated payroll master file and a report showing the additions, deletions, and changes to the file (see Illustration 2-2). When a file is updated on a regular basis (such as weekly or monthly), resequenced, or reports are created, the action is called *file processing*. Processing of the payroll master file occurs when the payroll time records are input to produce a payroll report, checks, and an updated payroll master file. The payroll time records serve as a transaction file.

A data processing system is likely to use a number of master and transaction files. The method of file organization and access used for each file will depend on how often the file is to be accessed, how quickly records need to be read, and the file storage media available in the data processing system.

DATA-RECORDING MEDIA FOR A DATA PROCESSING SYSTEM

For many years, business organizations used a wide variety of manual systems to process data. More recently, data processing systems involving various types of machines have been used to process data. Before the introduction of the computer, *punched-card data processing systems* were prevalent. These systems consisted of a series of electrically operated machines that processed data recorded on punched cards. The machines were electromechanical in nature and were called *tabulation* ("*tab*" for short) *equipment* because they were often used to perform tabulation functions. As a group, they formed a punched-card, or *unit-record*, data processing system. The system performed automatic data processing.

The punched card shown in Illustration 2-3 was introduced in the late 1800s when Herman Hollerith was hired by the Census Bureau to develop a punched-card data processing system for use in the 1890 census. In 1896, Hollerith resigned his job with the Census Bureau and started the Tabulating Machine Company, which specialized in the manufacture and sale of punched-card equipment for commercial use. After merging with two other firms, this company formed the Computing-Tabulating-Recording Company. Its name was changed to the International Business Machines (IBM) Corporation in 1924.

When Hollerith left the Census Bureau, he was replaced by James Powers. Powers furthered the use of punched cards by the Census Bureau by developing a number of electromechanical machines to process cards. These machines were used to calculate the 1910 census. In 1911, Powers left the Census Bureau to produce commercial equipment; he formed the Powers Accounting Machine Company. In 1927, this company merged with others to form the Remington Rand Corporation. In 1955, the Remington Rand Corporation merged with the Sperry Rand Corporation. Today the company is known as Sperry Univac.

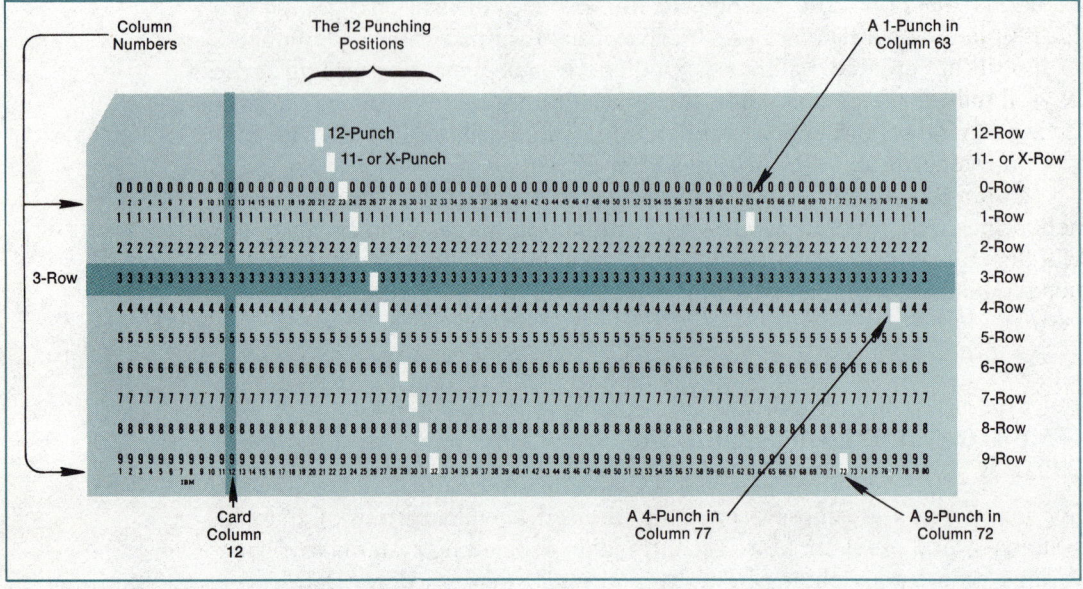

ILLUSTRATION 2-3 80-column punched card

The basic idea underlying punched-card data processing was to record source data as holes punched into cards, and then to process the data with the use of machines. Once data had been recorded on a machine-readable document, it could be processed repeatedly at machine speeds and with machine accuracy to prepare documents for a number of different departments and for a number of different business applications.

The punched card has been a very popular medium for recording source data to be entered into a data processing system. Although the punched card is still used to record source data for entry into a computer data processing system, other methods are becoming more popular. These methods of recording source data are examined in more detail in Module A.

Currently, two types of punched cards are used to record data for use in computer data processing systems. They are discussed below.

The 80-Column Punched Card

The punched card designed by Hollerith consists of 80 vertical *columns* and 12 horizontal *rows*. The columns are numbered from 1 to 80, starting from the left side of the card. The names of the rows from the top to the bottom of the card are the 12-row, the 11-row, the 0-row (zero row), and

CHAPTER 2: DATA PROCESSING APPLICATIONS

the 1-, 2-, 3-, 4-, 5-, 6-, 7-, 8-, and 9-rows. For ease of visual identification a corner of the card may be cut; the card may be colored; and the front, or face, of the card may contain printed information. The card in Illustration 2-3 has a left-corner cut.

Holes can be punched into any rows or columns of the card. In Illustration 2-3, there is a 1-punch in column 63, a 9-punch in column 72, and a 4-punch in column 77. The 12 punching positions are illustrated in columns 21 through 32.

When data is recorded in a punched card using the most common punched-card coding system, each letter, number, or special character occupies a separate column of the card. One punched card can contain up to 80 characters of data. These characters are represented by combinations of punches in the columns of the cards. For example, the combination of a 12-punch and a 1-punch stands for the letter A; the combination of a 0-punch and a 2-punch stands for the letter S. The punched-card coding system is called **Hollerith code**.

Illustration 2-4 shows all the combinations of punches in Hollerith code. It also introduces the two punching areas of the card: the **zone-punching area** and the **digit-punching area**. The zone punches are in the 12-, 11-, and 0-rows. The digit punches are in the 0- through 9-rows. (The 0-punch is therefore both a zone punch and a digit punch.)

In Illustration 2-4 the digits 0 through 9 (**numeric characters**) are punched in columns 15 through 24. Each number consists of a single digit

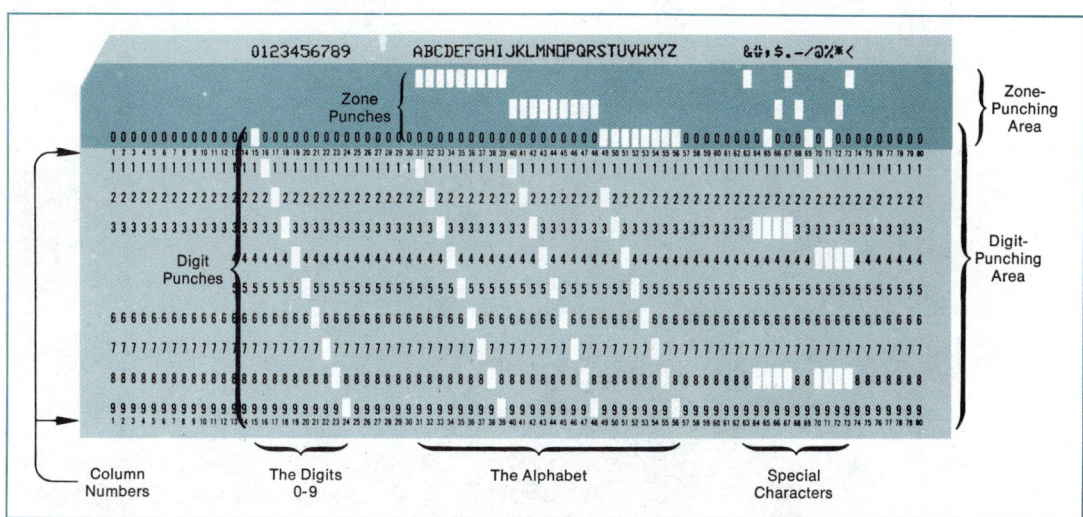

ILLUSTRATION 2-4 Hollerith code

punch. A letter (*alphabetic character*) consists of two punches in a column: a zone punch and a digit punch. The letters are recorded in columns 31 through 56. The letters A through I consist of the 12-punch and the digit punches from 1 through 9; letters J through R consist of the 11-punch and the digit punches from 1 through 9; letters S through Z consist of the 0-punch and the digit punches 2 through 9. The remaining characters (*special characters*) are represented by one, two, or three punches. They are punched in columns 63 through 73 in the illustration. As one can see, the ampersand (&) is represented by a 12-punch, the at sign (@) by a 4- and an 8-punch, and the asterisk (*) by an 11-, a 4- and an 8-punch.

The chart in Illustration 2-5 shows the zone and digit punches for every Hollerith-code alphabetic character in a convenient tabular form. The letter A consists of a 12-punch and a 1-punch; the letter B consists of a 12-punch and a 2-punch; and so on.

Before data is punched into a card, a specific number of consecutive columns is assigned to each item of data the card will contain. Each group of columns is called a *field* of the card. When alphabetic data is recorded in a field it is *left-justified*; that is, it starts in the leftmost position of the field. When the data that is being recorded in an alphabetic field does not fill the entire field, the unused portion of the field is left blank. The data in a numeric field is recorded *right-justified*; that is, it starts in the rightmost position of the field. When the data being recorded in a numeric field does not fill the field, leading zeros are often inserted in the field to insure that the numeric data is entered in the rightmost positions of the field.

The card in Illustration 2-6 is separated into many fields. Columns 2–6 are the order-number field, columns 13–14 the salesperson-number field,

ILLUSTRATION 2-5 Hollerith-code alphabetic characters

		Digit Punches							
		1	2	3	4	5	6	7	8	9
Zone Punches	12	A	B	C	D	E	F	G	H	I
	11	J	K	L	M	N	O	P	Q	R
	0		S	T	U	V	W	X	Y	Z

CHAPTER 2: DATA PROCESSING APPLICATIONS

columns 15–19 the customer-number field, and so on. Since the customer-number field is five columns wide, the customer number may be a value from 00000 through 99999. The item description may be up to 18 characters long.

The card in Illustration 2-6 contains data from the shaded areas of the shipping order source document. In this example, the order number 843

ILLUSTRATION 2-6 Data fields of a punched card

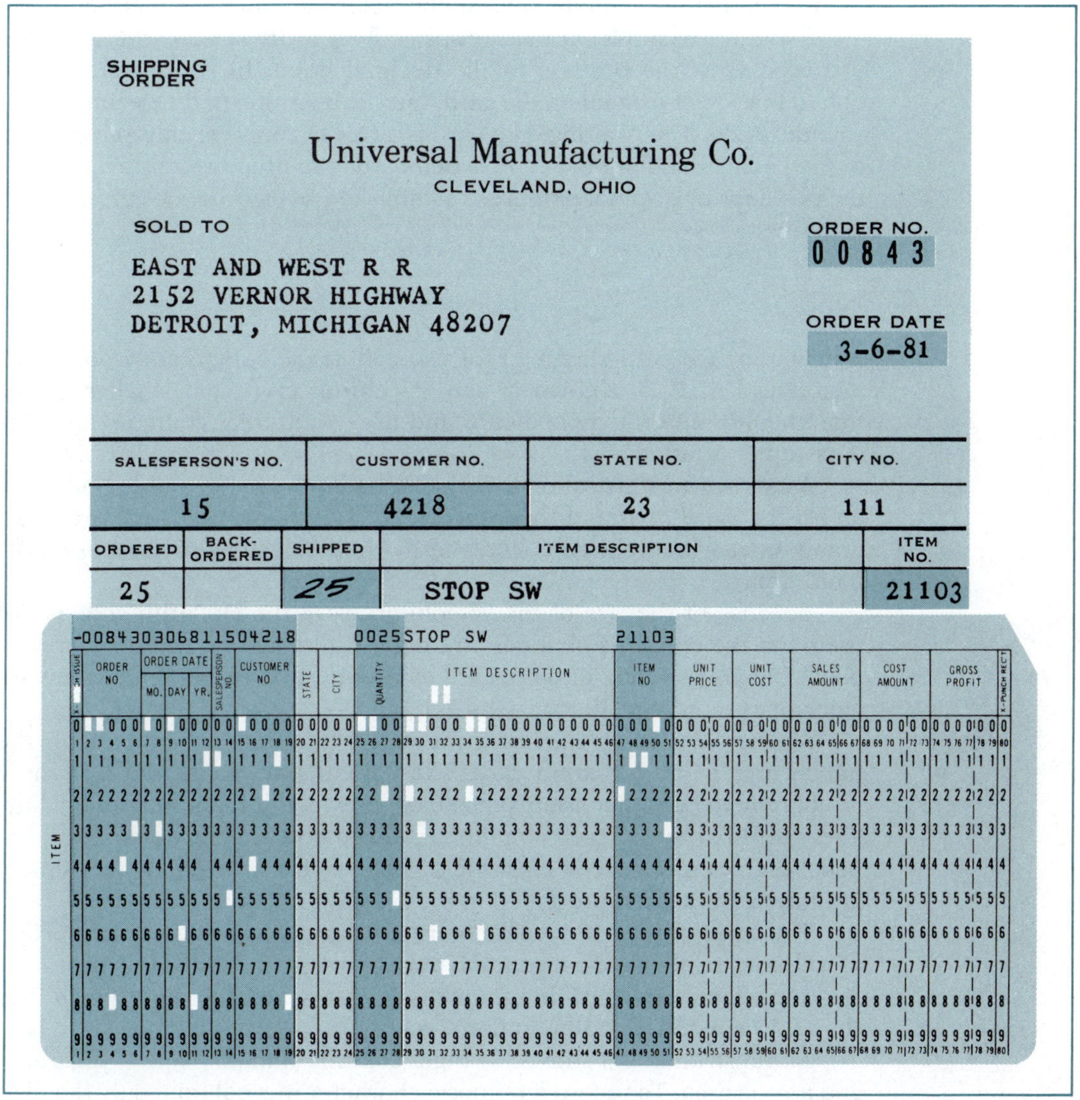

is recorded in the order-number field as 00843; it is right-justified. The customer number 4218 is recorded in the customer-number field as 04218; it is right-justified. The item-description field entry of STOP SW starts in column 29. It is left-justified. Columns 36–46 of the field are blank.

Note also that when numeric data containing a decimal point is punched into a card, the decimal point is not punched. It is omitted for two reasons: (1) to reduce the number of characters in a field, thus shortening the keypunching operation, and (2) to avoid input errors, since numeric data cannot contain special characters like the decimal point.

Look, for example, at the unit-price field in Illustration 2-6. A dotted line represents the position of the decimal point. In some systems, the dotted line is not printed on the card, but the postition of the decimal point is understood. The printing on a card is, after all, only for the convenience of the people handling the card. When cards are processed by a computer the positions of decimal points are established by instructions given to the computer.

The 96-Column Punched Card

A new punched card, designed for use with small computer systems, was announced in 1969. Known as the 96-column card, it is smaller in size than the 80-column punched card and uses a different coding system for data representation.

As shown in Illustration 2-7, the 96-column card is divided into two areas: the **print area** and the **punch area.** The 96-column card is considerably smaller than the 80-column card, but it can store almost 20 percent more data.

Because of the size of the 96-column card, the Hollerith code is not used, but the concepts of zones and digits and columns and rows are applied. Data is punched into the card as round holes rather than as rectangular ones (compare Illustrations 2-4 and 2-7).

As the term *96-column card* indicates, there are 96 columns in the punch area of a 96-column card. The columns are separated into three 32-column *tiers* rather than placed on one continuous horizontal line. There are six rows in each column, and each column can hold one alphabetic, numeric, or special character. Thus, each of the characters shown in Illustration 2-7 is represented in the six rows in one column of the card.

The two top rows in a column are used to represent the zone portion of a character; they are called the B and A zones. The alphabetic character B is represented by the zone punches B and A and the digit punch 2 as shown in column 1 in Illustration 2-8.

As Illustration 2-8 shows, a single column contains both a digit area and a zone area. To record a numeric character in a column, only the digit

CHAPTER 2: DATA PROCESSING APPLICATIONS

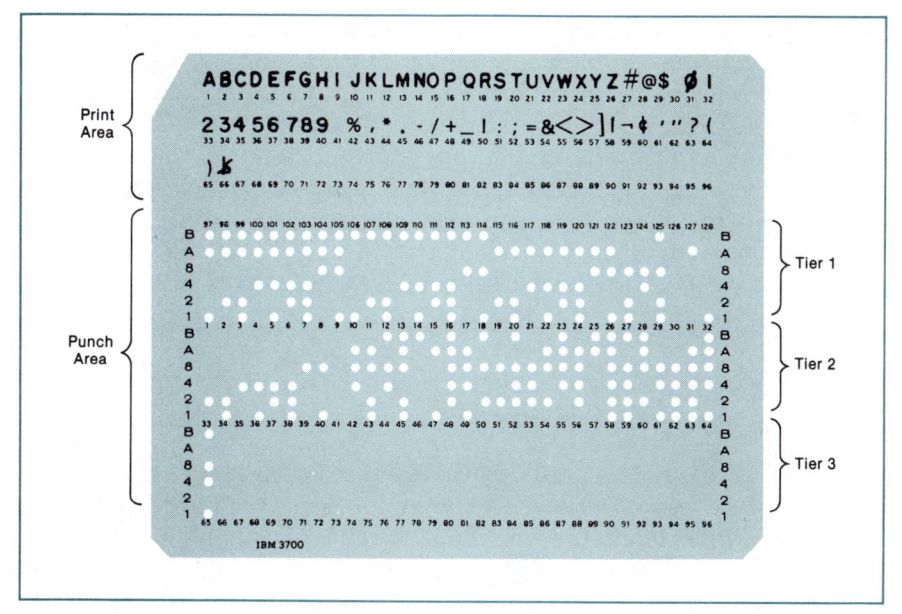

ILLUSTRATION 2-7 96-column card code

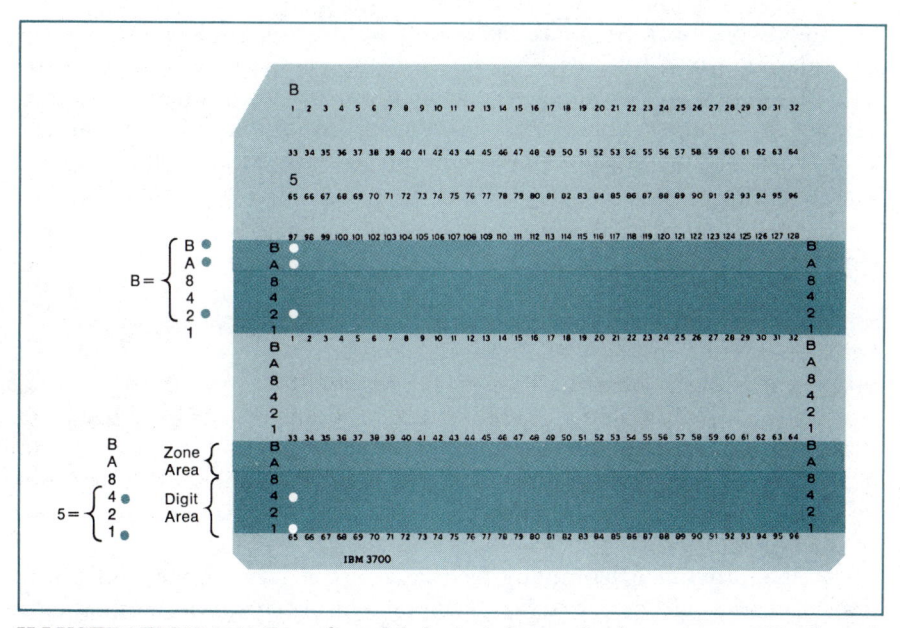

ILLUSTRATION 2-8 Recording alphabetic and numeric characters on a 96-column card

area of the column is needed. Any number from 0 through 9 can be represented by one or more punches in the digit rows 8, 4, 2, and 1. In Illustration 2-8 the number 5 is represented by punches in rows 4 and 1 in column 65.

The print area of a 96-column card is divided into four rows to provide print interpretation of characters punched in any of the 96 columns. There are 32 positions in each row, or a total of 128 print positions. The 32 extra print positions are provided so that spacing can be inserted between the printed characters to allow the card to be read easily by persons who use it.

THE USES OF A DATA PROCESSING SYSTEM

Data processing systems are used in a variety of business operations. These operations are called *data processing applications*. Billing is one data processing application. The operation of billing is accomplished by the data processing system applied to the billing of customers. Another example of a data processing application is inventory control. The objective of the inventory-control application is to keep track of inventory items so that they can be reordered or reproduced when necessary. The data processing system applied to inventory control prepares records and reports to help inventory-control personnel do their jobs.

In any business, there are many data processing applications. In fact, any operation of a business that requires information or paperwork is a data processing application. The applications vary from business to business just as the operations vary. Nevertheless, certain basic operations and data processing applications are common to most businesses.

THE BASIC BUSINESS OPERATIONS

A manufacturing company is a typical business. It carries out several basic operations in order to make its products, sell them, and realize a profit. These basic operations are: (1) *producing* the items in the product line, (2) *storing* these items, (3) *selling* the products, (4) *shipping* the products, (5) *billing* customers for purchases, (6) *collecting* payments from customers, (7) *purchasing* goods when needed, (8) *receiving* the purchased goods, (9) *paying* for the purchased goods, and (10) *paying* the employees of the company.

A manufacturing company also carries out other important operations. Accounting, for example, takes place in one form or another, as in all companies. In the accounting department, financial records are kept to indicate whether the company is making a profit and whether the total value of the company is increasing. Since accounting is not directly connected with making and selling a product, it is not considered a basic operation. Similarly, the research and development department, the legal department, and the personnel department may carry out operations that are not included in the list of basic operations of manufacturing.

Of course, not all companies manufacture products. Some companies are distributors. A distributor buys products and then sells the products to customers. A wholesale toy distributor, for example, buys toys from toy manufacturers and sells them to department stores and other retail outlets. A distributor does not need a production operation. However, the other basic operations are the same as those of a manufacturing company.

Other organizations, banks and insurance companies, for example, sell services rather than products. For this reason, their basic operations are somewhat different from those of a manufacturing company. A service company may not store material to be sold, but it does store material that it uses. Similarly, a service company bills its customer, collects from them, purchases goods and services from other companies, and so on.

Another variation of basic operations is seen in not-for-profit organizations, such as the government. Many of the basic operations of a manufacturing company may not occur in a government agency. For example, many government agencies do not bill customers or collect payments. They do, however, purchase material and pay employees.

Since the basic operations of a manufacturing company also take place in most other businesses, these operations are a useful background for studying the common data processing applications.

○ THE COMMON APPLICATIONS

Data processing can be applied to any operation of a company. The most common applications are: (1) *order writing,* associated with shipping; (2) *billing,* associated with customer billing; (3) *accounts receivable,* associated with collection; (4) *inventory control,* associated with stores (or stock-keeping); (5) *sales analysis,* associated with selling; (6) *accounts payable,* associated with paying for material; (7) *payroll,* associated with paying employees; and (8) *production control,* associated with producing manufactured goods.

This text deals primarily with five of these: order writing, billing, accounts receivable, inventory control, and sales analysis. The reader should learn the objective of each application and its basic forms and reports.

Order Writing

In the language of data processing, any report or form used by a company is called a *document*. The objective of a data processing application is to prepare output documents from source (input) documents. In the order-writing application, the objective is to prepare a document called the ***shipping order*** from the original ***sales order***. The input to the order-writing system is the sales order; the output is the shipping order.

Both a sales order and a shipping order are shown in Illustration 2-9. The sales order is filled out by the salesperson, the customer, or a clerk. It is often prepared as a single copy. The shipping order is then prepared in several copies, using the sales order as a source document. One copy of the shipping order is sent to the customer as an acknowledgment that the order has been received. One copy is used to tell the person who picks the order in the warehouse (the order picker) what items should be shipped. And one copy is packed with the shipment to tell the customer what items have been included in the shipment.

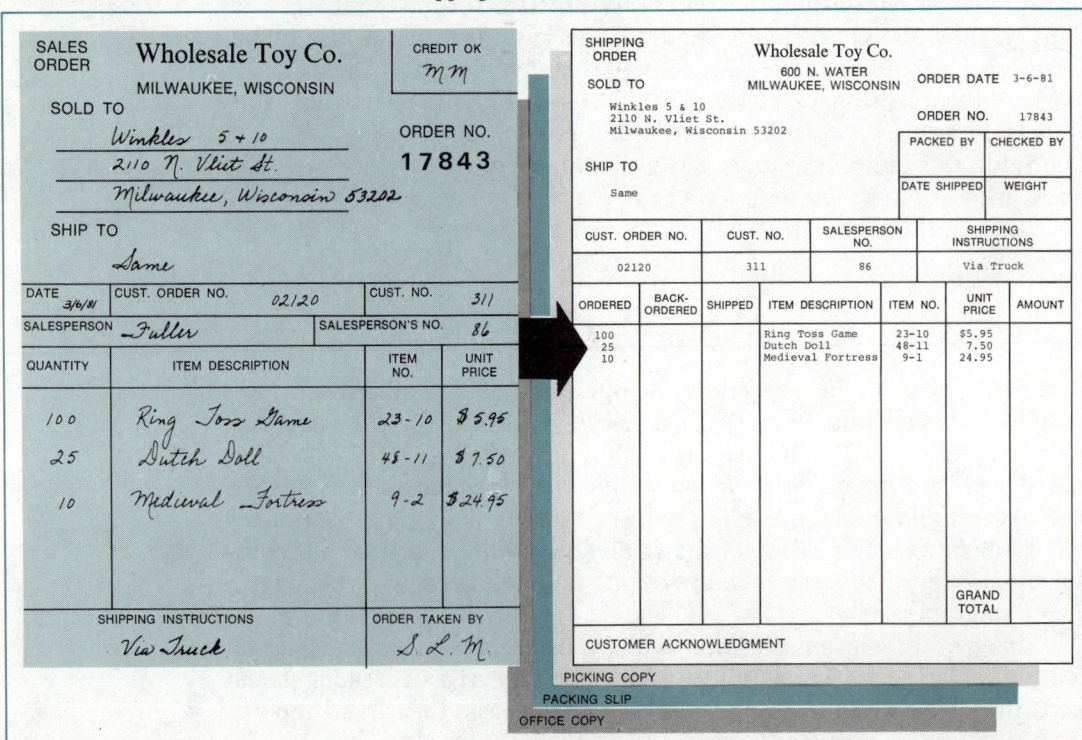

ILLUSTRATION 2-9   Sales order and shipping order

CHAPTER 2: DATA PROCESSING APPLICATIONS

In some companies, order writing (or *order entry,* as it is sometimes called) is the most important application. This is often true of distributors. The sales of a distributor may depend on whether orders can be shipped faster than sales can be made. On the other hand, in companies where speed in shipping an order is not critical, order writing is a less important data processing application.

Billing

Billing is an application similar to order writing. Once an order has been shipped, the customer must be billed. The input to the billing application is often the shipping order, which shows the items that were actually shipped. The output of the application is the bill, or *invoice*.

Illustration 2-10 shows a shipping order that has been marked by an order picker and the invoice prepared from it. The major difference between the two documents is that on the invoice the **line items** have been

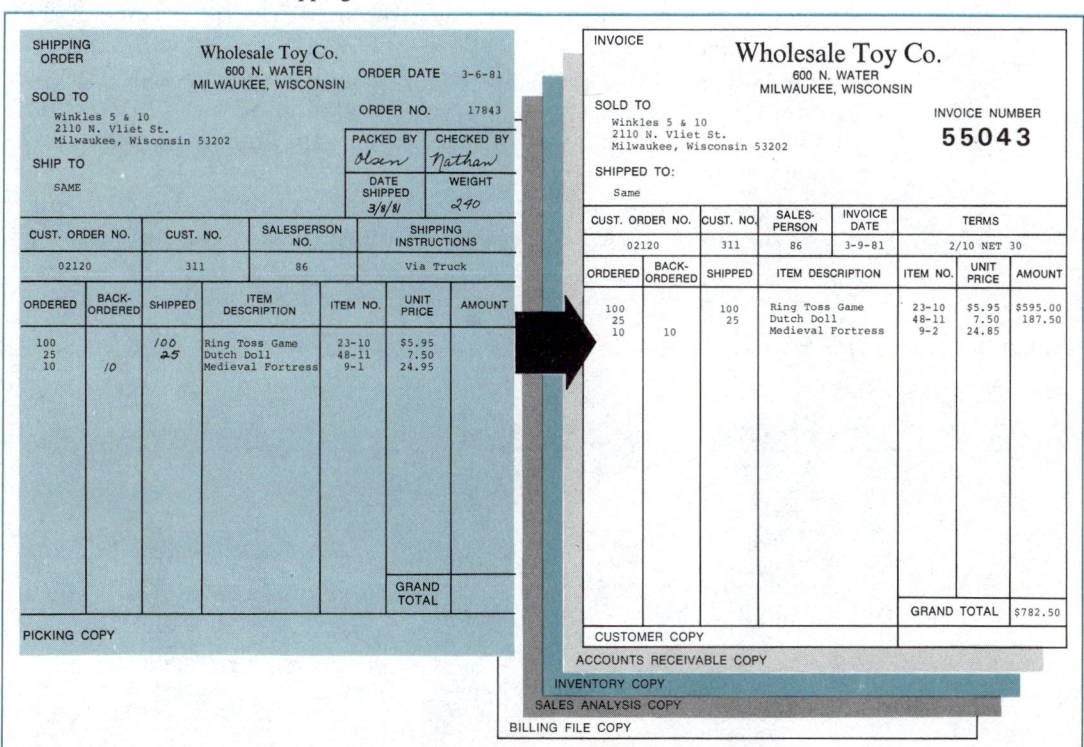

ILLUSTRATION 2-10   Shipping order and invoice

UNIT ONE: SOME FUNDAMENTALS OF DATA PROCESSING

extended. A line item is the information contained in one line in the body of the invoice. Each line item refers to one type of item sold. The invoice in Illustration 2-10 has three line items. Extending a line item means multiplying the unit price by the quantity to arrive at a total for the line item. In the illustration, the extension of the second item is $187.50.

Notice that not all of the items on the shipping order have been shipped. The items that were not shipped (because they were not in stock) have been indicated in the "Back-Ordered" column on the shipping order and on the invoice. As soon as these items are available, they will be shipped to the customer. In some systems, inventory records are checked and the items that must be back-ordered are detected before the shipping order is prepared. Then only the items that are available are extended on the shipping order. The invoice can be a copy of the shipping order.

Speed and accuracy are important in billing just as they are in order writing. Accuracy is important for obvious reasons: overbilling a customer is unsatisfactory customer service; underbilling a customer can mean lost income. Speed in billing is important because it affects the amount of money owed to the company. To appreciate this, look at Illustration 2-11. Each of two companies has an average daily billing of $10,000. One company sends its bills out two days after shipment. The other sends its bills out seven days after shipment. The customers of both companies pay their bills an average of fourteen days after the bills have been sent. How will the difference in billing speed affect the total amount owed to each company? To ask this another way, what is the average amount of money owed to each company at any given time?

Since customers pay their bills fourteen days after they are sent, a total of 14 times $10,000 or $140,000, is owed to each company before it

ILLUSTRATION 2-11 How speed in billing affects amounts owed to a company

	Average Daily Billing	Time Delay for Billing	When Paid	Total Days	Total Dollars
Company A	$10,000	2 days	14 days	16	$160,000
Company B	10,000	7 days	14 days	21	210,000
Difference				5	$ 50,000

starts receiving payments from customers. Since two days pass before the bills are prepared, an additional 2 times $10,000, or $20,000, is owed to the first company at any given time. The total amount of money owed to the first company, then, is $140,000 plus $20,000, or $160,000. Using this same reasoning, the total owed to the second company at any given time is $140,000 plus $70,000, or $210,000. The difference between the total amounts of money outstanding is $50,000. It results from the difference in the billing speeds of the two billing systems.

Why is the amount of money owed to a company important? Available cash, or capital, determines to what extent the company can develop new products, purchase new machinery, or build additions to buildings. If a company's capital tends to be tied up because of a slow billing system, improvement of the billing application may be advisable.

Accounts Receivable

The objective of an accounts receivable application is twofold: (1) to keep records of the amounts of money that are owed to the company, and (2) to provide information that helps collection personnel to collect outstanding debts. The inputs to a system for accounts receivable are usually invoices and documents indicating cash payments. The outputs of the system are accounts receivable records that indicate charges and payments to a customer's account, monthly statements to customers indicating what is owed, and management reports such as the Aged Accounts Receivable report in Illustration 1-3 (see Chapter 1).

Illustration 2-12 shows an accounts receivable record called a *ledger card*. It contains a record of all charges and payments to a customer's account. In a system that uses ledger cards as the basic accounts receivable record, one card is kept for each customer. The sum of the balances on all ledger cards is the total amount of money owed to the company. The difference between the ledger card and the monthly statement sent to the customer is that the card shows all charges and credits that have occurred since the card was originated. The statement shows only recent credits and outstanding charges.

Management information is a valuable output of an accounts receivable system. Many accounts receivable systems prepare management reports like the Aged Accounts Receivable. In other accounts receivable systems, preparing the Aged Accounts Receivable report may require so many person hours of work that a company has to decide whether the report is worth the cost of preparing it. The result of this decision varies from industry to industry. For example, a retail distributor (such as a large department store) is likely to have thousands of customers with charge accounts. Keeping track of overdue accounts is an important and sizable

UNIT ONE: SOME FUNDAMENTALS OF DATA PROCESSING

CUSTOMER NAME	CUSTOMER NO.	CREDIT LIMIT
ALBERT AND SONS 2911 SOUTH LANE PITTSBURGH, PA 15219	23891	$5,000.00

DATE	REFERENCE NO.	CHARGES	CREDITS	BALANCE
			BALANCE FORWARD	200.00
07/02/81	12368	187.72		387.72
07/21/81	12566	13.91		401.63
07/30/81	12671	304.11		705.74
08/07/81	56739		187.72	518.02
08/20/81	12802	156.12		674.14
09/04/81	13094	73.17		747.31
09/14/81	13308	75.00		822.31
10/04/81	73333		195.00	627.31
10/09/81	01299		20.00	607.31
10/16/81	15103	46.98		654.29
10/25/81	15487	141.71		796.00
10/29/81	15782	88.06		884.06

ILLUSTRATION 2-12   Accounts receivable ledger card

job. For such a distributor, aged credit information is often valuable. On the other hand, some manufacturers have no need for such information because they have a relatively small number of customers, few of whom let their accounts become delinquent.

Speed is important in the accounts receivable application. Accounts receivable records are more valuable when they are up to date. When customers ask how much they owe a company, personnel should be able to check their accounts receivable records and answer immediately. But if the charges and payments for the last week have not been recorded on the accounts receivable records, they cannot be used for this purpose.

Similarly, each monthly statement should represent the actual amount of money owed by a customer at the end of the billing period. Thus, the speed of the accounts receivable system is important in preparing customer records and monthly statements to aid in cash collection.

Inventory Control

Inventory control is often the data processing application that provides the greatest potential benefit to a company. In some cases, the needs of this application cause a company to install an automated data processing system. The objective of inventory control is to meet two basic goals. One of the goals is always to have on hand those items that are needed—in other words, to avoid *stockouts*. The other goal is to keep the value of inventory as low as possible. A complication is that these goals tend to work against each other.

A stockout occurs when a customer orders an item that is not available in inventory. The item is then back-ordered. Since the customer demand for an item varies, avoiding stockouts is not an easy job. If a large demand for an item occurs unexpectedly and exceeds the supply on hand, a stockout occurs. Of course, one way of avoiding stockouts is to keep large inventories of all items in the product line. If an item averages fifty units sold per month, and a thousand units are kept on hand, one can assume the company will not run out of the item. However, if this is done, the second inventory goal—keeping the inventory value low—is not achieved.

Inventory should be kept as low as possible because it costs money to store (or carry) inventory. First, warehouse space has to be provided, and handling, insurance, and tax costs must be paid. Second, action must be taken to prevent deterioration of the items in inventory; rust must be inhibited, handling abuses eliminated, and so on. Meanwhile, the money tied up in inventory, some of which may be borrowed at high interest rates, cannot be used for other purposes. Finally, a certain percentage of items in inventory becomes obsolete each year. When this happens, the obsolete items must be discarded or sold at a lower price. The costs of carrying inventory vary from industry to industry. However, one common estimate is that carrying costs are 25 percent of the average inventory value. Therefore, if a company's average inventory value is $100,000, the yearly cost of carrying the inventory is $25,000.

To reach a balance between the conflicting goals of inventory management, an inventory-control department must have certain information. This information can be provided by the inventory-control system. The information should be detailed enough to answer the following questions:

1. What items need to be reordered?
2. How much of each item should be reordered?

3. What items have had an unusual increase or decrease in sales?
4. What items account for the major part of the inventory investment?
5. What items have become obsolete?

By installing an inventory-control system that gives this kind of information, some companies have been able to make striking advancements toward both inventory goals. By improving inventory information, they have been able to control inventory levels and, at the same time, reduce stockouts.

The source data in an inventory-control system is the recorded transactions of items sold, issued, destroyed, received, or returned. This data appears on input documents such as invoices, scrap notices, packing slips from shipments received, and return slips. When this data is processed, it is converted into inventory records and inventory management reports.

One type of inventory-control document is a ledger card, such as the one shown in Illustration 2-13. There is one ledger card for each item in inventory. In addition to the transactions (receipts and issues) and balance on hand, each ledger card shows the item reorder point, the price of one item (unit price), and the cost of one item (unit cost). By looking at a ledger card, inventory-control personnel can tell whether the balance on hand for an item has fallen below the reorder point and whether the item should be reordered. They can also determine what the sales of the item have been for any given period. However, this information is not in a form that points out the items needing attention. To discover unusual sales patterns, inventory-control personnel may have to study many cards. Moreover, all of the cards must be examined if one wishes to determine all items that should be reordered. Since many of the ledger cards will not have changed since they were last reviewed, many of the items will not require attention.

One alternative to ledger-card examination is to provide a report indicating items that require attention and items whose sales have changed significantly since the immediately preceding report was provided. As indicated in Chapter 1, this kind of reporting is called management-by-exception. The idea behind it is to have management concern itself only with exceptional items (those that require attention) rather than with all items.

Illustration 2-14 shows three kinds of exception reports. The first report is called an *Inventory Action Report*. It lists items that have fallen below their reorder points and shows the transactions that have taken place since the last report, the current balances, and the amounts on order. Using this report, inventory-control personnel can verify (before passing the list on to the purchasing department) that the listed items should be reordered. The second report is a *Slow-Moving Items Report*. It is a list of items that have had little activity over the last twelve months. The report

CHAPTER 2: DATA PROCESSING APPLICATIONS

ITEM NUMBER
4561237
REORDER POINT
200
UNIT PRICE
$7.50
UNIT COST
$3.75

ITEM DESCRIPTION
TRANSFORMERS

DATE	REFERENCE NO.	RECEIPTS	ISSUES	BALANCE ON HAND	ON ORDER
03/02/81			BALANCE FORWARD	560	
03/11/81	12379		125	435	
03/18/81	12402		50	385	
03/26/81	12509		135	250	
04/02/81	12697		100	150	
04/03/81	5894			150	500
04/13/81	12774		15	135	
04/13/81	13007		25	110	
04/16/81	13277		75	35	
04/16/81	13308		10	25	
04/17/81	5894	500		525	
04/28/81	15003		75	450	
05/05/81	15233		80	370	
05/15/81	15324		175	195	
05/20/81	5999			195	500
05/21/81	15987		50	145	
05/26/81	16001		15	130	
06/01/81	16043		92	38	
06/03/81	5999	500		538	
06/11/81	16319		125	413	
06/18/81	16403		75	338	
07/01/81	16522		15	323	
07/02/81	16539		25	298	

ILLUSTRATION 2-13 Inventory ledger card

gives the date the item was last sold and shows how many months supply of stock is on hand, based on the sales for the last twelve months. According to the report, the seventh item on the list has a balance on hand that will last 135 months, or more than eleven years! The third report, a **Cumulative Percent of Sales Report**, is another kind of activity report. It lists the items of inventory in order of total dollar sales for the year. In addition, in the "Cumulative $ Sales" column, is a total for all items listed thus far. The cumulative percentage is developed on the same basis. This report helps inventory-control personnel identify the items that account for the greatest percentage of sales. One of the interesting things that often

INVENTORY ACTION REPORT

DATE 11/30/81   PAGE 7

PRODUCT NUMBER	OPENING BALANCE	+ RECEIPTS	— ISSUES	= BALANCE ON HAND	ON ORDER	REORDER POINT
7310921	150		150			100
3871123	1100		600	500		1000
4061397	200		200		500	400
4561237		300	200	100		200
0120125	50		25	25		25

SLOW-MOVING ITEMS REPORT

DATE 07/01/81   PAGE 37

STOCK LOCATION	STOCK NUMBER	DESCRIPTION	UNIT	DATE OF LAST ACTIVITY	NUMBER OF TRANSACTIONS	QTY.	AVERAGE PER MONTH	QTY.	MONTHS SUPPLY	VALUE
2715-237	127205	LIGHT RECEPTACLE	EA	07/80	2	4	.3	16	53.3	$4.32
2715-420	247389	SOLENOID, HEATER	EA	07/80	1	1	.1	7	70.0	4.43
2715-267	111462	SWITCH, STARTER	EA	08/80	1	4	.3	4	13.3	8.64
2715-601	896124	PINION STUD	EA	09/80	4	16	1.3	84	64.6	9.24
2716-234	59827	GASKET, MANIFOLD	EA	11/80	2	12	1.0	16	16.0	7.52
2716-320	614	WASHER, RUBBER	DZ	12/80	1	3	.2	14	70.0	2.52
2717-086	6213	BOLT, CARRIAGE	DZ	12/80	1	2	.2	27	135.0	32.40
2717-742	1032	BEARING,								
2717-748	148722	AXLE								
2719-147	2642	BRUSH, GE								
2719-382	222649	REGULATOR								
2720-416	421	VALVE								

CUMULATIVE PERCENT OF SALES REPORT

DATE 09/81   PAGE 1

ITEM COUNT	ITEM NUMBER	ANNUAL UNITS	UNIT PRICE	ANNUAL $ SALES	CUMULATIVE $ SALES	CUMULATIVE % OF SALES
01	T7061	51,553	3.077	158,629	158,629	25.5
02	S6832	243,224	.317	77,102	235,731	37.9
03	S7036	98,406	.470	46,251	281,982	45.4
04	G9655	6,768	4.876	33,001	314,983	50.7
05	T3320	4,250	7.369	31,318	346,301	55.7
06	K8946	44,560	.675	30,078	376,379	60.6
07	K5322	8,680	3.286	28,522	404,901	65.2
08	K2026	27,581	.930	25,650	430,551	69.3
09	16267	3,428	5.901	20,228	450,779	72.6
10	H1981	52,765	.379	19,998	470,777	75.8
11	G9282	1,105	14.676	16,217	486,994	78.4
12	N8565	23,908	.640	15,301	502,295	80.8
40	S6219	15,360	.050	768	618,897	99.6
41	K2068	3,494	.176	615	619,512	99.7
42	G7413	1,904	.282	537	620,049	99.8
43	H3772	2,842	.120	341	620,390	99.86
44	N9773	2,439	.123	300	620,690	99.91
45	T6613	2,670	.103	275	620,965	99.95
46	M2613	3,750	.048	180	621,145	99.98
47	G2605	198	.505	100	621,245	99.995
48	T6562	210	.143	30	621,275	100.0
49	S6132	0	.062	0	621,275	100.0
50	M3742	0	.073	0	621,275	100.0

ILLUSTRATION 2-14   Three inventory reports

shows up in this kind of report is that about 20 percent of a company's items account for 80 percent of its sales. When this is the case, the inventory-control department usually directs most attention to those items.

    One can see how information can be valuable in managing inventory. Effective inventory control can benefit a company in several ways. By reducing the average inventory, carrying costs are decreased. By reducing the number of stockouts, sales are increased.

Sales Analysis

The objective of the sales analysis application is to provide information that helps sales management increase sales. The inputs to the system are the invoices showing items sold and the return slips showing items returned by customers. The outputs of the system are management reports that show sales by salesperson, customer, item class, geographical area, branch, and any number of other classifications. Three sales reports were illustrated in Chapter 1 (see Illustration 1-2).

Unlike some application systems, the value of a sales analysis system is difficult to measure. The manager has to estimate how much sales will increase as a result of using the information provided by the system. This increase must be balanced against the cost of the system. Most companies today perform some sales analysis. The amount of information a company needs from its sales analysis system will vary with its size and product line. A company with many products and customers, a large sales force, and a number of sales offices is likely to have an extensive sales analysis application.

THE OTHER COMMON APPLICATIONS

Although the other common applications are not discussed in detail in this book, one should be familiar with their objectives. In accounts payable, the objective is to pay suppliers (vendors) for items and services. The output of the system is the payment check. The discounts that vendors offer for prompt payment of bills are an important source of savings in the accounts payable application. A common discount is 2 percent if bills are paid within 10 days of the time they are received. One of the goals of an accounts payable system is to take advantage of all such discounts, but pay each bill on the last day of its discount period.

Payment of employee salaries and wages is the objective of the payroll application. Payroll checks and payroll reports are the outputs of this application. The input is employee time cards. Because payroll expenses are usually one of the major costs of running a business, payroll information can be an important aid to the management of a company.

For a manufacturing company, the production-control application may offer great potential saving. A company has to control several resources—personnel, machines, and materials. The objectives of production control are to keep machines and people working efficiently at all times, and to keep the investment in production materials as low as possible without running out of them. To work effectively toward these goals, production-control personnel need current information that points out critical situations. Such information is the output of the production-control system.

UNIT ONE: SOME FUNDAMENTALS OF DATA PROCESSING

In addition to these common applications, there are others less common, but similarly related to basic operations. Vendor analysis, for example, is an application associated with the purchasing operation. In this application, reports are prepared to indicate which vendors have the lowest prices, the highest percentage of on-time deliveries, the lowest percentage of defective shipments, and so on.

There are still other applications peculiar to particular types of organizations. For example, grade reporting is associated with educational institutions, mortgage loan accounting is unique to financial institutions, and policy rating is done in the insurance industry. The point is that there are many applications besides those commonly associated with the basic operations. Any operation that takes place in a company can be the basis for a data processing application.

HOW THE APPLICATIONS ARE RELATED

To introduce the common applications one at a time may be misleading. It may imply that the applications are not related. Actually, the applications in a business are closely related, one to another. In fact, a group of related applications is often referred to as a *family of applications*. Order writing, billing, accounts receivable, inventory control, and sales analysis are members of a family that is sometimes called the ***distribution family of applications***. Within this family, the output of one application is the input to the next. The shipping order returned from the shipping department is the input to the billing system; the bill produced by the billing system is the input to the accounts receivable, inventory-control, and sales analysis systems.

Looking at it another way, the data on the original sales order is source data for the entire distribution family of applications. When data from customer and item files is added to this source data, and certain calculations are performed, the various outputs of this family are derived. As discussed above, the sales order is the source document for the shipping order. The invoice is the result of extending the line items on the shipping order, adding the extensions, and subtracting the customer discounts. Inventory records are the result of summarizing the line items by item number and, for each item, subtracting the total number sold from the previous on-hand balance. Sales analysis reports are the result of grouping the line items by salesperson, customer, or item and then summarizing them. In short, the applications in a family are related, not only through input and output, but also through use of the same source data.

One should keep in mind that a company's files, like source data, are often used by an entire family of applications rather than by just one. For example, a customer file usually contains permanent data such as each customer's name and address, number, credit limit, discounts, special terms, and shipping instructions. Such a file is used in the order-writing, billing, and accounts receivable applications. Similarly, an item file containing information such as unit price, unit cost, item number, reorder point, and reorder quantities is used in the order-writing, billing, inventory-control, and sales analysis applications.

Some companies organize all of the data needed by the various applications into a structured set of related files, known as a ***data base***. This eliminates the need for duplicate data and permits additions, updates, and deletions of records to be made to one file. A key to the success of the data base concept is that files are not duplicated in several applications. All applications use the same files, and changes made to the files are available to all applications. When a data base system is not used, updating of multiple files may not occur at the same time. This can sometimes cause data that is common to several files not to be current when needed by a family of applications. The basis for a management information system is a comprehensive data base or several well-planned data bases. Companies are developing management information systems using data bases to insure that data is current for all applications. (See Chapters 15 and 16.)

In evaluating the system for a given application, it is important to keep in mind how that application relates to others. It is a mistake, for example, to consider a billing system without considering the order-writing system. If the relationships between applications are not considered, the data processing system for one application may be improved at the expense of the system for a related application.

○ SUMMARY

1. The purpose of a data processing system is the collection, manipulation, and storage of data for reporting and analysis. To achieve this purpose, data is organized into files. Files consist of groups of associated records that pertain to one aspect of a business. Records are further subdivided into fields. Files of a permanent nature are called master files, while those of a temporary nature are referred to as transaction files.

2. File organization is the method of arranging the records in a file. Sequential file records are in order according to a record key within each record. Direct file records are placed in the file without regard to order.

3. File access is the method used to retrieve records from a file. When sequential file access is used, each record in the file is read, starting with the first record. Direct access to a file allows the retrieval of individual records that are to be manipulated. File manipulation includes file creation, and the adding, deleting, and updating of records in the file.

4. The most common punched card has 12 rows and 80 columns. The zone rows are the 12-, 11- and 0-rows; the digit rows are the 0- through 9-rows. When data is represented on a punched card, a specific field (group of card columns) is assigned to each item of data. In Hollerith code, a digit is represented by a single digit punch, a letter by the combination of a zone punch and a digit punch, and a special character by either one, two, or three punches in a column.

5. The 96-column punched card has 96 card columns. These columns are broken into three tiers, each having 32 columns. Each tier has six rows. The zone rows are the B- and A-rows; the digit rows are the 8-, 4-, 2-, and 1-rows. In the 96-column card code, a digit is represented by one or more holes in the digit rows, and a letter by a combination of holes in the zone and digit rows. A special character is represented by a combination of holes in the zone and digit rows (with one exception—a blank is represented by no punches in a column).

6. The common data processing applications are order writing (order entry), billing, accounts receivable, inventory control, sales analysis, accounts payable, payroll, and production control. These applications are closely associated with some of the basic operations of a company.

7. In the order-writing application, a document is prepared that can be used by the shipping department for picking and shipping the customer's order. This document is usually called the shipping order. In many industries, the speed of this application is very important because it determines in part how fast an order can be shipped.

8. Billing prepares the customer's bill (invoice) after the order has been shipped. Speed in billing is important because it affects the amount of money owed to the company.

9. In accounts receivable, monthly statements are prepared, records of customers' accounts are kept, and management information is prepared. A common form of accounts receivable information is a report called Aged Accounts Receivable.

CHAPTER 2: DATA PROCESSING APPLICATIONS

10. The goals in inventory control are to avoid stockouts and at the same time to keep down the amount of money invested in inventory. To meet both of these goals, an inventory-control system keeps inventory records and prepares management information. One useful type of inventory reporting is exception reporting.

11. The function of a sales analysis system is to prepare reports containing sales information. The importance of this application varies, depending on the size of the sales force, the number of products, and the number of sales offices within the company.

12. Although they are often talked about separately, the applications of a business are closely related—the source data and files for one are often used in others. Data base systems are being developed by companies because of this relationship.

REVIEW QUESTIONS

1. Name the subdivisions of a file.
2. What is the purpose of a record key?
3. What types of file access can be used to read records? Which is faster and why?
4. What is the purpose of file maintenance?
5. What are the common business data processing applications?
6. How can the speed and accuracy of the billing application affect a company?
7. What source document is likely to be used in the billing application?
8. Name several reports that are likely to be produced by an inventory control system.
9. Explain at least one advantage of using a data base.

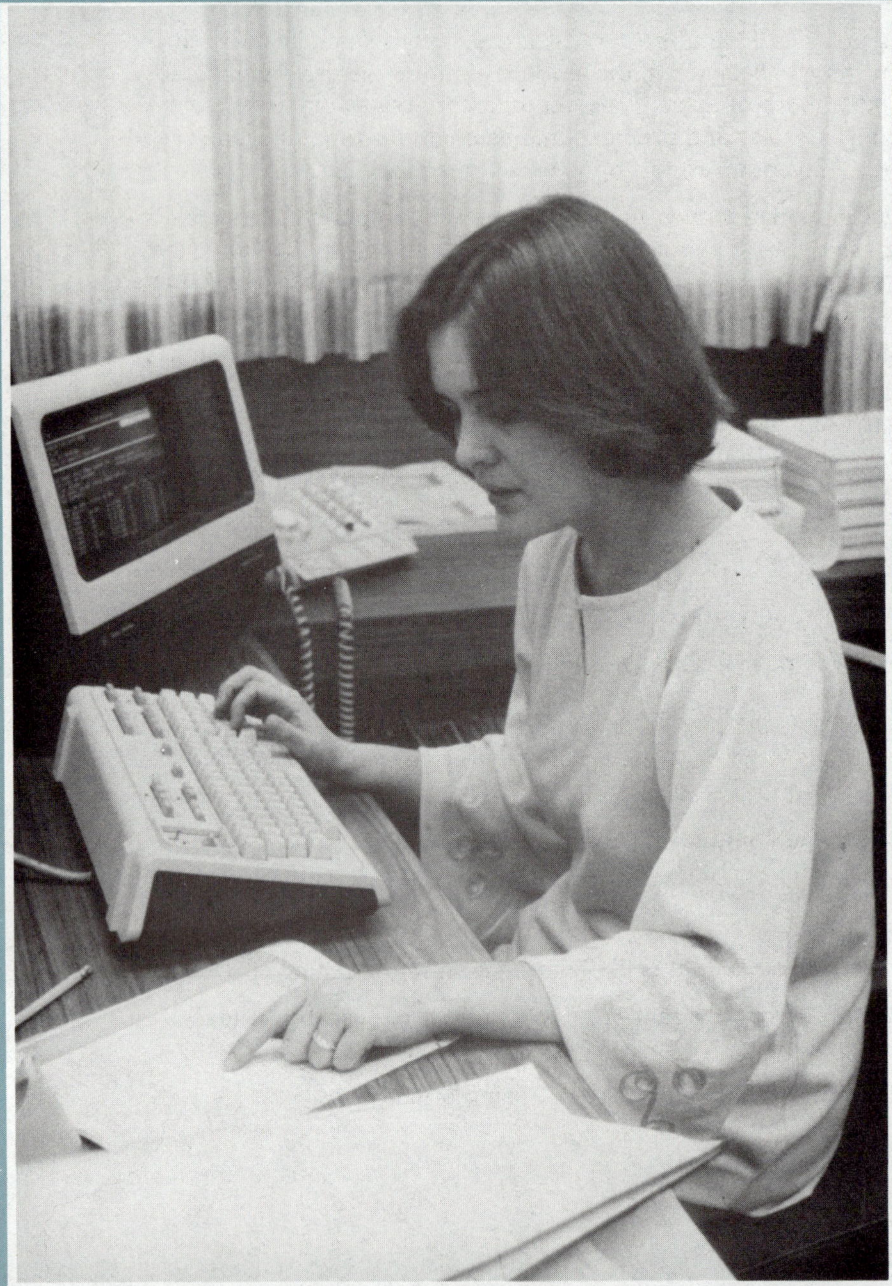

CHAPTER 3

SYSTEM ANALYSIS AND DESIGN

THE STEPS IN
SYSTEM ANALYSIS AND DESIGN

SYSTEM FLOWCHARTING

ALTERNATIVE WAYS OF PROCESSING DATA

THE RELATIONSHIPS
BETWEEN APPLICATIONS

EVALUATING ALTERNATIVES

Opposite: During a systems study, the systems analyst reviews the output from the current system.

A *system* is an assembly of methods, procedures, and techniques united by regulated interaction to form an organized whole. In effect, it is an organized collection of people, machines, and methods required to accomplish a set of specified objectives. At any time and for any number of reasons, a company may decide that all or part of its data processing system must be improved. It is the responsibility of the *systems analyst* to produce a detailed description of what the present system does and then to complete an analysis of the procedures, techniques, and methods employed in the part of the data processing system under review. This work is commonly referred to as a *system study*.

If the company is large, a systems analyst (or systems department) within the company may conduct the system study to decide what changes to make. A smaller company may hire a consultant or a consulting firm to perform the function. In either case, the objective is to develop a plan for a system that will provide maximum speed, accuracy, and useful management information at minimum cost.

THE STEPS IN SYSTEM ANALYSIS AND DESIGN

Several steps must be taken to revise or design a system once it has been recognized that there is a need to do so. These generalized steps include: (1) analysis of the present system; (2) analysis of the various data processing methods available; (3) design of a new data processing system, including its forms, records, reports, files, and processing methods; and finally, (4) determination of implementation procedures for the system.

The first task of the systems analyst is to analyze what is taking place in the existing system. This is not as easy as it may sound. A data processing system can involve many people in several departments, working with dozens of documents and a variety of machines, ranging from typewriters to computers. Furthermore, written descriptions of what takes place are often incomplete or nonexistent. In this case, the systems analyst must obtain information by interviewing the people who actually do the processing in each application being analyzed.

Interviews do not always yield the information that the systems analyst needs. People who are interviewed may forget to mention important steps or be too concerned about minor details. They sometimes include long descriptions about irrelevant matters. In some cases, even managers of departments are not in a position to explain how particular operations relate to the data processing system as a whole.

In addition to conducting interviews, the systems analyst studies all of the documents used in the present system. These may be manually or machine-produced. The analyst studies the steps used to create the documents, noting the interrelationship of data processing equipment, personnel, and documents.

SYSTEM FLOWCHARTING

The systems analyst uses a number of techniques in organizing the mass of information about an existing system and in planning a new one. One of these techniques is system flowcharting, the preparation of diagrams (called *system flowcharts*) that show the flow of data and the sequence of operations in a system. The set of symbols commonly used on system flowcharts is shown in Illustration 3-1.

There are several forms that a system flowchart may take. One form specifies the departments in which the operations take place. Illustration 3-2 is an example. It is a flowchart for an order-writing system. The symbol ⬜ represents a document; ⬜ represents a processing step (or operation); and ▽ represents a file. By studying this flowchart, one can determine what processing steps take place in preparing the shipping order, in what department each step takes place, where each document is sent, and what files are used.

Illustration 3-3 is an example of another form of system flowchart, showing the operations performed to produce a monthly sales report; it represents a system that uses a computer. The input is a deck of punched cards ⬜ that contains both customer cards and product cards. This deck is fed into the computer which then prepares the output document ⬜ in a processing step ⬜. After the processing step (**run**) is completed, the deck of input cards is separated △. The customer card and product cards are returned to their respective card files ▽.

One basic rule of flowcharting concerns direction. The sequence of data processing steps should proceed from top to bottom and from left to right. Arrowheads should be used on the lines connecting the symbols to indicate direction otherwise. In other words, one can assume that processing starts at the top (or left-hand corner) and goes down and to the right unless there are arrows that point up or to the left. This rule is especially important when designing or reading complex flowcharts.

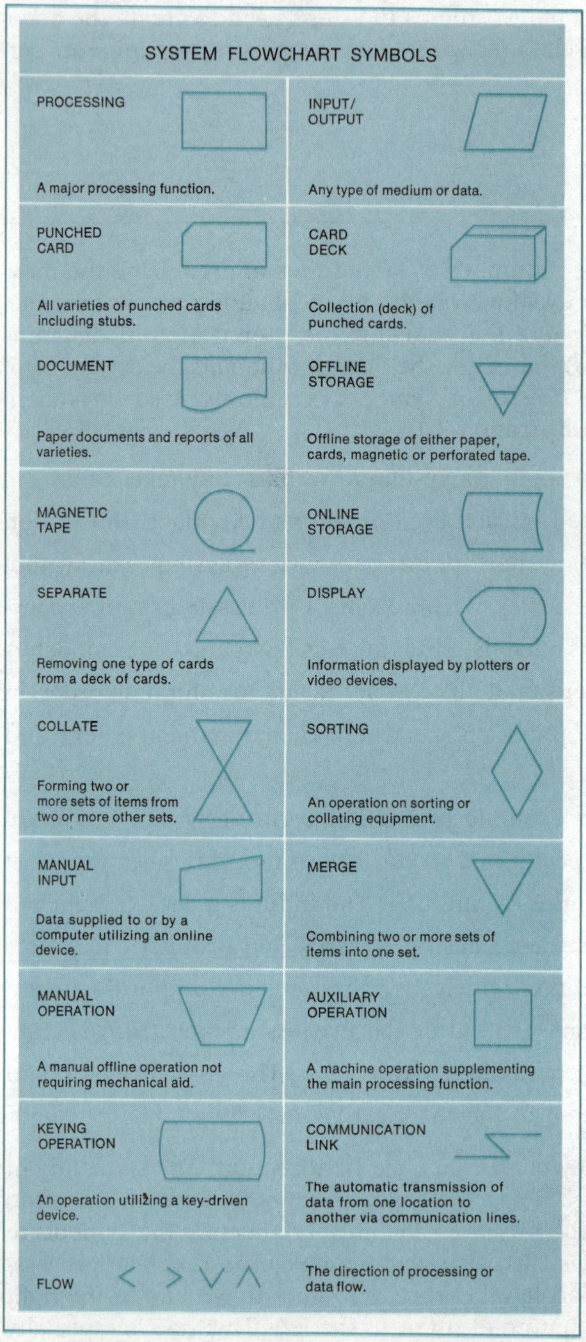

UNIT ONE: SOME FUNDAMENTALS OF DATA PROCESSING

SYSTEM FLOWCHART SYMBOLS

PROCESSING	A major processing function.
INPUT/OUTPUT	Any type of medium or data.
PUNCHED CARD	All varieties of punched cards including stubs.
CARD DECK	Collection (deck) of punched cards.
DOCUMENT	Paper documents and reports of all varieties.
OFFLINE STORAGE	Offline storage of either paper, cards, magnetic or perforated tape.
MAGNETIC TAPE	
ONLINE STORAGE	
SEPARATE	Removing one type of cards from a deck of cards.
DISPLAY	Information displayed by plotters or video devices.
COLLATE	Forming two or more sets of items from two or more other sets.
SORTING	An operation on sorting or collating equipment.
MANUAL INPUT	Data supplied to or by a computer utilizing an online device.
MERGE	Combining two or more sets of items into one set.
MANUAL OPERATION	A manual offline operation not requiring mechanical aid.
AUXILIARY OPERATION	A machine operation supplementing the main processing function.
KEYING OPERATION	An operation utilizing a key-driven device.
COMMUNICATION LINK	The automatic transmission of data from one location to another via communication lines.
FLOW	The direction of processing or data flow.

ILLUSTRATION 3-1 System flowchart symbols

CHAPTER 3: SYSTEM ANALYSIS AND DESIGN

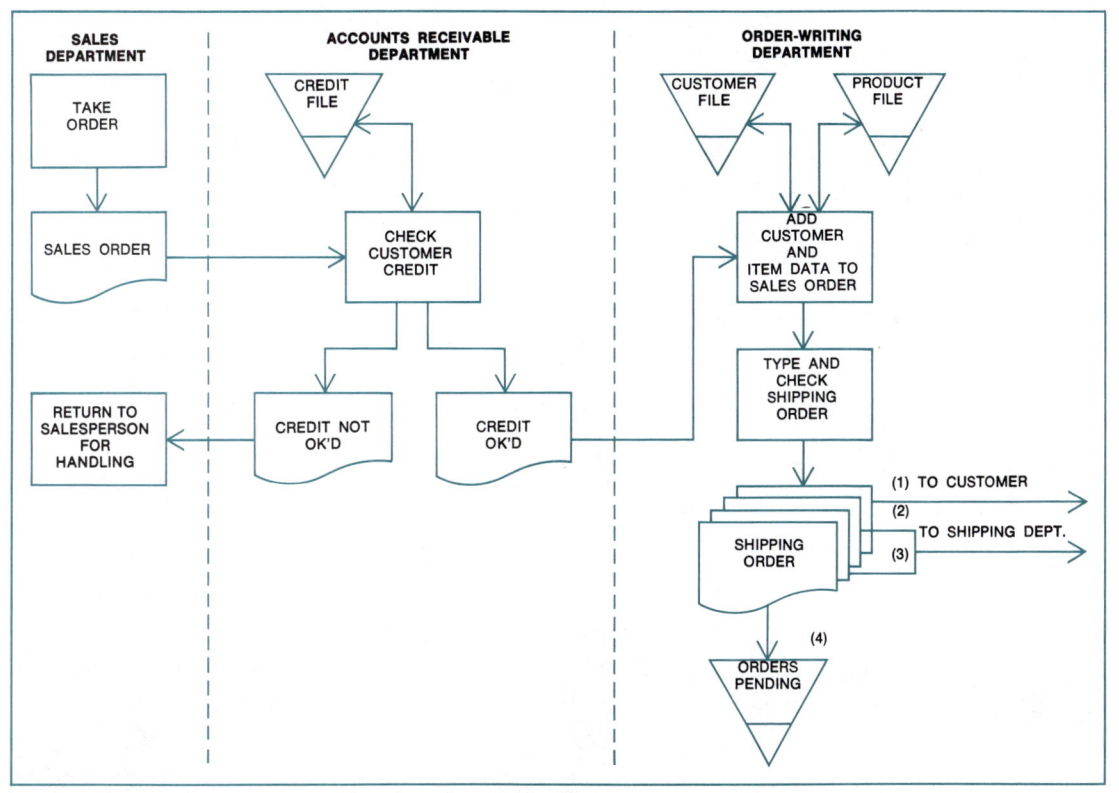

ILLUSTRATION 3-2 System flowchart for order writing

The value of a flowchart is that it represents, by use of symbols, relationships that are difficult to present in words. For example, it is easy enough to understand what a single clerical worker does in preparing a shipping order, but it is not always easy to visualize where that single clerical step fits into the sequence of an entire order-writing application. By preparing a flowchart like the one in Illustration 3-2, a systems analyst can show clearly that the application involves three departments, five separate clerical operations (the rectangles), and four different files (the triangles).

When the flowchart for a system is completed, the analyst can use it to analyze the relationships between the illustrated steps. The analyst can decide where errors might be taking place, whether or not some steps can be combined for greater efficiency, how interdepartment mailing can be reduced, and so on.

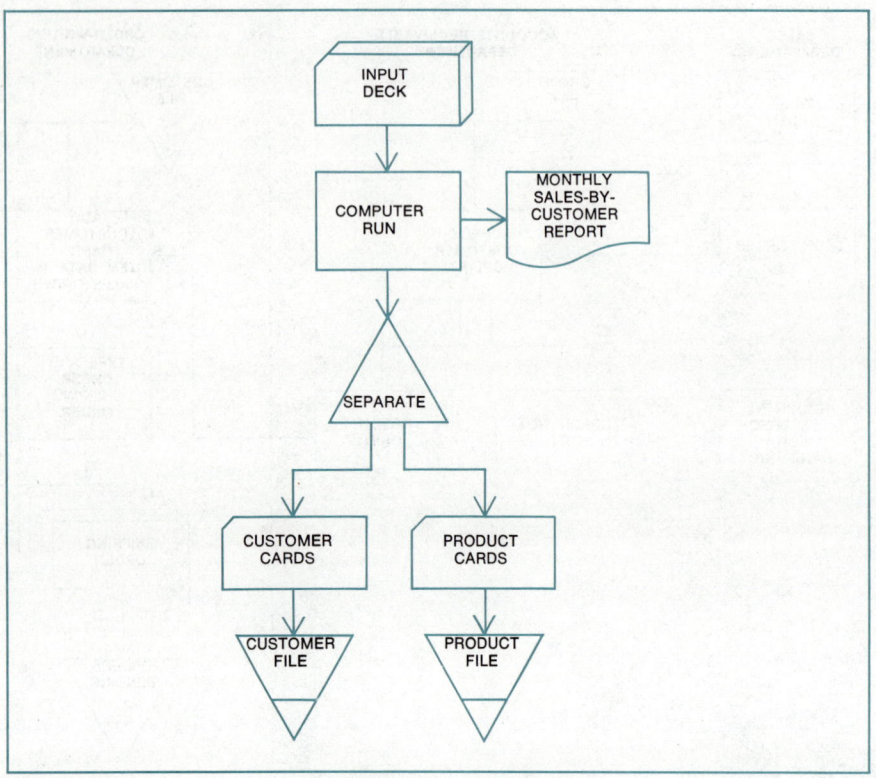

ILLUSTRATION 3-3 System flowchart for sales analysis

○ ALTERNATIVE WAYS OF PROCESSING DATA

Now the systems analyst is ready to tackle the problem of what equipment and procedures should be used in the new system. There are many different kinds of equipment that can be used in any application, and there are many different ways in which operations can be carried out. The analyst, therefore, has a large number of alternatives to choose from. Of course, many kinds of equipment can be immediately eliminated because of high cost or low capacity. A company that has gross monthly sales of $100,000 cannot afford a computer that rents for $5000 a month. A company that bills 10,000 items a day is not interested in a billing machine with a maximum capacity of 500 line items a day.

Even after satisfactory equipment is chosen, many alternative procedures must be considered. Can a checking step be eliminated without affecting the accuracy of the system? Can a procedure be improved by changing the sequence of steps? Can a processing step be simplified? Can the efficiency of a procedure be improved by combining steps? Because there are so many possible solutions to the problem of equipment and procedures, the systems analyst's job is a complex and continually challenging one.

THE RELATIONSHIPS BETWEEN APPLICATIONS

Another matter that concerns the systems analyst is the fact that applications in a business system are related. Because this is so, questions come up: Which applications in a family of applications should be analyzed? Should the systems analyst, in trying to improve the accuracy of a billing system, also consider the order-writing system? Should one also analyze the systems for accounts receivable and sales analysis? In fact, when considering any application, should one perhaps consider all related applications?

To analyze all applications every time one aspect of an application needs improvement is impractical. On the other hand, thinking in terms of only one specific improvement to only one specific application may be unjustifiably expensive.

Suppose the system flowchart in Illustration 3-4 represents a billing system that allows too many errors. The input to the system is the shipping order, after it has been used to pick the order and marked to show backorders and quantities shipped. The flowchart shows three processing steps: (1) the extensions and invoice totals are calculated and written on the shipping orders; (2) the arithmetic is checked; and (3) the invoices are typed. To pinpoint where errors are occurring, a number of shipping orders and corresponding invoices are studied. The study reveals that, although the calculations on the shipping orders are correct, errors frequently appear on the invoices. How can the accuracy of the system be improved?

By looking at the flowchart, the systems analyst can see that no checking is done to verify that the data on the invoice is typed correctly. This may indicate that one way to improve the system would be to add a comparison step after the typing of invoices. With this additional step, the data on the invoice could be compared with the shipping order. Any data that was not the same on both forms could be corrected. This solution is reasonable and probably would reduce the number of inaccurate invoices.

A better solution could perhaps be designed by thinking not only of the billing system but also of the order-writing system. For example, when the shipping order was prepared, one copy of it could be filed for later use

```
                    ┌─────────────┐
                    │ PICKER'S COPY│
                    │     OF      │
                    │  SHIPPING   │
                    │   ORDER     │
                    └──────┬──────┘
                           │       1
                           ▼
                    ┌─────────────┐
                    │  CALCULATE  │
                    │  EXTENSIONS │
                    │      &      │
                    │INVOICE TOTAL│
                    └──────┬──────┘
                           │       2
                           ▼
                    ┌─────────────┐
                    │    CHECK    │
                    │  ARITHMETIC │
                    └──────┬──────┘
                           │       3
                           ▼
                    ┌─────────────┐      ┌──────────┐
                    │ TYPE INVOICE│─────▶│ INVOICE  │
                    └─────────────┘      └──────────┘
```

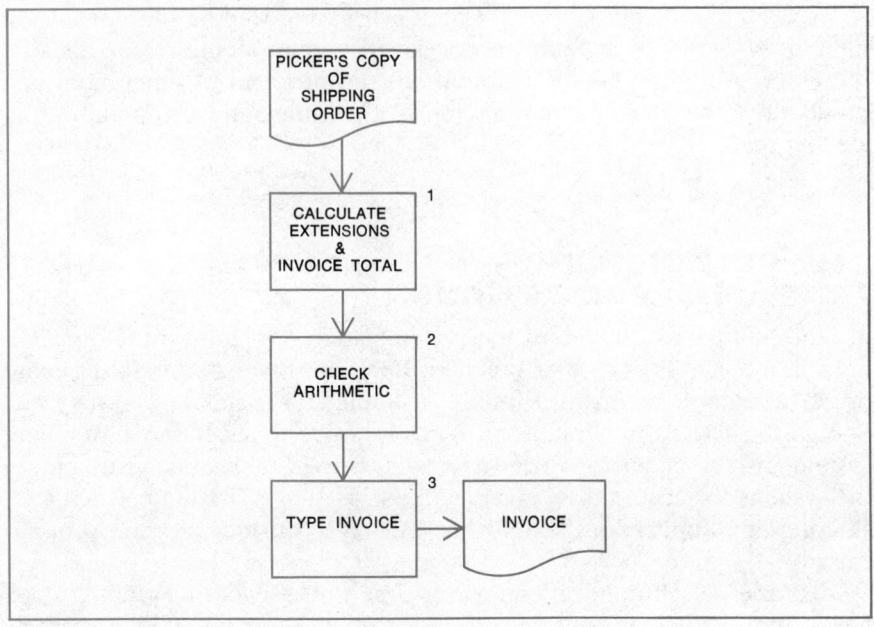

ILLUSTRATION 3-4 System flowchart for billing

as the invoice. By using a copy of the shipping order as the invoice, such data as customer name and address, quantities ordered, and item description would not have to be retyped when the invoice was prepared. Then, when the order picker's copies of shipping orders were returned from the shipping department, the billing procedures could take place as flowcharted in Illustration 3-5.

In steps 1 and 2, the extensions and invoice totals are calculated, written on the shipping orders, and checked. In step 3, the invoice copies of the shipping orders are pulled from the file. Since these copies already contain much information, only the quantities shipped and back-ordered, the extensions, and the invoice totals are typed from the shipping orders (step 4). This procedure reduces typing time and decreases the chance of error in the billing system. Then in step 5, only this typed information must be checked, again saving clerical time and reducing the chance of error.

This example is not intended to indicate that a systems analyst should always think in terms of more than one application. It simply illustrates one of the problems of system design. When starting a job, an analyst has to determine how much time can be allotted for system analysis and take as broad a view as possible within that limitation.

CHAPTER 3: SYSTEM ANALYSIS AND DESIGN

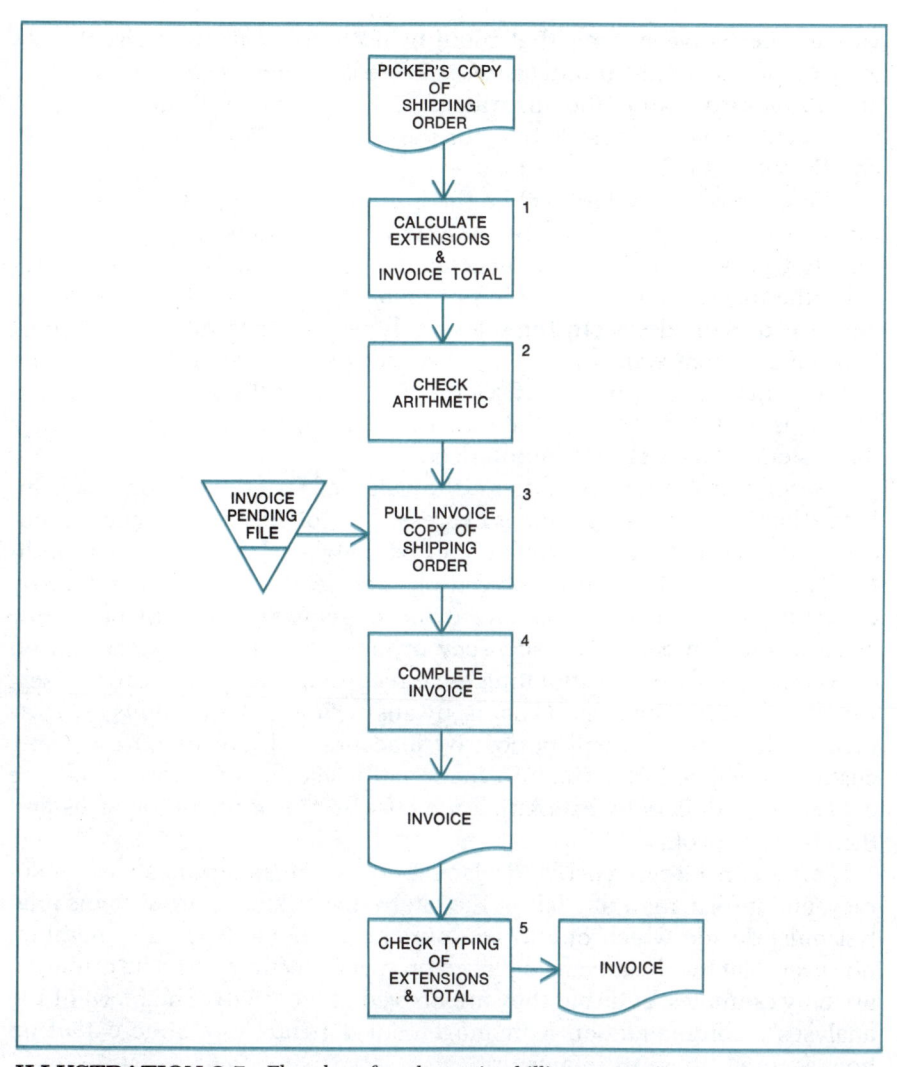

ILLUSTRATION 3-5 Flowchart for alternative billing system

○ EVALUATING ALTERNATIVES

After analyzing a business system by (1) using techniques such as flowcharting, (2) considering all varieties of equipment and procedures that could be used, and (3) taking into account the relationships between members of a family of applications, the systems analyst must evaluate the various alternative systems that could be used. All of them satisfy the objectives of the application; all vary in cost, speed, accuracy, and the amount of information they provide. The systems analyst's last job, then, is to decide which system is best for the company. This decision is influenced by two final considerations.

First, no single system will be the best in all respects. The most accurate one may not be the fastest. A system that is both fast and accurate may not provide sufficient management information. The one that provides the most usable information probably costs the most. A simple example is a manual system for sales analysis. For each additional report that management wants, additional procedures have to be designed. The result is that each report increases the total cost of the sales analysis system. This trade-off between the qualities of a system holds true whether the system is manual or computerized.

Second, it is hard to measure the value of speed, accuracy, and information. The cost of a system is expressed in dollars, but the speed, accuracy, and information of a system can be converted to dollars only indirectly. A dollar value can be placed on the speed of a billing system by estimating how much will be saved by reducing the amount of money owed to the company. The accuracy of an order-writing system can be converted to dollars by estimating the effect of accuracy on customer service and therefore on sales. (That is, by answering such questions as: How many dollars in sales will be lost by inaccurate shipments? How many customers will be lost?) The information of a sales analysis system can be converted to dollars by estimating the effect of information on sales and therefore on profits.

After considering cost, and placing dollar values on the speed, accuracy, and information of each of the alternative systems, the systems analyst must decide which one to recommend to management. Remember, however, that the dollar values placed on speed, accuracy, and information are only estimates, and that they are arrived at indirectly. The merit of the analyst's recommendation to management depends to a large extent on how accurate these estimates are.

○ SUMMARY

1. One of the first steps in system design is to analyze the system that is to be improved. This is often difficult because the system can consist of many people, many separate procedures, and many different kinds of equipment.

2. Flowcharting is a technique commonly used in system design and analysis. A system flowchart consists of symbols that represent the data flow and the operations performed. Flowcharts vary in form, depending on the purposes for which they are used, but all should be designed to be read from the top down and from left to right.

3. Many different kinds of equipment and procedures can be used in a business system. As a result, in designing a business system, the systems analyst has many alternatives from which to choose.

4. One of the major problems in designing a system is to determine how much of a family of applications should be analyzed. Since applications are related, it is often advantageous to look at the largest group of applications that can be analyzed in the time allotted to the project.

5. In choosing the best system from among a number of alternatives, a systems analyst assigns dollar values to the speed, accuracy, information, and cost of each alternative. This is difficult. It can be done by estimating the effect of each quality on operating costs and sales.

○ REVIEW QUESTIONS

1. What is the purpose of a system study?
2. List the basic steps necessary to design or revise a system.
3. Who is responsible for conducting a system study?
4. How can an existing system be analyzed?
5. In what ways might system flowcharts be used in conducting a system study?
6. Why is it important to consider the relationships between applications?
7. A system study may identify several alternative systems that could be used. What factors should be considered when determining which of these alternative systems is best for a company?

CAREER PROFILE

Eleanor Y. Gomez
Senior Systems Analyst
American Broadcasting Company

Background Experience

My career path was not a direct route! I dropped out of college, worked for several years, and got married. I returned to college to complete my undergraduate degree in Anthropology with a minor in Computer Science from California State University at Dominguez Hills. I completed the course work for an M.S. degree in Behavioral Science while working part-time for a software company specializing in financial applications. After deciding I wanted a career in the computer field, I completed a concentrated computer course at the Urban League Training Center. I then worked as a systems engineer for a computer vendor, selling, installing, and servicing computer systems. Among my accounts were two publishing companies: Los Angeles Magazine and National Insurance Law Service (NILS), both owned by American Broadcasting Company, where I now work.

Primary Job Responsibilities

As senior systems analyst, I am responsible for providing computer services and support for the two publishing companies. This includes doing system design and writing program specifications for various data processing applications. Both publishers have financial applications packages and subscription/billing programs; one also uses word processing applications. For example, as typesetting operations at NILS become computerized, I anticipate new challenges in helping users to convert to online composition for books, newsletters, and other publications.

About 80% of my job involves interpersonal skills. I see my role as one of helping others to understand what the computer can do to make their jobs easier and more effective. I work with all levels of management, including the president. This usually surprises people who think jobs in data processing are all technical or mathematical.

What Has Made You Successful?

Success is a state of mind—you have to decide you are going to be successful, and then do the work that prepares you to come through for your clients or supervisor. You have to be prepared to work long hours—especially getting oriented and organized for a new job. Luck is important, but you have to create your own luck by telling people what you want. Otherwise, most of the time you won't get it.

UNIT TWO

COMPUTER SYSTEMS

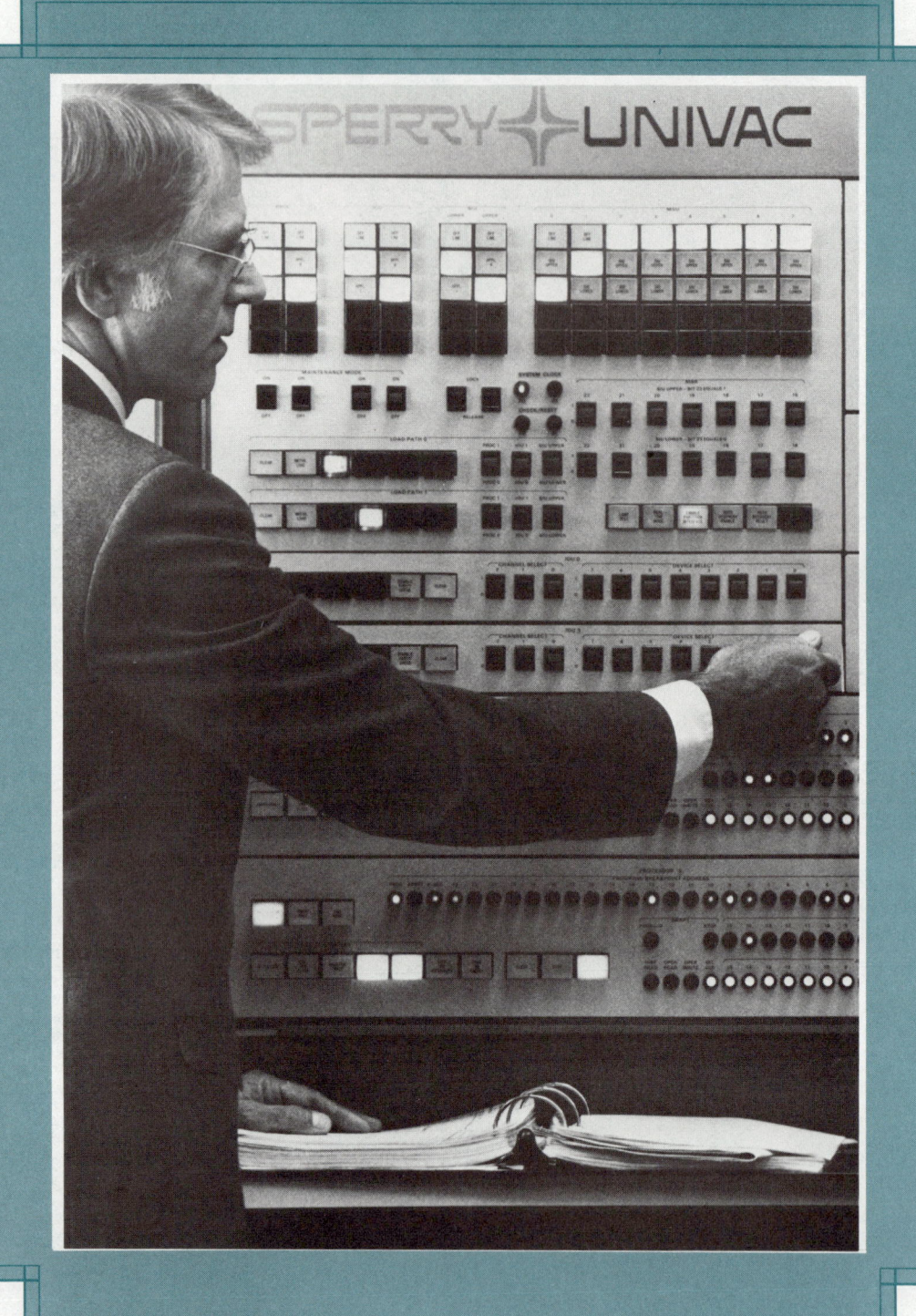
SPERRY UNIVAC

CHAPTER 4

INTRODUCTION TO COMPUTER SYSTEMS

THE EVOLUTION OF THE COMPUTER
Charles Babbage's Analytical Engine
The Mark I Computer
The ENIAC
The EDVAC

COMPUTER GENERATIONS

AN OVERVIEW OF COMPUTER SYSTEMS

A COMPARISON OF HUMAN
AND COMPUTER CAPABILITIES

Opposite: A computer console control panel is used by service personnel to perform maintenance functions.

As discussed in the preceding chapters, the processing of data is not a recent development. Rather, people have processed data, in an attempt to obtain timely and relevant information, for hundreds of years. What has changed is the means by which data is processed into information. Specifically, both organizations and individuals have continued to develop means by which data can be processed into information much faster and with greater reliability and accuracy.

THE EVOLUTION OF THE COMPUTER

Charles Babbage's Analytical Engine

The first major step in the evolution of the computer was taken by Charles Babbage, a professor of mathematics at Cambridge University in England. In 1830, Babbage began to design and build what was to be the first completely automatic, general-purpose, ***digital computer*** (a machine with characteristics explained more fully in the next chapter). He named this computer the "analytical engine" to reflect the fact that it was to be able to perform mathematical calculations on numbers in a storage unit within it. The arithmetic and storage units of the machine were to be governed by a control unit that coordinated and supervised the sequence of operations.

Babbage continued to work on the analytical engine until his death in 1871. Because his idea was beyond the technical capabilities at that time, he was not able to complete the engine; nevertheless, he must be given credit for having the foresight to design and attempt to build a machine that was approximately 100 years ahead of its time. Babbage is considered one of the great pioneers in the field of computation.

The Mark I Computer

After Babbage's death, no significant progress was made in the development of automatic computation until 1937. Professor Howard Aiken of Harvard University began to build an automatic calculating machine that would combine the technical capabilities of that time with the punched-card concepts developed by Hollerith and Powers (see Chapter 2). During the next several years, Aiken, with the assistance of graduate students and IBM engineers, worked on building the machine. In 1944 the project was completed. A machine known as the Mark I was formally presented to Harvard University. (See Illustration 4-1.)

The Mark I is considered to be the first successful general-purpose, digital computer. The machine was based on the concepts of accepting data from punched cards as input, making calculations by means of automatically controlled electromagnetic relays and mechanical arithmetic counters, and punching the results into cards. Thus, the Mark I was an *electromechanical computer.*

The Mark I was the first machine capable of solving various types of scientific-oriented problems and performing long series of arithmetic and logical operations. Each sequence of calculations was controlled by a punched paper tape. In many respects, the Mark I was the realization of Babbage's dream. Compared with modern computers, it operated quite slowly.

The ENIAC

The first *electronic digital computer* was designed and built in the early 1940s at the University of Pennsylvania's Moore School of Electrical Engineering. The project to design and build the computer was the result of a contract between the University of Pennsylvania and the United States government.

ILLUSTRATION 4-1   The Mark I computer

The team of John W. Mauchly and J. Presper Eckert, Jr. was responsible for the construction of the computer. They named it the Electronic Numerical Integrator and Calculator (ENIAC). The ENIAC was completely electronic in that none of its parts moved during the processing of data.

The ENIAC cost several million dollars to build, weighed approximately 30 tons, took up approximately 1500 square feet of floor space, and used 18,000 vacuum tubes instead of electromagnetic relays as were used in the Mark I. The fastest electromechanical machine of the time could perform only one multiplication per second. With the replacement of the slow electromagnetic relays by vacuum tubes, the ENIAC could perform 300 multiplications per second. It could do in one day what would have taken 300 days to do manually. When completed, the ENIAC was installed at the Aberdeen Proving Grounds in Maryland. In 1956, it was placed in the Smithsonian Institution because of its historical significance.

In 1946, John von Neumann, a well-known mathematician from the Institute for Advanced Study at Princeton University, became acquainted with the work of Mauchly and Eckert at the Moore School of Electrical Engineering. He wrote a paper in which he described the basic philosophy of computer design for the group of people connected with the ENIAC project at the Moore School of Electrical Engineering. Almost everything concerning computer design that von Neumann discussed in his paper has been incorporated in modern computers. Thus, it is often stated that the basis for the design of computers is the "von Neumann concept."

The EDVAC

The computer design considerations presented by von Neumann in his paper came too late to be incorporated in the ENIAC. However, with these design considerations as a basis, Mauchly, Eckert, and others at the Moore School of Electrical Engineering began to build the Electronic Discrete Variable Automatic Computer (EDVAC). Although the design of the EDVAC actually began prior to completion of the ENIAC, EDVAC was not completed until 1952.

EDVAC was smaller than either the Mark I or the ENIAC, but it had greater capability. Two design features that distinguished the EDVAC from the ENIAC were the use of binary numbers instead of mechanical arithmetic counters and the internal storage of instructions in digital form. (These design features are discussed in the next chapter.)

Up to this time, primary emphasis was placed on building computers for use on projects of a *scientific* nature. In 1946, Eckert and Mauchly founded the Eckert-Mauchly Computer Corporation to build computers for *commercial* use. The computers were to be *business-oriented*—designed primarily to process business data. The diversion of their attention to this company was one of the reasons why EDVAC was not completed until 1952. During these years, the Electronic Delayed Storage Automatic Computer (EDSAC) was built at Cambridge University in England. Completed in 1949, the EDSAC was the first **stored-program electronic digital computer**. (As above, this design feature is discussed in the next chapter.)

○ COMPUTER GENERATIONS

Generally, computer systems have been classified as belonging to specific "generations." The implication of the term *generation* is that a significant change in the design of a computer distinguishes it from computers classified as members of a preceding generation. The ***first generation*** of computers extended from 1951 to 1959. The computers of this generation were large, bulky machines characterized by the use of vacuum tubes. (See Illustration 4-2.)

The UNIVersal Automatic Computer (UNIVAC) I was the first commercially available computer (see Illustration 4-3). That is, the UNIVAC I was the first computer built with the assumption that several computers of the same type would be built and sold. Until the development of the UNIVAC I, computers were one of a kind.

The UNIVAC I was built by the company founded in 1946 by Eckert and Mauchly. The company became a subsidiary of Remington Rand in 1949. This subsidiary later became the Sperry Univac division of Sperry Rand Corporation.

The first UNIVAC I computer was installed at the United States Bureau of Census in 1951. The computer was used by the Bureau of Census until 1963, when it was classified as obsolete and placed in the Smithsonian Institution because of its historical significance.

In 1954, the first UNIVAC I acquired for business data processing was installed at General Electric's Appliance Park in Louisville, Kentucky. The introduction of the computer to business opened a new field and is the major factor behind the growth of the computer industry.

In 1953, IBM, which had not been particularly active in the development of computers, entered the computer field with the business-oriented IBM 701 computer. This computer was followed in late 1954 by the IBM 650 computer (see Illustration 4-4). The IBM 650, like the 701, was business-oriented. It was the most popular computer between 1954 and 1959. As a result of the popularity of the computer, IBM obtained a dominant position in the computer field. Since that time, the company has retained its position.

The ***second generation*** of computers extended from 1959 to 1964. The computers of this generation were characterized by the use of transistors

UNIT TWO: COMPUTER SYSTEMS

Computer Type	Date Delivered	Features
Mark I	1944	First successful general-purpose, digital, electromechanical computer
ENIAC	1946	First electronic digital computer; programmed by manual setting of switches
EDSAC	1949	Electronic digital computer; instructions (program) were stored in the computer
EDVAC	1952	First computer designed for the use of binary numbers and the internal storage of instructions in digital form
First Generation	1951-1959	Used vacuum tubes for the storage of data; large bulky machines
Second Generation	1959-1964	Used transistors for the storage of data; smaller machines requiring less power to operate; more reliable
Third Generation	1965—	Use miniaturized circuits (magnetic cores) for the storage of data; integration of hardware with software; data communication capability; capability to perform several operations simultaneously
Third + Generation	1971—	Increased miniaturization of circuits (semiconductors) for the storage of data; greater integration of hardware with software

ILLUSTRATION 4-2 The history of computers

CHAPTER 4: INTRODUCTION TO COMPUTER SYSTEMS

ILLUSTRATION 4-3   The UNIVAC I computer

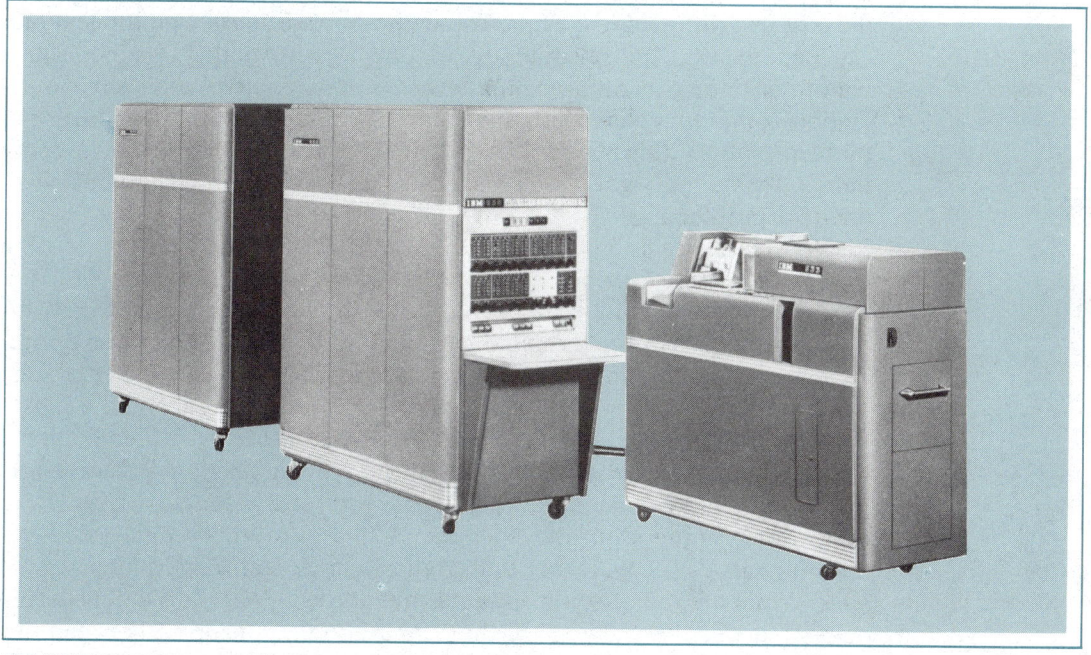

ILLUSTRATION 4-4   The IBM 650 computer

instead of vacuum tubes. The basis for changing from vacuum tubes to transistors was that transistors are smaller, less expensive, generate almost no heat, and require little power. Thus, second-generation computers were substantially smaller, required less power to operate, and were more reliable than first-generation computers. As in the first generation, a particular computer of the second generation was designed to process either scientific-oriented or business-oriented problems. For example, the most popular business-oriented computer was the IBM 1401; the most popular scientific-oriented computers were the IBM 1620 and the IBM 7090–7094 series.

The *third generation* of computers began in 1965, when IBM first delivered its System/360 computers. The computers of this generation are characterized by (1) miniaturized circuits, which further reduced the physical size of computers and increased their processing speed, reliability, and accuracy, (2) the integration of hardware with software (these terms are explained in the next chapter), (3) data communication capability (this term is discussed in Chapter 14), and (4) the capability to perform several operations simultaneously. Also, the prices of third-generation equipment are generally lower than those of comparable second-generation equipment. (The price of computers relative to performance has decreased an average of 20 percent per year since the UNIVAC I. For example, in 1952 it cost $1.26 to do 100,000 multiplications. By 1958 the cost had dropped to 26 cents, and by 1964 the cost was down to 12 cents. By 1970 the cost had dropped to 5 cents. Today those same 100,000 multiplications can be executed for seven-tenths of one cent.) Another distinguishing feature of third-generation computers is that while first- and second-generation computers were designed to process either scientific or business problems, most third-generation computers are general-purpose computers. They are designed to process both scientific-oriented and business-oriented problems.

Most individuals believe that computer systems introduced since 1971 should be classified as belonging to the *third+ generation*. The basis for this belief is a recognition that several evolutionary—in contrast to revolutionary—changes in the design of computers have occurred. These design changes involve the increased miniaturization of circuits and the greater integration of hardware with software.

There is general agreement on the distinguishing features of first-, second-, and third-generation computers. The distinction is based primarily on circuitry—vacuum tubes, transistors, and magnetic cores. However, the computers introduced since 1971 are improved and enhanced (evolutionary) systems rather than radically different (revolutionary) systems. While the use of semiconductor memories in 1971 was a new development, it was not a change of the magnitude that occurred between the first three generations of computers. Rather, semiconductor memories are an extension of third-generation circuitry.

Two results of the evolutionary changes are that (1) while a first-generation computer could perform 2000 multiplications per second, today a computer can perform 239,000 multiplications per second, and (2) while 400 cubic feet of physical space were required to store one million characters in first-generation computers, today's computer requires only three-tenths of a cubic foot to store one million characters.

AN OVERVIEW OF COMPUTER SYSTEMS

In one sense, a computer system is like any other data processing system. It takes input, processes it, and provides output. In other ways, a computer system is quite different from other data processing systems. For example, data is processed electronically, rather than manually, mechanically, or electromechanically. As noted in Chapter 1, computer systems are often called electronic data processing (EDP) systems.

The machines usually included in a basic computer system are a card reader, a computer, and a printer. A card reader reads data stored on punched cards; a computer processes the data; and a printer prints the results. A larger system may also include magnetic tape units and magnetic disk units, which are used to store data. (A computer system with all of these machines is shown in Illustration 4-5.) In addition to these machines, a variety of other machines can be used. The basic factor determining which machines are appropriate is the data processing required.

Although the machines in a computer system are developed as separate units, they are connected prior to operation of the system. Each of the input and output machines is attached to the computer by means of electric cables. When a card reader reads a punched card, the data is transferred to the computer. Similarly, after the computer has processed the data, the results are transferred from the computer to the printer to be printed out. Thus, the components of a computer system work together.

A COMPARISON OF HUMAN AND COMPUTER CAPABILITIES

Although humans have the ability to do anything a computer can do, the reverse is not true—a computer cannot do everything a human can do. A computer has two basic capabilities. First, it is extremely fast. Its speed is reflected in its capability to execute instructions in *nanoseconds*, or billionths of a second. Second, it is almost perfect in reliability and accuracy.

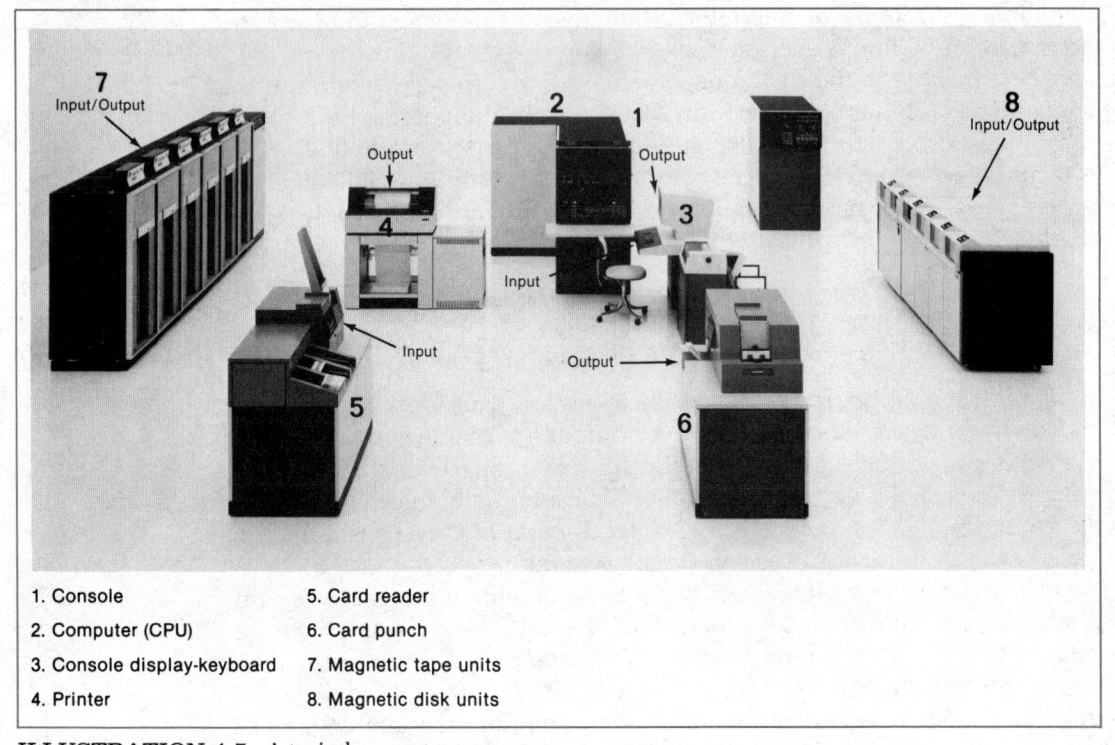

1. Console
2. Computer (CPU)
3. Console display-keyboard
4. Printer
5. Card reader
6. Card punch
7. Magnetic tape units
8. Magnetic disk units

ILLUSTRATION 4-5 A typical computer system

Studies of error rates indicate that, on an average, a computer makes one error per 1.25 million characters in processing data. A human is at a disadvantage when compared with the computer as a data processor. The human is slow and not completely accurate. Studies of error rates indicate that, on the average, a typist or clerk makes one error per 1000 characters in processing data.

Humans have two advantages over a computer. First, they can innovate or adapt during the process of solving a problem. Thus, they do not require a set of instructions that anticipates beforehand everything that may happen during the problem-solving process. They have the ability to relate the current situation to preceding ones and act accordingly.

Second, humans can reason heuristically. That is, they can learn by trial and error. Rather than solve a problem in a step-by-step manner, humans often make decisions based on incomplete information and the effect of past experiences. Humans are aware of their environment, and learning from past experiences is available to them. A computer has only the information that a stored program has made available to it.

CHAPTER 4: INTRODUCTION TO COMPUTER SYSTEMS

A human is best suited to think, reason, and discover; a computer is best adapted to calculate, manipulate, and compare. Thus, the computer can extend the power of the human being.

○ SUMMARY

1. The first major steps toward the development of an automatic, general-purpose, digital computer can be traced back to the work of Charles Babbage in 1830.

2. The first working model of a general-purpose, digital computer (the Mark I) was completed by Howard Aiken in 1937. It utilized the punched-card concepts of Hollerith and Powers, and it functioned by a series of electromagnetic relays and mechanical arithmetic counters. It was a scientific-oriented machine capable of performing long series of arithmetic and logical operations.

3. The ENIAC was the first electronic digital computer. Developed by John W. Mauchly and J. Presper Eckert, Jr. in the early 1940s, it used vacuum tubes and was able to do 300 multiplications per second.

4. The EDVAC, also developed by Mauchly and Eckert, employed the basic design philosophy described by John von Neumann in 1946. Known later as the "von Neumann concept," it proposed the use of binary numbers and the internal storage of instructions in digital form.

5. The UNIVAC I was the first commercially available computer. Its introduction was followed by the entrance of IBM into the computer field with the IBM 701 computer.

6. Computers can be classified by generations—each generation separated from the previous one by significant changes in the design of the computer. The first generation was characterized by the use of vacuum tubes; the second by the use of transistors; the third by miniaturized circuits and significantly enhanced functional capabilities; and the third+ by the increased miniaturization of circuits and the greater integration of hardware with software.

7. The computer has two advantages over humans—it is extremely fast and almost perfect in reliability and accuracy. Humans have two disadvantages and two advantages over the computer—they are slow and not completely accurate as data processors, but they can innovate or adapt and they can reason heuristically.

REVIEW QUESTIONS

1. Charles Babbage attempted to build a machine employing the concepts now used in computers. What was this machine called and why was it never built?

2. What was the first successful general-purpose, digital computer? How did this machine differ from first-generation computers?

3. What were the significant contributions and differences between the ENIAC and the EDVAC?

4. What was the significance of first-generation computers and what important contributions did they make in the data-processing field?

5. What was the significance of second-generation computers and how did they differ from first- and third-generation computers?

6. Compare and contrast human capabilities and limitations with those of computers.

CAREER PROFILE

Mary Ann Vargas
Computer Operations Supervisor
International Diamond Company

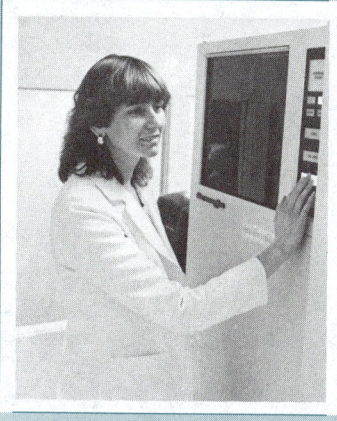

Background Experience

I started working in data processing operations at International Diamond about two years ago. Before joining International Diamond, I worked in accounting at another company. I dealt with data processing input and output, but my job was not a data processing job. I started here in the accounting department. At the time, the data processing department was expanding computer operations. I had some knowledge of data processing because I had taken several data processing courses while studying accounting at a community college. The data processing manager asked whether or not I would be interested in transferring to his department to learn computer operations. It appeared to be a great career opportunity for me, so I agreed to do so.

The company had a Hewlett-Packard 3000 computer that I had to learn to operate. My training has been primarily on the job. I have read all of the manuals about the computer system. The computer was fairly easy to operate, but it took me awhile to learn all of the applications. After working two years as a computer operator, I was promoted to my present job as supervisor of computer operations.

Primary Job Responsibilities

As the supervisor of computer operations, I must keep the computer operational 24 hours a day and insure that reports are produced on time. We have from 40 to 50 terminals, both here and at remote locations, from which users may require access to the computer at any time. Each user enters data through a terminal and requests the execution of a particular job.

I may reschedule some of the execution requests based on the estimated times to complete and on how important it is to complete a particular job by a given time. Much of my time is spent in setting priorities for running production reports and in insuring that users get the reports when needed. One of my more difficult tasks is supervising the operators who work the evening and night shifts. Because I seldom see these operators, I must rely primarily on written instructions. I am on call 24 hours a day to assist the operators if a system problem occurs or a written instruction needs clarification.

What Has Made You Successful?

For me, being successful in my career stems from a combination of determination, education, and willingness to spend the time necessary to learn a new job. I have spent a great deal of my own time studying computer manuals to learn more about our computer. My accounting experience and education have been very helpful. I believe that continuing my education is important to further advancement.

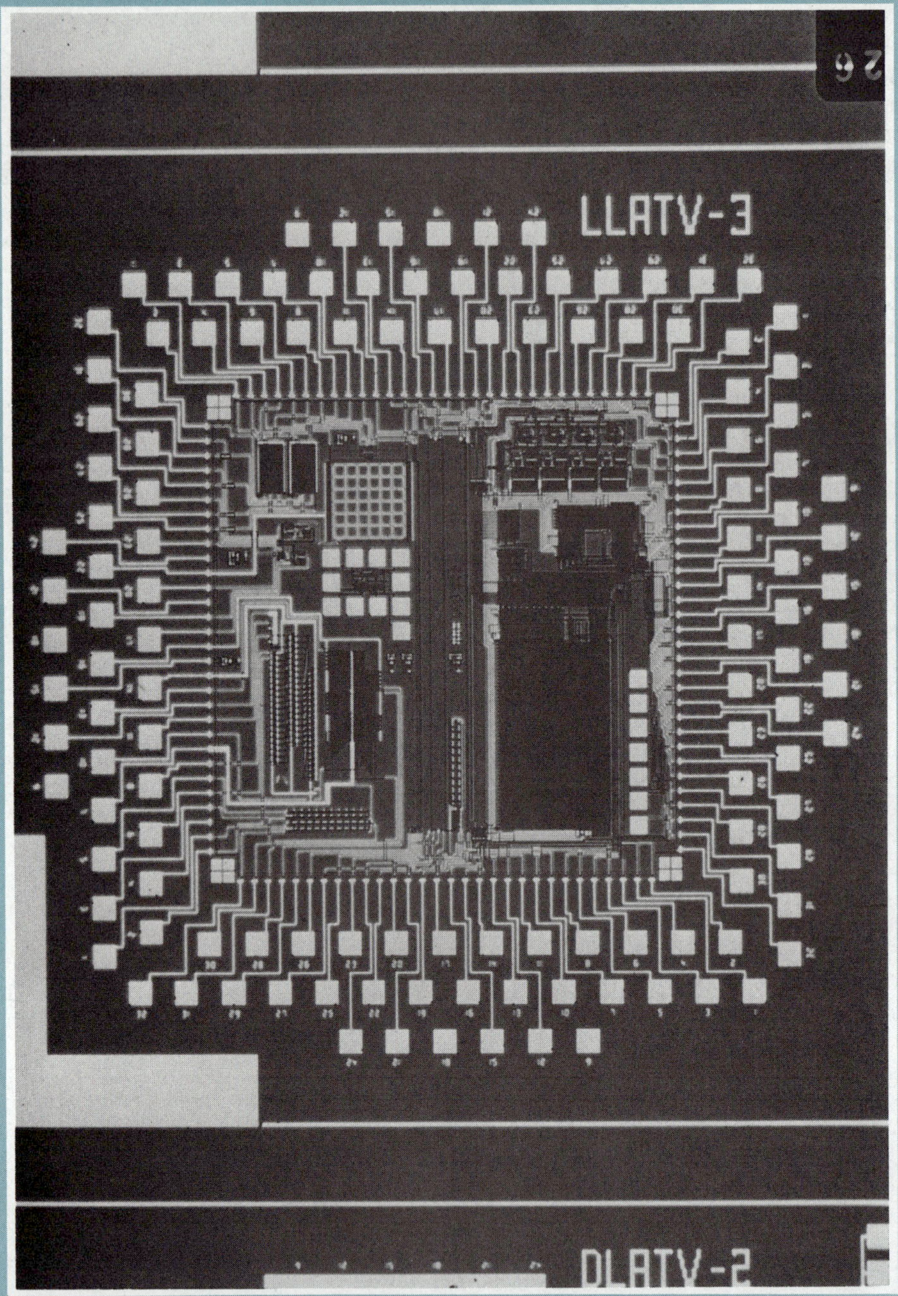
LLATV-3
DLATV-2

CHAPTER 5

COMPUTER CONCEPTS

THE CLASSIFICATION OF COMPUTERS
Analog and Digital Computers
Hybrid Computers
Special-Purpose and General-Purpose Computers

THE COMPONENTS OF A COMPUTER SYSTEM
Hardware
System Software
Application Software
Procedures
Data Processing Personnel

BINARY REPRESENTATION OF DATA
Magnetic Cores
Semiconductors
Magnetic Bubbles
Binary Codes
Parity Bits

HEXADECIMAL REPRESENTATION

THE EXECUTION OF PROGRAM STATEMENTS

Opposite: Experimental silicon chip $\frac{1}{6}''$ square that can contain 30,000 bytes of storage in the large rectangular area.

The evolution and general nature of the modern computer system were discussed in the preceding chapter. In fact, the term *computer* has been used several times in this book, but it has not been defined. Before the details of the computer are discussed, the key implications of this term should be pointed out.

The term *computer*, while applicable to any machine capable of arithmetic calculation, generally implies a machine with certain characteristics:

- ***Electronic.*** Achieves its results through the movement of electronic impulses rather than the physical movement of internal parts.
- ***Internal storage.*** Has the ability to simultaneously store programs and data. This ability enables the computer to consecutively execute program statements at a high rate of speed.
- ***Stored program.*** Follows a series of **statements** (also called **instructions**) in its internal storage. These instruct it in detail as to both the specific operations to perform and the order in which to perform them.
- ***Program-execution modification.*** Can change the course of the execution of program statements (***branch***) because of a decision based on data in its internal storage and/or the results of one or more arithmetic or logical operations.

In summary, a computer is an electronic machine possessing internal storage capabilities, a stored program of instructions, and the capability of modifying the course of execution of the instructions during processing.

○ THE CLASSIFICATION OF COMPUTERS

There are many useful ways in which computers can be classified. Among these are: (1) by the type of data they are capable of manipulating (digital or analog), (2) as a mixture of data-handling types (hybrid), and (3) by the purpose for which they were designed (special-purpose or general-purpose).

Analog and Digital Computers

There are two main types of computers: digital and analog. A ***digital computer*** operates directly on digits that represent either discrete data elements or symbols. It takes input and gives output in the form of numbers, letters, and special characters represented by holes in punched cards, magnetized areas on tapes, printing on paper, and so on. This is the type of computer most commonly thought of and referred to when the word *computer* is used either by itself or in context.

Digital computers are generally used for business and scientific data processing. Depending upon the particular characteristics of the digital computer and the precision of the data it is processing, the digital computer is capable of achieving varying degrees of accuracy in both intermediate and final results. Digital computers are the most widely used type of computers in business. Thus, unless stated otherwise, the discussion of computers in this book concerns digital computers.

An *analog computer*, in contrast to a digital computer, measures continuous electrical or physical magnitudes; it does not operate on digits. If digits are involved at all, they are obtained indirectly. Factors such as current, length, pressure, temperature, shaft rotation, and voltage are directly measured. The output of an analog computer is often an adjustment to the control of a machine. For instance, an analog computer may adjust a valve to control the flow of fluid through a pipe, or it may adjust a temperature setting to control the temperature in an oven. For these reasons, analog computers are often used for controlling processes such as oil refining and baking. Digital computers can also be used for controlling processes. To do so, they must convert analog data to digital form, process it, and then convert the digital results to analog form. A digital computer possesses greater accuracy than an analog computer, but the analog computer can process data faster than a digital computer.

Hybrid Computers

While digital and analog computers are the most extensively used types of computers in business, in certain situations (e.g., to simulate a guided missile system or a new aircraft design), a computer that combines the most desirable features of both is employed. A computer of this nature is referred to as a **hybrid computer**. Two major features incorporated into a hybrid computer that make it especially suitable for certain types of business problems are the ability to solve problems faster than digital computers with greater accuracy than analog computers.

Special-Purpose and General-Purpose Computers

Digital computers may be designed for either special or general uses. A *special-purpose computer*, as the name implies, is designed for a specific operation. It usually solves a particular type of problem. While a special-purpose computer may incorporate many of the features of a general-purpose machine, its applicability to a particular problem is a function of its design rather than of a stored program; the instructions that control it are built into the machine. This "specializing" of the machine leads to efficient, effective performance of a specific operation. One consequence of this specialization, however, is that the machine lacks versatility. That is, it cannot be used to perform other operations. For example, the special-purpose computers designed for the sole purpose of controlling a petroleum refinery cannot be used for other purposes without making major changes to the computers.

A *general-purpose computer*, as the name implies, is designed to perform a variety of operations. This capability is a result of its ability to store different programs of instructions in its internal storage. Unfortunately, the ability to perform a variety of operations is often achieved at the expense of certain aspects of speed and efficiency of performance. In most situations, the computer's flexibility, with respect to its being able to perform a variety of operations, makes this compromise an acceptable one.

THE COMPONENTS OF A COMPUTER SYSTEM

A computer system is composed of (1) machines, which are referred to as *hardware*, (2) programs and operating aids referred to as *system software*, (3) other programs known as *application software*, (4) procedures, and (5) data processing personnel.

Thus, the term *computer system* refers to the machines; the software that causes the machines to function; the procedures required to prepare and process the data and distribute the results of the processing; and the people who keep the hardware, software, and procedures efficiently and effectively functioning. Each of these components is discussed below. The remainder of the chapter centers around (1) how program statements and data are represented in the storage unit of a computer, and (2) the execution of program statements.

Hardware

The hardware of a computer system can be classified according to the five basic functions that the equipment performs. These functions are preparation, input, manipulation, storage, and output of data. Their typical relationships are shown in Illustration 5-1. (All of the input and output devices mentioned in the following paragraphs are discussed in Chapters 6, 7, and 8 and Module A.)

Data-preparation devices. Before data is transferred to a computer, it is usually transferred from source documents to an *input medium* that an input device can read. The most common input medium is the punched card. Consequently, the most common data-preparation device is the card punch. Because data preparation is time-consuming and expensive, how-

CHAPTER 5: COMPUTER CONCEPTS

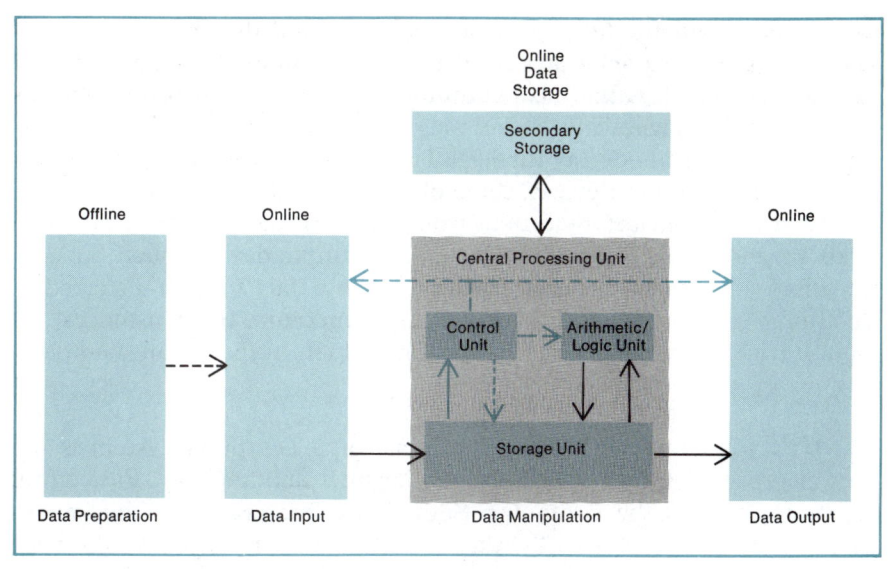

ILLUSTRATION 5-1 The five equipment functions in a computer system

ever, there is a trend toward elimination of this function by either encoding the data on the source document for direct input to the computer or creating device-readable input as a by-product during the process of creating the source document. For example, the bills mailed to customers by many utility companies are punched cards. The amount of a customer's bill and the information needed to process the account are punched into a card. Thus, the source document serves both as a bill and as a direct input medium to the computer. The direct input of data to the computer from an input device such as a console display-keyboard used as a terminal also eliminates the data-preparation function.

The broken arrow connecting the data-preparation function and the input function in Illustration 5-1 reflects the fact that all machines used during the data-preparation function are *offline* to the computer. Machines that are offline to the computer are not in direct communication with it; therefore, the computer cannot receive data directly from these machines. In contrast, the input devices and output devices are *online* to the computer, that is, in direct communication with it. Therefore, the computer can receive data directly from these machines. (The concepts "online" and "offline" are discussed more fully in Chapter 14.)

Input devices. A computer must receive both program statements and data to solve problems. The entry of program statements and data into a computer occurs by means of an input device, such as a card reader. A card reader reads the holes punched in cards, and the characters represented by the holes are transferred to the computer. In addition to the card reader, which is the most common input device, such machines as magnetic tape, magnetic disk, and magnetic drum units; console display-keyboards; and cathode-ray-tube (CRT) devices are used as input devices. There are many other devices, some of which are discussed in Module A.

Most input devices read data from an input medium (say, punched cards, magnetic tape, or magnetic disk). Other input devices, such as a console display-keyboard used as a terminal, allow data to be transferred to a computer without recording it on an input medium. In all instances, the input devices provide the means through which humans can communicate with the computer.

Central processing unit. The heart of a computer system is the central processing unit (CPU). Or, stating this another way, the central processing unit *is* the computer. Sometimes referred to as the "mainframe," this unit processes the data transferred to it by an input device and, in turn, transfers the results of the processing to an output device.

CPU speeds make input/output speeds seem slow by comparison. The speed of a computer depends on the speed at which its components operate plus the length of the interconnections between them. Current internal processing speeds are measured in nanoseconds. How fast is a nanosecond? Well, the speed of electricity is 186,000 miles per second, which is approximately 1 foot per nanosecond. (A practical processing speed is approximately 8 inches per nanosecond.) For example, on one large computer, 5 million additions can be executed in one second; this means that it can do one addition every 200 nanoseconds. One way to increase the processing speed of a computer is to reduce the length of the interconnecting wiring between the components of the central processing unit.

As shown in Illustration 5-1, the computer is composed of three units: (1) the control unit, (2) the arithmetic/logic unit, and (3) the storage unit. The storage unit can be in the same cabinet as the control and arithmetic/logic units or in a separate cabinet. As indicated by the dark solid arrows in Illustration 5-1, data is transferred from an input device to the storage unit, and from the storage unit to an output device.

Each of these units serves a specific function and has a particular relationship to the other units of the CPU. The *control unit*, as the name implies and as indicated by the colored solid arrow, selects one program statement at a time from the storage unit. It interprets the statement and, as indicated by the colored broken arrows, sends the appropriate electronic impulses to the arithmetic/logic and storage units to cause these units to carry out the operations required. Thus, the control unit does not perform the actual processing operations on the data. Rather, its function is to maintain order and direct the flow of operations and data within the computer. The control unit also tells the input device when to start and stop transferring data to the storage unit. It tells the storage unit when to start and stop transferring data to an output device.

All arithmetic calculations and logical comparisons are performed in the *arithmetic/logic unit*. As indicated by the dark solid arrows in Illustration 5-1, data flows between this unit and the storage unit during processing. Specifically, data is transferred as needed from the storage unit to the arithmetic/logic unit, manipulated, and returned to the storage unit. No processing is performed in the storage unit. Data may be transferred back and forth between the two units several times before manipulation is completed. When the manipulation of the data is completed, the resultant information is transferred from the storage unit to the output device, as indicated by the dark solid arrow extending from the storage unit to the output device.

The *storage unit* (sometimes called *primary storage*, or *memory*, because of its similarity to the human memory with respect to function) is the unit in which the program statements and data transferred from the input device are stored.

The storage unit is used for four purposes. Three of these purposes relate to the retention of data during processing. First, as indicated by the dark solid arrow in Illustration 5-1, data is transferred from an input device to the storage unit. It remains there until the computer is ready to process it. Second, a *working-storage area* within the storage unit is used to hold both the data being processed and the intermediate results of the arithmetic/logic operations. This is reflected by the dark solid arrows connecting the storage unit and the arithmetic/logic unit. Because of the nature of its use, the working-storage area is sometimes referred to as a *"scratch-pad" memory*. Third, the storage unit retains the result of the processing until it can be transferred to an output device. Fourth, in addition to these three data-related purposes just discussed, the storage unit retains the program statements transferred from an input device or a secondary storage medium (see below) to process the data. These statements are stored in the *program-storage area* and, as indicated by the colored solid arrow, upon request of the control unit are transferred one at a time to that area of the storage unit. They instruct the computer in detail as to the specific operations it is to perform and the order in which it is to perform them.

The storage unit of the computer can hold three types of characters—alphabetic, numeric, and special characters (as a group, these three types of characters are sometimes referred to as *alphameric characters*). The computer can be classified as either *fixed-word-length*, *variable-word-length*, or *byte-addressable*. This reflects the fact that the organization of the storage unit is either word-oriented, character-oriented, or both word-oriented and character-oriented, respectively.

A *word-oriented* computer storage unit is divided into sections called *words*. Each word is designed to hold several characters (the maximum number of characters that a word is designed to hold varies among computers). So that the computer can locate a particular word, each word is assigned an *address*. Thus, a reference to a particular address is a reference to a fixed number of character storage locations, whether or not all of them are needed to hold the data being retrieved or stored. Since the word-oriented computer can manipulate a word containing a large number in the same amount of time as a word containing a small number, it is especially suited to execute scientific and mathematical problems. Such problems generally involve the processing of numeric characters rather than alphabetic characters, and word-oriented computers are well designed with respect to processing this type of data.

Generally speaking, however, a business-oriented problem is processed inefficiently with respect to the use of the storage unit when a fixed-word-length computer is employed. This type of problem usually involves the processing of alphameric characters and fields of data composed of fewer characters than can be stored at an address. For this reason, business-oriented computers having *character-oriented* storage units have been developed. In contrast to the word addressing of a word-oriented storage unit, each storage location in a character-oriented storage unit is assigned an address. The unit of storage is one *byte* (generally, eight bits in length; the counterpart of a word in a word-oriented storage unit). Each byte can contain one character. Therefore, a data field can be from one to several characters in size. All of the data fields composing a record, whether of a uniform size or differing in size, can be stored and processed efficiently.

An addressable section of storage (a word or character storage location) may be compared to a mail box in a post office. Each box has a unique number (address) assigned to it. A person gets mail at each box. Similar to the fact that the contents of a mail box have nothing to do with the number of the box, the contents of storage have nothing to do with an assigned address.

Several manufacturers of computer systems have developed storage units with the characteristics of both word-oriented and character-oriented storage. In these computers, a byte-addressable organization of storage is used. Basically, the programmer can cause the computer to consider its storage unit as being either word-oriented or character-oriented. This is the primary reason why computers with a byte-addressable organization are called general-purpose computers; a computer with this type of storage unit can efficiently process both scientific and mathematical problems and business-oriented problems.

The storage unit of a computer can hold a specified number of characters. The capacity of a storage unit is indicated by a reference to its size. For example, the storage unit of a particular computer can be described as having a capacity of 512K. In data processing terminology, the letter *K* as used here represents 1024; thus, the exact size of a 512K computer storage unit is 524,288 storage locations.

Secondary storage media. Secondary storage media, often referred to as *auxiliary storage*, are used to store programs and data not currently being used by the computer. Secondary storage media thus extend the storage capabilities of the computer system. The two most commonly used secondary storage media are magnetic tape and magnetic disk.

Secondary storage devices (*auxiliary storage devices*) are online to the computer. However, secondary storage media may be online or offline. For example, programs and data stored on magnetic tape and magnetic disk are online if the magnetic tape and magnetic disk are mounted on their respective units. However, if the magnetic tape and magnetic disk are stored in a cabinet, they are offline. Programs and data stored on punched cards are usually offline in that the punched cards are generally stored in punched-card file cabinets, rather than in a card reader, when not being used.

Output devices. Just as the input of program statements and data occurs by means of an input device, the results of the processing of the data are received from the computer by means of an output device. These results are written from the storage unit onto an *output medium* such as printer forms or punched cards. The most common output device is the printer.

System Software

System software is the collection of programs and operating aids associated with a computer that facilitate its programming and operation and extend its processing capabilities. For example, a program called a *utility program* (which is one of several such programs) provides the means by which data is transferred from an input medium, such as punched cards, directly to an output medium, such as magnetic tape. The programs and operating aids are usually furnished by the computer manufacturer. System software can also be obtained from independent software companies.

Application Software

The processing of data occurs according to the program statements stored in the program-storage area of the storage unit. These programs are called application software. The computer manufacturer may supply programs for common processing tasks, such as payroll and billing. In some cases, users have to modify these manufacturer-supplied programs to meet their specific processing requirements. Often, the users of a computer must either write or obtain from other sources most of the programs required to accomplish their specific data processing objectives.

Procedures

A primary objective of a computer system is that the processing of data be accomplished in an efficient and effective manner. For this reason, it is imperative that procedures be developed to detail the exact manner in which such activities as the collection, preparation, and processing of data, and the distribution of results to managers or other individuals or groups, are to be accomplished. Procedures are also necessary for supervisory and operational control purposes, such as to indicate the action to be taken if an error is discovered in the collection, preparation, or processing of data and/or the distribution of results; or if one of the machines in the computer system fails to function properly.

Data Processing Personnel

Generally, a data processing system is housed within a prescribed area, commonly referred to as the data processing department or the computer center. The people working within the area are classified as data processing personnel. Basically, these personnel perform numerous activities required to prepare for and execute the data processing functions. Chapter 17 contains a discussion of the various job classifications, the educational and experience background required of the personnel occupying these job positions, and the fundamental activities performed within each job.

BINARY REPRESENTATION OF DATA

The storage unit of a computer consists of electronic components that can be made to represent either of two possible states: the off state or the on state. Because one component can represent only two different states, it takes several of them to form combinations that represent letters, numbers, or special characters. The use of two-state components to represent data is known as *binary representation*.

Magnetic Cores

One type of two-state component used to form the storage unit is the *magnetic core*. It is similar in shape to a doughnut and can be magnetized in

CHAPTER 5: COMPUTER CONCEPTS

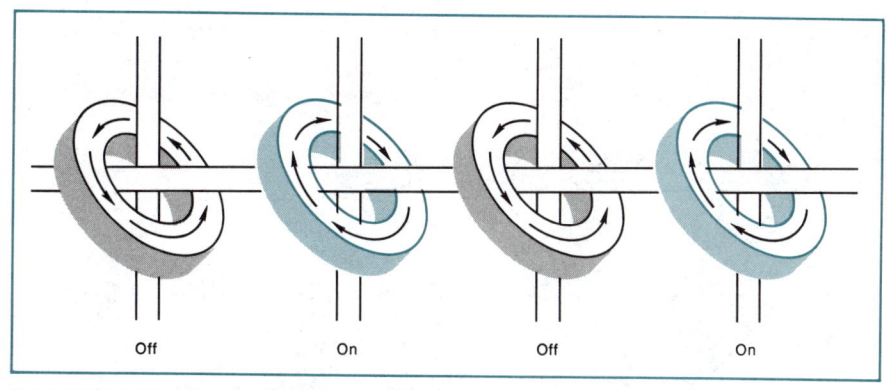

ILLUSTRATION 5-2 Four magnetic cores

either of two directions: clockwise or counterclockwise. When a core is magnetized in one direction, it is said to be "on"; when it is magnetized in the other direction, it is said to be "off." Illustration 5-2 shows four cores, two of which are on and two of which are off. The wires that are strung through the cores are used to set them on and off.

Computer storage that is made up of cores is called **core storage**. It consists of planes of magnetic cores. Illustration 5-3 shows nine planes of magnetic cores. Each vertical column of nine cores in the illustration constitutes one storage location. These nine planes represent 100 nine-bit storage locations (they are 10 × 10 core positions in size). The storage location that is highlighted in the illustration consists of cores that are (from top to bottom) parity bit, on-on-off-on-off-on-off-off. In one type of computer, this combination of on and off cores represents the letter M.

Magnetic-core storage units are **nonvolatile.** This means that once a character(s) is stored at an address, it remains at that address until another character replaces it. The term **destructive read-in** is used to indicate that any characters read (transferred) into storage locations replace any character(s) previously stored in those locations.

Semiconductors

A second type of two-state component used to form a storage unit is the **semiconductor**. The first major commercial system to use semiconductors was IBM's System/370 Model 145 computer, which was first installed in 1971. Semiconductor storage has replaced core storage as the major storage medium used to form storage units. Since semiconductors can be used to form very small, compact circuitry, a semiconductor storage unit is very small. The circuitry is made up of silicon chips, each containing memory

UNIT TWO: COMPUTER SYSTEMS

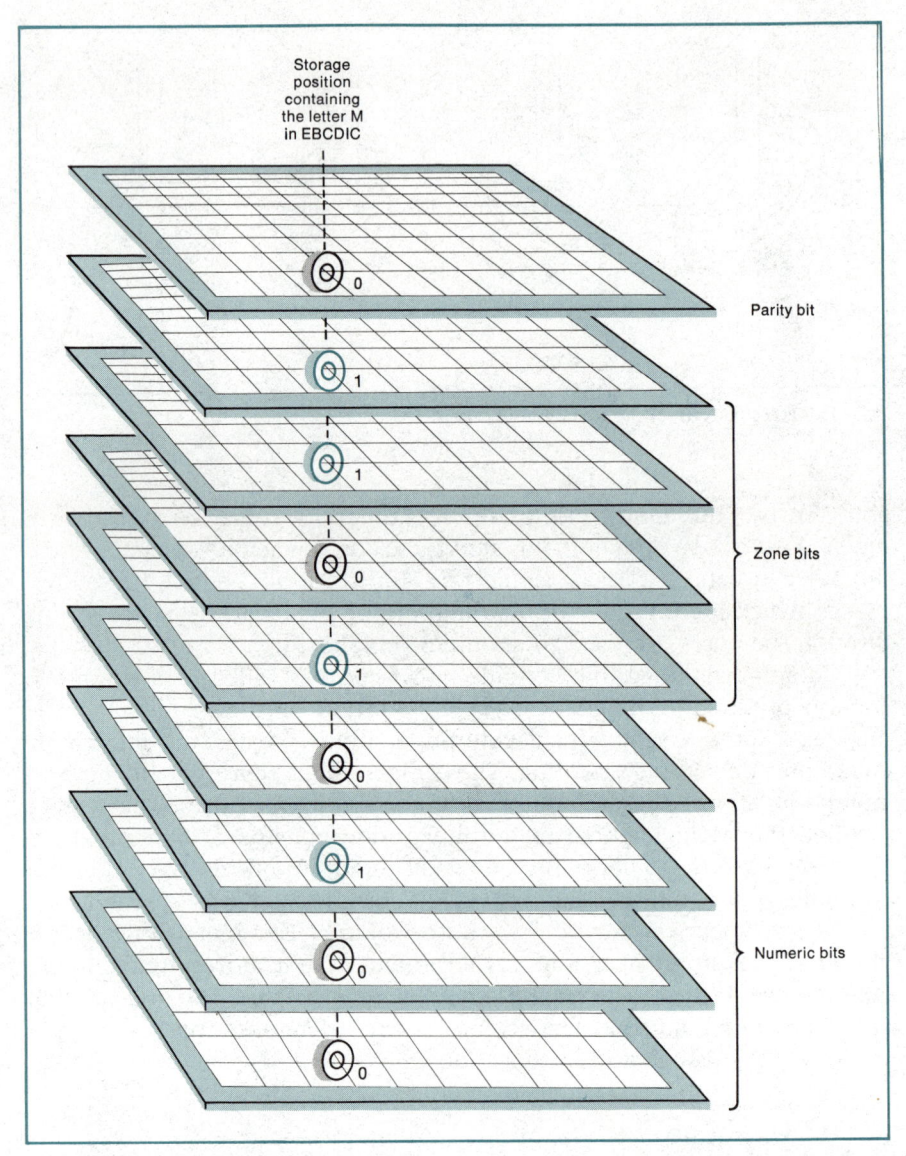

ILLUSTRATION 5-3 Planes of cores

"cells" built into its surface. The on or off position of each switch (analogous to a bit) is determined by the direction of the electrical impulse running through a cell.

There are two sizes of silicon chips. One size is a one-tenth-inch square silicon chip that can store either 2 thousand or 4 thousand characters. A second size is a one-quarter-inch square silicon chip that can hold 8 thou-

CHAPTER 5: COMPUTER CONCEPTS

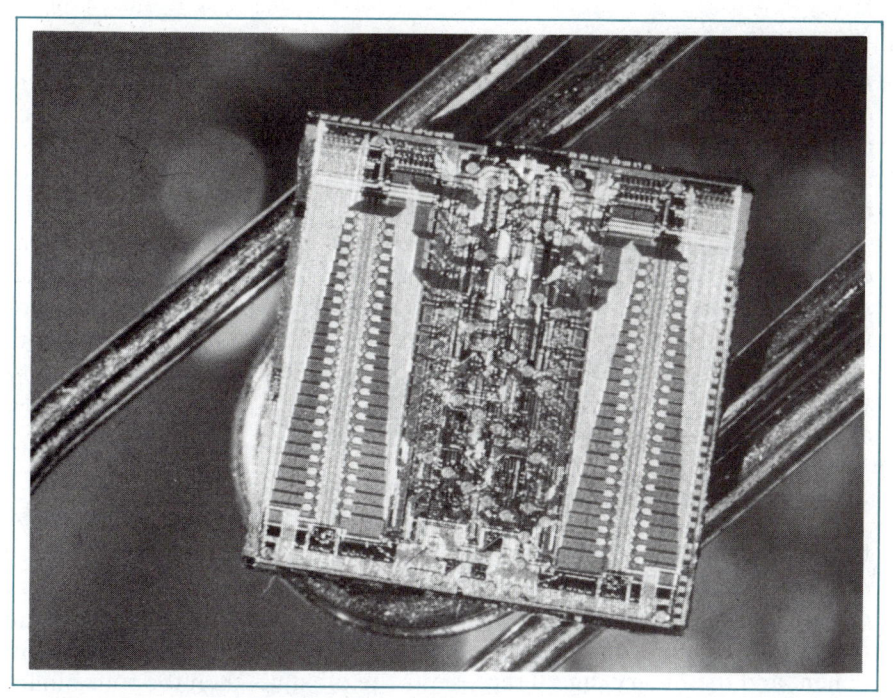

ILLUSTRATION 5-4 An 8000-character storage silicon chip on a paper clip (shown about eleven times actual size)

sand characters plus circuitry to support several processing functions (see Illustration 5-4).

In common practice, core storage circuits are referred to as "partially integrated" (hybrid) circuits because each module is composed of several combined components. Semiconductor storage circuits are called "monolithic" circuits because each chip is totally integrated (indivisible).

The advantages of a semiconductor storage unit over a magnetic-core storage unit are increased access speed and a large reduction in physical storage unit size. This reduction in storage unit size does not imply a reduction in storage capacity. Thus, while a large first-generation computer storage unit could retain up to approximately 20,000 characters, today's large computer storage unit can retain up to approximately 16 million characters (16 MB, or *megabytes,* of data).

A disadvantage of semiconductor storage is impermanence. Unlike magnetic-core storage, which retains the current settings of its bits even if the source of electrical power for the computer system terminates, a semiconductor storage unit is dependent on an ***uninterrupted power supply***. If the power supply for a computer system with semiconductor storage fails, the contents of storage are lost. Thus, semiconductor storage is said to be *volatile*.

UNIT TWO: COMPUTER SYSTEMS

Magnetic Bubbles

A third and promising approach to forming a storage unit is to use *magnetic bubbles.* The technology is based on tiny magnetic "bubbles" that appear in certain kinds of crystalline materials under the control of magnetic and electrical fields. The presence of a bubble signifies an on bit and the absence an off bit.

Magnetic bubble storage units have three advantages over semiconductor storage units: (1) extremely high storage capacity—a one-inch square chip can retain 125 thousand characters; (2) permanence, or nonvolatility; and (3) lower power consumption.

Magnetic bubbles, however, have two disadvantages compared to semiconductors. These disadvantages are (1) a slower access rate to the data, and (2) a slower transfer rate of the data.

Binary Codes

Each component used in a binary representation of data is called a *binary component*. The codes formed by these components are called *binary codes*. The states of the components can be illustrated by the use of the *binary digits* 0 and 1. If the binary digit 1 represents the on state of a component and the binary digit 0 represents the off state, then the four binary digits 0101 can be used to represent four cores that are off-on-off-on. Binary digits are also called *bits*, an *acronym* for *bi*nary dig*its*.

Different types of computers use different binary codes for representing data. For example, the binary code most commonly used to represent data requires 8 bits at each storage location. The binary code is called *Extended Binary Coded Decimal Interchange Code* (*EBCDIC*). In contrast another type of computer uses seven bits at each storage location. Its code is called *American Standard Code for Information Interchange* (*ASCII*). Binary codes formerly used were 4-bit BCD and 6-bit BCD. The binary codes currently used are EBCDIC, ASCII, and true binary. The following discussion traces the development and use of these five codes.

4-bit BCD. Since one bit can represent either of two conditions (0 and 1), two bits can represent four different conditions: 00, 01, 10, and 11. Similarly, three bits can represent eight different conditions. Four bits can represent sixteen different conditions (see below). Each time a bit is added, the total number of possible combinations is doubled.

0000	0100	1000	1100
0001	0101	1001	1101
0010	0110	1010	1110
0011	0111	1011	1111

CHAPTER 5: COMPUTER CONCEPTS

If a unique letter, number, or special character is assigned to each 4-bit combination, 16 (2^4) different characters can be represented. In 4-bit BCD, only 10 of the 16 possible combinations are used. These combinations represent the 10 decimal digits (0 through 9). Because binary codes represent decimal digits, the code is called **Binary Coded Decimal**, or **BCD**.

To convert a 4-bit BCD code to its decimal equivalent, each of the positions in the binary number is given a place value. From left to right in the number, the place values are 8, 4, 2, and 1. Therefore, the rightmost bit can be called the 1-bit, the second from the right the 2-bit, the next the 4-bit, and the leftmost the 8-bit. When the place values of the bits that are on (on bits) in a 4-bit BCD code are added, the result is the decimal equivalent. In the binary number 0101, for example, the 1-bit and the 4-bit are on. Therefore, the decimal equivalent is 1 plus 4, or 5. Illustration 5-5 shows the place values and the decimal equivalents of the 10 binary combinations used in 4-bit BCD.

To represent a decimal number of more than one decimal digit, more than one group of four bits is needed. To illustrate, the decimal number 183 can be represented in 4-bit BCD coding as follows: 000110000011. If

ILLUSTRATION 5-5   4-bit BCD coding

Decimal Equivalent	4-Bit BCD Code Place Values			
	8	4	2	1
0	0	0	0	0
1	0	0	0	1
2	0	0	1	0
3	0	0	1	1
4	0	1	0	0
5	0	1	0	1
6	0	1	1	0
7	0	1	1	1
8	1	0	0	0
9	1	0	0	1

this number is broken into groups of four bits, it is: 0001 1000 0011. Then if each of the groups is converted from BCD to decimal, the result is 183.

6-bit BCD. Another type of BCD coding is 6-bit BCD. It is sometimes called ***alphameric BCD*** because it can be used to represent alphabetic, numeric, and 28 special characters. All 64 (2^6) possible combinations of six bits are used in this coding scheme.

From left to right, the six bits in an alphameric BCD code are called the B-bit, the A-bit, the 8-bit, the 4-bit, the 2-bit, and the 1-bit. These bits correspond to the punches in the Hollerith (punched-card) code. The rightmost four bits (the 8-, 4-, 2-, and 1-bits) correspond to the digit punches in the Hollerith code. The leftmost two bits (the B- and A-bits) correspond to the zone punches in Hollerith code. This relationship is shown in Illustration 5-6.

The numeric bits in a 6-bit BCD code are converted to their decimal equivalent in the same way that 4-bit BCD codes are converted. The place values of the on bits are added. The one exception to this rule is that the numeric bits 1010 are converted to a decimal 0 in 6-bit BCD but they have

ILLUSTRATION 5-6 6-bit BCD compared with Hollerith code

Bit Positions in 6-Bit BCD					
Zone Bits		Numeric Bits			
B	A	8	4	2	1

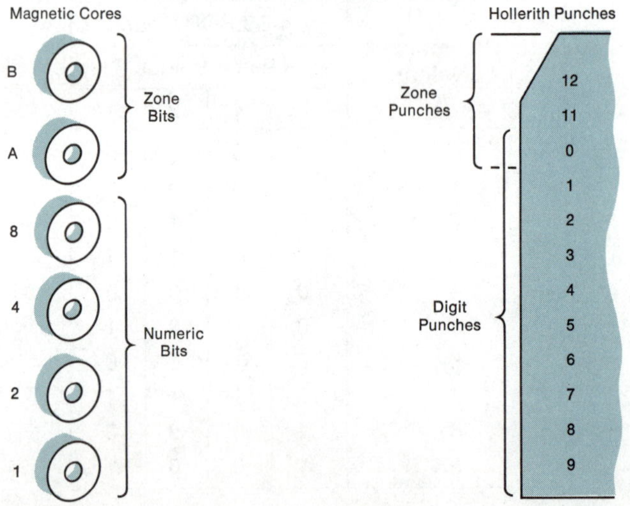

CHAPTER 5: COMPUTER CONCEPTS

Zone Bits BA	Zone-Punch Equivalents
11	12
10	11
01	0
00	No punch

ILLUSTRATION 5-7 Zone equivalents

no equivalent in a 4-bit BCD. Thus, the numeric portion of the code 111010 is equivalent to a 0-punch; the numeric portion of 110010 is equivalent to a 2-punch.

To convert the zone bits in a 6-bit code, the following rules are used. If both the B- and A-bits are on, the representation is equivalent to a 12-punch. If only the B-bit is on, it is equivalent to an 11-punch. If only the A-bit is on, it is equivalent to a 0-punch. Finally, if both the B- and A-bits are off, it is equivalent to no zone punch. These rules are summarized in Illustration 5-7. The zone portion of the code 110001 is equivalent to a 12-punch; the zone portion of the code 010010 is equivalent to a 0-punch.

By combining zone equivalents with numeric equivalents and relating them to Hollerith codes, the 10 decimal digits and the 26 letters of the alphabet can be decoded. For example, the 6-bit BCD code 110010 has a zone equivalent of a 12-punch and a numeric equivalent of a 2-punch; it is, therefore, the code for the letter B (the Hollerith combination of a 12-punch and a 2-punch). Similarly, the code 001010 is equivalent to no zone punch and a 0-punch; it represents the decimal digit 0. Illustration 5-8 gives all 64 BCD codes and their equivalent characters.

To represent four characters in 6-bit BCD requires four groups of six bits, or 24 bits. For example, 110010100000000010001001 can represent four characters. Broken into groups of six bits and decoded, it represents the characters B-29.

EBCDIC. The Extended Binary Coded Decimal Interchange Code, or EBCDIC (pronounced ee-'bee-dick or ib-'si-dick), is an 8-bit code for character representation. Since there are 256 (2^8) possible combinations of the eight bits, up to 256 different characters can be coded. In addition to

UNIT TWO: COMPUTER SYSTEMS

Character	Card Code	6-Bit BCD Code
b	No punches	
.	12-3-8	B A 8 2 1
□	12-4-8	B A 8 4
[	12-5-8	B A 8 4 1
<	12-6-8	B A 8 4 2
≠	12-7-8	B A 8 4 2 1
&	12	B A
$	11-3-8	B 8 2 1
*	11-4-8	B 8 4
]	11-5-8	B 8 4 1
;	11-6-8	B 8 4 2
△	11-7-8	B 8 4 2 1
−	11	B
/	0-1	A 1
,	0-3-8	A 8 2 1
%	0-4-8	A 8 4
⌒	0-5-8	A 8 4 1
\	0-6-8	A 8 4 2
⧧	0-7-8	A 8 4 2 1
ɞ	2-8	A
#	3-8	8 2 1
@	4-8	8 4
:	5-8	8 4 1
>	6-8	8 4 2
√	7-8	8 4 2 1
?	12-0	B A 8 2
A	12-1	B A 1
B	12-2	B A 2
C	12-3	B A 2 1
D	12-4	B A 4
E	12-5	B A 4 1
F	12-6	B A 4 2

Character	Card Code	6-Bit BCD Code
G	12-7	B A 4 2 1
H	12-8	B A 8
I	12-9	B A 8 1
!	11-0	B 8 2
J	11-1	B 1
K	11-2	B 2
L	11-3	B 2 1
M	11-4	B 4
N	11-5	B 4 1
O	11-6	B 4 2
P	11-7	B 4 2 1
Q	11-8	B 8
R	11-9	B 8 1
≠	0-2-8	A 8 2
S	0-2	A 2
T	0-3	A 2 1
U	0-4	A 4
V	0-5	A 4 1
W	0-6	A 4 2
X	0-7	A 4 2 1
Y	0-8	A 8
Z	0-9	A 8 1
Ø	0	8 2
1	1	1
2	2	2
3	3	2 1
4	4	4
5	5	4 1
6	6	4 2
7	7	4 2 1
8	8	8
9	9	8 1

ILLUSTRATION 5-8   Standard 6-bit BCD code

the alphabetic, numeric, and special characters that a 6-bit code allows, the alphabetic characters in lowercase (the 6-bit code allows only uppercase letters) and additional special characters, such as the question mark and quotation marks, can be represented. Not all of the 256 combinations of the eight bits have been assigned to characters.

A second major advantage of using an 8-bit code for character representation concerns the storage of numeric characters. Since a numeric character can be represented by only four bits, an 8-bit configuration allows the representation of two numeric characters. The representation of two numeric characters in eight bits is commonly referred to as *packing*.

As shown in Illustration 5-9, the rightmost four bits in EBCDIC coding are the 8-, 4-, 2-, and 1-bits. They often correspond to the numeric bits in

CHAPTER 5: COMPUTER CONCEPTS

Bit Positions in EBCDIC								
Zone Bits				Numeric Bits			
8	4	2	1	8	4	2	1

ILLUSTRATION 5-9 EBCDIC coding

6-bit BCD coding. The leftmost four bits of EBCDIC are the zone bits, various combinations of which are used in conjunction with the rightmost bits to represent letters, numbers, and special characters.

The EBCDIC representations for uppercase alphabetic characters and the numeric characters 0 through 9 are shown in Illustration 5-10. The bit pattern 1111 is the zone combination for the numeric characters; 1100 is the zone combination for the alphabetic characters A through I; 1101 is used for characters J through R; and 1110 is used for characters S through Z. Thus, for example, the EBCDIC code 11111001 is equivalent to the decimal digit 9; the EBCDIC code 11000001 is equivalent to the letter A. Other zone combinations are used for special characters. The EBCDIC representation of B-29 is shown below.

B	—	2	9
11000010	01100000	11110010	11111001

In EBCDIC, an unsigned digit is assumed to be positive and is represented by 1111 in the leftmost four bits. The 1111 combination was chosen to make certain that numeric characters would be the highest in the collating sequence (ordering) of characters. A plus sign is represented by 1100 and a minus sign by 1101. Usually, the sign of a number occupies the leftmost four bits of the least significant (low-order) digit of the number. The remaining digits of the number contain 1111 in the leftmost four bits. In the packed format, however, the sign occupies the rightmost four bits of the least significant digit and all other sign designations are eliminated.

ASCII. EBCDIC was developed by IBM. A 7-bit code, known as the **American Standard Code for Information Interchange**, or **ASCII**, is sponsored as a 7-bit standard code by the *American National Standards*

UNIT TWO: COMPUTER SYSTEMS

Character	EBCDIC Bit Representation
0	1111 0000
1	1111 0001
2	1111 0010
3	1111 0011
4	1111 0100
5	1111 0101
6	1111 0110
7	1111 0111
8	1111 1000
9	1111 1001
A	1100 0001
B	1100 0010
C	1100 0011
D	1100 0100
E	1100 0101
F	1100 0110
G	1100 0111
H	1100 1000
I	1100 1001
J	1101 0001
K	1101 0010
L	1101 0011
M	1101 0100
N	1101 0101
O	1101 0110
P	1101 0111
Q	1101 1000
R	1101 1001
S	1110 0010
T	1110 0011
U	1110 0100
V	1110 0101
W	1110 0110
X	1110 0111
Y	1110 1000
Z	1110 1001

ILLUSTRATION 5-10 EBCDIC codes for digits and uppercase letters

Character	ASCII Bit Representation
0	0 1 1 0 0 0 0
1	0 1 1 0 0 0 1
2	0 1 1 0 0 1 0
3	0 1 1 0 0 1 1
4	0 1 1 0 1 0 0
5	0 1 1 0 1 0 1
6	0 1 1 0 1 1 0
7	0 1 1 0 1 1 1
8	0 1 1 1 0 0 0
9	0 1 1 1 0 0 1
A	1 0 0 0 0 0 1
B	1 0 0 0 0 1 0
C	1 0 0 0 0 1 1
D	1 0 0 0 1 0 0
E	1 0 0 0 1 0 1
F	1 0 0 0 1 1 0
G	1 0 0 0 1 1 1
H	1 0 0 1 0 0 0
I	1 0 0 1 0 0 1
J	1 0 0 1 0 1 0
K	1 0 0 1 0 1 1
L	1 0 0 1 1 0 0
M	1 0 0 1 1 0 1
N	1 0 0 1 1 1 0
O	1 0 0 1 1 1 1
P	1 0 1 0 0 0 0
Q	1 0 1 0 0 0 1
R	1 0 1 0 0 1 0
S	1 0 1 0 0 1 1
T	1 0 1 0 1 0 0
U	1 0 1 0 1 0 1
V	1 0 1 0 1 1 0
W	1 0 1 0 1 1 1
X	1 0 1 1 0 0 0
Y	1 0 1 1 0 0 1
Z	1 0 1 1 0 1 0

ILLUSTRATION 5-11 ASCII codes for digits and uppercase letters

CHAPTER 5: COMPUTER CONCEPTS

Institute (*ANSI*). This code was developed through the cooperation of several computer manufacturers. Their objective in developing the code was to standardize a binary code, and thus provide a computer user with the capability of using the same data with several machines produced by a single manufacturer or by several manufacturers. The concept and advantages of ASCII are identical to those of EBCDIC. As shown in Illustration 5-11, the vital difference between the codes lies in the 7-bit combinations used to represent the various alphabetic, numeric, and special characters.

True binary representation. In some computers, numbers can be represented in true binary code. The number of bits used to form a true binary number varies. For example, some computers use 8-bit true binary numbers, others use 12-bit true binary numbers, and so on. Regardless of the number of bits, a true binary representation can represent numeric data only.

To convert a true binary number to its decimal equivalent, the place values of the on bits are added. These place values start at the rightmost bit position with a value of 1 and double for each position to the left. Thus, for an 8-bit true binary number, 128, 64, 32, 16, 8, 4, 2, and 1 are the place values. In a 36-bit true binary number, the place value of the leftmost bit position is 23,359,738,368! Illustration 5-12 shows how the 12-bit true binary number 111010111011 is decoded. Its decimal equivalent is the total of the place values of the on bits, or 3771.

True binary representation of numbers is useful because fewer bits are required to represent large numbers in true binary than in any of the BCD codes. For example, in the illustration, the decimal number 3771 requires 12 bits as a true binary number. However, it requires 32 bits in EBCDIC. A computer that has 36 bits at each storage location and uses

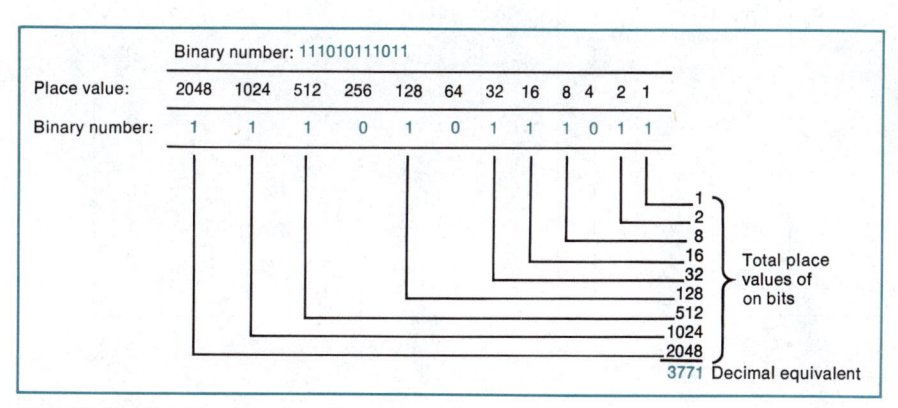

ILLUSTRATION 5-12 Decoding a true binary number

true binary representation can store the equivalent of 68,719,476,735 in one storage location. The largest number that it can store in 36 bits is 999,999.

Parity Bits

In addition to the bits used to represent data, most computers have one additional bit in each storage location. This bit is used to detect errors in circuitry. It is called a *parity bit*, or *check bit*. A computer that uses the ASCII 7-bit code has an eighth bit for parity; and a computer that uses EBCDIC has a ninth bit for parity.

The parity bit is used to make the number of on bits in a code location either odd or even, depending on whether the computer uses *odd parity* or *even parity*. Illustration 5-13 shows the EBCDIC code combinations for a computer that uses odd parity. When the parity bit is taken into account, each of the combinations has an odd number of on bits. In a computer that uses even parity, the number of on bits in each code location is even.

The parity of data is checked each time that the data is moved into or from the storage unit, or referred to while in the storage unit. To illustrate, suppose that the EBCDIC code (and parity bit) 11110011 has just been

ILLUSTRATION 5-13 4-bit BCD with odd parity

Decimal Equivalent	P	8	4	2	1	8	4	2	1
0	1	1	1	1	1	0	0	0	0
1	0	1	1	1	1	0	0	0	1
2	0	1	1	1	1	0	0	1	0
3	1	1	1	1	1	0	0	1	1
4	0	1	1	1	1	0	1	0	0
5	1	1	1	1	1	0	1	0	1
6	1	1	1	1	1	0	1	1	0
7	0	1	1	1	1	0	1	1	1
8	0	1	1	1	1	1	0	0	0
9	1	1	1	1	1	1	0	0	1

(EBCDIC Bit Representation columns under P)

moved into the storage unit of a computer that uses odd parity. Since the number of on bits in the code is even, a bit must have been set on or off due to error. This error is caught by the checking circuitry of the computer. The computer first attempts to re-read the bit. If necessary, it continues to retry the operation several times. If no retry is successful, the system informs the computer operator that an error has occurred.

Parity checking gives some assurance that the operations that take place in a CPU are accurate. If a bit is set on or off in error, the error is detected. In contrast, other types of data processing equipment—for example, accounting machines—may function improperly without giving any indication that an error has occurred.

○ HEXADECIMAL REPRESENTATION

In daily activities, humans generally use the decimal numbering system. In a computer storage unit, however, data is represented in binary form. It is often necessary for an individual, say a programmer trying to get a program to execute successfully, to determine the contents of particular storage locations. Suppose the programmer had to convert the data in these storage locations from binary to decimal. Doing so would be time-consuming and the chance of error would be high. Because of these two problems, most computer systems are designed to print out the contents of storage locations using a convenient and efficient representation for binary numerals: *hexadecimal (base 16) representation.*

A group of four binary digits can be represented by one digit of the hexadecimal numbering system. As the term *base 16* implies, 16 symbols are used in the hexadecimal numbering system—the digits 0 through 9 and the letters A through F. Equivalent binary, hexadecimal, and decimal numbers are shown in Illustration 5-14.

The decimal equivalent of $12F1_{16}$ can be found by (1) multiplying each symbol by the appropriate power of the base 16 and (2) adding the resultant products to get the decimal equivalent. Thus, 12F1 represents:

$(1 \times 16^3) + (2 \times 16^2) + (F, \text{ or } 15, \times 16^1) + (1 \times 16^0)$, or

$4096 + 512 + 240 + 1 = 4849_{10}$

○ THE EXECUTION OF PROGRAM STATEMENTS

When program statements or data items are moved into or from the storage unit, the contents of one or several storage locations are moved at a

UNIT TWO: COMPUTER SYSTEMS

Binary System (place values) 8 4 2 1	Hexadecimal System	Decimal System
0 0 0 0	0	0
0 0 0 1	1	1
0 0 1 0	2	2
0 0 1 1	3	3
0 1 0 0	4	4
0 1 0 1	5	5
0 1 1 0	6	6
0 1 1 1	7	7
1 0 0 0	8	8
1 0 0 1	9	9
1 0 1 0	A	10
1 0 1 1	B	11
1 1 0 0	C	12
1 1 0 1	D	13
1 1 1 0	E	14
1 1 1 1	F	15

ILLUSTRATION 5-14 Binary, hexadecimal, and decimal equivalent values

time, depending on the *access width* of the computer. The access width is the number of storage locations into or from which data is moved (or accessed) at a time. For example, if the access width of a computer is one byte (one storage location), one byte of data is moved at a time. If the access width is two bytes, two bytes of data are moved at a time.

An *access cycle* is a computer cycle during which one access width of data is moved into or from the storage unit. These cycles take place continuously as a computer operates. For instance, suppose that a computer with a one-byte access width executes a program statement that is four bytes long. As the program statement is moved to the control unit, four access cycles take place. Similarly, suppose a computer with a one-byte access width executes an add program statement that is six bytes long and that adds two five-byte fields and places the answer in one five-byte field. This program statement takes 21 access cycles: six access cycles to move the statement into the control unit, ten to move the five-byte data fields into the arithmetic/logic unit, and five to return the answer to the storage unit.

The *access speed* of a computer is the time required for one access cycle. This speed varies among computers, but it is constant for a particular type of computer. For example, one common type of computer has an access speed of 420 nanoseconds. The access speed of a computer is one indication of the overall speed of the CPU.

To calculate the total time it takes a computer to execute a program statement, one needs to know the number of access cycles required for that execution, the access speed of the computer, and the time required to carry out the function of the statement. For example, if the computer has an access width of one byte and a four-byte program statement is executed, four access cycles are required plus the time for carrying out the statement itself. Therefore, if the access speed of the computer is 420 nanoseconds, execution of the program statement takes 1680 nanoseconds plus the time to perform the statement. (Remember, there are approximately as many nanoseconds in a second as there are seconds in 30 years.) Similarly, if a program statement that takes 21 access cycles is executed on a computer with a 420-nanosecond access speed, it takes 8820 nanoseconds plus the time for performing the addition in the arithmetic/logic unit.

The time for carrying out the function of a program statement varies, depending on the type of statement and the computer. For instance, it may take less than the equivalent of one access cycle to carry out some types of statements. On the other hand, the equivalent of many access cycles may be required to perform the function of a multiplication program statement. Some computers can perform this and other arithmetic functions significantly faster than other computers.

In summary, the speed of execution of a program statement depends on the time required for access cycles and the time needed for carrying out the function of the statement. Although for some program statements the time required for carrying out functions can be significant, in most cases the time required for access cycles is a good indication of the speed of the computer.

○ SUMMARY

1. The term *computer* implies a machine capable of arithmetic calculation and having many other characteristics, the most notable of which are that it is electronic, has internal storage, is instructed by a stored program, and is capable of program-execution modification.

2. There are many useful ways in which computers can be categorized. Among these are classifications by the type of data they are capable of

manipulating (digital and analog), by the purpose for which they were designed (special and general), and as mixtures of types (hybrid).

3. Computer systems are composed of five basic components: hardware, system software, application software, procedures, and data processing personnel. Hardware is the machines used by a data processing department, including data-preparation devices, input devices, a central processing unit, secondary storage devices, and output devices. System software consists of the collection of programs and operating aids associated with a computer that facilitate its operation and programming. Application software consists of programs for tasks such as payroll and billing. These programs are usually written by the users of computers. Procedures are the rules, policies, and guidelines governing the operation of the computer center. Data processing personnel are the people responsible for keeping the data processing department functioning in an effective and efficient manner.

4. The central processing unit has three parts: the control unit, the arithmetic/logic unit, and the storage unit. The control unit controls the flow of data into and out of the storage unit of the computer. It also interprets program statements that it retrieves from the storage unit. The arithmetic/logic unit provides the arithmetic calculation and logical comparison capability of the computer. The storage unit stores program statements and data until called for by some other unit. It also acts as a temporary holding point for the intermediate results of calculations.

5. Computers are designed on a two-state (binary) coding system. Storage units of computers consist of two-state magnetic cores, semiconductors, or magnetic bubbles, each of which can be electromagnetically charged to either an on or an off condition. To represent the two-state coding system, binary digits, or bits, are used (0 corresponds to off and 1 corresponds to on).

6. The coding schemes employing binary code are referred to as Binary Coded Decimal (BCD) representations. These include the 4-bit BCD (used to code the 10 decimal digits); 6-bit BCD (capable of representing alphabetic, numeric, and 28 special characters); EBCDIC; and ASCII.

7. The BCD codes have one additional bit called the parity bit, or check bit, which is used to detect errors in circuitry so that no characters are changed inadvertently as they are transferred between units. Some computers use odd parity (an odd number of on bits per character) while others use even parity.

8. Representation of the contents of storage using the hexadecimal numbering system assists an individual in determining the contents of particular storage locations.

9. The time required for execution of a program statement depends on access width, access speed, and type of statement being executed. The access width determines the number of bytes of data that can be transferred from one unit to another at one time. The access speed is the time required for one access cycle (a computer cycle during which one access width of data is moved into or from the storage unit).

REVIEW QUESTIONS

1. Distinguish between analog computers and digital computers, giving examples of each.
2. What is a computer system? Identify its components.
3. What is the purpose of the storage unit?
4. What is the difference between offline equipment and online equipment?
5. Distinguish between system software and application software. Give examples of both types of software and explain why each belongs to the particular category.
6. What is the relationship between hardware and software?
7. Why are computer coding schemes needed? What advantages does EBCDIC offer as compared to 6-bit BCD?
8. What developments have occurred in primary storage media and what impact have these developments had on third-generation computers?
9. Identify the factors that must be considered when calculating how fast a computer can execute a program statement.

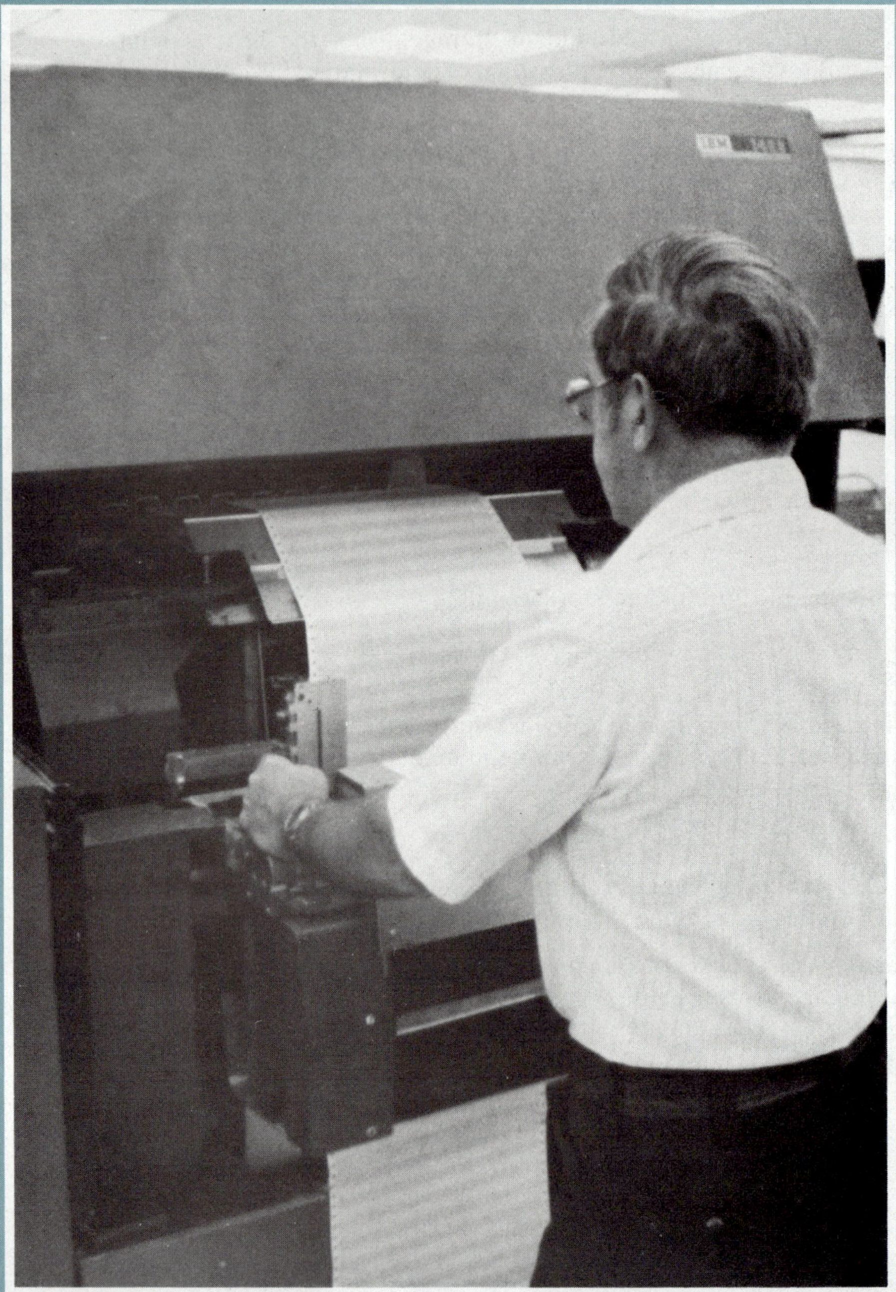

CHAPTER 6

BASIC INPUT AND OUTPUT DEVICES

CARD INPUT AND OUTPUT

CHECKING FOR ERRORS

ADVANTAGES AND LIMITATIONS
OF PUNCHED-CARD INPUT/OUTPUT

PRINTER OUTPUT
Impact Printers
Nonimpact Printers

ADVANTAGES AND LIMITATIONS
OF PRINTER OUTPUT

Opposite: A computer operator makes adjustments to a printer that uses continuous forms.

The speed of a data processing system depends in large part on the CPU and input and output (input/output) speeds of the computer. Remember, however, that before a computer can process data, the data must be read from an input device and stored in its internal memory; and after the data is processed, results must be written on an output device. In most business applications, the reading and writing operations require more time than the processing of data. Therefore, the speeds of input and output devices have a significant effect on the overall speed and efficiency of a computer system. Generally, the speed and efficiency of a system can be increased by reducing the time required to read data and write results. For instance, a system that has a 1200-cards-per-minute card reader and a 2000-lines-per-minute printer can process more data than a system that has a 1000-cards-per-minute card reader and an 1100-lines-per-minute printer—regardless of the speeds of operations that take place inside the CPU.

This chapter deals with the basic media of input and output: punched cards and printed documents. It also deals with the input/output devices that process these forms of data: card readers, card punches, and printers. The following two chapters and module discuss magnetic tape, mass storage, and special-purpose input/output devices. These and other devices are sometimes referred to as *peripheral equipment* (see Illustration 6-1). This reference is due to the fact that while they are not physically part of the CPU, they are often located in close proximity to it.

For each type of input or output device, there are a number of physical variations. The important thing to notice is how these physical characteristics can affect the design of a data processing system and how they can help to insure the reliability and accuracy of input and output operations.

○ CARD INPUT AND OUTPUT

The *card reader* is one of the most basic input devices through which data enters the computer. In addition to the various models produced by different computer manufacturers, there are two distinct methods of reading a punched card and there are two separate principles on which card readers are designed. One method used in reading a punched card is called the *serial method*. This technique is characterized by reading a card column-by-column starting with the first column (and ending with the eightieth column, on a standard punched card). A card reader employing the serial method, therefore, records (or causes the computer to recognize) one character at a time.

The second method of reading a punched card is called the *parallel method*. This method is characterized by the row-by-row reading of a punched card. On a standard punched card, this operation begins with the

CHAPTER 6: BASIC INPUT AND OUTPUT DEVICES

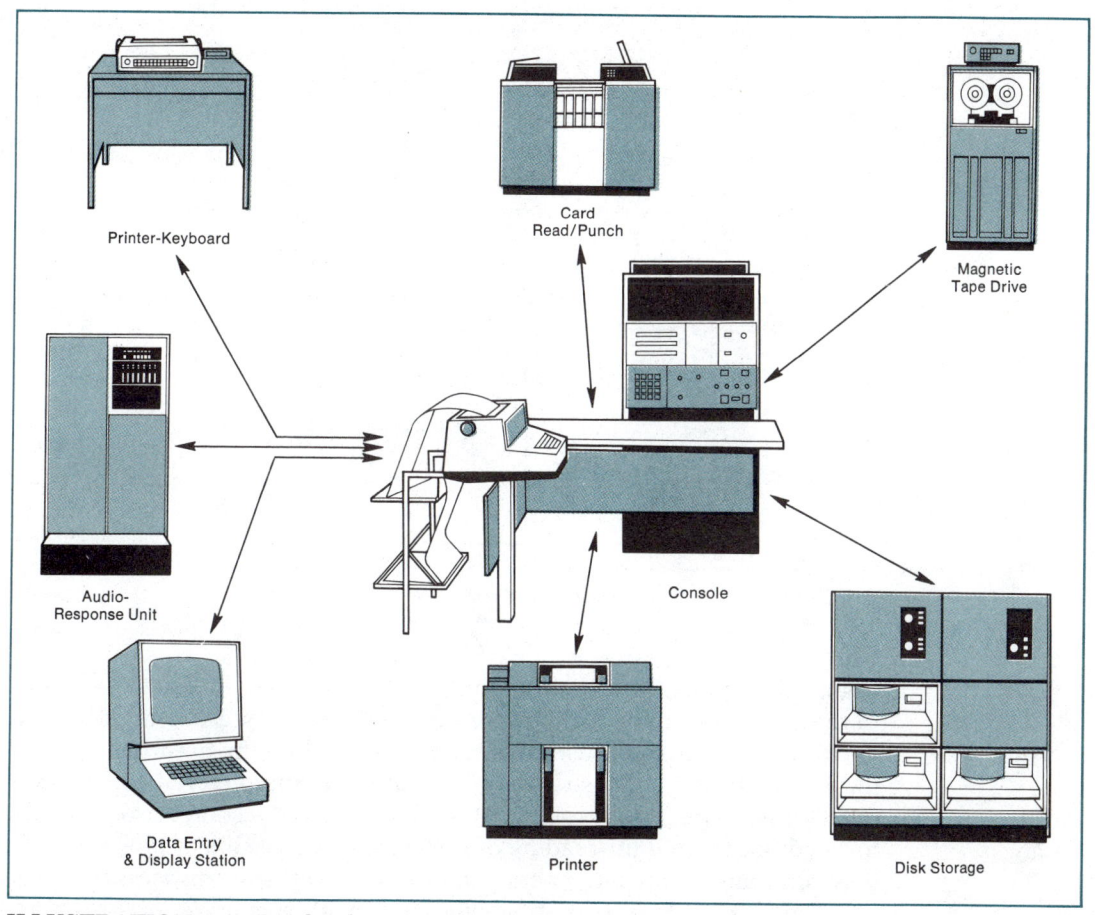

103

ILLUSTRATION 6-1 Peripheral equipment

top of the card (the 12-edge) and is completed with the reading of the last row on the card (the 9-edge). A character is recognized by the distance between the holes in the card. Therefore, a constant reading speed is required on this type of card reader. It is not until the last row is read that the computer can determine the characters on the card from the holes punched in the card. When the last row of the card has been read, all of the characters on the card (up to 80 on the standard card) are recorded.

The principle on which card readers are designed is a reflection of the physical characteristics of the reading process. Two types of card readers can be distinguished under this criterion, namely, the brush-type reader and the photoelectric reader. The ***brush-type reader*** employs small metal brushes to determine the positions of holes in a punched card. As the card

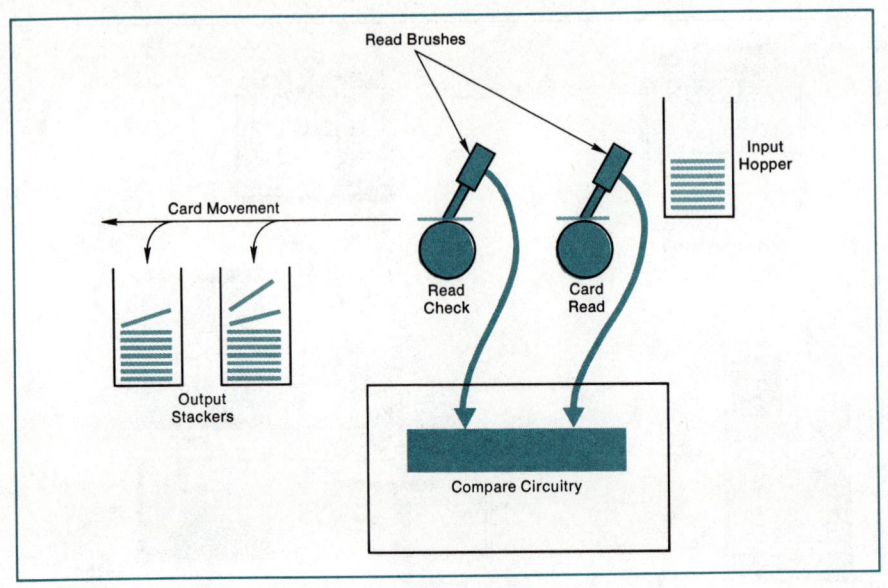

ILLUSTRATION 6-2 Parallel brush-type reading

passes through the *read station*, the metal brushes apply a slight pressure to the card. When the brushes pass over a hole, they cause an electrical circuit to be completed with the metal roller below the card. This procedure is illustrated in Illustration 6-2. As noted in the pictorial explanation of the brush-type reader, each card is read twice and a comparison is made to avoid undetected misreading of the card. If the results of the two reading operations do not correspond, the computer refuses to process the card.

The second type of card reader is the **photoelectric**, or **brushless**, **reader**. The photoelectric reader requires the use of a **light source** and a series of **photoelectric cells**. As shown in Illustration 6-3, this type of reader is characterized by the passing of each punched card under a luminous object that projects a beam of light through the holes in the card. The light is received by photoelectric cells positioned directly behind the hole positions in the card. When a photoelectric cell is activated by the light, an electrical circuit is completed; the card reader recognizes a hole in the card. These readers operate at higher speeds and with greater reliability than brush-type readers.

The **card punch** is an output device. The function of the card punch is to record results transferred from the computer onto punched cards. While the card reader transforms punched holes into electrical impulses, the card punch converts electrical signals into card punches. As Illustration 6-4 demonstrates, the card punch takes blank cards from the input hopper

CHAPTER 6: BASIC INPUT AND OUTPUT DEVICES

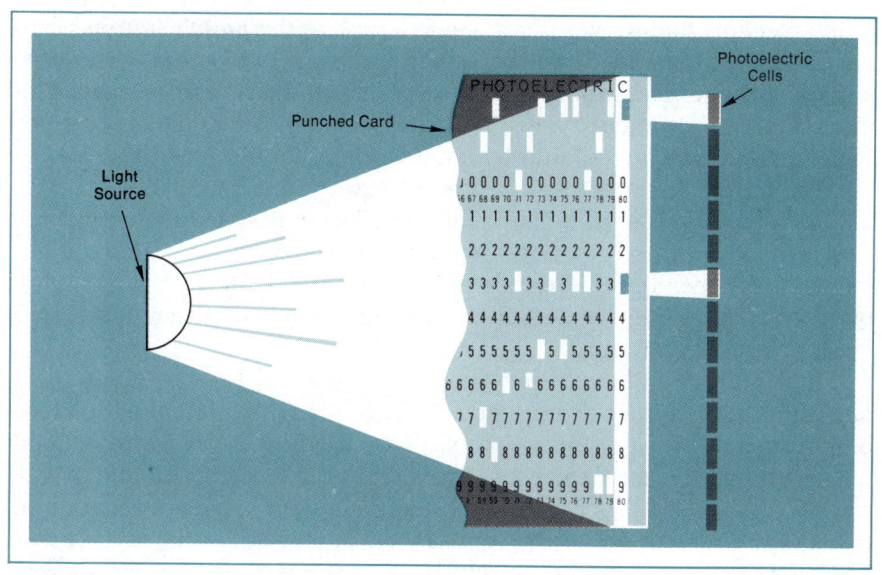

ILLUSTRATION 6-3 Serial photoelectric reading

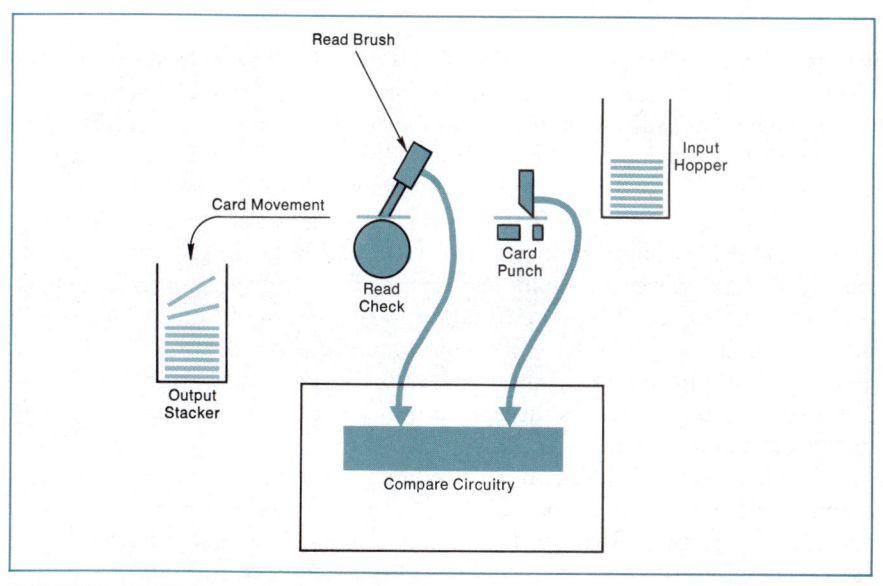

ILLUSTRATION 6-4 Card-punch operation

of the machine and moves them one at a time to the *punch station* where the holes are punched. Then the card passes to a *read station* where the punching is checked. Finally, the card passes to the output stacker. As in the reading of a punched card, the card-punching function may be performed either serially (column-by-column) or in parallel (row-by-row).

The physical characteristics of card readers and punches vary. They may be separate physical units, or they may be combined into a single unit. The combined units may have separate input hoppers for reading and punching, or they may have only one input hopper for both reading and punching. The design of a data processing system may vary because of these physical variations.

Illustration 6-5 shows one type of combined card read/punch. It has one input hopper for reading, one input hopper for punching, and five output stackers. Two of the stackers can be used for cards from the read-feed; two can be used for cards from the punch-feed; and the middle stacker can be used for cards from either feed. With this device, data from cards in the read-feed can be reproduced into cards in the punch-feed. Cards from either feed can be separated into any one of three stackers. And because the middle stacker is common to the read-feed and the punch-feed, cards from the punch-feed can be merged into a deck with cards from the read-feed.

CHECKING FOR ERRORS

To insure the accuracy of input and output operations, input/output devices carry out various types of checks for errors. If these checks were not carried out, computer system processing errors could occur even when CPU operations took place flawlessly. Several types of input/output checks are possible with card readers and punches.

One type of error checking in card reading is called *validity checking*. This is a check of all combinations of punched holes in the card to make sure that they represent valid characters. For example, suppose an 80-column punched card has a combination of a 3-punch and a 1-punch in one of its columns; this is not a valid character in Hollerith coding. Such an error is caught by the circuitry that checks for validity errors. The computer system stops or alerts the operator in some other way that a problem has been encountered.

A second type of check on card reading is shown in Illustration 6-2. As noted in the discussion of brush-type readers, cards that are read by this device actually pass through two read stations. The first reading of the cards is compared with the second reading. If the two readings are not the same, an error is indicated. The same principle of checking by comparison

CHAPTER 6: BASIC INPUT AND OUTPUT DEVICES

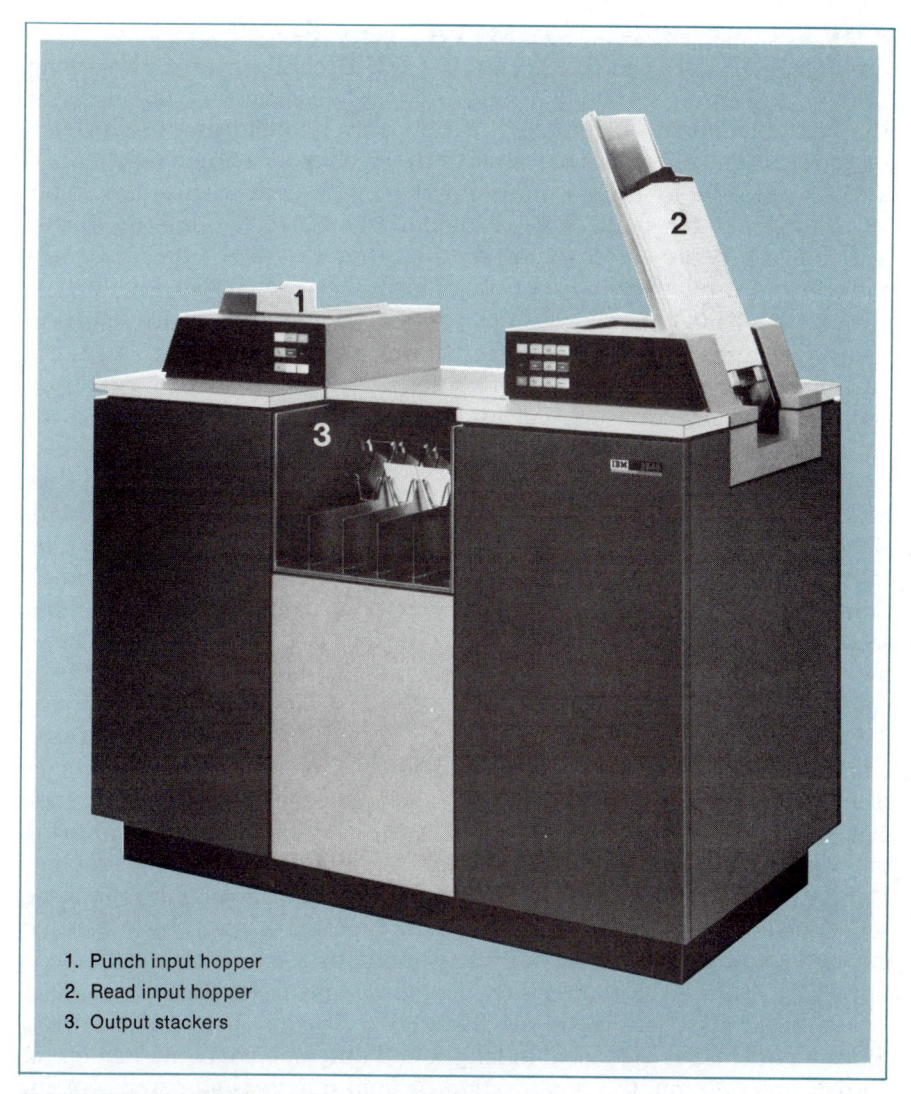

1. Punch input hopper
2. Read input hopper
3. Output stackers

ILLUSTRATION 6-5   Combined card read/punch

is used in many other input/output devices. Recall that, after a card is punched by the card punch in Illustration 6-4, the card passes through a read station. The data punched in the card is read and compared with the data that was intended to be punched. If they are not the same, an error is indicated.

○ ADVANTAGES AND LIMITATIONS OF PUNCHED-CARD INPUT/OUTPUT

The basic advantages of punched cards as an input medium stem from the physical characteristics of the cards themselves. First, data on punched cards is readable by humans, as compared with data on magnetic tape, for example, which is machine-readable only. Since the data on a card is visible, errors are easier to correct than they would be otherwise. Second, cards are relatively inexpensive. Third, they are a relatively durable form of input medium. Fourth, records can be added to or deleted from a card file without processing the remaining portion of the file. This is not possible with magnetic tape. Finally, since the major impetus of card input and output stems from original uses of punched-card equipment, cards are a compatible medium for any other punched-card equipment in use.

Although punched cards are a popular form of input and output, they have many limitations. A serious disadvantage of any card-oriented system is the slow speed of input and output. Card readers are capable of handling from 150 to 2667 characters per second (112 to 2000 cards per minute). Compared to the input speed of magnetic tape, even 2667 characters per second is relatively slow. Punched-card output is even slower because of mechanical movements required at the punch station. Typical speeds of card punches range from 80 to 650 characters per second.

A second disadvantage of punched cards is that they cannot be erased and reused. In contrast, a potential for reuse is one of the basic advantages of magnetic tape, disk, and drum storage. For example, a magnetic tape can be reused in six consecutive jobs, with its contents changing during every job. Third, decks of punched cards are subject to calamities such as being dropped or being inadvertently rearranged. Card records may be sequenced incorrectly or lost. A magnetic-tape file is not subject to such errors because the tape is a continuous medium; each record on a tape is physically attached to the records preceding and following it.

Another disadvantage is the fixed **data density** of a punched card. Since a punched card is fixed in length and only one character can be recorded in a column, the organization of data may be hampered. For instance, if 81 characters of data are to be entered on standard 80-column punched cards, two cards are required. In contrast, with magnetic tape, the data can be packed or the size of the record on tape can be increased to accommodate the data.

Finally, as an input or output medium, punched cards are bulky and require large amounts of storage space relative to other media. Thus, the handling and storage costs for punched cards are greater than the costs of keeping the same amount of data on another medium.

CHAPTER 6: BASIC INPUT AND OUTPUT DEVICES

In summary, there are a number of variations in card readers and punches that affect the functional capabilities and, therefore, the design of a system. In addition, there are some variations that affect the speed and reliability of the devices. Finally, circuitry that checks for errors is part of both reading and punching operations. This is necessary to insure the overall accuracy of the processing done by a computer system.

PRINTER OUTPUT

The common functions of a printer are to print one line at a time; to space one, two, or three lines at a time; and to skip to any of 12 punches in a *forms-control tape*. The four major variations in printers are: (1) varieties of forms a printer can print on; (2) number of print positions available on a single print line; (3) number of different characters that can be printed; and (4) type of printing mechanism used for printing. Of these, the first three can affect the design of a system. The fourth can affect the speed and reliability of a printer.

Perhaps the key variation in printers that affects the design of a system is the types of forms a printer can print on. Most printers print on *continuous forms*. Some can print on *cut forms* such as punched cards or postal cards. Illustration 6-6 shows a printer that can print on both punched cards and continuous forms. The punched cards are fed into and printed on the left side of the machine. Continuous forms are printed on the right side of the machine. When this type of printer is used, punched cards can be printed and used as output documents such as utility bills. Later, when a bill of this type is returned with a requested payment, it can be processed by the computer as a record of payment. The same punched card is both an output of, and an input to, the system.

The number of print positions that a printer has and the number of different characters that it can print affect the design of output forms. For example, if a printer has 100 print positions, it cannot print a report that is 140 print positions wide. Similarly, if a printer can print only the decimal digits, the alphabet, and certain special characters, it cannot print a report requiring many special characters. Although the characteristics of a printer are not normally a limitation in system design, they must be considered when designing reports.

Among the popular printers of today are those capable of printing 132 and 144 characters per line. The continuous-forms printer in Illustration 6-7, for example, is capable of printing up to 144 characters per line.

To insure accuracy, various checks on printer-output operations are performed. Some of the common checks are:

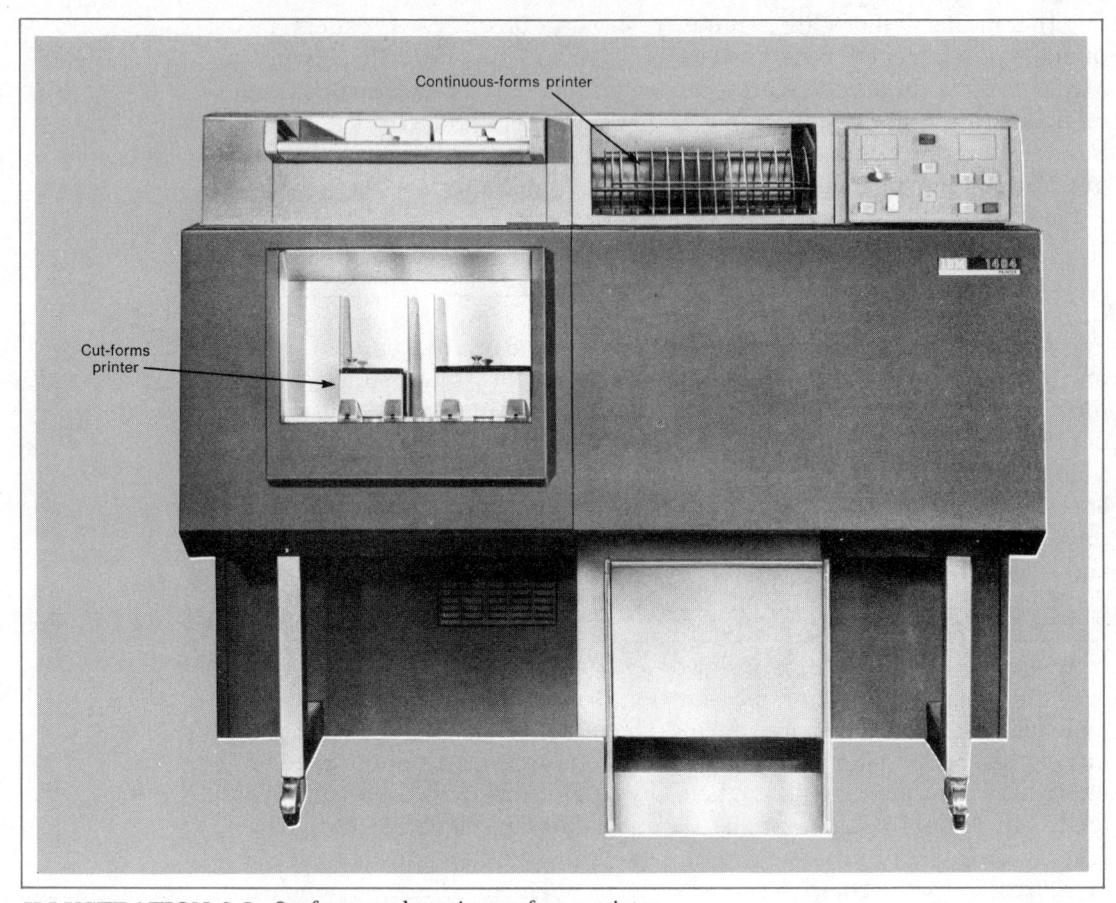

ILLUSTRATION 6-6 Cut-forms and continuous-forms printer

1. Characters to be printed are examined to make sure the printer is capable of printing them.
2. Movements of paper and of printing mechanisms are constantly checked to make sure they are synchronized.
3. Print hammers are checked to make sure they do not misfire.

If an error condition occurs, the computer system halts or alerts the operator in some other way that a problem has been encountered.

There are two principles on which printers are designed just as there are two principles for design of card readers. The distinction in the case of printers is one of character-at-a-time printing versus line-at-a-time printing. *Character-at-a-time printers* include console printers, teletype printers,

CHAPTER 6: BASIC INPUT AND OUTPUT DEVICES

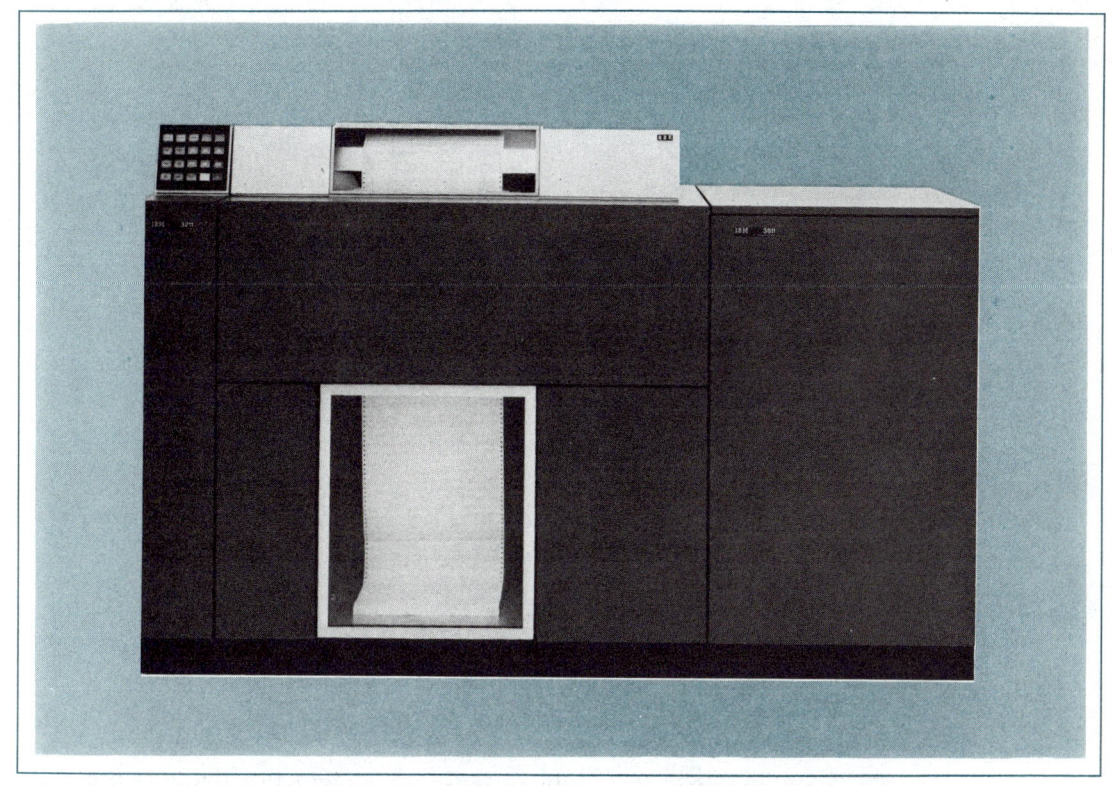

ILLUSTRATION 6-7 Continuous-forms printer

and matrix printers. Since the console printer provides a special function, it is discussed in Module A, which deals with special-purpose input/output devices. Typical *line-at-a-time printers* are bar, wheel, comb, drum, and chain printers. In this class, the drum printer and the chain printer are the most popular.

Impact Printers

The printing devices discussed below are known as ***impact printers***. They are typical printers used on computer systems. The term *impact* is appropriate because each printer uses some kind of mechanical printing element to strike the paper on which an output character is to be printed.

The ***teletype printer*** is used when limited amounts of printer output are expected. It consists of a square which contains the desired characters (see Illustration 6-8). The printing operation is initiated by moving the

UNIT TWO: COMPUTER SYSTEMS

A	B	C	D	E	F	G
H	I	J	K	L	M	N
O	P	Q	R	S	T	U
V	W	X	Y	Z		0
1	2	3	4	5	6	7
8	9		#	.	,	/
@	*	♯	&	-	%	$

ILLUSTRATION 6-8 Teletype square

square across the page from left to right and stopping to position a character. Then, a hammer behind the character strikes the square, causing the character to be imprinted on the page. Since the teletype printer stops for the positioning of each character, its printing speed is extremely slow, generally about 10 characters per second.

The *matrix printer* is based on a design principle similar to that of the scoreboard clock in many football stadiums. It consists of a 5 × 7 rectangle composed of pins, and certain combinations of the pins are activated to represent characters (see Illustration 6-9). As these pins are

ILLUSTRATION 6-9 Printer matrix

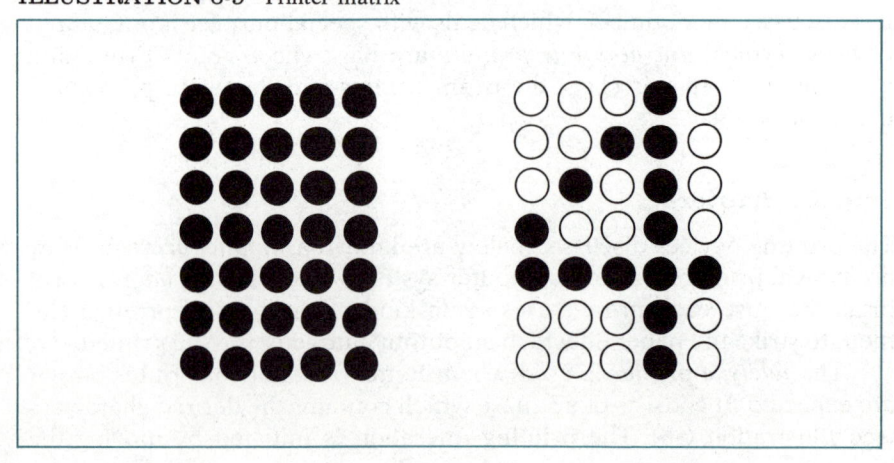

CHAPTER 6: BASIC INPUT AND OUTPUT DEVICES

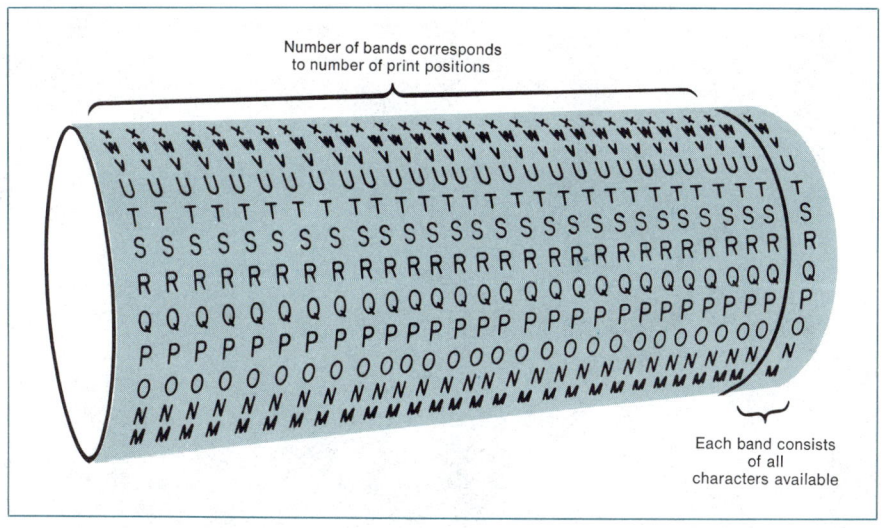

ILLUSTRATION 6-10 Print drum

pressed against the page, the composite of the character results. Typical speeds of matrix printers approach 120 characters per second.

The ***comb printer*** has one bar that moves horizontally along a line of print from left to right. As the bar moves, hammers behind the desired characters strike the bar to produce the desired characters at the required positions. After each pass, the bar returns to its original position for the next line of print. Typical speeds of the comb printer approach 150 lines per minute.

The ***drum printer*** has a cylinder with raised characters on its surface. At each print position, there is a circular band containing all the characters that the printer can print (see Illustration 6-10). The drum rotates at a constant speed, making one revolution for each line of print. As the appropriate character on the drum passes the print position, a hammer at the position strikes the paper against an inked ribbon and then against the character. Drum printer speeds range from 700 to 1600 lines per minute.

The design of a ***chain printer***, such as the IBM 3211 printer shown in Illustration 6-7, is based on the concept of a ***print chain***. The print chain consists of several sets of characters revolving horizontally past all print positions (see Illustration 6-11). As the characters pass the print positions, hammers behind the paper press it against an inked ribbon, which in turn presses against appropriate characters on the print chain, thus printing the characters. Chain printers are capable of producing from 600 to 2000 lines of print per minute.

UNIT TWO: COMPUTER SYSTEMS

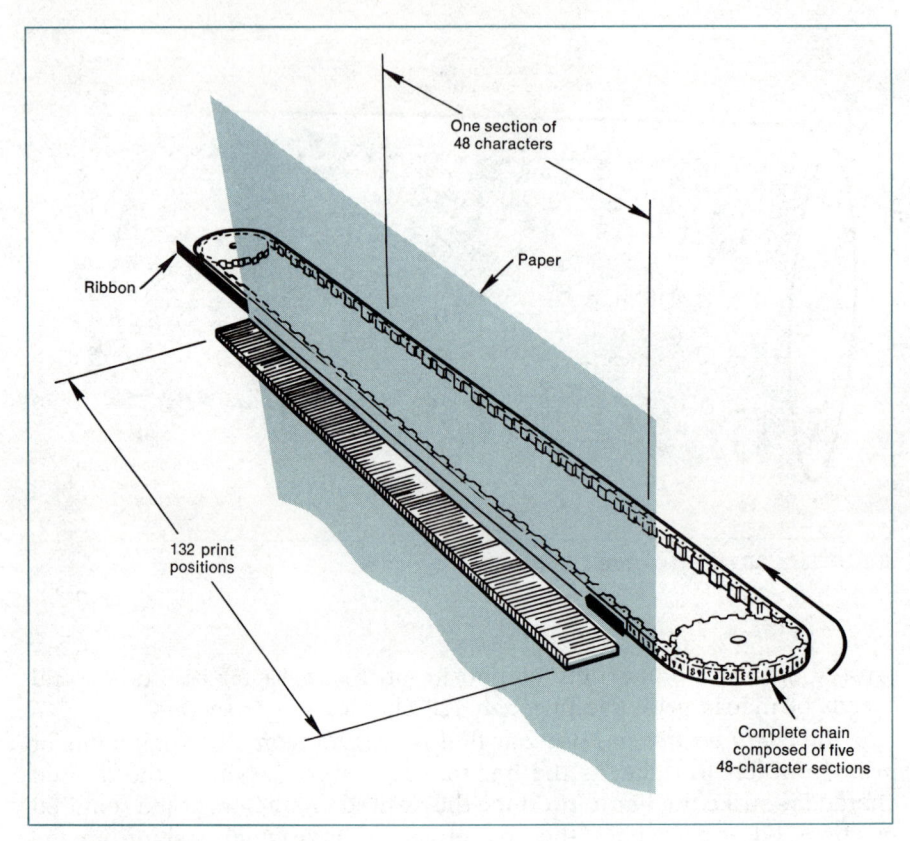

ILLUSTRATION 6-11 Print chain

Nonimpact Printers

A newer group of printing devices consists of *nonimpact printers*. Printers belonging to this group use a variety of methods to print output.

Electrothermal printers generate characters using heat to make an image on heat-sensitive paper. Character forms are generated by heating selected rods in a matrix. When the ends of the heated rods touch the heat-sensitive paper, the character image is transferred to the paper.

Electrostatic printers form character images on paper by means of charged wires which generate electrical charges in a desired dot-matrix character pattern. Some electrostatic printers require special paper. Others can print on ordinary paper.

The electrothermal or electrostatic printer is often used where a low-cost printer is needed. They are most commonly found on portable terminals and low-cost computers. Their silent operation is often a reason

CHAPTER 6: BASIC INPUT AND OUTPUT DEVICES

for their use, especially in applications where noise might be a problem. Although most electrothermal and electrostatic printers are relatively slow-speed devices, some are capable of producing 2000 to 5000 lines of print per minute.

Another type of nonimpact printer is referred to as an *ink-jet printer*. A nozzle is used to shoot a stream of ink toward the paper in this printer. As the ink passes through a dot-matrix electronic field, a character is formed.

The printer system in Illustration 6-12 can print at speeds as high as 20,000 lines per minute. This printer uses a laser and electrophotographic technology to attain high speeds. Such a high-speed printer overcomes the primary disadvantage of nonimpact printers: the inability to make carbon copies. Several original printings of a page can be made in less time than it takes an impact printer to print one page.

ADVANTAGES AND LIMITATIONS OF PRINTER OUTPUT

An advantage of employing a printer as an output device is that it produces human-readable output. However, printers have a number of disadvantages. First, somewhat like the punched card, printer output is of a fixed

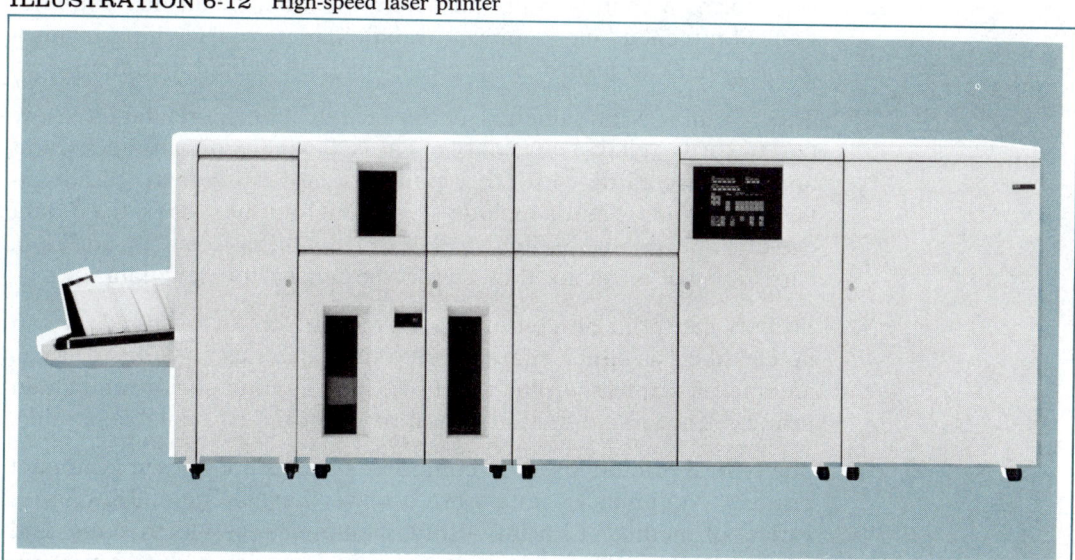

ILLUSTRATION 6-12 High-speed laser printer

size. If a report must be wider than the printer's capability permits, the output must be broken into separate segments and manually aligned. Second, printing is a relatively slow form of output. There are wide variations in printing speeds, but most printers print at speeds of 300, 600, 1200, or 2000 lines per minute.

The nonimpact printer is not used as widely as the impact printer for several reasons. Most of them are not able to make carbon copies of output. They often require special paper that is very expensive. The quality of the nonimpact printed image may not be as good as that produced on impact printers.

SUMMARY

1. Punched cards are a basic input/output medium of most computer systems. Card readers and card punches are the input/output devices (peripheral equipment) used to process them. The readers and punches are designed to read and punch data using either a serial (column-by-column) or a parallel (row-by-row) method. To read the holes in a card, some card readers use a brush-type mechanism while others use a brushless, or photoelectric, mechanism. In addition to reading and punching cards, a combined card read/punch may be capable of reproducing or merging.

2. A card reader performs two checks on data received as input. First, it performs a validity check to determine whether all the combinations of punched holes represent valid characters. Then it performs a second check to insure the accuracy of the reading operation.

3. The advantages of punched cards include human readability, low cost of cards, relative durability of cards, flexibility of card decks, and ability to use cards with other punched-card equipment. Disadvantages of punched cards include slow input/output speeds, fixed data density, and relatively high storage and handling costs. In addition, cards are not erasable; they cannot be reused for new data.

4. Printers can print on continuous forms and/or cut forms. They can be classified as either character-at-a-time, such as console, teletype, and matrix printers, or line-at-a-time, such as comb, drum, and chain printers. They also differ in the number of positions available per line.

5. The typical printers used on computer systems are known as impact printers. Nonimpact printers are a newer development. They use a variety of methods to print output, including heat, electrostatic, and laser techniques. Their low cost and silent operation make them popu-

lar for many applications. Their chief disadvantage is the inability to make carbon copies.

6. The principle advantage of printer output is that it is human-readable. The disadvantages of printers include fixed output size and relatively slow print speeds.

REVIEW QUESTIONS

1. Describe the operation of a card reader.
2. Discuss the two distinct methods of reading data from a punched card.
3. How does a card reader check the accuracy of a read operation?
4. Identify several advantages and limitations of punched-card input/output.
5. What is the primary function of the card punch?
6. What is a printer? Briefly describe the two types of printers.
7. Discuss the different kinds of impact and nonimpact printers.
8. What are the advantages and limitations of printer output?

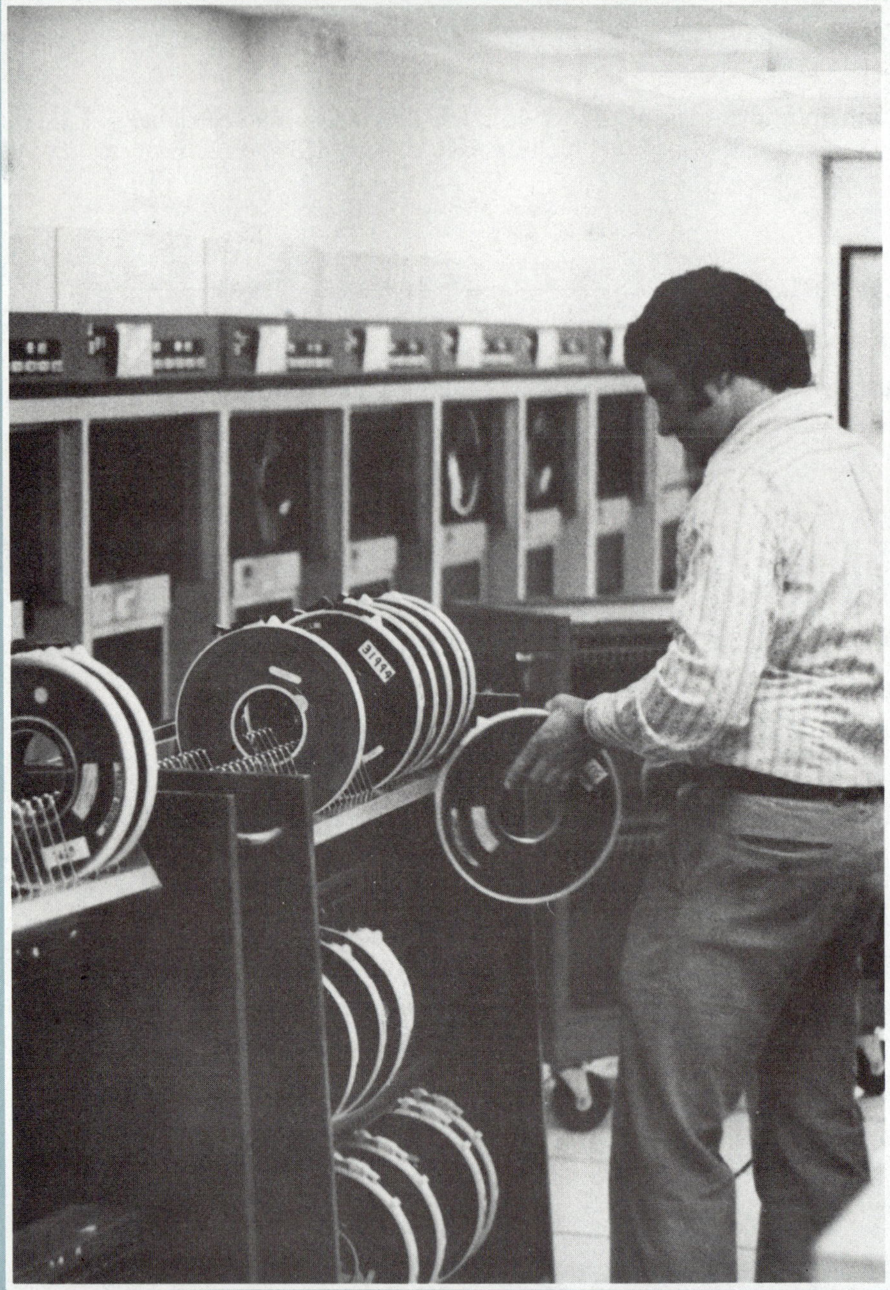

CHAPTER 7

MAGNETIC TAPE INPUT AND OUTPUT

DATA REPRESENTATION ON TAPE

THE TAPE DRIVE

THE SPEED OF
TAPE INPUT/OUTPUT OPERATIONS

THE CAPACITY OF TAPE REELS

ADVANTAGES AND LIMITATIONS OF TAPE
AS AN INPUT/OUTPUT MEDIUM

AN EXAMPLE OF
MAGNETIC TAPE UTILIZATION

DISCUSSION

Opposite: A computer system with many tape drives requires an operator just to load and unload tapes.

Magnetic tape, in appearance, looks much like the tape in a tape recorder. It has two major parts: the *base,* which is a plastic material, and the *magnetic coating,* which consists of a *ferric oxide.* These parts are bonded together by a thin layer of adhesive. While the plastic base of magnetic tape represents the bulk of the tape, the magnetic coating is the essential ingredient allowing magnetic tape to serve as an input/output medium. Data is recorded on the surface of the tape in the form of magnetized areas, combinations of which correspond to letters, numbers, and special characters. The areas are analogous to the holes that represent data in punched cards.

A reel of magnetic tape can hold as much data as can be punched into several hundred thousand cards. A typical speed at which a magnetic tape can be read is 320,000 characters per second—the equivalent of 4000 punched cards.

Magnetic tape is wound on a reel called the *file reel,* or *supply reel,* in much the same way that motion-picture film is placed on a reel. Generally, a reel of magnetic tape is ½ inch wide and 2400 feet long. However, there are magnetic tapes that are ¾ inch or 1 inch wide. The length of the tape can, of course, be determined by its purpose and may range from 50 to 3600 feet. Illustration 7-1 presents a reel of tape and a blow-up of a section of the tape showing its composition.

A small strip of reflecting material is placed at each end of a magnetic tape. The strip at the beginning of the tape is called the *load-point marker.* It indicates to the computer the beginning of the usable portion of the tape. The strip at the end of the tape is called the *end-of-reel marker.* It tells the computer where the end of the tape is located so that the tape is not run off the reel and processing delayed accordingly. These markers are on opposite sides of the tape to insure that the computer can distinguish between them. They are sensed when they pass under a light source, and they reflect light into photoelectric cells assigned to the markers. The file markers and the photoelectric cells are shown in Illustration 7-2.

DATA REPRESENTATION ON TAPE

Generally, there are two forms of coded data representation on tape. Illustration 7-3 shows one of them: 6-bit BCD code with a seventh bit for parity checking. The short vertical lines on the tape represent areas that are magnetized and are equivalent to on bits. The spaces represent areas on the tape that are not magnetized and are equivalent to off bits. Each of the seven horizontal rows on tape is called a *track*. The tracks correspond to the seven bits of BCD coding: B-, A-, 8-, 4-, 2-, and 1-bits plus the parity, or check, bit. Each character consists of the combination of bits in one

CHAPTER 7: MAGNETIC TAPE INPUT AND OUTPUT

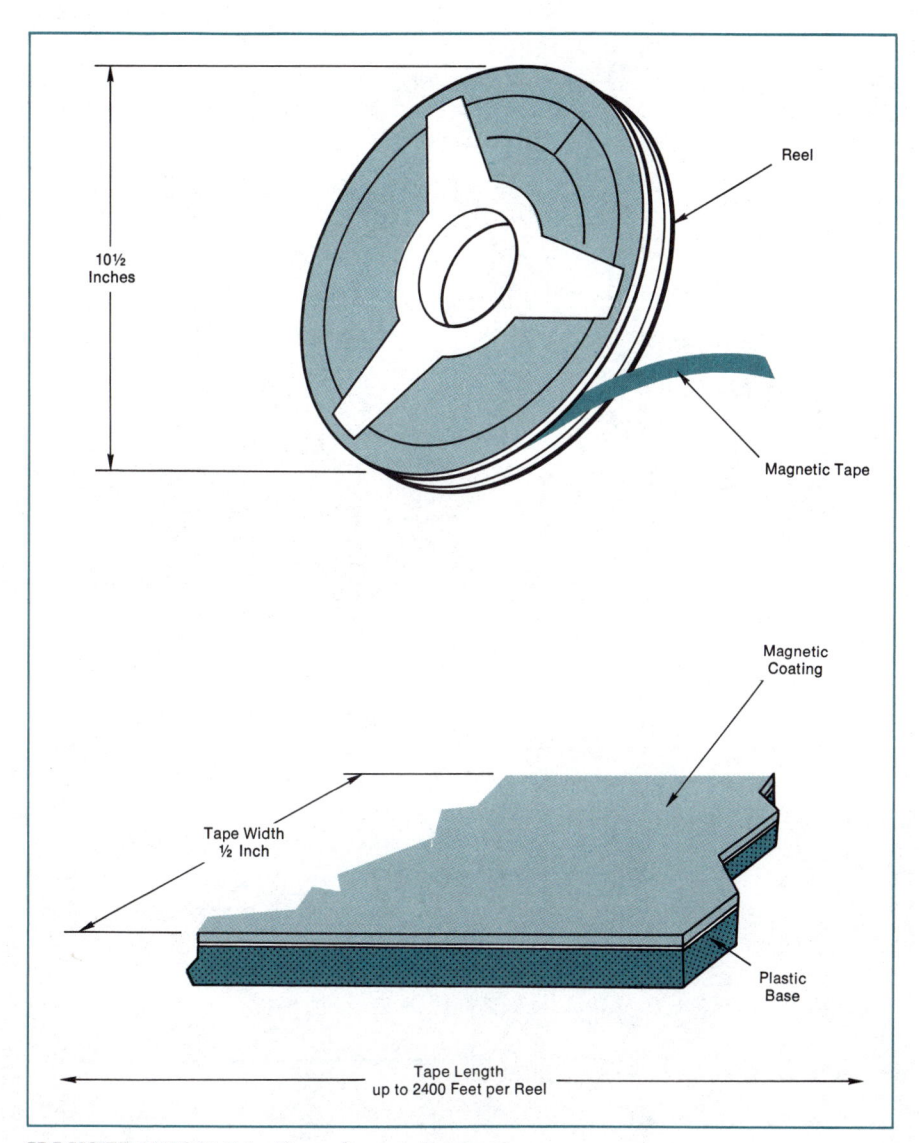

ILLUSTRATION 7-1 Tape characteristics

vertical column of the tape. For example, the first character in Illustration 7-3 is the number 0, which consists of an 8-bit and a 2-bit; the check bit is off because this tape uses even parity. Because there are seven vertical positions in which there can be on bits, this tape is known as *seven-track tape*.

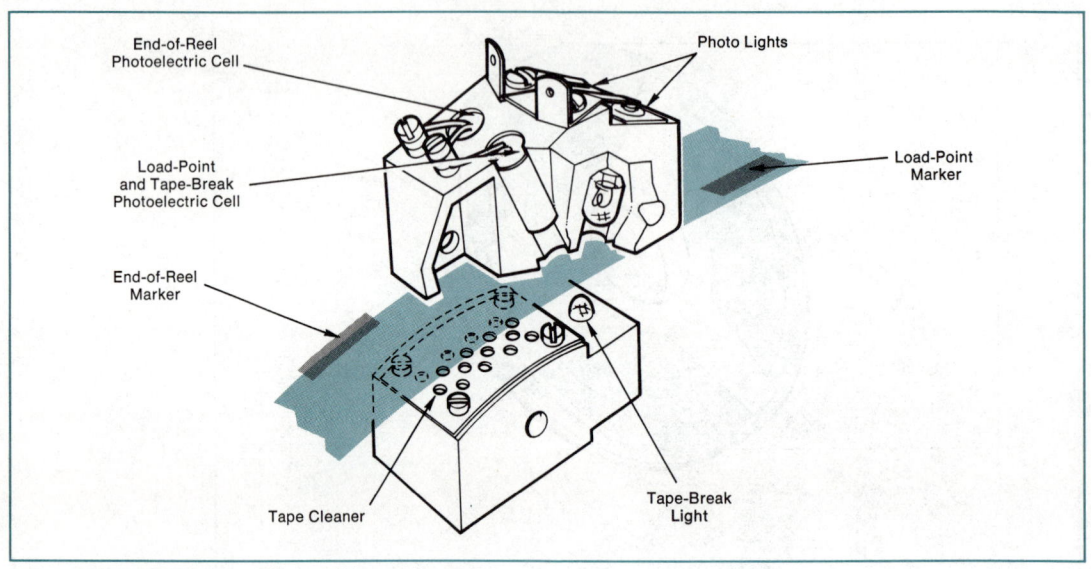

ILLUSTRATION 7-2 File marking and sensing

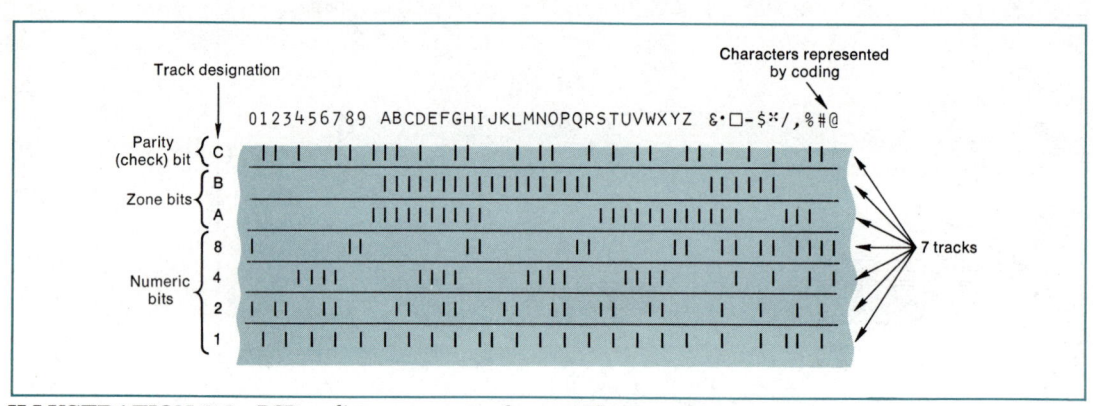

ILLUSTRATION 7-3 BCD coding on seven-track magnetic tape

In addition to seven-track BCD coding, **nine-track tape** codes are used. As the term *nine-track* implies, these codes are used with tapes having nine vertical positions, or tracks. They are the most common type of tapes. In each set of vertical positions (byte) on a nine-track tape, either one EBCDIC or ASCII character or two 4-bit BCD digits can be coded. Nine-track tapes are generally written in odd parity; the ninth track is used for a parity bit (see Illustration 7-4).

Data is stored on magnetic tape as groups of characters called **physical records**, or **blocks**. Each block, while composed of characters, also

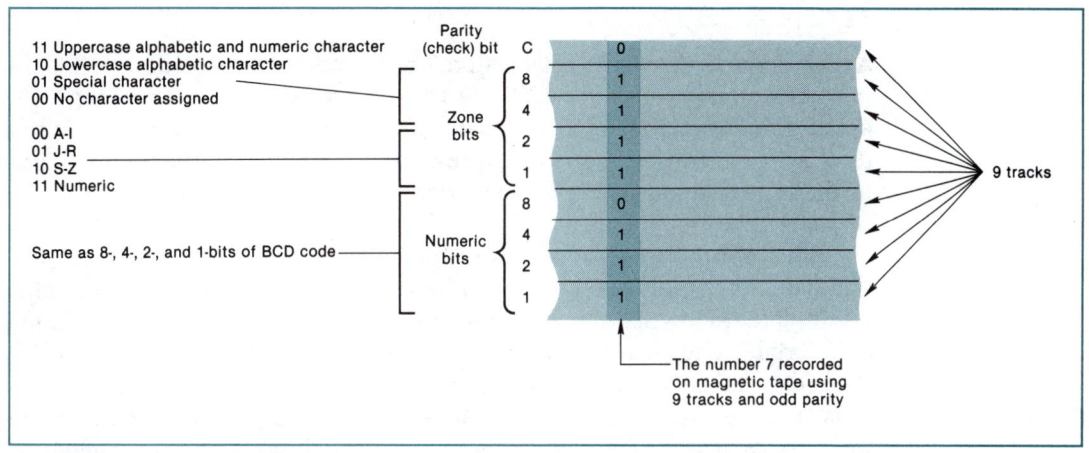

ILLUSTRATION 7-4   EBCDIC coding on nine-track magnetic tape

represents one or more *logical records*—the data grouping known to an application program.

The number of characters in a block can vary from few to many. Data storage on magnetic tape is not restricted to 80 characters as on the standard punched card. Consecutive blocks on the tape are separated by spaces in which no data is recorded. These spaces are called *interblock gaps*, or *IBGs*.

When a tape is read during the execution of a program, all of the data between two IBGs is read by a single read instruction. If each block is 100 characters (or bytes) long, a single read instruction reads 100 characters of data. The IBGs are necessary because of this start/stop type of operation. They provide the space required to stop the passage of tape over the read/write heads of the tape drive. Since reading and writing are performed at a constant speed, a portion of the IBG is used for the tape to gain speed when a read/write operation begins. The width of the IBGs varies from 0.6 inch to 0.75 inch, depending on the type of tape unit and whether the tape is seven- or nine-track. Illustration 7-5 shows four blocks of data and the gaps that separate them.

ILLUSTRATION 7-5   Section of tape with four blocks of data and interblock gaps

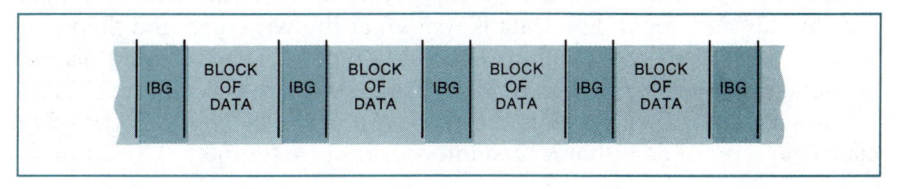

○ THE TAPE DRIVE

A tape drive is shown in Illustration 7-6. This device reads and writes the magnetized areas on a tape. When this device reads data from tape, the data is not affected. That is, the reading operation is not destructive. When data is written on tape, any data previously recorded on the affected area of the tape is replaced by the new data. Therefore, the writing operation is destructive.

Illustration 7-7 demonstrates the arrangement of reels on a tape drive. The file reel (supply reel) that is to be read or written has been mounted on the left side, while the *machine reel* (*take-up reel*) has been mounted on the right. The *vacuum column* for each reel (see Illustration 7-6) allows slack tape to be pulled from the reel. These columns are necessary because the reels rotate at such high speeds that the tape would snap if slack were not provided. The tape is threaded through a mechanism called the *read/write assembly* (an enlarged schematic of which appears in Illustration 7-7) and anchored on the machine reel. Some tape drives require manual threading of the tape, but other tape drives do this automatically.

When the tape is processed, it moves from left to right through the read/write assembly and onto the machine reel. On some tape drives, the tape is automatically rewound onto the file reel before it can be read or written on again. Most tape drives are capable of reading the tape while the reel is moving in the reverse direction (right to left) also, so no rewinding operation is required.

The reading operation is accomplished by individual *read/write heads*. There is one head for each track on the tape. The reading portion of the head senses the small magnetized areas and, in conjunction with the other reading assemblies, converts these areas into characters. Since data is recorded on the tape serially, the reading operation is performed serially. The writing operation follows a similar pattern. Instead of sensing magnetized areas, a write head places magnetized areas on the tape, replacing any data already there.

The basic programmed functions of a tape drive are to read and write data on a tape. In addition, the tape can be rewound, backspaced, and skipped ahead (over faulty sections of tape) under control of a program.

To insure the accuracy of tape reading operations, a computer system, in conjunction with its tape drives, carries out three checks for accuracy. One kind of check is dependent upon whether or not the read/write heads are single-gap or dual-gap. Many tape drives have a dual-gap read/write head capability. Data is written at the write gap and then read at the read gap for verification. Thus, this type of head offers a distinct advantage over the single-gap read/write head, which lacks this capability.

A second kind of check is the *vertical parity checking* performed on each character of data that is read into storage (see Chapter 5). In addition,

CHAPTER 7: MAGNETIC TAPE INPUT AND OUTPUT

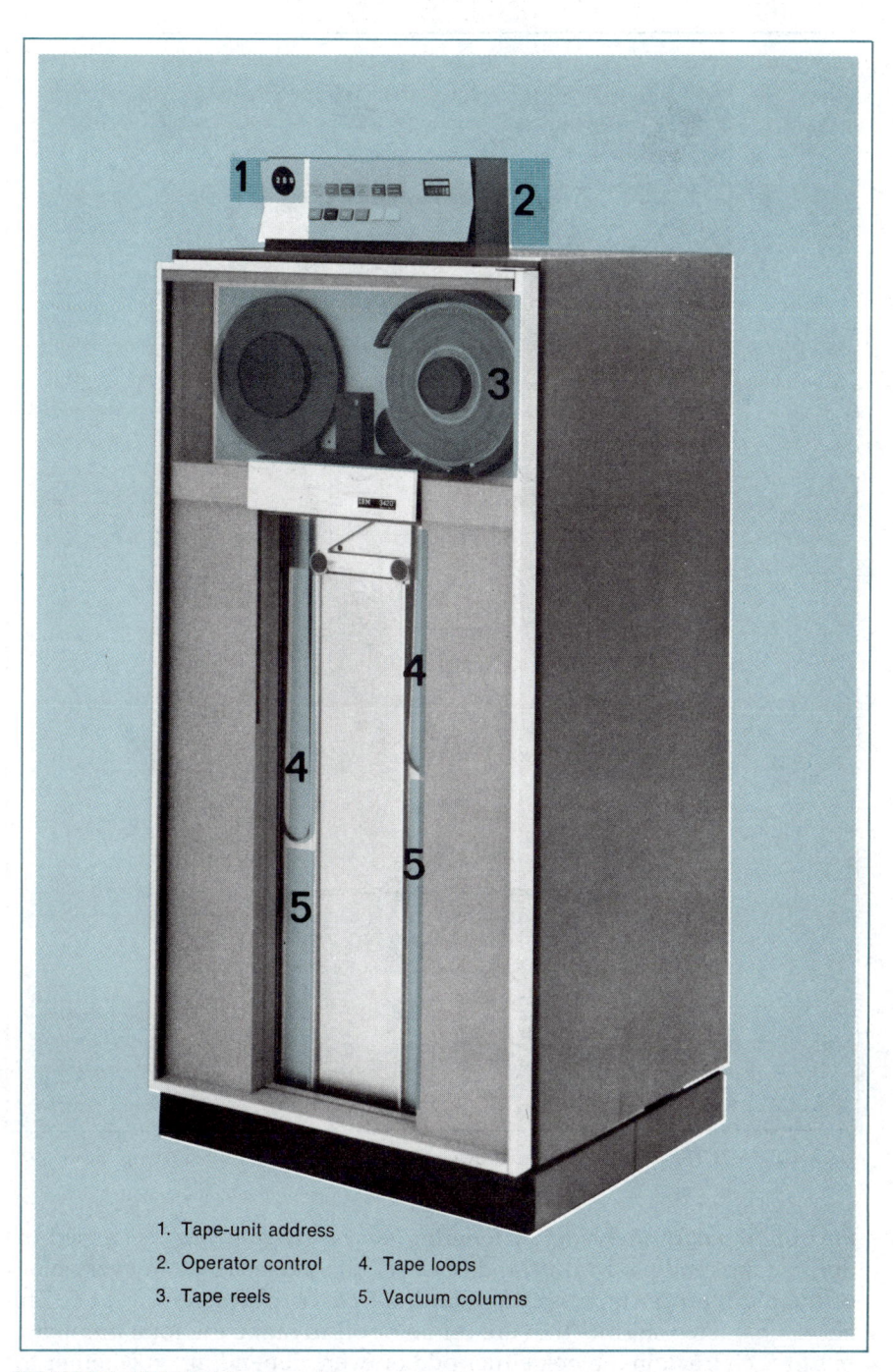

1. Tape-unit address
2. Operator control
3. Tape reels
4. Tape loops
5. Vacuum columns

ILLUSTRATION 7-6 Tape drive

126

UNIT TWO: COMPUTER SYSTEMS

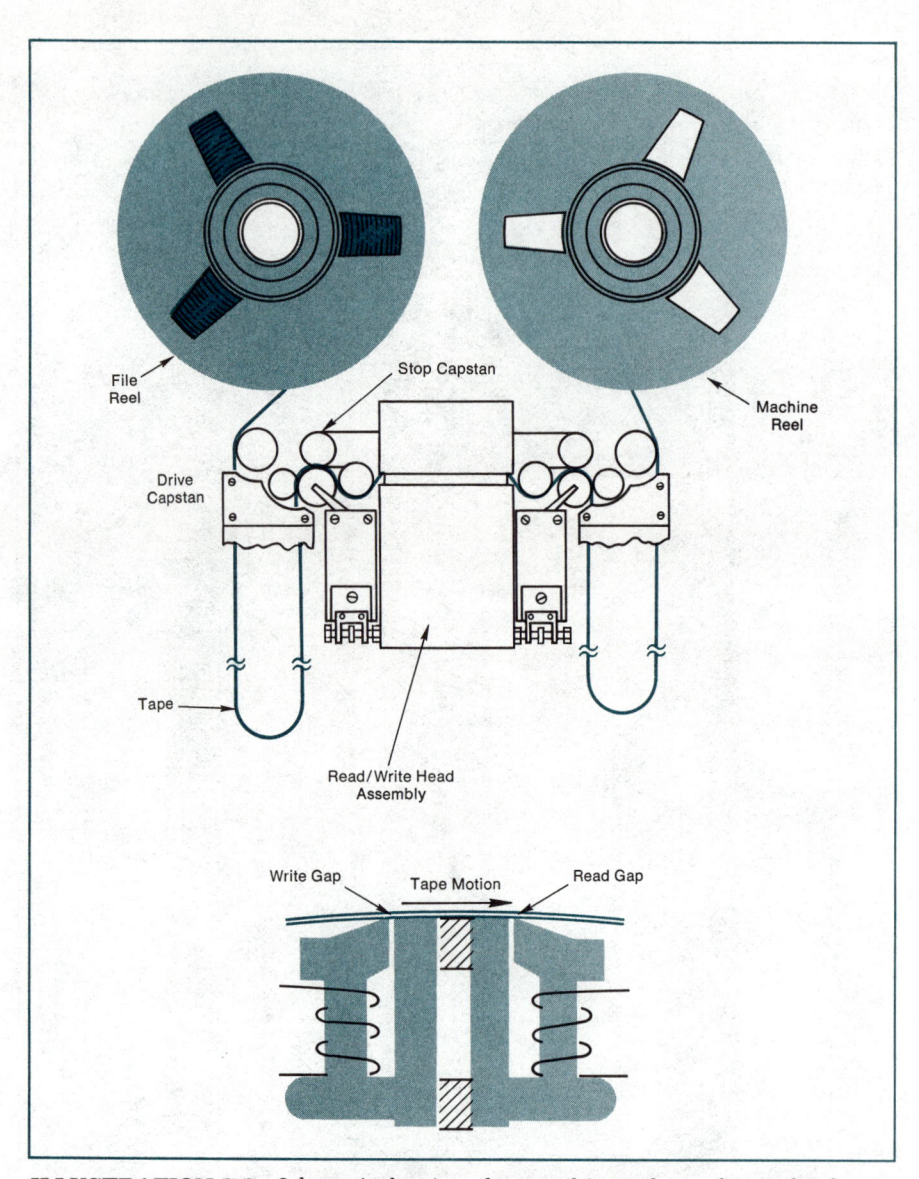

ILLUSTRATION 7-7 Schematic drawing of a tape drive and a read/write head

horizontal parity checking, or *longitudinal parity checking*, is carried out during tape reading. In this kind of checking, the last byte in every block of data written on tape is a *longitudinal check character*, or *LCC*. This check character has bits that are set on or off to make the total number of bits in each track in a block either odd or even, depending on whether the

CHAPTER 7: MAGNETIC TAPE INPUT AND OUTPUT

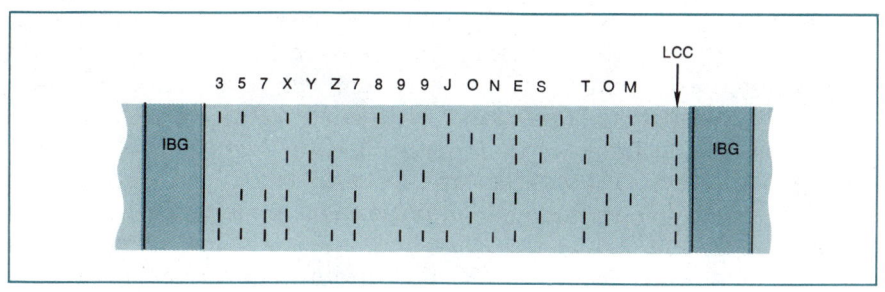

ILLUSTRATION 7-8 Vertical and longitudinal parity checking

check is for odd or even parity. Illustration 7-8 shows a block of 20 characters and the LCC for the block. The individual characters have odd parity and the LCC insures that each track in the block also contains an odd number of on bits. When data is read by a tape drive, the data is checked for both vertical and horizontal parity.

To insure accuracy of tape writing operations, data is read immediately after it is written. This is possible because the writing mechanism immediately precedes the reading mechanism in the read/write assembly. The data that is read is then compared with the data that was intended to be written on the tape. If they are not the same, an error is indicated.

Unlike input and output errors on a card system, tape reading and writing errors can sometimes be corrected without interruption of processing. When a reading error is detected, for example, the computer system branches to a programmed routine for handling errors. This routine causes the tape to be backspaced one block and read again. It is possible that on the first reading there was a piece of dust or dirt on the tape surface that caused an error. If it was wiped off in passing through the read/write assembly, the second reading may take place without interruption. If so, the computer continues to execute the program as if no error had been indicated. If not, the computer branches to the error routine again. This routine may backspace and re-read the tape as many as 100 times before alerting the computer operator that an error has occurred.

The same type of error procedure is followed when a writing error is detected. The tape is backspaced, and the computer system tries to write the block again. If the writing takes place without error on this second try, the computer continues to execute the program. Only after many tries does the error routine skip over the faulty section of tape that cannot be written on (this has the effect of making one long interblock gap) and continue farther down the tape. Because errors are corrected in this way, writing errors should not cause the computer system to stop unless a large portion of the tape's surface is damaged or otherwise unusable.

To prevent records from being destroyed in error, detailed written instructions for each processing step are prepared for the computer operator. Among other things, these instructions tell which tapes are to be mounted on which tape drives and whether the tapes are to be read or written on. The operator then checks the label on the outside of each reel to make certain that it holds the tape specified in the instructions. If the tape is to be written on, the operator places a *file-protect ring* on the back of the tape reel before mounting it (no ring—no write). Such a ring is shown in Illustration 7-9. If a program tries to write on a tape drive that does not have a file-protect ring, a writing error occurs and no writing takes place. The requirement for this ring helps to prevent records from being destroyed in error.

ILLUSTRATION 7-9   File-protect ring

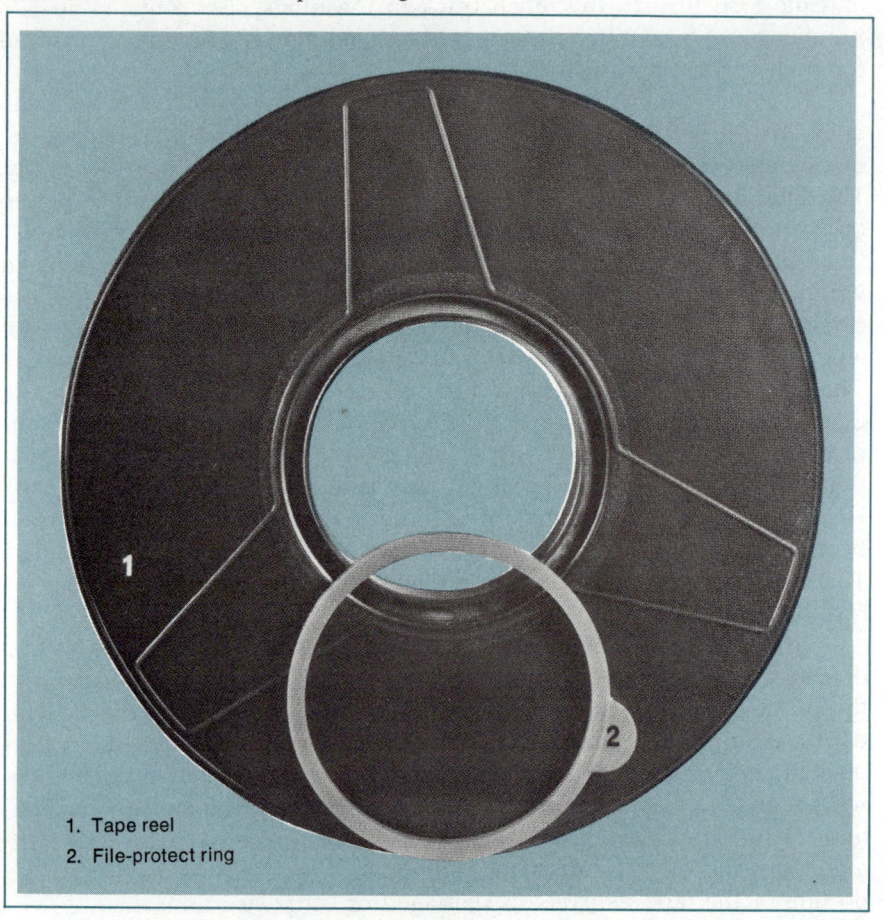

1. Tape reel
2. File-protect ring

Another technique to prevent the destruction of records is called *label checking*. In this case, the label is not on the outside of the reel; it is part of the tape itself (an 80-byte record preceding the first data record of a file.) This record, or *header label*, contains such items as file name, date the file was created, and date after which it is permissible to write on the file. The label is checked by a programmed routine that is executed before records are read or written. The routine reads the header label and checks to make certain that the tape is the right tape and that it is mounted on the correct drive. After the label check, if all is well, the program execution continues. If not, the program prints out an error message, and the tape is not processed.

The computer determines the end of a file by means of a *trailer label*, a special record following the last data record on the file. This 80-byte record contains control information, such as the number of records in the file.

THE SPEED OF TAPE INPUT/OUTPUT OPERATIONS

One measure of the speed of magnetic tape reading and writing operations is the *transfer rate* of the tape drive. This rate is the maximum number of bytes of data that can be read or written on a tape per second. It depends upon the speed at which the tape moves past the read/write heads (called the *transport speed*) and the number of characters, or bytes, that are recorded per inch along the length of the tape (called the *density*). A common transport speed is 200 inches per second. Some typical tape densities are 556, 800, 1600, and 6250 bytes per inch (BPI, or bpi). Many tape drives have a *dual-density* capability. If a tape drive has this capability, its read/write heads can write on a magnetic tape in either of two densities. A common dual-density is 1600/6250 BPI.

The transfer rate of a tape drive is calculated by multiplying the transport speed times the density. As an example, suppose that a tape drive, with a transport speed of 200 inches per second, reads tapes with a density of 1600 bytes per inch. The transfer rate of this tape drive is 1600 times 200, or 320,000, bytes per second. To appreciate this speed, consider that this book could be read by such a tape drive in less than 10 seconds.

Although the transfer rate of a tape drive is a good indication of its speed, this figure is somewhat misleading. Actually, when a tape drive reads blocks of data, it stops each time it comes to an interblock gap. Therefore, when blocks are being read or written, a certain amount of time is spent stopping and starting at each interblock gap. This is called *start/stop time*. The total amount of time required to read or write a given number of blocks is the sum of the time spent reading or writing the data plus the time spent starting and stopping at the interblock gaps.

To appreciate the effect of start/stop time on reading and writing speeds, assume that a tape drive has a transfer rate of 320,000 bytes per second and a start/stop time of three **milliseconds** (.003 second). If this tape drive is used to read 6000 blocks and each block is 100 characters long, how long will it take?

In this problem, a total of 6000 times 100, or 600,000, bytes of data are to be read. Since the transfer rate is 320,000 bytes per second, the total time for reading the data is 600,000 divided by 320,000, or 1.88 seconds. As for start/stop time, there are 6000 interblock gaps and passing over each takes .003 second. The total start/stop time is 6000 times .003, or 18, seconds. Therefore, 1.88 plus 18, or a total of 19.88 seconds, are required to read the 6000 blocks. To say it another way, 18 seconds are spent in stopping and starting the tape, and only 1.88 seconds are spent in reading the data.

Up to this point, each block (physical record) has been assumed to contain only one logical record. For reasons that will become obvious, normally more than one logical record is included within each block. For example, blocks of 10 logical records can be recorded on tape. In this case, the records are called **blocked records**. The tape is said to have a **blocking factor** of 10. Illustration 7-10 represents blocked records with a blocking factor of four. A tape may have a blocking factor of one (one logical record per block); the records on such a tape are unblocked.

In the example above, the reading of 6000 unblocked records, each 100 characters long, took 19.88 seconds. Suppose the 6000 records were blocked, 10 to a block. How would this affect the total input time? Since 10 records, instead of one, would be recorded between interblock gaps, the total number of gaps to be passed over would be reduced from 6000 to 600. Otherwise, the problem is the same as the preceding one. The total input time would be 1.88 seconds (for reading data) plus 1.8 seconds (600 times .003), or 3.68 seconds. In other words, by blocking the records in this manner, the input time would be reduced from 19.88 seconds to 3.68 seconds. If the blocking factor were increased to 100, the reduction in input time would be from 19.88 to 2.06 seconds.

ILLUSTRATION 7-10 Block of records with a blocking factor of four

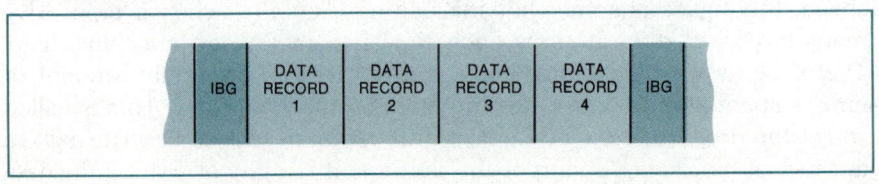

| IBG | DATA RECORD 1 | DATA RECORD 2 | DATA RECORD 3 | DATA RECORD 4 | IBG |

CHAPTER 7: MAGNETIC TAPE INPUT AND OUTPUT

While certain figures were used in the above illustration, they do not represent all of the capabilities of magnetic tape. The transport speed, which was given as 200 inches of tape per second, can also be 120, 320, 470, 780, or 1250 inches per second. The number of bytes that the tape drive is capable of reading or writing, which was stated as 320,000 bytes per second, may range from approximately 41,700 to 1,250,000 bytes per second. Finally, the density, which was given as 1600 bytes per inch, can also be 556 or 6250 bytes per inch. Therefore, when the speed of tape input/output operations is to be calculated, a primary consideration is the type of tape drive utilized.

Although blocking records improves tape input/output speeds, it has one major limitation. Since all of the data between two IBGs is read during a single operation, the input area of storage must be at least as large as the block of data. For example, if 100-character records are blocked 10 to a block, the input area in storage must be large enough to hold 1000 characters. If a program is to read two input tapes and write two output tapes and each block of data is 1000 characters in length, the program requires 4000 positions of storage for input and output areas. The amount of storage that can be set aside for input and output areas must be considered when determining whether (or how) records should be blocked.

THE CAPACITY OF TAPE REELS

To figure the maximum capacity of a reel of tape, one must know two characteristics of the tape: its length and its density. If, for example, a 2400-foot tape has a density of 1600 bytes per inch, the maximum capacity of the tape is 2400 feet times 12 inches times 1600 bytes per inch, or a total of 46,080,000 bytes of data. This total is roughly equivalent to the amount of data that can be recorded on 576,000 punched cards.

The capacity of a tape is reduced by the interblock gaps separating the data on the tape. As noted earlier, a typical length for interblock gaps is 0.75 inch. At a density of 1600 bytes per inch, each of these interblock gaps takes up the equivalent of 1200 bytes of data. To figure the total length of tape that a given number of records will take up, one must calculate the length of tape used for data and for interblock gaps. Since the gaps on tapes are wasted space, blocking records increases the capacity of a length of tape.

Suppose, for example, that 8000 unblocked records are to be recorded on tape and each record contains 100 characters. If the tape has a density of 1600 bytes per inch and an interblock gap of 0.75 inch, how many inches of tape will be required?

Since the total number of characters to be recorded is 800,000 and the density is 1600, the length of the tape used for data is 500 inches (800,000 divided by 1600). Since 8000 interblock gaps separate the 8000 records, 6000 inches will be used for interblock gaps (8000 times 0.75). Therefore, a total of 6500 inches of tape will be required for these 8000 records. Twelve times as much tape will be used for interblock gaps as for data.

If the records are blocked 10 to a block, the only thing that changes is the number of interblock gaps required; only 800 will be needed instead of 8000. Therefore, the total length of tape required for the same amount of data will be 500 plus 600, or 1100 inches. And if the blocking factor is 100, the data will require only 560 inches of tape. In other words, by increasing the blocking factor, the capacity of a tape is increased. Remember, however, that records can be blocked only within the limits of a computer's available storage.

○ ADVANTAGES AND LIMITATIONS OF TAPE AS AN INPUT/OUTPUT MEDIUM

The primary advantage of magnetic tape as an input or output medium is the speed with which data can be transferred. Tape provides a means through which data becomes extremely accessible to the computer. In conjunction with the input and output speeds, which are desirable in themselves, this additional capability also saves computer time. Since the computer performs better than any input or output device yet discussed, the closer the operating speeds of the input and output devices to the speed of a computer, the more time is saved. Second, magnetic tape possesses the advantage of low storage cost. In comparison to punched cards, magnetic tape is capable of storing a mass of data in a relatively small space. This is possible because of the high density that can be achieved on tape. Third, magnetic tape is reusable. Even though data has been written on a tape, the tape can be completely erased, or updated data can be written over old unwanted data. Fourth, the cost of tape is less than that of punched cards. A single 2400-foot length of magnetic tape costs approximately $15. To record the amount of data that can be placed on a single tape on cards would require several boxes of cards. Fifth, the header label placed at the beginning of a tape can be used as a security device. Normally, a serial number is included in the header label. It is difficult to access the tape without knowing this number. Therefore, if this number is not made available, the chances of gaining access to the data on the tape or of destroying its contents are reduced. Finally, magnetic tape can be used either online or offline. When online, the tape is under the direct control of the computer. Offline means that, while the tape may be stored in the computer room, the computer does not have access to it. Thus, an online tape may contain frequently used programs or data; an offline tape may contain information saved for historical purposes.

There are three primary limitations of magnetic tape. First, the data coded on magnetic tape is not readable by humans. Since the contents of a tape cannot be read by a programmer or an operator, the data on a tape may have to be printed before an error can be located. Second, data on tape can be organized only in a sequential manner. This means that individual items on a tape cannot be accessed in a direct fashion. The tape must be scanned from its beginning to locate a specific data item. Generally, processing data in this fashion is relatively slow when compared to processing data on magnetic disk or drum. Finally, magnetic tape may be influenced by environmental factors. Such problems as dust, dirt, high or low temperatures, humidity, and electrical fields cause errors in the processing of data on tape. Dust and dirt on magnetic tape may cause the read head to misread characters. Temperature fluctuations and humidity may cause distortions of the tape or cause it to become brittle so that breakage occurs. Electrical fields or magnetic currents may alter the magnetized areas on the tape. Even static electricity caused by the soles of a person's shoes rubbing a nylon carpet, if discharged into a reel of tape, can cause the tape to be erased. Therefore, extreme care should be exercised in the handling and storage of magnetic tape to insure the accuracy of its contents.

AN EXAMPLE OF MAGNETIC TAPE UTILIZATION

A typical tape-oriented system can perform processing that is impossible on a typical card-oriented system. Many of the functions that are carried out by punched-card equipment in a card system are done by the computer itself in a tape system. The system design for tape processing is significantly different from that for card processing.

Illustration 7-11 is a system flowchart for the basic processing of an order-writing, billing, inventory, and accounts receivable application. It represents six processing steps during which a combined invoice and shipping-order form is printed, and inventory (item) and accounts receivable (customer) master records on tape are brought up to date. The first step is keypunching and verifying; the other five steps are computer processing runs. In the system flowchart, the ▢ symbol indicates a computer run, and the ◯ symbol represents a magnetic-tape file.

UNIT TWO: COMPUTER SYSTEMS

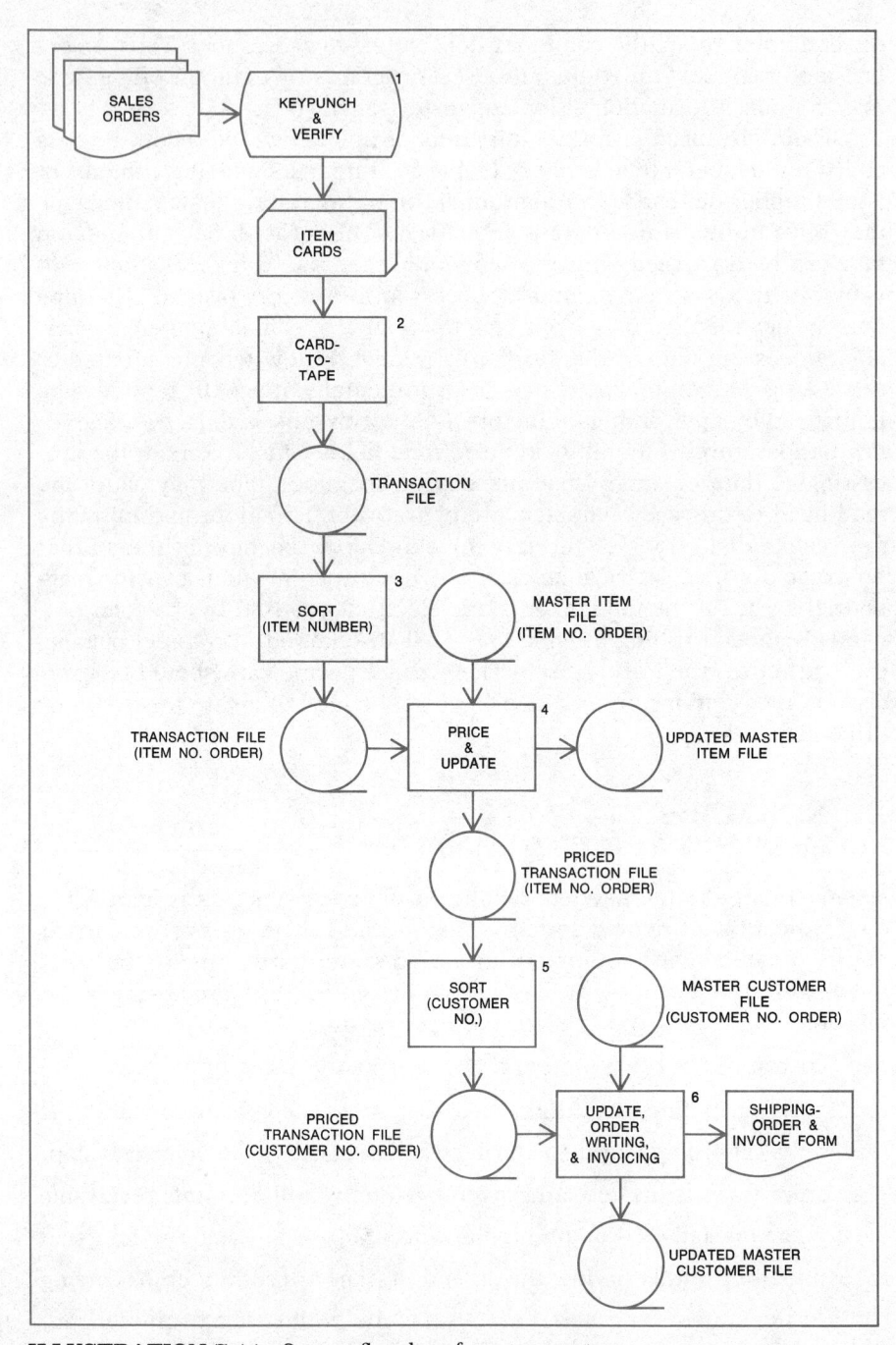

ILLUSTRATION 7-11 System flowchart for a tape system

CHAPTER 7: MAGNETIC TAPE INPUT AND OUTPUT

Sales orders serve as the source documents in this system; they are used in the keypunching and verifying of item cards. The intent is to record in punched cards the data pertaining to the line items on the orders. This includes the customer number and other identifying information plus quantity ordered and item number for each item. It does not include item description or unit price because this data can be added to the transaction records from master records during subsequent processing.

Although this transaction data can be punched one line item to a punched card as it would be for a punched-card system, it can also be punched several line items to a card. When this method is used, the punched cards are called *spread cards* and the volume of cards to be processed by the system is reduced. Illustration 7-12 is an example of a spread card in which customer number, order number, and order date are punched in the first three fields of the card as identifying information. Thereafter, quantity ordered and item number are punched for up to six line items. If more than six line items are ordered by a single customer, additional spread cards must be used.

Regardless of which type of punched card is used (the unit-record or the spread card), the second step in the system is to convert the punched-card data to data on tape. This is done in a *card-to-tape-run*. At the end of this step, each record on the tape will have five fields: customer number, order number, and order date (these identify each record); and quantity ordered and item number (these represent the transaction). The records may be either blocked or unblocked on the tape. Illustration 7-13 shows a portion of the tape with a blocking factor of four.

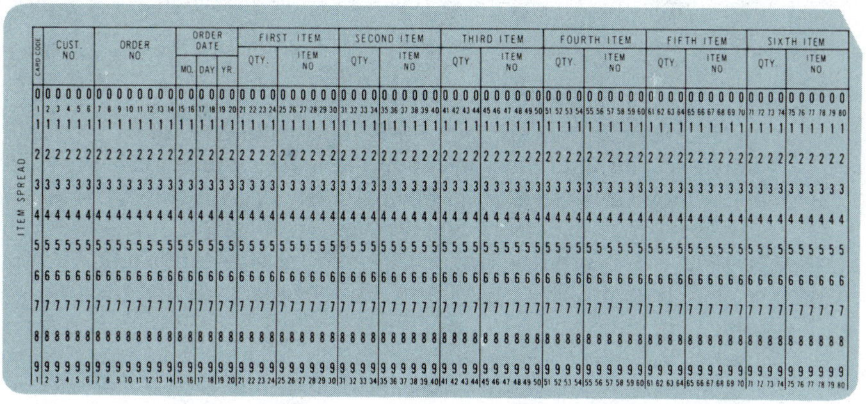

ILLUSTRATION 7-12 Spread card

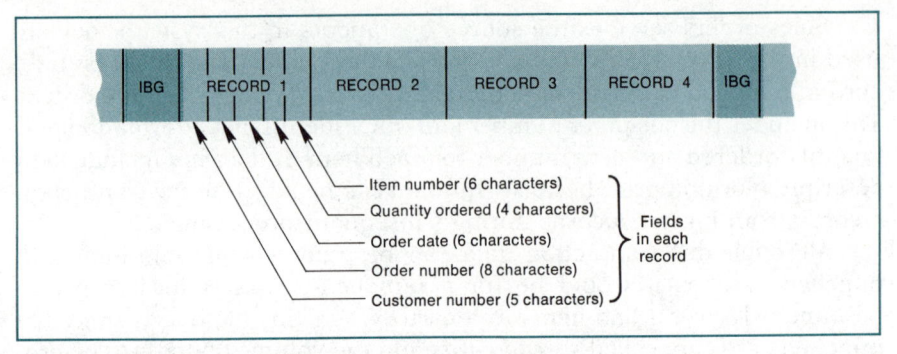

ILLUSTRATION 7-13 Blocked transaction records

Step 3 is a sort run. Although a single input tape and a single sorted output tape are shown, more than two tape drives are required for sorting. It is possible to use only three tape drives, but four are normally used, to increase the speed of the sorting operation. The input tape with the records in the original sequence is mounted on one of the drives. During the sort, each of the tapes on the four drives may be written on, or read from, several times. On completion of the sort, one of the drives holds the output tape with records in item-number order. This sorting process may be very complex from a programming point of view, but the programming effort is easily justified; the ability to sort tape records into a desired sequence is a very important characteristic of tape systems.

Step 4 in the system is designed to do two things. First, additional data is added to the transaction file so that it can be used to print the line items of the shipping-order and invoice form. This additional data includes item description, unit price, and whether the items will be shipped or back-ordered. Second, the master item file (inventory file) is brought up to date. The records in the master item file have the format indicated in Illustration 7-14. The fields in each master item record that may be affected during this update process are the on-hand field (it will be reduced by the number of items shipped) and the back-ordered field (it will be increased by the number of items ordered when no inventory is available to be shipped).

It should be clear now why step 3 in Illustration 7-11, the sorting operation, is required before step 4 can be accomplished. The transaction records have to be sorted into item-number order so that they are in the same sequence as the master item records before they can be processed against the master item file.

Step 4 has two input tapes and two output tapes. The input tapes contain the transaction records (the transaction file) and the master item records (the old master file). The output tapes contain the priced transaction

CHAPTER 7: MAGNETIC TAPE INPUT AND OUTPUT

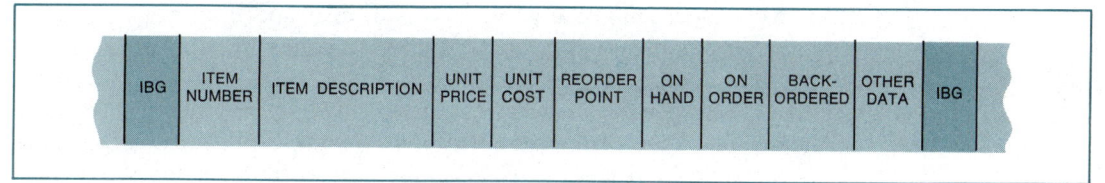

ILLUSTRATION 7-14 Master item record

records (the priced transaction file) and the updated master item records (the new master file). After this processing run, the new master file is the same as the old master file except that the on-hand and/or back-ordered fields in certain records are brought up to date. The priced transaction records (one of which is shown in Illustration 7-15) have the same basic data as the sorted transaction records plus five fields derived from the master item records. The priced transaction records now contain all of the data needed to print the line items of invoices.

The processing in step 4 takes place by reading into storage both a master item record and a transaction record. If the master item record has the same item number as the transaction record, any affected fields in the master record (on-hand and/or back-ordered) are brought up to date. A priced transaction record is assembled and written on the priced transaction file. Then the next transaction record is read into storage. When all transactions for a master record have been processed, the updated master record is written on the master file. On the other hand, if there are no transactions for a master record, the record is written on the new master file exactly as it was on the old one. Because a relatively small percent of the master records may be affected in an update run, many master records may simply be copied from the old master file to the new one.

In step 5 the priced transaction records are sorted into customer-number order in preparation for the processing run of step 6. Since the master

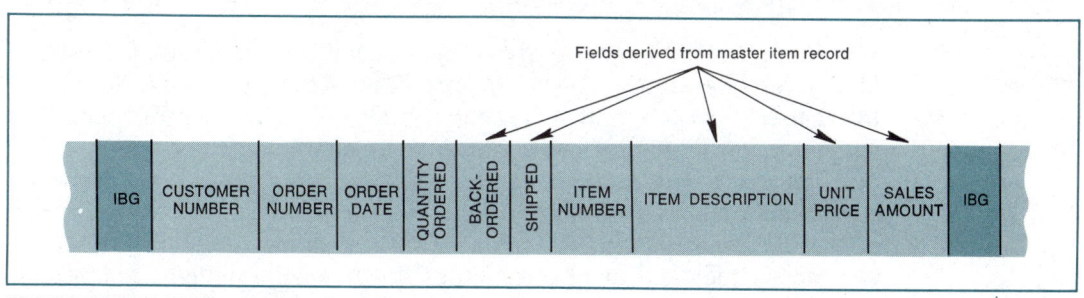

ILLUSTRATION 7-15 Priced transaction record

customer file (accounts receivable file) is in customer-number order, the priced transaction file must be sorted into that same sequence. Once again, although only one input tape and one output tape are shown on the flowchart, all tape drives on the system are normally used by the sort program.

The inputs to the processing run of step 6 are a master customer file (old master) and the priced transaction file. The outputs of this run are the shipping-order and invoice form, plus an updated master customer file (new master). The master customer records contain data needed to print the heading of the shipping-order and invoice form (such as customer name and address, terms, and shipping instructions) plus accounts receivable data (such as total amount owed, and amounts owed over thirty, sixty, and ninety days). After the heading of the output form is printed from the data in the master customer record, the line items are printed from the data in the priced transaction file. At this stage, the invoice total is calculated, printed on the shipping-order and invoice form, and used to bring up to date the customer's accounts receivable data. Then the updated customer record is written on the new master file. Because many customers will not have ordered any items, many customer records can simply be read from the old master file and written, unchanged, on the new master file.

Restating this point, card records are converted to tape records in card-to-tape runs. The tape records are first sorted into the order of the master files to be updated and then processed against these master files. Printed reports can be prepared during master updates or later in separate processing runs. At the end of the six steps illustrated in the flowchart, the updated master item file, the updated master customer file, and the priced transaction file are ready for further processing. For instance, the master item file could be processed by the computer to prepare inventory-management reports. Similarly, the master customer file could be used to prepare an Aged Accounts Receivable report. The priced transaction file could be used to prepare sales analysis reports.

○ **DISCUSSION**

When tape and card systems are compared, it is obvious that tape systems have several advantages. First, tape records can be read and written faster than card records. Second, a tape can contain a large number of characters while a card is limited. If more than 80 or 96 characters must be recorded, additional cards are required. Third, a tape system usually requires fewer steps than a card system for comparable amounts of processing. For example, the tape system in Illustration 7-11 requires six steps to update two master files and print one output document. A similar card system might require eight or more steps for this processing. Fourth, data and programs can be handled more easily when recorded on tape. Consider, for example, the difference between putting 8000 cards in a card reader and mounting one reel of tape on a tape drive. An experienced operator can mount a tape on a drive in 10 to 15 seconds.

On the other hand, tape systems present complications that are not found on card systems. First, programming for a tape system is more difficult than programming for a card system. Because tape-processing runs often involve multiple input and output files, the processing within the program is not as simple as reading a card, processing it, and writing a line on the printer. Multiple input and output areas are required, as well as more complex programming logic. In addition, error-handling routines are required for tape input and output operations, but not for card opertions. Remember, for example, that if a tape reading error is detected, the tape is backspaced and the operation is retried. Finally, if logical records are blocked—say, 10 to a block—they must be assembled in an output area in storage before a write operation is performed. Similarly, when a block of logical records is read into storage, the program must keep track of which logical record in the block is next to be processed.

A second complication of tape processing was mentioned earlier: Data on tape cannot be read or decoded by an operator. If an error occurs during a processing run, it is difficult to determine whether the error resulted from programming or from inaccurate data. A program that prints the contents of tapes on the printer must be available. Such programs are called *tape-to-printer programs*. Because an operator can decode data that is punched in cards, such programs are not necessary for card systems.

Third, adding, changing, or deleting records in a tape file requires the creation of a new file. In a card system, a master record in a card file can be changed by keypunching a new record and replacing the old record in the card file with the new record. In a tape system, special programs, called *file-maintenance programs*, must be executed to add, change, or delete records from a file. The change records are sorted and then processed against the master file by the file-maintenance program to produce a new master file containing the changes. This approach is flowcharted in Illustration 7-16.

Also mentioned earlier was the fact that records on tape can be influenced by environmental factors. Because the surface of a tape can become damaged or dirty, records on tape can become unreadable. In addition, tape records can be destroyed by writing other data over them. Suppose, for example, that a company's current accounts receivable master tape was mounted by mistake on a tape drive used for the output of an inventory-update program. When inventory data was written on the tape, the accounts receivable master records would be destroyed. Can you imagine the loss to the company?

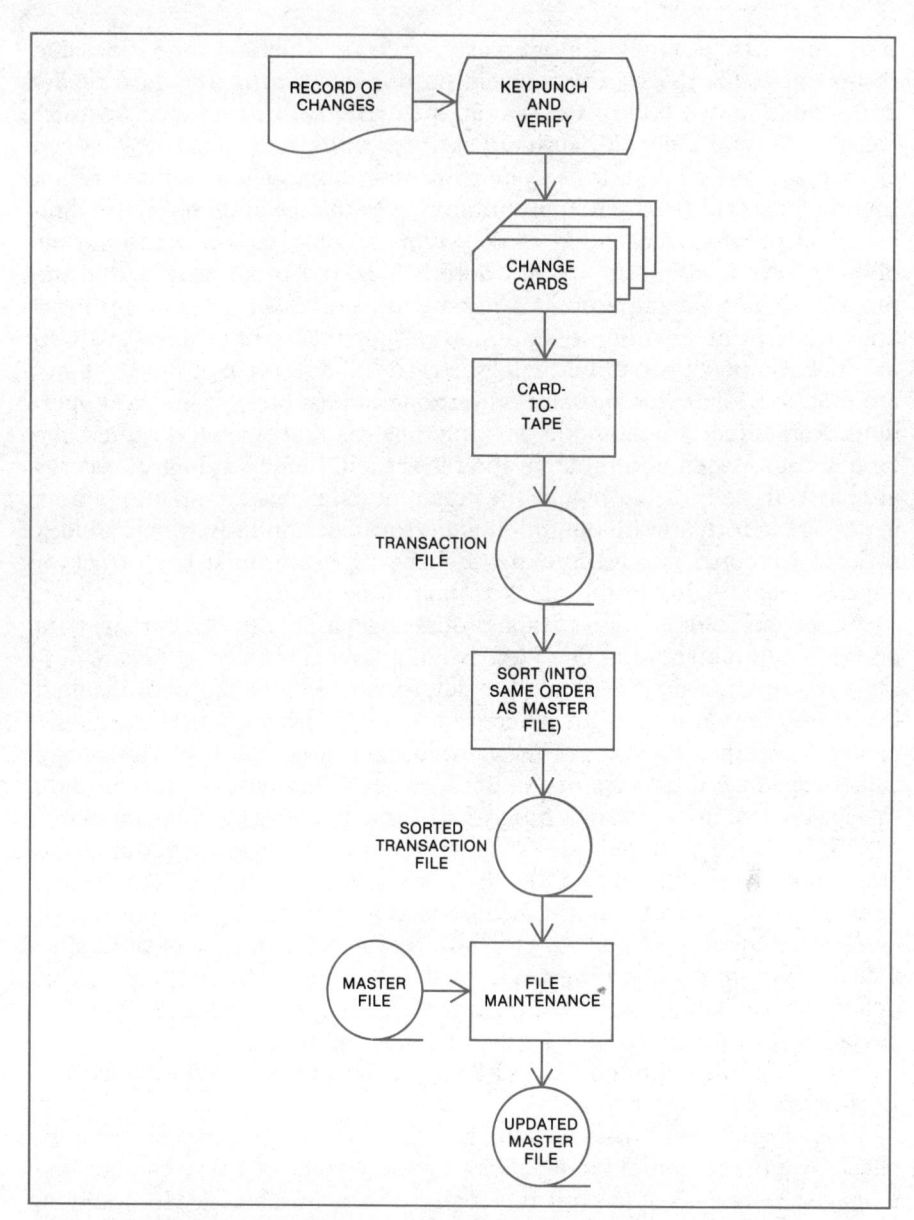

ILLUSTRATION 7-16 System flowchart for file maintenance

    Regardless of the precautions taken, records are destroyed or do become unreadable. To handle this problem, a system designer plans for ***backup***—some way of creating again records that have been lost. In a tape system, the most common backup procedure is to keep the old master and the transaction tapes when a new master tape is written. Then, if the new master tape is destroyed, it can be re-created by repeating the processing of the transactions against the old master records. For greater security, the two preceding master files and transaction tapes for each master file used in a system are kept. Then, even if the two most recent master files are destroyed, they can be re-created from the earlier versions of the files. This method of backup is called the ***grandfather-father-son method*** because, for every up-to-date master file (the son), the two preceding master files (the father and the grandfather) are kept.

In summary, a tape system can be an efficient system because of the speed, record flexibility, system design, and ease of handling data. However, the tape system introduces certain complications for the operator, programmer, and systems analyst. In addition, since most tape systems have multiple tape drives, the total cost of the system tends to be significant. To facilitate the additional tape input/output operations, more internal storage for input/output areas is generally required. This often leads to a search for a method of utilizing the entire system, computer storage as well as magnetic tape capacity, efficiently.

SUMMARY

1. A magnetic tape is similar in appearance to the tape used in a tape recorder. It is composed of a base and a magnetic coating bonded together with an adhesive. Areas on the tape's surface can be magnetized.

2. Data is represented on magnetic tape in two ways. A seven-track tape employs a 6-bit BCD code with a seventh bit as a parity bit. Nine-track tape uses a code such as EBCDIC with a ninth bit as a parity bit. The vertical columns on a tape are used to represent characters; the horizontal rows, spanning the length of the tape, are called tracks.

3. When data is recorded, it is recorded as groups of characters called blocks. Blocks are separated from each other by interblock gaps (IBGs).

4. A tape drive is the device that employs magnetic tape as an input/output medium. It has a file reel, vacuum columns, a read/write assembly with a read/write head for every track and photoelectric cells that sense file markers, and a machine reel.

5. To insure that data is properly recorded within a block, a longitudinal (horizontal) parity check is performed. At the end of each block, the bits of a longitudinal check character are set on or off to create either an even parity or an odd parity in all tracks in the block. Since each character is checked vertically as well, all data is checked both horizontally and vertically within each block.

6. To provide security, a file-protect ring is inserted on the back of the tape reel when data is to be written on a tape and removed when data is not to be written. Label checking is performed on the first record (header label) of the tape to verify that the tape is the one desired.

7. The speed of tape reading and writing is called the transfer rate and is measured in number of bytes per second. The number of bytes that can be recorded per inch of tape is called density and is measured in bytes per inch (BPI). The transfer rate is determined by multiplying the density by the transport speed, which is the number of inches of tape passing the read/write heads per second. The start/stop time of a tape drive is the time required to stop and start again at an interblock gap between blocks of records.

8. The major advantages of magnetic tape are the input/output speeds with which data can be transferred, low storage cost, reusability, the cost of tape versus the cost of punched cards, labels as security devices, and the online/offline capability of tape. Disadvantages include lack of human readability, the requirement for sequential organization of data, and the susceptibility of tape to environmental factors influencing its ability to retain the data recorded on it.

REVIEW QUESTIONS

1. Explain the operation of a magnetic tape unit.
2. How is data recorded on magnetic tape?
3. Explain the purpose of a parity check. How is it accomplished?
4. What is meant by the term *density*?
5. How are records written to magnetic tape? What is the purpose of the interblock gap?
6. What are the advantages and limitations of magnetic tape?
7. Why is magnetic-tape backup important, and how can it be accomplished?

CAREER PROFILE

Julie Ann Goff
Tape Librarian
IBM Corporation

Background Experience

After graduation from high school, I soon discovered that the job opportunities available to a person who possessed secretarial skills but no college degree were very limited. Then I read an ad from a company willing to train typists to become data transcribers. I was hired as a trainee and quickly became familiar with a 3277 CRT terminal. I was a data transcriber for a year and a half before coming to work for IBM as keypunch operator. I was trained by IBM to use the 129 card punch, and I did so for six months. I became very interested in the data processing career path. I observed that the field of data processing has unlimited career potential.

Next, I became a computer operator trainee. Through the company's on-the-job training and education programs, I learned how to do many operator tasks—involving printers, microfiche production, tape mounts, console monitoring, and so on. After becoming a computer operator, I completed more IBM classes, went through more training, and was promoted to my present position of tape librarian.

Primary Job Responsibilities

As a tape librarian, I am responsible for the tracking of all magnetic tapes and disks. I interface with all users of the library and help solve their problems. I also coordinate the work schedule of all three shifts in the library and help plan for the future growth and changing needs of the library. Being a tape librarian can be very satisfying because of the variety of skills and abilities I am called upon to use.

On a typical day, the first thing I do is to communicate with the preceding shift personnel to learn what happened during the evening. It is important to know what is happening with the various systems. It is a challenge to understand the many ways they affect the library. Next, I verify that my computer job, which tracks all tapes, has run successfully. Some time ago I attended a class on JCL and utilities. I use what I learned there to correct my library job definitions, to update some old job definitions, and to write new ones. I receive as many as 25 inquiries a day from users seeking assistance. A lot of my day is spent helping them to correct tape or disk problems. Working with the users is also a learning experience for me. I gain exposure to their jobs. I help them to understand my responsibilities and the services my area provides. Finally, I coordinate the work of the three shifts and turn over to the next shift what needs to be done. In free moments I work on future needs—looking for better ways to control the ever-changing requirements for data storage.

What Has Made You Successful?

Success in my work is based on a combination of things. It has come from the excellent education and opportunities that IBM has given me. It has come from people who were willing to help me and who took the time to train me. It has come from choosing a career path in which qualified people willing to work hard can excel. But I believe more than anything else, true success comes from team effort—from helping others and learning from others.

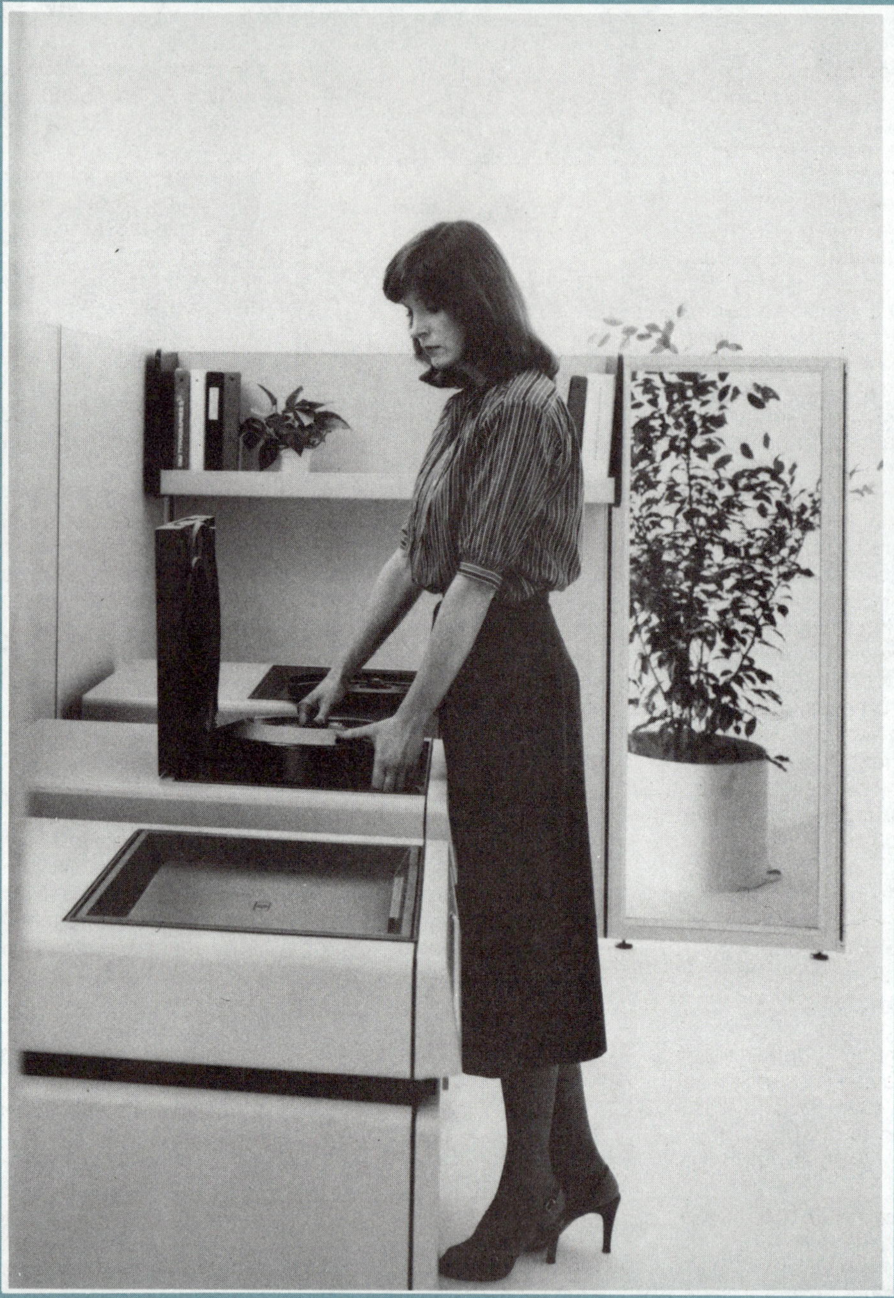

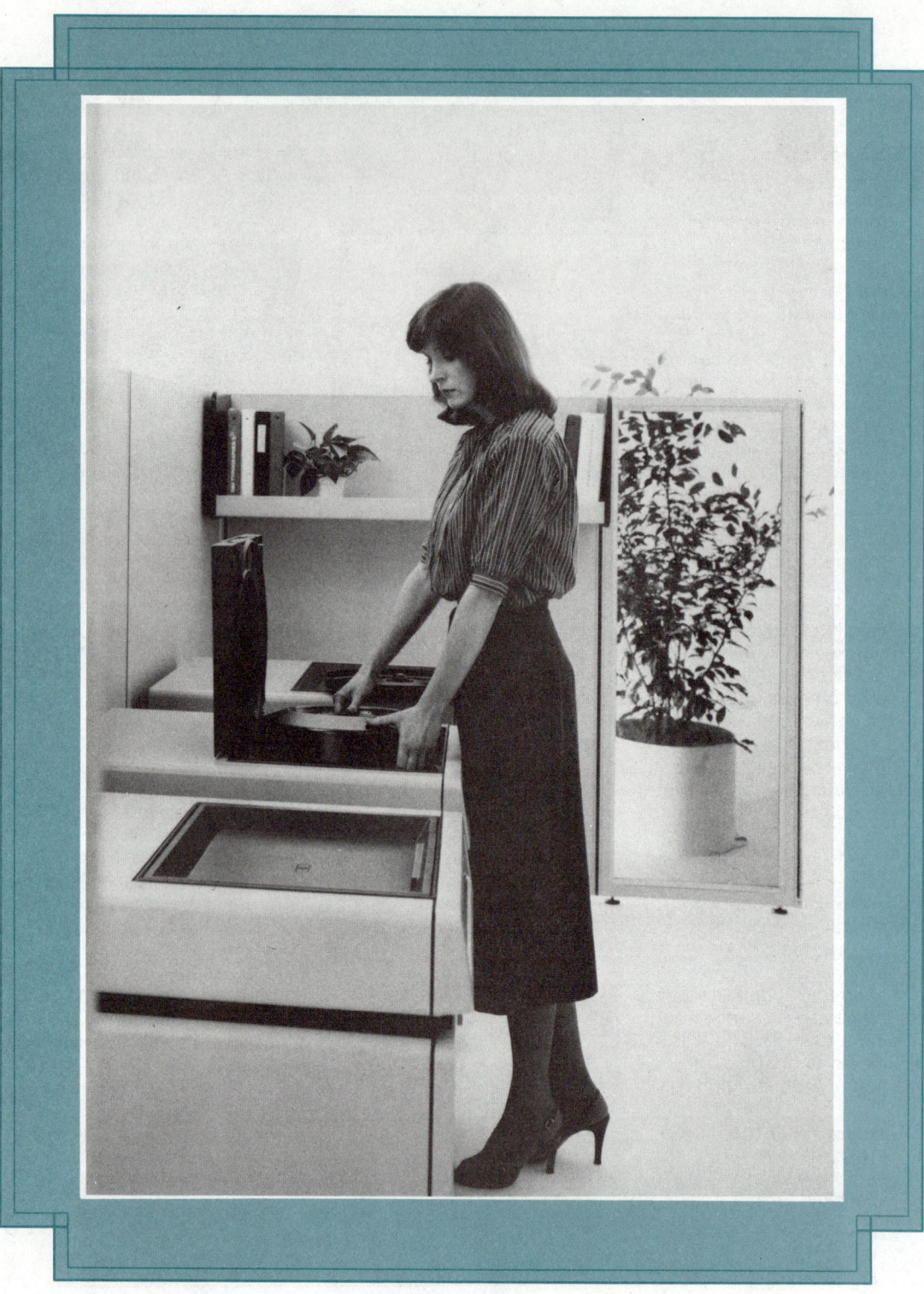

CHAPTER 8

MASS STORAGE DEVICES

THE DISK PACK

DATA REPRESENTATION ON DISK

THE SPEED OF DISK
INPUT/OUTPUT OPERATIONS

AN EXAMPLE OF
MAGNETIC DISK UTILIZATION

ADVANTAGES AND LIMITATIONS
OF DISK INPUT/OUTPUT

OTHER DIRECT ACCESS INPUT/OUTPUT DEVICES
The Magnetic Drum
The Mass Storage Subsystem

Opposite: An operator at a disk storage unit
that uses removable disk packs.

Although tape systems can process large amounts of data at high speeds, they have two major limitations. First, because the records in a tape file must be in sequence before they can be processed, a tape system requires many sorting steps. For example, before a master file can be updated by a transaction file, both files must be in the same sequence. Therefore, one or both of the files may have to be sorted before processing. Second, when a tape master file is updated, all of the records in the file must be read from the old master tape and written on a new one. Therefore, if a tape master file has 1000 records and only 100 of them are affected by a day's transactions, 900 records must be read and written simply because they are in the file.

As noted in Chapter 7, a computer can access a record in a tape file only after scanning all preceding records in the file. In contrast, it can locate a record in a file on a direct access device without reading all preceding records in the file. With the *direct access method*, it is possible to go directly to desired records and thus process only affected master records during a master-file update. The requirement for sorting is reduced or eliminated. For example, if 100 records of a 1000-record master file are to be updated by a day's transactions, only 100 master records need be read and written. The time required to execute the update program depends on the number of records affected by transactions, not on the number of records in the master file.

One *mass storage device* that can be used in direct access processing is the magnetic disk storage unit. While this mass storage device does not represent all of the devices that can be used in direct access processing, it does represent the most commonly used devices. This chapter deals primarily with magnetic disk, but the concepts and characteristics presented apply to all direct access devices and systems. In the latter part of the chapter, other direct access devices are mentioned to demonstrate other techniques employed in mass storage.

○ **THE DISK PACK**

Illustration 8-1 shows a single disk pack (top) and the mounted disk packs and the disk drives (bottom) of a magnetic disk storage unit. A disk drive is the part of the device that reads and writes data; a disk pack contains the data that is read or written. When it is in operation, this disk drive holds one or more disk packs that rotate continuously at a constant speed. Each disk pack can be removed, and another disk pack can be mounted in its place. Thus, the illustration depicts one of a class of disk drives with removable disk packs (that is, of the *removable-disk* variety). There are models of disk drives to which disks are permanently attached. This class of disk drives is said to be of a *fixed-disk* variety. Many users use only

CHAPTER 8: MASS STORAGE DEVICES

removable disk packs because the number of magnetic disk storage units they have available is much less than the number of disk packs required to store their data. Other users do not have this data storage problem and thus rarely change disk packs. These users prefer either some or all fixed-disk storage units because currently available fixed disk packs are capable of storing up to 4 times more data per disk than comparable removable disk packs. This increased data density per disk pack reduces the storage

ILLUSTRATION 8-1 Disk pack (top) and disk storage unit (bottom)

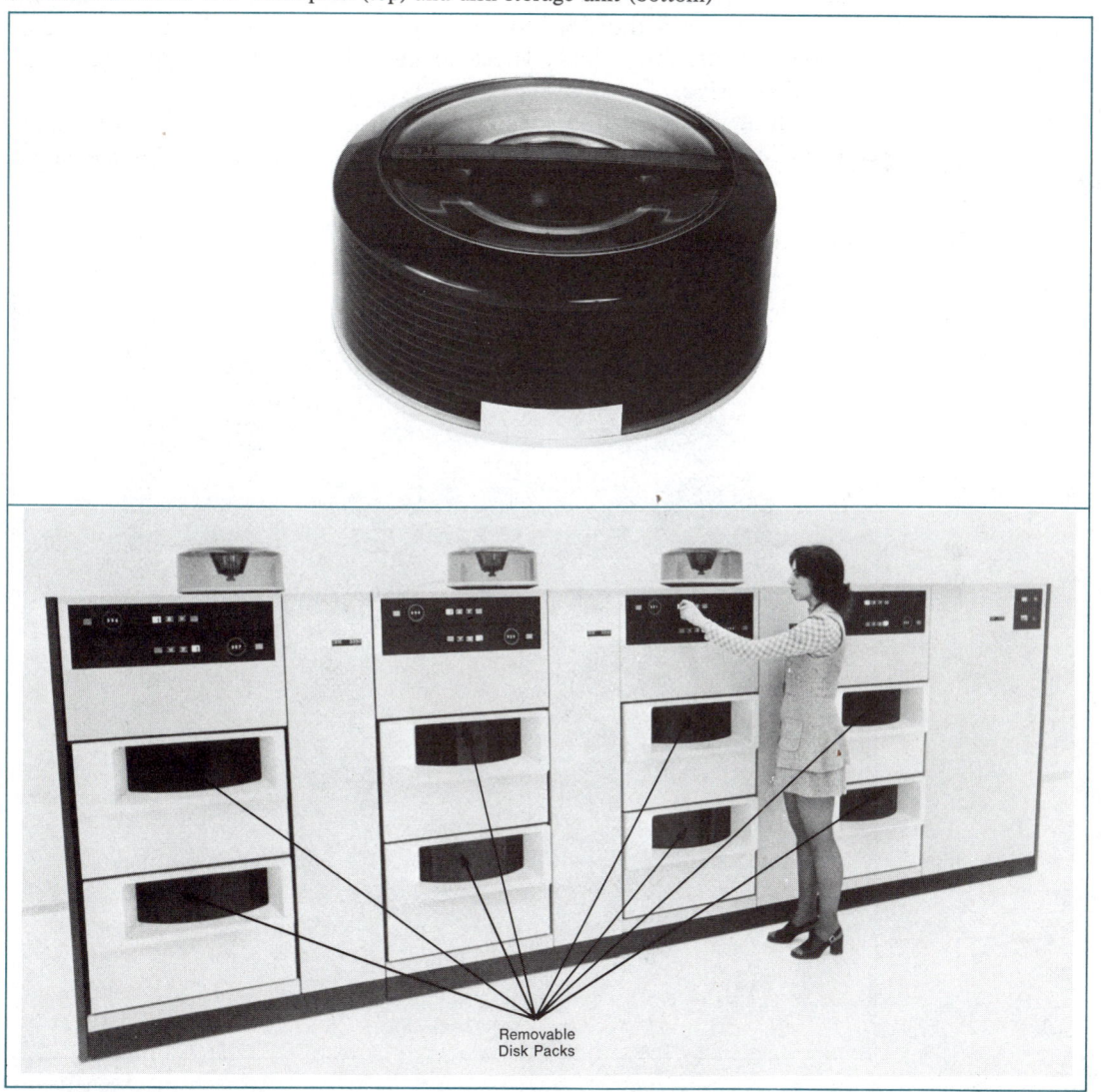

cost per byte from 50 to 70 percent of earlier removable disk pack storage costs.

The disk pack in Illustration 8-1 consists of 11 metal disks mounted on a central spindle. Twenty of the 22 surfaces of these 11 disks are coated with a material that can be magnetized. Data can be recorded on all surfaces of the disks except the top surface of the top disk and the bottom surface of the bottom disk. The top and bottom surfaces are blank for protection purposes and because they are apt to be scratched. The number of disks and the number of recording surfaces in a disk pack vary, depending upon the particular model. For example, there are some disk packs with only six disks, and there are others with eleven disks. There are spaces between the disks in a pack. These spaces allow for the read/write heads of the disk drive.

Each of the recording surfaces of a disk is divided into 200 or more concentric circles on which data can be recorded. These circles are called

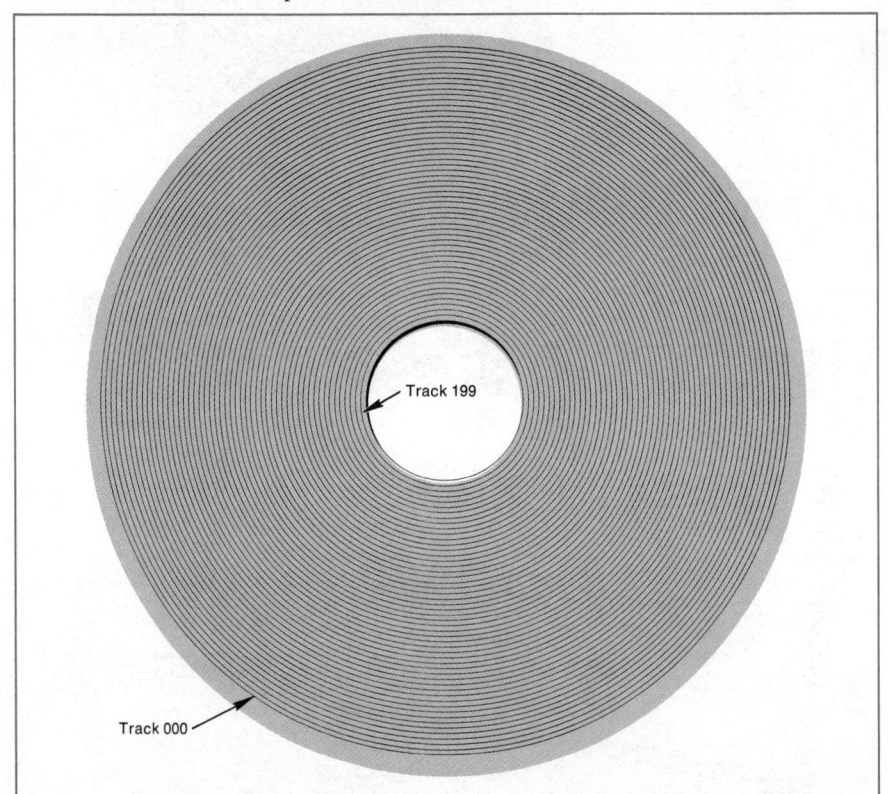

ILLUSTRATION 8-2 Top view of a disk surface

CHAPTER 8: MASS STORAGE DEVICES

tracks. Illustration 8-2 is a schematic top view of a recording surface that comprises 200 tracks. When a removable disk pack is to be used by a certain program, it is mounted on the appropriate disk drive and the drive is switched on. The disk pack then begins to rotate. When it reaches the appropriate speed, it is ready to be read from or written on. When data is read from the pack, the data is unaffected. When data is written on the pack, it replaces any data previously stored on the same area of the pack.

To read from or write on the disk pack, the disk drive uses an *access mechanism* with multiple *read/write heads*. However, only one of the heads can operate at a time. Each head can either read or write, but no head can do both at once. Illustration 8-3 shows the read/write heads and access mechanism of a disk drive. Most disk drives are designed to employ only one read/write head per disk surface. It positions itself on the disk as required.

To operate on all tracks of the recording surfaces, the access mechanism moves back and forth either hydraulically or electrically on a line

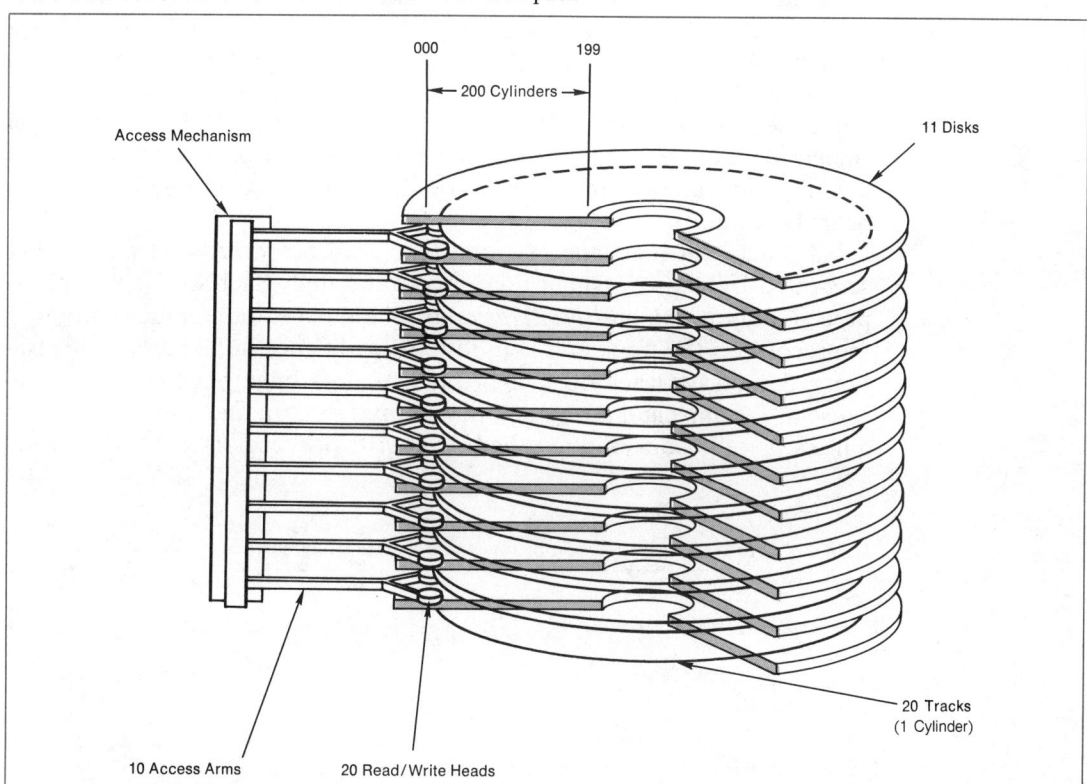

ILLUSTRATION 8-3 Access mechanism and disk pack

UNIT TWO: COMPUTER SYSTEMS

toward the center of the disk pack. All of the read/write heads of a multiple-head mechanism move at once. At one setting of the access mechanism, all of the read/write heads are on the same tracks of the recording surfaces. For example, the access mechanism could be positioned at the seventieth track on each of the recording surfaces. Then each of the read/write heads could operate on data in the seventieth track of the corresponding disk surface. The tracks that could be operated on at one time make up the seventieth *cylinder* of the disk pack. To say it another way, a cylinder consists of all tracks that can be read or written on in a single setting of the access mechanism. The access mechanisms on some disk drives allow each read/write head to be positioned independent of the others. With a single read/write head or independent read/write heads, the concept of a cylinder is not as well defined.

DATA REPRESENTATION ON DISK

Characters, and records composed of the characters, are recorded on a single track as strings of magnetized bits. Illustration 8-4 represents a section of one track of a recording surface in which several characters are recorded. The 1s indicate magnetized areas, or on bits. The 0s represent unmagnetized portions of the track, or off bits. Although the tracks get smaller as they get closer to the center of the disk pack, each track can hold the same amount of data because the data density is greater on tracks near the center.

A track can hold one or more records. The records on a track are separated by gaps in which no data is recorded. Each of the records is preceded by a *disk address*. This address indicates the unique position of the record on the track and is used to directly access the record. Illustration 8-5 shows a track on which three records have been recorded. Because of the gaps and addresses, the amount of data that can be stored on a track is reduced as the number of records per track is increased. How-

ILLUSTRATION 8-4   Section of one track of recording surface

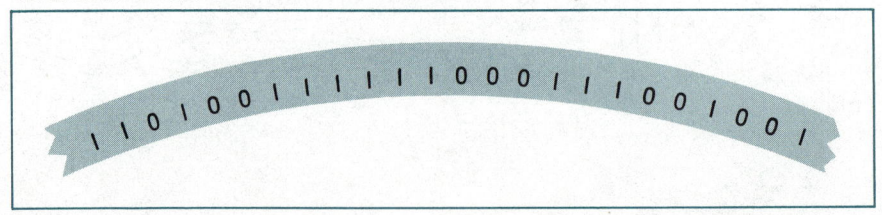

1 1 0 1 0 0 1 1 1 1 1 1 0 0 0 1 1 1 0 0 1 0 0 1

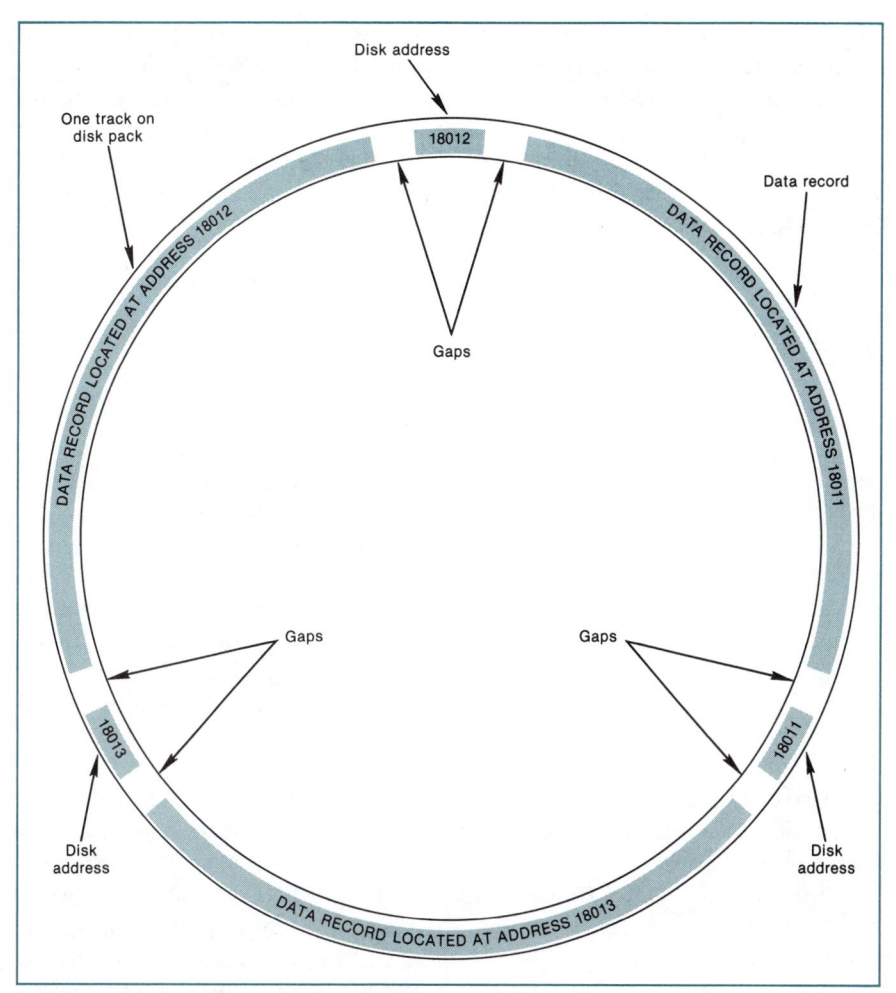

ILLUSTRATION 8-5 Three records on a track

ever, as with tape, records on disk can be blocked. Only one disk address is needed per block, and fewer gaps occur. Hence, this technique increases the amount of data that can be written on one track.

Some disk drives use parity bits on the individual bytes of data and a longitudinal check character after each record or block of records as a check on the accuracy of disk input. Other disk drives do not use either of these parity checks. Instead each record or block of records is followed by two 8-bit bytes called *cyclic check characters*, or **CCs**. These characters are generated when a record is written on the disk pack, based on the bit combinations of the data in the record. Later when the record is read, new cyclic check characters are generated and compared with those on the disk pack. If the compared characters are not equal, an error has occurred. This method of checking input data catches at least as many errors as the combination of individual parity bits and longitudinal check characters. It may catch more.

THE SPEED OF DISK INPUT/OUTPUT OPERATIONS

The speed at which a magnetic disk operates (*access time*) depends on three factors: (1) head positioning, (2) head switching, and (3) rotational delay. When a specific record is requested, the first response by the disk drive is to position a read/write head over the track at which the record is located. The speed with which this **head positioning** is performed depends on the number of read/write heads, the number of tracks that each head can access at a single position, and the distance the access mechanism has to be moved. Of course, the ideal situation so far as speed is concerned is to have a read/write head for every track on the disk. Some disk drives have this capability. This eliminates the time required to position the head, but it involves much hardware.

Head switching is the process of activating the appropriate read/write head so that data can be transferred from or written on the disk. Since this action takes place at the speed of electricity, the time required for it is considered to be negligible.

Rotational delay is the amount of time that it takes the disk drive to locate the desired data on a track. The time required depends entirely on the rotational speed of the disk, which can be up to 3600 revolutions per minute. An average of one-half revolution is used for the amount of rotation, because, in reality, one complete rotation, part of a rotation, or zero rotations may be required to find the data. If the read/write head is positioned directly over the record that contains the data, no rotation is necessary.

After a read/write head has been positioned over the required record, the **data transfer speed** becomes the focal point. Data transfer speed is measured in terms of the amount of time required to read or write a record, that is, to transfer data to or from the central processing unit. Average access times for typical magnetic disk drives range from 20 to 60 milliseconds (thousandths of a second). Data transfer speeds range from 156,000 to 1.86 million bytes (characters) per second. The storage capacities of these disk packs vary widely—from 7.25 million to 571 million characters.

○ AN EXAMPLE OF MAGNETIC DISK UTILIZATION

Suppose, in this example, a computer system having direct access capabilities is to prepare a combined shipping-order and invoice form from an original sales order and maintain inventory and accounts receivable master files. What steps are required to prepare the form and to update records of the inventory (item) and accounts receivable (customer) master files?

Illustration 8-6 is a system flowchart for the basic processing in this system. It consists of two steps and requires two master files: the item file and the customer file. A master item record contains such data as item number, item description, unit price, unit cost, reorder point, stock on hand, stock on order, and items back-ordered. A master customer record contains such data as customer number, customer name and address, shipping instructions, payment terms, and amount owed. These files can be stored on the same disk pack or on two disk packs. One or two disk drives may be needed, depending on whether one or two packs are used. The processing steps are the same in either case. (Note the symbol for disk input/output: .)

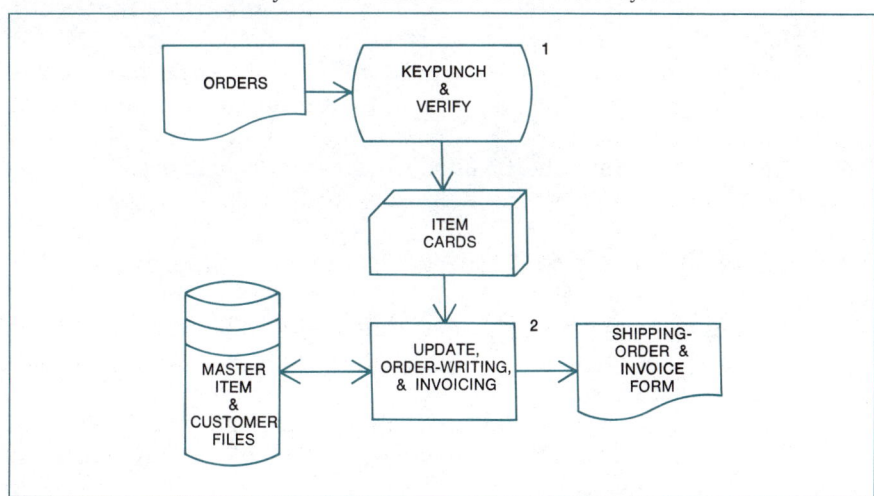

ILLUSTRATION 8-6 System flowchart for a direct access system

In step 1 of the system, item cards are keypunched from the original sales orders, then verified. These cards can be unit-record cards (one card per line item) or spread cards (several items per card). If spread cards are used, the number of cards required by the system is less than it would be otherwise. The data that is keypunched is the identifying information for each item ordered (item number and quantity ordered).

In the second step of the system, the keypunched item cards are processed by the computer. These cards do not have to be sorted before they are processed. In this single processing run, the item records are checked to see whether the items ordered are in stock. The combined shipping order and invoice is printed with back-ordered items so indicated, and the item (inventory) and customer (accounts receivable) records on disk are updated. Because of the direct access capabilities of the disk, only the master records affected by transactions are processed. If the item cards are spread cards, the basic processing steps in the program are as follows:

1. An input card is read.
2. The master customer record with the same customer number as the input card is directly accessed and read from disk.
3. The heading on the shipping-order and invoice form is printed from data in the customer record and in the input card (customer name and address, customer number, order number, order date, shipping terms, special instructions, and so on).
4. The master item record corresponding to an item named on the input card is directly accessed and read from disk.
5. The data for the first line item on the invoice is printed. Item number, item description, and unit price are taken from the master item record. Quantity ordered for the item is taken from the input card. However, if there is not enough stock on hand, the quantity ordered is printed in the back-ordered portion of the shipping form. To calculate the price for this line item, quantity shipped is multiplied by unit price.
6. The new stock-on-hand balance for the item is calculated. The updated master item record is written on the disk in its original location.
7. If more than one item is ordered by the customer, processing, like that for the first item on the order, is repeated for each of the remaining items. In short, the master item record is read, data for the line item is printed, and the updated master item record is written back onto the disk.
8. When there are no more line items to be processed for the customer, the invoice total (and any discounts) is calculated, and the total line of the invoice is printed.

9. At this point, the balance owed by the customer is increased by the amount of the invoice. The updated master customer record is written on the disk in its original location. Then processing continues with the next spread card in the input deck.

In short, both master item (inventory) and master customer (accounts receivable) records are updated as the shipping-order and invoice form is printed. Only the master records affected by the item cards are read and written. On the other hand, any master item record may be read a number of times during program execution. If, for example, one item is ordered by 100 different customers, the corresponding master item record must be read 100 times.

○ ADVANTAGES AND LIMITATIONS OF DISK INPUT/OUTPUT

As previously mentioned, magnetic disk drives offer the potential of directly accessing data stored on a magnetic disk. This is the primary advantage of the magnetic disk over input media such as punched cards and magnetic tape, which are sequentially organized and processed. Without this capability, online realtime processing cannot be effectively achieved. (The realtime concept is discussed in Chapter 14.)

Another basic advantage of magnetic disk is the speed at which data can be transferred to and from the central processing unit. While magnetic disk units have not yet achieved the transfer speeds of the magnetic drum (discussed below), they have surpassed magnetic tape devices in this respect.

Perhaps the most critical disadvantage of magnetic disk is that it does not usually provide for backup. When data is recorded on a magnetic disk, only one copy is normally made. In comparison, when magnetic tape is used as an input/output medium, an extra copy of the tape can be provided with relative ease, thus insuring that the data is protected from accidental erasure or destruction. Further, the magnetic tape cannot be written on unless a file-protect ring is properly installed.

Another disadvantage of magnetic disk is its cost. Consider, for example, the relative costs of magnetic disk and tape. As stated previously, a reel of magnetic tape costs approximately $15. Most disk packs cost between $400 and $1150.

Another limitation (or possibly, advantage, depending on how one views the problem) is one of system design and the difficulties that may be encountered in programming a system to operate according to its design.

File organization is a major system design consideration. A file can be organized in any one of three ways on a direct access device. Besides the *direct* organization, records can be stored in sequence on a direct access device. For example, on a disk device, record number 1 of a *sequential* file is stored in the cylinder 1, track 1, and record 1 location; record number 2 is stored in the cylinder 1, track 1, and record 2 location; and so on. When reading records from a sequential file, access-mechanism movement is minimal because all of the records in one cylinder are read before records are read from the next cylinder. Since direct access devices normally have fast transfer rates, records arranged sequentially can be read and written at relatively high speeds. Sequential records on a direct access device can be sorted using only that device, in contrast to a tape system where three tape drives are required to sort data, even when the records to be sorted are initially contained in one file on one tape drive.

A third kind of file organization, called *indexed sequential*, allows records to be retrieved sequentially or by direct access, depending on the program. In this method, the records are stored sequentially on the direct access device. In addition, a table (index) is kept that indicates the approximate location of each of the records stored on the device. To process the records on a direct access basis, a program looks for a record number in the table, determines the approximate location of the record on the device, and searches for the record at that location.

The problem of the system designer is to choose the best of these methods (direct, sequential, or indexed sequential) for each file stored on a direct access device. Since each method has advantages and disadvantages, the choice is difficult. For example, although direct organization may be best for an invoicing run such as the one shown in Illustration 8-6, it may be difficult to prepare management reports from directly organized master files. (How could an inventory report in item-number sequence be prepared from the directly organized master inventory file?)

In addition, a directly organized file requires additional storage space on the direct access device because of the problems in computing unique device addresses for records. In contrast, a sequential file permits full use of the storage allocated for it on the device. However, such a file has the disadvantages of other sequential files: (1) sorting is a common requirement, and (2) if only a few of the records in a master file are affected in a processing run, many records are processed unnecessarily.

Indexed sequential file organization combines the advantages of both direct and sequential organizations. However, run times for direct access processing of an indexed sequential file are likely to be longer than they would be if the file were organized on a direct basis. In any event, the problem of the system designer is to choose an organization that keeps processing times down, not just for a single processing run, but for all of the runs in which the file will be used.

In summary, direct access systems offer advantages not found in sequential processing systems. Direct access systems also require programming and systems considerations that are not required for sequential systems. Perhaps the most significant difference between direct access and sequential systems is that a direct access system can retrieve records from a master file more quickly than a sequential system can. Managers can "inquire" into files in a direct access system for current information. For instance, if a credit manager wants information on a customer account, the customer's number can be keyed on an input/output device that resembles a typewriter. Under program control, the computer system can, in milliseconds, retrieve the customer's record from a direct access device and print the contents of the record on the typewriterlike unit. Because of its inquiry capability, the direct access system makes possible a management information system. In contrast, in a sequential system, before the desired record could be retrieved for processing, all records preceding that record in the file would have to be read. Such an approach would be highly impractical.

OTHER DIRECT ACCESS INPUT/OUTPUT DEVICES

The Magnetic Drum

The magnetic drum is another type of direct access device (see Illustration 8-7). Although it was developed before magnetic disk storage, the use of the magnetic drum as a secondary storage device has dwindled in recent years. The primary reason for this dwindling usage is that the drum has a limited storage capacity—a result of the design of the device. The recording medium of the device is a *drum*, or *cylinder*, which is coated with a magnetically sensitive material. This drum is permanently fixed to the device. A magnetic disk pack may be removable, allowing additional data to be written or read, but a magnetic drum is not. The magnetic drum is still employed in some installations because of its primary advantage: the fast input/output speeds at which the device operates.

The drum is similar to a magnetic disk in that its surface is divided into tracks (see the schematic diagram in Illustration 8-8). These tracks form circular bands around the drum, which rotates at a constant speed. The coded representation of data in Illustration 8-8 follows a pattern similar to that used on a seven-track magnetic tape. The tracks can be assigned to *channels* as in the illustration. This illustration can be compared with Illustration 8-7 to observe one of the basic differences in various types of

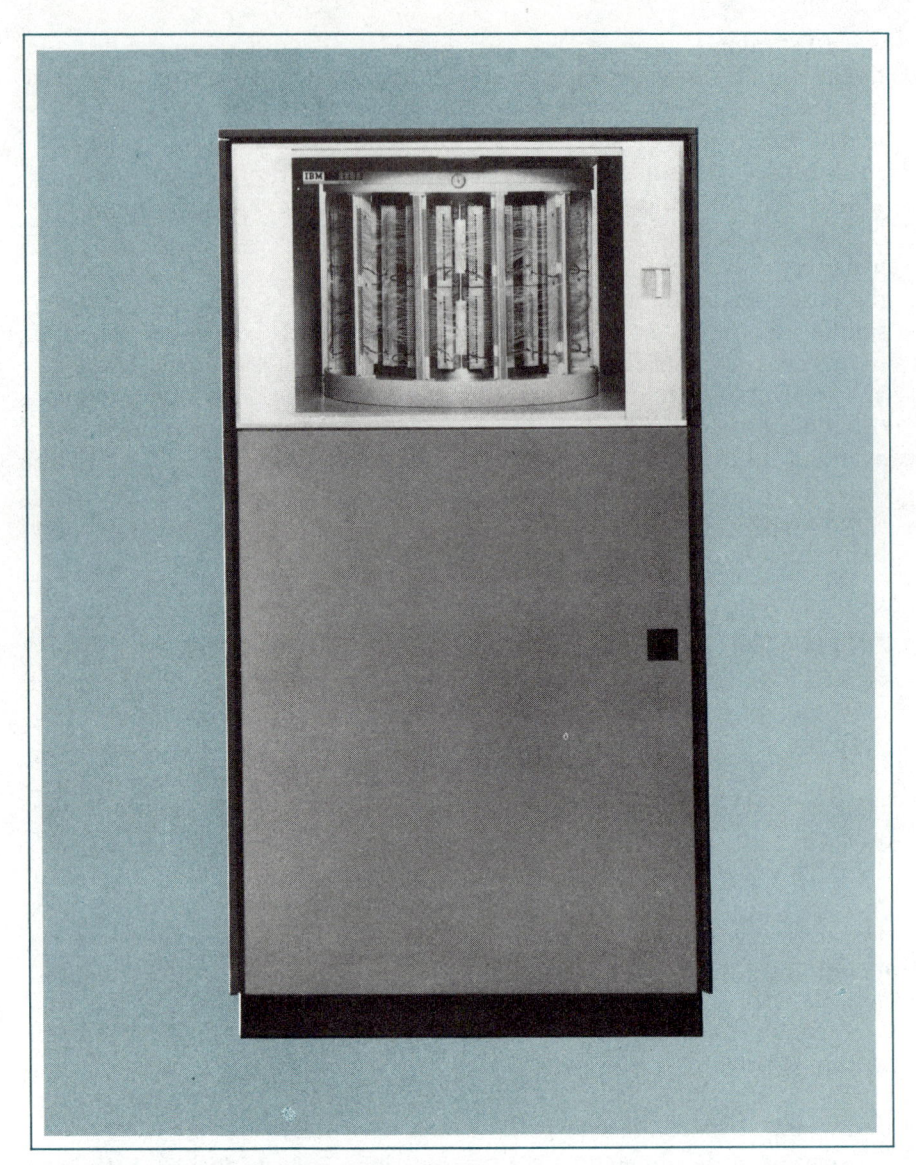

ILLUSTRATION 8-7 Drum storage device

magnetic drum devices: The drum in the schematic diagram is in a horizontal position; the drum in the previous illustration is vertical.

The basic functions of the read/write heads of a magnetic drum (see Illustration 8-9) are to place magnetized areas on the drum during the writing operation and to sense these areas during the reading operation in

CHAPTER 8: MASS STORAGE DEVICES

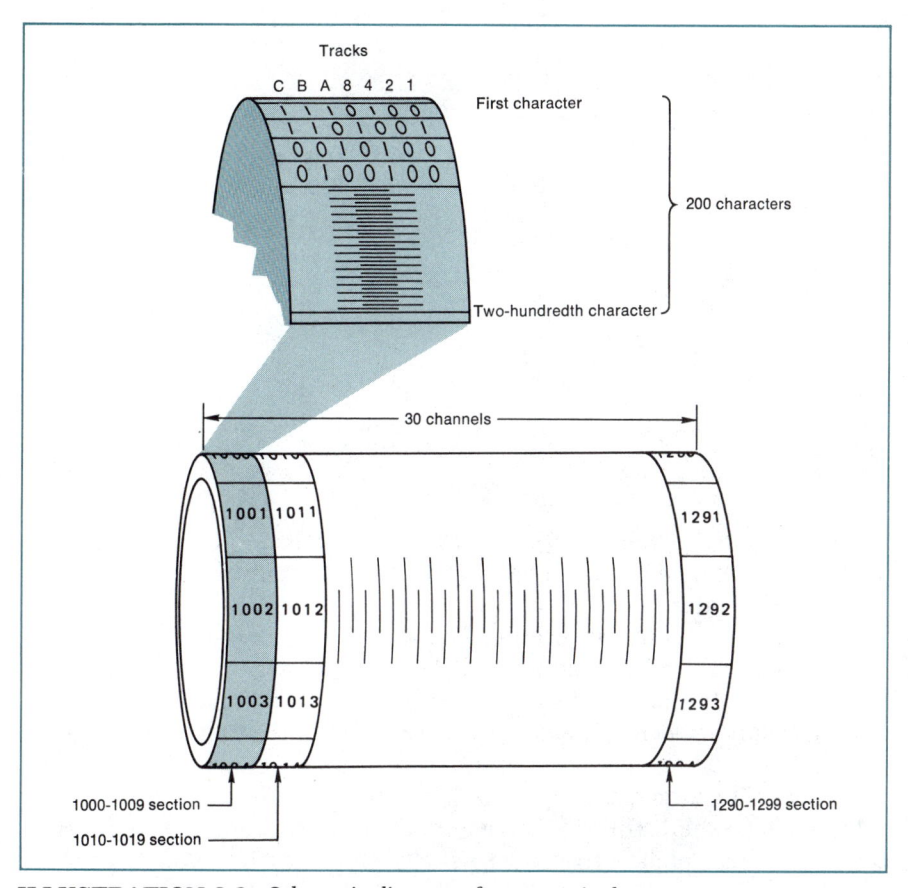

ILLUSTRATION 8-8 Schematic diagram of a magnetic drum

the same general manner that these functions are performed when magnetic tape or disk is used. A second major difference in the design of magnetic drums is the number of read/write heads employed. Some drums employ only one read/write head which services all tracks on the drum. The head moves back and forth (or up and down) over the surface of the drum as required. Other drums employ multiple read/write heads. They have one principle advantage over drums of the single-head type: Since one read/write head is assigned to each track, no read/write head movement is required. That is, the time required for head positioning is zero. The only significant time required when reading or writing is the rotational delay that occurs in reaching a desired record location.

Data can be recorded on a magnetic drum by either of two methods: serial or parallel. A drum on which data is written in parallel is read in

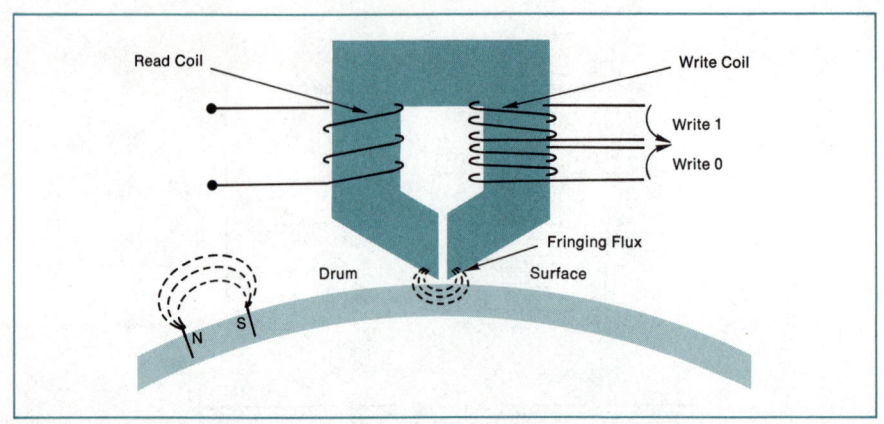

ILLUSTRATION 8-9 Magnetic drum read/write head

parallel; another type of drum uses serial reading and writing. These methods are similar to the two ways of reading punched cards, as discussed in Chapter 6.

Since there is wide variation in the design of magnetic drums, the speeds at which the writing and reading of data can be performed vary greatly as well. The speed of drum rotation ranges from approximately 6000 revolutions per minute (10 milliseconds per revolution) for high-speed drums to about 600 revolutions per minute (100 milliseconds per revolution) for larger drums. Since the faster rotating drums are usually smaller than other drums, less data can be recorded on their surfaces. In addition, these smaller drums are usually more expensive because of the mechanics required to achieve accurate data transfers at high speeds. Some of these high-speed drums are capable of transferring over one million characters of data per second. This is roughly equivalent to reading a stack of cards 8 feet high in one second. The storage capacities of magnetic drums range from 20 million to more than 130 million characters.

The Mass Storage Subsystem

A third type of direct access device is the mass storage subsystem, such as the IBM 3850, which was introduced in 1974. The 3850 uses fist-sized data cartridges to store data. Each cartridge is about 2 inches in diameter and 4 inches long. It can hold up to 50 million bytes of data. (See Illustration 8-10.) Inside the system, the cartridges are stored in a honeycomblike arrangement of cells. (See Illustration 8-11.)

When a program calls for a certain file or a portion of a file, one of two cartridge accessors is automatically instructed to retrieve the needed car-

CHAPTER 8: MASS STORAGE DEVICES

ILLUSTRATION 8-10 Data cartridge

ILLUSTRATION 8-11 3850 "honeycomb"

tridge from its cell and mount it at a read/write station if it is not already mounted at the station. The cartridge is opened, and the contents of the 3 × 770 inch tape strip contained therein are transferred to a disk pack for computer use. This process is called *staging*. After processing is completed, only altered records are written back to the tape strip.

Perhaps the greatest advantage of the 3850 Mass Storage Subsystem is economy of data storage. The subsystem can store from 35 billion to 472 billion bytes of data; the maximum is roughly equivalent to the data stored in a 47,200-reel tape library. The system can end practically all manual handling of tape reels and disk packs and greatly lower the cost of maintaining a library. An important security aspect is that extensive data files can be kept in one place. The 3850 can be located up to 200 feet away from the computer and can be equipped with special features to detect the presence of any foreign magnetic device, to sense fire and fumes, and to trigger a fire suppression system (if the user chooses to provide one). Access to data in the 3850 subsystem is controlled through password-protection programming.

Perhaps the largest potential for the 3850 exists among the multitude of magnetic-tape users. Although the 3850 subsystem provides direct access capabilities, it is not well suited to random retrieval. The staging process described above involves a significant amount of physical movement.

Access times are long when such movement is required. For records stored and processed sequentially, the frequency of staging is lower than it might otherwise be. But some users have determined that they can transfer data from 6250-BPI magnetic tapes faster than from the disk packs that provide online access to 3850 data. For organizations with massive amounts of data, economies of storage media and storage space may be determining factors.

○ SUMMARY

1. Magnetic disk drives, magnetic drum units, and mass storage subsystems are direct access devices employing slightly different recording media. Data is recorded on a disk pack by a disk drive, on a magnetically sensitive cylinder by a magnetic drum unit, and on a magnetic strip retrieved from a cartridge in a mass storage subsystem.

2. Disk drives are characterized as either fixed-disk or removable-disk drives, depending on whether or not the recording medium (magnetic disks) can be removed. Each disk is composed of concentric circles called tracks. Disk packs for removable-disk devices come in many varieties. They differ in number and size of disks employed as well as in number of tracks per disk. The data recorded on these tracks by one or more read/write heads of an access mechanism is composed of a disk address and a record or block of records. The corresponding tracks of each disk in a disk pack are called a cylinder.

3. The speed at which a magnetic disk operates (access time) depends on three factors: head positioning, head switching, and rotational delay. Head positioning is the time required to position a read/write head over the required track. Head switching is the time expended to activate the read/write head in preparation for an input/output operation. Rotational delay is the time required to locate a record once the head has been positioned and activated. To maintain the accuracy of data on magnetic disk, cyclic check characters are placed at the end of each record or block of records.

4. Mass storage devices permit a variety of file organizations, including direct, sequential, and indexed sequential arrangements.

5. While the magnetic disk is the most commonly used mass storage medium, both magnetic drums and mass storage subsystem devices have especially useful functions. Magnetic drums are noted for their speed while mass storage subsystem devices are known for their low cost and large storage capacity.

REVIEW QUESTIONS

1. What are direct access storage devices?
2. Compare and contrast magnetic tape and magnetic disk as secondary storage media. Identify applications for which each is suitable.
3. What factors must be considered in determining the access time for a magnetic disk?
4. Under what conditions is direct access more effective than sequential access (magnetic tape) processing?
5. Identify the advantages and limitations of magnetic disk as an input/output medium.
6. What is a magnetic drum? What is it ideally suited for?
7. When is it desirable to use a mass storage subsystem instead of magnetic disk(s)?

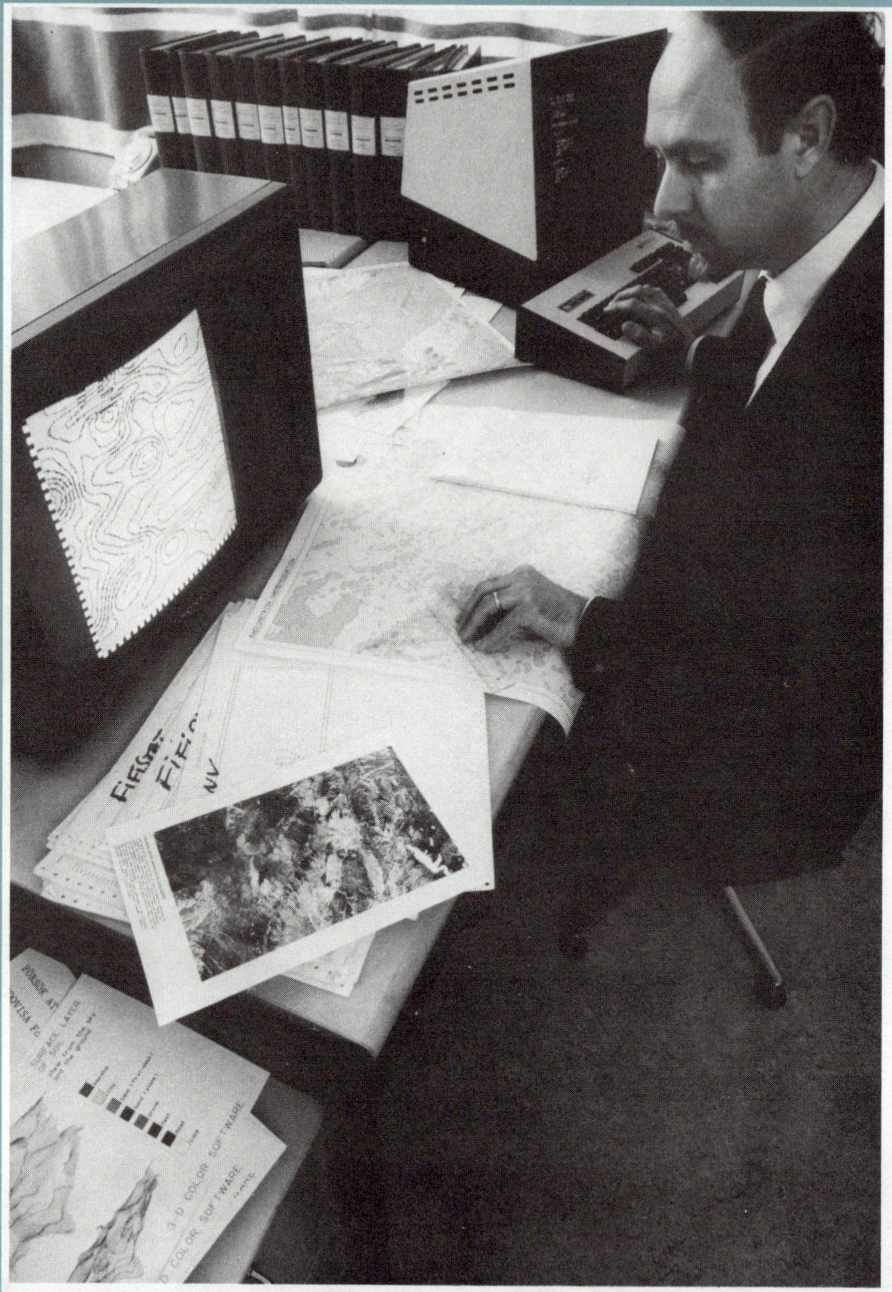
3-D COLOR SOFTWARE

MODULE A

SPECIAL-PURPOSE INPUT AND OUTPUT DEVICES

CHARACTER RECOGNITION INPUT DEVICES
Magnetic Character Readers
Optical Character Readers

DATA COMMUNICATIONS

TERMINALS
Touch-Tone Devices
Audio-Response Units
Visual Display Devices
Hard-Copy Devices
Point-of-Sale Devices
Intelligent Terminals

KEY-ENTRY DEVICES
Key-to-Tape Devices
Key-to-Disk Devices
Key-to-Diskette Devices

OTHER INPUT/OUTPUT DEVICES
Paper Tape and Paper Tape Devices
Console Display-Keyboard
Plotters
Computer Output Microfilm
Word Processors
Floppy Disk Devices

Opposite: Preparation of topographical maps with the use of a graphic display device.

In Chapters 6, 7, and 8, several of the more commonly used input/output media and devices are discussed. Other input/output devices, although not as commonly used, are more appropriate in certain situations. Some of these devices are discussed in this module.

CHARACTER RECOGNITION INPUT DEVICES

With the development of electronic data processing systems, there came a realization that wide use could be made of input devices capable of reading data that could also be read by people. The processing of billions of checks and an inestimable volume of other notices—insurance billings, magazine subscription renewals, invoices, manufacturing routing slips, utility bills, and so forth—could be simplified by the use of characters recognizable by both people and machines. Two input devices that can read such characters are magnetic character readers and optical character readers.

Magnetic Character Readers

In 1955, the American Bankers Association (ABA) began to study the problem of how to automate the processing of a continuously increasing volume of checks. A major consideration of the individuals studying the problem was the realization that any approach to the electronic processing of checks had to be widely supported by the banking industry. A bank may handle a check written on an account in another bank. The check then may be handled by one or two Federal Reserve Banks. Finally, it is processed by the bank handling the account.

After considering several alternatives, the individuals studying the problem proposed that certain data be coded on checks in *magnetic ink*. This approach had three advantages:

1. A check could be used as an input medium to the computer, or the data on it could be transferred to another medium for later processing.
2. The data required in processing could be coded on checks of varying lengths, widths, and thicknesses.
3. The coded data would be easily readable by people.

The proposal to use magnetic ink was accepted by the American Bankers Association membership. Three committees (one representing the American Bankers Association, another representing the Federal Reserve System, and a third representing the computer manufacturers) were formed to study the problem of what *type font* (a complete set of type

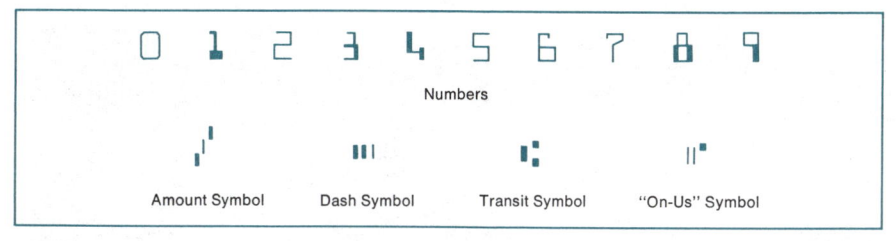

MODULE A: SPECIAL-PURPOSE INPUT AND OUTPUT DEVICES

ILLUSTRATION A-1 E-13B type font

of one size and face) should be adopted. After several months of study, the E-13B type font was adopted, primarily because it was easily readable by people as well as by machines. As reflected in Illustration A-1, the E-13B type font is composed of 14 characters. Since no alphabetic characters are included, the kind of data that can be processed using this type font is limited. However, the type font serves a significant purpose: It allows the banking industry to efficiently and effectively process billions of checks each year.

The first bank to receive a check must copy the amount of the check on the check in machine-readable form. (See Illustration A-2.) This is accomplished by means of a *magnetic character inscriber* (**MCI**) like the one shown in Illustration A-3. A *magnetic character reader* (**MCR**) reads

ILLUSTRATION A-2 Use of the E-13B type font on a check

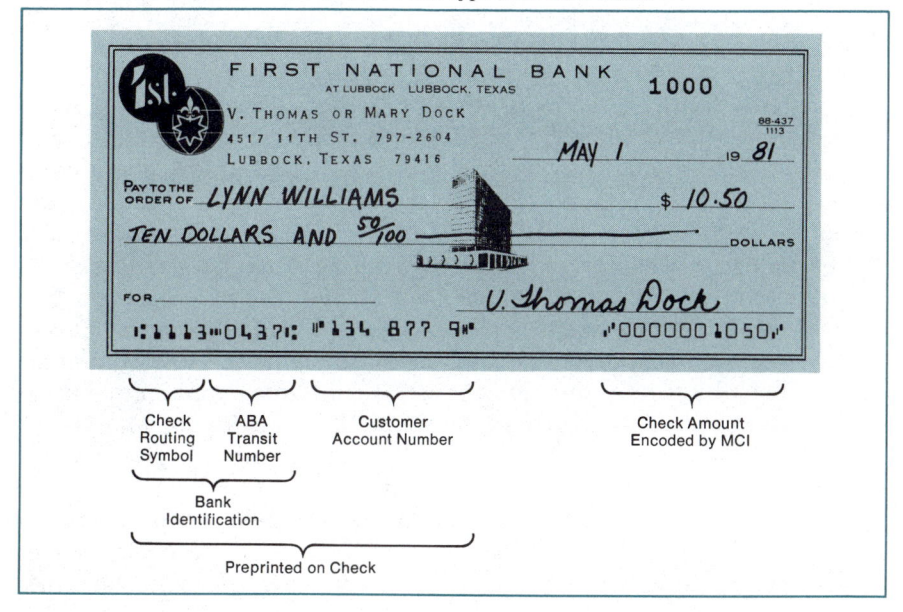

ILLUSTRATION A-3 Magnetic character inscriber

the E-13B type font characters inscribed on a check. (See Illustration A-4.) A second important labor-saving feature of this specialized input device is its ability to sort magnetically inscribed checks by account number in off-line operations. The characters composing each account number are magnetized as the checks are fed through the MCR. These characters are then read by a sensing mechanism. During a sorting operation, the reader sorts the checks into sort pockets. By repeated passes of checks through the machine, the checks can be grouped and routed to their sponsor banks. In each sponsor bank, a MCR is used as an input device to a computer system. Thus, the sorting function of the MCR assists a bank in updating customer accounts and returning checks to the individuals who wrote them. This device is basic to the banking industry's timesaving method of processing large volumes of daily transactions.

 The MCR is used by most banks today. Many savings and loan associations are also using this machine. The extensive use of this device is due to (1) the coordinated efforts of the American Bankers Association and the

MODULE A: SPECIAL-PURPOSE INPUT AND OUTPUT DEVICES

1. Sort pockets
2. Sensing mechanism

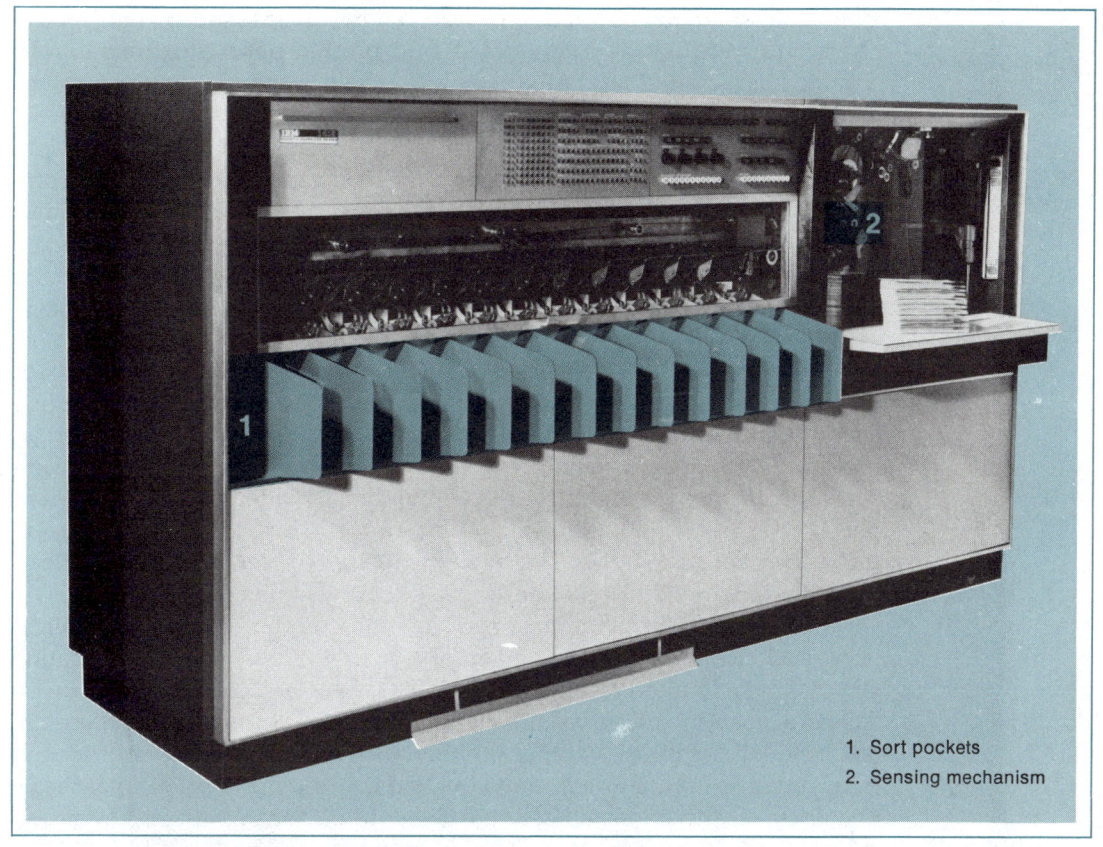

ILLUSTRATION A-4 Magnetic character reader

various manufacturers of magnetic character readers, and (2) the fact that the Federal Reserve Banks will not handle checks through regular bank channels unless they are inscribed with magnetic ink characters. The British Bank Association has also accepted the E-13B type font as a standard.

Optical Character Readers

The input of data to the computer is one of the least efficient steps in data processing. The speed, accuracy, and efficiency of a computer system can be significantly improved if data is collected in computer-readable form at its source. The collection of data at its source in a computer-readable form is referred to as *source-data automation*. The *optical character reader* (*OCR*) is a second type of device that helps to make such automation possible. Optical character readers can read printed uppercase and lowercase alphabetic characters, numeric characters, bar codes, and certain special characters from handwritten, typed, and printed paper documents. The specific characters that can be read and whether the characters must be handwritten, typed, or printed depend upon the type of OCR being used. The purpose of the reading operation is to translate the source data into machine language. The data may be either entered directly into the computer or transferred directly to punched cards or magnetic tape for later processing by the computer. Thus, no special step to transcribe data from source documents to an input medium is needed; the time between receipt of data and entry of that data into the computer system is accordingly less.

Optical-mark recognition. Optical marks are commonly used for scoring tests. Illustration A-5, for example, shows a typical test-scoring sheet. It is marked by the person taking the test and can be read by an *optical-mark page reader*. The test-scoring sheet is exposed to a light source as it is run through the optical-mark page reader. Wherever a heavy pencil mark has been made on the form, the light is reflected, thus causing the scoring action to occur. When online to a computer system, an optical-mark page reader can read up to 2000 documents an hour.

Besides test scoring, optical-mark documents can be used for applications such as order-writing, inventory control, insurance policy rating surveys, questionnaires, and payroll. Illustration A-6, for example, shows a source document for an order-writing application. In this application, the order clerk marks the customer number and salesperson number for each order, and the item number, unit size, and quantity for each item ordered. The document then has all of the data required for processing the order. It can be read and processed by the computer system.

One of the problems in designing a system that uses an optical-mark document is designing the document itself. It must be understood and completed easily by the people who use it. If it is not, errors may result—more perhaps than would occur using a traditional source document and keypunch. These errors may then be spread throughout any master files updated during subsequent processing.

Optical-character recognition. Other kinds of optical character readers can read optical characters. These characters have a slightly irregular typeface as shown in Illustration A-7. They consist of the letters of the alphabet, the 10 decimal digits, and several special characters. The characters can be printed by accounting machines, computer printers, cash registers, adding machines, and typewriters.

Optical character recognition devices can read data on either cut forms (for example, sales slips) or continuous forms (such as cash-register tapes), depending on the model. Usually, the machines that can read cut

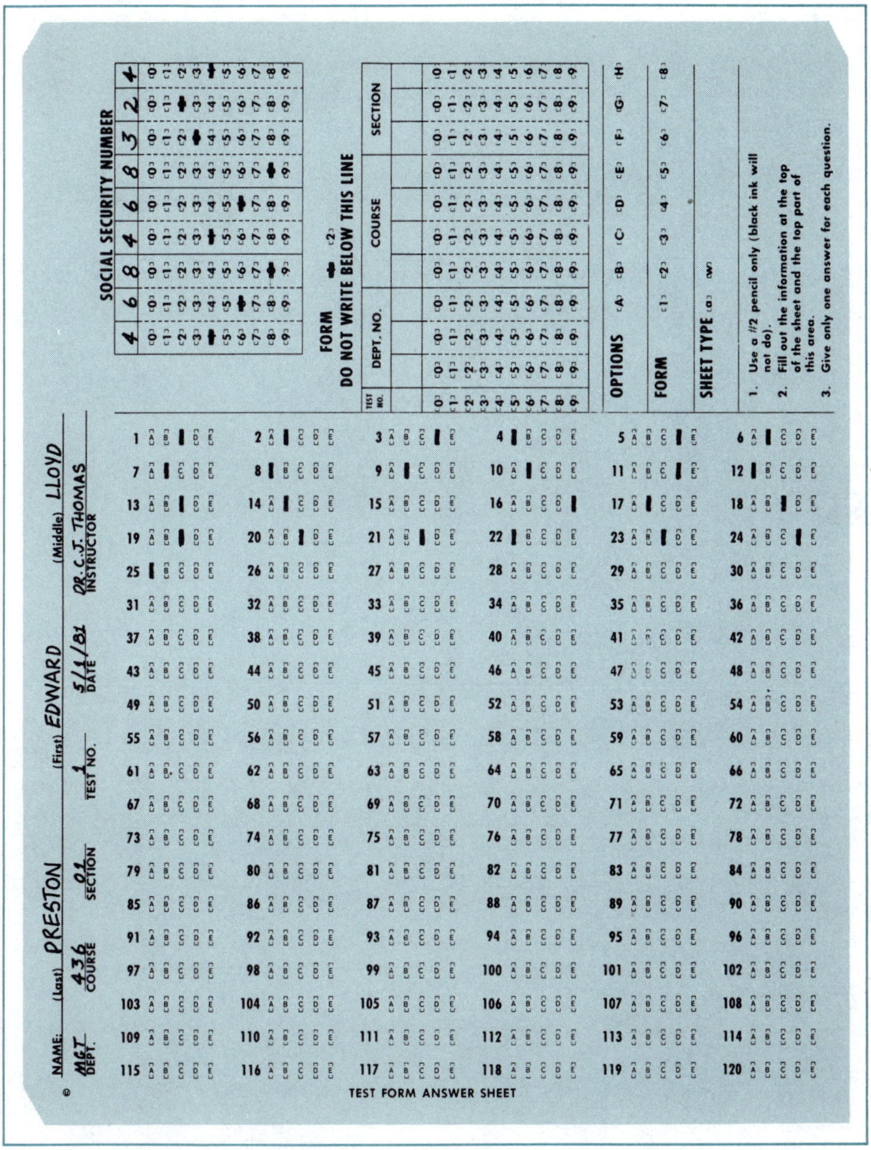

MODULE A: SPECIAL-PURPOSE INPUT AND OUTPUT DEVICES

ILLUSTRATION A-5 Test-scoring sheet with optical marks

forms can be used offline to sort them. Some optical character recognition devices can read optical marks as well as optical characters. In this case, the source documents can contain both forms of representation.

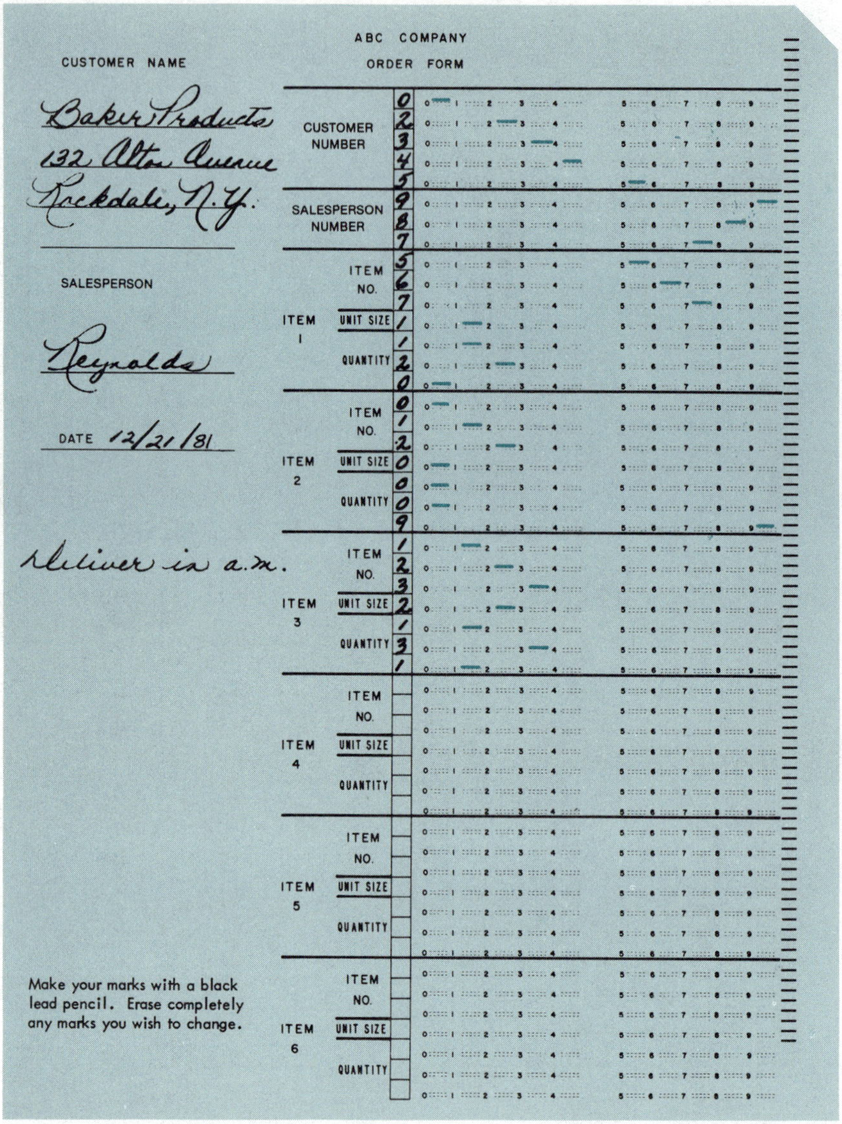

UNIT TWO: COMPUTER SYSTEMS

ILLUSTRATION A-6 Order-writing form

    An application well suited for optical character recognition is accounts receivable. For example, Illustration A-8 shows a utility bill with printed optical characters. On the left side of the bill are spaces for optical marks. If the bill is returned with full payment, the document is processed as

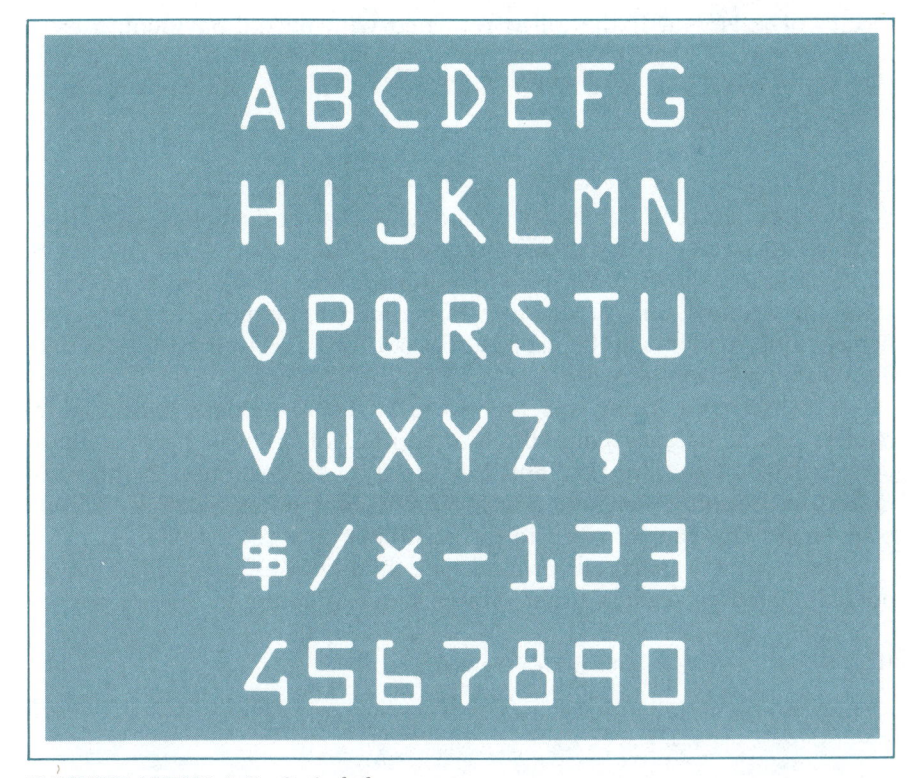

MODULE A: SPECIAL-PURPOSE INPUT AND OUTPUT DEVICES

ILLUSTRATION A-7 Optical characters

ILLUSTRATION A-8 Utility bill with optical characters and optical marks

receipt of payment. If the bill is returned with partial payment, a clerk marks the amount of the partial payment on the left of the document before it is processed. Use of this document eliminates the need for manual keying of data.

Handwritten characters. Finally, some optical character recognition devices can read handwritten data as well as optical characters. Specifically, they can read certain precisely written letters and numbers. Illustration A-9 shows some handwritten characters that can be read and some that cannot. Like other optical character recognition devices, most handwriting-readers can be used to sort cut forms as well as to read data into computer storage.

Because handwriting is a basic form of recording data, handwriting-readers can be used in many different applications. For instance, a handwritten sales slip can be read and processed by the computer as the basic input to accounts receivable and inventory-control applications. A copy of the sales slip can be given to the customer as a record of sale.

The diversity in typed, printed, and handwritten characters causes optical character readers to encounter some difficulty in reading source

ILLUSTRATION A-9 Handwritten characters

Rule	Correct	Incorrect
1. Write big	0 2 8 3 4	0 2 8 3 4
2. Close loops	0 6 8 8 9	0 6 8 8 9
3. Use simple shapes	0 2 3 7 5	0 2 3 7 5
4. Do not link characters	0 0 8 8 1	0 0 8 8 1
5. Connect lines	4 5 T	4 5 T
6. Block print	C S T X Z	C S T X Z

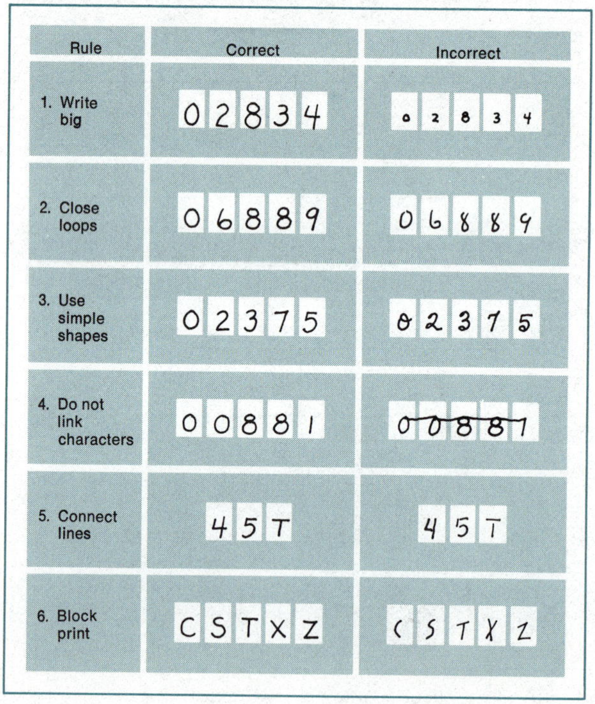

MODULE A: SPECIAL-PURPOSE INPUT AND OUTPUT DEVICES

documents. This is reflected by the fact that a small percentage of the source documents are rejected. Also, characters are read but incorrectly identified in a very small percentage of the source documents. Fewer and fewer of these errors are occurring for two reasons: (1) the expanding use of a standard type font (OCR-A), which is recognized by the American National Standards Institute (ANSI), on source documents, and (2) improved optical scanning techniques.

Optical character readers are used in many diverse areas. For example, they are used in credit card billing, utility billing, and the reading of adding machine and cash register tapes, and by the post office. The use of optical character readers should continue to increase and expand as improved scanning techniques result in fewer source documents being rejected, fewer characters being identified improperly, the reading speed of readers increasing, and the cost of readers decreasing.

Optical bar codes. Optical bar codes were first used by railroads in 1967 for automatic rail car identification. Similar bar codes were introduced in grocery stores in 1973. The bar codes usually included characters readable by people (see Illustration A-10). Many retailers are installing optical character readers that can read special bar codes that identify merchandise. One code is called the ***Universal Product Code***, or ***UPC***. When marked on an item, it consists of 10 pairs of vertical bars representing the manufacturer's identity and the identity code for the item. Over 85 percent of the products sold in supermarkets bear this code. The code can be read by a hand-held wand reader or by passing the coded item over a fixed scanner. (See Illustration A-11.) The data that is read is entered into a computer system that prices and identifies the item. Its output is then displayed or printed by the cash register terminal. As a by-product of this

ILLUSTRATION A-10   Optical bar codes

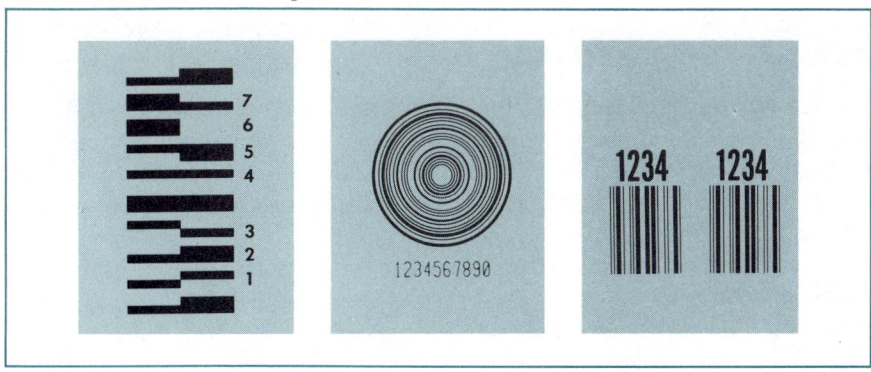

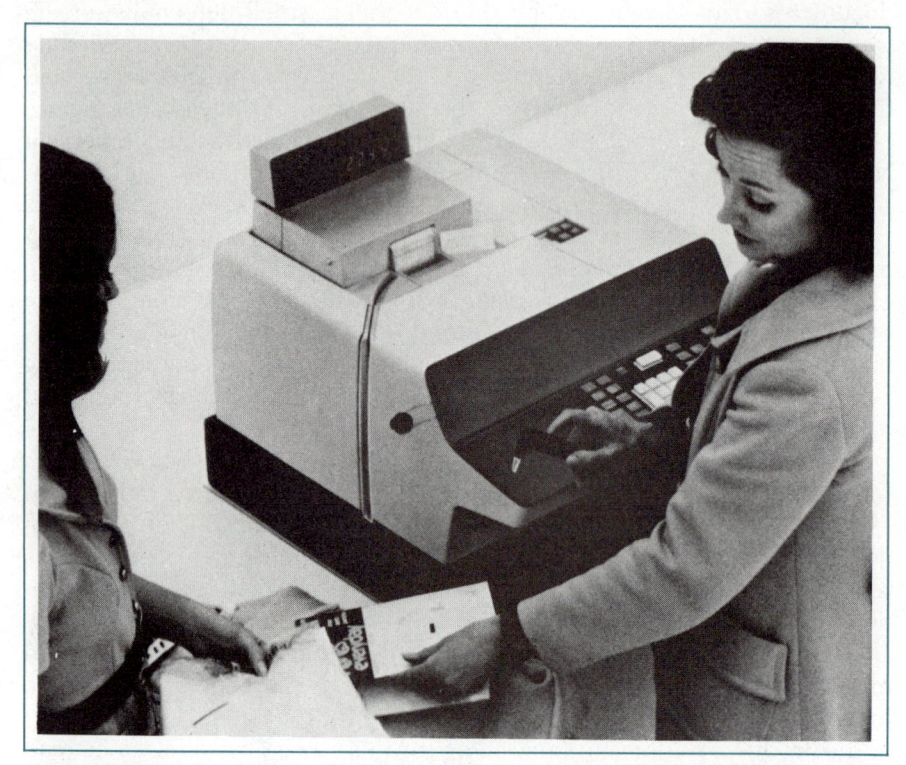

ILLUSTRATION A-11 Reading a bar code with a wand reader

operation, the computer system keeps track of each item sold for inventory control purposes. Other types of bar codes are used on merchandise tags attached to retail items. The processing is similar: A clerk passes a wand reader over the tag and a coded description of the item is recorded.

DATA COMMUNICATIONS

The devices used to enter data into a computer are often close to it. However, under some circumstances this arrangement may not be efficient; it may even be impossible. Consider the assembly line operation of an automobile manufacturer. Assume data concerning the progress of specific steps in the operation must be provided as input to a computer. Obviously, it is impractical to have the computer near the assembly line. It is also impractical to physically transport the data to a computer facility elsewhere every time the steps are performed. If the computer facility is located in a

MODULE A: SPECIAL-PURPOSE INPUT AND OUTPUT DEVICES

city several hundred miles away, such a procedure is impossible. It takes too long. Thus, a means of relaying data to the computer (and in some cases, receiving a reply) is needed. The data must be entered into the computer as it is generated, regardless of the distance between the point of origin and the computer.

The addition of these kinds of capabilities to computer systems did not necessitate a vast redesign of computers. Existing telephone, telegraph, and microwave installations were suitable for data transmission with only minor modifications of existing hardware. In most cases, all that was required was the implementation of devices to convert data at the point of origin into electrical impulses that could be transmitted over telephone lines. Then the impulses could be modified at the computer facility for input to the computer. The data could be transmitted in either *serial* (one bit at a time) or *parallel* (one character at a time) mode. As further explained in Chapter 14, *data communication* is simply the electrical transfer of data from one point to another. This type of data transmission can occur at rates of 300 to 3000 cycles per second.

A *data set* is the device that converts data to either transmit it from its point of origin or receive it at its destination. The encoding of data for transmission as electrical impulses is called *modulation*. The decoding of data when it reaches the computer facility is called *demodulation*. Therefore, data sets are sometimes called *modems* (*mo*dulation-*dem*odulation devices).

○ TERMINALS

As the number and variety of computer applications increase, the need to communicate with the computer from remote locations becomes more evident. To satisfy this need to "converse" with the computer, a variety of *remote devices*, or *terminals*, have been developed. These devices allow the input of data to the computer facility and/or the output of information to the user.

The number and type of remote devices in a system depend upon the number of points from which transmission of data is required, the volume of data to be transferred, the transmission quality desired, the timing of transmissions (peak and slack periods of transmission), and the transmission speed required. The remote devices can be connected to the computer through a channel (discussed in Chapter 12). Touch-tone devices, audio-response units, visual display devices, hard-copy devices, point-of-sale terminals, and a group of devices commonly known as "intelligent terminals" are discussed below.

Touch-Tone Devices

Touch-tone devices are designed to use existing telephone communication links. Perhaps for this reason, business organizations have readily adopted these devices. However, as a group, the touch-tone devices are low-speed devices.

A touch-tone terminal is shown in Illustration A-12. This terminal has audio capabilities to take advantage of touch-tone telephone dialing. It is triggered by sound frequencies that are converted into electrical pulses when data is keyed on a keyboard or entered by a magnetic strip on a plastic card. The data transfer rate of this device averages 5 to 7 characters per second.

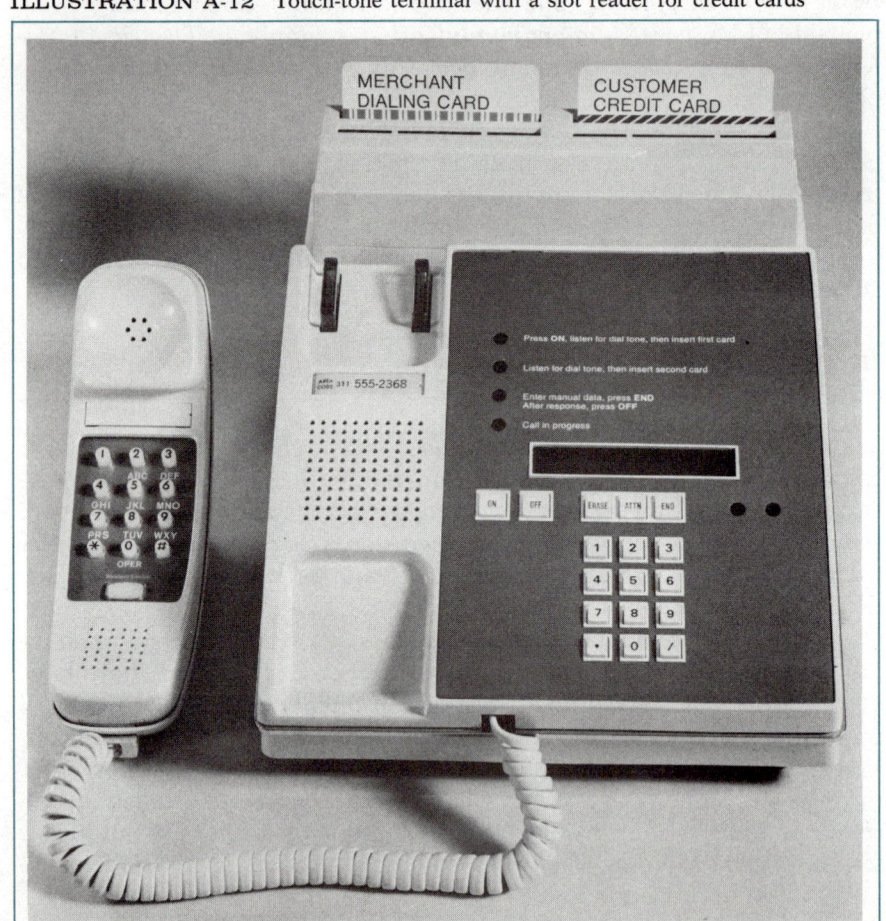

ILLUSTRATION A-12 Touch-tone terminal with a slot reader for credit cards

MODULE A: SPECIAL-PURPOSE INPUT AND OUTPUT DEVICES

Audio-Response Units

An audio-response unit can be connected to telephone lines or to lines especially installed for the audio-response unit. This unit is typically used as an output device. However, voice data entry terminal systems that are computer based and can be programmed to recognize voice input are available. As an output device, the audio-response unit is limited only by the coded vocabulary preselected for it by the system designer.

Audio-response units are used in a number of applications. Common examples are: banking, weather reports or credit verification via telephone, order entry, and inventory control.

A portable terminal used for order entry is shown in Illustration A-13. The terminal consists of a touch-tone input device and an audio-response unit. A salesperson can call the computer from any telephone by placing the telephone head set into the back of the terminal. Order data is entered on the touch-tone input unit by the salesperson in response to the computer-generated voice from the audio-response unit. The computer guides the salesperson through the ordering procedure.

Visual Display Devices

The visual display device, commonly referred to as a **CRT** (cathode-ray-tube), is used in many computer systems for both input and output. The

ILLUSTRATION A-13 Audio-response terminal

display unit in Illustration A-14 has a screen similar to that of a television set. This device can display both alphameric and special characters. It also has a keyboard similar to a typewriter for data entry.

CRT devices may be equipped with light pens. The operator of such a device directs a beam of light from the light pen onto the CRT screen to enter data. The operator either points the light pen at a certain spot on the screen or draws on the screen to enter the data. If data is entered into one of these devices from the keyboard, each character is displayed on the screen for visual checking by the operator. This allows the operator to make corrections to the data before forwarding it to the computer.

ILLUSTRATION A-14   Visual display device

MODULE A: SPECIAL-PURPOSE INPUT AND OUTPUT DEVICES

These units do not produce printed output. They are often called *soft-copy devices*. In contrast, devices that produce printed output are often called *hard-copy devices*. CRT devices have several advantages over hard-copy devices. They are silent in operation and have a much higher display speed (up to 10,000 characters per second). In some applications, a quick response to an inquiry is needed but a printed record is not necessary. The CRT is well suited for this type of use. In cases where a printed copy of the display on the screen is needed, a microfilm unit or a printer can be attached to the CRT. When used in such applications as airline reservations, car rental reservations, and credit card verification, CRTs are often called *inquiry/response stations*.

Another type of CRT is the *graphic display device*. (See Illustration A-15.) It can perform all of the functions mentioned for the visual display device. It can also present graphs and line drawings. Some graphic display devices have color display screens. The use of color graphics is increasing because of its versatility. As many as 4, 7, or 16 colors may appear on a single screen, depending on the capabilities of the device. The user has many options to choose from when presenting information.

ILLUSTRATION A-15   Graphic display device

CRT devices may be located at a central computer facility with connections to the computer made by cable. They may be at locations several thousand miles away. The major disadvantage of visual display devices is that no permanent record is written when information is received or data is transmitted. This can be overcome by attaching a microfilm unit or a printer to the CRT as suggested above.

Hard-Copy Devices

As mentioned in the previous section, devices that produce printed output like that of a typewriter are referred to as hard-copy devices. They are used in applications where printed output is needed. As a class they are much slower than CRTs. They may be noisy in operation. There are many different types of these devices, and they use a variety of printing methods. Some do impact printing similar to a typewriter. Others do nonimpact printing using a thermal process.

Portable hard-copy devices are becoming increasingly popular. A portable terminal like the one in Illustration A-16 can be connected directly to the computer or communicate with it via a telephone line. Such a device is especially useful when it is necessary for the user to communicate with the

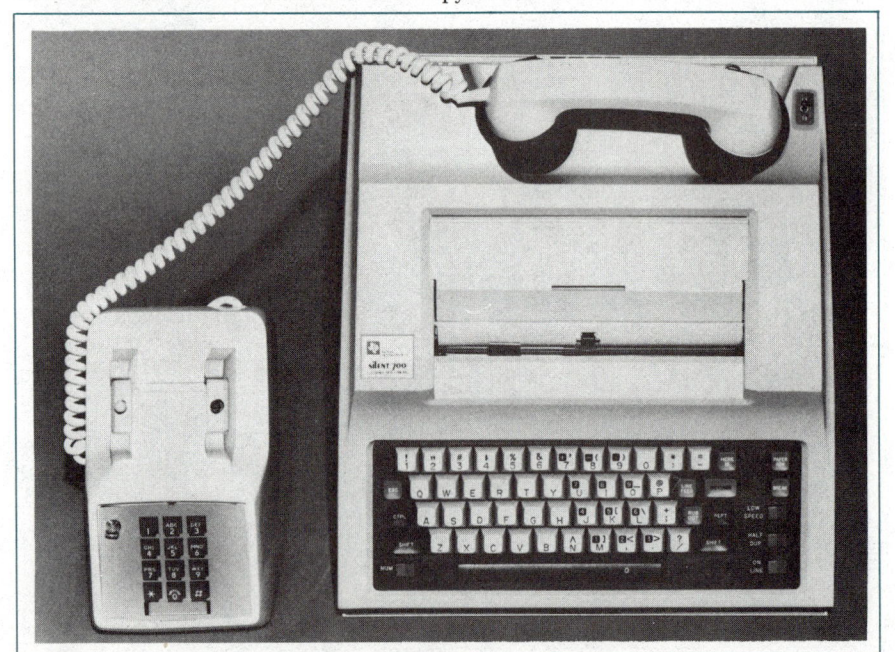

ILLUSTRATION A-16 Portable hard-copy device

computer from remote locations. For example, a business representative may need information from a central computer while on a business trip. The representative can dial the number of the computer from a telephone, and then insert the telephone handset in a special holder in the terminal to communicate with the computer.

Point-of-Sale Devices

Many retail operations use remote terminals capable of performing the functions of a cash register while recording sales data. These terminals are commonly referred to as *point-of-sale* (*POS*) *terminals*. A typical terminal is shown in Illustration A-17. Such devices usually include a keyboard for entry of sales data, a display panel to show the price, a cash drawer, and a cash receipt printer. All POS terminals are designed to allow operators to use them without much training. A message panel or a series of lighted keys directs the operator when entering a transaction. Often a wand reader is included and used by the operator to read either the Universal Product Code on boxes, cans, and packages or other bar code on merchandise tickets, thus eliminating keyboard entry. The POS terminals are an essential part of a source-data collection system that provides important inventory and sales information for the retailer. When the POS terminals are connected to a central computer, this information is immediately available.

Intelligent Terminals

A terminal that can be instructed, or programmed, and that contains an internal storage unit to hold the instructions is referred to as an *intelligent terminal*. Intelligent terminals are used for a wide variety of data entry functions. They can be used to collect and edit data prior to transmitting it to a central computer. They can also be used to collect data from a number of nonprogrammable terminals, edit the data, and then transmit it to a central computer. The specific data entry functions that can be performed are controlled by the program in the internal memory of the terminal. (Terminals that cannot be programmed are limited primarily to inquiry/response applications. Such terminals were discussed earlier in this module.)

One of the newest types of intelligent terminals uses magnetic bubble storage to store up to 80,000 characters of data before it is transmitted to a central computer. The magnetic bubble storage is contained in a small module (see Illustration A-18). It stores digital data by changing the magnetic polarity of a thin, crystalline film. Because this storage works magnetically, it retains data when power is turned off (is nonvolatile). Therefore, it is especially suitable for portable intelligent terminals. It is likely

184

UNIT TWO: COMPUTER SYSTEMS

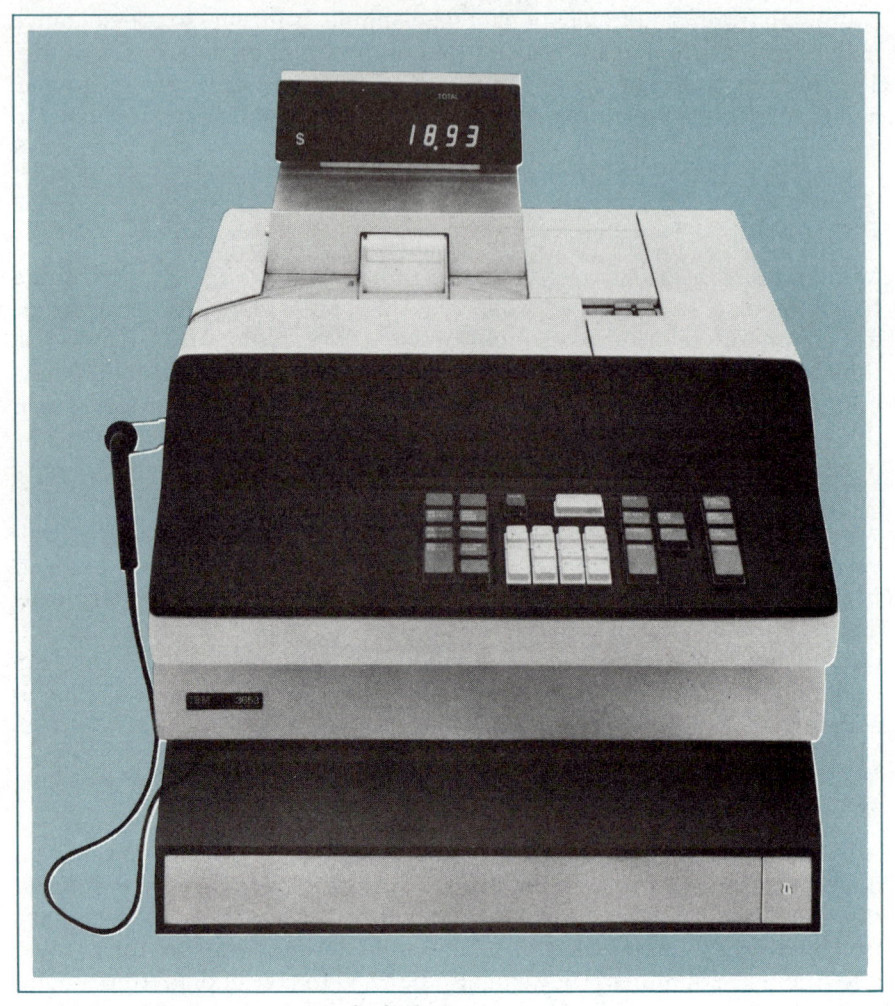

ILLUSTRATION A-17   Point-of-sale device

that magnetic bubble storage will replace other types of storage now being used for intelligent terminals because it is nonvolatile and is smaller than other types of internal storage units used in intelligent terminals.

A typical application of this type of terminal is sales order entry. A salesperson can enter sales data over a period of time. It is stored in the bubble storage. Later, the salesperson can print the sales orders, make any necessary changes, then transmit the sales data to a central computer over a dial-up telephone line.

Many applications now use intelligent terminals. One of the most widely used applications is the POS system mentioned above. Among the

MODULE A: SPECIAL-PURPOSE INPUT AND OUTPUT DEVICES

ILLUSTRATION A-18 Magnetic bubble storage module

newer uses of intelligent terminals are the automatic tellers or cash-dispensing terminals used by some banks. Terminals like the one in Illustration A-19 can be placed at various locations in a community. For example, many banks provide 24-hour deposit and withdrawal services by means of these terminals.

The remote CRT terminal is one of the most widely used computer input/output devices. As more transaction-oriented computer systems are installed, the use of intelligent CRT terminals will increase. More and more communications with computers will be handled this way, and more and more data will be captured as transactions occur. The development of low-cost processors has made it feasible to make most terminals intelligent. This in turn will help to make data entry and retrieval easier for the user.

○ KEY-ENTRY DEVICES

The most widely used method of data entry today involves key-to-storage devices. There are two basic types of key-to-storage devices: key-to-tape and key-to-disk. A *key-to-tape device* can be a single unit that replaces a keypunch machine. A *key-to-disk device* typically comprises several keyboard units. Both of these devices are used to record data that will be processed by a computer at a later date; that is, they are used to prepare the

ILLUSTRATION A-19 Automatic teller terminal

data offline. This is in contrast to the terminals just discussed, which can operate online. As they record data, they also transmit it directly to the computer.

Key-to-Tape Devices

Magnetic tape can be produced as a by-product of some operation (typing or keypunching) or directly by a keying operation. A key-to-tape device consists of a keyboard for entering data, a buffer storage area that temporarily holds the data for an accuracy check, and a magnetic tape unit. After data is keyed onto the tape, the tape is rewound. The same device can be used to verify the data. The verified data can then be read by a computer system

Although keying data onto tape does not reduce or eliminate the keying of source data, it has several advantages over keypunching and verify-

MODULE A: SPECIAL-PURPOSE INPUT AND OUTPUT DEVICES

ing cards. First, there is no movement of cards to slow the key-to-tape operation; the operator can work faster when using this device than when using a card punch. Second, the handling of cards is eliminated. Third, magnetic tape units have higher input speeds than card readers do.

Key-to-Disk Devices

The key-to-disk devices are another popular method for key entry of data. A key-to-disk system includes multiple keyboard terminals connected to a computer and a magnetic tape unit and magnetic disk drive. (See Illustration A-20.) The number of keyboard terminals can range from 2 through 64. They usually have display screens to assist operators in entering data

ILLUSTRATION A-20   Key-to-disk data entry system

correctly. As data is entered at a keyboard, it goes through the computer, which edits and validates the data and then stores it on a magnetic disk. Key-to-disk systems use the magnetic disk as temporary storage to allow more effective operator control in formatting and editing the data. The computer then writes all of the data on magnetic tape for later input to another computer for processing. In most cases, the final output of the key-to-disk system is a magnetic tape. These systems are most often used to prepare large amounts of data for processing on either medium-size or large computers.

Key-to-Diskette Devices

A second type of key-to-disk system allows one or more operators to key data directly onto a *flexible disk*, more commonly called a *floppy disk* or *diskette*. The floppy disk is a single flexible disk contained in a plastic envelope.

A key-to-diskette device is shown in Illustration A-21. Such a device can be connected directly to a computer while the data is keyed, or keying

ILLUSTRATION A-21   Key-to-diskette data entry device

can be done as a separate function. This type of device is often used with minicomputer systems (discussed in detail in Chapter 9). The floppy disk is commonly used for data storage.

OTHER INPUT/OUTPUT DEVICES

Paper Tape and Paper Tape Devices

Punched paper tape is a continuous strip of paper that is wound on a reel and punched with combinations of holes that represent data. There is similarity between this method of representing data and the coding of data on magnetic tape. Illustration A-22 shows one of the punched-hole coding schemes that can be used with paper tape. In this coding scheme, each column of punches represents one character. The coding scheme corresponds closely to 6-bit BCD (see Chapter 5). Paper tape can be read at speeds ranging from 350 to 2000 characters per second. Historically, paper tape has been used in terminal applications that require the transmission of data over communication lines. Today, the use of paper tape is diminishing. It is most often used where it is punched as a by-product of some other operation. A paper tape punch is shown in Illustration A-22.

Console Display-Keyboard

The display-keyboard in Illustration A-23 is both an input device and an output device. It is usually close to a panel of lights and switches called the *console*, from which overall control of the computer system and executing programs is exercised. Because the console display-keyboard is an extremely slow input/output device, it is used primarily for communication between the operator and the computer system. Programmed messages to the operator are displayed as output. Responses from the operator are keyed as input.

When the display-keyboard is used as an input device, data is keyed on the keyboard and then read into computer storage under control of an executing program. It is used as an output device when an executing program displays output on the CRT. Suppose, for example, that a tape needed by a payroll program is not mounted on a tape drive. The program directs the computer to display PLEASE MOUNT PAYROLL TAPE on the console display and then waits for a reply from the operator. The operator mounts the payroll tape and keys a response on the keyboard. The response is read and processed by the executing program. If the response is an acceptable one, the program continues processing. This same type of communication can be used to alert the operator of other error or exceptional conditions in the system.

190

UNIT TWO: COMPUTER SYSTEMS

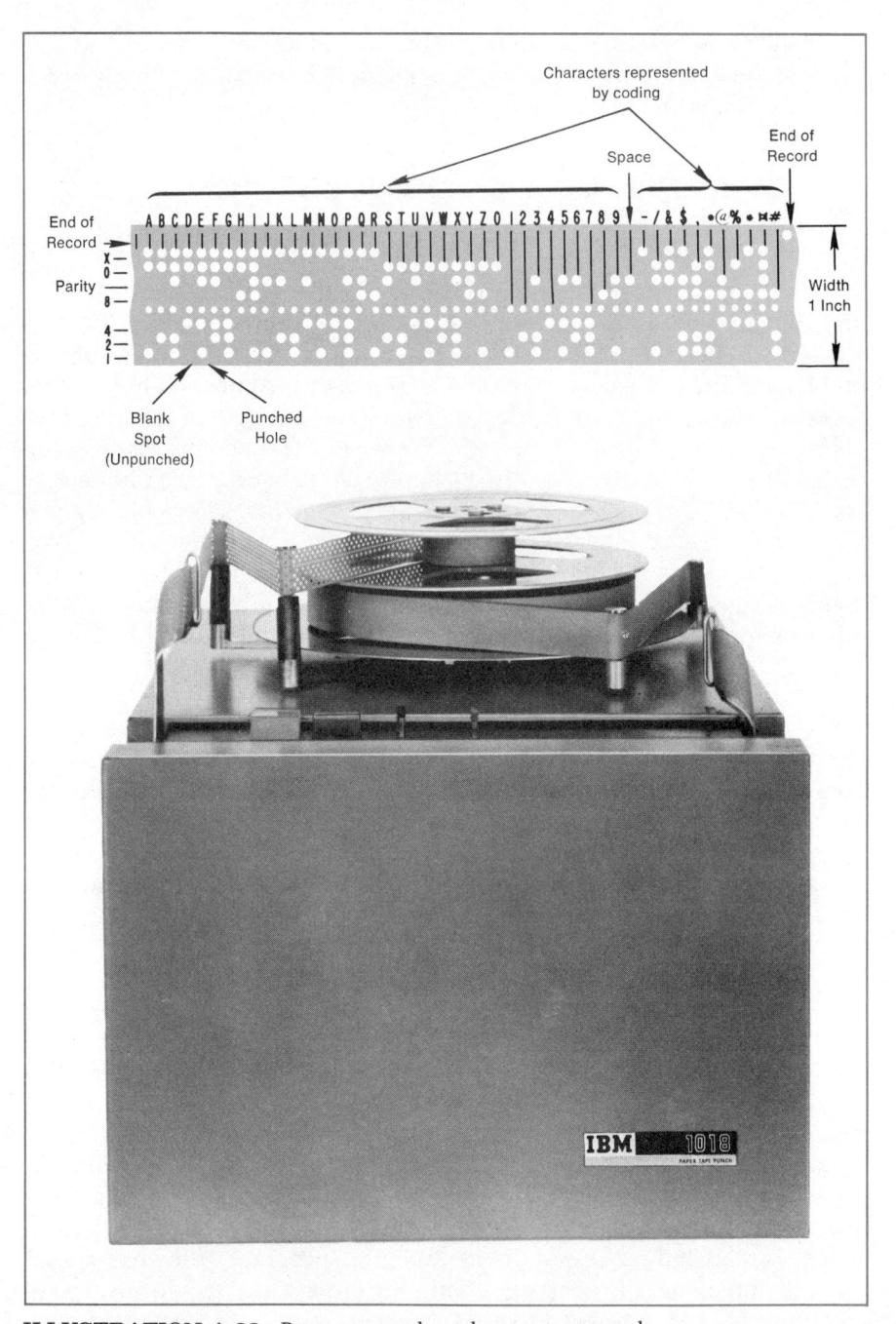

ILLUSTRATION A-22 Paper tape code and paper tape punch

MODULE A: SPECIAL-PURPOSE INPUT AND OUTPUT DEVICES

ILLUSTRATION A-23 A console display-keyboard

On some computer systems, the console output device is a printer and/or a CRT. The CRT allows relatively fast display of messages to the operator. If a low-speed printer is also available, the operator can cause items to be printed when hard copy is wanted.

Plotters

A *plotter* is an output device that creates graphic output on paper. It can be used to produce bar graphs, pie charts, line charts, and complex pictorial shapes such as topographical and weather maps. Low-cost plotters that can be attached to intelligent graphic terminals to produce hard-copy output of screen displays are available (see Illustration A-24).

One type of plotter consists of a movable carriage, which holds one or more pens, and a chart paper holder. Output is produced as the carriage moves back and forth across the paper as directed by a computer program. The color of the output varies according to the pens that are held in the carriage. Pictures with very good detail may by produced. The pens can be positioned in any of over 40,000 points in each square inch of paper on some plotters. Another type of plotter uses a matrix-type printer to produce single-color output.

ILLUSTRATION A-24 Use of a plotter to produce graphic output

Several factors have increased the use of plotters in business applications. First, a plotter produces pictorial output that can be understood easily. Second, the costs of plotters have decreased. They are more appealing to businesses because they can be used to reduce the cost of preparing charts, graphs, and other pictorial output. As noted above, a plotter is directed by a computer program to produce the desired output. Plotter manufacturers often provide software that programmers can use to produce plotter output. In other cases, the programmers of the user organization write all of the programs necessary to produce the desired output.

Computer Output Microfilm

Photographing and placing computer output on microfilm, referred to as *computer output microfilm*, or *COM*, is being used by an increasing num-

MODULE A: SPECIAL-PURPOSE INPUT AND OUTPUT DEVICES

ber of organizations. Using COM can reduce the costs of producing reports in several ways. There are reductions in paper costs and in the costs associated with handling and storing computer reports. The costs of producing computer reports have accelerated over the past few years due to rising paper costs and increasing numbers of reports. Printing an increasing number of reports consumes increasing amounts of computer time. This can be reduced significantly using COM. Reports placed on microfilm take much less storage space, and less handling is required when a report needs to be retrieved.

The increased cost of mailing computer reports has also been a major reason for companies to switch to COM. Microfilm can be mailed at a fraction of the cost of printed reports. The reports on microfilm can be printed at the receiving end if needed.

One type of process to place reports on microfilm is shown in Illustration A-25. Computer reports are placed on a magnetic tape that serves as input to a microfilm recorder. COM can also be produced by a microfilm processor attached directly to the computer as an output device. The microfilm can be viewed with a microfilm reader or used to produce printed reports as needed.

The use of COM will continue to increase as organizations continue to seek ways to reduce costs and yet meet the need for additional reports.

Word Processors

Word processing (***WP***) is the manipulation of words (textual data) to produce letters, reports, and other types of printed documents. Word pro-

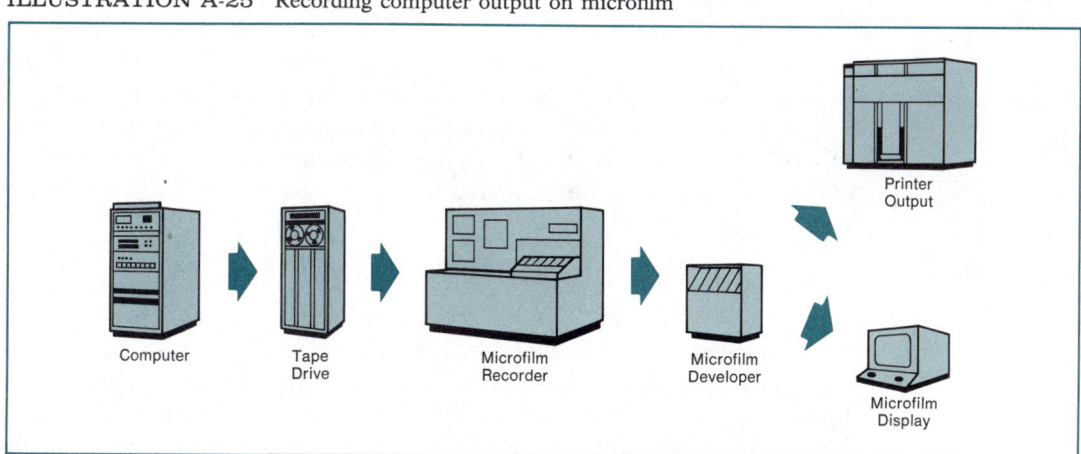

ILLUSTRATION A-25 Recording computer output on microfilm

cessors are equipment that produces this type of output. Word processing started with the introduction of electric typewriters that could store a typist's keystrokes and allowed the correction, modification, and duplication of keyed material. Word processors are now used for a variety of purposes. Their uses include the preparation of administrative calendars and schedules, and of other printed materials that support communication within an organization.

Word processing systems are available in a variety of configurations, ranging from standalone systems to shared-logic systems (see Illustration A-26). A standalone system is shown in the upper portion of Illustration A-26. It consists of a CRT, one or more floppy disks, a printer, and an internal processor. On the most basic system, the internal processor can do a set of fixed functions that are executed through keyboard entries. The user cannot alter these functions. More advanced systems have programmable internal processors. Standard software packages for use with these systems are supplied on floppy disks by their manufacturers.

Shared-logic systems consist of several CRTs attached to the same processor and data storage unit. In such a system, a common data base, say up to 40,000 pages of data, may be available to all users. This type of system can be used in a word processing center, or the CRTs can be dispersed, with users at various locations sharing the common data base. These systems allow multiple users to enter, display, or print text at the same time. A shared-logic system equipped with communication capabilities can be tied in with other word processing systems or computers. Software packages to perform math functions, data sorting, and password security checking to limit user access to data are usually available.

A word processing system is used in the following way to produce textual material. The user keys in words on the keyboard. As the words are keyed, they are displayed on the CRT. The user can correct, insert, delete, copy, or move words within text. After the text has been corrected to the user's satisfaction, it can be printed or saved to be used later. The user can also combine several sets of text saved previously to produce new text. This allows the rapid production of reports or letters that vary only in some respects. The user can also direct the system to produce any number of printed copies of stored text. This allows the production of any number of "original documents."

Floppy Disk Devices

The floppy disk was introduced in 1973 for use in key-to-diskette systems as discussed previously. Soon after, manufacturers began making floppy disk devices for use with minicomputers. The floppy disk drive is now one of the most popular input/output devices on minicomputers (see Illustration A-27). It is also used with intelligent terminals, word processors, and

ILLUSTRATION A-26 Two examples of word processing systems

ILLUSTRATION A-27 Minicomputer with floppy disk input/output

POS terminals. The small business computers and microcomputers to be discussed in Chapter 9 frequently use floppy disks for data storage. The floppy disk comes in two sizes: 5¼ inches and 8 inches. The 8-inch disk is used primarily with minicomputers. The smaller disk is used with microcomputers. The number of characters that can be stored on a floppy disk depends on whether one or both sides of the disk are used for data storage and on the specific computer in use. Considering these factors, the smaller disk may store from 75,000 to over 250,000 characters. The larger disk may store from 200,000 to 1.2 million characters. Both offer the advantage of direct access storage at a very low cost. A floppy disk can be purchased for as little as $5.00.

MODULE A: SPECIAL-PURPOSE INPUT AND OUTPUT DEVICES

○ SUMMARY

1. Character recognition input devices fall into two categories: magnetic character readers and optical character readers. Magnetic character readers are capable of distinguishing magnetically inscribed characters of the E-13B type font. In addition, documents on which magnetic characters are inscribed can be sorted offline. The result is faster processing of documents. Optical character recognition equipment can be used to read handwritten, typed, and printed documents, optical marks, and bar codes. This allows data to be entered into a computer system without the intermediate step of transcribing it from source documents to an input medium.

2. The advantages of character recognition input are: (1) data can be input directly from documents or stored on some other medium for later processing; (2) the characters can be recorded on documents of varying widths, lengths, and thicknesses; and (3) the coded data is easily read by humans.

3. Data communication devices became necessary because of the time required to physically transport data from its point of origin to the computer facility. These devices allow data to be transmitted over existing transmission media such as telephone or telegraph lines. To accomplish this, data sets (modems) were devised to transmit the data as electrical pulses from the point where it is created (modulation) and to decode the data at the computer facility (demodulation).

4. There are many devices that may serve as remote terminals to provide input to or receive output from a computer. Among the devices are touch-tone devices, audio-response units, visual display devices, hard-copy devices, point-of-sale terminals, and intelligent terminals. Each satisfies distinct needs for data entry and transmission.

5. Key-to-tape, disk, and diskette devices are the most widely used form of data entry. They allow formatting and editing of data as it is recorded.

6. Paper tape is an input/output medium that has been in use for some time. Paper tape output is often produced as a by-product of some other operation.

7. A console display-keyboard is used directly with the computer to relay information to the operator from the computer, and to the computer from the operator, while a program is being executed.

8. A plotter is an output device that can produce pictorial output on paper. It is used to create charts and graphs and other types of graphic output.

9. Computer output microfilm is being used by an increasing number of organizations to reduce the costs associated with computer reports. Microfilm offers several advantages as an output medium. It requires less storage space; mailing costs less; and paper usage is less. Printed reports can be generated from microfilm when needed.

10. Word processors provide the capability to edit textual material and to produce as many printed copies of the output as needed. A basic word processing system consists of a CRT, a printer, and one or more floppy disks for data storage. Text editing functions include the insertion, deletion, correction, moving, and copying of words.

11. The floppy disk drive is a very popular input/output device on small computer systems. It offers direct access storage capability at a low cost. Many low-cost computer systems use floppy disks as their only data storage medium. The floppy disk is in widespread use in a number of data entry applications including key-to diskette devices, intelligent terminals, and word processors.

○ REVIEW QUESTIONS

1. Identify the two basic types of character recognition equipment.
2. When is it necessary to have data communication as well as data processing capabilities in a system?
3. In what ways can audio-response units be used?
4. Give several applications for which CRT terminals are especially suitable.
5. Why are key-entry devices popular for data entry?
6. What is the purpose of the console display-keyboard?
7. List the types of output that can be produced by a plotter.
8. What are the advantages and limitations of computer output on microfilm?
9. Explain the basic functions of word processors.
10. How are floppy disks used?

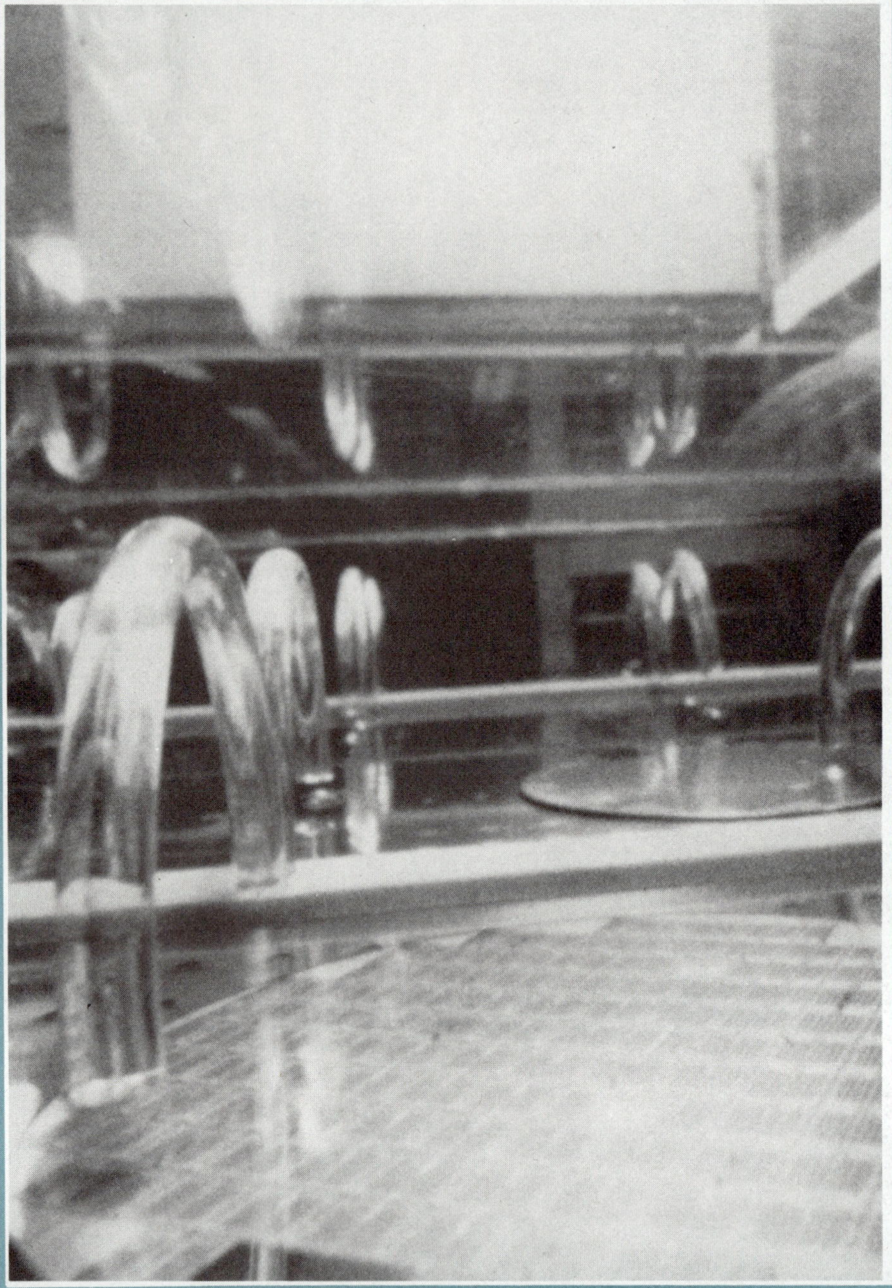

CHAPTER 9

COMPUTER SYSTEMS

MAINFRAME SYSTEMS
Large Computers
Medium-Size Computers
Small Computers

MINICOMPUTER SYSTEMS

MICROCOMPUTER SYSTEMS

THE SIZE OF COMPUTERS AND SCOPE
OF THE COMPUTER INDUSTRY:
A RESTATEMENT AND COMPARISON

Opposite: Silicon wafers containing 64K bit (8000 byte) storage chips are moved by air along a production line.

The past decade has seen a tremendous growth in both the types of computers being produced and the number of manufacturers making them. There are now over 50 manufacturers producing a wide variety of computers. Their product lines range from small systems that cost less than $750 to large computers that cost millions of dollars.

In the past decade, there has been a tenfold increase in the number of computers installed. A good percentage of this total has been due to the minicomputer. (This term is defined later in this chapter.) The introduction of the minicomputer has led many new companies to enter the computer manufacturing field, and, by contrast, General Electric and RCA have stopped manufacturing computers.

As technological advances are made, the size and cost of computers continue to drop while their capabilities increase. A computer job that cost $14 to process and took 375 seconds of computer time in 1955 can now be processed for less than $.15 and in three seconds.

In the past few years there has been a tremendous increase in the density of electronic circuits and in the number of bytes of memory that can be placed on a silicon chip. These recent advances in microelectronics have significantly reduced the time needed to design and build new computer systems, thus accelerating the development of computers. Because of these improvements in computer cost and performance, computers are being used in many new applications. Many of these new applications involve the newest development in computers, the microprocessor. The *microprocessor* is a development of microelectronics, a miniaturized version of a computer central processing unit. When combined with input/output devices, a storage unit, and an internal clock for timing operations, it becomes a *microcomputer system*.

Traditionally, computer power has been centralized. Data has been collected and brought to a central computer for processing. A major reason for this approach has been the high cost of the computer and the special facilities needed to house it. With the introduction of the microcomputer and the minicomputer, there has been a move toward increased decentralization of computer power. This has been possible because of the low cost of these computers and because they do not require special facilities.

It has become increasingly difficult to distinguish between the various classes of computer systems. Size, cost, and processing capability are the characteristics that have separated them but they now frequently overlap. The most generally accepted classes of computers are large, medium, and small computers, minicomputers, and microcomputers. The computers in the large, medium, and small classes are commonly referred to as *mainframes*. The purpose of this chapter is to identify the characteristics of the various classes of computers and to discuss their typical business applications.

CHAPTER 9: COMPUTER SYSTEMS

○ MAINFRAME SYSTEMS

Large Computers

A large computer system offers the ultimate in operating speed and storage capacity. A typical system has a main storage capacity of from 4 to 16 megabytes. It operates at speeds measured in nanoseconds and uses from 2 to 4 billion bytes of secondary storage. These systems rent for $40,000 to $250,000 or more per month; they cost millions of dollars. The costs and capabilities of these systems vary greatly depending on the number of input/output devices used. A large computer can support many magnetic disk and magnetic tape drives, printers, card readers, plotters, terminals, and other input/output devices. These types of systems have traditionally been used by large organizations to provide all data processing services from a centralized location. The large computer system in Illustration 9-1 has 8 megabytes of main storage, multiple disk drives, and a high-speed laser printer. It can support several hundred terminals.

ILLUSTRATION 9-1 IBM 3033 large computer system

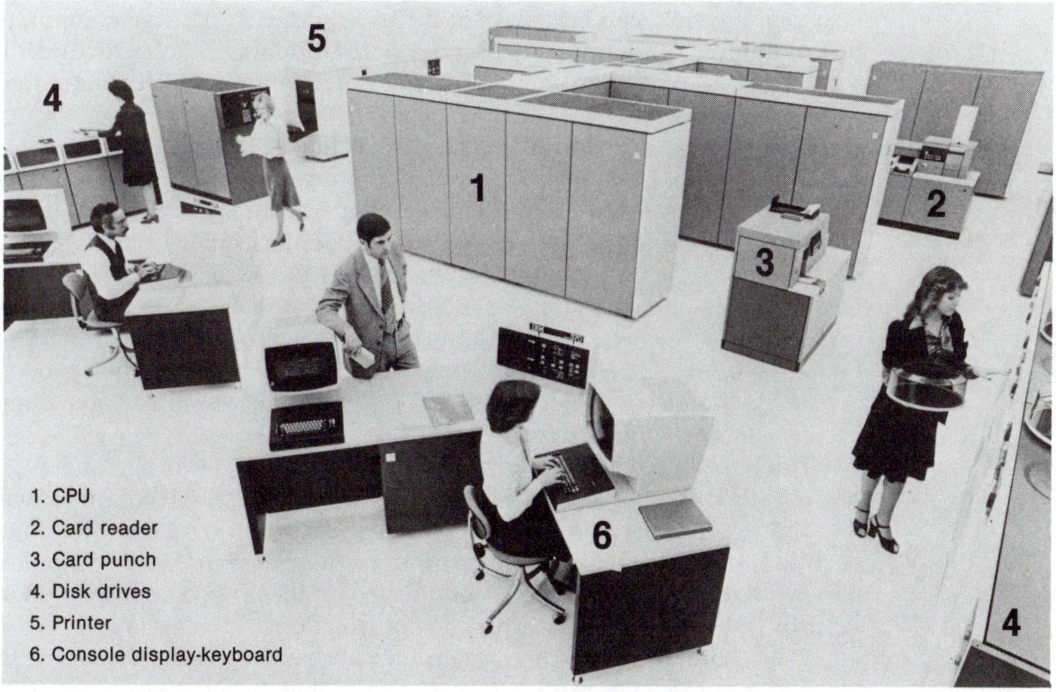

1. CPU
2. Card reader
3. Card punch
4. Disk drives
5. Printer
6. Console display-keyboard

The software needed to support large computers is very sophisticated. It is one of the major distinctions between this class of computers and others. This software may support virtual storage, multiprocessing, multiprogramming, and terminals. A combined hardware and software feature called *virtual storage* (or *virtual memory*) makes it appear that the computer has more main storage than is actually physically present. This allows the computer to execute programs that would otherwise be unacceptable because they are too large to fit into main storage. When a programmer is writing a program to be run on a computer with virtual storage, the program size need not be limited to the amount of main storage actually available. *Multiprogramming* allows several programs to be stored in one CPU at the same time. Each program takes its turn in executing. A large computer may run 50 or more programs concurrently under the direction of software that supports multiprogramming. (Both virtual storage and multiprogramming will be discussed further in Chapter 13.)

There can be two or more central processing units within a system. Such a configuration allows simultaneous running of programs. This is called *multiprocessing*. In addition to providing faster processing, the system can be set up to allow one processor to take over for another if one fails. Both processors may share the available resources to provide optimum system performance and reliability. Multiprocessor systems are often used for applications that are time-dependent such as airline and car rental reservation systems and credit card verification systems. Large computers that multiprocess can also support multiprogramming. Each processor in a multiprocessing system can act like a single computer and run a number of jobs concurrently.

Management decision-making tools, such as *simulation*, can be used on large computer systems. Through mathematical techniques, for example, various activities of a business that would normally occur over many months or years can be simulated in hours. For example, a business may be considering the installation of a new inventory-control system to achieve better control of items in stock. Before conversion to the new system is undertaken, several years of inventory activity can be simulated to verify that the system will be an improvement over current methods of handling inventory. A large computer system may support a very sophisticated management information system.

The large computer system is also well suited for scientific and engineering work. Its speed and size allow it to do mathematical computations that are not practical or possible on other computer systems. The engineering research and development processing necessary for the creation of new products can often be accomplished on the large computer system used for other business data processing functions.

A distributed processing system can be based on a large computer that has a number of minicomputers or small computers attached. (Distributed processing systems are discussed in detail in Chapter 14.) The large computer processes jobs that are too large for the other computers and maintains the data base of the organization. In many cases, the large computer acts as a routing agent to interconnect smaller computers so they can share information.

Often business organizations initially install large computer systems to handle the processing of large volumes of data. Such large-volume processing may be required by: a bank that processes 10 to 20 million checks, 5000 to 10,000 loan applications, and several hundred thousand loan payments each day; an insurance company that processes several thousand insurance applications and claims daily; a utility company that bills several million customers each month; and a credit reporting agency that provides credit checks for several million persons in its files. Each of these businesses is likely to use more than one large computer when either the processing volume increases or it is necessary to provide a backup computer in case their primary system fails. These large computer systems may also be used to support management information systems and management decision-making tools like simulation in addition to the processing of large volumes of business transactions.

Medium-Size Computers

The medium-size computer has a smaller main storage capacity than a large computer. A typical medium-size computer has a main storage capacity of from 500,000 to 4 million bytes. It operates in nanoseconds, but it may be from 4 to 10 times slower than a large computer. It uses from 1 to 2 billion bytes of secondary storage. These systems are likely to support multiprogramming and virtual storage. All of the major programming languages are usually supported, and extensive software is usually available. If multiprogramming is supported, a number of jobs can be run at one time. For example, a group of jobs running concurrently may include: a payroll program, an inventory master file update, a customer billing program, and an accounts receivable program. These programs can be accessing files on different magnetic disk and/or magnetic tape units at the same time.

These systems are capable of supporting batch processing along with multiple users at terminals, at the same time. Under batch processing, the data is collected over a period of time and in a separate step before it is submitted to the computer for processing. This is the traditional way in which computers have been used for business data processing.

The medium-size computer can also support a management information system and its associated data base. The data base requires extensive storage. It should be maintained on a magnetic disk for fast access. Terminals may be set up in management offices so that executives can make inquiries to obtain current information. Distributed data processing may also be supported. These systems can also support research and development and scientific applications requiring large amounts of disk storage and fast processor speeds.

Such systems cost from $5000 to $20,000 a month to rent and up to $1,000,000 to purchase. This wide range in price results partially from the expandability of the systems. For example, a business may start with a system that has 500,000 bytes of main storage, 500 megabytes of secondary storage on disks, a card reader, and a 2000 lines-per-minute printer. As the data processing needs of the business increase, the system may be expanded to include 2 megabytes of main storage, 1 billion bytes of secondary storage, and terminals.

Illustration 9-2 shows a medium-size computer system with tape and disk storage. The disk storage capacity of this system is 384 megabytes. It is expandable to over 2 billion bytes. The main storage capacity can be up to 4 megabytes. Such a system can be rented for about $12,000 to $15,000 per month; it can be purchased for about $800,000.

ILLUSTRATION 9-2   IBM 4341 medium-size computer system

1. Disk drives
2. Tape drives
3. CPU
4. Console display-keyboard
5. Card punch
6. Card reader
7. Printer

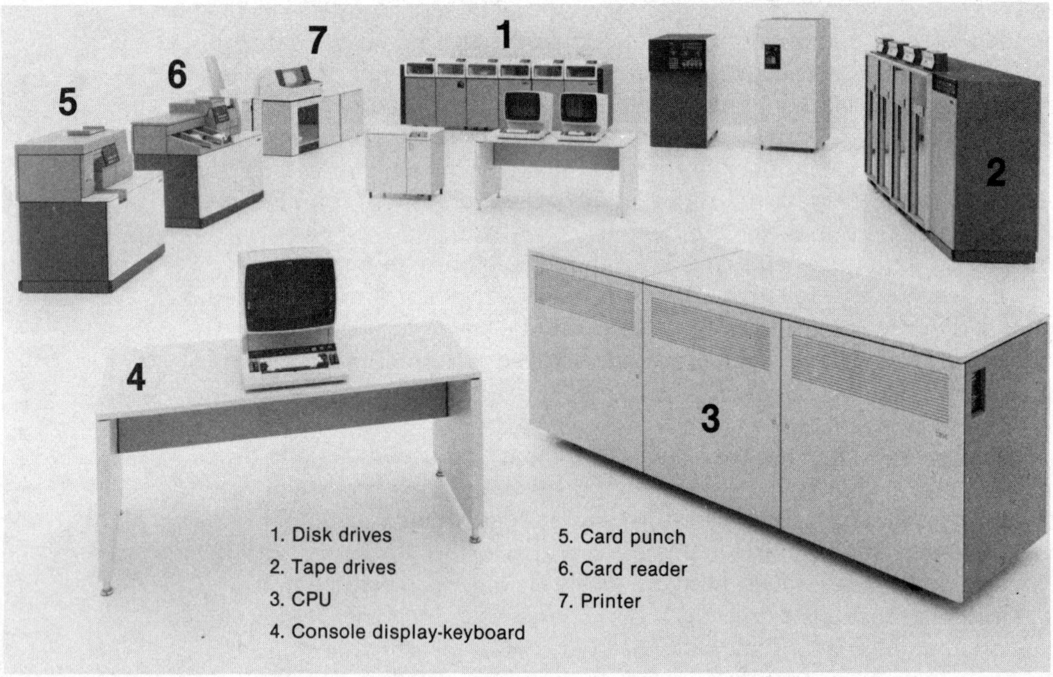

A business is likely to acquire a medium-size computer after outgrowing the processing capability of a small computer. A medium-size computer is needed when either the number of jobs to be processed in a given time period exceeds the capacity of the small computer or the type of processing required cannot be supported by the computer or the software available. For example, a business may be using a small computer to process sales orders on a batch basis after they have been collected from a number of sales branches. As sales and competition increase, it may be determined that sales orders must be processed more rapidly to serve customers and remain competitive. To process sales orders more rapidly, the business may install terminals at each branch so that sales orders can be entered directly into the computer. Such a system requires a computer with a large amount of secondary storage, data communication capability, increased main storage, and software to handle the terminals. A medium-size computer can handle this type of processing.

Small Computers

A small computer system typically includes a general-purpose digital computer with a storage capability slightly larger than that of a minicomputer. It can support a variety of input/output devices. There is a wide price and performance range within small computer systems. Small computers usually have from 64,000 to 500,000 bytes of main storage, and use from 20 to 100 megabytes of secondary storage.

The small computer system may replace a punched-card or manual data processing system. Punched-card input and output are commonly used by companies who had punched-card systems in the past and then upgraded to small computers. Batch processing is often used.

For the business that is using a punched-card system for data processing, the small computer can offer an increase in system processing speed, greater flexibility in the use of the system, and better management information. It may offer a reduction in equipment cost. Often a small computer system can be justified in a business using punched-card data processing just by its potential for reducing data processing costs. Additionally, such a system could make available more accurate and timely management information.

A business acquiring a computer for the first time may choose a small computer. Often a decision is made on the basis of the applications to be processed and the cost. It is more likely today, however, that a business will choose a minicomputer as its first system. A very small business may consider a microcomputer. A business with a small amount of data entry in relation to processing may start with a minicomputer system using a terminal attached to the system for data entry. When data entry begins to consume a major portion of processing time, the system may be replaced with a small batch computer. In a small batch system, the data can be recorded on punched cards, magnetic tape, and/or magnetic disk, independent of the computer, using data entry equipment like that discussed in Module A. The recorded data then can be processed on the computer when it is available.

A typical small computer system is shown in Illustration 9-3. Many users who previously used punched-card data processing have selected small computers that use 96-column cards for input and output. This system uses the 96-column card, the first new punched-card design in over 50 years when it appeared in 1969. The system has a card reader and card punch unit that handles the functions necessary for card processing. These functions include reading, punching, sorting, combining two decks of cards, and printing on each card its contents. The system also includes disk and tape storage, two printers, and a console with a display and keyboard.

ILLUSTRATION 9-3   IBM System/38 small computer system

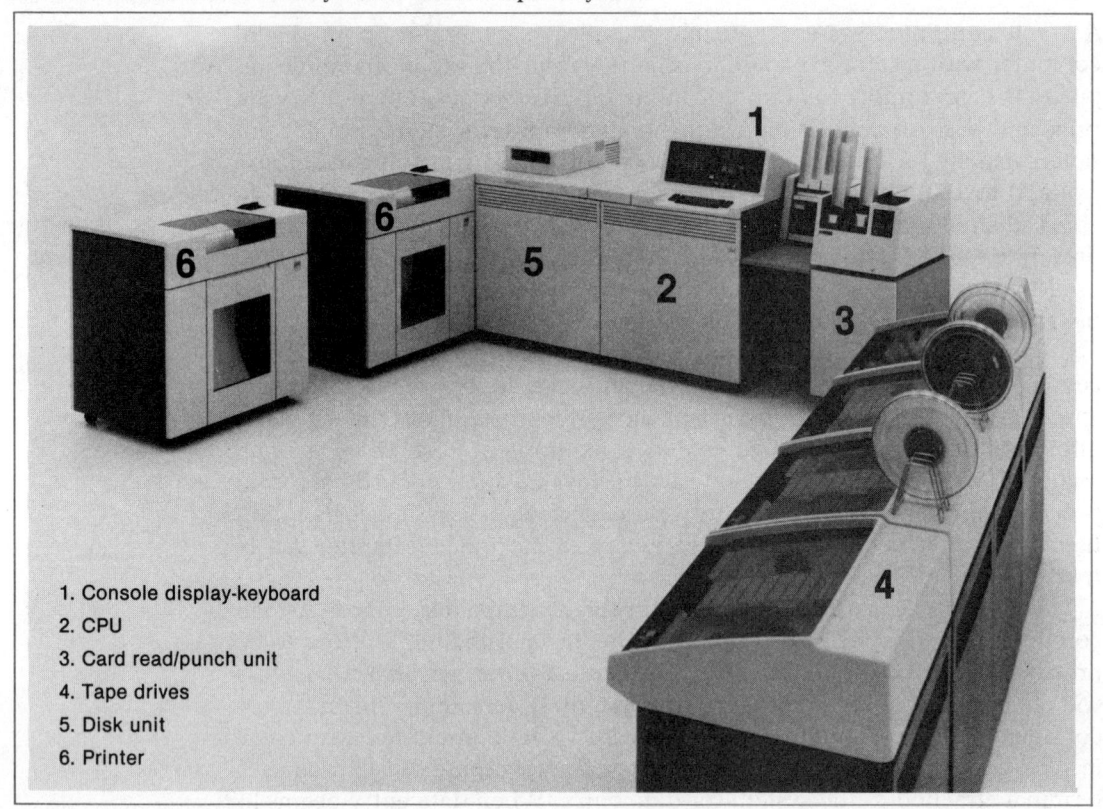

1. Console display-keyboard
2. CPU
3. Card read/punch unit
4. Tape drives
5. Disk unit
6. Printer

A terminal-oriented small computer system is shown in Illustration 9-4. This type of system has CRTs for data entry. On this type of system, several CRT operators may be performing data entry functions while the computer is processing one or more additional jobs. Data entered from the terminals can be stored on magnetic disk until it is processed.

The software available for small computer systems is less powerful than that available for medium-size and large computer systems. It may support virtual storage and multiprogramming, and both batch processing and online data entry. Most computer manufacturers also provide several high-level programming languages such a RPG II, COBOL, and FORTRAN for program development. Any additional programming needed is often obtained from an outside programming service on a contract basis. It is common for the cost of these application programs to exceed the cost of the computer.

How does a business decide whether it needs a minicomputer or a small computer system? If a small business changed to computer data processing in the 1960s, it may have started with a minicomputer. The point

ILLUSTRATION 9-4   IBM System/34 terminal-oriented small computer system

at which a small computer should be acquired is not fixed. A business must determine its processing needs and then select a system that best meets those needs, with consideration given to cost and performance.

Selecting the right computer can be a difficult task for a small business. Often such a business does not have a computer staff who can do the analysis necessary to choose the best system. In this situation, a computer consultant should be hired to analyze the processing needs of the business and recommend the best system.

The small computer has a place in the large business. Since the need for computing power is not always easy to satisfy with one large computer, it is often necessary to install several small computers within branches or divisions of a business. A small computer can be used at each branch or division for all of its major data processing needs. When necessary, the small computer can be used as a terminal to a larger computer.

MINICOMPUTER SYSTEMS

The minicomputer market began to develop in the early 1960s when a few manufacturers provided a rather limited line of systems. The large increase in manufacturers in the late 1960s resulted from the demand for a low-cost computing machine capable of performing functions ranging from those of a desk-top calculator to the control of production processes in manufacturing. A typical minicomputer is a digital computer, compact in size, with limited internal storage, and a purchase price of from $20,000 to $50,000. The characteristics of minicomputer systems vary widely depending on their cost and application. Many of the characteristics of the minicomputer equal those of larger mainframe computers. The technology that made possible the development of the minicomputer is called *large scale integration*, or *LSI*. LSI is the process of placing thousands of electronic components and transistors on chips. This high density of electronic components has made it possible to produce minicomputers that are small in physical size and that do not require special temperature-controlled computer rooms. Through the use of LSI circuits and new memory technology, designers have been able to achieve processor speeds and data rates close to those of medium-size computers. A typical minicomputer system like the one in Illustration 9-5 includes a display screen, printer, and magnetic disk storage. A minimum system may be purchased for under $20,000, but systems are often higher.

In manufacturing plants, the control of production processes and quality-control testing by minicomputer makes it possible to produce better products more economically. Many manufacturing plants produce products through a continuous production process. Where such products are developed, minicomputers can be installed to control the production process, monitoring it and making any changes necessary to insure a uniform product. In a steel mill, for example, the continuous production of sheet steel can be monitored by a minicomputer. It detects any changes in the thickness of the steel and makes corrections in the production process accordingly.

Businesses use minicomputers in several ways in addition to process control applications. These include: (1) replacement of manual or mechanical data processing systems; (2) remote data entry devices to large computers; (3) replacements for a large computer; and (4) to supplement a large computer.

Many small businesses that have used traditional manual methods of data processing or accounting services are installing minicomputer systems. The continual drop in the cost of minicomputers has made them a

ILLUSTRATION 9-5 Hewlett-Packard 300 minicomputer system with magnetic disk storage

UNIT TWO: COMPUTER SYSTEMS

feasible alternative to manual data processing systems. In many cases, a minicomputer system can reduce data processing costs and/or provide more relevant information for business decision making. An increasing number of minicomputer manufacturers are making systems specifically designed for small businesses. These manufacturers commonly call the systems *small business computers*. The small business system may contain a minicomputer or a microcomputer, but it is still referred to as a small business computer.

The lowest-cost small business computers are usually *transaction-oriented systems*. Data is entered through a keyboard and processed concurrently; that is, data entry and processing are a combined operation. A typical transaction-oriented system like the one in Illustration 9-6 includes: a keyboard for data entry; a display screen for operator verification of data entered and for display of processing results; a printer to

ILLUSTRATION 9-6 Wang 2200 transaction-oriented minicomputer system

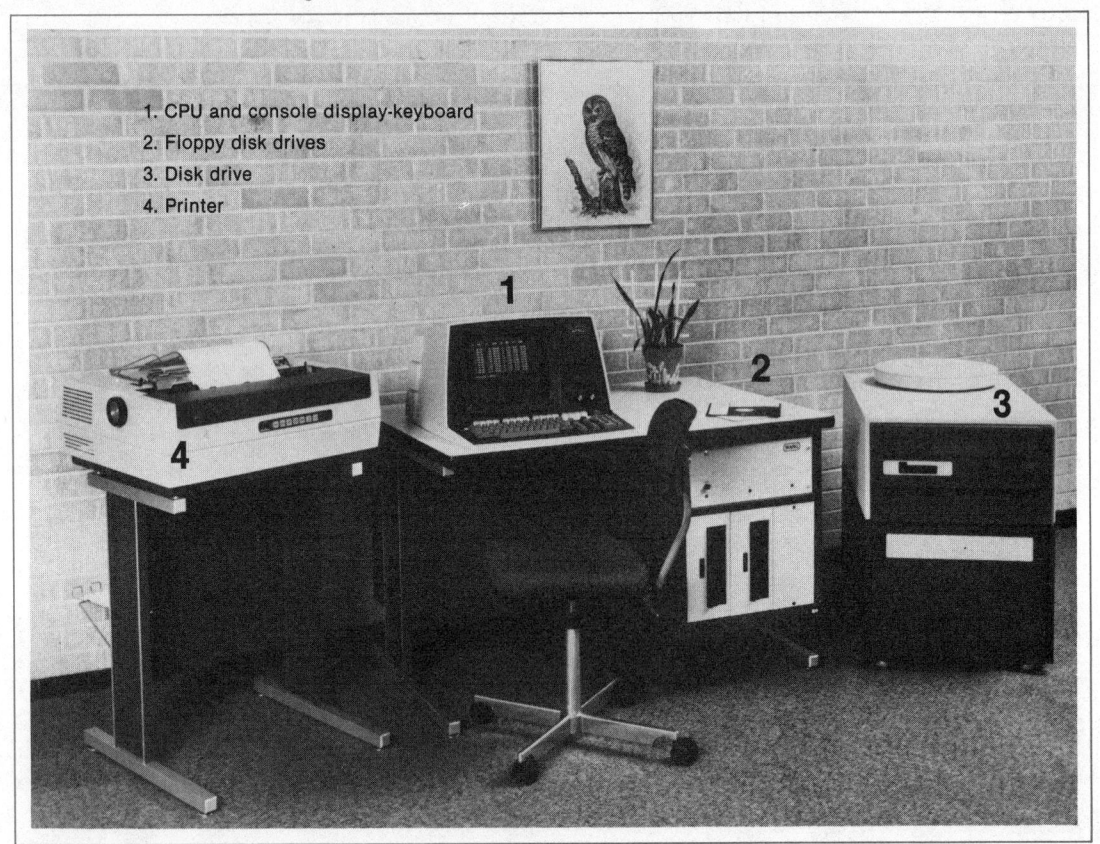

1. CPU and console display-keyboard
2. Floppy disk drives
3. Disk drive
4. Printer

provide a copy of the results; and a magnetic disk unit for secondary storage. Both floppy disks and a disk pack are used as secondary storage on this system. The main disadvantage of these systems is their slow operating speed. Because data is entered by an operator at a keyboard, this operation is limited by the keying speed of the operator. The overall speed of the system is limited accordingly. Typically, low-speed printers are attached to these systems to keep costs down. They are adequate, given the operator's data entry speed.

Transaction-oriented systems are designed to be operated by individuals who have little data-processing background, but who are familiar with the applications being processed. The computer manufacturer or a vendor often provides all of the computer programs needed to perform the common applications of small businesses. These include packages for such applications as invoicing and billing, order entry, accounts receivable, and payroll. The small business may use these programs rather than hire programmers. However, if programs are needed for specific applications, the cost of developing them or of having them developed may exceed the cost of the computer. Several computer manufacturers are addressing this need by providing programming packages for specific types of small businesses. A small business computer system may include a number of special industry application programs. Examples are programs for the construction industry, food and paper wholesaling, office product suppliers, hospitals, and membership organizations and associations.

The increased capability of small business computers, along with lower processing costs and simpler operating procedures, will accelerate the use of computers in small businesses in the years to come. As the costs of a business continue to rise and governmental reporting requirements continue to increase, more businesses will turn to the small business computer to remain competitive and profitable.

As a remote device for a large computer, a minicomputer in a branch location of a business can refine and condense data to be entered into a central computer by means of a data-transmission facility. Remote input/output devices linked to a central computer have been used for *remote job entry* for some time. Remote job entry allows the transfer of large amounts of data to a central computer and the return of the results of processing to the remote location. In many systems, the minicomputer acts as the remote job entry terminal and is used also for *local processing* (that is, some processing is done at the remote location).

A business that is using a central computer to serve the needs of several branches may find that it is more practical and economical to replace the central computer with minicomputers at the branches. This is especially likely if the functions of the branches are not closely related. However, the complete decentralization of computer power in a business is not as likely to occur as is another method of data processing called *distributed processing*. In a distributed processing system, small computers or minicomputers are placed at points in the organization where data originates. The data can be processed and retained locally, or it can be passed to a central computer. (Distributed processing is discussed in more detail in Chapter 14.)

As new data processing applications in a business require additional computing power, adding minicomputers may be preferable to increasing the size of the central computer. The minicomputers can be dedicated to specific functions, yet linked to the central computer if needed.

Some computer professionals believe that completely distributed processing, which eliminates the central computer and links all of the minicomputers in a system so that they can exchange data and programs, will appear in the future. While this may be possible in a few years, it is likely that a central computer supplemented by minicomputers will be used in many businesses for some time.

The minicomputer can support many of the input/output devices found on larger computers. Typically, slower, lower-cost versions of printers, magnetic tape units, and magnetic disk units are used.

The lower-priced minicomputers and small business systems often use floppy disks for secondary storage. The floppy disks offer many of the advantages of larger disk units at a much lower cost; they are an increasingly popular storage medium.

The overall processing capability of the minicomputer is far less than that of a large computer. One reason for this is the small set of instructions that the minicomputer can perform. The basic set of instructions built into the minicomputer may not include functions like division and multiplication. Instead, these functions may be performed by software called *subroutines*. Under this approach, more processing time is required for the functions than would be needed if the functions were performed directly by the hardware.

A number of minicomputer manufacturers offer *microprograms* to overcome the lack of certain basic instructions. Microprograms can be placed in a special storage area in the central processing unit to perform functions not available directly in the hardware. The purpose of such a microprogram is to carry out some function that would otherwise be accomplished by a subroutine. The primary advantage of using a microprogram is that it can perform the function much faster than would be possible if a subroutine were used.

The special storage area for microprograms may be either a *read-only memory* (*ROM*) or a *programmable read-only memory* (*PROM*). The ROM is programmed by the manufacturer and cannot be altered by the user. The PROM is programmed by the manufacturer, but it can be reprogrammed for special functions. Users do not normally write microprograms, but it is possible. Microprograms will continue to be used in minicomputers for some time. They greatly increase system versatility.

By the mid-1970s, the minicomputer had become one of the fastest growing computer markets. With the maturing of the minicomputer, manufacturers began to place more emphasis on customer support. Early users of minicomputers often found themselves with a computer, a set of instruction manuals, and little else. Support services now include extensive system software, high-level programming languages, application programs (so users need not write all their own programs), and customer education on system use.

The cost and size of minicomputers continue to drop at significant rates, while capability increases, because of the use of LSI chips. Many minicomputers have microprocessors as internal components. The microcomputer is replacing the low end of the minicomputer market. Over the next three years, the fast-growing minicomputer market is expected to triple in size. Sales will exceed $10 billion with the business user contributing the main portion of this growth.

Without question, the minicomputer will play an important role in computer applications over the next decade. It will become more difficult to tell the difference between minicomputers and larger computers. Already the top-of-the-line minicomputer has as much computing power as many small and medium-size computers.

MICROCOMPUTER SYSTEMS

The development of the microcomputer began in 1971 when the first computer processor based on microelectronics was introduced. Since that time there have been a number of improvements in the microcomputer, and it has had a tremendous impact on the computer industry. Today over 30 active manufacturers are offering some 50 different models. It is predicted that by 1983 over 2.6 million units will have been installed. A microcomputer uses a processor that is from 100 to 1000 times smaller than a comparable central processing unit built in 1970. Its primary advantage besides size is its low cost in comparison to other processors.

Illustration 9-7 is an enlarged view of a microprocessor chip, which is actually about one-tenth-inch square. An entire computer using this chip could be placed on this page. A typical microprocessor consists of a chip of silicon containing over 20,000 electronic components. It is capable of performing more than 100,000 operations per second and has about the same processing power as the central processing unit contained in a first-generation computer costing over $500,000. Yet the cost of this microprocessor is

ILLUSTRATION 9-7 Microprocessor chip

less than $10. A complete microcomputer system using the microprocessor costs less than $700. A microcomputer and its CPU, a microprocessor, are shown in Illustration 9-8. Input/output devices can be attached to form a complete microcomputer system.

The internal storage of a microcomputer is generally made of semiconductor chips. It includes *random-access memory* (**RAM**) and may also include *read-only memory* (**ROM**). Random-access memory is used to store both data and programs when the microcomputer is operating. Random-access memory is volatile; therefore, it does not retain its contents when the microcomputer is turned off. Read-only memory is not

CHAPTER 9: COMPUTER SYSTEMS

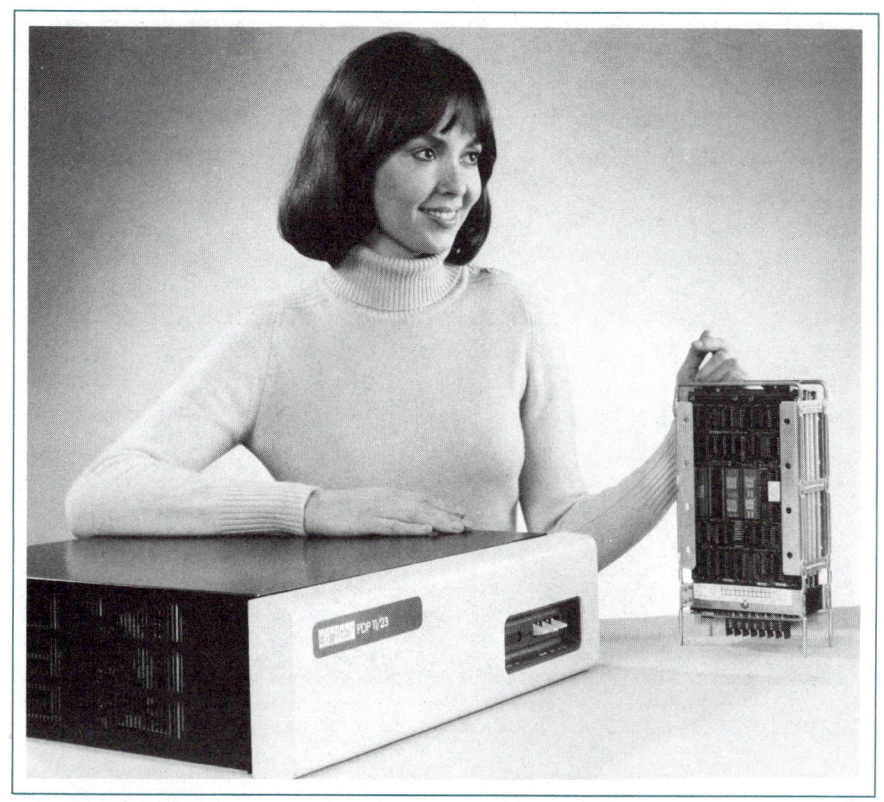

ILLUSTRATION 9-8 Digital Equipment Corporation PDP-11/23 microcomputer (left) and its CPU, a microprocessor (right)

volatile; thus, it is used to store some system software and permanent data. Usually the software that supports the programming languages available for a microcomputer is stored in read-only memory.

The low cost of microprocessors is due not only to their size but also to the method by which they are produced. The wafer in Illustration 9-9 is about four inches in diameter. Each square on the wafer is a microprocessor. The LSI technology that made the minicomputer possible is also the basis for the microprocessor.

The number of components contained on a microprocessor chip continues to increase. Manufacturers have used this increased density to achieve significant advances in the performance of microcomputers.

While the microprocessor is a direct descendant of the LSI technology used in the minicomputer, it is not likely to replace the minicomputer processor for some time. The average microprocessor is 3 to 10 times slower than the processor of a minicomputer. It has less internal storage

ILLUSTRATION 9-9 Wafer containing a number of microprocessors

capacity and supports fewer input/output devices. These limitations are major disadvantages in many application areas. However, there are applications for which microprocessors can be used. Since its introduction, the microprocessor has appeared in a variety of computer hardware and business equipment.

The desk-top microcomputer system in Illustration 9-10 is designed for small companies, offices, and individuals requiring personal computing power. It is not much larger than an office typewriter, yet it is a complete computer. A variety of input/output devices are often used on these computers. A typewriterlike keyboard is provided for the entry of data and programs. It is also used to control the system. Such a system can be linked to a larger computer as a terminal when additional computing power or access to other data files is needed. The desk-top system illustrated uses dual 5¼-inch floppy disk drives to provide about 135,000 bytes of data storage. A typical desk-top computer utilizing 64,000 bytes of main storage, two 5¼-inch floppy disk drives, and a hard-copy printer ranges in price from $3000 to $5000.

CHAPTER 9: COMPUTER SYSTEMS

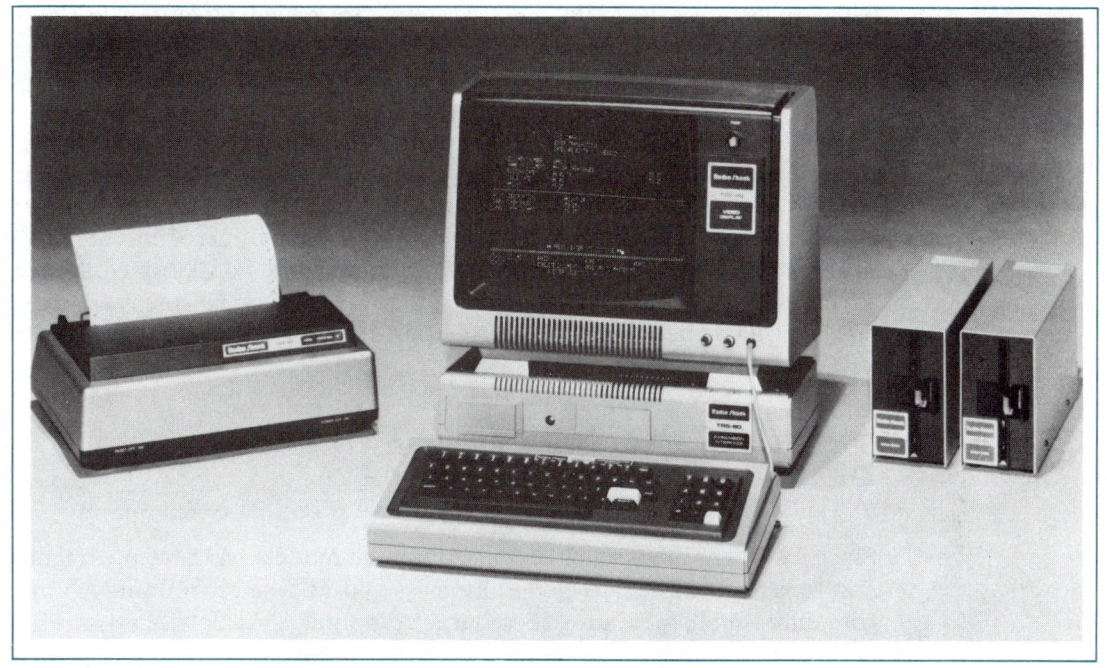

ILLUSTRATION 9-10 Radio Shack desk-top microcomputer for business use

Most desk-top computers designed for business are offered with a variety of ready-to-use computer programs for such applications as customer billing, accounts receivable/payable, payroll, inventory control, order entry, and word processing. These programs are often sold separately. Their cost may exceed the cost of the computer. Many small organizations are using these systems to replace manual record keeping and data processing systems, to provide word processing, and for specific applications such as the preparation and maintenance of mailing lists. Many larger organizations already using other types of computers are using desk-top computers. Departments and employees gain direct access to computing power (which they are not always able to obtain from the other computers).

In addition to being used in microcomputers, microprocessors are found in pocket calculators, office copiers, telephone systems, cash registers, typewriters, check processors, credit card verification systems, and computer input/output devices such as printers and terminals. One popular system uses microprocessor-based cash register terminals to collect and refine data before it is transmitted to a central computer. Each terminal performs the functions of a cash register and also verifies credit cards while collecting sales data. Such systems are called point-of-sale (POS) systems. They are being used by many large retailers to lower inventory costs, improve customer service, and provide timely sales information for management. Module A discusses these systems in more detail.

The rate at which the microcomputer is used in business data processing applications will accelerate along with the trend toward decentralized processing. Organizations using terminals for the entry of data into a central computer can replace the terminals with a microcomputer that provides the functions of an intelligent terminal and a desk-top computer. As the microcomputer becomes easier to use, lower in cost, and more powerful, it will be used increasingly in small organizations and businesses.

○ THE SIZE OF COMPUTERS AND SCOPE OF THE COMPUTER INDUSTRY: A RESTATEMENT AND COMPARISON

Since 1954, hundreds of different computer models have been designed and built. A computer is generally classified as a microcomputer, minicomputer, small, medium-size, or large computer. This classification is not necessarily an indication of physical size. Rather, it is usually a general price and performance categorization. Average monthly rental prices and purchase prices are accepted by the computer industry as means to classify computers. The average prices to rent or purchase computers in various classifications are shown in Illustration 9-11. Basic models in each computer size classification can be purchased within the price range shown. The total cost of a computer system in any of these size classifications increases as more hardware and/or software are added.

Through 1955, several hundred computer systems were installed. In contrast, through 1965, 23,000 computer systems were installed; through 1970, 90,000 computer systems were installed; through 1975, 210,000 were

ILLUSTRATION 9-11 Rental and purchase price ranges of computer systems

Computer size	Average monthly rental price range, including maintenance	Purchase price range
Microcomputers		$ 500- 10,000
Minicomputers	$ 300- 1,200	2,000- 50,000
Small	1,200- 5,000	50,000- 200,000
Medium	5,000- 20,000	200,000-1,000,000
Large	25,000-200,000	1,000,000-7,000,000

installed; through 1980, 600,000 were installed; and by 1983 it is estimated that 750,000 computer systems valued at $100 billion will have been installed. These figures represent the commercial use of computers. They do not include microcomputers, because the majority of microcomputer systems are owned by individuals who have bought them for personal use. The total number of microcomputers sold through 1980 was over 300,000 units.

Many computer companies are engaged in the design, construction, and installation of computer systems. The industry leaders for mainframe systems and for the minicomputer market are shown in Illustration 9-12. The leading supplier of mainframe computers is IBM. Digital Equipment Corporation is the leading supplier of minicomputers.

In recent years, emphasis has been placed by United States computer firms on the building of minicomputers and small computers. As a result, most of the mainframe manufacturers have started making minicomputers. This emphasis is primarily a response to the strong desire of small and

ILLUSTRATION 9-12 Industry leaders for mainframes and minicomputers

1979 INFORMATION PROCESSING RELATED REVENUES

Mainframe Computer Manufacturers

	Sales in millions of dollars	Market share
IBM	$18,338	60.6%
NCR (National Cash Register)	3,000	9.9
Burroughs	2,780	9.2
Sperry Univac	2,400	8.0
CDC (Control Data)	2,273	7.5
HIS (Honeywell)	1,453	4.8
TOTAL	$30,244	100.0%

Minicomputer Manufacturers

DEC (Digital Equipment)	$ 1,850	39.4%
Hewlett-Packard	750	16.0
Data General	540	11.5
HIS (Honeywell)	290	6.2
Perkin Elmer	140	3.0
Texas Instruments	130	2.7
General Automation	113	2.4
Others	887	18.8
TOTAL	$ 4,700	100.0%

Source of statistics: International Data Corp.

medium-size businesses to change to electronic data processing. The result of this emphasis is reflected by the fact that in terms of the distribution of computers, about 3 percent are large systems, 14 percent are medium-size systems, and small and minicomputer systems make up the remainder.

○ SUMMARY

1. Computer systems come in a variety of sizes and price ranges. Each can satisfy the data processing needs of numerous business applications. Computers that are classified as large, medium, or small are referred to as mainframe systems. The other classes of computers are minicomputers and microcomputers.

2. Large computer systems are used by big businesses to process large amounts of data on a regular basis. They are capable of supporting extensive management information systems. In addition to the types of applications performed by other computer systems, large computer systems can be used for mathematical simulations and scientific applications where the internal operating speed of the computer is critical. A large computer can serve as the main computer in a system that includes minicomputers or small computers that do distributed processing.

3. Medium-size computer systems, because of their internal storage capabilities and the use of virtual storage, can support a wider range of business data processing applications than either minicomputers or small computers. They often support batch processing and users at terminals at the same time. Also, they are capable of supporting a wide variety of high-speed input/output devices.

4. Small computers have greater storage capacities and faster operating speeds than minicomputers. They use a variety of input/output devices. Small computers supporting devices that handle punched cards are well suited for batch processing.

5. Minicomputers are compact in size. They vary greatly in price and performance. The minicomputer is used in such ways as: the control of production processes; as a replacement for manual or mechanical data processing methods; as a remote data entry device to a large computer system; as a transaction-oriented small business system; and in a distributed processing system. Microprograms are now offered on some minicomputers to overcome limitations in the hardware. The floppy disk is a popular low-cost storage medium used with these computers. One of the fastest growing markets for the minicomputer is the small business system.

6. Microcomputers are based on microprocessors that are constructed on chips less than one-tenth-inch square. Microprocessors are used in a variety of equipment including office copiers, minicomputers, desktop computers, and intelligent terminals. The business use of microcomputers will increase as they become more powerful, lower in cost, and easier to use.

○ REVIEW QUESTIONS

1. State some distinguishing characteristics of large computers.
2. What types of applications are likely to use large computers?
3. Why is multiprogramming used on medium-size computers?
4. What are the characteristics of a small batch-oriented computer?
5. How are minicomputers used in business?
6. What are the characteristics of a transaction-oriented small business computer?
7. What is the purpose of remote job entry?
8. How are minicomputers used for distributed processing?
9. What is the purpose of microprograms?
10. In what ways may a business use desk-top computers?

CAREER PROFILE

Monte F. James
Senior Account Manager
NCR Corporation

Background Experience

My first experience with electronic data processing occurred when I took a programming course in COBOL at Middle Tennessee State University. I majored in Business Administration because I wasn't yet certain that I wanted a career in data processing. During four years in the Air Force, I gained some experience as a remote terminal operator. I decided to combine my business education with my interest in computers.

I started at NCR as a programmer trainee and began taking evening classes at a local technical institute. These courses, along with NCR's internal training program, helped me to get promoted to systems analyst. As I gained experience, I advanced to larger computer systems. Four years ago, I was offered a position in sales. I decided it was a good opportunity. I have since moved from sales trainee to marketing representative, to account manager, and to my present position of senior account manager.

Primary Job Responsibilities

I work primarily with financial institutions. While my major task is selling mainframe computer systems, I also promote the associated hardware and software. In other words, I "manage" the account, both before and after the sale. I coordinate the actual installation of the system. In many ways I serve as a business consultant for my customers. Any system is good only if it meets the client's needs. My largest customer is a bank with assets exceeding $120 million; the bank handles some 50,000 accounts with an average daily transaction volume of 55,000 items. Most of my client firms are much smaller.

My typical work day begins with a few minutes in the office. I follow up on problems, schedule installations, and get information that I may need for customers. I spend the rest of the day working with customers and prospecting for new accounts.

What Has Made You Successful?

First, you must have the desire to succeed. The second key to success is knowledge. The more knowledge you have of your product, the more you can help your customers and earn their trust. My experience as an analyst was beneficial in helping me to understand computer installations from the user's point of view. To suceed in sales, probably the most important criterion is to have genuine concern for your customer's continuing success and well-being. Of course sales training and technical education are important. You acquire useful knowledge and techniques and increase your self-confidence.

UNIT THREE

COMPUTER PROGRAMMING AND DESIGN

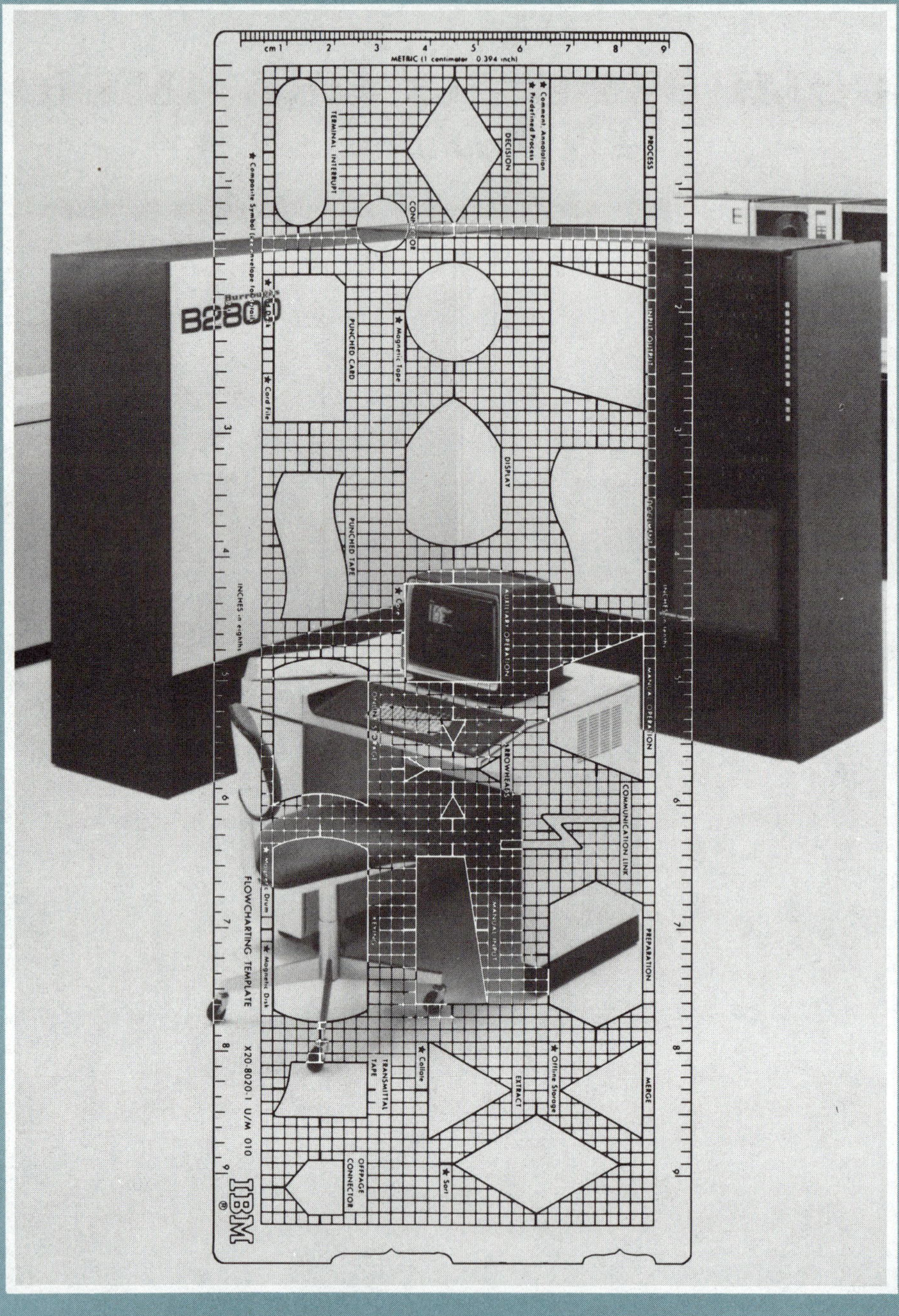
B2800
IBM
FLOWCHARTING TEMPLATE
X20-8020-1 U/M 010
PROCESS
DECISION
TERMINAL, INTERRUPT
PUNCHED CARD
PUNCHED TAPE
DISPLAY
MANUAL OPERATION
COMMUNICATION LINK
PREPARATION
MERGE
EXTRACT
TRANSMITTAL TAPE
OFFPAGE CONNECTOR

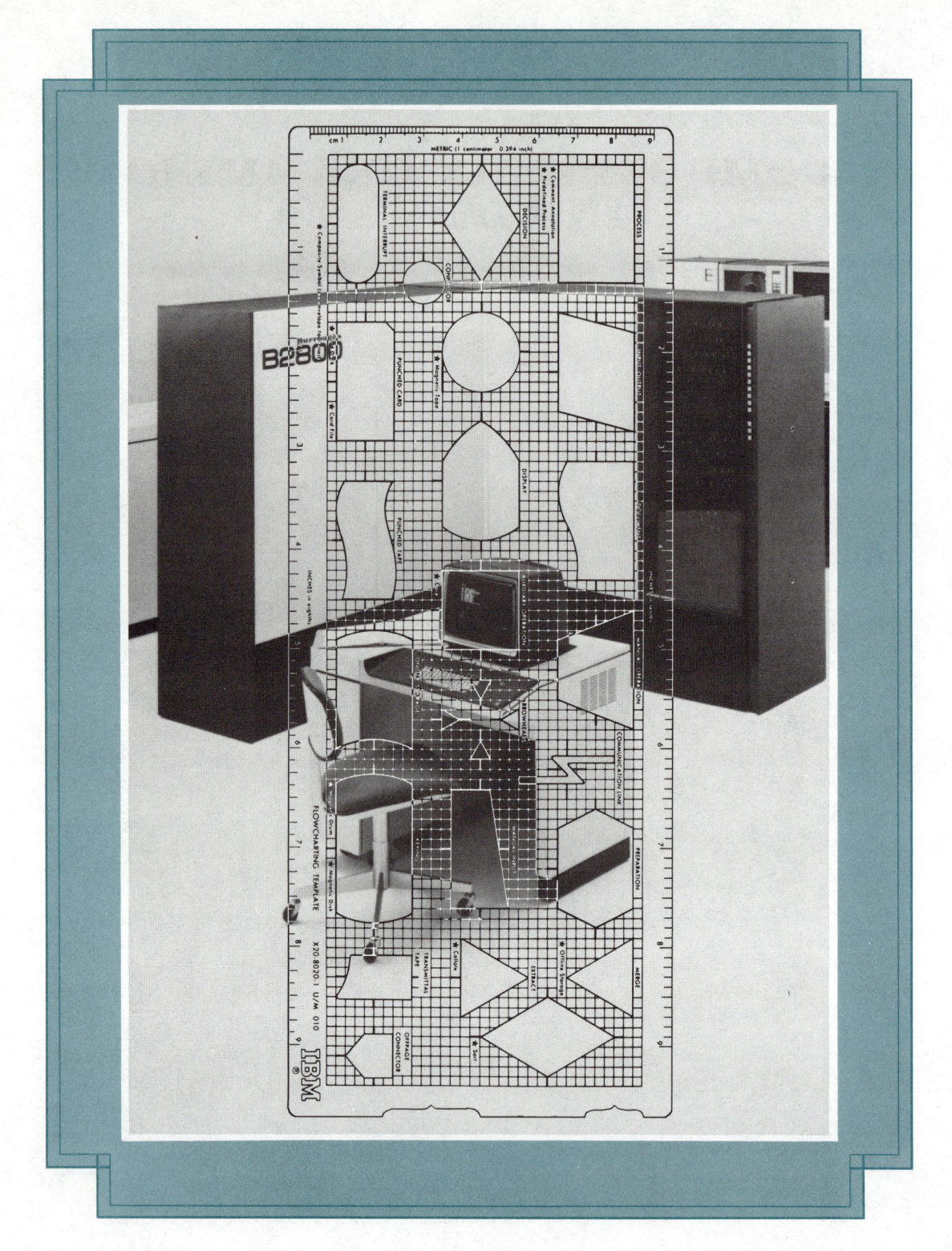

MODULE B

PROGRAM FLOWCHARTING

PROGRAM FLOWCHARTS
PROGRAM FLOWCHART SYMBOLS AND USAGE
PROGRAM LOOPS
USE OF CONNECTORS
SPECIALIZED FLOWCHART SYMBOLS
FLOWCHARTING AIDS

Opposite: The standardized symbols contained on the template aid in the preparation of flowcharts.

The use of a computer to solve business data processing problems requires that a procedure be developed for the computer to follow in solving the problem. A computer is a powerful machine; however, it is capable of doing only what it is directed to do. This direction is provided by a *computer program*, a series of instructions that the computer executes, or carries out.

The preparation of a computer program also involves following a procedure. The problem must first be defined. This definition must include an analysis of the data elements within the source documents that will be used by the program and of the data elements that will constitute the desired reports or other output from the program.

Once the problem has been defined and sample layouts of any reports or records have been created, the program that will produce these reports or records must be prepared. As seen in Chapter 3, the *system flowchart* is a tool that can help clarify the relationships that exist between several applications in a business system; it is a graphic representation of the system and the flow of data through the system. But details as to how processing will occur in the system are not specified in a system flowchart. Rather, processing details are provided in *program flowcharts*. The general relationship between system and program flowcharts is shown schematically in Illustration B-1.

Normally, a detailed program flowchart is prepared for each program required for an application. There are no standards as to the amount of detail to be included in program flowcharts. If an application is complex, two levels of program flowcharts may be prepared. One flowchart describes the main processing steps. Several others provide more exacting details of these steps.

The flowchart that describes the main processing steps in a data processing application is often called a *modular program flowchart*. Each major step is considered a *module*. A module can represent a complete program or a part of a program, say, a subroutine, depending on the complexity of the application. Each module can be represented by a *detailed program flowchart*. It describes the individual steps that are necessary for the solution of the problem. The modular flowchart provides a clear picture of the application without the clutter of the detailed processing steps. This makes it easier for the programmer to determine whether or not all of the major processing steps have been identified before creating any detailed flowcharts.

Compare the modular flowchart in Illustration B-2 with the detailed flowchart. The main steps needed for a customer billing application are shown in the modular flowchart. The detailed flowchart shows the steps for calculating a customer bill. There are advantages in flowcharting and designing programs in this manner. Large programs can be divided into manageable sections. Several programmers can be assigned to complete

229
MODULE B: PROGRAM FLOWCHARTING

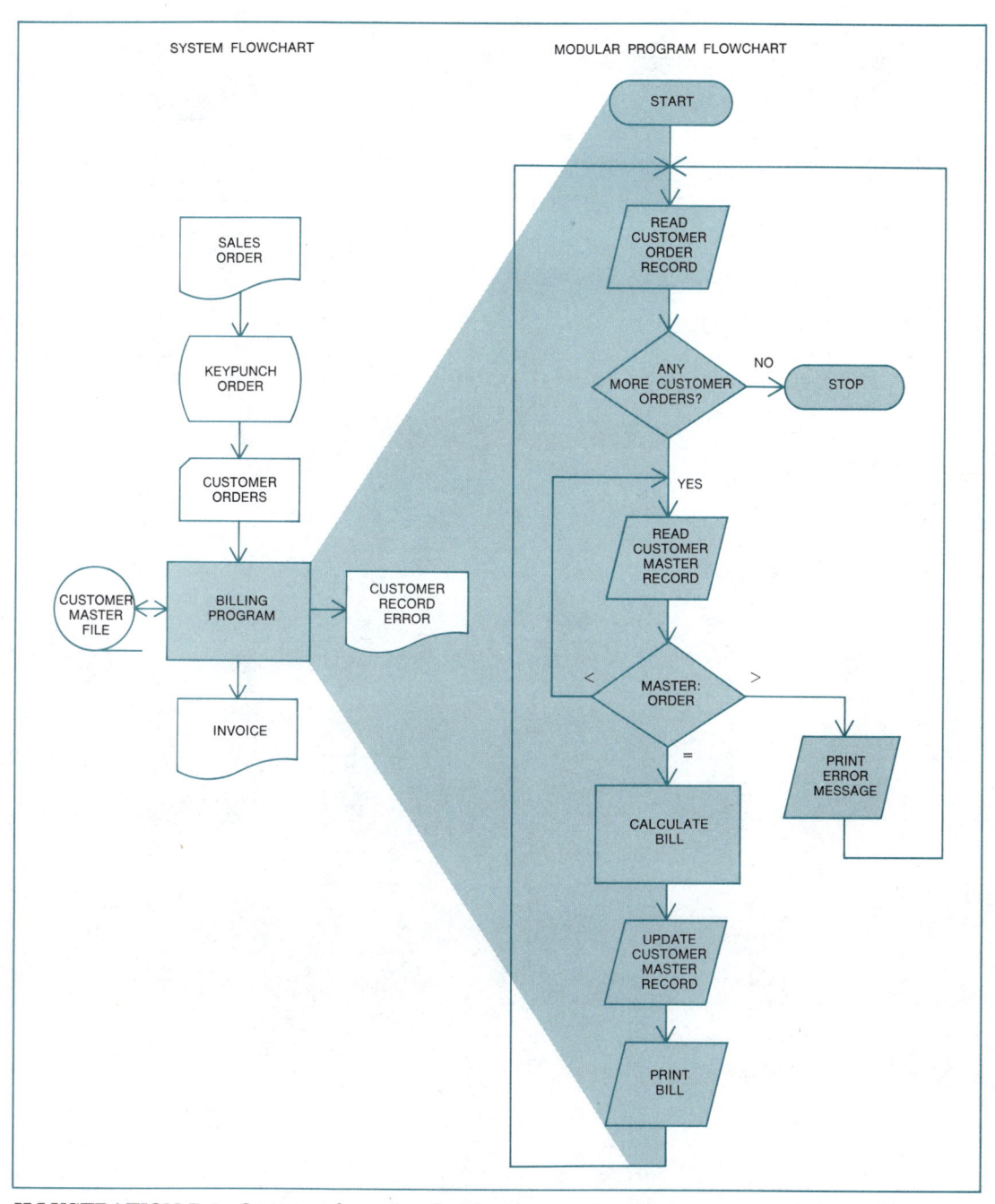

ILLUSTRATION B-1 System and program flowcharts

UNIT THREE: COMPUTER PROGRAMMING AND DESIGN

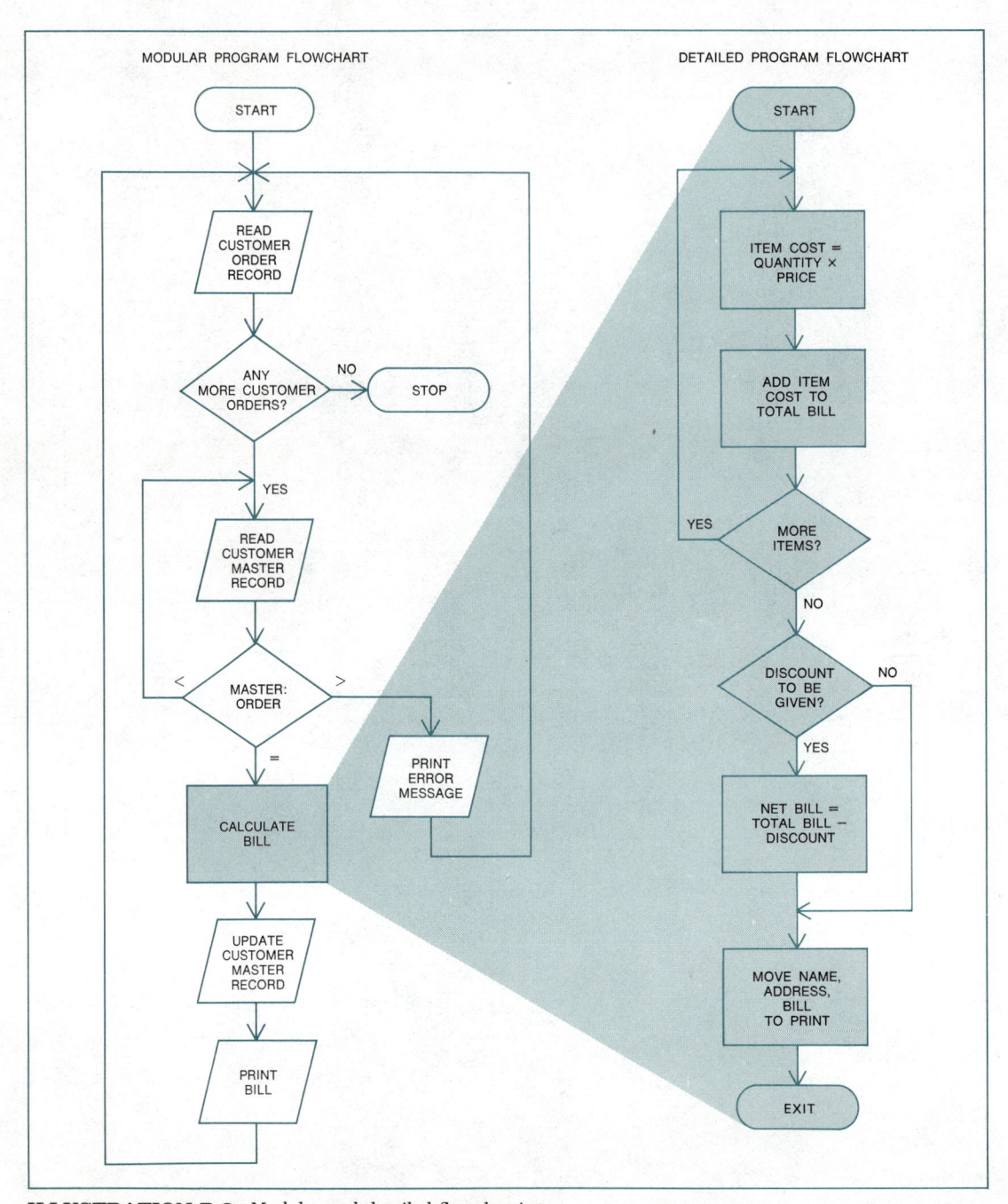

ILLUSTRATION B-2 Modular and detailed flowcharting

specific processing modules. Each of these modules can be flowcharted, developed, and tested to insure it is correct before it is combined with other modules.

The programmer uses a program flowchart to prepare a program (in effect, a series of instructions representing the steps in the flowchart). After the programmer has written the program, and it has been recorded on an input medium, it is ready to be compiled, tested, and debugged. **Compiling** is the process of translating the programming language into a machine-readable language. **Debugging** is the process of finding program errors and correcting them so that the program runs correctly. This is often a very challenging and time-consuming activity. **Testing** consists of running the program with input data that simulates, or is a representative sample of, the real data that will be processed by the program.

PROGRAM FLOWCHARTS

A program flowchart, the pictorial representation of the steps necessary to solve a problem, is sometimes called a *logic diagram* or *block diagram*. The detailed steps of problem solution can be seen clearly when displayed on a program flowchart. The purpose of a program flowchart is to represent by use of symbols the processing that should take place in a program. In other words, a program flowchart shows the detailed steps within the program and the order in which the steps are to be performed. It indicates the "logic" of a program. By studying the flowchart, a programmer can analyze the logic and determine whether a reasonable plan for the solution of the problem has been developed. The flowchart must be detailed enough to serve as a guide when coding the program and as a reference when testing and debugging it. The flowchart also serves as documentation of the program, either for future modifications of the program or for use by other personnel in the business.

Flowcharts contain symbols that represent basic functions or opertions. Each symbol represents an instruction or a series of instructions that the computer must execute to solve a problem. In an attempt to standardize these symbols, the *American National Standards Institute* (*ANSI*) has adopted a set of symbols that are widely used and accepted by programmers. Some variations exist in data processing installations that have developed their own sets of symbols. The ANSI system flowchart symbols were shown in Illustration 3-1 of this book. The ANSI program flowchart symbols are shown in Illustration B-3.

PROGRAM FLOWCHART SYMBOLS AND USAGE

The *terminal symbol* (the leftmost symbol in Illustration B-4) is used to indicate the beginning or end of a program. Additionally, it is used to show

UNIT THREE: COMPUTER PROGRAMMING AND DESIGN

PROGRAM FLOWCHART SYMBOLS

PROCESSING
A group of program instructions which perform a processing function of the program.

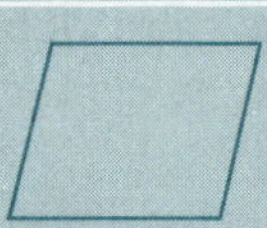

INPUT/OUTPUT
Any function of an input/output device (making information available for processing, recording processing information, tape positioning, etc.).

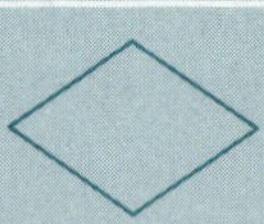

DECISION
The decision function used to document points in the program where a branch to alternate paths is possible based upon variable conditions.

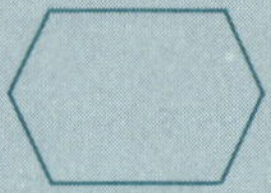

PREPARATION
An instruction or group of instructions which changes the program.

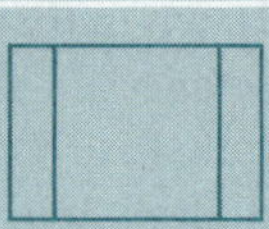

PREDEFINED PROCESS
A group of operations not detailed in the particular set of flowcharts.

TERMINAL
The beginning, end, or a point of interruption in a program.

CONNECTOR
An entry from, or an exit to, another part of the program flowchart.

OFFPAGE CONNECTOR*
A connector used instead of the connector symbol to designate entry to or exit from a page.

FLOW DIRECTION
The direction of processing or data flow.

SUPPLEMENTARY SYMBOL FOR SYSTEM AND PROGRAM FLOWCHARTS

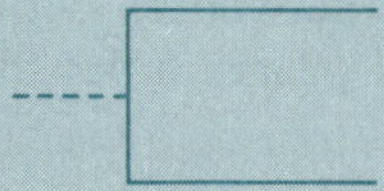

ANNOTATION
The addition of descriptive comments or explanatory notes as clarification.

*IBM usage only

ILLUSTRATION B-3 Program flowchart symbols

MODULE B: PROGRAM FLOWCHARTING

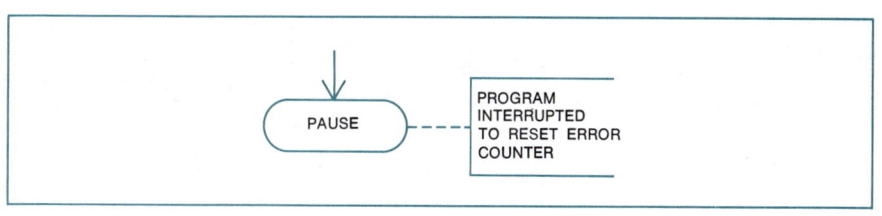

ILLUSTRATION B-4   Terminal and annotation symbols

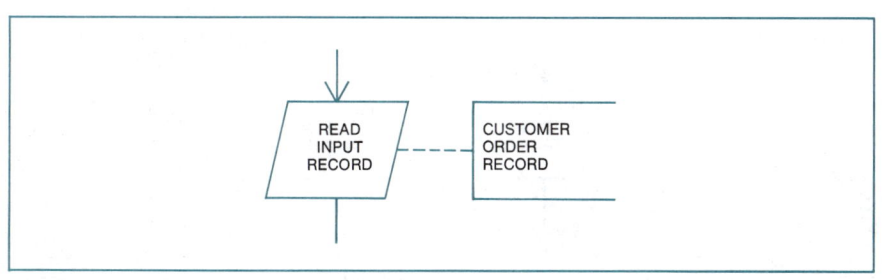

ILLUSTRATION B-5   Input/output symbol

any pause in a program because of an error condition or for operator action.

Within the terminal symbol (or any other flowchart symbol) is a brief comment about the function or activity that is to take place. When additional comments are needed for clarification, an *annotation symbol* is used as shown at the right in Illustration B-4. It is connected to the symbol for the function by a broken line as in the illustration.

Any input or output function is represented by the *input/output symbol* (Illustration B-5). For input this symbol usually represents reading a record from some input device. For output the symbol represents writing the results of processing on an output device. Only one input/output function should be represented by one symbol. On most flowcharts, there are at least two input/output symbols.

Direction of flow is indicated by a *flowline* and an arrowhead (Illustration B-6). Generally, the flowchart is drawn from the top of the page to the bottom, starting at the left of the page and continuing to the right if needed. The symbols on the flowchart are connected by flowlines. An arrowhead must be used on any flowline providing for a direction of flow other than from the top or the left. Arrowheads can be used on all flowlines to improve clarity.

A processing step completed by the computer is represented by the *process symbol* (Illustration B-6). Any data manipulation, such as a calculation or moving data from one location to another, is processing. One

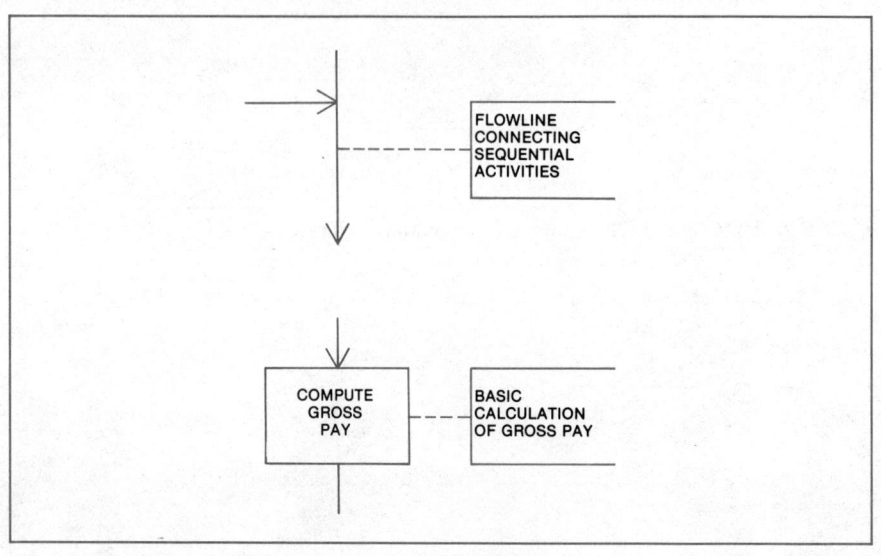

ILLUSTRATION B-6 Flowline and process symbols

process symbol may represent one operation, for example, "Multiply hours by rate." More than one operation can be represented by a process symbol when the operations are related; for example, the symbol containing "Compute gross pay" in Illustration B-6 may represent several calculations.

The steps in a program flowchart are executed in order unless the sequence is altered by a decision process. This alteration of program sequence by branching, or transfer of control, allows great flexibility. The program logic may be quite complex in applications where extensive branching is used.

Testing for one or more specific conditions that may be encountered during program execution is represented on a program flowchart by the

ILLUSTRATION B-7 Decision symbol

MODULE B: PROGRAM FLOWCHARTING

decision symbol (Illustration B-7). Generally, one decision or test is represented by a decision symbol; however, multiple alternatives can be indicated. As shown in Illustration B-7, two or three flowlines may exit the decision symbol. The flowlines must be labeled to identify the outcomes of the test that they show.

Given two numeric quantities, X and Y, their possible relations can be expressed as follows:

X is equal to (=) Y
X is not equal to (≠) Y
X is less than (<) Y
X is less than or equal to (≤) Y
X is greater than (>) Y
X is greater than or equal to (≥) Y

Tests are often stated in terms of relationships that may exist between two numeric quantities, or data items. Some examples are shown in Illustration B-8.

ILLUSTRATION B-8 Relational tests

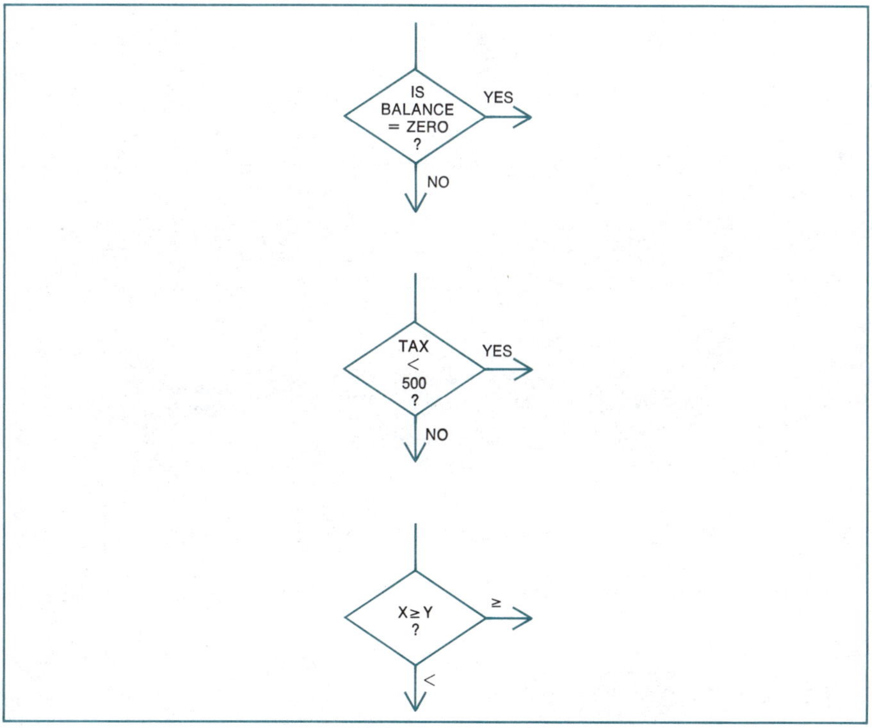

PROGRAM LOOPS

The ability of the computer to repeat a series of instructions that it executes is called *looping*. As an outgrowth of the repetitive execution, a *program loop* is formed. Such a loop is shown in Illustration B-9. The flowchart describes a program that prepares a printed listing of an inventory file on punched cards. It repeats a series of instructions by branching back to the first instruction.

Every program loop should contain an exit point so that the repeated execution of the loop can be terminated, either to continue with other processing or to stop. In Illustration B-9, the exit point is the test that determines whether the last record has been read. If so, the loop is terminated. Using a last record test to terminate processing is a common practice when the number of records to be processed is unknown. Generally, the last record in the file contains, not data, but rather some indication that it is the last record. Since it is not a data record, it is not processed as one. For this reason, the last record read by the program in Illustration B-9 is not written to the output file.

The flowchart in Illustration B-10 uses the same inventory file to prepare a listing of current inventory balances for items in stock. Each card

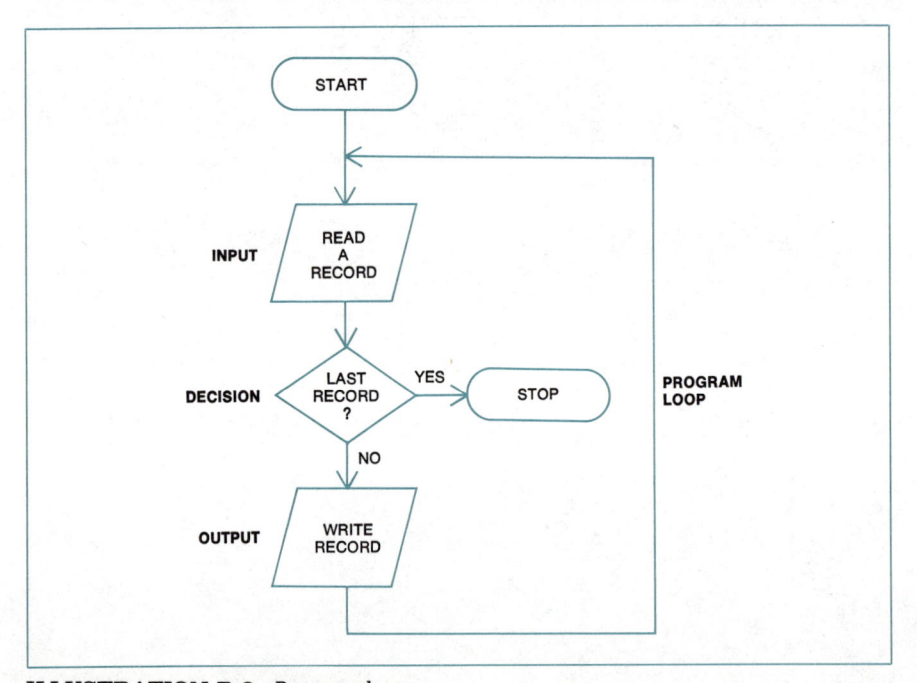

ILLUSTRATION B-9 Program loop

237

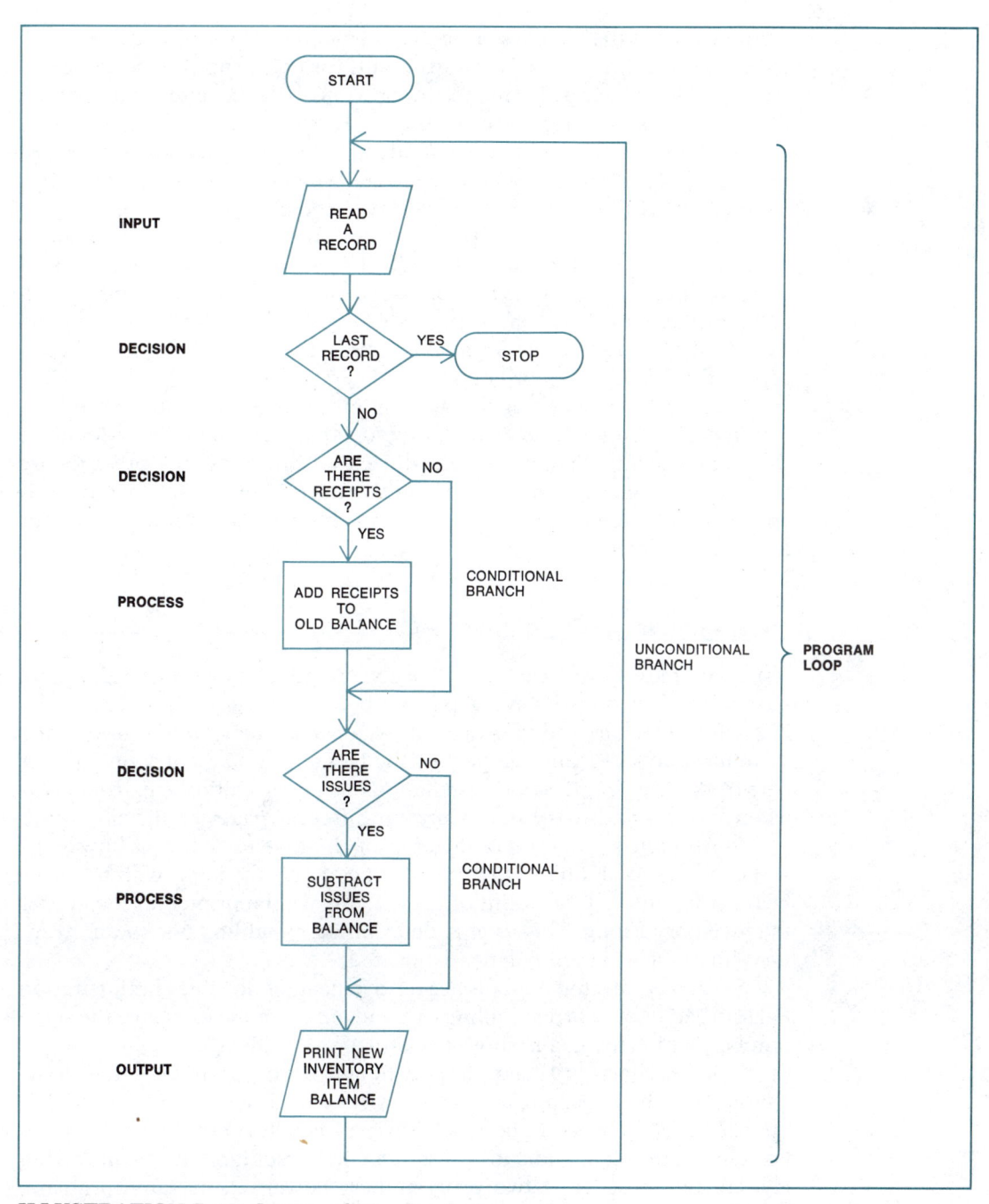

MODULE B: PROGRAM FLOWCHARTING

ILLUSTRATION B-10 Inventory listing flowchart

record contains the old balance on hand from the previous month and any issues and receipts for the current month for one item. It is necessary to add all of the receipts, if any, to the previous balance, and then subtract any issues to arrive at a current balance for the item.

A record is read, and a test is made to see whether it is the last record in the file. If it is not, a test is made to see whether there are any receipts for the item. If there are, they are added to the previous balance in a process step. If there are not, the process step is omitted; a branch is made to the next test. A test for issues is made, and a similar process step is executed or branched around. The last step prints the current inventory balance for the item. This completes the processing cycle for a record. A return to the read step occurs at this point. The entire loop sequence is repeated if any data records have not been processed.

Two types of branching are used in this example: conditional and unconditional. A **conditional branch** requires that a condition be met before the branch occurs. In this example, the tests for receipts and for issues are conditional branches. An **unconditional branch** is always taken when it is encountered. Here an unconditional branch occurs after the balance for an item is printed.

USE OF CONNECTORS

More complex flowcharts often involve multiple loops and additional branching. They may be several pages long. To reduce the number of flowlines on a flowchart and improve clarity, a **connector symbol** is often used to connect an exit from one part of the flowchart to an entry on another part of the flowchart. Some installations use a special **offpage connector** when the exit and entry points are on different pages of the flowchart.

Illustration B-11 is a modification of the inventory listing flowchart. It shows the logic required to print a listing of only the items with balances below 500 units. A total count of these items will be printed at the end of the inventory listing. This total is determined by adding one to an inventory count each time a balance is printed.

Several connector symbols are used instead of flowlines in Illustration B-11. In each case, corresponding exit and entry connectors have the same number, and arrowheads show the direction of flow.

The flowcharts in Illustrations B-10 and B-11 are similar. Other flowcharts could have been drawn to show how to provide the same output but use different steps in doing so. There is usually more than one way to flowchart a problem and still arrive at a correct solution. Problem solving is a creative process. If two programmers flowchart the same problem, their flowcharts are likely to differ even if they provide identical results.

239

MODULE B: PROGRAM FLOWCHARTING

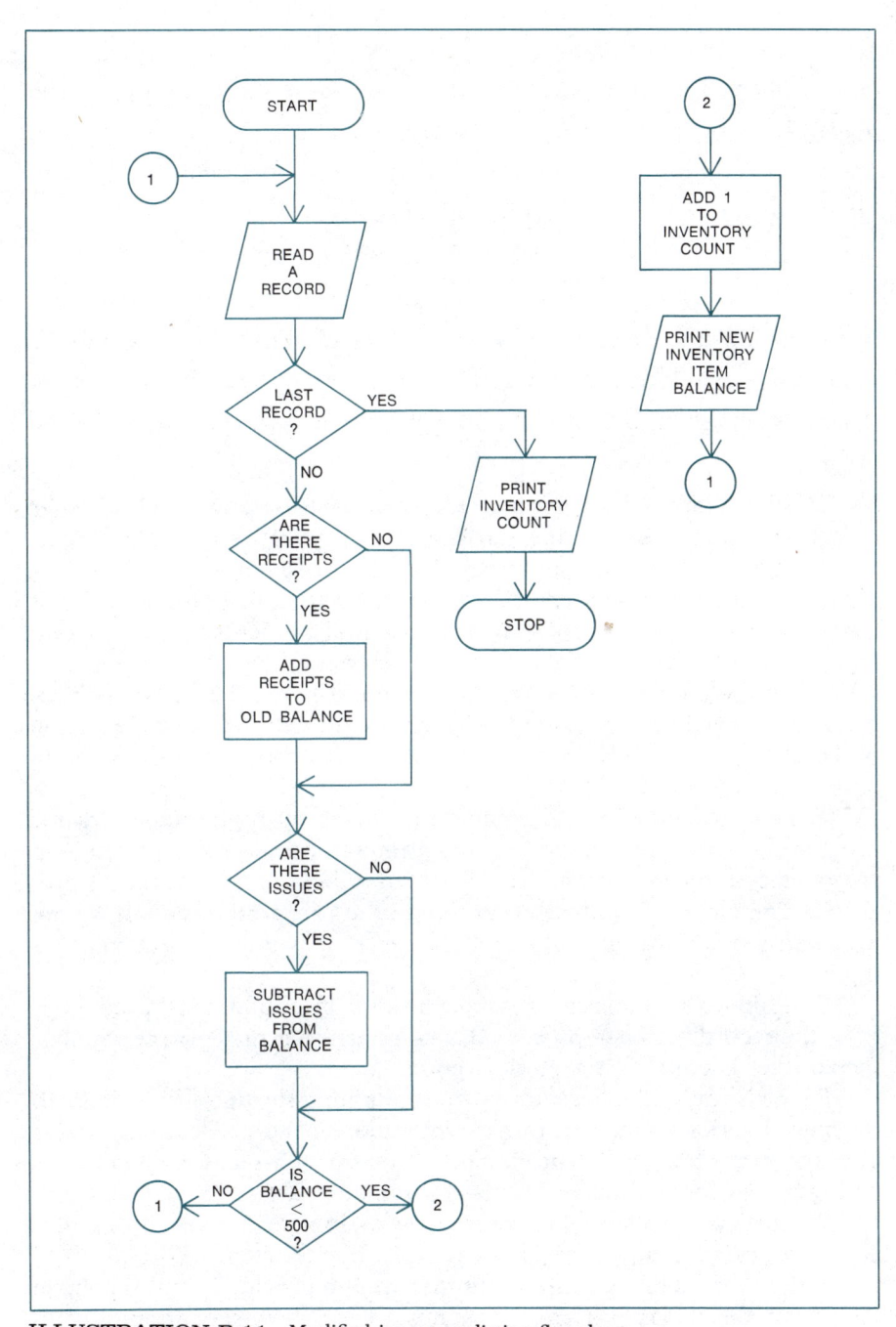

ILLUSTRATION B-11 Modified inventory listing flowchart

UNIT THREE: COMPUTER PROGRAMMING AND DESIGN

○ SPECIALIZED FLOWCHART SYMBOLS

Several specialized flowchart symbols are shown in Illustration B-12. The ***predefined process symbol*** represents a group of operations that are not defined on the program flowchart. These operations may be another program that is used by the main program. They may be a subprogram, which is simply a series of instructions that may be executed several times but is not part of the main program. The ***preparation symbol*** is used to indicate a step such as setting a location to zeros or to a maximum value, or setting a binary digit position to 1 or 0 for use as a switch that determines whether or not a branch is made during execution of the program.

The flowchart in Illustration B-12 shows how to determine: (1) whether or not a student is eligible for enrollment, and (2) if a student is eligible, what tuition the student should pay, based on residence considerations. This flowchart contains a counter that is used to control the number of times a program loop is repeated. The essential elements of the program loop are: (1) initializing the counter, (2) incrementing the counter, and (3) testing the counter to see whether or not a particular limit has been reached. Either incrementing or testing may directly follow initialization of the counter. The logic sequence is set up by the programmer who constructs the flowchart.

The use of counters is a common practice in programming. In this program, the counter that controls the number of times the program loop is executed, at the same time, controls the number of student records processed. The counter is initialized to zero in the preparation step. It is then tested to see whether its value equals the limit (student count) read as input.

Each time a student record is read, a value of 1 is added to the counter. After the record has been processed, a comparison is made to see whether the counter is equal to the student count.

Records for students requiring special billing for tuition are handled by special series of instructions represented by the predefined process symbols on the flowchart. The connectors on this flowchart contain letters and numbers for reference. This is a common practice.

When a counter is used to control processing, the limit of the counter can be provided in any of several ways. The flowchart in Illustration B-12 uses a limit that is read as input. Another way to provide a limit is to state the limit in the program. This approach is used in the flowchart in Illustration B-13.

241

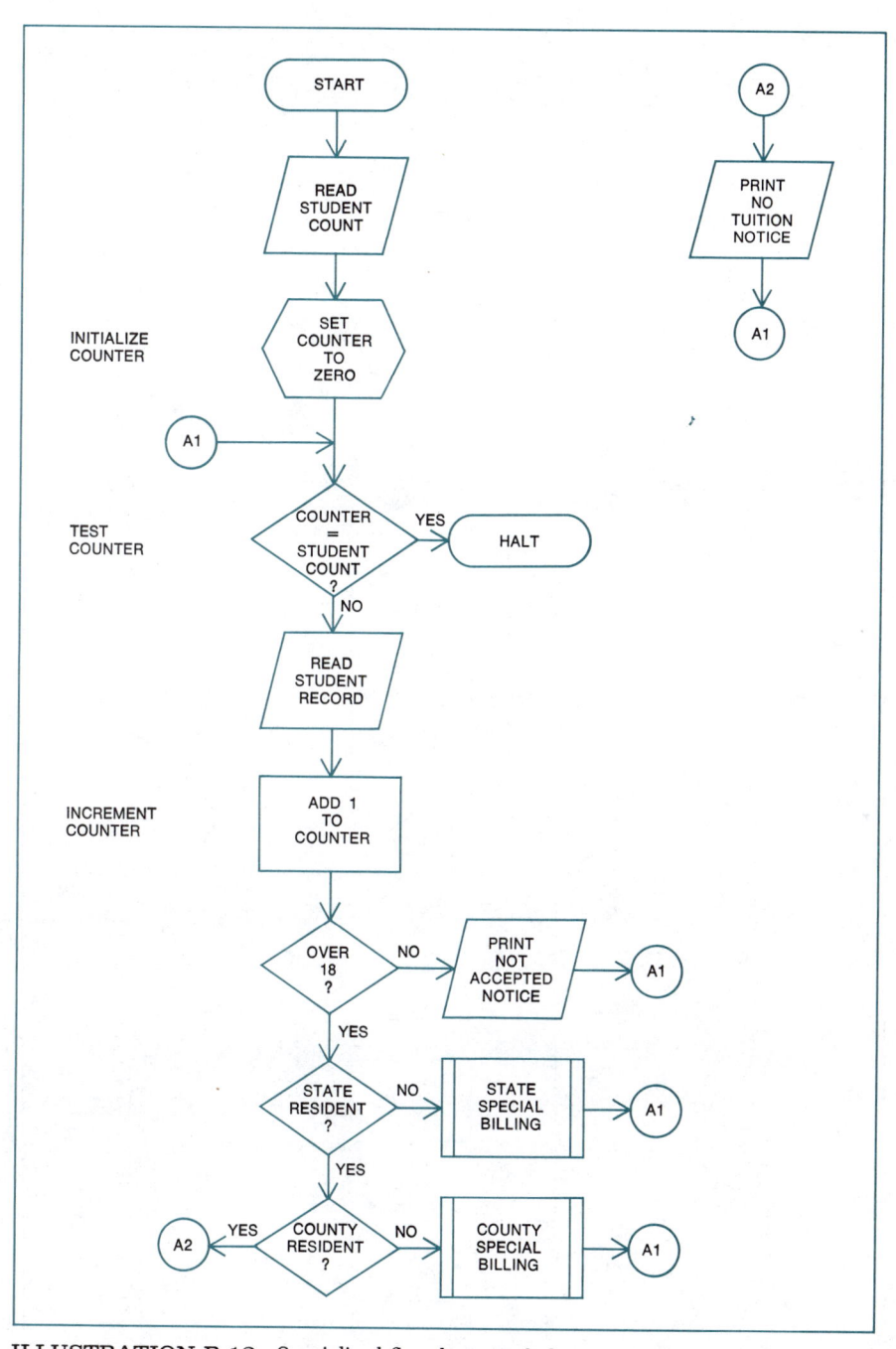

MODULE B: PROGRAM FLOWCHARTING

ILLUSTRATION B-12 Specialized flowchart symbols

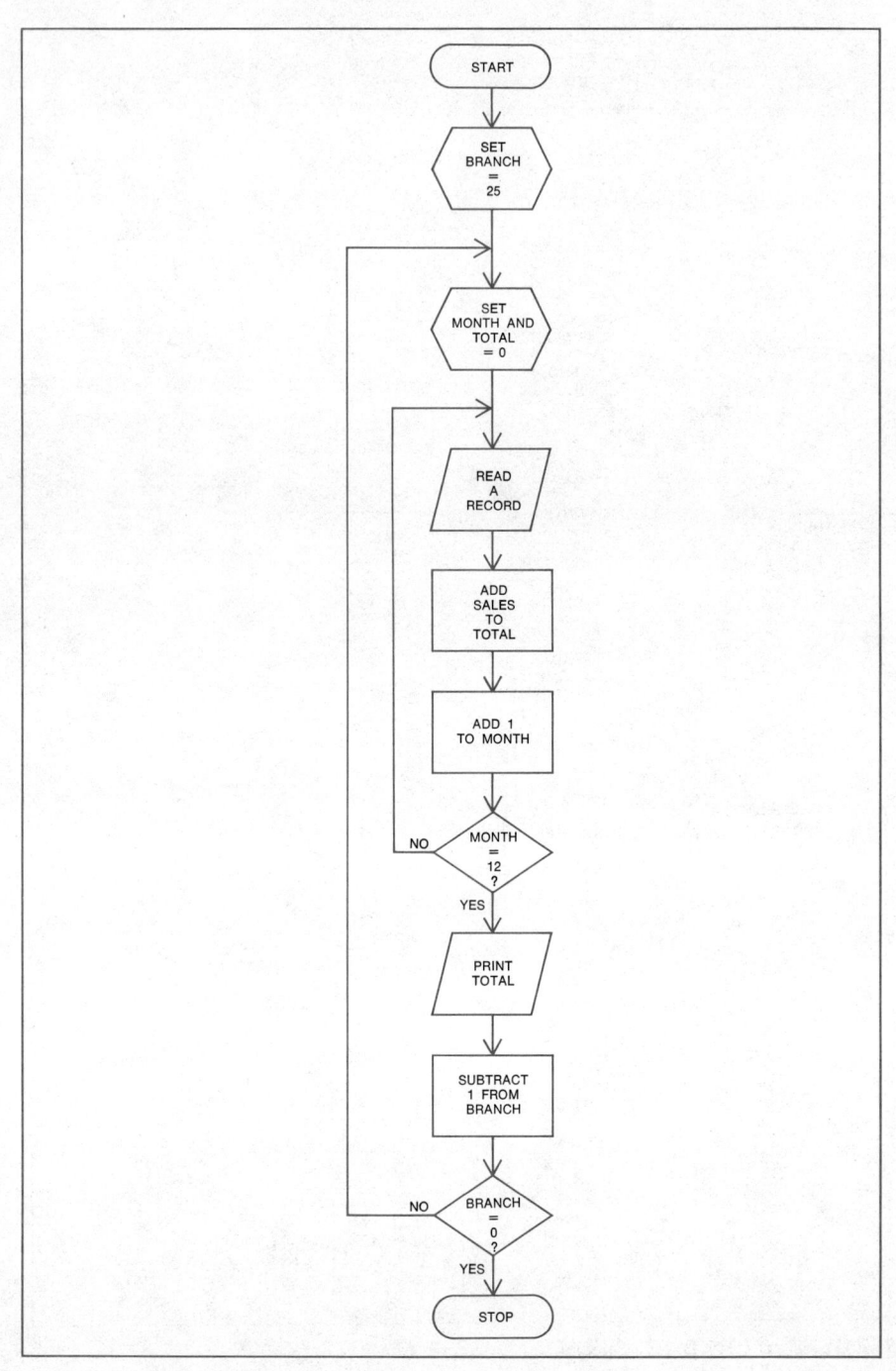

ILLUSTRATION B-13   Nested loop

The flowchart in Illustration B-13 shows how to process a file of records containing monthly sales in sequence by branch office to determine the annual sales total for each of 25 branches in a retail chain. Twelve monthly sales records are to be processed for each branch. The counter used for the branch limit is set to 25 and the counter used for months is set to zero in preparation steps; both of these counters are used to control program loops. The data field used to accumulate the annual sales total for a branch is also set to zero. Its content is added to repeatedly in determining each branch total.

After a record has been read and the monthly sales added to the annual sales total for a branch, the counter for months is incremented by 1 and then tested for a value of 12. This program loop is repeated 12 times. Then the annual sales total for the branch is printed.

The counter for the branch limit is reduced by 1 after each branch total is printed. The loop controlled by this counter is repeated until the counter equals zero. Then processing halts.

The program described in Illustration B-13 contains one loop that is entirely within another; that is, all steps in the loop controlled by the counter for months are also within the loop controlled by the branch counter. Such a loop is called a ***nested loop***.

FLOWCHARTING AIDS

Several flowcharting aids are available to the programmer. The *flowcharting template* contains all of the flowchart symbols as cutout forms that can be traced neatly on a flowchart. Flowcharts can be prepared on any type of paper; however special *flowcharting worksheets* are available for this purpose. Illustration B-14 shows a flowchart on such a worksheet.

When the flowcharting worksheet is used in preparing a flowchart, certain conventions should be followed. Each rectangle is identified by a letter and number so that connectors can point to specific rectangles. If a connector symbol refers to a rectangle on another page, the number of the page is written to the left of the connector. There are no such references on the flowchart in Illustration B-14, because this flowchart is contained on only one page. However, if such a reference were needed, it could be written as shown in Illustration B-15. Together, the symbol and text indicate that this particular path of a program continues at B5 on page 6 of the flowchart.

In preparing a modular program flowchart on a flowcharting worksheet, individual modules can be cross-referenced as shown in Illustration B-16. All of the main processing steps or modules are represented by symbols that use striping at the top to show the names of detailed flowcharts.

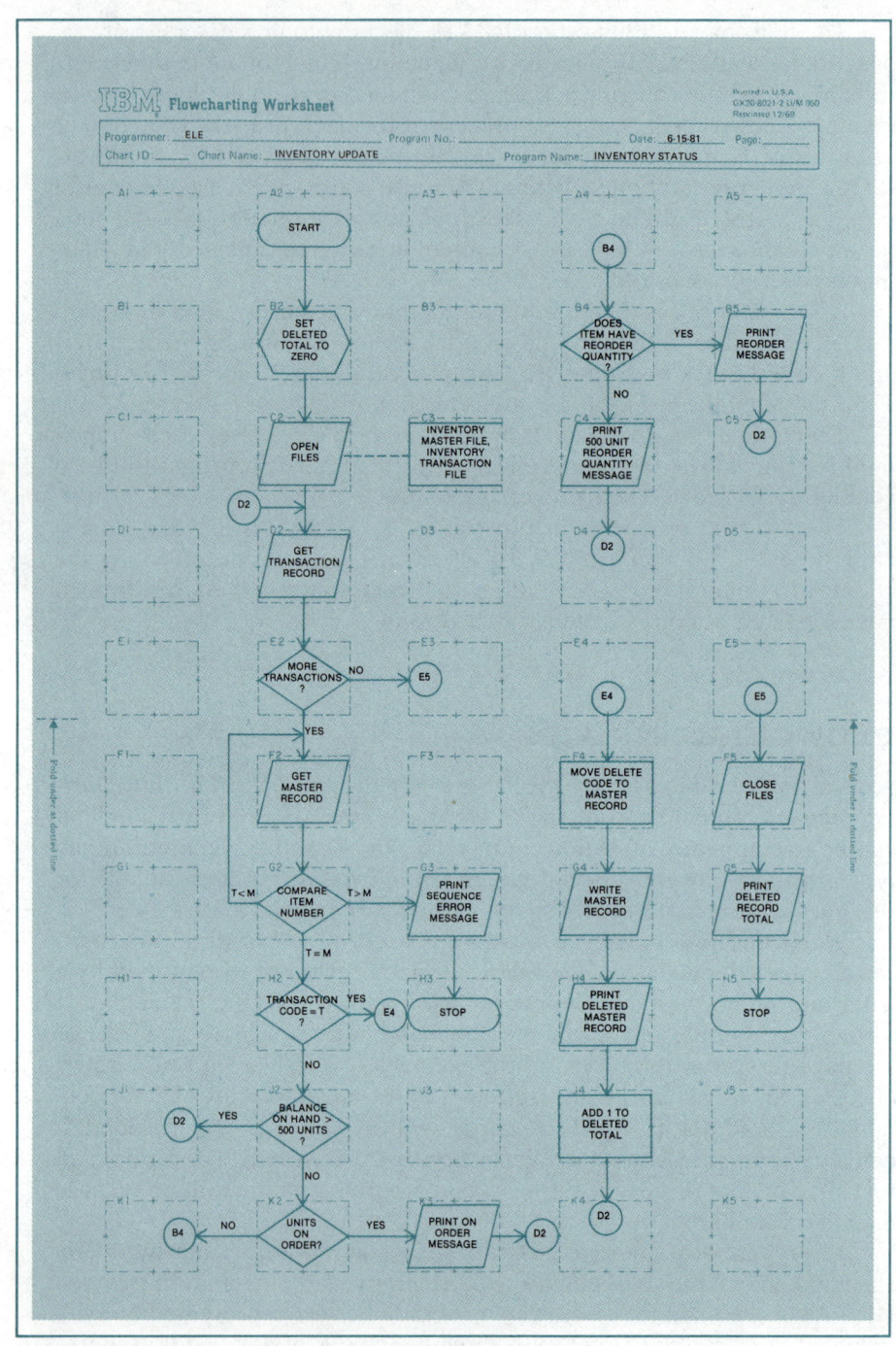

ILLUSTRATION B-14 Flowcharting worksheet

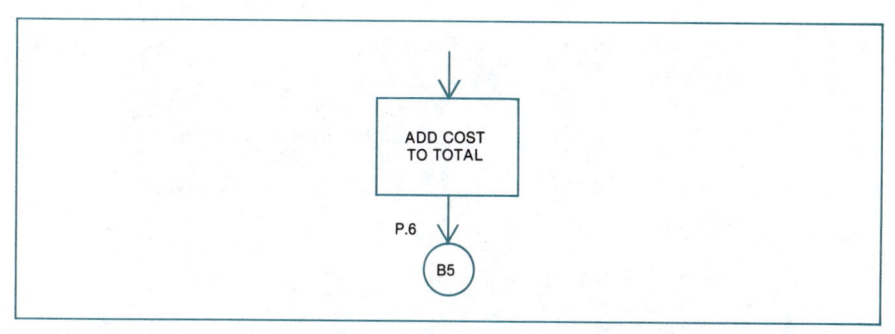

ILLUSTRATION B-15 Reference to a step on another flowchart page

The page on which the detail begins is indicated above the upper left corner of each symbol. The modular flowchart for the main module refers to all of the major processing routines, but ideally it consists of not more than one flowcharting worksheet. A detailed flowchart consisting of one or more flowcharting worksheets is required for each referenced module. (For another example, look back at Illustration B-2. The "Calculate bill" module would normally be represented with striping like the modules in Illustration B-16.)

Computer programs that prepare flowcharts from detailed instructions are available. Generally, the programmer sketches out the basic logic to be described on the flowchart. This is expressed in a form acceptable as input to the flowchart program. The flowchart program produces a flowchart complete with machine versions of the flowchart symbols as output. Such automated flowcharting allows revisions to the flowchart to be made by a computer. Manual redrawing is eliminated. This saves considerable time and makes it easier to keep the flowchart current.

SUMMARY

1. System and program flowcharts are tools used in defining procedures for solving problems in business data processing. A system flowchart is a graphic representation of the flow of data and work through a business data processing system. A program flowchart is a graphic representation of a series of steps necessary to solve a problem.

2. A modular flowchart can be used to describe the major processing steps in an application. Each major step, or module, can be described on a detailed flowchart.

3. The basic symbols used on most program flowcharts are the terminal, input/output, flowline, process, decision, and connector.

UNIT THREE: COMPUTER PROGRAMMING AND DESIGN

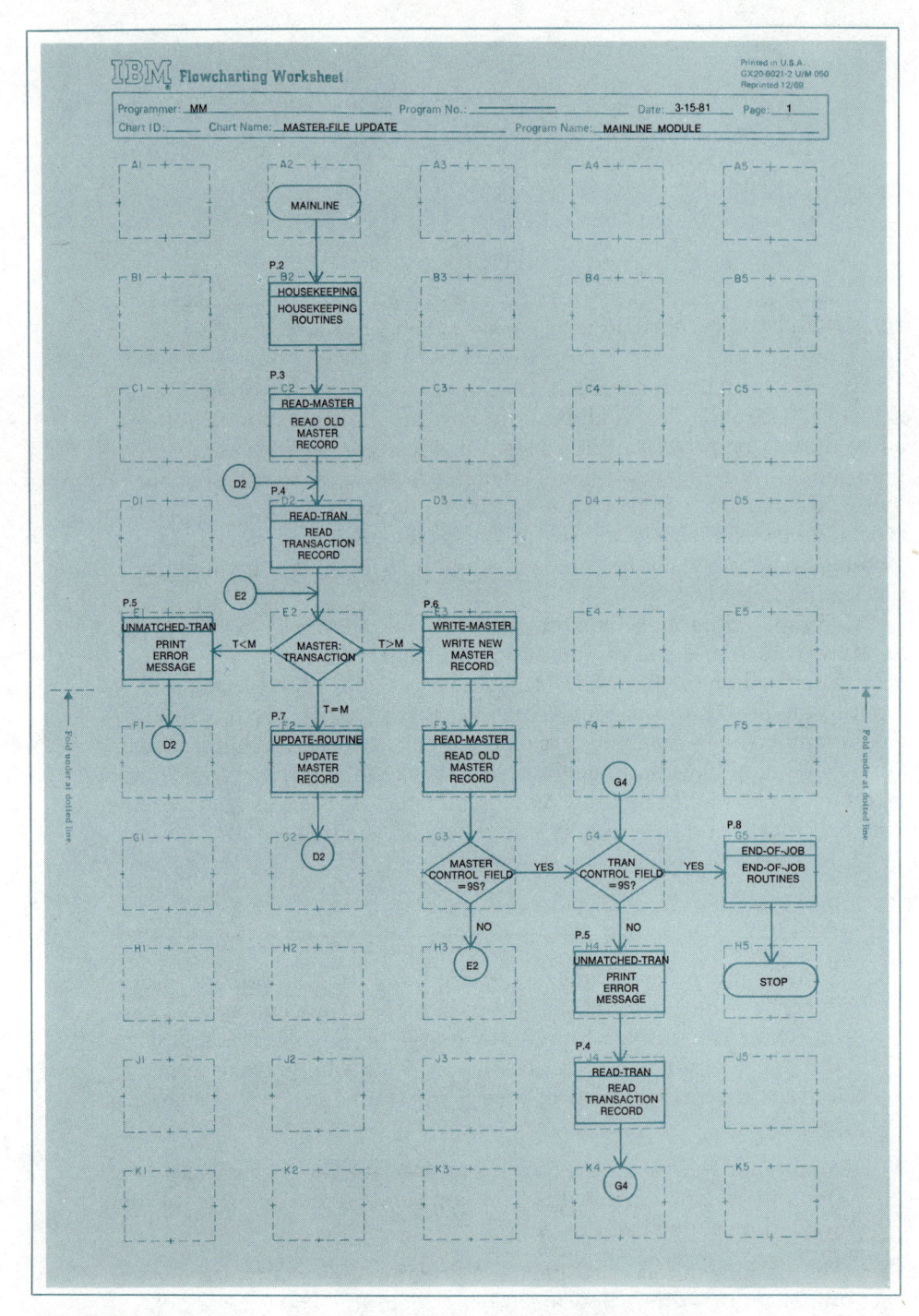

ILLUSTRATION B-16   Modular flowchart for a master-file update program

4. Each symbol on a program flowchart contains a brief description of the function or activity to be performed. The annotation symbol should be used when additional comments are needed for clarification.

5. A program or subprogram that is not defined on a program flowchart can be represented by the predefined process symbol.

6. The preparation symbol is used to indicate processing steps that change the program.

7. The flow in a flowchart should be from top to bottom and from left to right. Where flowlines are numerous, connectors should be used for clarity.

8. Program testing is represented by the decision symbol. It allows for alternate paths of flow. A change in direction of flow based on a decision is called a conditional branch. When program testing is not involved in a branch, the branch is unconditional.

9. Program loops are often based on conditional branching. One type of program loop uses a counter to control the number of times the loop is executed. The counter is initialized, then tested for a limit and modified within the loop. The processing steps in the loop are repeated until the limit of the counter is reached.

10. Several flowcharting aids are available to the programmer. These include flowcharting templates, flowcharting worksheets, and computer programs for flowchart preparation.

REVIEW QUESTIONS

1. How are program flowcharts used during the programming process?
2. Explain the purposes of modular and detailed program flowcharts as they are used in program design.
3. What is the meaning of the preparation symbol?
4. How is the annotation symbol used?
5. What is the meaning of the predefined process symbol?
6. What is the general direction of flow in a flowchart?
7. What is a program loop?
8. Explain how connectors are used in a flowchart.
9. Identify two flowcharting aids and explain how they are used.

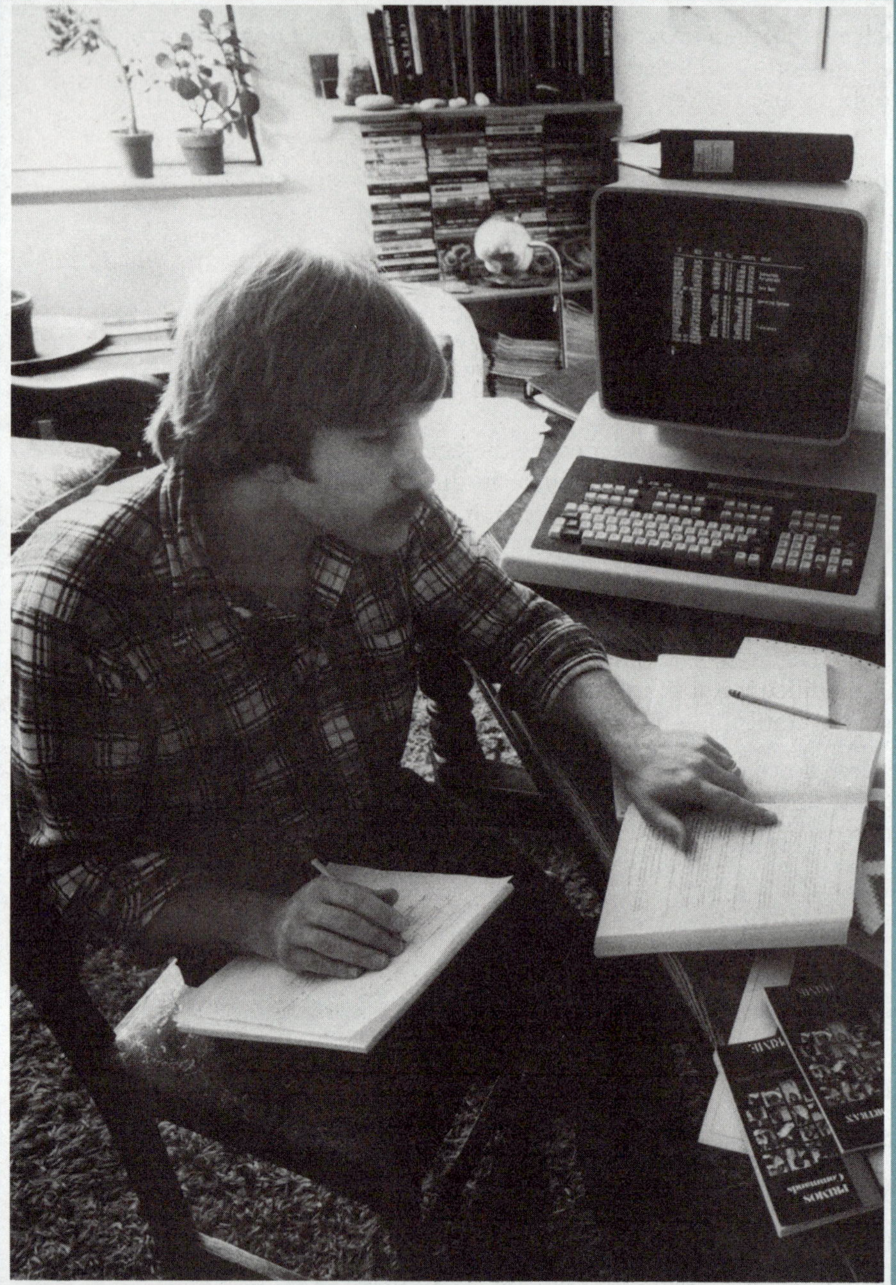

CHAPTER 10

THE PROGRAMMING CYCLE

RECOGNIZING AND DEFINING THE PROBLEM
The Problem Statement
Acquiring Data
Establishing Formats
The Structure of the Problem
Establishing Procedures

PLANNING THE SOLUTION TO THE PROBLEM

SELECTING A PROGRAMMING LANGUAGE

PROGRAM CODING

PROGRAM DEBUGGING AND TESTING
Debugging
Testing

PROGRAM DOCUMENTATION
AND MAINTENANCE

Opposite: Computer terminals are making it possible for programmers to work outside an office environment.

When a programming project has been agreed upon, a number of rather well-defined steps should be taken to create a useful and efficient program. Among the steps that should be taken are: (1) recognizing and defining the problem, (2) planning the solution to the problem, (3) selecting an appropriate language, (4) coding the program, (5) debugging and testing the program, and (6) program documentation and maintenance. The flow of these steps is shown in Illustration 10-1. In most cases, the required tasks are the responsibilities of several individuals, such as the manager, the systems analyst, and the programmer. Each performs a different function. In some instances, however, the majority of the tasks fall to a programmer or a team of programmers. In an educational environment a student may perform all of them.

○ RECOGNIZING AND DEFINING THE PROBLEM

Before a problem can be defined, there must be a realization that the problem exists. Often, the problem stems from the desires of management personnel to obtain more information with which to make better decisions. For example, the production supervisor may request information related to the efficiency of the present configuration of machinery. In another case, the corporation president may ask for a breakdown of the financial standing of the firm. In each of these situations, the existence of a problem is realized; if a decision is made to use the computer to solve the problem, the programming cycle is initiated.

The definition of the problem, sometimes called **system analysis and design** (see Chapter 3), comprises a number of interrelated tasks. The first task is to lay out a clear and concise statement of the problem. Second, if required data is not readily available, a method for acquiring the data must be devised. Third, the basic formats of input and output should be established, as should the structure of related files. Fourth, if necessary, the problem should be divided into component parts. Finally, the basic procedures for the project should be outlined.

The Problem Statement

Developing an accurate statement of the problem is probably the most important step in problem definition and in the development of a program. In an educational setting, most of the problems encountered by students are well defined. In a business environment, this is not usually the case. If the problem is loosely or improperly defined, the resulting program may not solve the problem at all; it may serve only as a waste of time and money. However, if good judgement is exercised, and a clear definition established, a solution to the problem can usually be obtained.

CHAPTER 10: THE PROGRAMMING CYCLE

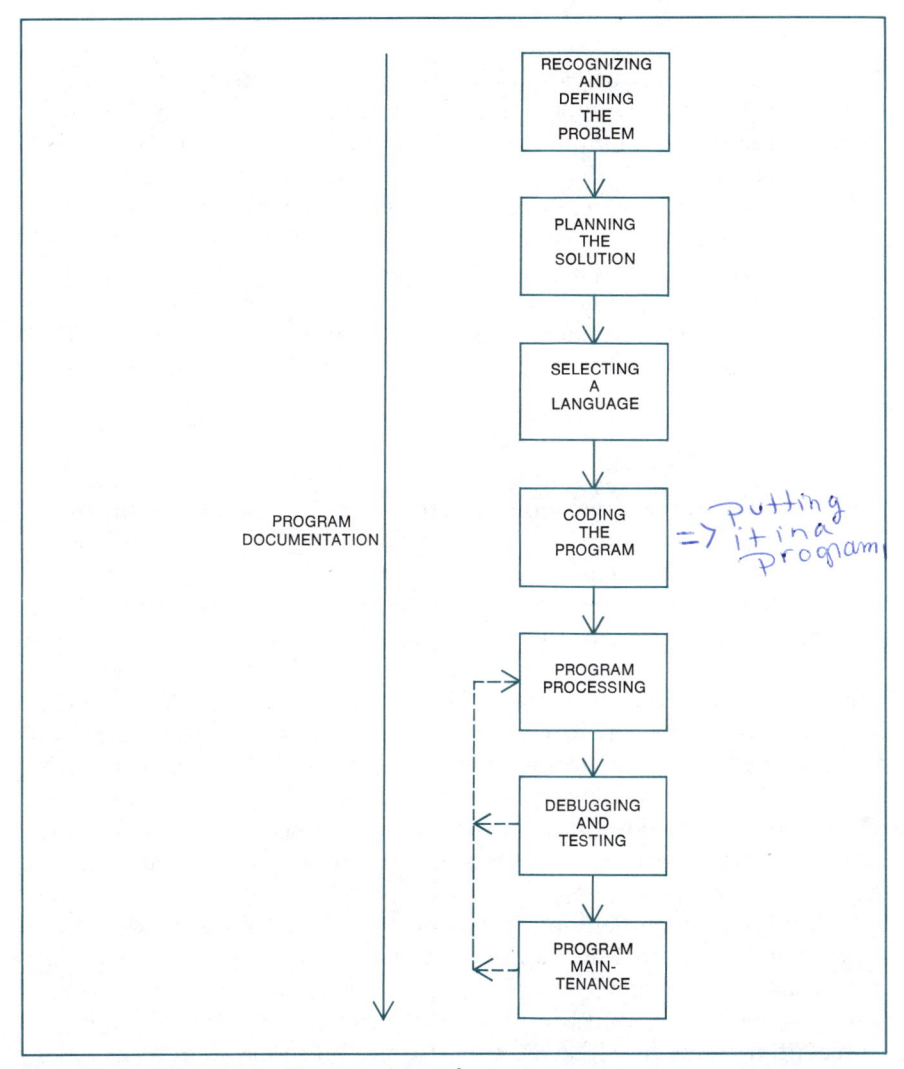

ILLUSTRATION 10-1 Programming cycle

In addition to the problem statement, the objectives and goals of the program that is to satisfy the problem requirements should be set forth in a clear and concise manner. In this way, misinterpretation is minimized. After the programmer or analyst (depending on the structure of the firm) has developed a complete statement of the problem, he or she should consult with the individual or group who is to use the information, or results. If the definition satisfies the problem requirements, the next phase of program development can begin.

UNIT THREE: COMPUTER PROGRAMMING AND DESIGN

Acquiring Data

The next stage in the analysis of a problem is the acquisition of data. This phase depends entirely upon the problem to be solved. If the objective is market research, for example, the source of the data is external to the firm. The important point is that some plan for collecting, recording, editing, organizing, and processing the data must be established. Caution must be exercised in collecting the data so that the resulting data base accurately depicts the actual situation. If the data that is accumulated is irrelevant to the problem, no program—not even an accurate, precise one—can arrive at a correct answer. In such a situation, a simple truth applies: **GIGO** (*garbage in/garbage out*).

Establishing Formats

The next stage in the development of the program is to design functional input, output, and file formats. The input form should be designed for ease of recording as well as ease of processing. The output should be designed to accurately present the results to the user in a way that enhances the information and promotes understanding.

Illustration 10-2 shows two documents used by programmers in designing input and output formats. The top document is a **Multiple-Card Layout Form**. It gives the formats of the input cards for a program. In this example, the format for the one type of card used as input to an Inventory Status Program is given on the form. Columns 1–20 of each card are the name field, columns 21–25 are the balance field, and columns 26–30 are the cost field. If necessary, one Multiple-Card Layout Form can be used to give the formats for up to six types of cards.

The second document in Illustration 10-2 is the left-hand portion of a **Print Chart**. It shows 75 of the 144 print positions representable on a complete chart of this type. The Print Chart indicates the specific horizontal print positions to be used for information printed on a report. In this example, print positions 11–30 are used for the inventory item designation; 36–40 are used for the balance (on-hand quantity) of each item; and 45–50 are used for the cost of each item. Print position 48 of 45–50 is reserved for a decimal point.

In designing the layout of files, a number of requirements must be dealt with. For example, if a file is to be maintained on magnetic tape, such items as the recording mode, the block size, the number of characters per record, the retention cycle, the number of items to be maintained, and the volume number of each reel should be stated. Illustration 10-3 shows a document called a **Record Format**. The Record Format is one kind of storage layout form. When used properly, it provides information relevant to the organization and handling of the file.

The Structure of the Problem

The fourth phase of problem definition is to determine the component parts of the problem. Under some circumstances, a problem solution can be divided into segments. Each segment solution becomes part of the final solution. The problem, and its solution, may be structured either *serially* or *in parallel*. With serialization, the output of one segment serves as the input to the next. With parallelism, some or all segments are designed to be executed simultaneously. If a problem can be subdivided, the final results may be achieved more quickly, assuming that personnel are available to code the various segments. Some problems cannot be subdivided.

ILLUSTRATION 10-2 Multiple-Card Layout Form and Print Chart

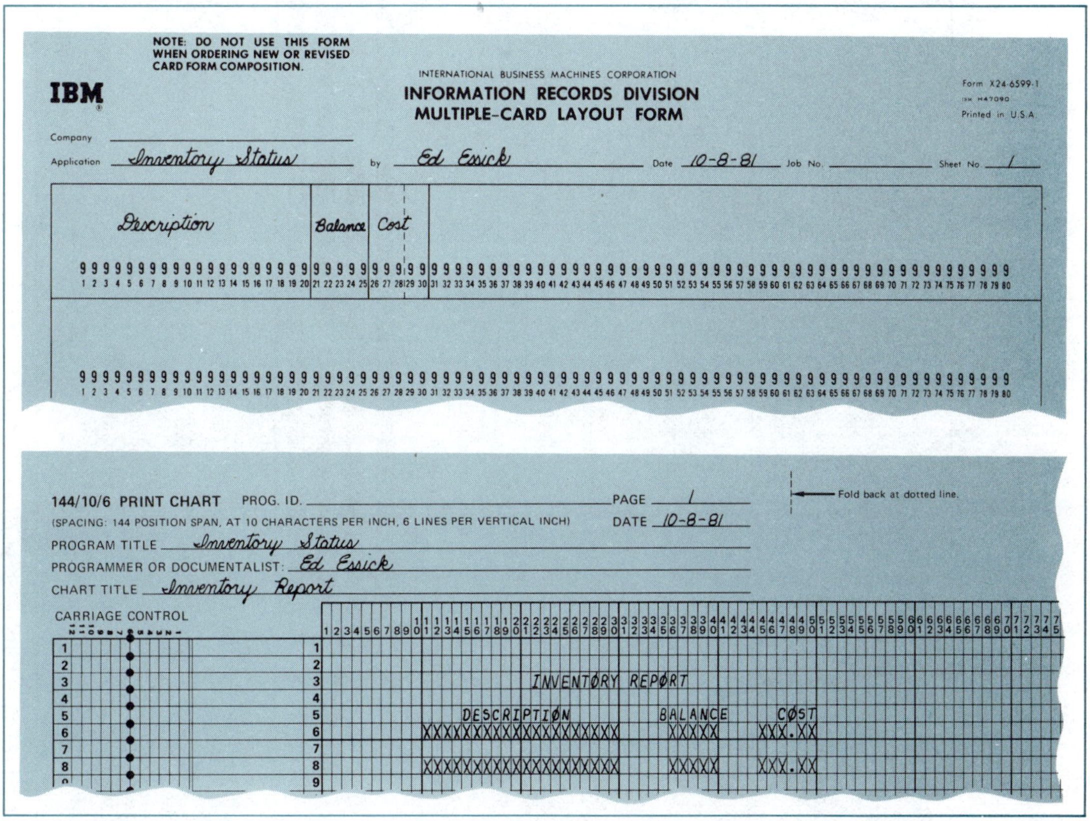

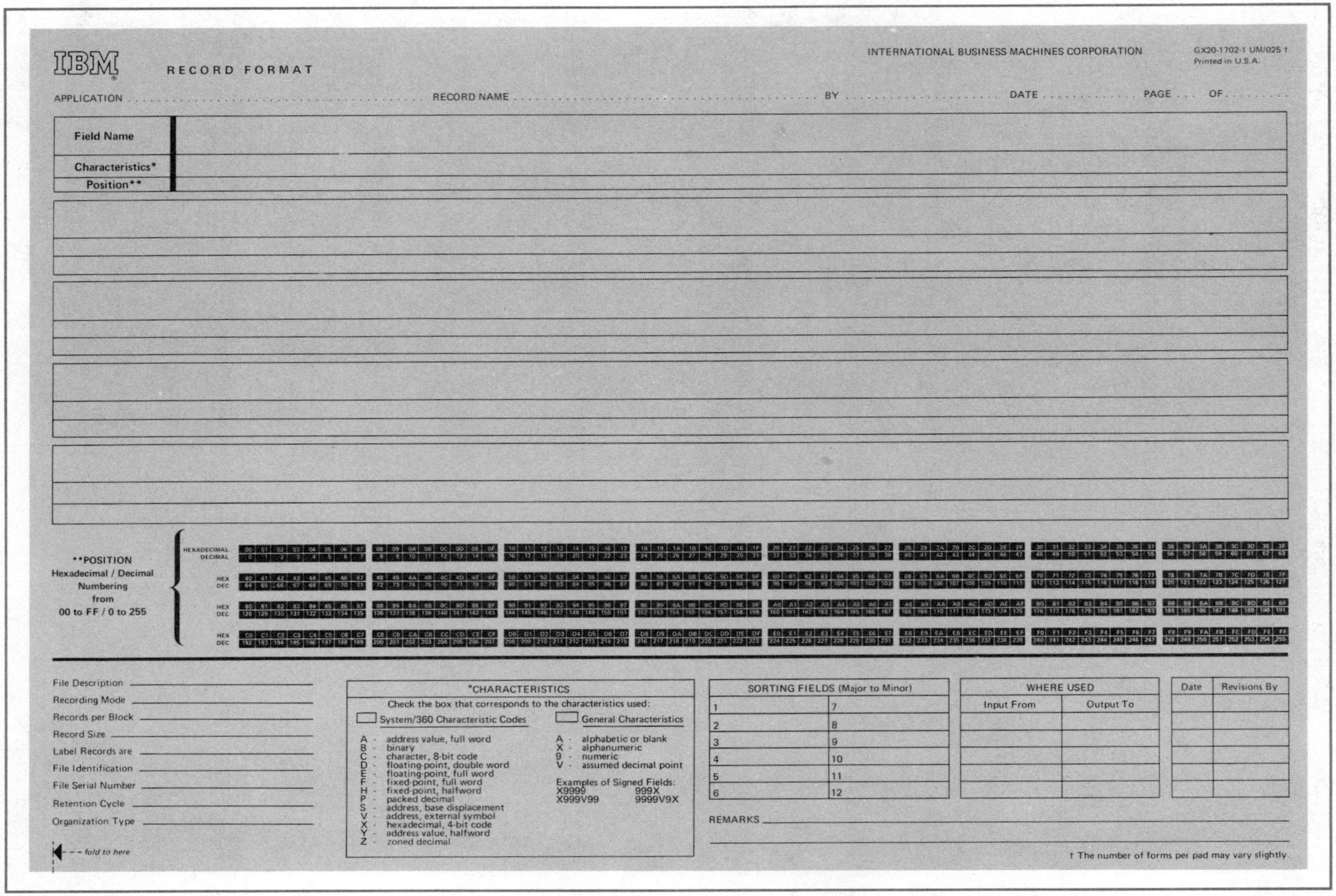

254 UNIT THREE: COMPUTER PROGRAMMING AND DESIGN

ILLUSTRATION 10-3 Storage layout form

Establishing Procedures

The final phase of problem definition is the establishment of procedures. The procedures may pertain to several diverse items, each of which is important to the final results. For example, a special form may be devised to preserve the accuracy of data that is gathered. A staffing projection assigning the responsibility for each segment to a specific individual or team may be developed. Finally, a timetable for program (and project) completion may be established. Thus, the procedural phase considers the project organization. Its purpose is to determine how to make continued, efficient progress toward stated objectives.

○ PLANNING THE SOLUTION TO THE PROBLEM

After the problem has been defined, the planning for its solution can begin. In this step, the layout of the program is determined. It should coincide with the next step, in which the language to be used in programming is determined. The language should be selected at this point because it is one of the factors determining the ease or difficulty with which a solution can be worked out.

In the planning stage, the programmer finalizes the design of the input and output records. From this, the programmer determines the logical processes by which the program will accept and produce the records. Then, how the program will provide the desired final results is planned out.

The programmer employs many tools to describe the sequence of steps in the program. Probably the most commonly used aid is the *program flowchart*. The purpose of the program flowchart is to represent, by use of symbols, the processing that should take place in the program. It indicates the instructions that should be executed repeatedly by looping and the conditions under which branches should be made. By constructing a program flowchart and then studying it carefully, a programmer can analyze the logic of a program and determine whether a reasonable plan for the solution of the problem has been worked out.

A simplified flowchart for an Overtime Program is shown in Illustration 10-4. The basic symbols on this flowchart are the essence of flowcharting. The parallelogram ▱ represents an input or output operation. It normally appears where a read or write operation should occur. The rectangle ▢ stands for a processing operation. It may be either an arithmetic or a data-movement operation. The diamond ◇ represents a decision. The flowlines represent the direction of flow, which is generally

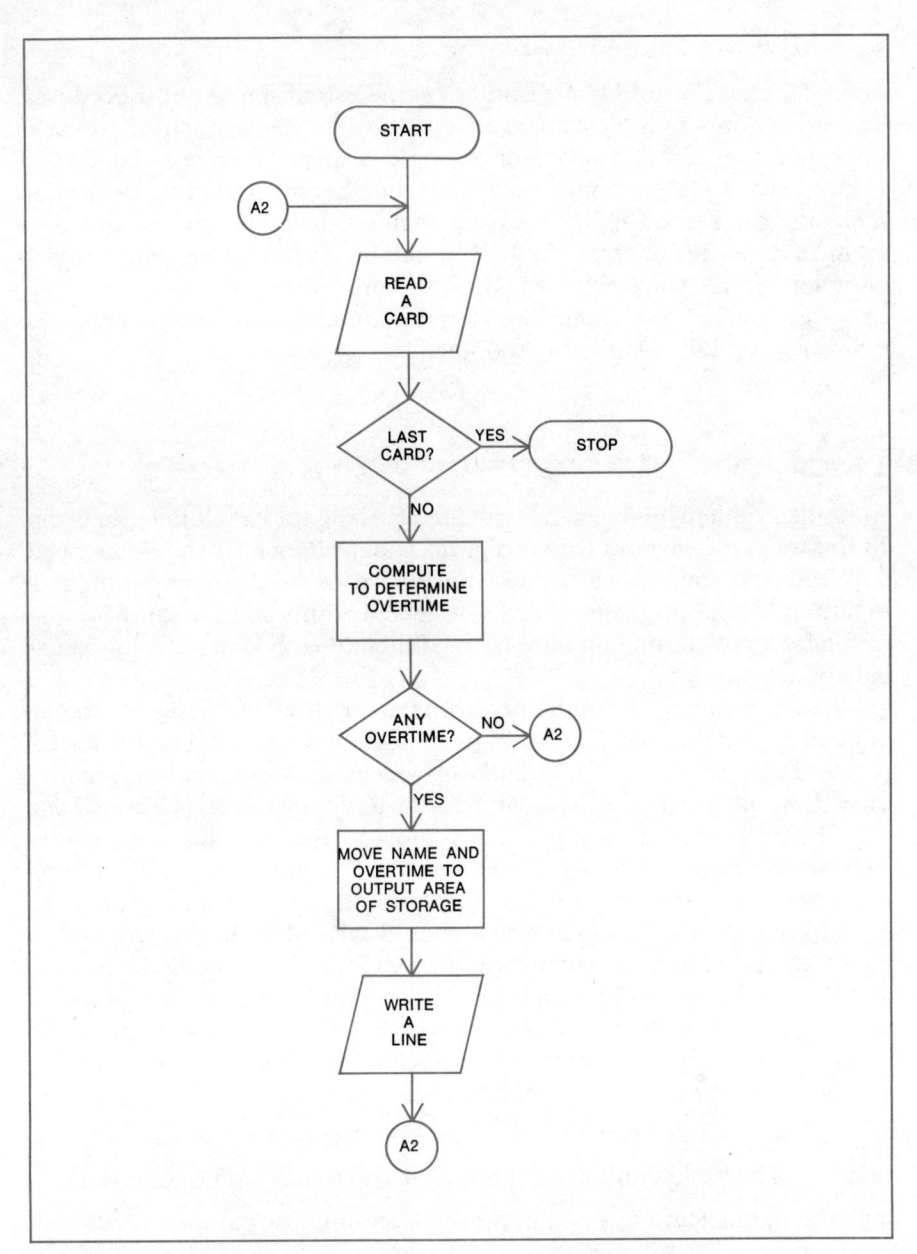

ILLUSTRATION 10-4 Program flowchart for an overtime program

from top to bottom and left to right on a flowchart. One symbol on a flowchart can represent one or more instructions of the program. (An extended discussion of program flowcharts is given in Module B.)

CHAPTER 10: THE PROGRAMMING CYCLE

This planning activity is the final step before the actual preparation of the program. If any alterations are to be made to the basic definition of the problem, they should be made at this point. Delaying such changes beyond this point creates major difficulties and seriously impedes the completion of the project.

○ SELECTING A PROGRAMMING LANGUAGE

Coinciding with the plan for the solution of the problem should be a survey to determine which language should be used in programming. A selection must be made in the planning stage because the language choice often affects the solution to the problem. The program flowchart for a solution in one language may differ from that for another. The specific considerations in selecting a language are discussed in detail in Chapter 11.

○ PROGRAM CODING

After the solution to the problem has been planned and an appropriate language has been selected, the program can be coded. Program coding is the process of translating the planned solution to the problem, depicted in a program flowchart, into statements of the program. The program flowchart acts as a guide to the programmer as he or she describes the logical processes involved in the problem through the medium of a programming language.

The program is usually written on a *coding form*. Several forms are shown as examples in Illustration 10-5. These coding forms are designed to simplify the task of coding. The basic advantages of proper use of coding forms are:

1. They depict the basic structure and some of the characteristics of the language for which they are designed.
2. They tend to reduce clerical errors in coding.
3. They make the keying task easier.
4. They assist in the organization and identification of the program.

During the coding phase, the programmer may encounter an operation depicted on the program flowchart for which there is no practical implementation in the chosen language. If so, program development must regress to the planning stage so that an alternative solution can be proposed. If the program is to be entered on punched cards, it is now keypunched (one card for each line of code on the coding form) and desk checked (see below). Then it is submitted to the computer. Today, a program is often created by entering it directly into the computer from a

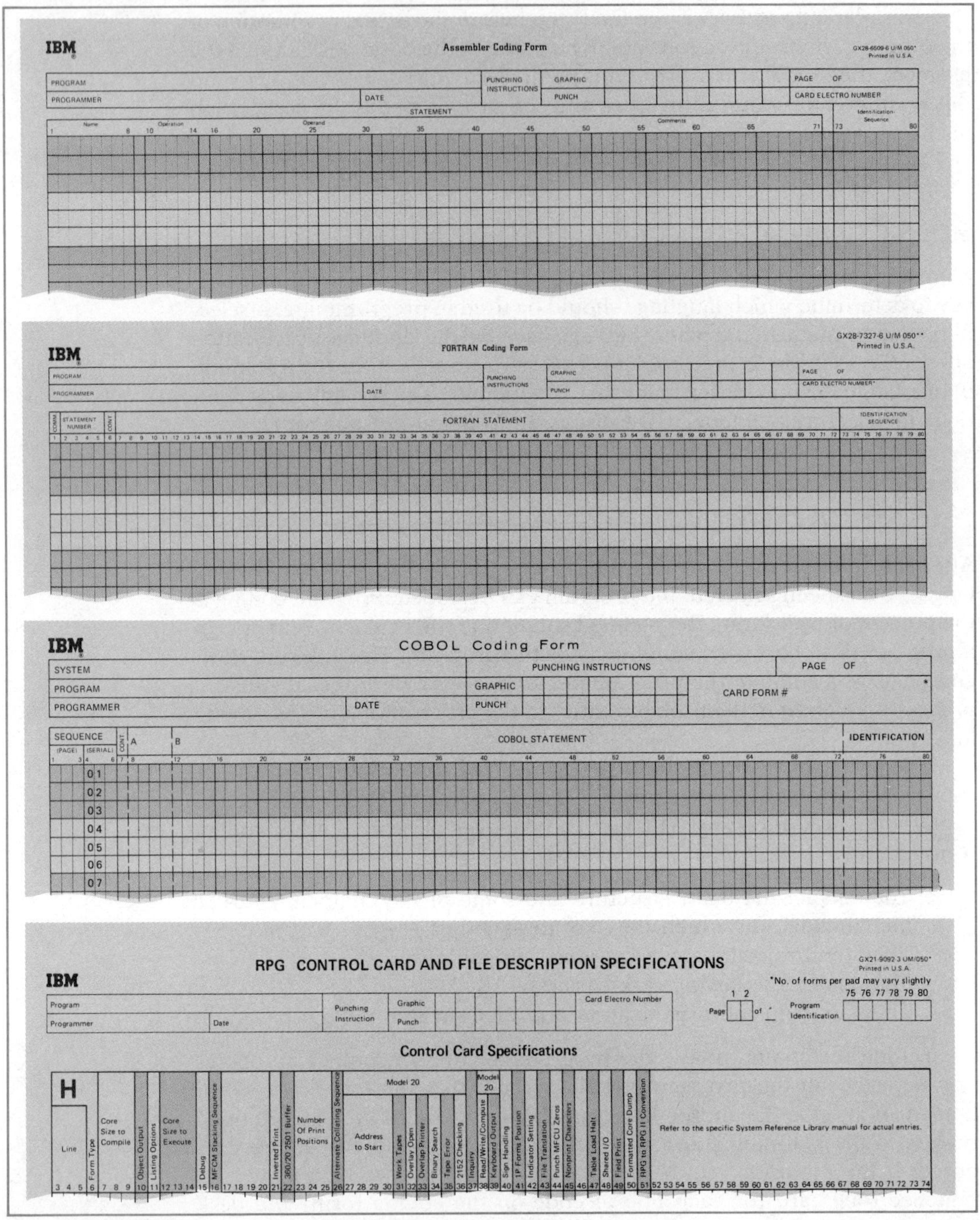

ILLUSTRATION 10-5 Some commonly used coding forms

terminal. The program is keyed at the terminal by the programmer or a data entry operator. If the programmer has the responsibility for keying the program at the terminal, coding forms may not be used at all. In this kind of development environment, the programmer may code, debug, and test the program at the terminal.

PROGRAM DEBUGGING AND TESTING

No program development task is complete until debugging and testing procedures have been carried out. The care exercised in this step (or the lack of it) may significantly affect the worth of the program.

Debugging

A program is seldom executed successfully the first time. If the program contains any degree of complexity, it normally contains a few errors (bugs) as well. Debugging is the process of locating and correcting programming errors. These errors may be due to faulty logic in the design of the program. They may also be caused by mistakes in coding.

There are two basic levels of debugging. The first level is called **desk checking**. Its purpose is to locate and remove as many logical and clerical errors as possible. When the program is keyed in from a terminal, desk checking can be performed as the program is keyed. If the program is punched on cards, each card is checked for errors after it is punched. Then the program is read into the computer and processed by a **language translator**. The function of the language translator is to convert the program statements written by the programmer into the binary code of the computer. As a part of this translation step, the program statements are examined to verify that they have been coded correctly. If errors are detected, a series of **diagnostics** referred to as an **error message list** is generated by the language translator (see Illustration 10-6). With this list in hand, the programmer enters the second level of debugging.

The error message list helps the programmer to find the causes of errors and make the necessary corrections. At this point, the program may contain keying errors, as well as other clerical errors and logical errors that were not detected in the desk-checking process. The diagnostics provided by the language translator should enable the programmer to eliminate most, if not all, of the clerical errors and some of the logical errors.

After the corrections have been made, the program is again read into the computer. If the program still contains errors, the language translator again generates diagnostics. Corrections are made, and the program is resubmitted. This procedure continues until an error-free run (a run in which

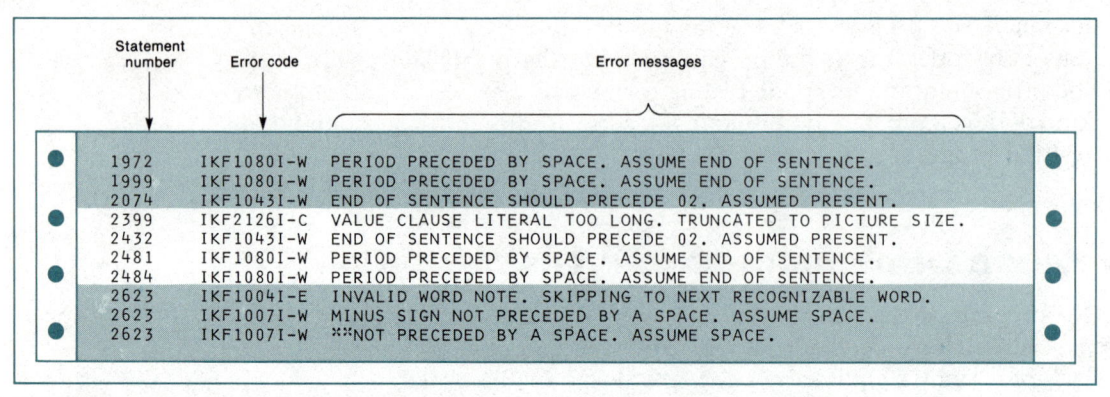

Statement number	Error code	Error messages
1972	IKF1080I-W	PERIOD PRECEDED BY SPACE. ASSUME END OF SENTENCE.
1999	IKF1080I-W	PERIOD PRECEDED BY SPACE. ASSUME END OF SENTENCE.
2074	IKF1043I-W	END OF SENTENCE SHOULD PRECEDE 02. ASSUMED PRESENT.
2399	IKF2126I-C	VALUE CLAUSE LITERAL TOO LONG. TRUNCATED TO PICTURE SIZE.
2432	IKF1043I-W	END OF SENTENCE SHOULD PRECEDE 02. ASSUMED PRESENT.
2481	IKF1080I-W	PERIOD PRECEDED BY SPACE. ASSUME END OF SENTENCE.
2484	IKF1080I-W	PERIOD PRECEDED BY SPACE. ASSUME END OF SENTENCE.
2623	IKF1004I-E	INVALID WORD NOTE. SKIPPING TO NEXT RECOGNIZABLE WORD.
2623	IKF1007I-W	MINUS SIGN NOT PRECEDED BY A SPACE. ASSUME SPACE.
2623	IKF1007I-W	**NOT PRECEDED BY A SPACE. ASSUME SPACE.

ILLUSTRATION 10-6 Error message list

no diagnostics are generated) is achieved. The programmer should not assume that the program is truly error-free because logical errors and clerical errors of a nature that the language translator cannot detect may still exist. But, at this point, testing begins.

Testing

The purpose of testing is to determine whether a program consistently produces correct or expected results. A program is normally tested by executing it with a given set of input data, for which correct results are known. However, one run represents only one test of the program. The extent of testing may depend on the amount of time available for testing (the recipient of the information may be willing to forgo complete testing because he or she desperately needs the results). In addition, there may be little money available for testing. In short, the amount of testing is usually determined by balancing the cost of testing against the penalties of acting on incorrect information.

In a typical test of a program, the test procedure is broken into three segments. First, the program is tested with inputs that one would normally expect for an execution of the program. If the results of this test run correspond to the expected results, the second test run is made. Valid but slightly abnormal data is injected to determine the capabilities of the program to cope with exceptions. For example, the minimum and maximum values allowable for a sales-amount field may be provided as input to verify that the program processes them correctly. In the third segment, invalid data is inserted to test the program's error-handling routines.

When a program is designed to replace an existing system or procedure (whether it is another program or a manual operation), *parallel runs* may be set up as a part of the test procedure. Each parallel run entails using both the old and the new systems and determining whether the systems yield identical results. Generally, several of these runs are made over a period of time. For example, if a company is preparing to shift from a manual accounting operation to a computer program designed to perform the same function, both systems may be used for six months to verify that the program is capable of replacing the manual operation.

Now, suppose that the results of test runs are not adequate. If the distortions are rather minor in nature, minor bugs may be the cause. The programmer may use any of three alternatives to locate minor errors. First, the programmer may trace the processing steps manually to find the errors. In effect, the programmer may pretend to be the computer, following the execution of each statement in the program and noting whether or not results are as expected. For example, if a statement multiplies hours worked by rate of pay, is the field reserved for the result defined correctly and large enough to hold any result that may be calculated?

As a second alternative, the programmer may use *tracing routines* if such routines are available for the language in which the program is coded. This approach has at least one advantage over the first one: It takes less time. Furthermore, the computer performs the tracing operation. Machine steps are not susceptible to human error as manual procedures are.

Finally, the programmer may use a *storage dump*, which is a printout of the contents of computer storage locations. In most systems, this storage dump is printed out in hexadecimal representation as shown in Illustration 10-7. Practice is required to become skillful in reading such a listing; however, most programmers soon learn to use this debugging tool. By examining the contents of various storage locations, the programmer can determine the instruction at which the program halted. This information is an important clue to finding the error that caused the halt to occur.

If major inadequacies are noted during test runs, a return to the planning stage may be necessary. A program may never be completely error-free because some routines may never be executed, some branches may never be taken, or the data provided as input may never cause a malfunction. To test all possibilities may be next to impossible. Even so, testing is a necessary and useful process. The debugging and testing step in the programming cycle may be as costly and time-consuming as both the planning and coding steps, but it is an essential one.

PROGRAM DOCUMENTATION AND MAINTENANCE

Documentation of the program should be developed at every step of the programming cycle. Documentation in the problem-definition step should include a clear statement of the problem. The objectives of the program

0E4900	18F14110	B2CA05EF	12114780	B0CED207	B2DA1000	5810B2E2	5800B2E6	1BFF0A3E
0E4920	4100B2CA	4110B2B9	98EFD3A0	58B0B2C6	0A020510	58B011D4	D603B2DA	B2DA4780
0E4940	B14A5810	B2DA5910	B2DE4720	B14AD603	10001000	4770B11A	41110006	47F0B100
0E4960	58010060	5000B2D2	4A010004	5000B2D6	41110006	5010B2DA	4100B2D2	4110B2B9
0E4980	58B0B2C6	0A020510	58B01180	47F0B0FC	4110B422	4500B156	000E4B68	0A0291C0
0E49A0	D3F24710	B2045820	D1881222	4780B204	58320000	12334780	B2041BFF	9120302D
0E49C0	4710B18A	9110302D	4780B192	41F0000C	98473000	45AF7000	58103010	12114780
0E49E0	B1A495F0	10004770	B1F89180	302947E0	B1C44100	000858F0	300841FF	000012FF
0E4A00	4780B1F8	05EF47F0	B1F89120	30314780	B1F89110	302A4710	B27E5810	300891E0
0E4A20	30304780	B1E65810	30340700	5010B1F2	4110B42A	4500B1F6	00000000	0A0294DF
0E4A40	30314122	000447F0	B16A9101	D3C74780	B2189120	D3C74710	B23C47F0	B27091C0
0E4A60	D3F24710	B2329120	D3C74710	B236910C	D3F24710	B2320A0E	1B000A06	9801D1DC
0E4A80	0A1041F0	00019680	D3C7910C	D3F24780	B27041F0	00E795F0	D5264770	B27058E0
0E4AA0	D1FCD504	E00BB2B4	4780B270	F274D048	E00B4FF0	D04858D0	D004980C	D01458ED
0E4AC0	000C07FE	58503008	41400003	58150000	12114780	B2A80700	5010B29E	4110B42A
0E4AE0	4500B2A2	00000000	0A0294DF	30314155	00044640	B28647F0	B1F8F0F0	F0F0F05B
0E4B00	5BC2D7C4	E4D4D700	500E4846	000E3F88	000E1000	000E5044	000EF7FF	00000000
0E4B20	00000000	00000000	000F0280	00004FFF	5CC9D5C9	E3404040	5CC7C5E3	C9D54040
0E4B40	5CD6C6D3	40404040	5CC4C5E3	C3404040	5CC4C5E3	D3404040	5CE3D6E3	C3404040
0E4B60	5CE3D6E3	D3404040	00008000	08000003	000E4BC0	00000000	000E4CB0	3380C4E4
0E4B80	D4D4E840	40000000	00000000	00000800	002020F3	240E4C58	80000000	00000000
0E4BA0	000000FF	000000FF	00000000	00000000	3B000020	00000000	00000001	47000000
0E4BC0	070E4BA2	40000006	310E4BA4	40000005	080E4BC8	20000001	1D0E4BB4	A0000008
0E4BE0	050E4C58	60000001	310E4BA4	40000005	080E4BE8	20000001	1E0E4BF8	30000009
0E4C00	00000000	--SAME--						
0E4C40	00000000	00000000	00000000	00000000	47FF001C	47FF001C	40000000	F9C3F14E
0E4C60	D9D7C7C9	C4F0F0F0	5B5BC2D6	D7C5D540	5B5BC2C3	D3D6E2C5	00000000	00000000
0E4C80	00000000	--SAME--						
0E4CA0	00000000	00000000	00000000	000000D3	0A320000	47F0F000	47F0F032	47F0F032
0E4CC0	47F0F000	47F0F000	47F0F036	47F0F1E0	C9D1D1C6	C3C2E9C4	3402FFFF	D9E5FFFF
0E4CE0	34029026	F3145860	100895FF	101E4780	F0464A60	104A9103	102B4710	F2024740
0E4D00	F1949140	102C4780	F06294BF	102C4530	F1865846	00000640	9180102A	4780F0A2
0E4D20	4B60104A	96606004	D2006000	104195E6	40004780	F09AD200	60001040	95E54000
0E4D40	4780F09A	D2006000	40004A60	104A47F0	F1949200	F34891F0	40004710	F0EA95C1
0E4D60	40004780	F0EA95C2	40004780	F0EA95C3	40004780	F0EA4800	F3664130	F36F4133
0E4D80	0012D500	40003000	4780F0EA	06304600	F0D29201	F34847F0	F1161830	43040000
0E4DA0	41400012	4334F36F	19304780	F1024640	F0F44940	F36447B0	F112920B	60004530
0E4DC0	F1864144	F3829108	102A4710	F1369541	40004780	F1369581	40004780	F1369201
0E4DE0	600047F0	F13CD200	60004000	D6006000	10289108	102C4780	F1949180	10024710
0E4E00	F1540A07	91101003	4780F166	18314110	F3680A02	1813D200	10401038	D2001038
0E4E20	1030D24F	10981048	58301030	D24F1048	300047F0	F1940A00	91801002	4710F192
0E4E40	0A0707F3	4530F186	9108102A	4780F1B0	9501F348	4780F1B0	92016000	4530F186
0E4E60	91011004	4710F1CC	91401005	4710F2CA	91101003	4710F2E2	47F0F1E0	9108102A
0E4E80	4710F1E0	9102102C	4710F2B8	58E01040	9826F314	9506101D	4770F200	91801003
0E4EA0	4780F200	96406000	97801003	47F0F032	07FED200	10401050	D5001040	10484770
0E4EC0	F2A85820	103C4A20	F3601842	43401047	192447D0	F22E5A20	F3604320	10355020
0E4EE0	103CD503	103C1036	4740F29C	4780F24C	9506101D	4770F15C	4780F254	9506101D
0E4F00	4770F29C	91801026	4780F268	9180102C	4780F27E	47F0F1CC	4120F350	50201008
0E4F20	0A004530	F1884120	10585020	10089006	F32C92FF	F3344100	F3304110	F3580A02
0E4F40	9200F334	9806F32C	47F0F194	D2001040	1049D203	104C103C	43401040	41440001
0E4F60	47F0F194	42401050	18214802	00064110	10160A02	181247F0	F1E094BF	102C9147
0E4F80	10E84710	10E850E0	F32858E0	10E847F0	F2F694DF	102C9147	10EC4710	10EC50E0
0E4FA0	F32858E0	10EC90F1	F32C5816	00009826	F3140700	070005EE	98F1E024	58E0F328
0E4FC0	47F0F032	00000000	00000000	00000000	00000000	00000000	00000000	00000000
0E4FE0	00000000	--SAME--						
0E5000	170E5000	00000001	5B5BC2D6	D7C5D540	00010000	000D0006	5B5BC2C5	D9D9E3D5
0E5020	F1F2F3F4	F5F6F7F8	F9C1C2C3	4EE5E660	F0400B8B	939BA3AB	B3BBC3CB	D3DBE303
0E5040	01411B13	0B000000						

ILLUSTRATION 10-7 Storage dump

(what the program is designed to accomplish) should be indicated. The source of the request for the program and the persons approving the request should be identified. The date of the request submitted and the date of approval should be listed for reference purposes.

Documentation in the second step (planning the solution to the problem) should include flowcharts or other descriptions of the program logic, and descriptions of input, output, and file formats. The language selected and why it was selected should be pointed out. Documentation in this stage should also include a full and complete statement of the hardware requirements for the program.

Documentation in the program-coding step should include the number of personnel involved, their names, the segment of coding for which each is responsible, and the amount of time spent in coding the program.

The documentation of a program may include two additional components. First, a *user's manual* may be prepared to aid persons who are not familiar with the program in applying it correctly. This manual should contain a description of the program and what it is designed to accomplish, the details of the input records, and the essence of the output produced. A second component, an *operator's manual*, may be developed to assist the computer operator in successfully running the program. This manual contains (1) instructions about starting, running, and terminating the program, (2) messages that may be printed on the console display-keyboard and their meanings, and (3) setup and takedown instructions for files.

The documentation should be such that it provides all necessary information for anyone who comes in contact with the program. First, it may help supervisors in determining the program's purpose, how long the program will be useful, and future revisions that may be necessary. Second, it simplifies program maintenance (revising or updating the program). Third, it provides information as to the use of the program to those unfamiliar with it. Fourth, it provides operating instructions to the computer operator.

Although program maintenance is not a part of documentation, it is heavily dependent on it. The programmer is likely to use the documentation of a program whenever program maintenance is required. Changes in programming staff often necessitate that programmers maintain programs they did not write. The lack of proper program documentation can add considerable time to the program maintenance function in such cases. Good program documentation helps to insure that programs can be maintained even when programming staff changes occur. As an example, assume that a company uses a payroll program to calculate the wages of its workers. Further assume that the income tax rates, the basic wage rate, the premiums for life insurance, and the base for computing social security tax (FICA) are included as constants in the program. Program maintenance is required whenever any of the constants must be changed. If the program has been documented properly, the location of each of the constants is easy to determine. From this, it is a rather simple task to alter the program by replacing an old rate with a current one, thus updating the program. However, if the program is not documented properly, the programmer may spend hours searching through the program for one of the rates. The importance of documentation cannot be overemphasized because the long-range success or failure of the program may depend on it.

○ SUMMARY

1. The programming cycle consists of a set of rather well-defined steps. Among them are: (1) recognizing and defining the problem, (2) planning the solution to the problem, (3) selecting an appropriate programming language, (4) coding the program, (5) debugging and testing the program, and (6) program documentation and maintenance.

2. Defining the problem, sometimes called system analysis and design, includes making a clear and concise statement of the problem; devising a scheme for acquiring the necessary data; establishing the basic formats for input, output, and related files; breaking the problem into component parts; and outlining the basic procedures for the project.

3. Planning the solution to the problem consists of identifying the basic logical processes required to solve the problem. One basic tool employed in this area is the program flowchart. It outlines what is to be done by the program.

4. Selection of an appropriate programming language is a crucial step; it must not be taken lightly. A language selection must be made in the planning stage because it often affects the solution to the problem.

5. Program coding is the process of translating the planned solution to the problem, which may be depicted in a program flowchart, into statements of the program. Often, programmers use coding forms to simplify the coding process.

6. Program debugging and testing are the means by which the program is checked for correctness. This may be done by executing the program with test data. If an existing system is being replaced, parallel runs may be made.

7. Program documentation is essential throughout the programming cycle. With proper care, it can contribute to the continuing success of the program.

8. Program maintenance is a continuing process whereby existing programs are revised or updated to meet current needs. Programmers usually refer to program documentation when performing program maintenance. Their work is much easier when proper documentation is provided.

REVIEW QUESTIONS

1. Discuss the six steps needed to create a useful and efficient program.
2. Discuss the five interrelated tasks performed in recognizing and defining a problem.
3. Discuss the two basic levels of debugging.
4. What is the purpose of program testing?
5. How is a storage dump used?
6. What are the uses of program documentation?

```
DSNUCBRP:
  PROC ( SYSBLKSI ) ;
    save SYSBLKZI ;                       /* save SYSPRINT block size    */
    build outparm ;
    SET outparm_commit_flag = YES ;
    SET final_return_code = ok ;
    CALL CBRPCBLK ;                       /* SET up first message block  */
    SET outparm_USBL_address ;            /* SET ptr to first message block
                                                                         */
    SET UCM pointer to first UCM ;
    DO thru UCM stack
      IF UCM is for LOCATE THEN
        CALL CBRPLOC1 ;                   /* process LOCATE statement    */
      ELSE
        IF UCM is for VERIFY THEN
          CALL CBRPVER1 ;                 /* process VERIFY statement    */
        ELSE
          IF UCM is for REPLACE THEN
            CALL CBRPREP1 ;               /* process REPLACE statement   */
          ELSE
            IF UCM is for DUMP THEN
              CALL CBRPDMP1 ;             /* process DUMP statement      */
      IF return_code > final_return_code THEN
        final_return_code = return_code ;
    END ;
    SET UCM pointer to first UCM ;
    DO thru UCM stack IF final_return_code = ok ;
      CALL CBRPNMSG ( U650 ) ;            /* send normal message 'CONTROL
                                             STATEMENT:'                 */

      IF UCM is for LOCATE THEN
        CALL CBRPLOC ;                    /* process LOCATE statement    */
      ELSE
        IF UCM is for VERIFY THEN
          CALL CBRPVER ;                  /* process VERIFY statement    */
        ELSE
          IF UCM is for REPLACE THEN
            CALL CBRPREP ;                /* process REPLACE statement   */
          ELSE
            IF UCM is for DUMP THEN
              CALL CBRPDMP ;              /* process DUMP statement      */
      IF return_code > final_return_code THEN
        final_return_code = return_code ;
    END ;
    set address of outparm in DSNR1 ;
    RETURN CODE ( final_return_code ) ;

CBRPLOC :
  PROC ;
    IF UCMLTPG = YES THEN                 /* IF UCM for LOCATE           */
      DO ;
        SET URRMPTR to UCMLURRM ;         /* get URRM ptr from first pass
                                                                         */
        SET BBRNO from URRMPAGE ;         /* SET page number             */
        IF REPLACE follows LOCATE THEN    /* URRMFREP = YES              */
          DO ;
            lock URRMPAGE , 'X' , COMMIT ;
          END ;
        ELSE
          DO ;
            lock URRMPAGE , 'S' , COMMIT ;
          END ;
        ?DSNBGETP BB ( URRMBB ) ;         /* read in page                */
        IF any error during DSNBGETP then
          DO ;
            CALL CBRPEMSG ( U386 ) ;      /* send 'tttttt I/O ERRORS'    */
            RETURN CODE ( xx ) ;
          END ;
        SET URRMRECA = BBPADDR ;          /* get address of page         */
        SET URRMRECL to length of page ;
        SET URRMFGPG = YES ;              /* indicate page was read      */
      END ;
  END CBRPLOC ;

CBRPVER :
```

MODULE C

TOP-DOWN PROGRAM DESIGN AND STRUCTURED PROGRAMMING

TOP-DOWN PROGRAM DESIGN

PSEUDOCODE

STRUCTURED PROGRAMMING
Sequence Structure
Selection Structure
Loop Structure

DISCUSSION

Opposite: Pseudocode is a program design aid used to express the detailed logic of a program.

UNIT THREE: COMPUTER PROGRAMMING AND DESIGN

In recent years, data processing personnel have been searching for new and improved program design techniques, ways to reduce the costs of program development and maintenance. With the use of traditional methods of program design, programming costs have continued to rise in relation to computer hardware and software costs. Many programmers consider programs to be personal creations. Programmers with this viewpoint often write programs that are complex and obscure. Such programs are hard for other programmers to understand. Even the original programmers may find their own programs difficult to understand months later. Such programs are also difficult to maintain, especially if they become the responsibility of other programmers. One approach to program design and coding that is receiving widespread attention is called *top-down program design*. It can provide the following benefits:

1. Program standardization should improve because design is emphasized.
2. Programmers are more productive; they write more program instructions per day and make fewer errors.
3. Program complexity is reduced; as a result, programs are easier to read, write, debug, and maintain.

TOP-DOWN PROGRAM DESIGN

When top-down program design is used, a program is divided into segments called *modules*. Each of these modules is independent of other modules in the program and performs a separate function. Emphasis is placed on the main functional modules first because they contain the highest-level control logic and are the most critical to the success of the program. These modules are designed, coded, and tested. Then the next-lower-level modules are created in the same manner. In this way, most of the details of the solution plan are left until the lowest-level modules are designed. Thus, a program developed by using a top-down design consists of modules created and related in a treelike (hierarchical) structure.

The treelike structural relationship between modules in a top-down-designed program can be shown in a *structure chart*. The structure chart shows each module and its functional relationships to other modules. The flow of control is from the highest-level module to the lowest-level modules (top-down). Each module is called, or invoked, by a next-higher-level module.

Illustration C-1 shows a structure chart with one level of processing modules. This structure chart is based on the update, order-writing, and invoicing portion of the system flowchart for the tape system shown in

MODULE C: TOP-DOWN PROGRAM DESIGN AND STRUCTURED PROGRAMMING

Illustration 7-12. The main module controls the execution of each processing module directly below it in the hierarchy. Thus, after the execution of each processing module ("Read master record" through "Print shipping order and invoice"), control returns to the main module.

There can be as many levels of processing modules as needed in a program. Two lower levels of processing modules have been added to the update, order-writing, and invoicing program in Illustration C-2. Notice that the "Update master record" module is now both a processing module and a control module; it causes execution of the "Read master record"

ILLUSTRATION C-1 Structure chart for update, order-writing, and invoicing program

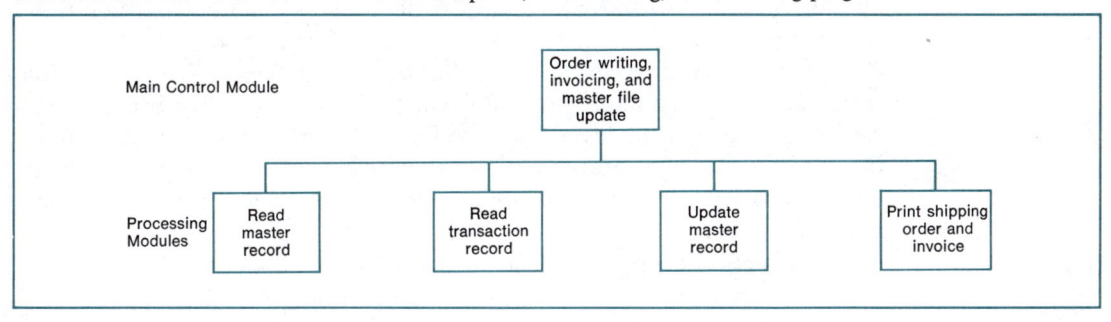

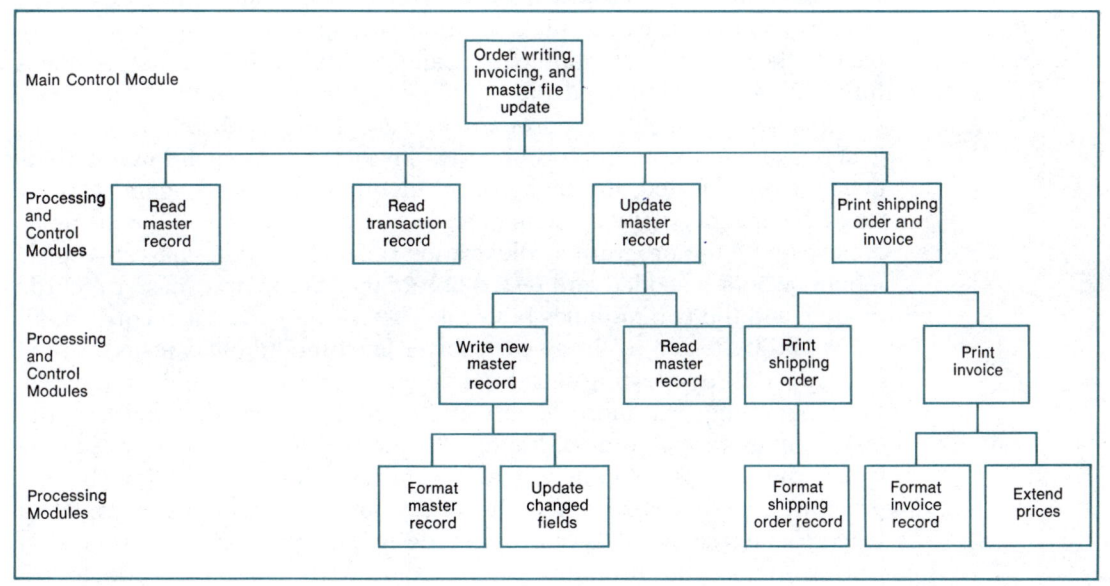

ILLUSTRATION C-2 Structure chart for update, order-writing, and invoicing program with three levels of processing modules

and "Write new master record" modules. The "Write new master record" module is also a processing and control module; it controls two processing modules directly below it. As this example suggests, a structure chart can be an effective alternative to a system flowchart when top-down program design is used.

Some basic guidelines should be followed when using top-down design to develop program modules. Each module should have only one entrance and one exit point so that the flow of control is easy to follow. The segmentation of a program should be done so that the program modules relate to each other in a treelike manner with control passing from the top down. Each module should represent a single program function. For example, each module in Illustration C-1 does a single stated function (read master record, read transaction record, and so forth). A module should not exceed one page of program code, that is, about 50 lines. When a module is contained on one page, program readability is enhanced. It is not necessary to look through several pages of code to understand the function of the module. Many programmers find that modules limited to a single page each are easier to test and debug than programs coded in the traditional manner.

The higher-level modules of a program are coded and tested first. These are followed by the next-lower-level modules. When a module is tested, it calls (attempts to execute) the modules that it controls (the modules directly below it in the hierarchy). Since these lower modules are not yet coded, *dummy modules* must be created for testing purposes. Each dummy module takes the place of an actual module and passes control back to the higher-level module that calls it so that testing of that module's function can be completed.

By coding and testing a program in this manner, each level of modules is debugged and tested before the next lower level. As each lower level is debugged and tested, the higher-level modules are tested again. This insures that the most critical, main modules are tested the most. For instance, in developing the program in Illustration C-2, the "Update master record" module would be coded and tested before the "Write new master record" module and the two modules below it. The "Update master record" module would be tested again as each lower-level module was tested.

By coding and testing each module separately and from the top down, the programmer can more readily isolate errors to specific modules. The task of finding errors is also simplified because the programmer need only look at the one page of code for each suspect module. The result is that the program is fully tested when the lowest-level modules are completed. Using traditional methods of program design, the programmer often must work with an entire program, possibly thousands of lines of code, to isolate, locate, and correct errors.

PSEUDOCODE

During the initial design phase of a program development project, each major module is identified and then further subdivided into lower-level modules. It has already been shown that a structure chart can be used to identify and show relationships between program modules. After the structure chart has been completed, and possibly redrawn several times, the detailed program design must be completed. This means that each module shown in the structure chart must be designed in enough detail to allow it to be coded in a programming language. A program flowchart could be used for this purpose. Several other design aids are also available. One of these is pseudocode.

Pseudocode is a program design aid that serves the same function as a program flowchart in expressing the detailed logic of a program. Many persons have insisted for some time that a program flowchart is often an inadequate tool for expressing the control flow and logic of a program. When using pseudocode, programmers express their thoughts as English-language statements. These statements can be used as a guide when coding and testing the program. Because there are no rigid rules to follow when using pseudocode, programmers can express the logic of programs in a natural manner. There is no need to conform to the rules of a particular programming language at this stage. For clarity, certain capitalized "structured words" (DO, ENDDO, IF-THEN-ELSE, ENDIF, DOWHILE, DOUNTIL) are used to express the major program functions. All other pseudocode is written in lower case. The structure words become the basis for writing the program using a technique called *structured programming* (see below).

An important point to remember is that the pseudocode is usually thrown away once the program is coded and tested. In other words, pseudocode is only used as a guide for coding and testing a program. Because the code for a structured program should be easy to read and understand, the final documentation for a structured program should consist of the structure chart plus the program code itself.

STRUCTURED PROGRAMMING

Structured programming is an approach to programming that (1) facilitates program development, (2) improves program clarity—the ease with which a person unfamiliar with the program, including possibly the original programmer, can read the code and determine what is occurring, and (3) simplifies program debugging.

A structured program is written using only three basic control structures: sequence, selection, and loop. Each of these structures has a single entry point and a single exit. The program listing is easy to read because there is no random branching (forward or backward) from one part of the program to another part. Since control flows from top to bottom, the listing can be read more or less like a book. The program logic is easy to follow.

Sequence Structure

The *sequence structure* (DO pattern) is simply recognition of the fact that program statements are generally executed in the order in which they are stored in the computer. Thus in Illustration C-3, the statements in function A will be executed before the statements in function B.

As indicated in Illustration C-3, control simply flows from function A to function B in this program segment. This is good programming practice. Branching to another function should be avoided. One of the objectives of structured programming is to eliminate branches out of a sequence structure. When there are branches, it is more difficult for the programmer to follow the program logic. Therefore, program debugging and maintenance are harder.

Selection Structure

The *selection structure* allows a choice between two program paths based on the outcome of a test, as shown in Illustration C-4. If the test condition is true, function A is done. If it is false, function B is done. The selection structure is also called the IF-THEN-ELSE pattern. It can be expressed directly in many programming languages.

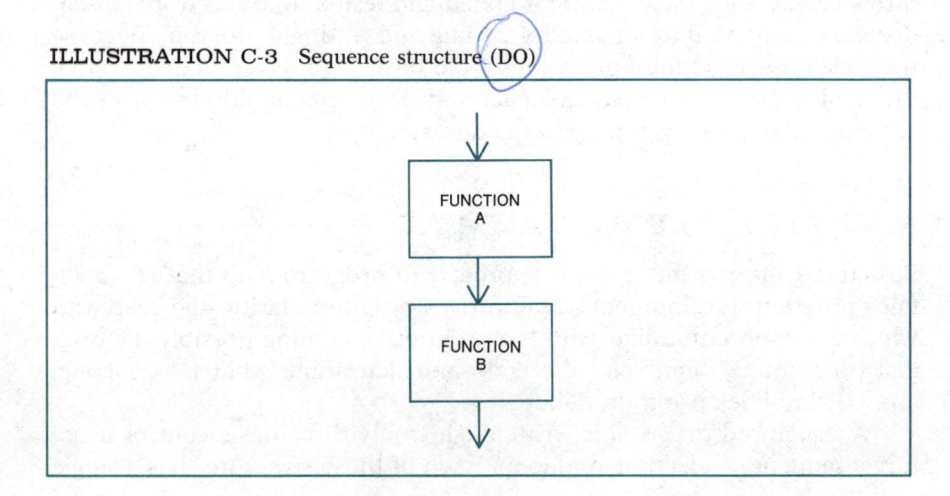

ILLUSTRATION C-3 Sequence structure (DO)

Loop Structure

The *loop structure* provides for performing a function *while* a condition is true.

The basic form of this structure is called the DOWHILE pattern. It is shown in Illustration C-5. The flow of control in the DOWHILE loop can be described as *"do* function A *while* condition B is true." In this type of structure, function A may never be executed because condition B may be false when it is first tested.

ILLUSTRATION C-4 Selection structure (IF-THEN-ELSE)

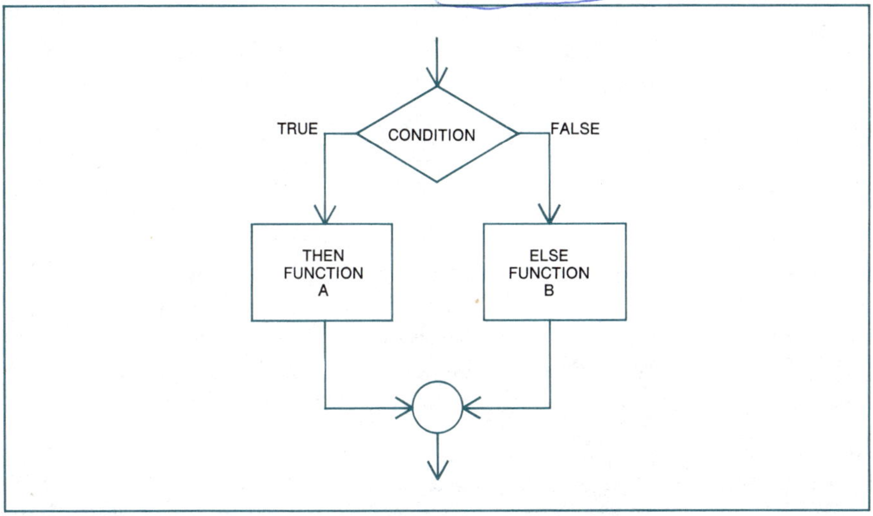

ILLUSTRATION C-5 Loop structure (DOWHILE)

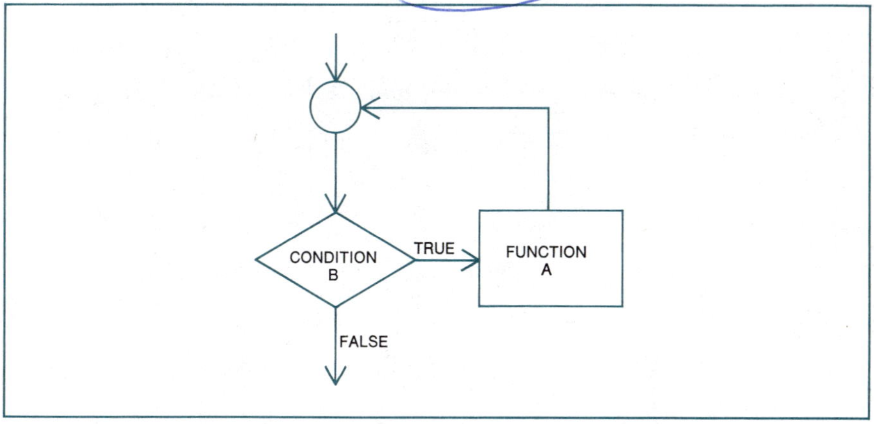

A variation of the loop structure is the DOUNTIL pattern. In this pattern, the processing steps in the loop are executed at least once (see Illustration C-6). The pattern here is *"do* function A *until* condition B is true."

Structured programming can be used with programming languages available today. It is easier to implement the basic patterns of structured programming in some languages than in others. These languages include statements that represent directly some or all of the patterns. In the other languages, a number of statements may be required to represent each pattern.

Illustration C-7 is an example of program logic expressed in pseudocode form. The structured-programming control structures are pointed out by the capitalized structured words. The functional details are written in lower case. A portion of the Procedure division of a structured COBOL program coded from this pseudocode is shown in Illustration C-8.

○ **DISCUSSION**

Structured programming has come to mean more than the use of the control structures just discussed. Most programmers find that to use structured programming effectively, they must design their programs using a top-down approach. A goal of top-down program design is to create independent program modules. Each module is to have one entry point and one exit point. This goal can be achieved using structured program-

ILLUSTRATION C-6 Variation of the loop structure (DOUNTIL)

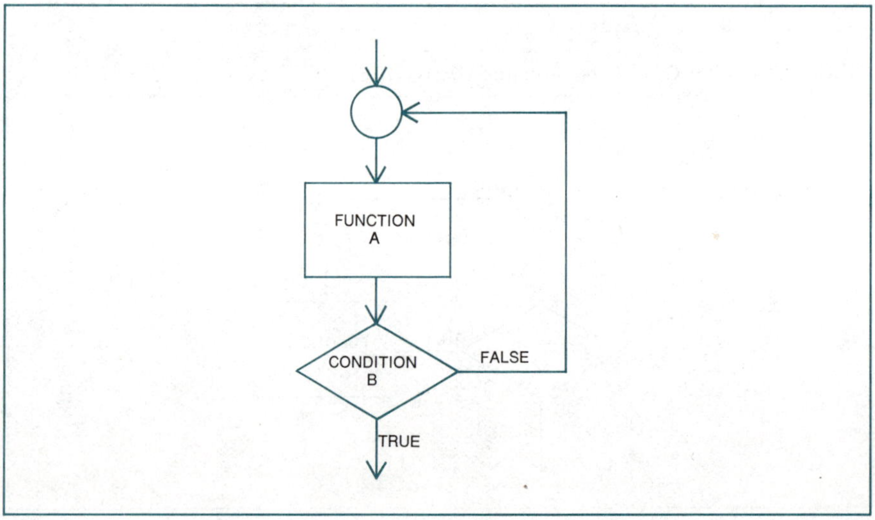

MODULE C: TOP-DOWN PROGRAM DESIGN AND STRUCTURED PROGRAMMING

```
Open files
Read first record (heading)
Initialize program variables
DOUNTIL no more text records
    Read text record
    DOUNTIL no more words in text record
        Extract next text word
        Search word table for extracted word
        IF extracted word found
        THEN
            increment word's occurrence count
        ELSE
            insert extracted word in word table
        ENDIF
        Increment words-processed count
    ENDDO (end of words in text record)
ENDDO (end of text records)
Print word table and summary information
Close files
Terminate program
```

ILLUSTRATION C-7 Pseudocode for word-frequency analysis program

[handwritten note: indentations shows where Loops begin ete!!!]

ming. Thus, these techniques are often used together. Top-down program design, top-down coding, top-down testing, the use of pseudocode for documentation, and structured coding are a set of techniques that programmers generally refer to as structured programming. The goal of all of these techniques is to make programs easier to write, read, debug, and maintain, thus making programmers more productive. The techniques are being used with positive results at many data processing installations.

○ SUMMARY

1. Traditional methods of program design and coding rely primarily on the creativity of the programmer. They have often resulted in programs that are complex and difficult to read. New program design and coding techniques have been developed in an effort to reduce program development and maintenance costs. Among these techniques are top-down program design and structured programming.

2. The focus of top-down program design is to divide a program into functional modules. The programmer designs the main module first and then designs lower-level modules. The programmer uses structure

```
PROCEDURE DIVISION.
WORD-FREQUENCY-MAIN-ROUTINE.
    PERFORM INITIALIZATION.
    PERFORM TEXT-PROCESSING
        UNTIL LAST-RECORD-PROCESSED.
    PERFORM PRINT-TABLE.
    PERFORM TERMINATION.
    STOP RUN.

INITIALIZATION.
    OPEN INPUT  INPUT-FILE,
         OUTPUT PRINT-FILE.
    READ INPUT-FILE INTO HEADING-LINE-TEXT.
    MOVE 0 TO WORDS-PROCESSED.
    MOVE 0 TO UNIQUE-WORDS.
    PERFORM INITIALIZE-WORD-TABLE.

TEXT-PROCESSING.
    READ INPUT-FILE,
        AT END MOVE '1' TO LAST-RECORD-PROCESSED.
    PERFORM EXTRACT-NEXT-WORD
        UNTIL LAST-WORD-PROCESSED.

PRINT-TABLE.
    MOVE WORDS-PROCESSED TO HI-WORDS-PROCESSED.
    MOVE UNIQUE-WORDS TO HI-NUMBER-OF-WORDS.
    MOVE 99 TO PRINT-LINE-COUNTER.
    PERFORM TABLE-PRINT-LOOP
        VARYING TABLE-INDEX FROM 1 BY 1
            UNTIL TABLE-INDEX = NUMBER-OF-ENTRIES.

TERMINATION.
    CLOSE  INPUT-FILE,
           PRINT-FILE.

INITIALIZE-WORD-TABLE.
    •
    •
    •

EXTRACT-NEXT-WORD.
    •
    •
      PERFORM TABLE-SEARCH
        UNTIL HIT-OR-EOT.
    •
    •

TABLE-PRINT-LOOP.
    •
    •

TABLE-SEARCH.
    •
    •
```

ILLUSTRATION C-8 COBOL Procedure division coding of the higher-level modules of the word-frequency analysis program

charts to show the program modules and their relationships. The purpose of a structure chart is to provide a clear view of the flow of control in a program and the purpose of each program module.

3. When using a top-down approach, the programmer codes the higher-level modules first and tests them. Then lower-level modules are coded and tested. Program debugging is easier because errors can be isolated to specific modules.

4. A program can be developed using pseudocode as a guide. The program is first written in pseudocode. In this step, the programmer represents the structured logic of a program but avoids the details of a specific programming language. The pseudocode then serves the same function as a program flowchart when the program is written in a programming language (the actual code).

5. Structured programming is a set of techniques using control structures for program coding. The control structures simplify program coding and establish coding standards that make programs easier to read. The three basic control structures are sequence, selection, and loop.

REVIEW QUESTIONS

1. List three benefits of top-down program design.
2. What is a program module?
3. What is the purpose of a structure chart?
4. Explain the guidelines that should be followed when top-down program design is used.
5. Why does top-down design make it easier to locate program errors?
6. Why are the most critical program modules the most frequently tested when top-down program design is used?
7. How is pseudocode used in program design?
8. What is structured programming?
9. What are the three basic control structures used in structured programming?

```
10  REM INVENTORY PROBLEM WHICH CALCULATES SALES, ENDING INVENTORY AND LOST
20  REM SALES KNOWING BEGINNING INVENTORY AND DEMAND.
30  REM X = PRODUCT
40  REM B = BEGINNING INVENTORY
50  REM D = DEMAND
60  REM E = ENDING INVENTORY
70  REM L = LOST SALES
80  PRINT SPA(17);"BEG";SPA(26);"END";SPA(5);"LOST"
90  PRINT SPA(5);"PRODUCT      INV      DEMAND      SALES      INV      SALES"
100 PRINT SPA(5);"-------      ---      ------      -----      ---      -----"
110 FOR I=1 TO 3
120 READ X,B,D
130 IF D>B THEN 160
140 S=D
150 GOTO 170
160 S=B
170 E=B-S
180 L=D-S
190 PRINT TAB(5);X;SPA(3);B;SPA(3);D;SPA(5);S;SPA(3);E;SPA(3);L
200 NEXT I
210 DATA 1001,80,27,1002,70,82,1003,30,30
220 END
```

| | BEG | | | END | LOST |
PRODUCT	INV	DEMAND	SALES	INV	SALES
1001	80	27	27	53	0
1002	70	82	70	0	12
1003	30	30	30	0	0

CHAPTER 11

AN OVERVIEW OF PROGRAMMING LANGUAGES

MACHINE LANGUAGE

MACHINE-ORIENTED ASSEMBLER (SYMBOLIC) LANGUAGE

MACRO-INSTRUCTIONS

HIGH-LEVEL PROGRAMMING LANGUAGES
Procedure-Oriented and
Problem-Oriented Languages
FORTRAN
COBOL
BASIC
RPG

LANGUAGE SELECTION

Opposite: BASIC is a popular language that may be used on most minicomputers.

Now that the reader has a basic understanding of the components of a computer system and of the programming tasks required to direct it, the types of computer languages and their characteristics should be discussed. If computer languages did not exist, a computer would be nothing more than a relatively expensive piece of machinery. The computer hardware must be applied in conjunction with computer software before the major benefits of this tool can be realized.

As noted in Chapter 4, the development of computers can be divided into generations that roughly correspond to specific developments of computer hardware. The same division can be applied to the development of specific types of computer languages. The first generation of computer languages is represented by *machine languages*, which are closely tied to the design of the computer. In the second generation, *machine-oriented assembler* (*symbolic*) *languages* were developed and *macro-instructions* came into use. The third generation was marked by the creation of several *high-level programming languages*. These languages can be divided into (1) *procedure-oriented languages* such as FORmula TRANslator (FORTRAN), COmmon Business Oriented Language (COBOL), and Beginners' All-purpose Symbolic Instruction Code (BASIC); and (2) *problem-oriented languages* such as Report Program Generator (RPG).

MACHINE LANGUAGE

Machine languages were first developed during the infant stage of computer development. They are closely tied to specific machines (that is, types of computers). Thus, the term *machine language* denotes the principle characteristic of these languages. A machine language consists of instructions that vary with the requirements and the design of the machine being used.

A machine-language instruction includes an *operation code* (*op code*) and an *operand* (usually, the address(es) of data on which an operation is to be performed). Since the computer stores every instruction in binary form, in absolute terms, a machine-language instruction consists of a string of zeros and ones (although an octal, hexadecimal, or binary coded decimal equivalent may be used in coding). The programmer must write an instruction to control each operation to be performed. Therefore, a one-to-one relationship exists between the instructions coded by the programmer and the performance of operations by the computer. The complete list of instructions is known as an *object program*.

The relationship between machine-language instructions (the object program) and the computer is shown in Illustration 11-1. An object program can be executed by a computer without first being translated; it is

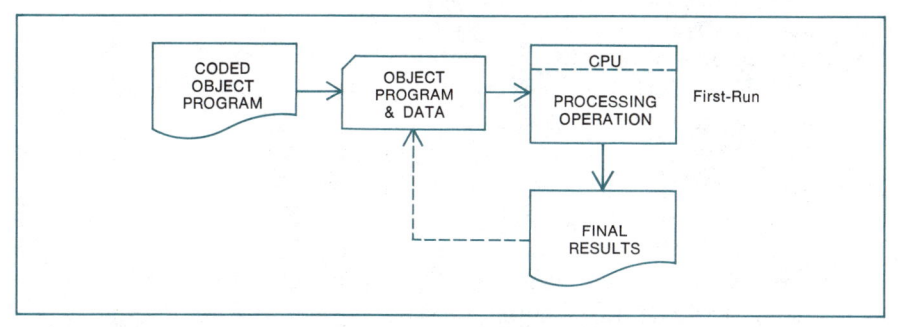

ILLUSTRATION 11-1 Processing cycle for a machine-language program

machine-understandable. The instructions are keyed and loaded into main storage to control subsequent processing steps. No translation process is necessary because the object program can be acted upon by the computer.

There are, however, a number of obvious disadvantages in the use of machine language. First, the programming aspects of a machine-language program are extremely tedious. As a programmer writes the program, the addresses of storage locations containing data to be operated on, as well as the addresses of instructions in the program, must be recorded. Such clerical details, in addition to the design of the program itself, take much of the programmer's time and attention.

Second, besides keeping track of addresses, the programmer has to remember numeric op codes. The programmer has to write the numeric op code for each operation that the computer must perform.

Third, if an error is discovered in the results produced by the program, the programmer has to tediously examine each instruction in order to find the point where the error occurred. If a correction entails more than removal of keying errors, any addition to, or deletion from, the program may mean that all instructions from the location of the error to the end of the program have to be changed. Since machine-language instructions are normally executed sequentially, from first to last, without interruption, the address of each instruction from the point of the insertion or deletion must be altered to reflect the modification. Any references to these instructions throughout the program must be changed.

Fourth, the programmer is not able to use any parts of previously written programs when coding a new program. Each program is written totally independent of any other program with which the programmer is familiar. If this were not the case, considerable time could be saved in coding.

Finally, the programmer must have a detailed knowledge of the computer on which the program is to be executed. If the type of computer is changed, the programmer must become familiar with the new machine. Any existing programs must be rewritten for the new machine.

All of these disadvantages can probably be summed up by saying that the design and development of a machine-language program is very time-consuming and, consequently, extremely expensive. The use of machine language for today's applications is impractical.

There are two basic advantages in using machine language. First, it can be an extremely efficient method of using the storage capacity of a computer. Second, the speed of processing is aided by the fact that no conversion (from another computer language to machine language) is necessary. However, the disadvantages of machine language so outweigh its advantages that little if any coding of programs in machine language is done today.

MACHINE-ORIENTED ASSEMBLER (SYMBOLIC) LANGUAGE

Because machine-language programming was tedious, time-consuming, and costly, efforts were made to alleviate the coding problem. In the early 1950s, the problem was partially solved by the introduction of a machine-oriented assembler (symbolic) language. The use of assembler language was possible because of a software aid called an *assembler program*, or *assembler*. The assembler program performed the task of recording (remembering and using) the address of each unit in the program, thus relieving the programmer of many clerical chores. In addition, the assembler allowed the use of *symbolic names*, or *mnemonics* (abbreviations of Englishlike words and acronyms), instead of numerical designations, for machine operations.

An assembler-language instruction is broken into three distinct segments. The first segment is the *label*, or tag (see Illustration 11-2). It rep-

ILLUSTRATION 11-2   Parts of an assembler-language instruction

A COMPLETE INSTRUCTION		
LABEL	OP CODE	OPERAND

resents the first storage location of the instruction to which it is attached. The label serves two purposes: (1) as an aid to the programmer in locating specific instructions in the program coding, and (2) as a point of reference when branching within the program is required.

The second segment of an assembler-language instruction is the op code (operation code). While labels can be mnemonics, the major advantage of the use of mnemonics is in the area of op codes. A set of mnemonics to be used as op codes is explicitly defined within the assembler language. These symbolic names replace their numerical counterparts in machine language. READ, ADD, and COMP (rather than strings of digits) may represent the input of data, the addition of data, and the comparison of two data fields, respectively. The programmer soon becomes familiar with the mnemonic op codes. The burden of memorizing and writing numerical representations of operations is removed.

The third part of an assembler-language instruction is the operand. It contains the addresses that are relevant to the op code of the instruction. In machine language, the addresses are given in binary form, but in assembler language, the addresses are stated in decimal or mnemonic form. Since the programmer does not have to write actual (also called absolute) addresses, this task is much easier. The programmer specifies (or reserves) the first storage location used for the program. The assembler assigns other addresses sequentially from the given point of reference.

The one-to-one relationship between an instruction and an operation exists in assembler language as in machine language. However, the one-to-one relationship takes on an additional meaning in assembler language: There is only one line of coding for each instruction. A single machine-language instruction may require many lines of coding.

One additional technique is used to provide the program with data and constants. It is called a ***declarative operation***, or simply a ***declarative***. It is similar to the assembler-language instruction described above (sometimes called an ***imperative***) in that it contains a label and operands. But it differs from an imperative instruction in that it contains a declarative op code. The op code signals the computer that data is to be placed in storage at the address stated in the operand. No action is performed on the data until it is referred to by an imperative instruction in another part of the program.

All of the instructions of an assembler-language program, organized into one unit, are called a ***source program***. A source program differs from the object program derived from machine-language instructions in that it must be translated into machine language before it can be executed by the computer. As Illustration 11-3 shows, the source program enters the central processing unit (CPU) and is translated into its object-program counterpart under the supervision of an assembler program.

UNIT THREE: COMPUTER PROGRAMMING AND DESIGN

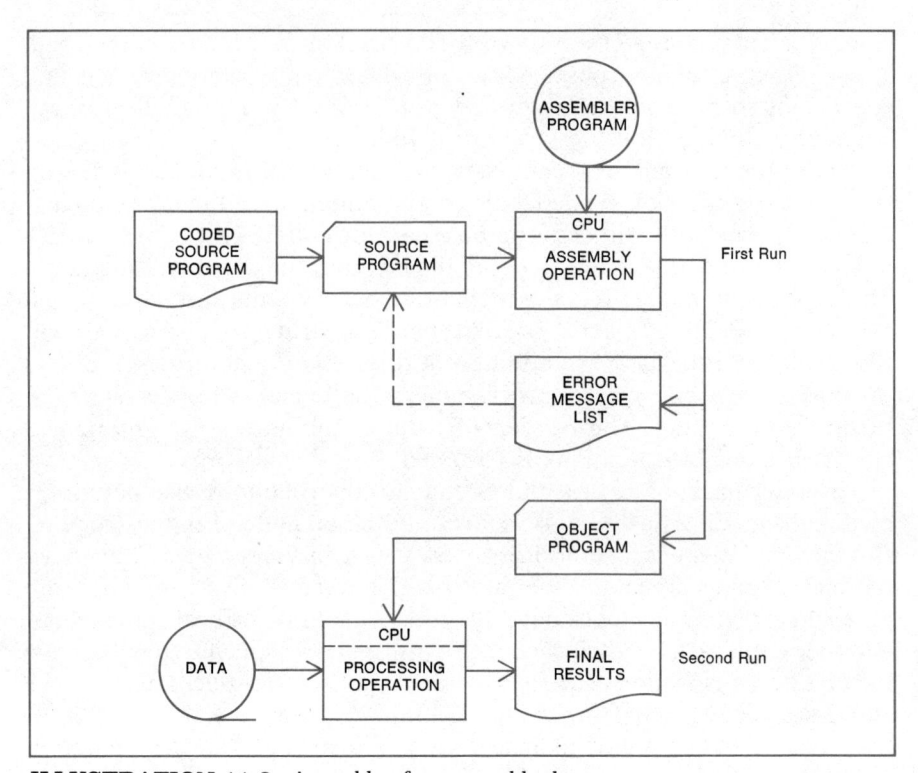

ILLUSTRATION 11-3 Assembly of an assembler-language program

The conversion from assembler language to machine language takes place in two parts. First, the mnemonic op codes used in the source program are replaced by machine-language equivalents. The assembler performs this step by referring to a table composed of all available mnemonic op codes and the corresponding machine-language operations. Second, the addresses used in the source program, which are stated as decimal digits or mnemonics, are transformed into equivalent actual addresses.

In addition to the object program, the assembler provides an error message list (recall "Program Debugging and Testing" in Chapter 10). It can detect errors due to violations of *syntax* (the grammatical correctness of instruction structure), instructions that are out of sequence, references to nonexistent parts of the program, and illegal mnemonic op codes. In some cases, the assembler is designed to overlook minor errors such as one wrong letter in a mnemonic op code. The assembler either corrects or accepts these minor errors. It continues to scan the source program and

CHAPTER 11: AN OVERVIEW OF PROGRAMMING LANGUAGES

detects other possible errors, but it may not generate an object program. Under most conditions, the errors are of such a nature that the object program, if generated, would be worthless to the programmer. The error message list provides a means by which the programmer is alerted to errors. The programmer can correct the errors and resubmit the source program.

When the source program satisfies all checks made by the assembler during translation, the object program is generated. It can be used in the second stage of attaining final results. (See the second run in Illustration 11-3.) This time the object program is executed; that is, problem-related data is provided as input, and processing takes place. The computer enacts the machine-language operations and generates the final results, or output.

There are a number of advantages to using machine-oriented assembler language rather than machine language. First, the programmer can employ easy-to-remember symbolic names, or mnemonics, in place of machine-language operation codes. In addition, the use of labels, or tags, makes the task of referring to instructions (say, for branching) easier. Second, the assembly operation provides an error message list that can be used in making corrections to the source program. Finally, since the computer adjusts addresses automatically when the source program is translated (assembled), the program can be modified without having to rewrite many instructions as is often required when a change is made to a machine-language program.

Although assembler language saves vast amounts of programmer time and effort previously required for clerical tasks, it shares one major disadvantage with machine language. The programmer is still not able to use parts of previously written programs in a new program. Each instruction has to be written individually.

○ MACRO-INSTRUCTIONS

To eliminate the necessity to write one line of coding for each operation, macro-instructions were introduced. Programmers noticed that many series of instructions appeared repeatedly in different programming projects. These instructions were always in the same sequence and were designed to accomplish the same objective in each use. As a result, a specific sequence of assembler-language instructions, or *routine*, was established for each objective and placed in a library of *macros* (macro operation codes). Then when a specific routine was required in a program, the programmer inserted a certain macro-instruction to cause the routine in the library to be referred to. The macro-instruction generated a number of assembler-language instructions. This broke the one-to-one relationship between the programmer's lines of coding and computer operations that existed previously.

A basic advantage of macro-instructions is that the use of a macro reduces the duplication of instructions and, therefore, the amount of coding required on the part of the programmer. A second advantage, derived from the reduction in coding, is that there is less chance of error.

Of course, there may be some highly repetitive routines for which no macro-instructions exist, but the programmer is not at a complete loss in this situation. The programmer can write new macros and insert them into the library of macro operation codes. The macro-instructions defined in this manner can be used just like others, whenever they are required.

○ HIGH-LEVEL PROGRAMMING LANGUAGES

Assembler language represents the second stage in the development of programming languages. It is closely related to machine language and is thought of as a *low-level programming language*. After assembler language and macro-instructions, a number of languages were developed. The designers of these languages took the idea of macro-instructions one step further; they created complete macro-instruction languages. Every statement (instruction) in these languages generates one or more routines to perform needed operations. As a group, the languages are known as *high-level programming languages*. They are not closely related to machine instructions. In fact, a programmer does not have to have a detailed knowledge of a computer to write programs in a high-level language.

Recall that an assembler-language program (also called a source program) is translated into machine language (an object program) by an assembler (see Illustration 11-3). The procedure of translating a source program coded in a high-level language into machine language (an object program) is very similar. It is shown in Illustration 11-4. The assembler is replaced by a *compiler* or *generator*, depending on the high-level language used. A compiler examines a program statement written by the programmer and converts it into one or more machine-language instructions. When using a generator language, the programmer does not write program statements; rather, the programmer describes what is needed in more general terms, through specifications. The generator creates the instructions needed to provide the final results.

Since a specific compiler or generator is developed for each high-level programming language, the language may also be called either a *compiler language* or a *generator language*. Like an assembler, both compilers and generators are software aids. They are often written by computer manufacturers and made available with computers.

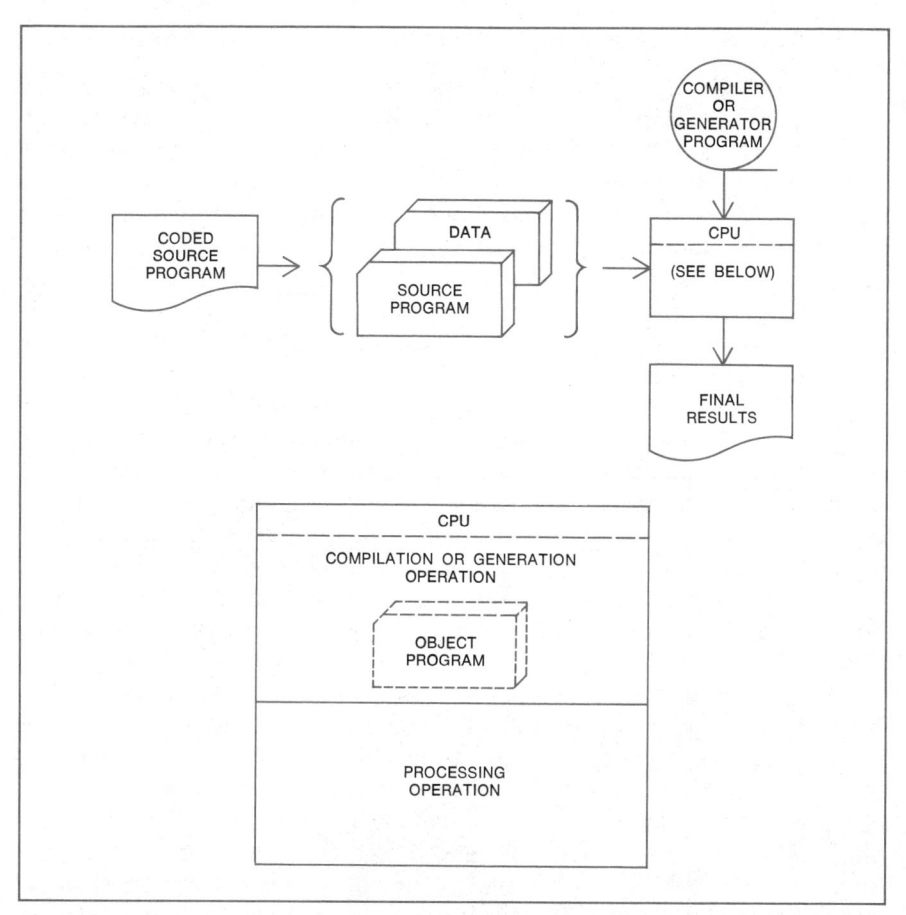

CHAPTER 11: AN OVERVIEW OF PROGRAMMING LANGUAGES

ILLUSTRATION 11-4 Compilation or generation of a high-level-language program

The processing steps of high-level languages differ from those of assembler language. The basic difference is that the data for a high-level-language program is often submitted with the source program, whereas it is maintained separately for an assembler-language program. The translation process also differs. While it is possible to compile or generate the source deck (data and source program, punched into cards) and produce an object deck (object program, punched into cards), the object program is usually stored within the CPU for subsequent use rather than punched into cards. Thus, with one submission of the program, assuming that all serious errors have been eliminated, the final results of program execution can be obtained.

Procedure-Oriented and Problem-Oriented Languages

The separation of high-level languages into procedure-oriented languages (such as FORTRAN, COBOL, and BASIC) and problem-oriented languages (such as RPG) was noted at the beginning of this chapter. Basically, a procedure-oriented language consists of a system of computational procedures designed to solve a problem. A problem-oriented language is descriptive in nature; it is used to describe problems. All high-level languages that require a compiler are procedure-oriented languages. As a group, however, high-level languages are sometimes referred to as problem-oriented (in contrast to machine-oriented). They are designed for ease of use in problem solving.

There are many basic advantages of high-level programming languages. First, as previously mentioned, these languages reduce the amount of coding. Second, they are easy to learn. Third, they are *machine-independent*; that is, programs written in any of these languages can be executed on a wide range of computers with little or no alteration. Fourth, the programs are easy to document since special provisions for documentation accompany each language. Finally, they are easy to update or maintain because revisions are possible without extensive rewriting of affected code.

High-level languages possess at least two disadvantages. First, high-level-language programs usually take longer to execute than comparative low-level-language programs. The translation process is extensive and generates many machine-language instructions. Second, some of the machine operations that a computer is capable of performing are not implemented in high-level languages. The languages were designed around basic, commonly employed routines. Some operations have been deemed impractical to implement thus far because of a general lack of need. But, these languages are constantly undergoing updates and changes. Therefore this disadvantage may be less critical in the future.

FORTRAN

In the mid 1950s, a group was organized to create a computer language that would easily lend itself to arithmetic computation. The group was headed by John Backus of IBM. By 1956, they had developed a language known as FORTRAN (an acronym for FORmula TRANslator). A FORTRAN compiler consisting of 25,000 lines of coding was ready to be tested. More than two years of effort and an estimated investment of over $2 million had been expended on the project.

In 1957, the first tests of the new compiler were conducted. By the end of that year, a number of minor errors had appeared. This prompted IBM to release a new version of the language, called FORTRAN II, in 1958. The same year, IBM also released a new FORTRAN compiler system as a complement to new hardware developments. Other computer manufacturers began to develop versions of FORTRAN to accompany their machines. Among these were FORTRAN IV, FORTRANSIT, and FORTOCOM. It became obvious that standardization was necessary to bring uniformity into programmer training and to aid in the interchange of programs. In 1962, the United States of America Standards Institute (USASI), now called the American National Standards Institute (ANSI), took on the task of standardization. Out of this, in 1966, came two standard versions of FORTRAN. First, ANSI Basic FORTRAN, which is similar to FORTRAN II, was proposed. Second, ANSI FORTRAN, which is similar to FORTRAN IV, was introduced. The computer manufacturers followed this lead. Compilers capable of translating ANSI Basic FORTRAN and ANSI FORTRAN have been developed for most computers. In 1977, ANSI released a new version of ANSI FORTRAN. This version is commonly referred to as FORTRAN 77. Significant properties of both the subset FORTRAN 77 and the full FORTRAN 77 versions of the language, collectively referred to as FORTRAN, are discussed below.

The initial purpose of FORTRAN has not changed even though many versions of the language have been offered. The original definition of the language, *THE FORTRAN Automatic Coding System of the IBM 704 EDPM*, is as valid today as it was when stated in 1956:

> "The FORTRAN language is intended to be capable of expressing any problem of numerical computation. In particular, it deals easily with problems containing large sets of formulas and many variables, and it permits any variable to have up to three independent subscripts. However, for problems in which machine words have a logical rather than numerical meaning it is less than satisfactory, and it may fail entirely to express some such problems. Nevertheless, many logical operations not directly expressible in the FORTRAN language can be obtained by making use of provisions for incorporating library routines."

Thus, FORTRAN has evolved into a scientific-mathematical language, basically algebraic or algorithmic in nature. As such, the language is especially adaptable to research applications or analysis of problems in engineering, science, and business (for example, operations research or statistical analysis). However, there are some applications, especially in business, to which FORTRAN is not particularly well suited. In situations where large volumes of input and output must be dealt with, or extensive file maintenance is required, other languages should be considered.

The basic element in a FORTRAN program is the ***statement***. It corresponds to an instruction in assembler language. The types of statements that can be included in a FORTRAN program are divided into four categories: (1) input, (2) assignment, (3) output, and (4) control.

An ***input statement*** causes data recorded on an external medium, such as punched cards, magnetic tape, or magnetic disk, to be accepted by the computer. One basic type of input statement—the READ statement—is available in FORTRAN.

An ***assignment statement*** causes the computer to perform some computational or logical operation. Normally, a statement of this type consists of at least three parts: a receiving field, the symbol =, and an expression containing one or more operators and operands. Consider the arithmetic assignment statement A = B + C. Here A is the symbolic name which acts as a receiving field; B and C are symbolic names used as operands; and the symbol + is an operator. Obviously, many different assignment statements can be created by varying the expression portion of the statement (B + C). Other symbolic names, operators, or constants such as 1.0, 22., and the like, can be included. The receiving field can also be changed.

An ***output statement*** causes data that is stored internally to be recorded on some external medium, such as printer paper, punched cards, or magnetic tape. There are three basic types of output statements, the WRITE, PRINT, and PUNCH statements, that perform this type of operation.

Finally, FORTRAN ***control statements*** include the GO TO, IF, DO, and STOP statements. These statements cause the computer to branch from the normal sequence of operations, make comparisons of values, perform looping operations, and stop executing the program, respectively.

A FORTRAN program to process up to 100 employee pay records and print a listing of the results is shown in Illustration 11-5. The program contains at least one statement from each of the four basic types (input, assignment, output, and control). The numerals 1 and 2 are placed in column 6, the continuation column, of continuation lines for statements that are longer than one coding line.

COBOL

Up to the late 1950s, no computer language particularly suited to business applications had been developed. Assembler language and various special languages valid with specific computers were being used to solve business problems. In May of 1959, the Federal government of the United States, through the Department of Defense, decided to sponsor a committee to develop a language especially applicable to problems in a business environment. At first, this idea met with opposition. But the government stood firm in its determination to create such a language and pointed

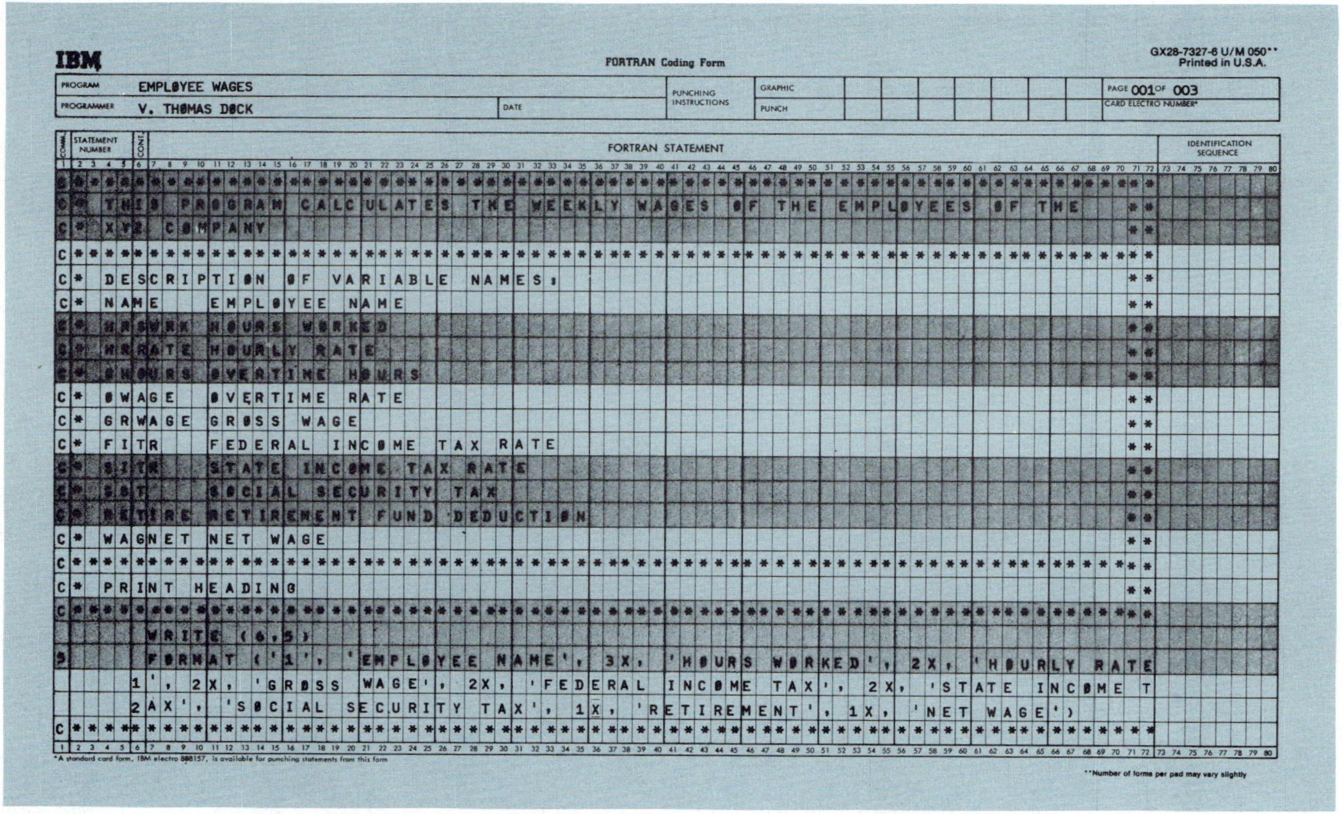

CHAPTER 11: AN OVERVIEW OF PROGRAMMING LANGUAGES

291

ILLUSTRATION 11-5   A FORTRAN program

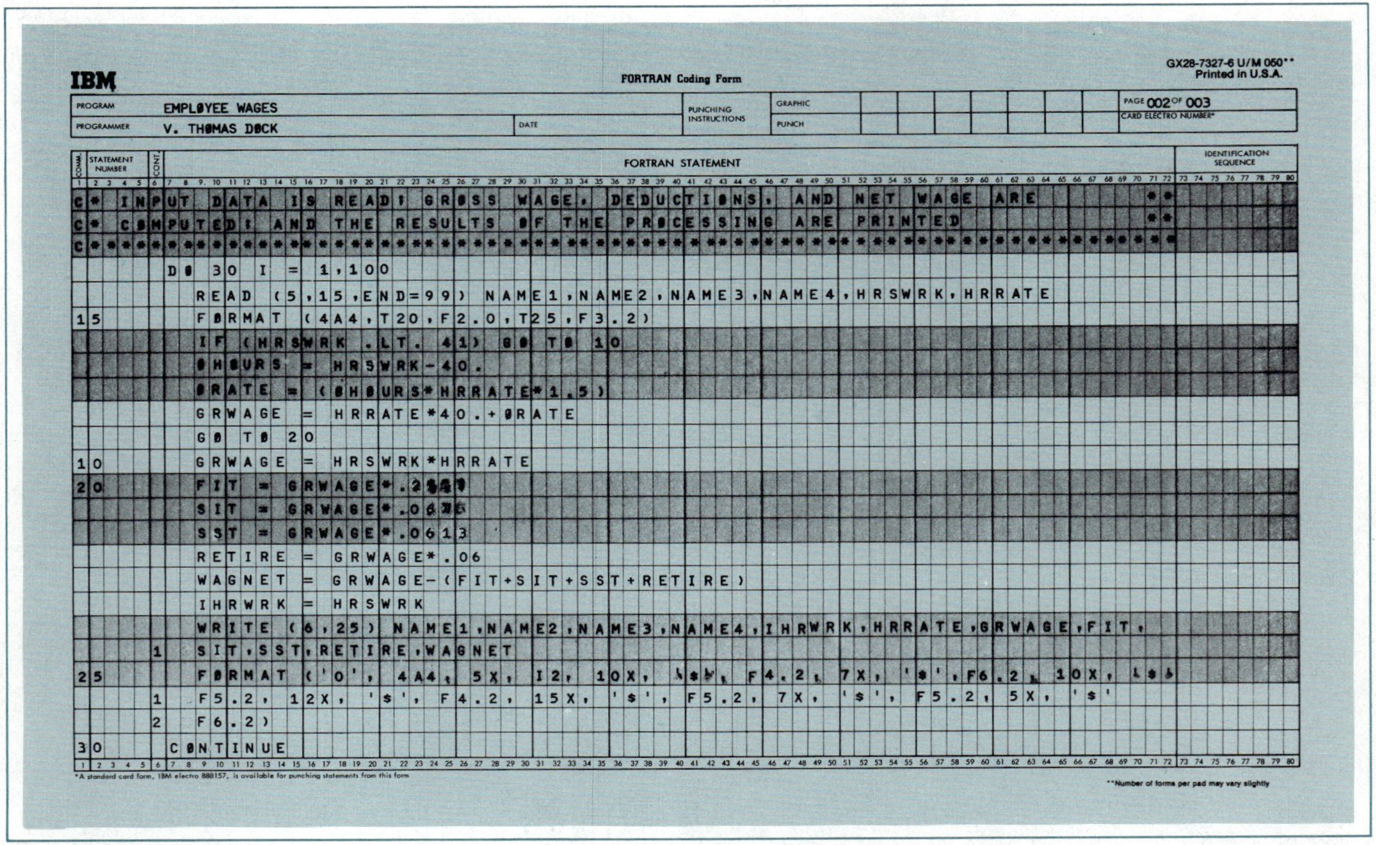

IBM FORTRAN Coding Form GX28-7327-6 U/M 050** Printed in U.S.A.

PROGRAM: EMPLØYEE WAGES
PROGRAMMER: V. THØMAS DØCK
PAGE 002 OF 003

```
C*  INPUT DATA IS READ; GRØSS WAGE, DEDUCTIØNS, AND NET WAGE ARE      **
C*  CØMPUTED; AND THE RESULTS ØF THE PRØCESSING ARE PRINTED           **
C*******************************************************************
      DØ 30 I = 1,100
        READ (5,15,END=99) NAME1,NAME2,NAME3,NAME4,HRSWRK,HRRATE
15      FØRMAT (4A4,T20,F2.0,T25,F3.2)
        IF (HRSWRK .LT. 41) GØ TØ 10
        ØHØURS = HRSWRK-40.
        ØRATE = (ØHØURS*HRRATE*1.5)
        GRWAGE = HRRATE*40.+ØRATE
        GØ TØ 20
10      GRWAGE = HRSWRK*HRRATE
20      FIT = GRWAGE*.2[illegible]
        SIT = GRWAGE*.06[illegible]
        SST = GRWAGE*.0613
        RETIRE = GRWAGE*.06
        WAGNET = GRWAGE-(FIT+SIT+SST+RETIRE)
        IHRWRK = HRSWRK
        WRITE (6,25) NAME1,NAME2,NAME3,NAME4,IHRWRK,HRRATE,GRWAGE,FIT,
     1  SIT,SST,RETIRE,WAGNET
25      FØRMAT ('0', 4A4, 5X, I2, 10X, '$', F4.2, 7X, '$',F6.2, 10X, '$'
     1  F5.2, 12X, '$', F4.2, 15X, '$', F5.2, 7X, '$', F5.2, 5X, '$'
     2  F6.2)
30    CØNTINUE
```

*A standard card form, IBM electro 888157, is available for punching statements from this form

**Number of forms per pad may vary slightly

ILLUSTRATION 11-5 A FORTRAN program (*continued*)

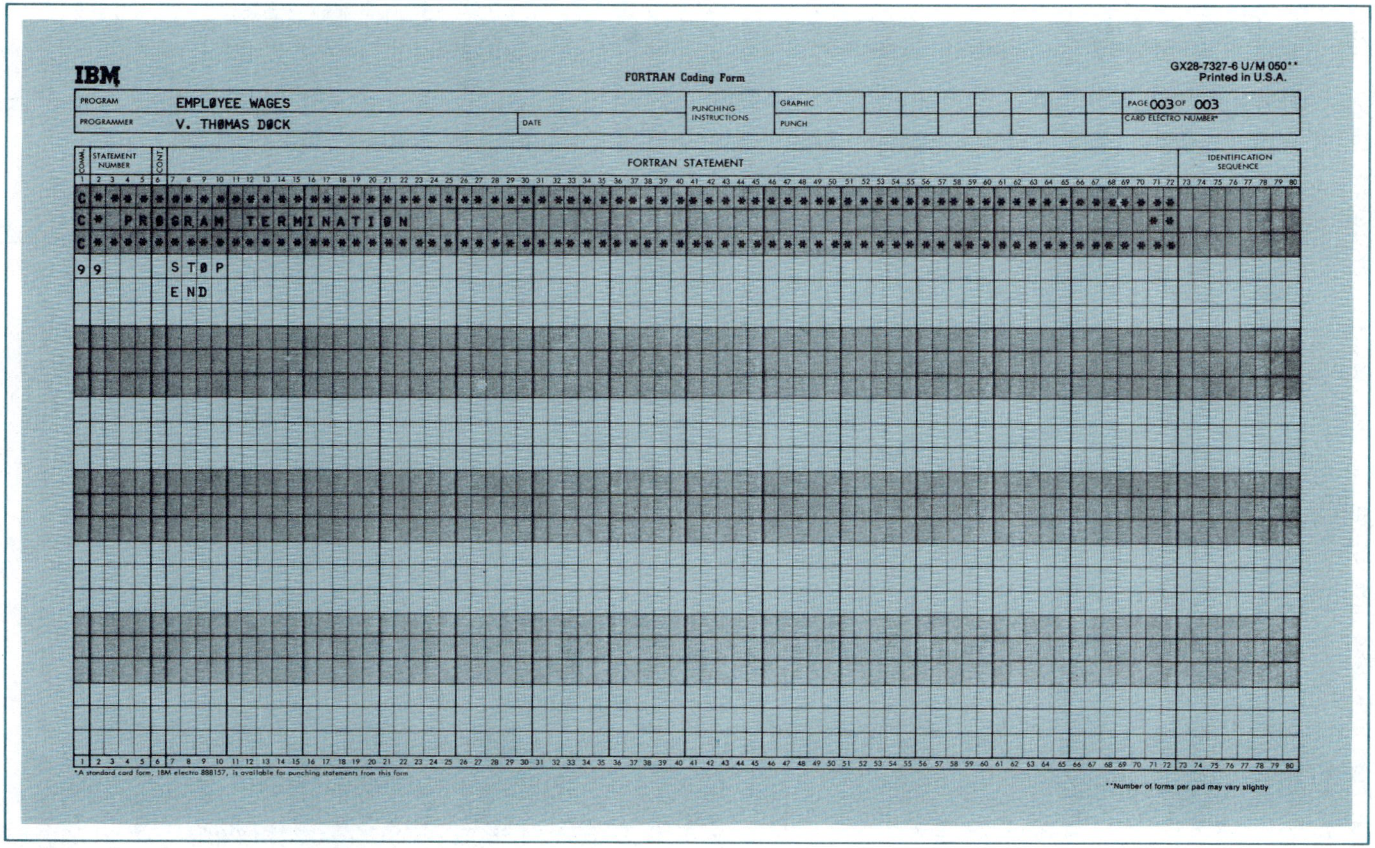

CHAPTER 11: AN OVERVIEW OF PROGRAMMING LANGUAGES

ILLUSTRATION 11-5 A FORTRAN program (*continued*)

out to computer manufacturers that the government was the largest single purchaser of computing equipment.

Under the guidance of the government, a committee was formed in 1959 to study the needs of business and develop an appropriate computer language. Representatives of business and of universities served as committee members. By December of 1959, the original specifications for COBOL (an acronym for COmmon Business Oriented Language) were completed. They were printed by the Government Printing Office in 1960. The design committee became known as **CODASYL** (*COnference of DAta SYstems Languages*). The first version of the language became known as COBOL-60.

To encourage full compliance with the project, in 1960, the Department of Defense announced that no lease or purchase contracts would be made for computers that did not possess the characteristics required for a COBOL compiler. Therefore, through some governmental pressure, computer manufacturers adopted a policy of designing their equipment so that COBOL compilers could be used.

Succeeding versions of COBOL were labeled by the year in which CODASYL made updates to the original specifications (1961, 1964, and 1965). Because of the many versions of COBOL available at different installations, the development of COBOL approached the same state as the development of FORTRAN. Therefore, ANSI again took on the challenge of setting up standards for a computer language. In 1968, ANSI (in conjunction with computer manufacturers and users) released American National Standard (ANS) COBOL. In 1974, a revised ANS COBOL standard was released.

COBOL offers several advantages. It is considered to be machine-independent. It employs much of the vocabulary of the business world and is written in Englishlike terms. Since it is Englishlike in nature, it tends to be self-documenting. No additional comments are necessary in a COBOL program. The program can be understood by programmers and by other business personnel as well. The language is relatively easy to learn. The COBOL compiler reduces the programming burden and provides diagnostics (error messages) that make program debugging easier. COBOL is well suited for the input and output operations commonly associated with business enterprises. Finally, the language can process alphabetic or alphameric information; this capability is extremely important because a significant portion of business data comprises other than numeric characters.

In keeping with the Englishlike nature of COBOL, the structure of the language is comparable to that of a book. The basic element of a COBOL program is the *sentence*. It is the COBOL counterpart to the statement in

FORTRAN. The next level in the structural hierarchy of the COBOL language is the *paragraph*. It is followed by *sections* and *divisions*, in order as named.

There are four divisions in a COBOL program. They are, in order of their occurrence in a program: (1) the IDENTIFICATION DIVISION, (2) the ENVIRONMENT DIVISION, (3) the DATA DIVISION, and (4) the PROCEDURE DIVISION. The IDENTIFICATION DIVISION identifies a program by requiring that, at a minimum, it be assigned a name. Additional information such as the author of the program, the installation at which it was written, the date it was written, the date it was compiled, security requirements, and remarks concerning the program may be provided. The COBOL program in Illustration 11-6 reads input and writes output similar to that of the FORTRAN program in Illustration 11-5. The IDENTIFICATION DIVISION of the program contains valuable program documentation.

The ENVIRONMENT DIVISION has two primary functions. First, it describes the type of computer that will compile and execute the program. Second, it relates each file used in the program with the input device from which the file is to be read or the output device on which the file is to be written. The DATA DIVISION describes in great detail all of the data to be processed by the program. It also shows the relationships that exist between data items. The PROCEDURE DIVISION contains the statements that instruct the computer in detail as to the specific operations it is to perform and the order in which it is to perform them.

BASIC

The acronym BASIC is derived from Beginners' All-purpose Symbolic Instruction Code. BASIC is similar to FORTRAN in many respects. It is an easy-to-learn high-level programming language, offering both numeric and alphabetic capabilities. The language was originally developed in the middle 1960s at Dartmouth College. It can be used for a variety of educational, engineering, mathematical, statistical, and business applications. The language is widely used by problem solvers working at terminals.

BASIC is an *interactive* (*conversational*) *language.* This feature of the language has several implications. First, a program and data can be entered into the computer, in parts, from a terminal. Second, the computer can request additional data during execution of the program. Third, one or more of the program statements can be changed from the terminal before execution of the program is completed. Thus, program statements and data can be changed, added, or deleted during execution of a program. Finally,

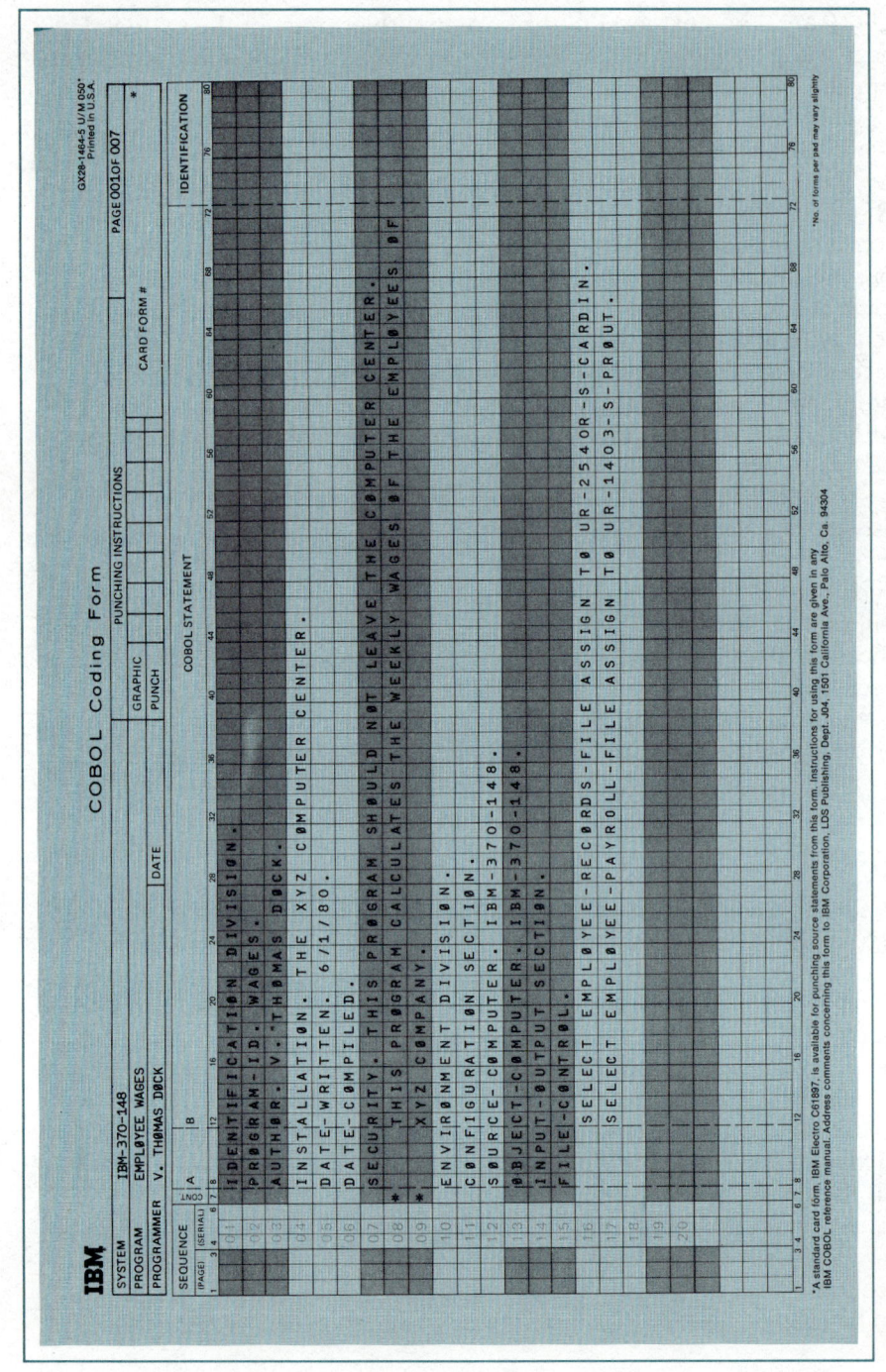

ILLUSTRATION 11-6 A COBOL program

CHAPTER 11: AN OVERVIEW OF PROGRAMMING LANGUAGES

```
DATA DIVISION.
FILE SECTION.
FD  EMPLOYEE-RECORDS-FILE
    LABEL RECORD IS OMITTED.
01  CARD-RECORD.
    02  EMPLOYEE-NAME       PICTURE A(15).
    02  FILLER              PICTURE X(4).
    02  HOURS-WORKED        PICTURE 99.
    02  FILLER              PICTURE XXX.
    02  HOURLY-RATE         PICTURE 9V99.
    02  FILLER              PICTURE X(53).
FD  EMPLOYEE-PAYROLL-FILE
    LABEL RECORD IS OMITTED.
01  PAYROLL-RECORD.
    02  FILLER              PICTURE X.
    02  EMPLOYEE-NAM        PICTURE A(15).
    02  FILLER              PICTURE X(6).
    02  HOURS-WORK          PICTURE 99.
    02  FILLER              PICTURE X(8).
    02  HOUR-RATE           PICTURE $9.99.
    02  FILLER              PICTURE X(8).
    02  GROSS-WAGE-OUT      PICTURE $$99.99.
    02  FILLER              PICTURE X(11).
    02  FEDERAL-INCOME-TAX-OUT  PICTURE $$9.99.
```

ILLUSTRATION 11-6   A COBOL program (*continued*)

298

UNIT THREE: COMPUTER PROGRAMMING AND DESIGN

SEQUENCE				COBOL STATEMENT		
01		02	FILLER	PICTURE X(13).		
02		02	STATE-INCOME-TAX-OUT	PICTURE $$9.99.		
03		02	FILLER	PICTURE X(12).		
04		02	SOCIAL-SECURITY-TAX-OUT	PICTURE $$9.99.		
05		02	FILLER	PICTURE X(9).		
06		02	RETIREMENT-OUT	PICTURE $$99.99.		
07		02	FILLER	PICTURE X(3).		
08		02	NET-WAGE-OUT	PICTURE $$99.99.		
09		02	FILLER	PICTURE X(133).		
10	01		PRINT-LINE			
11			WORKING-STORAGE SECTION.			
12	77		GROSS-WAGE	PICTURE 999V99.		
13	77		OVERTIME-HOURS	PICTURE 99.		
14	77		OVERTIME-RATE	PICTURE 99V99.		
15	77		OVERTIME-WAGE	PICTURE 999V99.		
16	77		FED-INCOME-TAX-RATE	PICTURE V99	VALUE .25.	
17	77		FEDERAL-INCOME-TAX	PICTURE 99V99.		
18	77		ST-INCOME-TAX	PICTURE V99	VALUE .06.	
19	77		STATE-INCOME-TAX	PICTURE V9999.		
20	77		SOC-SECURITY-TAX-RATE	PICTURE V9999	VALUE .0613.	
	77		SOCIAL-SECURITY-TAX	PICTURE 99V99.		
	77		RETIREMENT-RATE	PICTURE V99	VALUE .06.	
	77		RETIREMENT-TAX	PICTURE 99V99.		
	77		MORE-DATA-CARDS	PICTURE AA	VALUE SPACES.	

ILLUSTRATION 11-6 A COBOL program (*continued*)

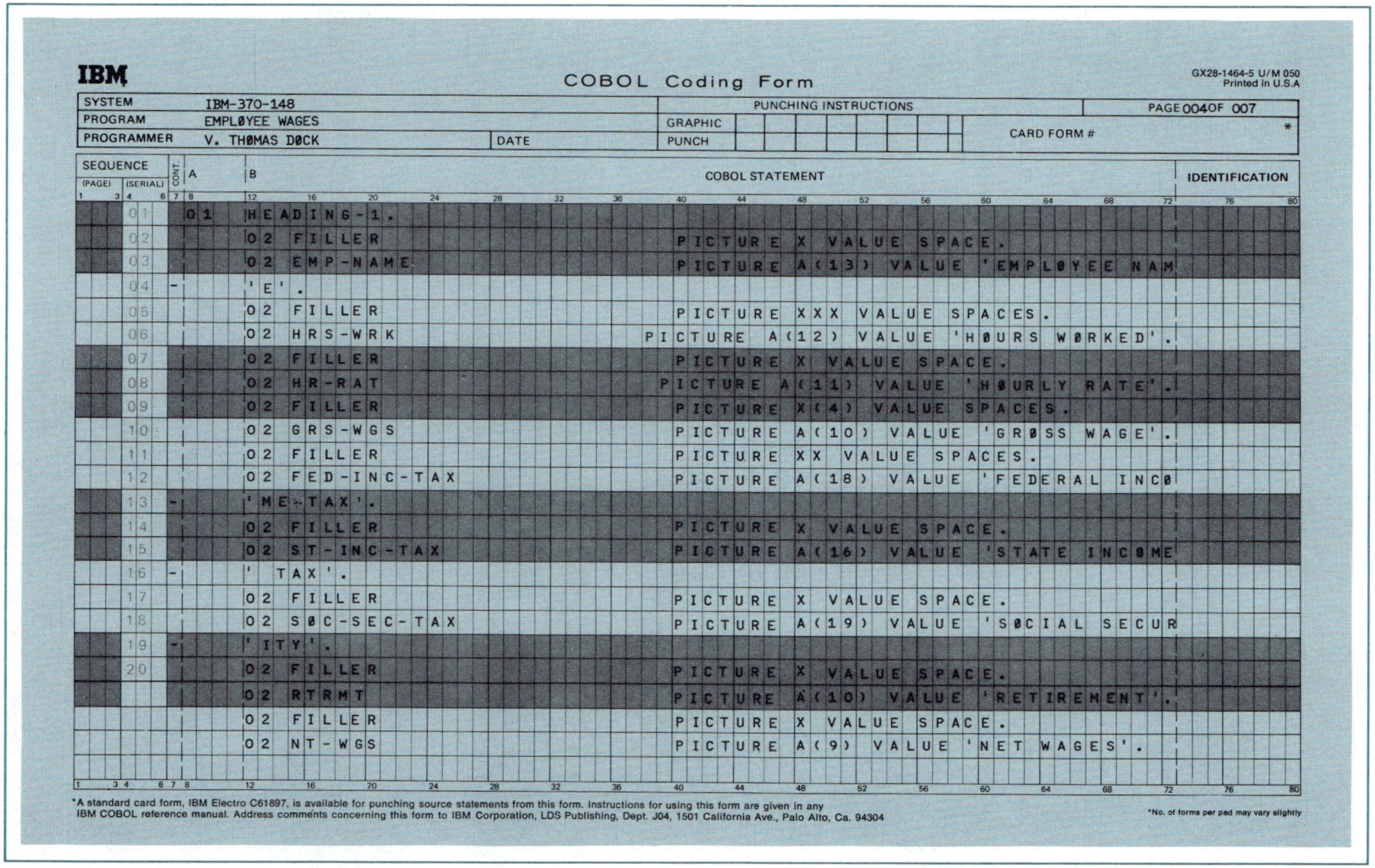

CHAPTER 11: AN OVERVIEW OF PROGRAMMING LANGUAGES

299

ILLUSTRATION 11-6 A COBOL program (continued)

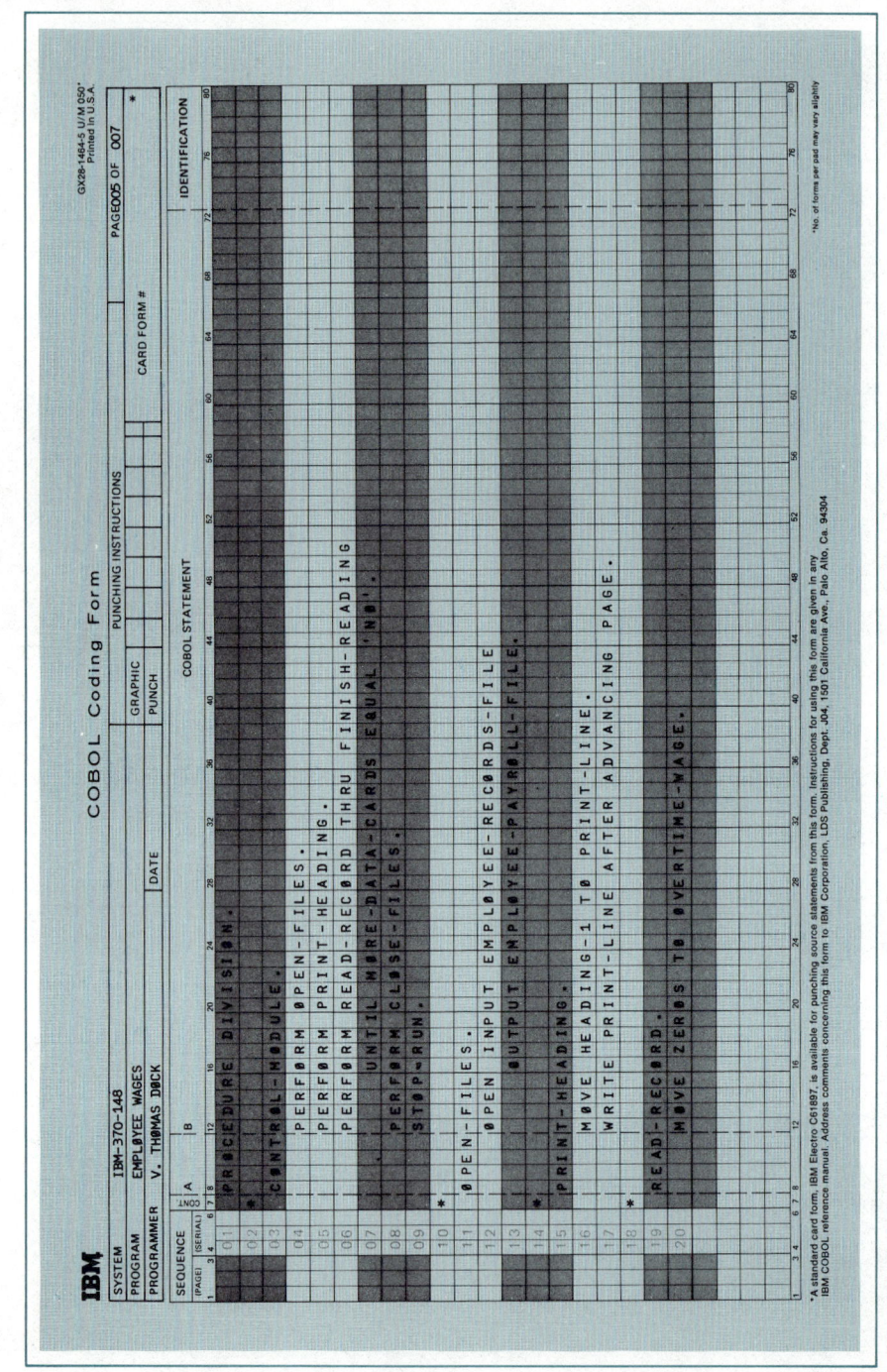

ILLUSTRATION 11-6 A COBOL program (continued)

301

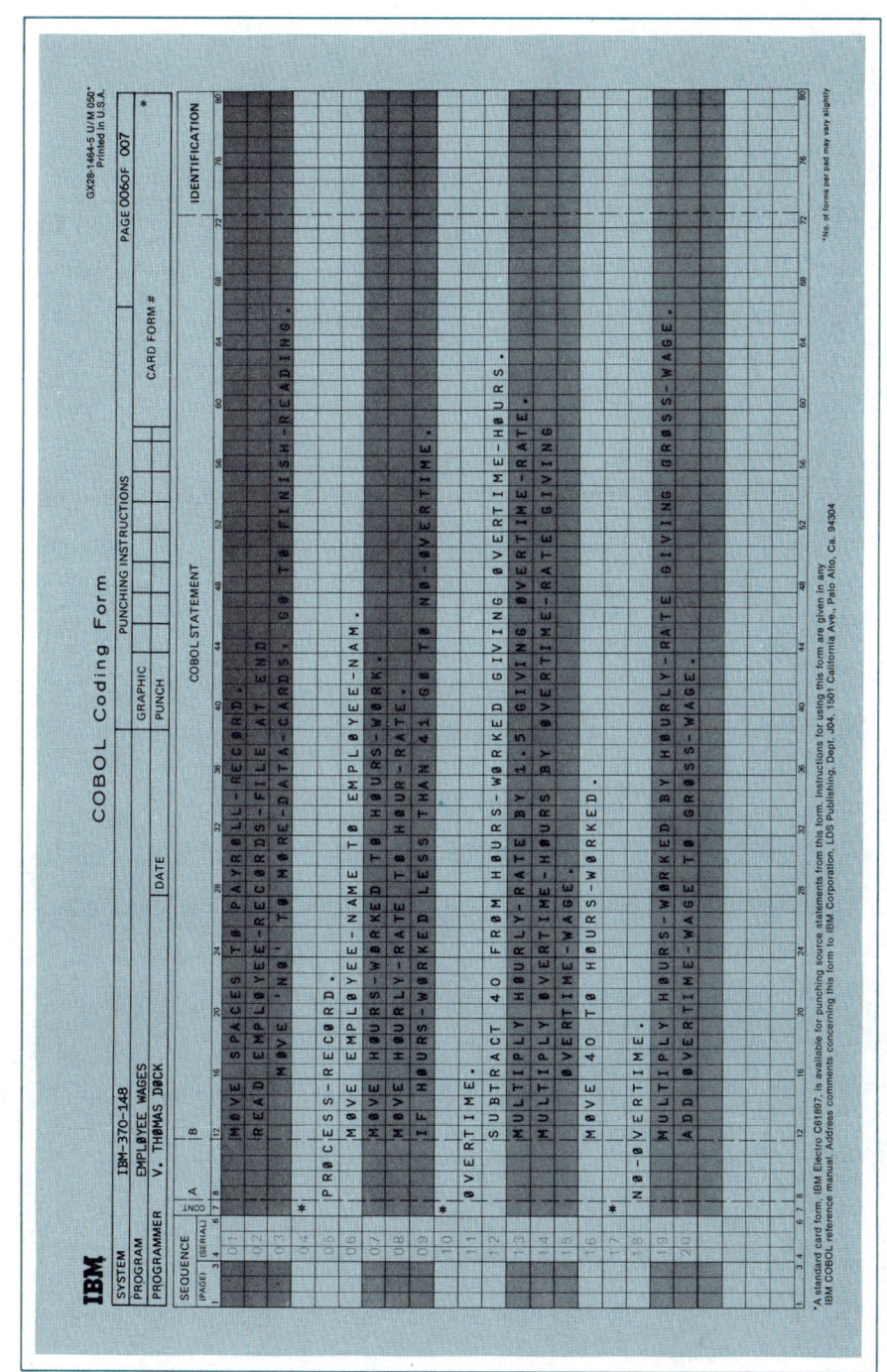

CHAPTER 11: AN OVERVIEW OF PROGRAMMING LANGUAGES

```
IBM                          COBOL Coding Form
SYSTEM    IBM-370-148                    PUNCHING INSTRUCTIONS                    PAGE 006 OF 007
PROGRAM   EMPLOYEE WAGES          GRAPHIC                    CARD FORM #          *
PROGRAMMER V. THOMAS DUCK    DATE PUNCH                                           IDENTIFICATION

SEQUENCE  A  B                                COBOL STATEMENT
01          MOVE SPACES TO PAYROLL-RECORD.
02          READ EMPLOYEE-RECORDS-FILE AT END
03               MOVE 'NO' TO MORE-DATA-CARDS, GO TO FINISH-READING.
04       *
05          PROCESS-RECORD.
06          MOVE EMPLOYEE-NAME TO EMPLOYEE-NAM.
07          MOVE HOURS-WORKED TO HOURS-WORK.
08          MOVE HOURLY-RATE TO HOUR-RATE.
09          IF HOURS-WORKED LESS THAN 41 GO TO NO-OVERTIME.
10       *
11          OVERTIME.
12          SUBTRACT 40 FROM HOURS-WORKED GIVING OVERTIME-HOURS.
13          MULTIPLY HOURLY-RATE BY 1.5 GIVING OVERTIME-RATE.
14          MULTIPLY OVERTIME-HOURS BY OVERTIME-RATE GIVING
15               OVERTIME-WAGE.
16          MOVE 40 TO HOURS-WORKED.
17       *
18          NO-OVERTIME.
19          MULTIPLY HOURS-WORKED BY HOURLY-RATE GIVING GROSS-WAGE.
20          ADD OVERTIME-WAGE TO GROSS-WAGE.
```

ILLUSTRATION 11-6 A COBOL program (continued)

COBOL Coding Form

SYSTEM: IBM-370-148
PROGRAM: EMPLOYEE WAGES
PROGRAMMER: V. THOMAS DOCK

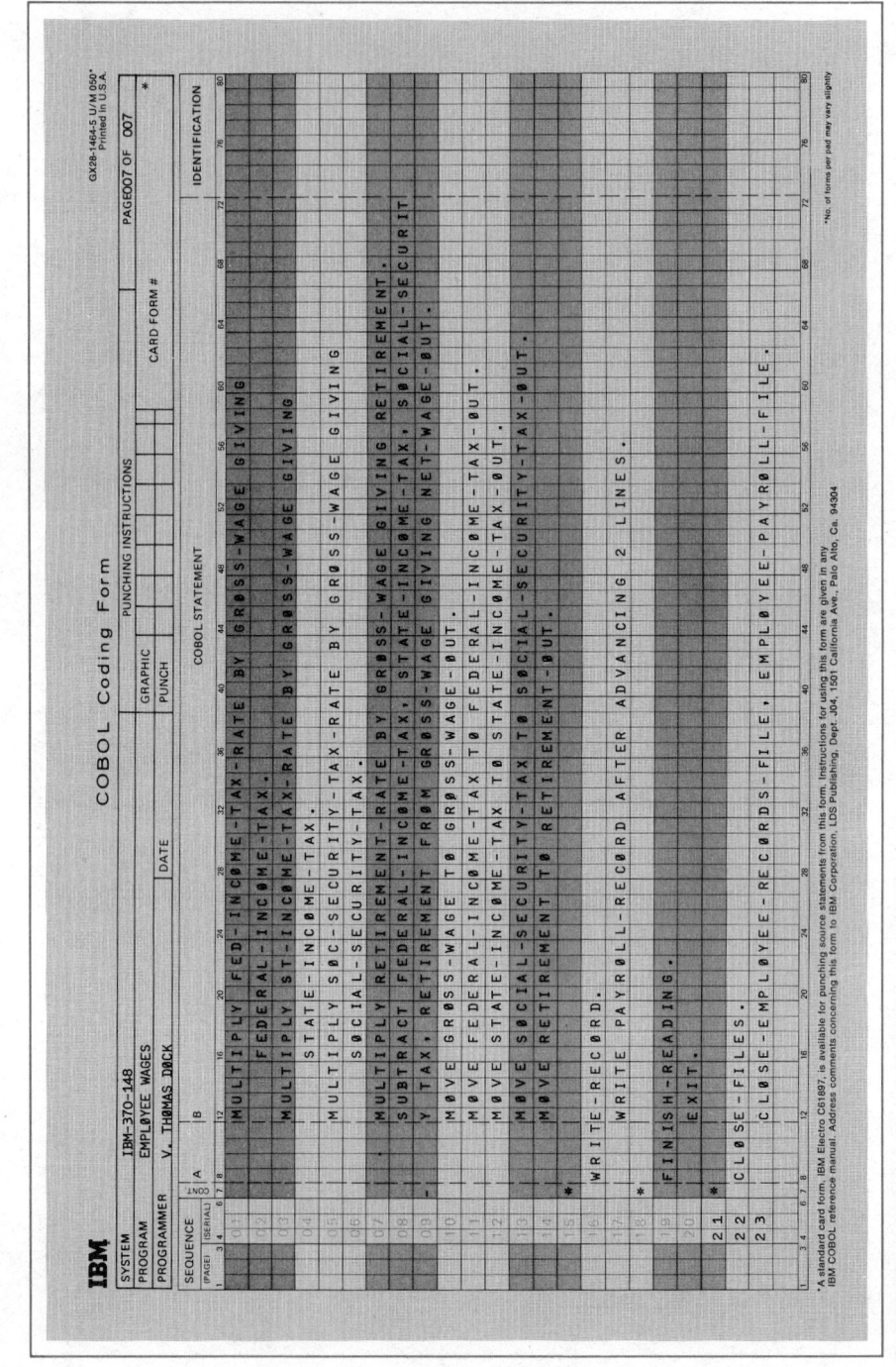

Seq	A/B	COBOL Statement
01		MULTIPLY FED-INCOME-TAX-RATE BY GROSS-WAGE GIVING
02		FEDERAL-INCOME-TAX.
03		MULTIPLY ST-INCOME-TAX-RATE BY GROSS-WAGE GIVING
04		STATE-INCOME-TAX.
05		MULTIPLY SOC-SECURITY-TAX-RATE BY GROSS-WAGE GIVING
06		SOCIAL-SECURITY-TAX.
07		MULTIPLY RETIREMENT-RATE BY GROSS-WAGE GIVING RETIREMENT.
08		SUBTRACT FEDERAL-INCOME-TAX, STATE-INCOME-TAX, SOCIAL-SECURIT
09	-	Y TAX, RETIREMENT FROM GROSS-WAGE GIVING NET-WAGE-OUT.
10		MOVE GROSS-WAGE TO GROSS-WAGE-OUT.
11		MOVE FEDERAL-INCOME-TAX TO FEDERAL-INCOME-TAX-OUT.
12		MOVE STATE-INCOME-TAX TO STATE-INCOME-TAX-OUT.
13		MOVE SOCIAL-SECURITY-TAX TO SOCIAL-SECURITY-TAX-OUT.
14		MOVE RETIREMENT TO RETIREMENT-OUT.
15	*	
16		WRITE-RECORD.
17		WRITE PAYROLL-RECORD AFTER ADVANCING 2 LINES.
18	*	
19		FINISH-READING.
20		EXIT.
21	*	
22		CLOSE-FILES.
23		CLOSE EMPLOYEE-RECORDS-FILE, EMPLOYEE-PAYROLL-FILE.

ILLUSTRATION 11-6 A COBOL program *(continued)*

the programmer is in continuous direct communication with the computer. Because the BASIC language is most often used in a system having data communication capabilities, the language is discussed in more detail in Chapter 14.

RPG

As stated earlier in this chapter, Report Program Generator (RPG) is a problem-oriented language. The language was initially designed to generate programs whose outputs are business-oriented printed reports. An RPG program is a description of a report to be produced. Based on the description (specifications), a generator program (normally, provided by the computer manufacturer) creates a program to produce the report. Today, a more powerful implementation of the RPG language, known as RPG II, can also be used for other types of processing.

The RPG language was orginally designed to duplicate the logic of punched-card equipment. Thus, it was the primary programming language for small computer systems that were typically installed as replacements for punched-card data processing systems. An early example was the IBM System/3. The RPG language is also used on medium-size and large computer systems. In general, the RPG language is **upward compatible**; that is, with only minor modifications, an RPG program can be translated and executed on a computer system that is faster and has more internal storage than the computer system for which it was written. While RPG is not the primary programming language for medium-size and large computer systems, it is often used in business data processing applications for which it is particularly suitable.

The programmer who uses RPG must describe the input and output files to be used in the program, define the significant fields of input records, set up any calculations or logical operations to be performed, and define the report or output records to be created. To prepare an RPG program, five forms may be used. These are: (1) File Extension Specifications, (2) Control and File Description Specifications, (3) Input Specifications, (4) Calculation Specifications, and (5) Output Specifications. An RPG program to read input and provide output similar to that of the FORTRAN and COBOL programs discussed earlier is shown in Illustration 11-7.

Several entries are common to all RPG specifications forms: Page, Program Identification, Line, Form Type, and Comments. The page entry (punched-card columns 1 and 2) is located in the upper right corner of each form; it can be used with the line number assigned to each specification line (columns 3, 4, and 5) to provide program sequence information. A program code name can be entered in the program identification field (columns 75–80). Comments can be entered on any specifications form by

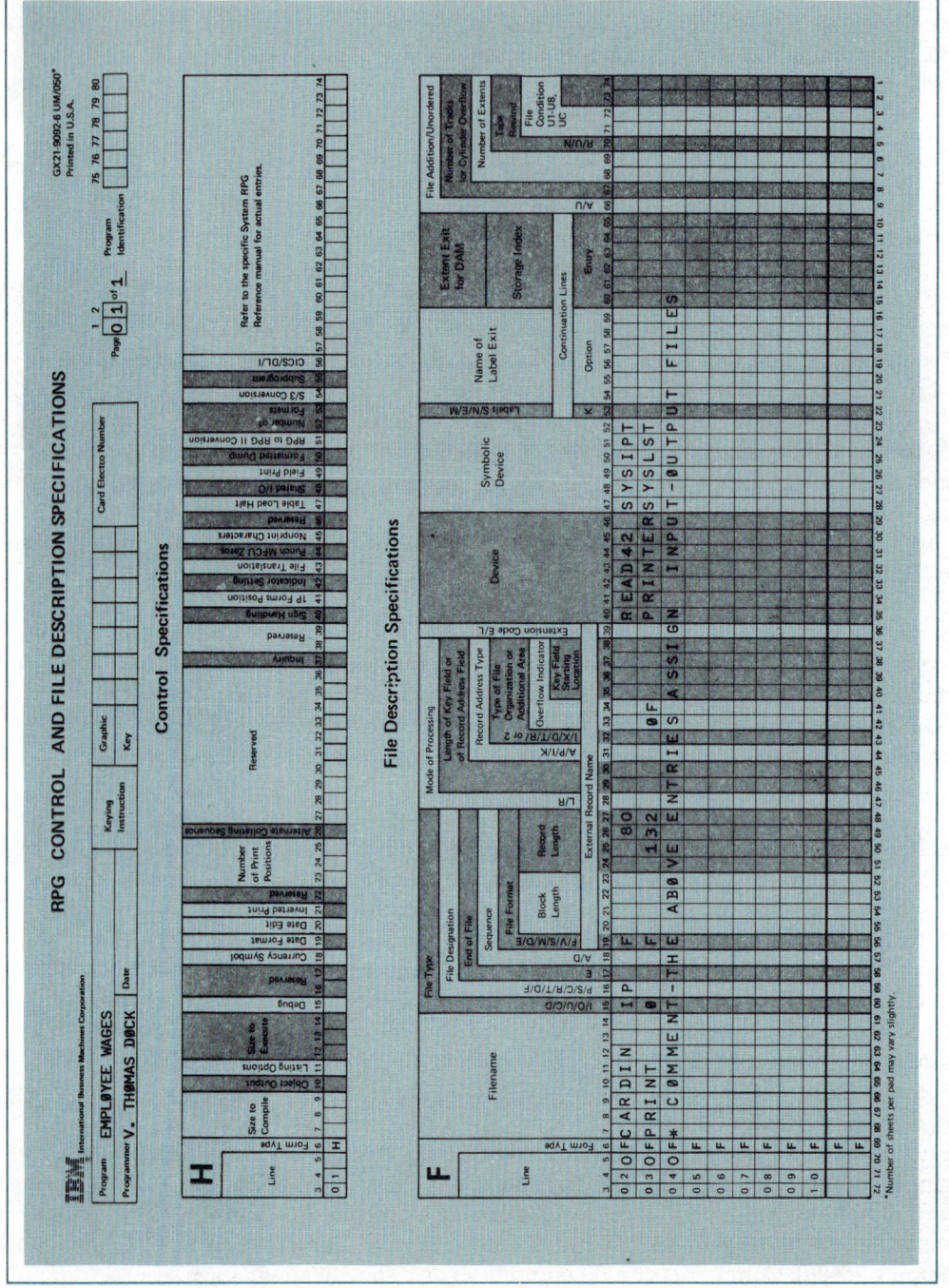

ILLUSTRATION 11-7 An RPG program

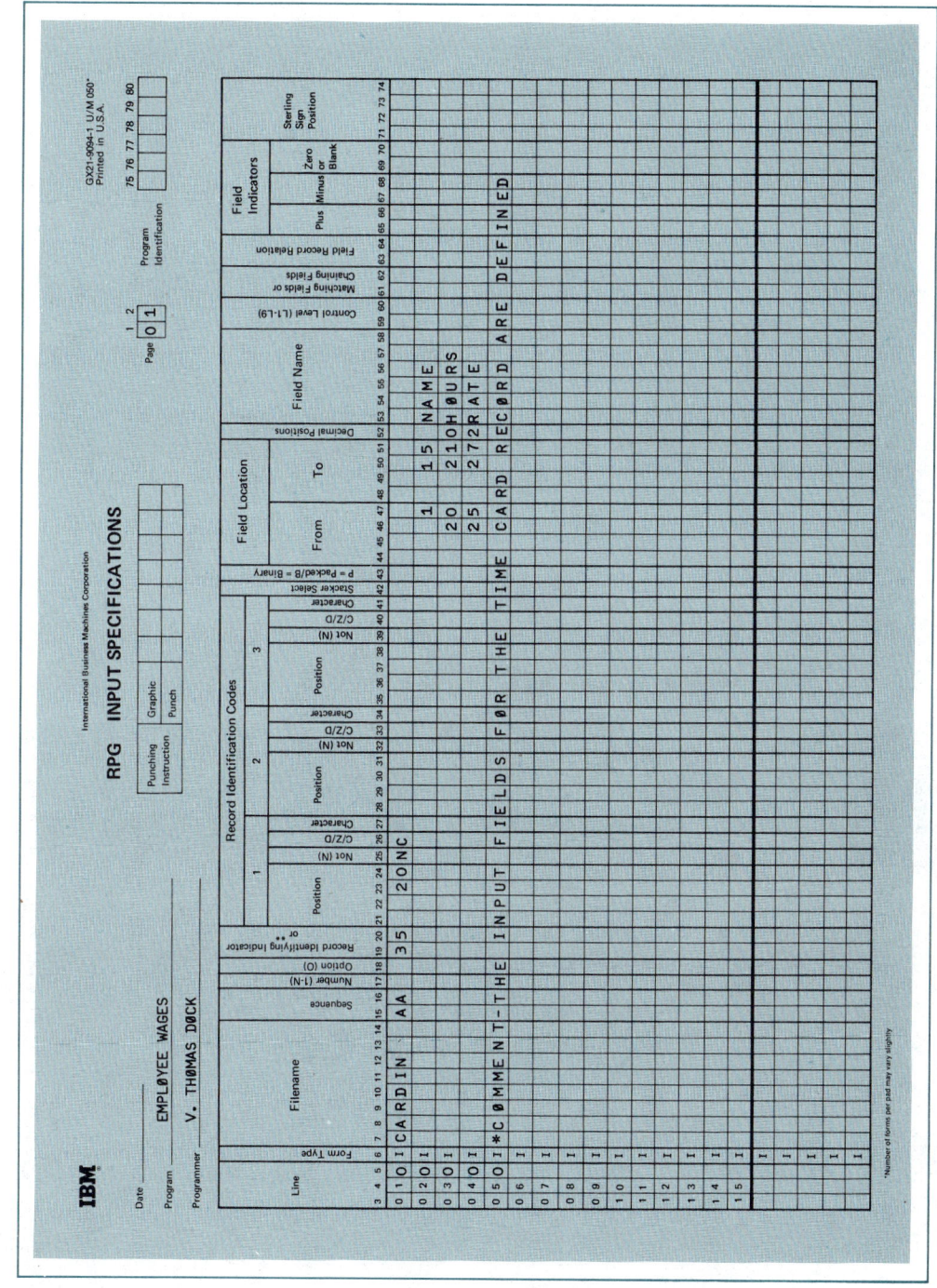

CHAPTER 11: AN OVERVIEW OF PROGRAMMING LANGUAGES

ILLUSTRATION 11-7 An RPG program (*continued*)

ILLUSTRATION 11-7　An RPG program *(continued)*

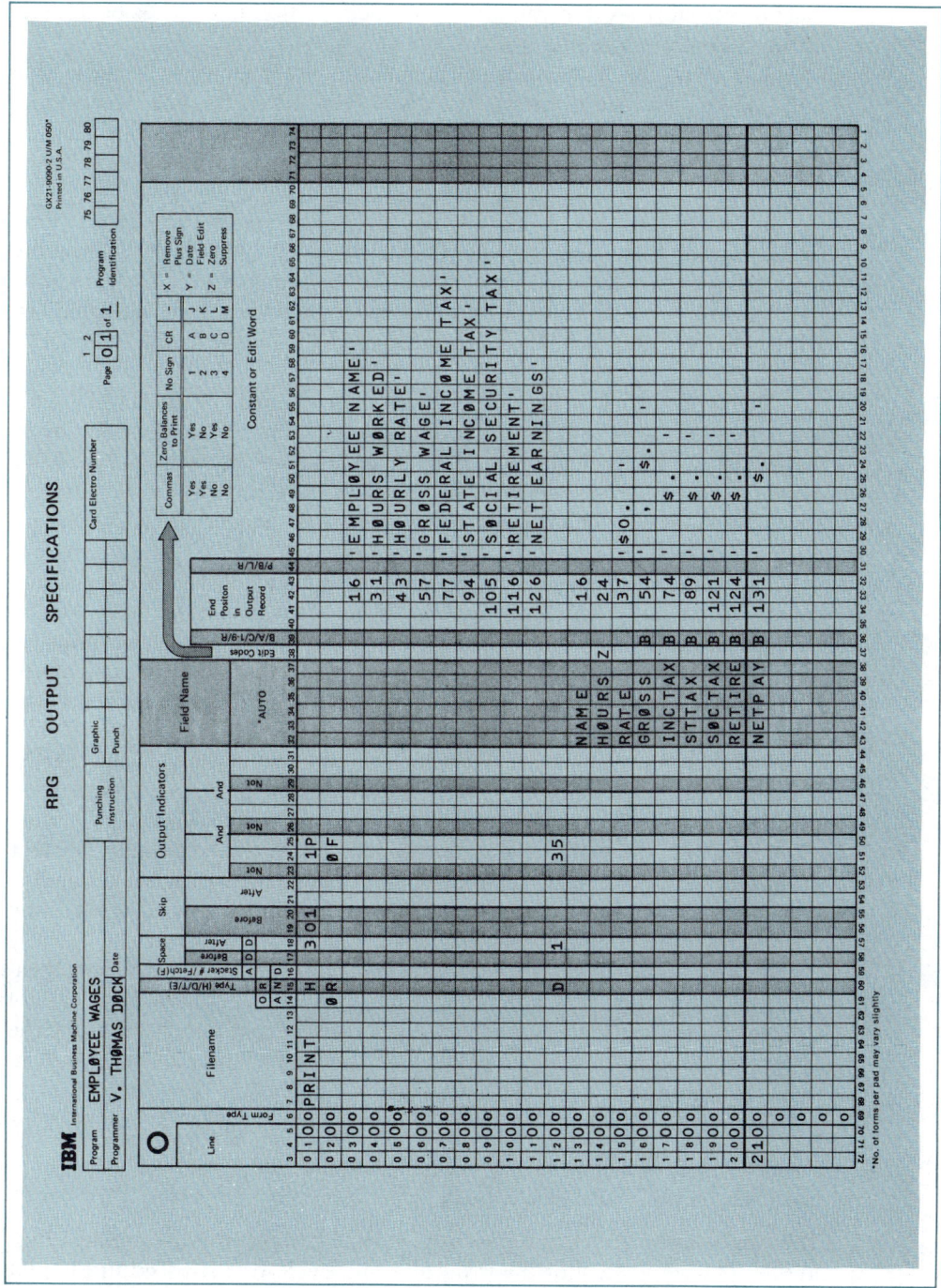

ILLUSTRATION 11-7 An RPG program (continued)

placing an asterisk (*) in column 7 of a specification line as has been done in the example program.

Generally, the RPG specifications forms are coded in the order that they will be arranged in the source deck: File Extension, File Description, Input, Calculation, and Output Specifications. The File Extension Specifications are prepared only when tables or disk files are to be used by the program.

In the example program, two files are defined on the File Description Specifications form. The first file (CARDIN) is the card input file containing employee pay records. The length of the records in the file is defined (80) and the type of input device that will read the file is indicated (an IBM 1442 Card Reader). The output file (PRINT) will be printed on a 132-characters-per-line printer.

The specific fields that will be used from records in the CARDIN file are defined on the Input Specifications form. Each field is identified by its starting and ending locations and is given a name. The coding on line 010 causes each input record to be checked to see whether or not it contains a character in column 20. If it does not, no further processing of the record occurs.

The calculations needed to determine values for the output report are described on the Calculation Specifications form. None of these calculations occurs until an input record is read. This is specified by the indicator 35 (columns 10 and 11), which also appears on the Input Specifications form (columns 19 and 20). These corresponding numbers indicate that the data to be used in the calculations comes from records in the CARDIN file. If the hours worked (HOURS) exceed 40, the overtime pay (OTEARN) is calculated. Otherwise, only regular pay (GROSS) is calculated. Then deductions are calculated to determine net pay (NETPAY).

The specifications for the output report to be created from the PRINT output file are given on the Output Specifications form. Each heading line (constant) and each field that is to be printed are defined. The editing needed for each field is specified.

By now it should be evident that RPG is not *free-form*. Each specification line entry must be placed in certain columns of the line. RPG cannot be free-form because the specifications that the programmer writes are the generator program's only guidelines in creating a complete program to perform the processing steps required.

○ **LANGUAGE SELECTION**

The importance of selecting an appropriate programming language during the planning stage of the programming cycle was stressed in Chapter

10. How does one decide whether an assembler language, FORTRAN, COBOL, RPG, or some other programming language should be used in coding? Generally, the basic question of which language to select can be viewed from three aspects: (1) the purpose of the program and the frequency of execution, (2) the time and money required to design and code a program in a particular language, and (3) the availability of a particular language.

The purpose of the program and the frequency of execution are considerations that emphasize the speed with which a program can be executed. Under most circumstances, if two programmers of equal talent were to write programs to solve the same problem, one using an assembler language and the other a compiler language, the program written in assembler language would be executed faster and require less storage space. Although the coding of an assembler-language program often requires more time and money than the coding of an equivalent program in a compiler language, if the program is to be run repeatedly, the savings in computer time and storage requirements may more than compensate for the extra coding costs. Furthermore, many factors indicating specific machine operations are easily programmed in an assembler language but are either not available or impractical to program in a compiler language. Therefore, if the nature of the program is such that a number of executions of the program are expected or if particular features of machine operations are needed, an assembler language is normally the best choice for the program. If program efficiency is the deciding factor, an assembler language is usually adopted.

The second aspect of the selection question is basically one of the preparation cost of a program. As suggested above, one of the basic weaknesses of assembler language is the amount of time required for coding. Compiler languages do not share this weakness. The effort involved in coding, correcting, and documenting a program is minimized when a compiler language is used. This implies that if the nature of the program is such that it is likely to be revised from time to time, a compiler language has an advantage over an assembler language. Any alteration of an assembler-language program may necessitate extensive rewriting.

An additional advantage of a compiler language is that it is somewhat machine-independent. This means that it can be employed on any of several types of computers. In contrast, an assembler language is machine-oriented (and, therefore, machine-dependent); it is designed for one particular type of machine. If a program is coded in an assembler language and then the computer is changed, but the need for the program continues, the entire program must be rewritten for the new machine.

The final aspect of the selection question is one of language availability. This question is primarily concerned with compiler or generator languages (since a particular assembler language can be used on only a certain type of computer). Before a particular high-level programming language is chosen, the capability to execute programs written in that language on the computer in use should be verified. If the purchase (or rental) of a compiler or generator program is anticipated, the costs should be weighed relative to the benefits of being able to use the language in programming.

The familiarity of programmers with any language that is considered for selection should be assessed accurately for the particular installation. If involved programmers have not had previous experience with a language, the training costs and the ease of adapting to the language should be estimated. The time required for such training and adjustment should be factored into the selection process.

Although choosing a language for a program may seem to be a relatively simple task, it is not as straightforward as one might assume. A great deal of effort should be expended in the selection of a language because, ultimately, it may determine the worth of the program.

SUMMARY

1. Programming languages, much the same as computer hardware, were developed in phases, or generations. Machine language was the first to be introduced. Assembler language and high-level programming languages followed.

2. Machine languages are machine-dependent; programs written in a machine language can be executed only by computers for which the language was designed. Thus, a program written for one computer cannot be executed by another computer unless it is of the same type. Machine languages are very tedious and time-consuming to use. However, once written, programs in machine language can be executed quickly and use a minimum amount of internal storage

3. Assembler languages represent the next development. They are structurally similar to machine languages but they permit the programmer to use symbolic names rather than numerical representations of operations. This reduces coding time and the amount of information the programmer has to remember. Assembler-language programs are processed by an assembler, which translates the assembler-language (source) program into a machine-language (object) program.

4. The third level of development of computer languages involved macro-instructions. These instructions contain macro operation codes.

They are used by the programmer to cause often repeated series of assembler-language instructions to be inserted in a program. This reduces the amount of coding necessary on the programmer's part.

5. The next level of computer languages includes high-level programming languages such as FORTRAN, COBOL, BASIC, and RPG. While some of these languages are considered to be procedure-oriented, they may all be called problem-oriented languages. These languages are generally machine-independent and satisfy specific needs. For example, FORTRAN and BASIC were designed to satisfy engineers' and scientists' needs for mathematical computation. COBOL and RPG are more suited to business data processing. All these languages reduce the amount of coding necessary for programs, compared with assembler-language programs. The programmer needs little in-depth knowledge about the computer on which the programs are to be executed. Programs do, however, take longer to execute (after translation) than equivalent programs initially written in machine or assembler language. Despite this handicap, high-level programming languages are in widespread use today.

REVIEW QUESTIONS

1. Distinguish between machine-oriented languages and procedure-oriented languages, giving examples of each.
2. How do high-level languages differ from machine languages?
3. Distinguish between a source program and an object program. In doing so, explain why translators are required.
4. Name the four divisions of a COBOL program. What is the function of each division?
5. Explain the special features of FORTRAN. For what types of applications is FORTRAN preferred and why?
6. Identify some applications for which RPG is appropriate. Explain why you selected these applications.
7. Briefly explain the characteristics of the BASIC language. What similarities and differences are there between BASIC and FORTRAN?

CAREER PROFILE

David Lui
Senior Programmer
(Systems) Analyst
Dakota County,
Minnesota

Background Experience

I graduated from St. Cloud State University with a B.S. degree in Quantitative Methods Information Systems. In my junior and senior years I worked as a student consultant at the University Computer Center. My job was to help students debug programs. During my senior year, I interned as a programmer at the Dakota County Government Center in Hastings, Minnesota. I designed, coded, and documented the 4-H Club enrollment system for the University of Minnesota Extension Service. The system was run on an IBM System/370 computer with DOS/VS.

Upon graduation, I accepted a position as a programmer analyst with Dakota County. While in that position, I designed the county Fixed Asset Accounting system. I also worked on the Payroll and Child Support Recovery systems. After that, I became systems programmer. I worked with a variety of commercial software packages such as DOS/VSPT, DYNAM/T, and WESTI. I made statistical studies of teleprocessing performance and completed some data base package evaluation projects. I worked as a systems programmer for two years and recently became a senior programmer analyst.

Primary Job Responsibilities

I am one of three systems analysts working for Dakota County. We coordinate the operation of a computer system that provides information needed to administer the County Taxation system. I am responsible for the whole computing process; that is, I prioritize, schedule, and help plan the jobs for three programmer analysts; assist in writing debugging programs when necessary; and work with the end uses of the information. Part of my job is quite technical. We must respond quickly and accurately to sudden changes. For example, changes in real estate laws or tax rates can have a dramatic impact. I am hoping the implementation of a data base/data dictionary system will improve our response to changes and also cut our maintenance costs.

What Has Made You Successful?

I like the challenge of solving both human and technical problems. I enjoy seeing how much the computer system can help the users, from the standpoint of the information we provide.

I enjoy the challenge of keeping our computer system in step with the latest technology. I like being involved in a dynamic, ever-changing field with unlimited potential capability.

# UNIT FOUR

AN OVERVIEW OF SYSTEMS

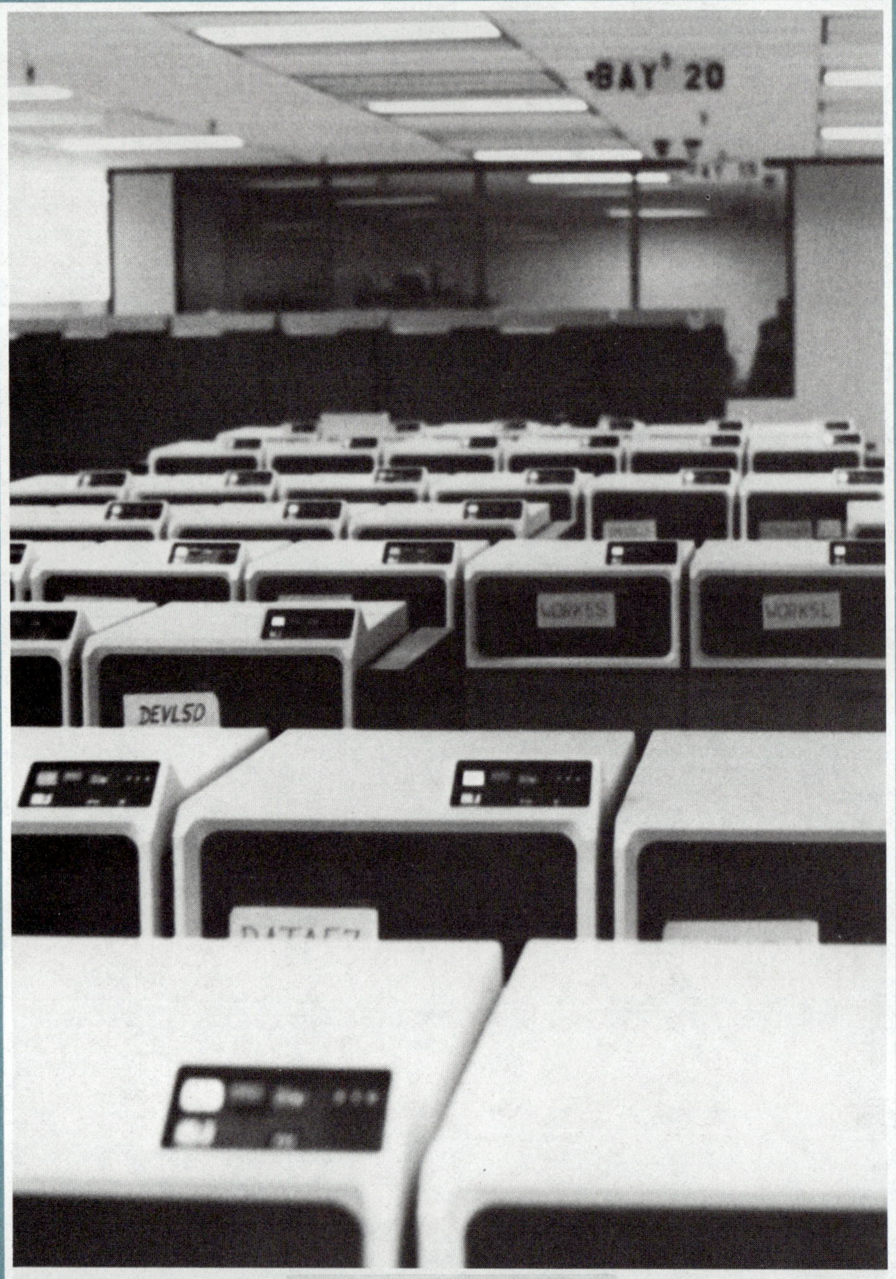
BAY 20
DEVL5D

CHAPTER 12

OVERLAPPED SYSTEMS

OVERLAPPED PROCESSING

TYPES OF OVERLAPPED PROCESSING
Multiprogramming
Spooling

Opposite: Multiple channels are required to attach a bank of disk drives to a large computer system.

UNIT FOUR: AN OVERVIEW OF SYSTEMS

Prior to the introduction of third-generation computers, computer systems could perform only one operation at a time. Thus, one of the inefficiencies of first-generation and second-generation computer systems was that some of their components were idle for long periods of time, even while the systems were running. As shown in Illustration 12-1, a typical card system read a card, processed it, and printed an output line on the printer. It then repeated this sequence for the next card. Assume a 600-cards-per-minute reader and a 600-lines-per-minute printer were included in the system. Allow .05 second to process each record, or card. The line graph in the illustration shows the relative amounts of time required for each of the operations. At these rates, the card reader and the printer were each used 40 percent of the time. The CPU—the most expensive component of the system—was used only 20 percent of the time.

In an effort to reduce the idle CPU time, third-generation input/output devices were buffered. A *buffer* is a storage device used to compensate for the difference in rates of flow of data from one device to another or from an input/output device to the central processing unit.

With faster input/output components, the input/output percentages may change, but the components still are idle part of the time. Illustration 12-2 shows similar processing for a tape system with 320,000-characters-per-second tape drives (1600 BPI × 200 inches per second). In this program, an 80-character record was read, processed, and written on a tape. Allow .002 second for processing each record (a faster CPU than the one on the card system described). The line graph in the illustration shows the relative amounts of time the components of the tape system were in use. In this case, the CPU was used about 80 percent of the time, but each tape drive was used only about 10 percent of the time.

To reduce the time that components are idle, third-generation computer systems are designed to *overlap* input and output operations with processing. For example, an overlapped card system can read a card,

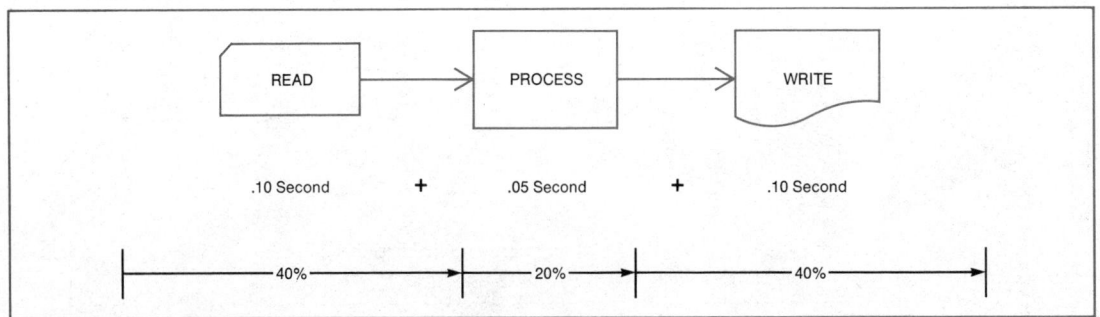

ILLUSTRATION 12-1   Card-system processing

READ → PROCESS → WRITE

.10 Second   +   .05 Second   +   .10 Second

|—— 40% ——|—— 20% ——|—— 40% ——|

process data from a card read earlier, and print a line—all at the same time. Similarly, an overlapped tape system can read a tape record, process the content of a tape record read earlier, and write another tape record—all at the same time. With overlapped operations, the components of a computer system are used a greater percentage of time and the computer system can do more processing in less time.

OVERLAPPED PROCESSING

Illustration 12-3 demonstrates the difference between nonoverlapped and overlapped processing. Nonoverlapped processing is shown in part A, and overlapped processing is shown in part B. In both cases, equal amounts of time (one time interval) are required to read a card, to process the data, and to print a line. At the end of the nine time intervals, then, three records have been read, processed, and written by the nonoverlapped system. Each of the components of this system (card reader, CPU, and printer) is in use 33 percent of the time. In the same amount of time (nine intervals), nine records have been read, eight have been processed, and seven have been written by the overlapped system. After the first two time intervals, each of the components is used 100 percent of the time.

Overlapping is possible because many of the access cycles that take place during an input/output operation are not used by the computer system. Take, for example, a card reading operation on a computer with a 1-byte access width and a 2-microsecond access speed. When the card reader reads an 80-column card, 80 access cycles (or 160 microseconds) are required to transfer the data from the card reader to main storage (one access cycle for each character of data read). However, at 1200 cards per minute, a card reader takes .05 second for each card read, the equivalent of 25,000 access cycles. During the reading of one card, then, 25,000 minus

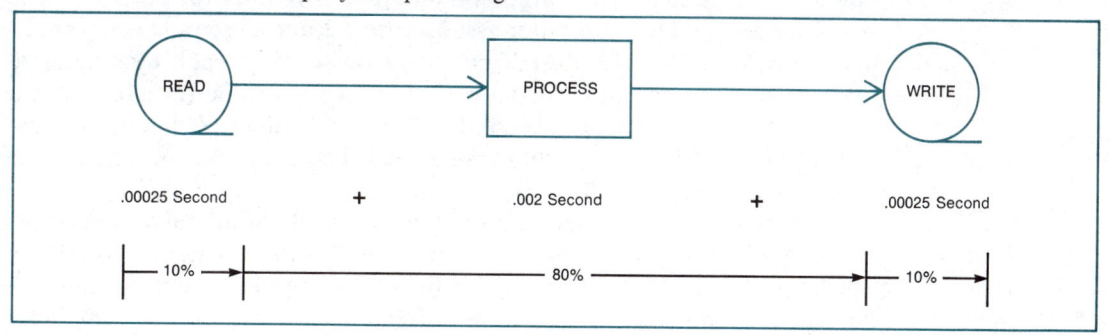

ILLUSTRATION 12-2 Tape-system processing

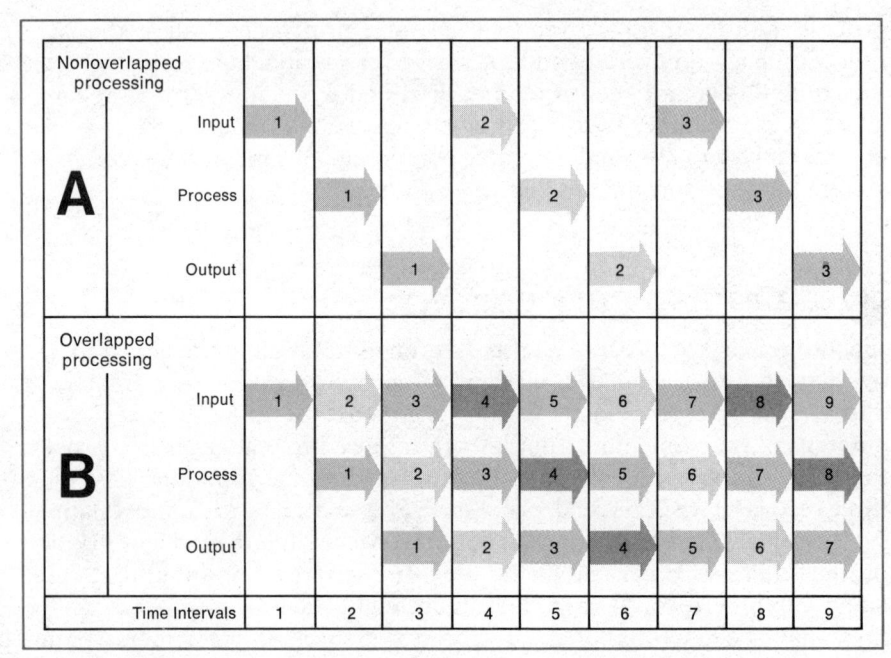

ILLUSTRATION 12-3 Overlapped and nonoverlapped processing

80, or 24,920, access cycles are not used by the computer system. The idea behind overlapping operations is to use these wasted access cycles for other input/output or CPU operations. For example, 100 access cycles could be used for printing a line while the card is being read. The remaining access cycles could be used for executing instructions in the CPU. (To review access cycles, see "The Execution of Program Statements" in Chapter 5.)

This idea of wasted access cycles applies to high-speed input/output operations in the same way that it applies to card input/output or printing operations. Suppose, for example, that a tape is read at the rate of 50,000 bytes per second on a computer system with a 2-microsecond access speed and a 1-byte access width. At 50,000 bytes per second, each byte takes 20 microseconds to be read, but only 2 microseconds to be transferred into storage. Therefore, 18 microseconds, or the equivalent of nine access cycles, are wasted for each byte of data read. These cycles can be used for other input/output or CPU operations.

A nonoverlapped system does not make use of additional access cycles because it has no way of executing more than one instruction at a time. The control unit of the CPU controls the execution of instructions (including input/output instructions), one after another. In contrast, an overlapped system has special devices, called *channels*, that control the execution of input/output instructions, thereby freeing the CPU's control unit to execute other instructions of a stored program. Thus, at any given time, the control unit of the CPU can control the execution of internal operations; one channel can control the execution of an input/output operation; and another channel can control the execution of another input/output operation. In this way, some of the access cycles that are wasted on a non-overlapped system can be put to use.

Illustration 12-4 represents the components of a card system that has two channels. Although the storage unit is often considered part of the CPU, it is shown here as separate from the CPU. The CPU consists of the control unit and the arithmetic/logic unit and is connected to the storage unit. The channels are between the storage unit and the input/output devices. During overlapped processing, each channel moves data to and from storage as it executes input/output instructions. The control unit of the CPU moves data to and from storage as it executes instructions. If a channel and the control unit require an access cycle at the same time, the channel has priority. Suppose, for example, that a channel has to move a byte of data from a card reader to the storage unit, but the CPU is in the midst of accessing an instruction into its control unit. The CPU stops for one access cycle; the byte of data is moved from the channel to storage; and the CPU resumes operations where it left off. During overlapped processing, then, access cycles can be used alternately by the channels and the CPU.

A channel can have one or more input/output devices attached to it, and a computer system can have one or more channels attached to it. The number of operations that can be overlapped depends on the number of channels on the system. Each channel can control only one input/output

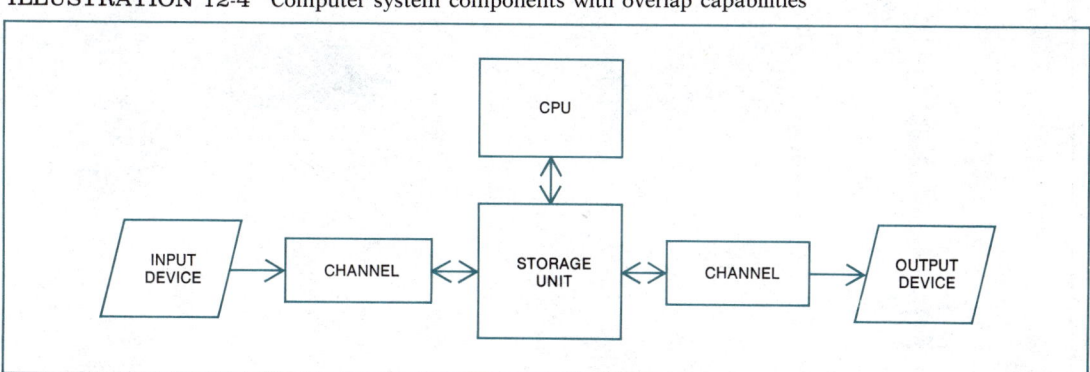

ILLUSTRATION 12-4   Computer system components with overlap capabilities

operation at a time. The types of operations that can be overlapped depend on the arrangement of the input/output devices on the channels.

Illustration 12-5 shows a system that has two channels and can, therefore, overlap two input/output operations with processing. For example, card reading and writing on tape 3 can be overlapped, but card reading and printing cannot be overlapped. In contrast, Illustration 12-6 represents a system with three channels. It can overlap three input/output operations with processing. Card reading can be overlapped with printing. Tape operations on tapes 1, 2, and 4 can take place at the same time. However, a tape reading operation on tape 2 cannot be overlapped with a tape writing operation on tape 3. The input/output devices must be on different channels if their operations are to be overlapped.

Because an overlapped system requires channels, it costs more than a nonoverlapped system. In addition, an overlapped system raises special programming considerations. For instance, instead of reading an input record, processing it, and writing an output record, a program for overlapped processing must start by reading two input records. This means that two input areas must be assigned in storage. The first input record is read into one input area. Then, while the second input record is read into the other input area, the first input record can be processed. Throughout program execution, the computer must switch back and forth between the two input areas. Since these same ideas apply to output areas in stor-

ILLUSTRATION 12-5 Overlapped tape system

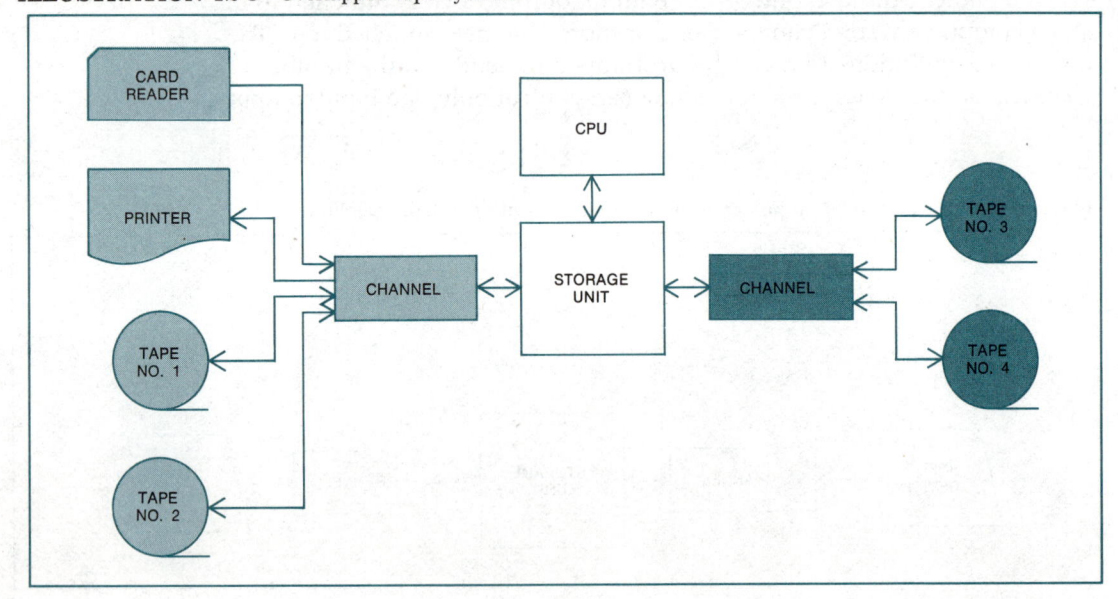

CHAPTER 12: OVERLAPPED SYSTEMS

age, the overlapped program is not a simple, straightforward program. The additional expenses (equipment and programming) are justified by the increased processing potential of the overlapped system.

TYPES OF OVERLAPPED PROCESSING

Although Illustration 12-3 shows equal times for input, processing, and output, this representation is unrealistic. Actually, input, processing, and output times would probably not be equal. In this case, even though a system overlapped operations, some of the components of the system would be idle part of the time—sometimes the CPU, sometimes one or more of the input/output devices.

Illustration 12-7 represents overlapped processing for a program that: (1) reads unblocked tape records as input; (2) processes the records; and (3) prints lines of output (one for each record) on a printer. In this system, the printer operations take twice as long as the tape operations and four times as long as the CPU operations. As a result, after seven intervals, the printer is in use 100 percent of the time, the tape drive 50 percent of the time, and the CPU 25 percent of the time. Because the speed of program

ILLUSTRATION 12-6 Three-channel computer system

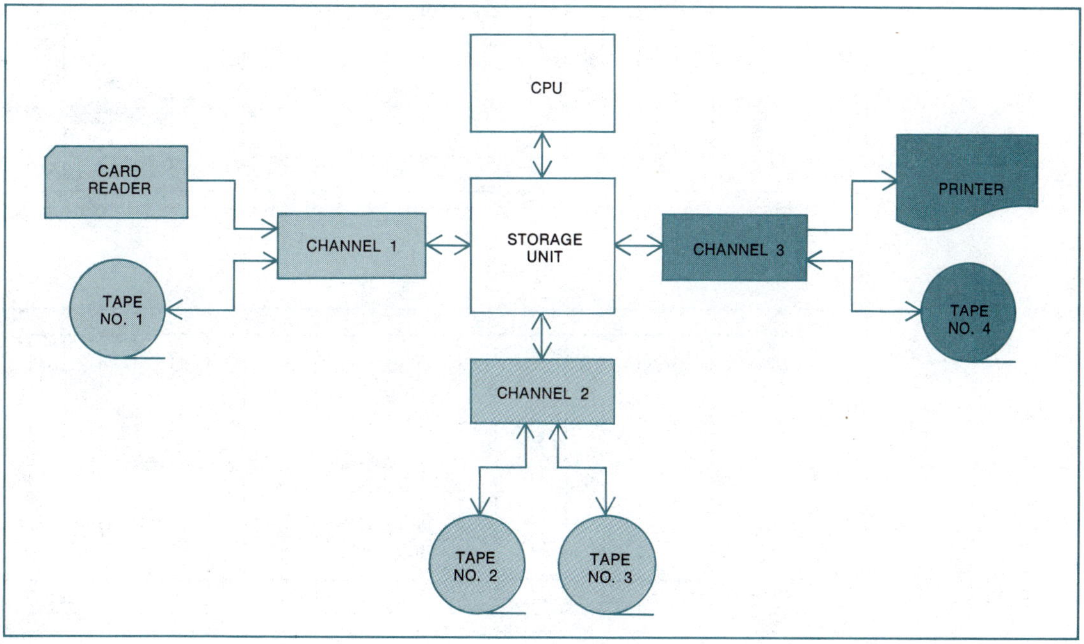

UNIT FOUR: AN OVERVIEW OF SYSTEMS

execution depends on the speed of the slowest input/output device, such a program is said to be *input/output bound*. If output is changed from the printer to a tape unit, the program is still input/output bound, but to a lesser extent. Illustration 12-8 shows the amount of overlap when a second

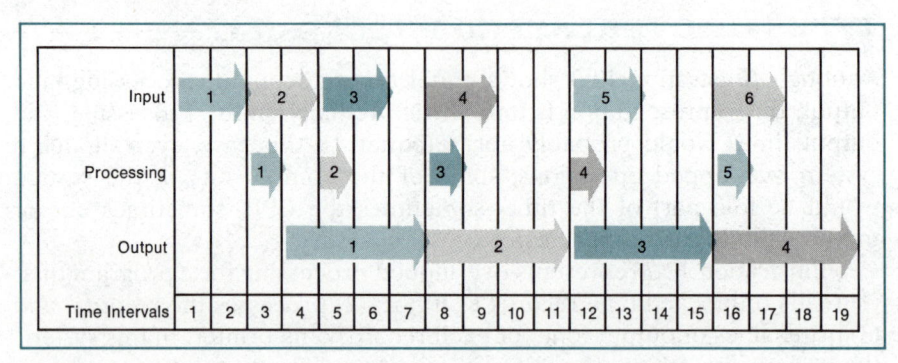

ILLUSTRATION 12-7 Input/output-bound tape-to-print program

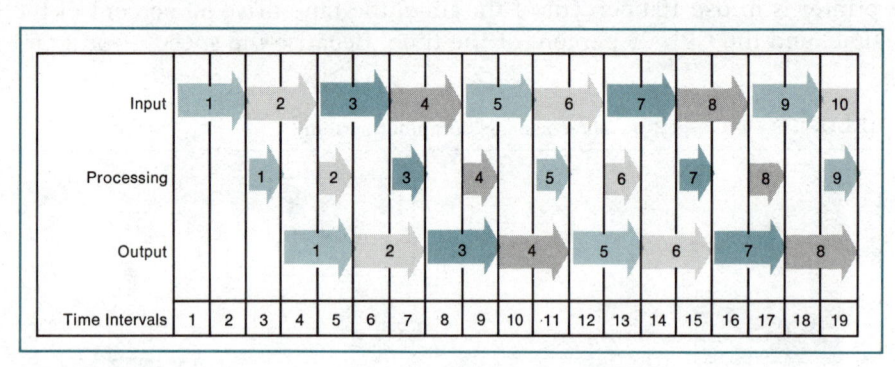

ILLUSTRATION 12-8 Input/output-bound tape-to-tape program

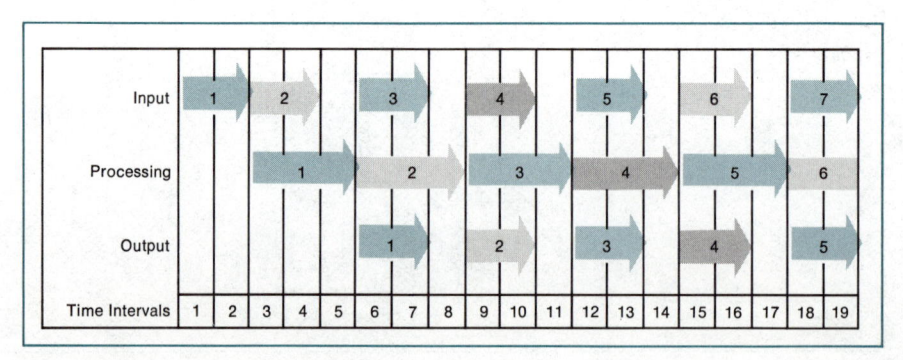

ILLUSTRATION 12-9 Process-bound program

tape unit is used instead of the printer. Eight output records have been written, in the amount of time that the printer in Illustration 12-7 completed only four. Since most business programs read and write relatively large amounts of data and perform relatively little processing, most business programs are input/output bound.

If the speed of program execution is limited by the speed of the CPU, the program is said to be ***process bound***. The process-bound program in Illustration 12-9 can be speeded up only by increasing the speed of the CPU operations. In this program, each of the input/output units is in use about 66 percent of the time, while the CPU is in use 100 percent of the time.

Multiprogramming

To increase the use of the components of a computer system during execution of an input/output-bound program or a process-bound program, some systems are designed to run two or more programs in internal storage concurrently. This is called ***multiprogramming***. The idea is to combine the execution of two input/output-bound programs, or of one input/output-bound program with a process-bound program. Then, whenever the CPU is idle during the execution of one program, it can branch to an instruction in the second program. Illustration 12-10, for instance, shows the execution of two input/output-bound programs on a multiprogramming system. At the start, the first two input records for each program are read into the

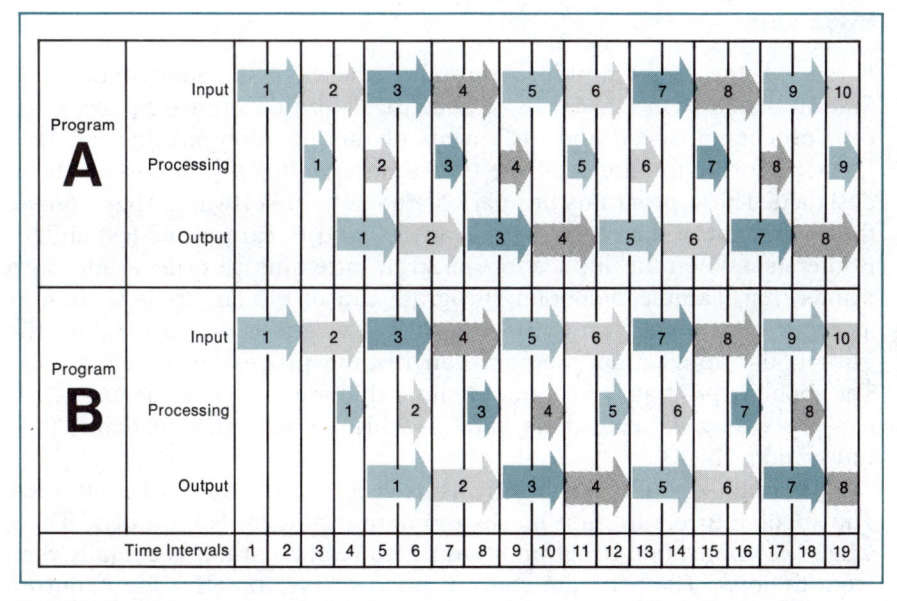

ILLUSTRATION 12-10 Multiprogramming two input/output-bound programs

storage unit. After the first input record for program A is in the storage unit, the CPU begins processing this record. The CPU finishes this processing at the end of interval 3. It would have to wait until the end of interval 4 if program A were the only program in the storage unit. Because program B is also in the storage unit, the CPU branches to this program and processes its first input record. The computer system continues switching back and forth between the programs throughout the execution of the programs. Because of multiprogramming, the two programs are executed in about the same amount of time as would otherwise be required to execute only one of them.

An added cost of a multiprogramming system is additional channels. In Illustration 12-10, for example, the input/output operations for two programs are overlapped rather than the input/output operations for one program. Twice as many channels (in this case, four) are required. A second added cost is additional storage capacity. Because two or more programs are read into the storage unit at one time, the multiprogramming system must have more storage capability than a computer system that executes single programs. In addition, multiprogramming requires extra system programming considerations. Specifically, routines must be written to branch back and forth between the programs in the storage unit. If, by multiprogramming, the computer system can do proportionately more processing than it could otherwise do, these additional costs are justified.

Spooling

Even with the use of multiprogramming, there is still usually more CPU time available than can be used because of the difference between the CPU processing speed and the speeds of the input/output devices. In a further effort to use the available CPU time, *spooling programs* have been designed. These programs are part of the system software. They control the movement of data from card reader(s) and to card punch(es) and/or printers(s). When an application program attempts to print a line on a printer, for example, a spooling program causes the line to be written as a record on a disk instead. Since a disk device is much faster than the printer, the application program can resume processing much sooner. The spooling program prints out the lines that are stored on the disk when less processing is being done and/or a printer becomes available. (See Illustration 12-11.)

The same spooling procedure is used in reverse for card input files. The spooling program first places the data in the cards on a disk. Then, when the application program attempts to read a card, it is actually read from the disk. The program waits a much shorter time for input/output completion.

CHAPTER 12: OVERLAPPED SYSTEMS

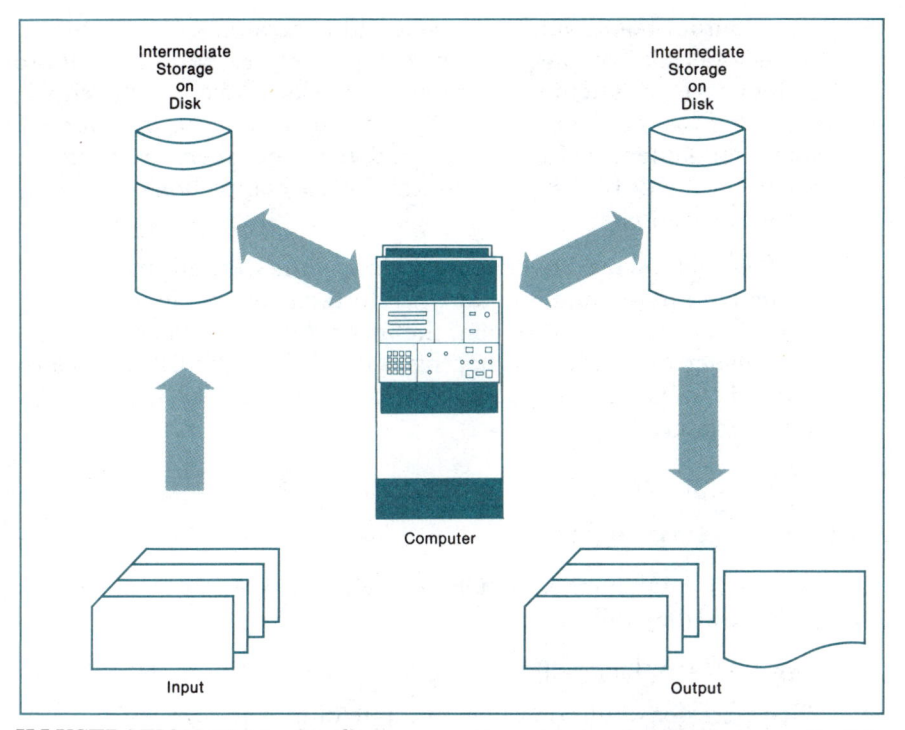

ILLUSTRATION 12-11 Spooling program stores input and output on magnetic disk

Spooling takes place even though the programmer may be completely unaware of it. An application program is written as though it is using card input and printer output, while it actually uses disk input and output. The system software makes the necessary adjustments so that spooling takes place automatically.

○ SUMMARY

1. Even when a computer system is running, it may have components that are in use only a fraction of the time. For this reason, overlapped systems were developed.

2. The idea underlying overlapped processing is to use the access cycles that are normally wasted during input/output operations. Channels control input/output operations and thus free the CPU for other processing. Input, processing, and output can be overlapped. The number of operations that can be overlapped depends on the number of channels on the system.

3. Input/output-bound and process-bound programs (even when overlapped) permit computer-system components to be idle. Multiprogramming is an attempt to increase the use of idle components by executing two or more programs at the same time. In this case, the computer system switches back and forth between the programs whenever the CPU is required to wait for the completion of an input/output operation.

4. Another method used to increase the use of the CPU during execution of input/output-bound programs is referred to as spooling. Under the control of a spooling program, the input data is transferred from a card reader to a disk and then from the disk to the CPU. Similarly, output is transferred from the CPU to a disk and then from the disk to the printer.

○ REVIEW QUESTIONS

1. What is a data channel? What are the main types of channels? Explain how they differ.
2. How does overlapped processing differ from serial processing?
3. What part does buffering play in input/output processing?
4. What is spooling?
5. Distinguish between multiprogramming and multiprocessing.
6. What factors must be taken into account in a multiprogramming environment?

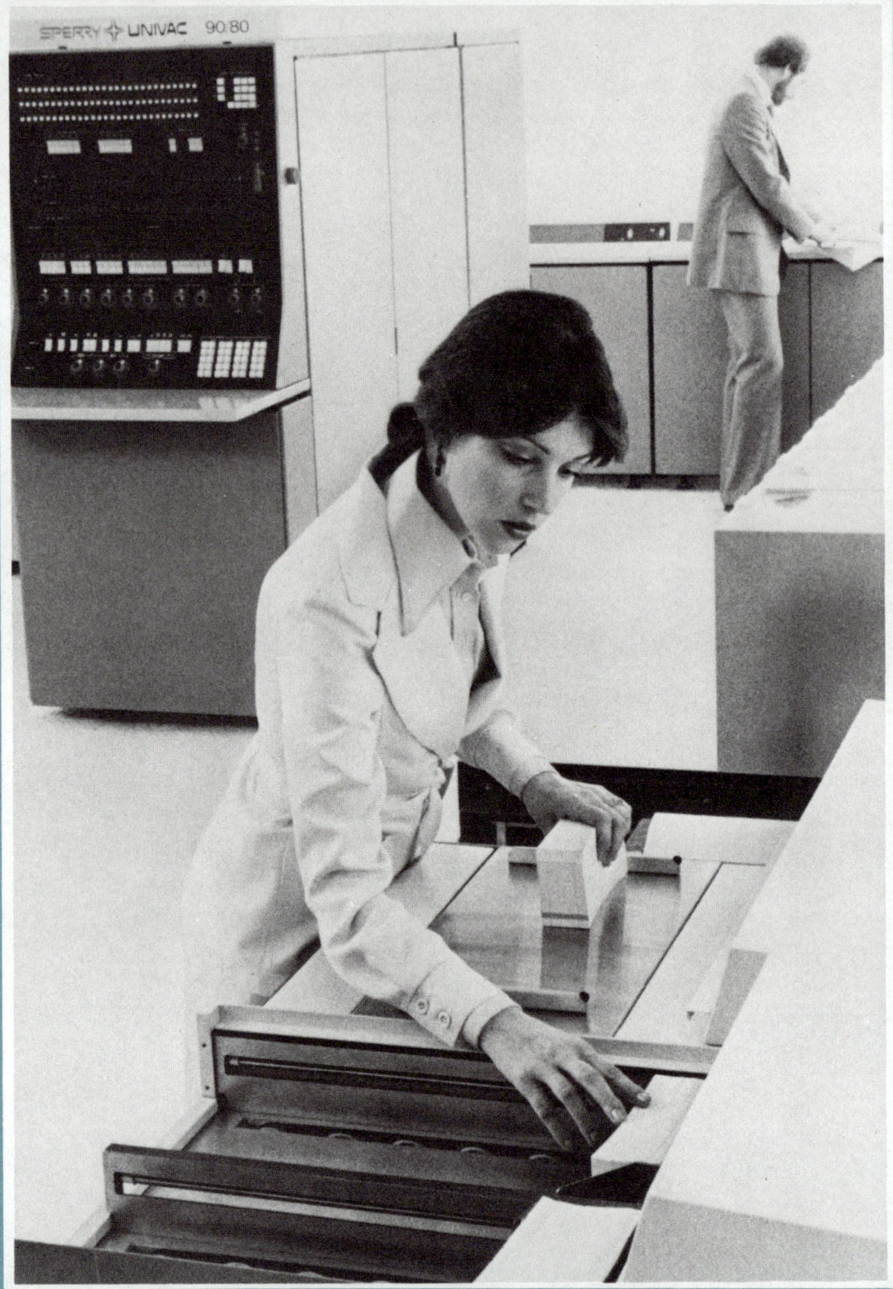
SPERRY UNIVAC 90/80

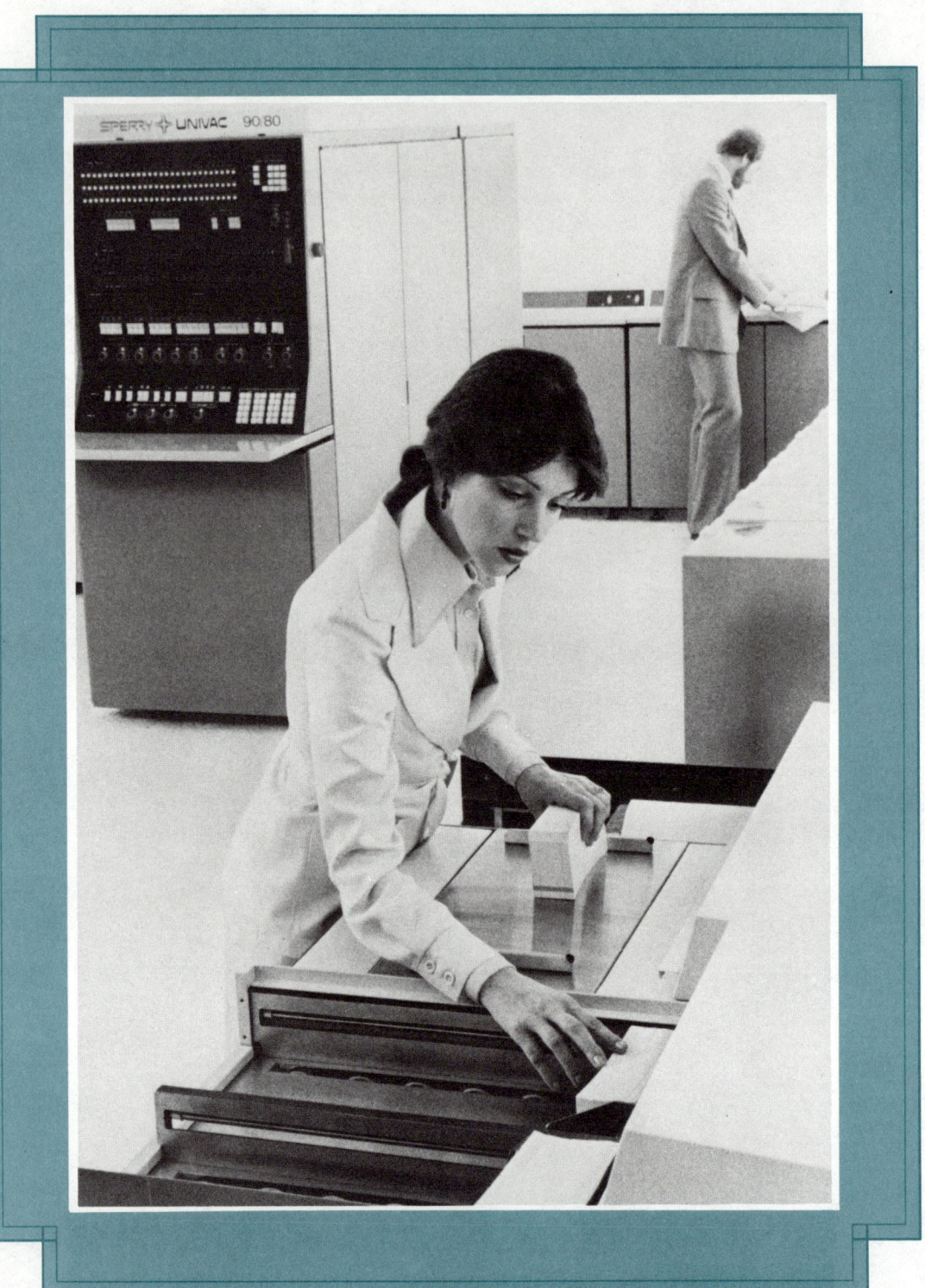

CHAPTER 13

INTRODUCTION TO OPERATING SYSTEMS

AN OPERATING SYSTEM
AND STACKED-JOB PROCESSING

AN OPERATING SYSTEM
AND THE PROGRAMMER

VIRTUAL STORAGE
Sharing the Internal Storage Unit
Sharing the Computer

Opposite: The operator begins the execution of a series of jobs by placing a deck of job cards in the card reader.

At one time, computer manufacturers designed a computer, then decided what programming support, such as assemblers or compilers, should be supplied with it. When designing third-generation computer systems, however, manufacturers faced the fact that the programming support, or software, was almost as important as the equipment, or hardware. They began to design software in conjunction with hardware. The result is that the hardware of a system and an *operating system* to support it are now developed together. The operating system is a group of programs designed to maximize the amount of work the system can do. Specifically, the operating system is designed to reduce the amount of time that the computer and other system components are idle. The programs are usually written by the computer manufacturer. They reduce the amount of programming required on the part of a computer user.

AN OPERATING SYSTEM AND STACKED-JOB PROCESSING

Before operating systems were developed, a computer system stopped when it finished executing a program. The operator then made ready the input/output devices to be used by the next program and loaded the program into main storage. During this time, the computer system was idle. If a computer system ran many programs during a day, it was likely to be idle a large part of the time. For example, if 40 programs were scheduled per day, with a 3-minute delay between programs, the computer system was idle two hours per day.

With an operating system, the operator does not load the programs that are to be executed. Instead, the operator places a deck of *job cards* in the card reader at the start of the day. Thereafter, the computer system loads and begins executing programs (jobs) according to the job cards. The computer system does not stop after executing a program. Instead, it reads the job cards for the next program. It loads the program into storage, usually, from tape or disk. Then it branches to the first instruction of the program. These operations are done under the direction of *control programs* that are part of the operating system. In short, the computer assists the operator. It reduces the time required to load programs and increases the amount of time the computer system can do productive work. This processing of a stack of jobs, rather than one job at a time, is called *stacked-job processing*.

Illustration 13-1 shows job cards for a stack of five jobs to be processed. For each job, two or more cards in the stack indicate which program is to be run and which input and output units are to be used (for example, the reels of tape required for the particular job and the tape

CHAPTER 13: INTRODUCTION TO OPERATING SYSTEMS

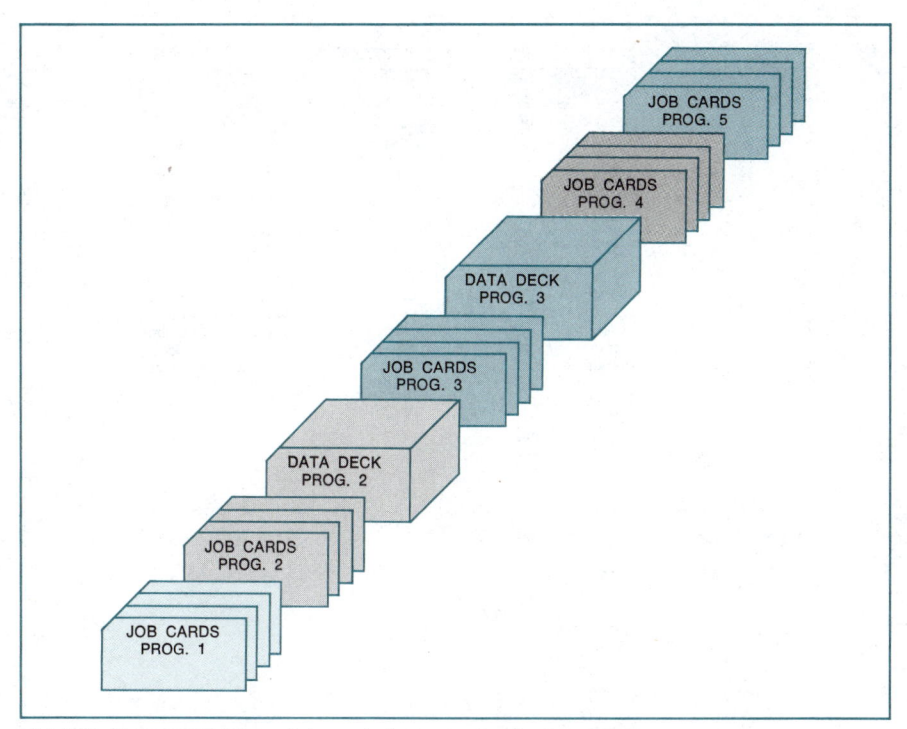

ILLUSTRATION 13-1 Job cards for a stack of jobs

drives on which they should be mounted). If a job is going to read data from punched cards, the data deck is placed behind the job cards for the job in the stack of jobs. For example, jobs 2 and 3 in Illustration 13-1 read data from cards.

During stacked-job processing, a control program called the *supervisor* (or *monitor*) resides in main storage. After a program has been loaded and executed, the computer branches to the supervisor program. At this stage, the supervisor could read the job cards for the next program, process them, and load the next program into storage. However, a supervisor program does not usually do all this. Instead, the supervisor loads a *job-control program* into storage. (See Illustration 13-2.) The job-control program reads and processes the job cards for the next program. When this processing is finished, control passes back to the supervisor program. The supervisor loads the next program identified by the job cards. The computer branches to it. By using a job-control program, instead of having the supervisor do all of the work, operating-system designers have reduced the number of main storage locations required for the supervisor. The

UNIT FOUR: AN OVERVIEW OF SYSTEMS

SUPERVISOR	SUPERVISOR	SUPERVISOR	SUPERVISOR	SUPERVISOR
Program 1	Program 1	Job-Control Program	Job-Control Program	Job-Control Program

The supervisor program and program 1, which is being executed, are in storage.

Program 1 is completed and branches to an instruction in the supervisor program.

The supervisor program loads the job-control program into storage and branches to the first instruction of the job-control program.

The job-control program processes the job cards that are in the card reader.

When finished, the job-control program branches to an instruction in the supervisor program.

SUPERVISOR	SUPERVISOR	SUPERVISOR
Program 2	Program 2	Program 2

The supervisor loads the next program to be executed into storage.

The supervisor branches to the first instruction of program 2.

Execution of program 2 begins.

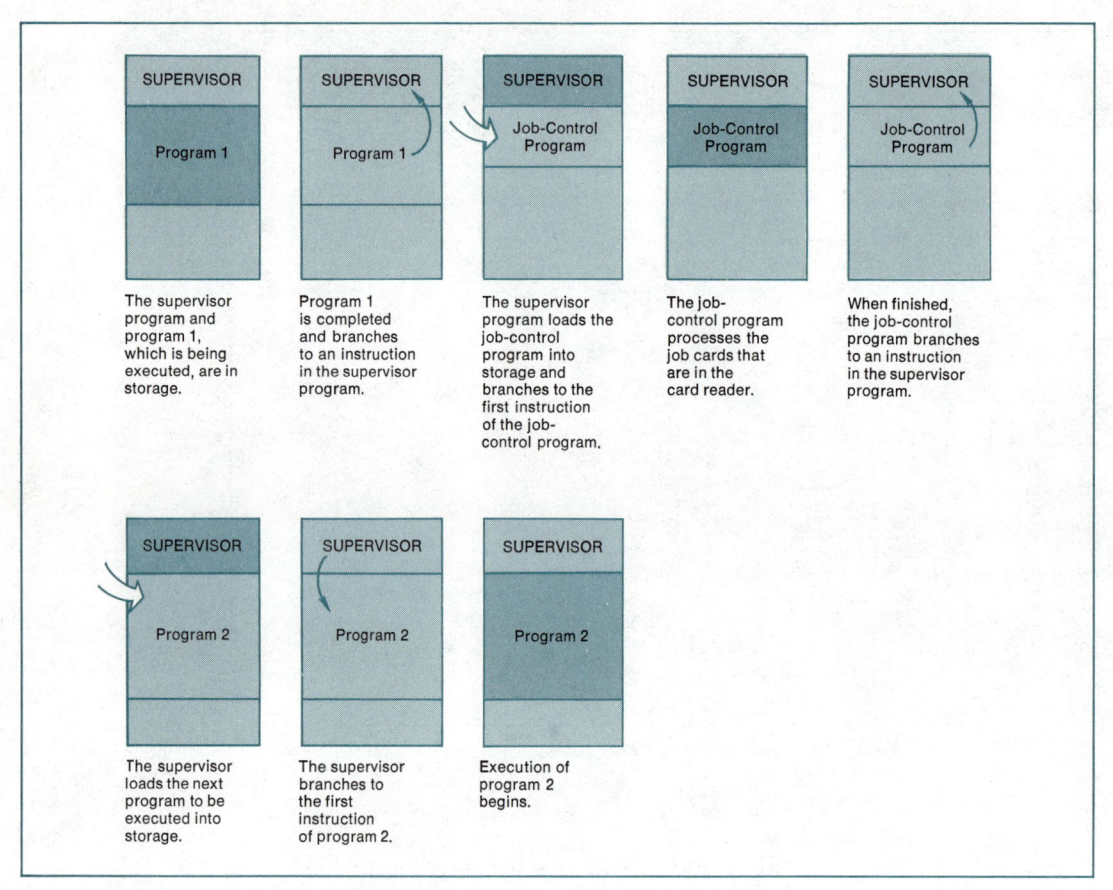

ILLUSTRATION 13-2 Job-to-job transition using control programs

job-control program occupies main storage only when loaded to read and process job cards.

The input/output device from which programs are loaded into main storage is often called the **system residence device**. This device must be directly available (online) to the computer at all times. It contains all programs to be run by the computer—both application programs (billing, sales analysis, and so on) and programs that are part of the operating system. Although the system residence device can be a magnetic tape unit, it is more commonly a direct access storage device. Because of its direct access capability, a direct access device eliminates the need to sequentially search for programs as is required when the programs are stored on tape. In addition, a direct access device has a relatively fast transfer speed. Therefore, less time is required to load programs into storage.

To see how stacked-job processing can eliminate idle computer time, consider the execution of six jobs as described in Illustration 13-3. They are to be executed on a system that consists of a CPU, a card reader, a card punch, a printer, six tape drives, and two disk drives, one of which is the system residence device. The purpose of scheduling these six jobs is to enable the operator to make ready the input/output devices for one job while another job is running. By so doing, the operator helps make it possible for the computer system to execute all six jobs without stopping.

The operator begins by placing cards for the six jobs in the card reader, mounting a tape on tape drive 1, and starting the computer system. While the first program (a card-to-tape program) is running, the operator mounts tapes on tape drives 2, 3, 4, 5, and 6 in preparation for the second job in the stack. At the end of the first job, the operating system reads program 2 (a sort program) and begins executing it. This program sorts the records originally mounted on tape drive 1, using the five tape drives 2 through 6. During execution of the program, the operator mounts the inventory disk pack on disk drive 2 in preparation for job 3. The computer system can then go to job 3 without having to stop. Continuing in this manner, the computer system can execute all six jobs without stopping.

In some cases, it is impossible to schedule jobs so that the operator can make ready the input/output devices for one job while another job is running. Then the computer system must stop, regardless of stacked-job processing. Similarly, the computer system must stop if an operator mounts the wrong tape on the wrong drive or fails to make ready an input/output device required by a program. In this case, the supervisor generally prints a message to the computer operator indicating which device requires attention. For example, the message

M 182,A12345,PAYROLL

may mean that a reel of tape with the label A12345 is required by the program named PAYROLL, and should be mounted on tape drive 182. As soon as the operator responds to this message, the computer system can resume processing.

The principles of stacked-job processing apply to multiprogramming systems as well as to systems that handle only one job at a time. In a multiprogramming system, however, the supervisor and other control programs of the operating system do more than has been shown so far. For example, various control programs keep track of available main storage and determine whether some of the programs in a stack of jobs can be multiprogrammed. Then, when programs are run simultaneously, programmed routines in the supervisor program handle the switching from one program to another. Because of this operating system help, multiprogramming is less difficult than it would be if each computer user had to control these tasks through user-written programs.

UNIT FOUR: AN OVERVIEW OF SYSTEMS

COMPUTER USES

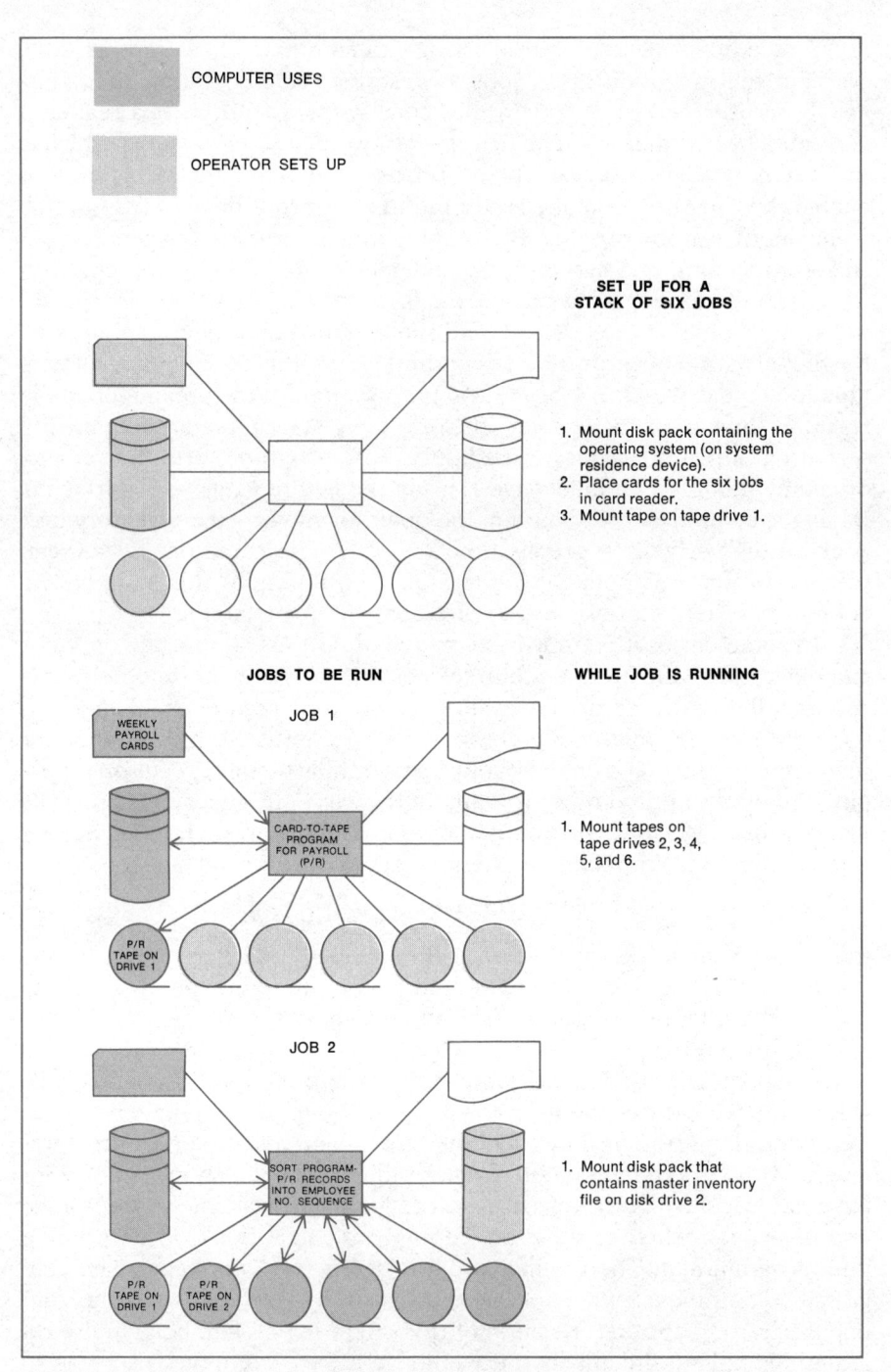

OPERATOR SETS UP

SET UP FOR A STACK OF SIX JOBS

1. Mount disk pack containing the operating system (on system residence device).
2. Place cards for the six jobs in card reader.
3. Mount tape on tape drive 1.

JOBS TO BE RUN   **WHILE JOB IS RUNNING**

JOB 1

WEEKLY PAYROLL CARDS

CARD-TO-TAPE PROGRAM FOR PAYROLL (P/R)

P/R TAPE ON DRIVE 1

1. Mount tapes on tape drives 2, 3, 4, 5, and 6.

JOB 2

SORT PROGRAM— P/R RECORDS INTO EMPLOYEE NO. SEQUENCE

P/R TAPE ON DRIVE 1

P/R TAPE ON DRIVE 2

1. Mount disk pack that contains master inventory file on disk drive 2.

ILLUSTRATION 13-3 Six jobs run without operator intervention

335

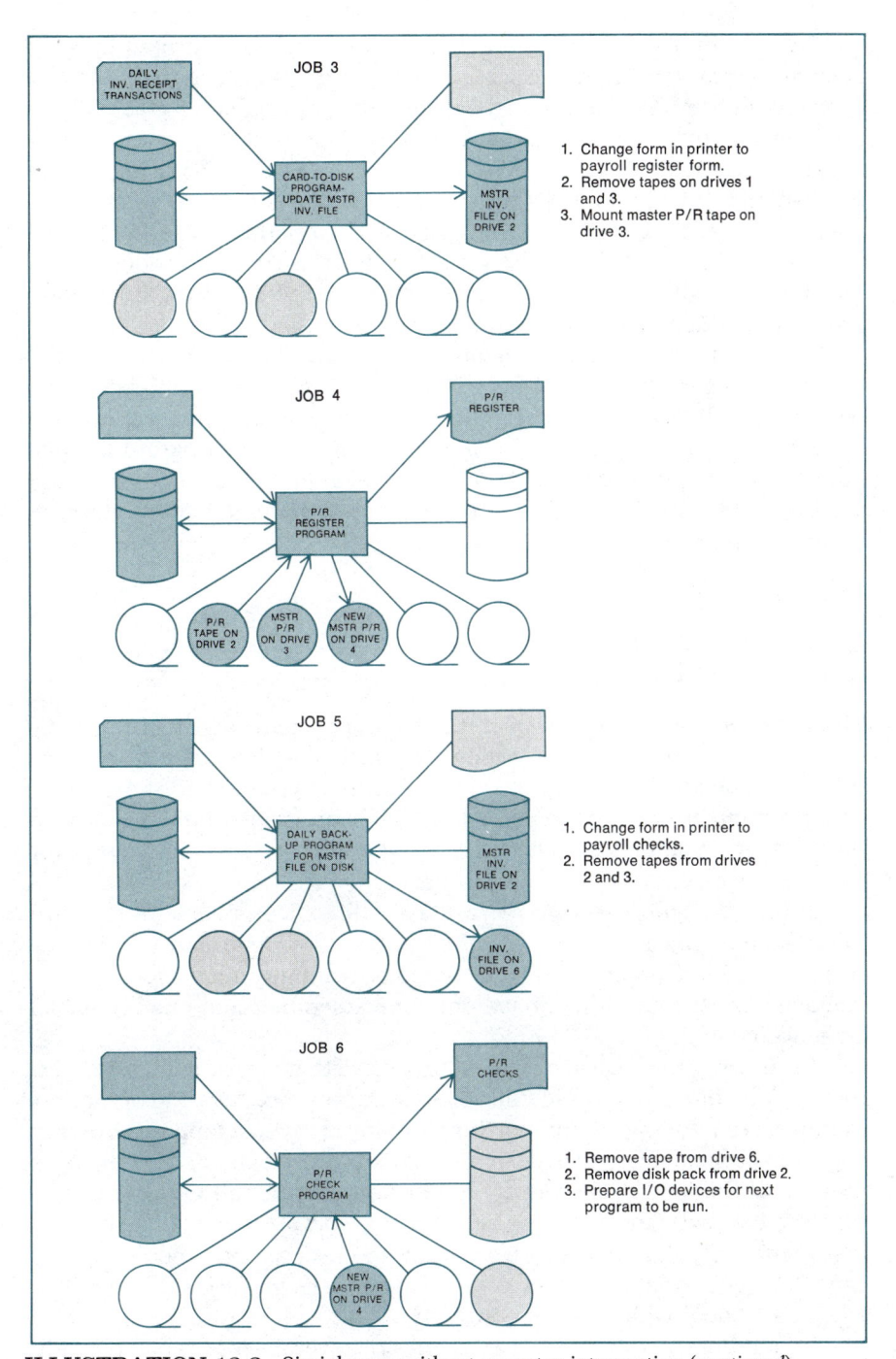

CHAPTER 13: INTRODUCTION TO OPERATING SYSTEMS

ILLUSTRATION 13-3 Six jobs run without operator intervention (*continued*)

In addition to the type of stacked-job processing illustrated thus far, an operating system can do much more. For example, it is possible for one card to indicate to the operating system that it should run a stack of jobs for which job information is already stored as part of the operating system. This means that the operating system, rather than data processing personnel, can schedule the jobs. As the programs in the stack are executed, the operating system can print out messages to the operator indicating which input/output devices should be made ready. The computer does the detailed work of keeping track of which programs are to be run and in what order, and which input and output files are needed.

Clearly, the amount of detail handled by control programs for stacked-job processing is significant. Nevertheless, the cost of these programs must be considered. For instance, a system residence device is required. So is enough additional main storage to hold the supervisor program and any other programs or routines that must be resident in main storage. These additional costs must be justified by the increased productivity of the computer system.

AN OPERATING SYSTEM AND THE PROGRAMMER

The programs and routines of an operating system help to reduce the time and expense of programming. In particular, language translators, utility programs, and an Input/Output Control System (IOCS) are stored in a *program library* for general use. Such programs and routines are provided on computer systems without operating systems, but programs are not processed on a stacked-job basis.

Typical *language translators* are assemblers, compilers, and generators. As discussed in Chapter 11, they reduce the programming time required to prepare object programs. Some operating systems include many language translators; others have only one assembler and one high-level-language compiler.

Utility programs are generalized programs that perform necessary but routine jobs in an electronic data processing system. A sort program, for example, is a utility program. Sorting is required in most tape systems, and only a few specifications vary from job to job (for instance, record length, location of the field to be sorted on, blocking factor, and number of tape drives to be used). Therefore, one generalized sort program can be used for many sort jobs. To use the sort program, the user supplies coded specifications for the variable factors, or *parameters*. The generalized program is adjusted to deal with them accordingly.

In addition to sort programs, there are several other types of utility programs. Programs that transfer data from one data-recording medium

CHAPTER 13: INTRODUCTION TO OPERATING SYSTEMS

to another are usually utility programs. Examples of these are card-to-tape, card-to-printer, tape-to-printer, and card-to-disk programs. (The use of such programs was introduced in Chapter 5 and mentioned in other chapters.) In addition, some utility programs are used for testing purposes. Others are used to keep programs on the system residence device up to date.

An *IOCS* contains programming for input and output operations, particularly operations involving tape and direct access records. This programming is valuable because input and output routines make up a large portion of a program (commonly as much as 40 percent). One type of input/output routine, for example, checks for tape-reading errors. Such a routine commonly backspaces the tape and attempts to re-read the record when an input error is detected. A typical routine may attempt to re-read the record up to 100 times before it gives up and prints an error message indicating that the record cannot be read. This type of error-checking routine must be executed for every program that uses tape input. Besides this type of routine, routines are needed to check labels on tapes and direct access records, to block and deblock records and, as described in Chapter 12, to keep track of input/output operations on an overlapped system. When an IOCS is available, the programmer does not need to write programs or routines to do these functions.

To use an IOCS, a programmer must specify, at the start of a program, the characteristics of the files and records that the program uses. Thereafter, the program is coded to accept input records as though they are read from simple sequential files. Whenever a read or write operation is necessary, the programmer codes a one-line macro-instruction (recall Chapter 11). Later, the program is translated into machine language and executed. Dozens of machine-language instructions may be included in the program and executed, in place of each single macro-instruction.

In summary, the language translators, utility programs, and IOCS routines of an operating system are designed to relieve the programmer of common programming chores. This increases the amount of time that the system is available for production by reducing the amount of computer time required for preparing object programs. It allows the programmer to concentrate on applications rather than on programming details.

○ VIRTUAL STORAGE

Sharing the Internal Storage Unit

Prior to the introduction of the IBM System/370 computer series, programmers generally had to be concerned with internal storage capacity. Each programmer had to make sure that a program and the data for it would fit into the available storage space. If the program was too large, the programmer had to split it into sections. This allowed the first section to be loaded into primary storage and the rest to be kept on secondary storage. After the first section was executed, the second section was written over (overlaid—commonly referred to as *overlaying*) the first section. Additional sections were executed in a similar manner.

Shortly after the introduction of System/370, in 1971, IBM announced that its medium-size and large computer systems would have ***virtual-storage*** (also called ***virtual-memory***) capability.

There are two principal methods of implementing virtual-storage capabilities. Generally, both software and hardware are involved. One method is ***segmentation***, in which each program's address space (range of storage locations referenced by the program) is split into variable-sized blocks ("segments"). The other method is ***paging***, in which physical-memory space is divided into fixed-size blocks ("page frames") and programs and data are divided into blocks ("pages") of the same size. Thus, one page of information can be loaded into one page frame.

Segmentation involves breaking a program into logically separable units. For example, one segment may be a subroutine; another may be a data area. An instruction or a data item within the program is identified by a two-part address which specifies the name of a segment and the relative location, or displacement, of the instruction or data item within the segment. The system constructs these addresses and keeps track of the various segments in a segment table established for the program in the storage unit. If an executing program tries to refer to a segment that is not in the storage unit, the system intervenes and brings the segment into it. (See Illustration 13-4.) Burroughs uses the segmentation technique to implement virtual-storage operations.

A computer having paging capability is automatically capable of breaking a program into the sequences of instructions called pages. The size of a page may range from that required to store a fairly small number of instructions to that required for a large segment. But all pages in a system are the same size. When a program is to be executed, a single page (or a small number of pages) of that program is brought into the storage unit from the virtual storage area, which is on direct access storage. Pages from several programs can be in the storage unit simultaneously. The computer executes instructions from one program, then from another, and so on. (See Illustration 13-5.) This ability is especially important if the computer system is operating in a time-sharing mode (about which more is said in Chapter 14).

When a page or segment (depending upon the implementation) not in the storage unit is referenced during program execution, a missing-item fault occurs. One method of minimizing the number of faults is by a prepaging or presegmentation technique. When one page or segment is trans-

CHAPTER 13: INTRODUCTION TO OPERATING SYSTEMS

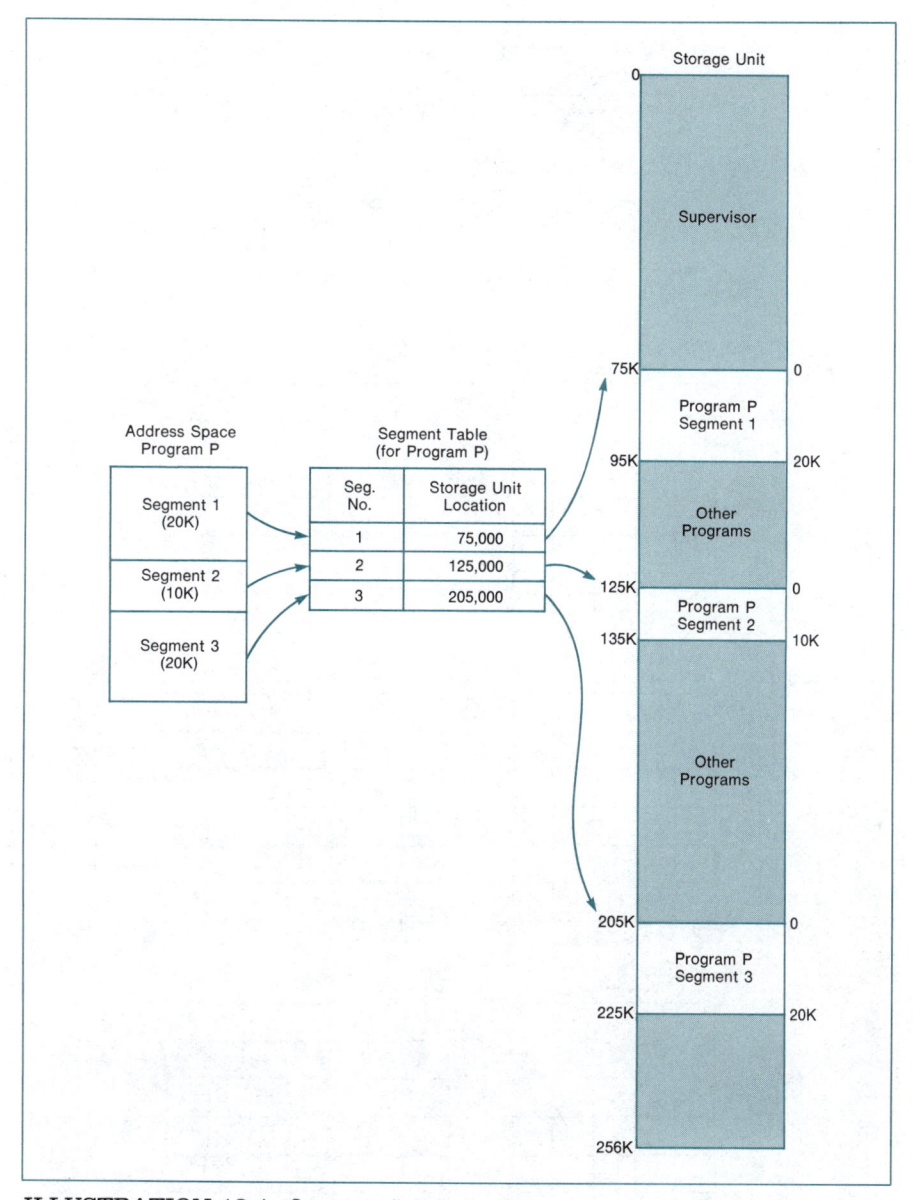

ILLUSTRATION 13-4 Segmentation

ferred into the storage unit, certain other pages are transferred as well, with the expectation that they are likely to be referenced. Only one page-in or segment-in operation is needed for the entire group, whereas a separate page-in or segment-in operation would be needed for each referenced page

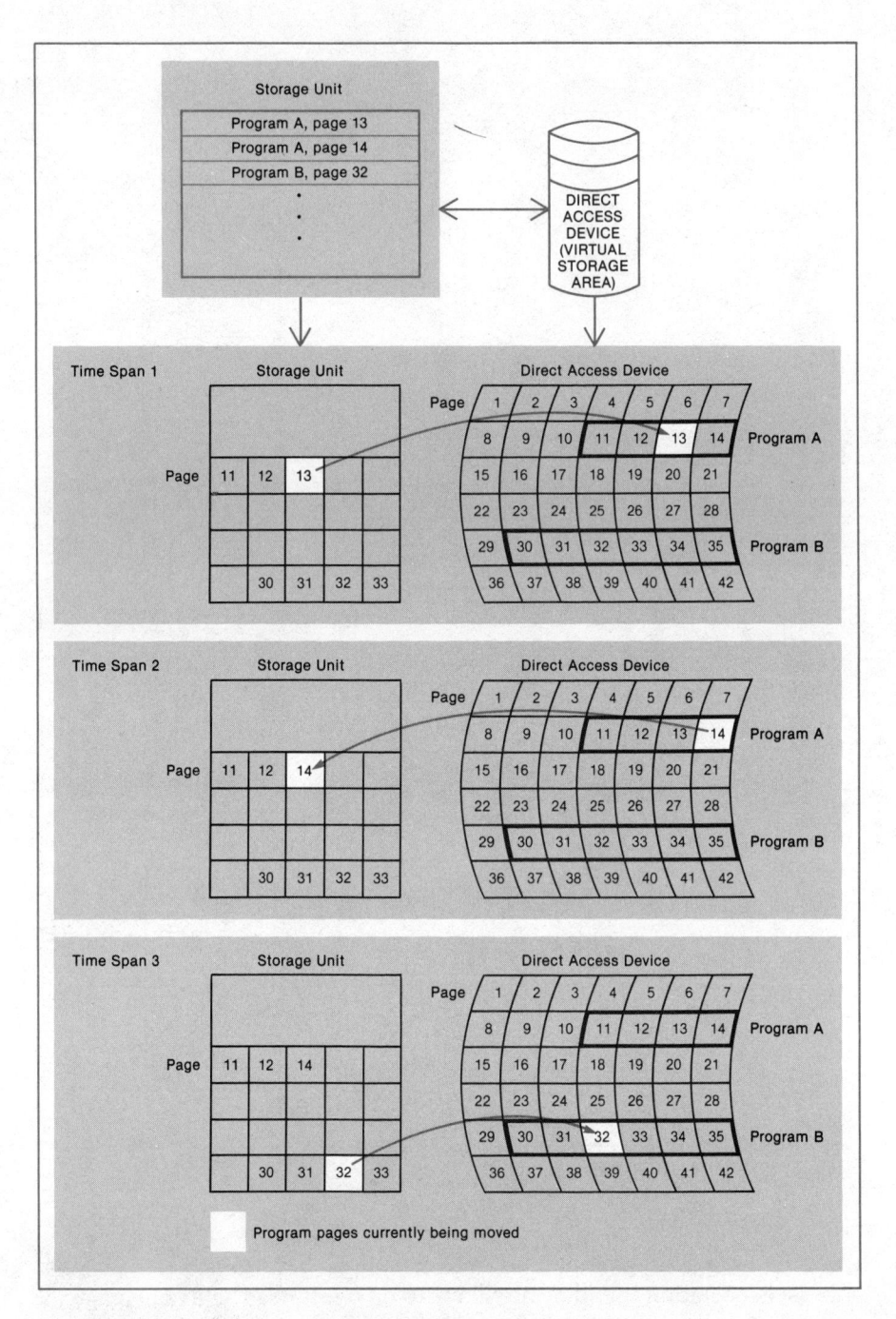

ILLUSTRATION 13-5 A method for sharing a storage unit

or segment if they were brought in singly. A second method of minimizing the number of faults is by the use of a demand paging or demand segmentation technique. Each page or segment is loaded into the storage unit only when called for as the result of a missing-item fault. No pages or segments are loaded unless referenced. There may be more page-in or segment-in operations, and the system may operate more slowly because of them, but no pages or segments are brought into the storage unit unnecessarily.

Virtual storage does not provide the user with an actual super-large storage unit. If all of the storage unit is in use when another page or segment is referenced, a replacement operation is necessary. Then, in System/370, for example, the least recently used (LRU) page in the storage unit is replaced. If that page was not modified while occupying the storage unit, it can be overlaid by the needed page, because a copy of the page being replaced exists in the virtual storage area. If the page was modified, however, a page-out operation must occur before replacement. This insures that a valid copy of the page will be available on virtual storage the next time it is referenced during program execution.

There is no concise, well-established rule for determining the amount of storage unit space that must be available to support a certain amount of virtual storage space. However, if an executing program is not allocated enough storage unit space, many of the references within it are likely to generate missing-item faults. If a similar situation exists for numerous programs in execution, the system is forced to spend most or all of its time moving pages or segments between virtual storage and the storage unit. This phenomenon is known as *thrashing*. The more thrashing occurs, the more inefficient the execution of programs.

The primary advantage of segmentation, paging, and virtual storage is better utilization of the storage unit. Less space is wasted because no contiguous portion of the storage unit large enough to hold a complete program waiting to be executed is available. The result is that potentially more programs can be executed. This in turn leads to greater utilization of the CPU and other system components. The greatest disadvantage is increased system overhead. The increased overhead involves: (1) the *increased* time it takes to transfer segments or pages from direct access storage, and (2) the *increased* storage unit space required for the sophisticated software needed to supervise the segmentation or paging operations.

Sharing the Computer

In either a segmentation or a paging system, several programs are in the storage unit at the same time. The computer can be programmed to share processing time among them. That is, multiprogramming can be used.

Either of two methods can be used in deciding when control should be transferred from one program to another in this kind of an environment. One method is to switch control at the end of a very short predetermined period of time, known as a *time slice*. Each program in turn gets its slice of time, if it can use it. This method is very useful for scientific-oriented applications where the time required to solve any one problem is unknown.

An alternative method is to switch control whenever a program currently having control has to wait for an input/output operation to be completed (recall Chapter 12). The program may thus be executed and then wait many times before its execution is completed. Since business-oriented applications commonly require frequent input/output, and input/output operations are slower than internal processing operations, this method is often used in business data processing.

SUMMARY

1. An operating system is a group of programs designed to increase the productivity of a computer system. Some of the programs reduce the amount of idle computer time. Others reduce the amount of programming that must be done by a computer user.

2. The idea behind stacked-job processing is to process many jobs in sequence by letting the computer load and begin execution of programs. This is done by control programs that load programs from a system residence device based on job cards placed in the card reader of the system. By careful scheduling of jobs and processing on a stacked-job basis, the idle computer time between the execution of programs can be reduced or eliminated.

3. The language translators, utility programs, and IOCS routines of an operating system reduce the amount of programming that must be done by a computer user. Because the programmer is relieved of common programming chores, less time and expense are required for programming.

4. To further increase the amount of useful work that can be accomplished by a computer system, virtual-storage capabilities based primarily on segmentation and paging techniques have been developed for current computers.

○ REVIEW QUESTIONS

1. How can an operating system improve the performance of a computer system?
2. What are the major components of an operating system? Briefly explain the functions of each component.
3. Explain how an operating system assists the computer operator.
4. Who is most likely to use utility programs and why?
5. Why were virtual-storage systems developed?
6. What is the difference between paging and memory swapping?

CAREER PROFILE

Darcy J. McCulloch
Manager, Point of Sale
Systems Development
American Express
Company

Background Experience

After high school, I joined the Air Force. I worked with the SAGE (Semi-Automatic Ground Environment) System. I knew I wanted a career in the computer field, so I enrolled in a technical school after leaving the Air Force. My first job was as a junior programmer for a small service bureau. In an organization of that size, you don't have the advantages of training programs or close supervision. You have to learn a great deal in a very short time.

I began at American Express as a programmer in a new realtime effort. I started taking college courses at night. First I completed the Phoenix College data processing program. I then finished undergraduate work at Arizona State University, majoring in Management. I'm currently pursuing an MBA with emphasis in Finance. During this time, I progressed from programmer to systems analyst, senior analyst, project leader, and project manager, and then to my present position as Systems Manager, Point of Sale Systems Development.

Primary Job Responsibilities

As a manager, I supervise and work with a large staff of programmers and systems analysts. Our task is to develop and refine systems for point-of-sale activities. This includes the use of realtime terminals to conduct business activities involving credit authorization, financial transcations, and the like. We have terminals all over the world. We are involved with all types of industries such as airlines, hotels, and department stores. It's a dynamic environment. We are at the leading edge of both technology and the application of technology. For example, our worldwide Credit Authorization System approves credit 24 hours a day, 365 days a year handling over 5½ million transactions per month. Our dispensing services permit the issuance of traveler's checks to persons who are thousands of miles from their homes—a form of electronic funds transfer. These are the types of computer applications we are developing—not just the more usual accounting types of applications.

What Has Made You Successful?

To my mind, success has two factors—one is talent, and the other is opportunity. I've been fortunate in studying from and working with some very competent people. I am part of a company that encourages education and is innovative in developing and applying new technology.

As I have progressed in my career, I find I do less of the work myself and more of it through others. It is important to understand the team concept and to develop a respect for the different talents and work styles of others.

I have always looked at what I am doing as a total learning experience. I have not separated academic pursuits from the work environment. It is easy to become too specialized. Too many data processing professionals are overly dependent upon one programming language, or one operating system, or one type of application. I believe that flexibility and professional curiosity are important and that there is always a need to learn more.

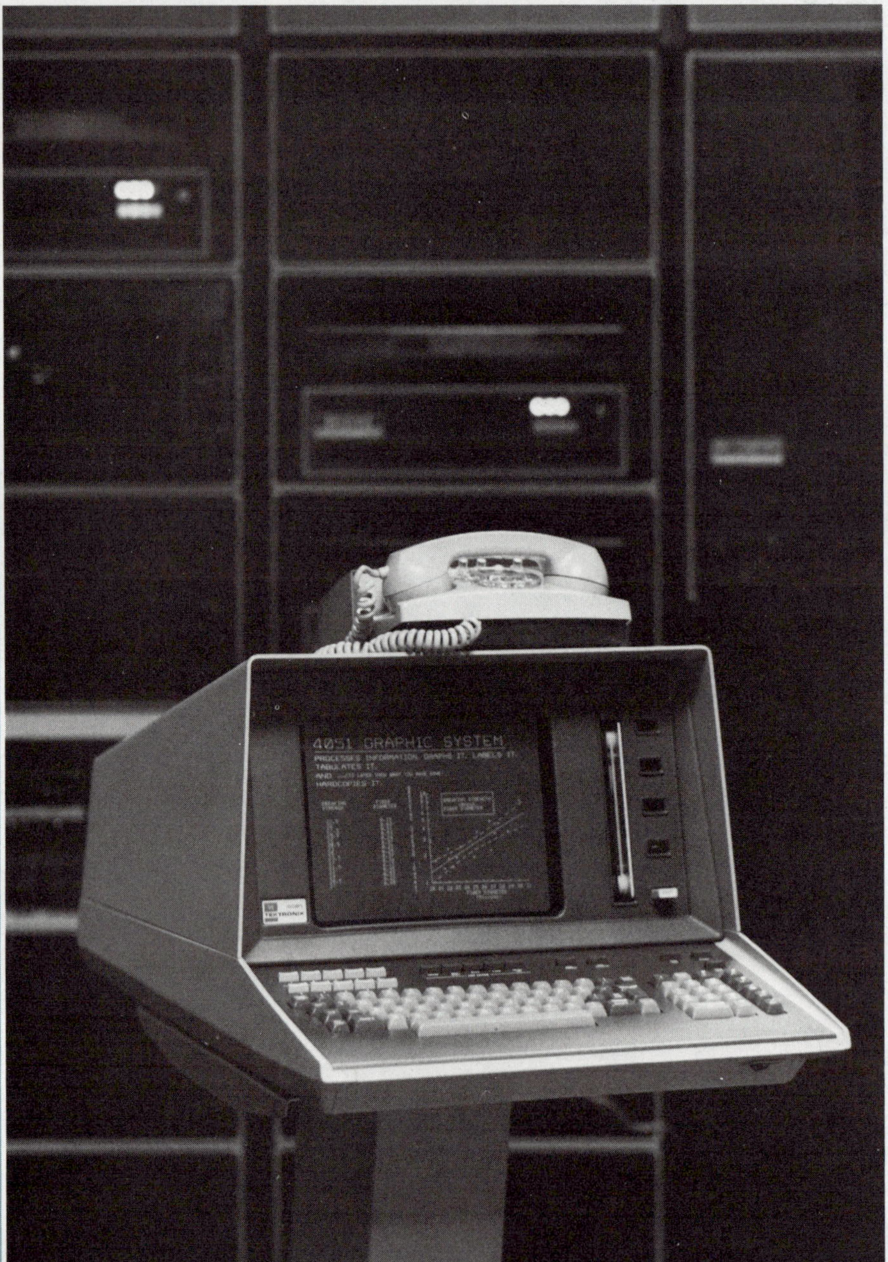
4051 GRAPHIC SYSTEM
TEKTRONIX

CHAPTER 14

INTRODUCTION TO DATA COMMUNICATIONS

ONLINE COMMUNICATION SYSTEMS

ONLINE REALTIME
COMMUNICATION SYSTEMS

TIME-SHARING SYSTEMS

DISTRIBUTED SYSTEMS

Opposite: A graphic display device and a data set
are used to access a timesharing system.

Significant developments in computer hardware and software have reduced the time required for processing data. However, processing is only one part of the data processing cycle. The total cycle consists of data collection, processing, and distribution. It is not surprising, then, that a data processing system may be slow even when the processing portion is fast.

The collection and distribution of business data is often complicated. Many companies have offices in several locations. Suppose, for example, that a company has five branch sales offices in various cities around the country and a warehouse across town from the home office. Also assume that the branch offices receive customer orders and mail them twice a day to the home office to be processed. The resultant shipping orders are printed as output. They are then delivered to the warehouse, where the ordered items are packed for shipping. In this system, the time required for collecting, processing, and distributing the order data may break down like this:

Data collection
    Waiting for batch of orders in branch office .... 4 hrs.
    Mailing orders to home office .... 24 hrs.
Data processing
    Keying order data .... 4 hrs.
    Processing keyed order data .... 1 hr.
Data distribution
    Delivery of shipping orders to warehouse .... 2 hrs.

Data collection and distribution require 30 hours. Data processing takes only 5. Even if no time were required for processing, 30 hours would still be required for an order to reach the warehouse.

A *data communication system* is one solution to this problem. It is designed to reduce the time required to collect and distribute data. Specifically, a system with data communication capability provides for the electrical transfer of data from a point of origin, such as a terminal in an office, to a computer, and from the computer to an output device, such as a terminal or a printer. (For details, see also Module A.)

Data communication is being used increasingly by organizations. The transmission of data is expected to increase by 35 percent each year between 1980 and 1985 because of the increased implementation of time-sharing and distributed systems (these terms are discussed later in this chapter). Part of this increase in data communication capability will be fostered by a significant reduction in data transmission costs. These costs are expected to be reduced by up to 50 percent by 1984.

Four commonly used types of data communication systems are: (1) online systems, (2) online realtime systems, (3) time-sharing systems, and (4) distributed systems. The capabilities available with these systems are described in this chapter.

CHAPTER 14: INTRODUCTION TO DATA COMMUNICATIONS

ONLINE COMMUNICATION SYSTEMS

An online data communication system periodically sends data directly between a terminal and a computer system. The online data communication system requires (1) terminals, (2) communication lines, (3) data sets, and (4) secondary storage. Terminals are attached to communication lines to send and/or receive data. Intelligent terminals with visual display screens or hard-copy devices are used in these systems. Communication lines are commonly telephone lines. These lines can be leased so that the communication system has 100 percent use of them, or they can be used on a dial-up basis and paid for at an hourly rate. Data sets are devices that convert data from a data processing code to a code that can be sent over communication lines, and convert the coded data back to a form acceptable for data processing.

An online data communication system for order entry is shown in Illustration 14-1. It includes an intelligent terminal with a visual display screen. During the day, orders are keyed on the terminal at the branch office. The terminal checks each data field for validity as it is entered by the operator. The validity checking is the enforcement of data standards

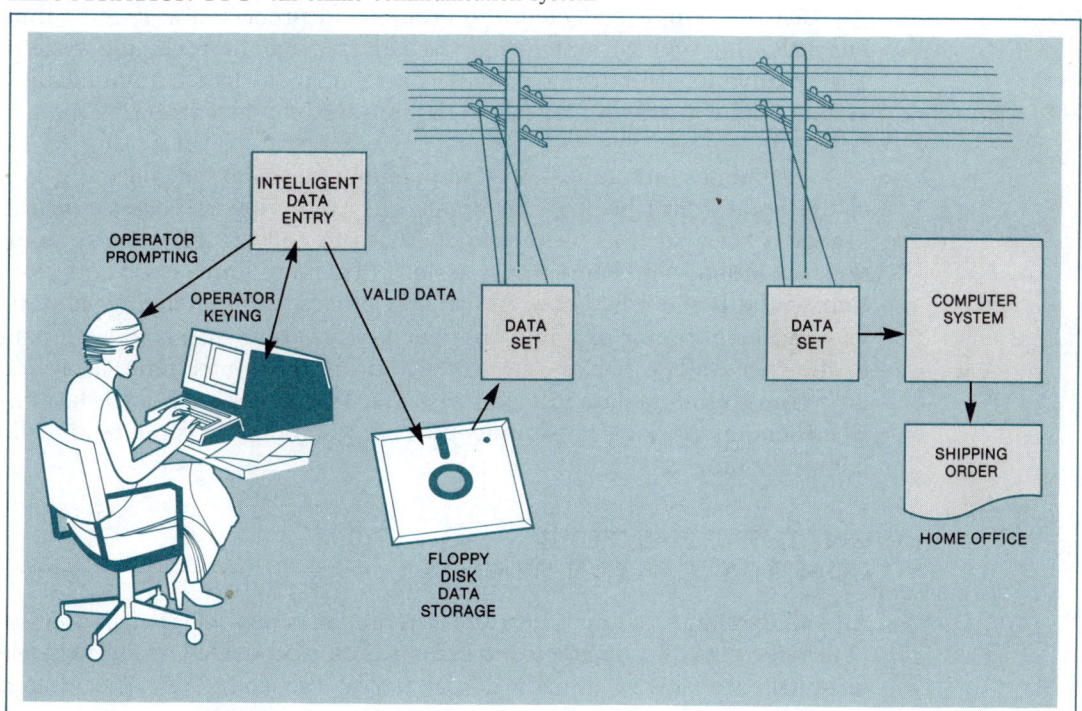

ILLUSTRATION 14-1 An online communication system

programmed into the intelligent terminal. For instance, if the operator enters an alphabetic character in a field that has been defined as numeric, the terminal will signal the operator that a data error has occurred. The correctness of the entered data cannot be checked fully by the terminal. Therefore the operator must visually check such factors as the spelling of names and addresses. At scheduled times (twice a day, for example), the data that has been accumulated on floppy disks is transmitted over communication lines to the computer in the home office.

Because the data in an online communication system is sent in batches, both the terminal and the computer must have some form of secondary storage. The CRT and typewriterlike terminals are likely to use cassette tapes, floppy disks, or bubble memory. A remote-job-entry station will transmit the data directly to an online secondary storage device. The computer generally uses magnetic tape or magnetic disk to store the incoming data and the processed results. For example, assume several branch offices make scheduled transmissions to the home office throughout the work day. The transmitted data is stored on magnetic tape by the computer in the home office. Then, one major processing run is made during the evening. The processed results are stored on magnetic tape and then transmitted to each of the appropriate branches in turn in time for the opening of business the following day.

Because data is collected into groups and processed at specific time intervals, this type of system can be called a batch-processing system. The disadvantage of using batch processing in a data communication system is that the data files in the system are only as current as the last run to update the files.

The online communication system eliminates delays in collecting data at the home office because terminals are used. However, delays at the branch offices, such as waiting for batches to collect, still exist. In addition, scheduling the online transmissions of data requires close coordination of the home office and the branch offices. Computer time may be wasted. Suppose, for example, that each of five branches is to send data to the home office twice a day. To avoid idle computer time, a branch office must send its data immediately after the preceding branch has finished sending its data. If, when its turn comes, a branch is not ready, idle computer time can result.

○ **ONLINE REALTIME COMMUNICATION SYSTEMS**

An online realtime communication system makes possible the elimination of all delays in collecting data and in distributing processed results because terminals are always directly connected to the computer. The system provides immediate two-way communication, processes transactions as

CHAPTER 14: INTRODUCTION TO DATA COMMUNICATIONS

they occur, and can respond to unusual processing conditions.

Illustration 14-2 represents the major components of an online realtime communication system for processing orders submitted by five branch offices. In this communication system, each branch office has a terminal that can both send and receive data. Such a system need not include intelligent terminals with data storage. The data can be transmitted directly to the computer and validated by it. When the terminal is used to send data, the operator keys the data on the terminal keyboard. The keyed data is either displayed on a screen or printed on paper at the terminal so that the operator can check it. When the terminal is used to receive data, the data is displayed or printed under control of the computer system.

There are two terminals in the warehouse. The first is a visual display device used for communication with the computer system. The second receives data from the computer and is used to print shipping orders. It may be a character-at-a-time printer similar to a typewriter or a high-speed line-at-a-time printer. In the home office, a data set converts the data sent over the communication lines into a data processing code that can be

ILLUSTRATION 14-2 A realtime communication system

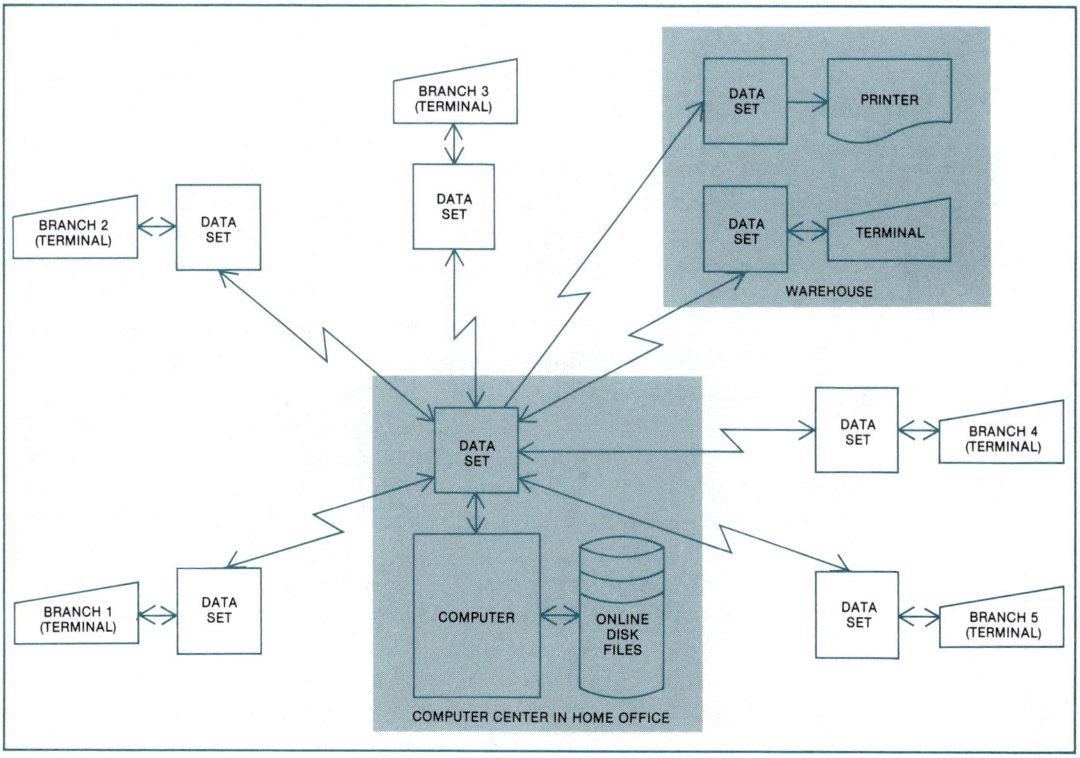

processed by the computer. A magnetic disk contains the inventory and accounts receivable files of the company.

In this type of communication system, when an order is received at a branch office, there is no waiting. The terminal operator keys the order data (customer number, item numbers, and quantities of items ordered) on the terminal. This data is sent over the communication lines to the computer in the home office. After the operator has keyed data, he or she presses a key to indicate to the computer that the data is ready for processing. If the data is not correct, the operator re-keys the data that is in error before signaling to the computer that the data is ready. The computer checks the inventory file on magnetic disk to determine whether the items ordered are in stock. If they are available, the computer sends a response to the branch-office terminal indicating that the order will be filled immediately. If any items are not in stock, the computer supplies the date when the items are likely to be available. Then the branch office can contact the customer (who may be waiting at a phone) to indicate the status of the order. After communicating with the branch office, the computer system processes the order data and prints a shipping order on the terminal in the warehouse.

There are definite advantages to this online realtime communication system. The time between receiving an order at a branch office and learning of it at the warehouse is reduced to minutes. In addition, because transactions are processed as they occur, the computer system can respond immediately to unusual situations such as stockouts.

In evaluating an online realtime communication system, the additional costs of operating the system must be weighed against the increased value it provides. In general, a realtime communication system necessitates additional equipment, programming, and system design. Among the equipment requirements are communication lines, data sets, terminals, and magnetic disk devices.

As a practical consideration, an online realtime communication system should have multiprogramming capabilities. (See Chapters 10 and 12.) Consider, for example, that an online realtime communication system for order processing must be available throughout the day to process incoming orders. Without multiprogramming capabilities, other processing programs such as payroll and inventory control can be run only on a second shift or by a second computer. Furthermore, although the realtime system must be available continuously, there are times when it is likely to be idle. During the lunch hour, for instance, few orders are likely to be received. Finally, because typewriterlike terminals are slow input devices, thousands of instructions can be executed by the computer system between the periods when any two characters of data are transmitted. Without multiprogramming capabilities, there is no way to use this available computing power (unused access cycles); hence, it is wasted.

CHAPTER 14: INTRODUCTION TO DATA COMMUNICATIONS

With a large computer system that offers multiprogramming capabilities, the realtime program (in this case, the order-processing program) and one or more other processing programs can be executed at the same time. Illustration 14-3, for instance, shows the contents of main storage while a typical realtime communication system is running. The primary program, called the *foreground program*, is the realtime program. It has priority over any other programs in main storage. Whenever data is being sent from a branch office, this program has control of the computer system. However, whenever data is not being sent, the secondary program, called the *background program*, is executed. In the illustration, this program is a payroll check-writing program. To handle the switching back and forth between the two programs, a supervisor program remains in storage throughout processing. As in other multiprogramming systems, the CPU executes the instructions of one of the programs while channels carry out input/output operations. With the use of multiprogramming, processing programs such as payroll, inventory-control, and sales analysis can be executed by the computer system that is available all day for realtime processing.

○ TIME-SHARING SYSTEMS

Time sharing is a technique that allows several users of a computer system to use that system on what appears to be a simultaneous basis. Each user is connected to the system via a terminal and operates independently of any other user. The time-sharing system gives almost immediate re-

ILLUSTRATION 14-3 The use of main storage in a realtime system

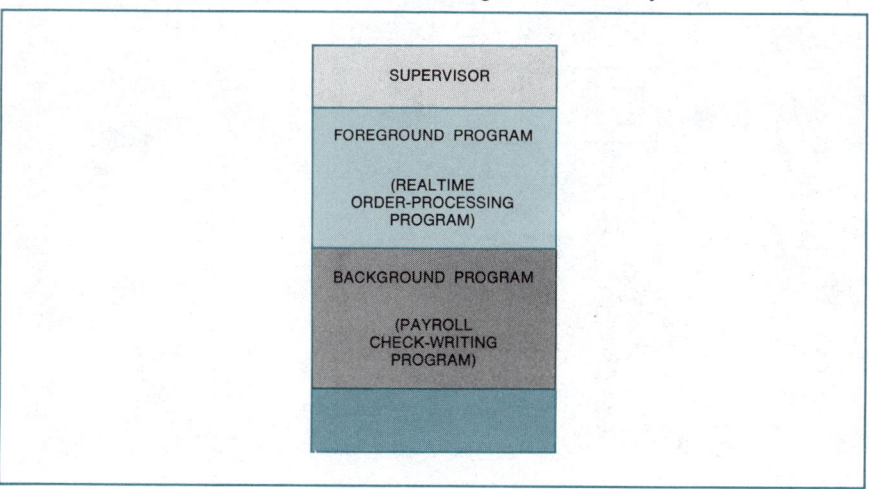

UNIT FOUR: AN OVERVIEW OF SYSTEMS

sponses to each user; therefore, the users are seldom aware that the system is being shared.

A time-sharing system is generally a multiprogramming system. Several programs are executed concurrently. Typically, a time-slicing algorithm as described in Chapter 13 is set up. Under this approach, each user is allocated a fixed portion of CPU time for execution of his or her program. Because each time slice (*quantum*) is very short, many users can share the system without having to wait for extended periods. As shown in Illustration 14-4, users of one time-sharing system may be inquiring into files, writing computer programs, preparing reports, and entering data from geographically separated terminals at the same time.

An organization may install a time-sharing system on its computer or use time-sharing facilities available for a fee from a computer services company. For some organizations, the latter choice may be more economical than installing a system; a decision favoring one approach or the other

ILLUSTRATION 14-4 A time-sharing system

must be based on an organization's data processing requirements. The advantage of using a computer services company is that, although certain fixed costs, such as those for acquisition and installation of terminals and communication lines, must be paid by the user, the user is charged for the central processing facilities of the computer system only when they are used to do the user's work. Thus, the user obtains access to a large computer system at a fraction of the cost of installing one internally.

Depending on the data processing requirements of an organization, only one terminal or many may be installed; in the first case, the organization becomes one time-sharing user, together with other organizations using the system. If there is a need for multiple terminals in an organization, such as one for each department, each terminal is, in effect, a time-sharing user.

Various types of time-sharing systems are used in organizations. Some have a series of application programs that can be executed by the user, but not altered; some allow the user to create and use programs; some have one main application and the user merely provides input data for that application; and others are a combination of all of these types with the main application having first priority.

An example of an application that can be executed but not altered is a payroll program for which a clerk enters weekly employee time-card data into a terminal and then requests program execution to print checks. In a second request, the payroll clerk may call for execution of a program to print a weekly payroll report.

An example of a single-purpose system is one that involves teller terminals designed for savings-account applications. When a customer goes into a bank to make a deposit or withdrawal, his or her passbook is placed in a terminal. The keyboard is used to enter such data as the customer account number, amount, and type of transaction. This data is transmitted to the computer. It processes the transaction, computes any accumulated interest, and prints the updated balance in the customer's passbook. Many of these terminals may be online to a computer at the same location or many miles away. Each terminal is operated by a time-sharing user of a realtime communication system designed for the primary purpose of maintaining customer savings accounts.

Time-sharing systems that allow users to create and use their own programs usually provide several progamming languages for this purpose. Some of these languages are *interpretive*; that is, they check each program statement as it is entered and point out any errors in the statement. This allows the programmer to edit and debug a program as it is being created. Once the program has been created, it can be executed and/or stored for future use.

One of the most popular time-sharing languages in use today is called BASIC (Beginners' All-purpose Symbolic Instruction Code). As noted in

UNIT FOUR: AN OVERVIEW OF SYSTEMS

Chapter 10, this language can be learned easily and used to solve many types of business problems. It is usually implemented as an interactive, or conversational, language, which means that it permits interaction between the user at a terminal and the computer during execution of a program.

Illustration 14-5 shows how a BASIC program can be created on a terminal, stored for future use, and then recalled and executed on one kind of time-sharing system. This program computes the compound interest on a user-specified sum of money for a user-specified period of time. The following steps are performed:

1. The user identifies himself or herself to the time-sharing system, giving an account number and some coded identification item, both of which are automatically typed over to protect the user's account.
2. The program is created and stored under the program name INTEREST.
3. The program is called for, and execution is requested.

ILLUSTRATION 14-5 A BASIC program

```
                    NAME? martin holland
                    ACCOUNT? ▓▓▓▓
       User         KEYWORD? ▓▓▓
   Identification   TERMINAL? p35
                    COMMAND ? clear text
                    COMMAND ? basic
                   :ENTERING STANFORD/BASIC.
                    COMMAND ? collect 10 by 10
                        10.   ? rem computes compound interest on a sum of money for any number years.
                        20.   ? print ' '
                        30.   ? print 'after the # prints, type in input data separated by commas'
                        40.   ? input p , i ,n
                        50.   ? print ' '
                        60.   ? let s = p * ( 1 + i ) ** n
                        70.   ? print p 'dollars compounded annually for' n 'years'
      Program        80.   ? print 'at' i 'percent interest gives' s 'dollars'
      Creation       90.   ? print ' '
                       100.   ? print 'if you wish to try other values type a 1, if not a 9'
                       110.   ? input z
                       120.   ? if z = 9 then 140
                       130.   ? go to 20
                       140.   ? print '*****     end of "interest" program      *****'
                       150.   ? print ' '
                       160.   ? end
                       170.   ? ***
      Program        #***
       Saved         COMMAND ? save interest on sys19
                    "INTEREST" SAVED ON SYS19
      Program        COMMAND ? use interest on sys19 clear load
       Called        COMMAND ? go

                    AFTER THE # PRINTS, TYPE IN INPUT DATA SEPARATED BY COMMAS
                    # 1000.00 , .05 , 10
      Program
      Executed       1000 DOLLARS COMPOUNDED ANNUALLY FOR 10 YEARS
                    AT .05 PERCENT INTEREST GIVES 1628.877 DOLLARS

      Program
      Terminated     9
```

4. The program requests the amount of money, interest rate, and time period. After this data is entered, the compound interest is computed and printed.
5. The user signifies the end of processing.

DISTRIBUTED SYSTEMS

When several geographically *dispersed,* or *distributed,* computers are connected in a communication network, the term *time-sharing system* is no longer appropriate. The term *distributed system,* or *network,* is used to describe this kind of an environment. A **distributed system** is like a time-sharing system in that it can be used within a single organization or by several organizations. In either situation, there is a decentralization of processing activity within the framework of a network with systemwide rules. A hierarchy of computers allows much processing and storing of data to be done at or near the origin of the data. But the important advantages of large, centralized computer systems, such as organizationwide access to basic operational data, are present as well.

Distributed processing decentralizes the processing and storage of data to wherever they are needed, for use wherever they are needed, to satisfy end-user requirements. The users have access to a central (commonly referred to as *host*) computer, under either loose or tight central management control. The emphasis is on the end user and central management flexibility for interfacing with that user.

Most organizations do not want to set up data processing staffs at end-user locations. The distributed computer systems are needed either to permit end users to develop their own relatively simple application software locally, utilizing procedure-oriented languages they can deal with, or to develop the application software centrally and then to distribute and maintain it centrally, or to allow both.

The lowest level of processors in a distributed system includes minicomputers or small computers. They have some local data storage and perform local processing. Tasks that are too large or that require data not available in local files are transmitted to a higher-level regional or centralized computer. The highest level in the hierarchy of computers has the capability to process large-scale problems.

Illustration 14-6 shows a basic distributed system. All terminals are interfaced with a small computer, which, in turn, is directly linked to a large computer. Additional devices can be linked to the small computer to permit data retrieval from files on secondary storage when needed. Such a system can be (and usually is) a realtime system. This capability depends on the availability of direct access storage devices.

As shown in Illustration 14-7, more than one small computer can be attached to one large computer. For example, a state university system

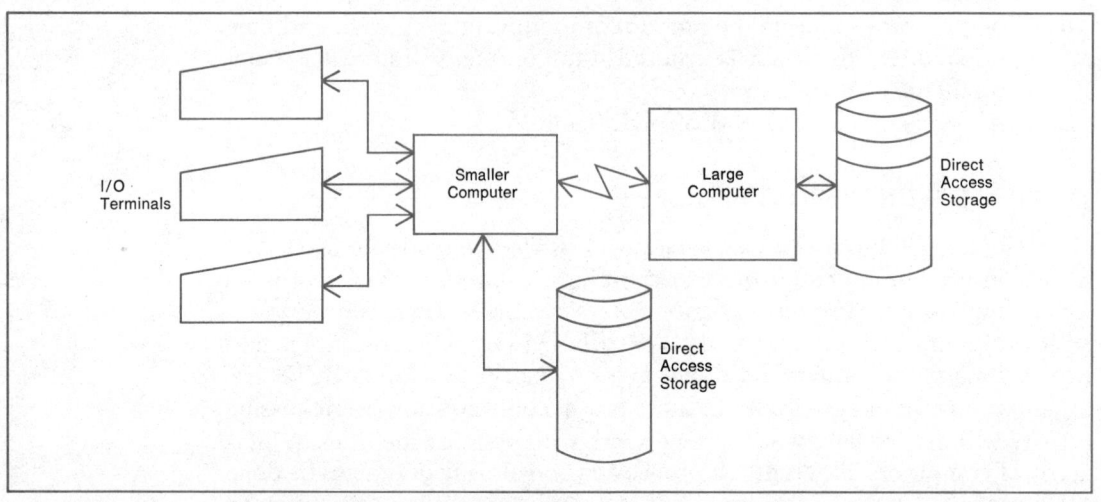

ILLUSTRATION 14-6 A basic distributed system

may have a small computer at each campus which can be either used alone or linked with a large central computer to operate as part of a distributed system. (See Illustration 14-8.)

System design and programming costs are relatively high for a distributed system because of the greater complexity of the system. A system like the one in Illustration 14-6 or 14-7 requires a complex routine to determine which communication line to deal with next and how to handle input when several terminals are ready to send data. The systems analyst must determine such things as the maximum number of terminals that the computer system can handle at one time, and the probability that all remote locations will want to send data at the same time. The systems analyst must evaluate the possibility of system overload and provide for any conditions that may occur. In addition, the systems analyst must provide an alternative method of handling input that can be used when the computer system is not working because of mechanical failure.

Assume Illustration 14-6 shows an order-processing system. Offsetting the costs of the system are benefits such as improved customer service. In addition to faster order processing, this type of system makes other types of customer service possible—specifically, quick and accurate responses to inquiries. Suppose, for example, that the system were also used for answering accounts receivable inquiries against a master file accessible to the large computer. In this case, a terminal user could key in the customer's account number and transmit it to the large computer. That computer could access the customer's accounts receivable record and send a response back to the terminal. The terminal user could quickly answer the customer's inquiry with up-to-date information.

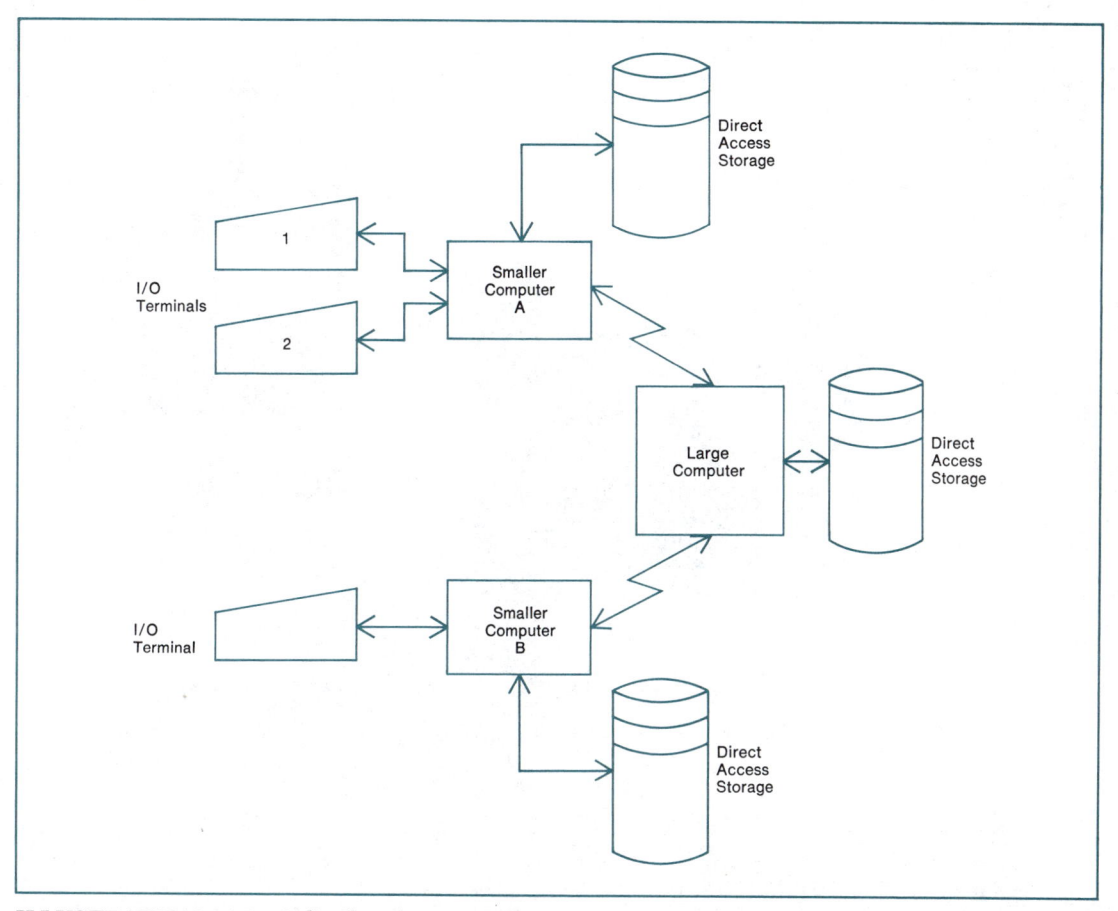

CHAPTER 14: INTRODUCTION TO DATA COMMUNICATIONS

ILLUSTRATION 14-7 A distributed system with two small computers

A distributed system can also make greater management effectiveness possible through updated management information. For example, consider how a distributed system can be used for inventory control. A terminal in each warehouse is used to record receipts of items into inventory. The inventory file on magnetic disk always contains the current inventory balances in the warehouse, not the balances as they were at some time in the past. When an inventory balance falls below its reorder point, a warning is printed out on a terminal in the inventory-control department. Thus, inventory-control personnel know about exceptional conditions when they happen—that is, in realtime. Similarly, distributed systems can be used to provide current information for sales management, production-control management, and any other area of operation where the value of the information justifies its cost.

UNIT FOUR: AN OVERVIEW OF SYSTEMS

ILLUSTRATION 14-8 Small computer in a distributed system

○ SUMMARY

1. Processing is only one part of the data processing cycle. The other parts, collecting and distributing data, may be far more time-consuming. Data communication systems are designed to reduce the time required for the collection and distribution of data.

2. Online data communication is the direct transmission of data from a terminal to a computer system. Online data communication systems require terminals, secondary storage, communication lines, and data sets. Data is keyed, validated, and held in the secondary storage of intelligent terminals, until it is transmitted to the computer. The data is usually transmitted in batches, one or more times each day. Once transmitted, it is often held in secondary storage at the central com-

puter location until all terminals have completed data transmission. Then all the data is processed. Scheduling the online transmission requires close coordination of branch locations with the central computer location to reduce the likelihood of idle computer time.

3. Online realtime systems process transactions as they occur and respond to conditions as they develop with immediate two-way communication. In an online realtime system, the terminals are always connected to the computer. In addition to terminals, communication lines, and data sets, realtime systems require direct access storage devices. For practical reasons, they should have multiprogramming capabilities.

4. Time sharing is a technique that permits several users to share a computer system on what seems to be a simultaneous basis. Each user is connected to the system via a terminal and is allocated a portion of CPU time. Access to a time-sharing system can be on a fee basis through a computer services company or on a system within the organization.

5. The term *distributed system,* or *network,* is used to describe several geographically dispersed, or distributed, computers connected in a communication network. Besides equipment costs, programming and system design costs are relatively high for such a system. These costs may be offset by the value of the information provided.

○ **REVIEW QUESTIONS**

1. What is data communication and what are its main characteristics?
2. What is an online realtime system?
3. What is the importance of online realtime processing in eliminating delays in transmitting data?
4. Describe the major components of an online realtime system.
5. What is time sharing?
6. What is conversational time sharing?
7. List the important advantages of conversational time sharing.
8. What is remote job entry?
9. What is the concept and primary function of distributed data processing?
10. What are the roles of host and satellite computers in distributed data processing?

CAREER PROFILE

Nancy Taylor Flanagan
Systems Designer
Keydata Corporation

Background Experience

I graduated from Bentley College with a B.S. degree in Computer Information Systems. Within that degree, I specialized in Accounting to learn more about computer applications, and in Management to learn more about the information needs of managers. While taking computer-related courses, I learned four languages: BASIC, FORTRAN, COBOL, and DBMS 10, which is a data base language for Digital Equipment Corporation's DEC 10 computer. I'm currently learning RPG. I completed the B.S. degree program at night while working full-time for the university during the day. I plan to start an MBA program, both to gain new information for my present job and to prepare for future career advancement.

Primary Job Responsibilities

My job as systems designer requires developing and implementing business computer systems for client companies. Once a salesperson secures a contract for a system, we work with the customer in designing the new system. That means several weeks of systems analysis—meeting with a company's management to determine the business application requirements, observing present procedures, and documenting the computer system we propose for the company. Using this information I prepare a system design proposal, which is formally presented to the customer for written approval. Once that is approved, I work with the customer in converting their records for the computer, write the detailed specifications for any special programming required, help in setting up the hardware, train the customer's staff in operating the system, and generally guide the overall implementation of the new system. So, at any one time, I may be working with one company in designing a system, with another in a training phase, and with yet others in support followup. While this may sound difficult, the diversity is one of the things I like about this job.

What Has Made You Successful?

I think, first of all, my education. I acquired a good understanding of computer concepts, systems fundamentals, and programming. I also developed human relations skills. I think my own enthusiasm for this field has been very important. A big part of my job is realizing that many people still mistakenly view computers as threats. By helping people to better understand the benefits of computers and by conveying my own excitement for this field, I encourage people to dig in and learn what they need to do. I enjoy working with people. This is an important factor because I meet and work with so many different people.

UNIT FIVE

MANAGEMENT INFORMATION SYSTEMS

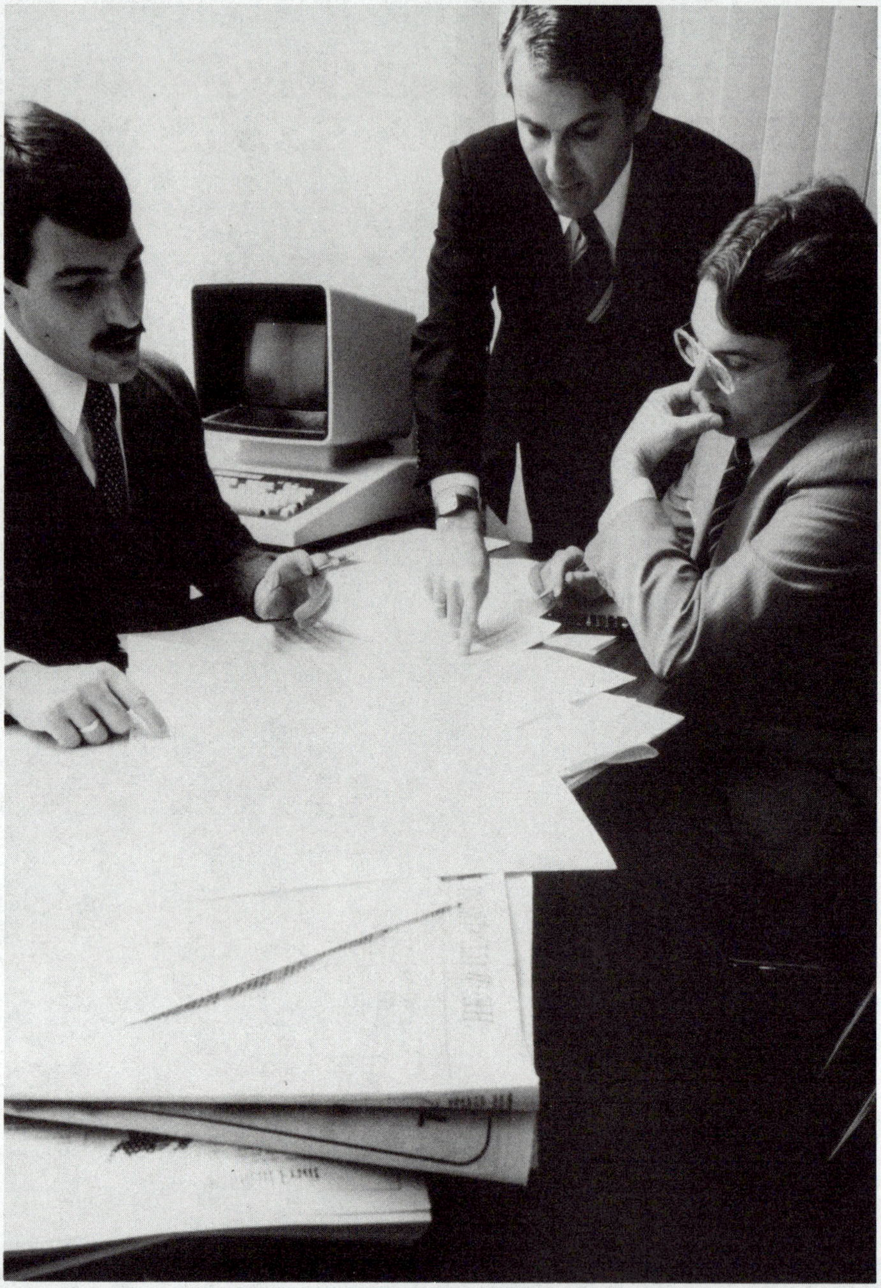

CHAPTER 15

MANAGEMENT INFORMATION SYSTEMS

THE NEED FOR MANAGEMENT INFORMATION
What Information Is Needed?
Desired Properties of Management Information

DISTINCTION BETWEEN
DATA PROCESSING SYSTEM AND
MANAGEMENT INFORMATION SYSTEM

THE INFORMATION THAT AN MIS PROVIDES
Information for Planning
Management Control Information

THE CONCEPT OF AN MIS

MIS AS SEEN BY THE USER
Functional Subsystems

DESIGN OF THE MIS
Top-Down Design Approach
Bottom-Up Design Approach
Combination Design Approach

INSTALLATION OF THE MIS

OPERATION AND CONTROL OF THE MIS

THE BEHAVIORAL SIDE OF THE MIS

EVALUATION OF THE MIS

Opposite: Both printed reports and visual display devices can provide information from an MIS.

It has been shown in preceding chapters that the managers of an organization need information at a reasonable cost. It is essential that managers be provided this information. They need it to make effective and efficient decisions regarding the operation of their organizations. The function of management is to use available resources to accomplish the objectives of the organization. This requires that managers guide and direct the efforts of others. One of the key resources they need in doing so is information. The information should be accurate, timely, complete, concise, and relevant.

Computers have had a tremendous impact on both the methods of processing data and the analysis of it to provide information for decision making. As organizations first began to use computers to process data, they were likely to transfer many of the business applications discussed in Chapter 2 onto the computers. The way in which the application was processed was changed, but in many instances the information provided was not changed. Although the application was processed faster, more accurately, and at a lower cost, little, if any, additional management information was provided for decision making.

Managers who used the information provided by computer data processing systems began to make requests for additional information and for analysis of it for decision making. As these new demands were placed on the data processing systems, the characteristics of the systems began to change. More attention was placed on the analysis of data for decision making; less emphasis was placed on the collection and organization of data solely for reporting purposes.

It is the objective of this chapter to examine the information needs of management and to show how management information systems can meet the needs.

○ THE NEED FOR MANAGEMENT INFORMATION

The computer has instigated significant changes in the techniques used by management to plan and control the activities of an organization. Managers who possess relevant information are better equipped to make decisions regarding the activities of the organization.

One of the most important processes in managing the activities of an organization is making decisions about alternatives. When the information available is not sufficient to make a decision, the manager needs to gather more information about the alternatives, compare them, and then choose an alternative. Decisions made without sufficient information are at best only estimates and typically lead to poor management performance. As shown in Illustration 15-1, quality information in the hands of those who

CHAPTER 15: MANAGEMENT INFORMATION SYSTEMS

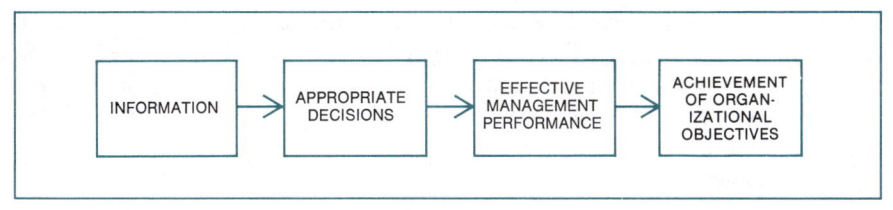

ILLUSTRATION 15-1   The role of information

can make good use of it supports appropriate management decision making. The resulting management performance should then lead to the successful achievement of organizational objectives.

Thus, information is the common element that holds an organization together. The relationship of the information systems of an organization to the decision making within that organization is shown in Illustration 15-2.

What Information Is Needed?

What information is needed by the manager to manage effectively and efficiently? A basic need common to all managers is an understanding of

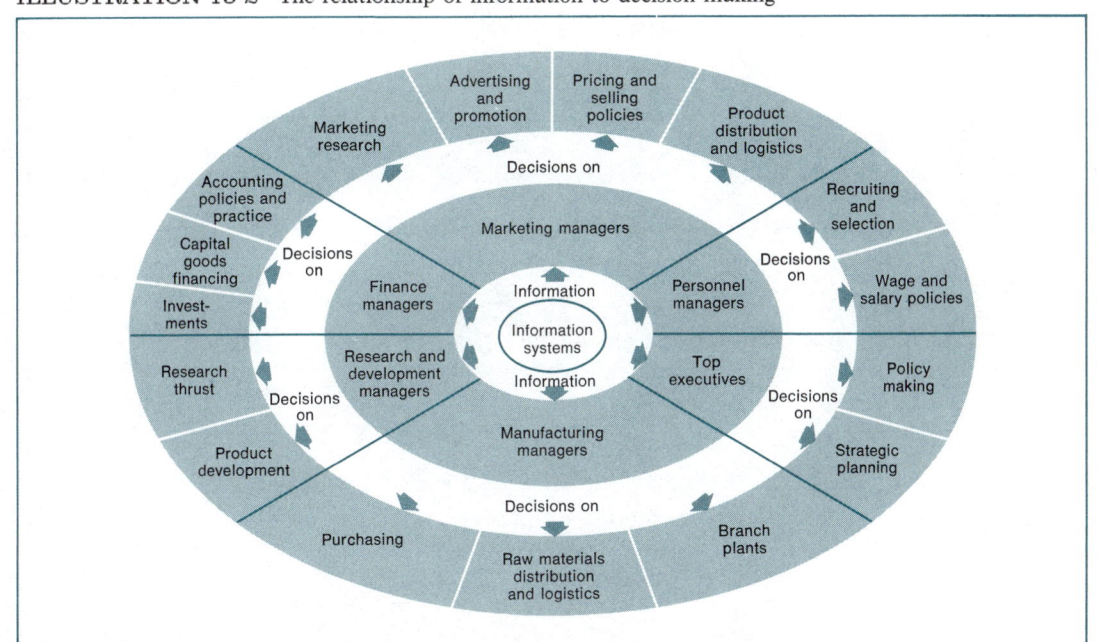

ILLUSTRATION 15-2   The relationship of information to decision making

the objectives of the organization. Individual managers differ in the manner in which they view information, in their analytical approaches in using it, and in their conceptual organization of the relevant facts. For this reason, the question of what information is needed by managers (beyond the basic informational requirements of every manager) can only be answered in broad, general terms.

The level of the manager in the organization is also a key factor in determining the kind of information needed in a specific managerial position. Lower-level management needs information with which to make daily decisions about the operations of the organization. Their activities are mainly control functions. At higher levels of management, concerns are more long-range. These managers require summarization of information from a variety of sources within the information systems of the organization. Top management needs information that summarizes trends and identifies whether the objectives of the organization are being met. This relationship is shown in Illustration 15-3.

The higher a person is in the management structure, the more likely he or she is to need and use information obtained from external sources (see Illustration 15-4). For example, a plant manager needs information to

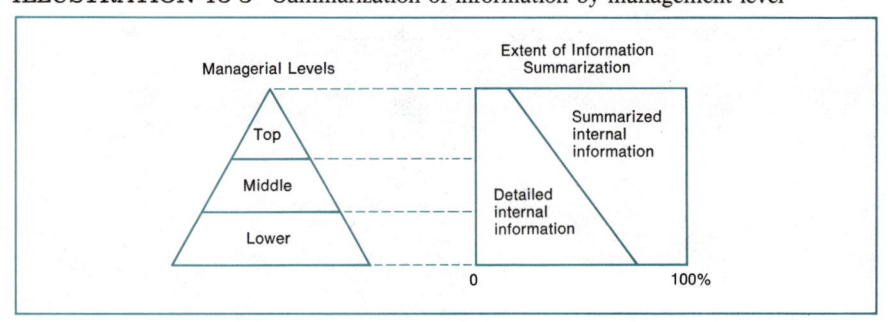

ILLUSTRATION 15-3   Summarization of information by management level

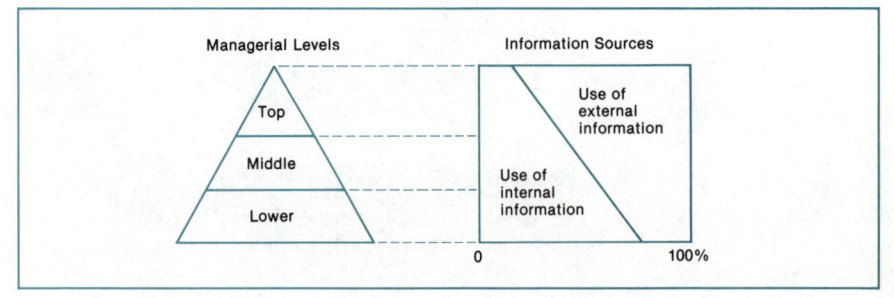

ILLUSTRATION 15-4   Sources of information by management level

control operational activities such as production schedules and plant maintenance; the president of the company needs information to make decisions about the introduction of new products, the location of new plants, and the sources of new capital for expansion. The plant manager can obtain the information he or she needs from within the organization. The president needs to consider information from a number of external sources to make the decisions for which he or she is responsible.

Desired Properties of Management Information

Every organization is dependent upon information for its survival. In order for managers to take action that will yield effective results, they need information that is accurate, timely, complete, concise, and relevant. There is no assurance that the manager will use this information effectively; however, it must be available to be used. In most cases, the availability of information to a manager will have a strong influence on the rationale applied in decision making.

Managers are often required to make decisions with information that lacks one or more of the properties above. This can have an undesirable impact on the effectiveness and efficiency of their decisions.

The *accuracy* of information is the ratio of correct information to total amount of information produced over a period of time. For example, if the monthly sales forecasts provided to a plant manager are not consistently accurate, it is difficult for the manager to make effective decisions concerning production schedules.

Timeliness of information is a reflection of whether or not the information arrives in time to be used by a manager in making a decision. The plant manager must receive the monthly sales forecast in time to make a decision about the monthly production schedule.

Completeness of information requires that a manager be provided with all of the information needed to make a decision. If sales forecasts cover only two-week periods, it is difficult to make decisions about monthly production schedules.

Conciseness of information is obtained through the summarization of relevant data. Such data may point out exceptions to normal or planned activities. A manager who receives concise information is saved a great deal of time otherwise spent in analysis of information for decision making. One type of summarization of information is provided in exception reports, as discussed in Chapter 1.

For information to be *relevant*, it must provide to each involved manager what he or she "needs to know." Information should not be given to a manager who does not have the authority to make the decision(s) that should be based on the information.

UNIT FIVE: MANAGEMENT INFORMATION SYSTEMS

DISTINCTION BETWEEN DATA PROCESSING SYSTEM AND MANAGEMENT INFORMATION SYSTEM

In Chapter 1, the data processing functions of data collection, manipulation, and storage as used to report and analyze business activities were discussed. The data processing system is oriented primarily to processing transactions for day-to-day operations. The transactions include sales orders, shipping orders, inventory orders, and payroll data. For most of these transactions, routine procedures can be established and carried out repetitively to do the processing required. The procedures become part of the data processing system.

A management information system (MIS) performs the processing functions of a data processing system. In addition, an MIS performs substantial processing functions beyond those of a data processing system. The MIS involves a person/machine system that provides information for managers to use as they perform their managerial functions of planning, organizing, staffing, directing, and controlling. Such a system supports basic transaction processing as does a data processing system. It also provides information about the past, present, and future (forecasts) as each relates to the operations within the organization and within its environment.

A data processing system is not an MIS. Two major distinctions between these types of systems are: (1) the characteristics of the information they require, and (2) the decisions that are made, based on this information. Illustration 15-5 summarizes these differences.

THE INFORMATION THAT AN MIS PROVIDES

An MIS that functions properly processes and analyzes data to provide, in particular, planning and control information that supports the decision-making role of management.

Information for Planning

Information for planning is needed at the strategic, tactical, and operational levels. The long-range or strategic planning in an organization involves making decisions about long-range objectives, and setting policies to meet them. Tactical planning involves securing resources and using them in an effective manner to reach these objectives. Operational planning involves determining the actual short-range tasks that must be performed. Lower-level managers are primarily concerned with operational planning. Their needs for information are more limited than those of managers at higher levels who are doing tactical or strategic planning.

CHAPTER 15: MANAGEMENT INFORMATION SYSTEMS

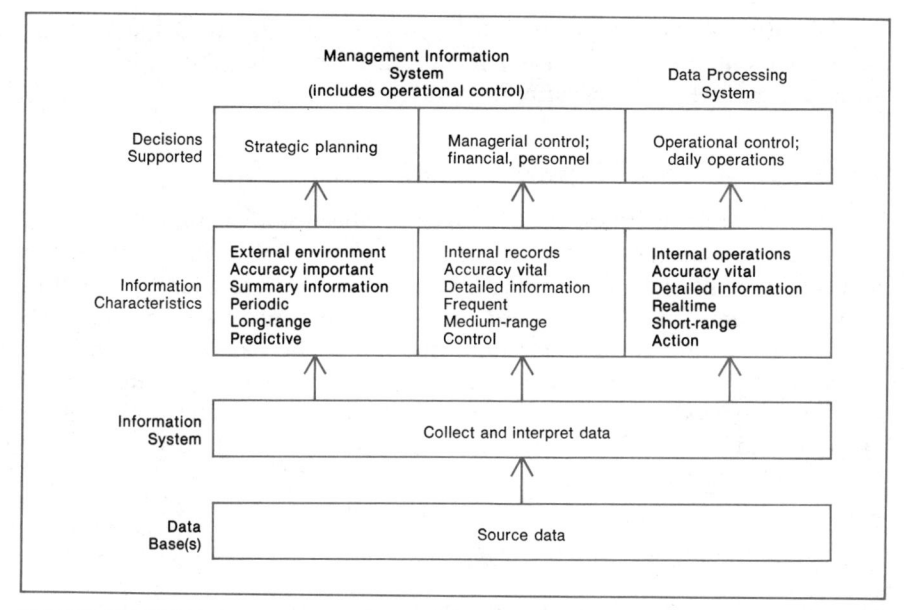

	Management Information System (includes operational control)		Data Processing System
Decisions Supported	Strategic planning	Managerial control; financial, personnel	Operational control; daily operations
Information Characteristics	External environment Accuracy important Summary information Periodic Long-range Predictive	Internal records Accuracy vital Detailed information Frequent Medium-range Control	Internal operations Accuracy vital Detailed information Realtime Short-range Action
Information System	Collect and interpret data		
Data Base(s)	Source data		

ILLUSTRATION 15-5 A comparison of data processing and management information systems

The basic types of information needed for planning are environmental, competitive, and internal. Therefore, planning information comes from three basic sources: (1) within the organization, (2) the competition, and (3) other environmental sources.

Organizational information is obtained internally from both the formal information system and informal sources. This internal information must describe the organization in enough detail so that the planner is aware of both the strengths and the weaknesses of the organization as it relates to the competition and to the environment.

Competitive information should indicate the nature of competing organizations—their past, present, and expected future activities. Such information about the competition can be obtained from a number of sources that are available to the general public. These include annual reports, product announcements, statements accompanying additional stock and bond issues, and public statements by company officials.

Environmental information should take into account the factors in the economy, the government, and the society which may impact the organization. Governmental regulations, such as health and safety standards for new plants, minimum wage legislation, and tax rates, are factors that often need to be considered in planning. Economic trends and forecasts, and changes in societal trends in education, age, and mobility, may also be essential information for planning.

All three of these types of information should be available through a management information system intended to support planning at the strategic, tactical, and operational levels.

Management Control Information

In order for a management control system to be effective, it must be based on a plan that can be used as a standard. Then, any variances from the plan can be identified and corrected. The system that provides information for management must be able to measure and report the performance of the organization compared to the plan. Periodic performance reports are typically provided by a data processing system for this purpose. In addition to periodic reporting, exception reports should be provided on an as-needed basis, whenever immediate action is required.

THE CONCEPT OF AN MIS

There is no universal agreement as to what constitutes an MIS; however, it is generally agreed that an MIS can only be supported with a modern computer system that has ample storage capacity. The concept of an MIS is not new, but MIS has been successfully implemented in business organizations only in the past several years. Generally, these are organizations whose size allows them to acquire the medium-size or large computer system needed to support an MIS.

An *MIS*, then, is a computer-based system that provides both the routine data processing of transactions and the information required by managers to perform their managerial functions in an integrated manner. There have been attempts to create *total* management information systems. Because of the complexity of such a task and the resources required, few, if any, organizations have achieved this objective.

No system is static. As time passes, the usage of an MIS and the requirements imposed on it change. Thus, a total MIS is difficult, if not impossible, to achieve.

No system planners can anticipate all future management information needs, next year or five years from now. The ways in which managers provide and use information also change over time and as the individuals change. This human element is another reason why the concept of a total MIS will probably remain primarily a concept.

An organization is more likely to install an MIS that falls short of a total MIS, yet meets most of the needs of management for planning, controlling, and decision making. Such a system should provide for a data base, comprehensive data analysis capabilities, and models. Operationally, it should provide for file definition, file maintenance, transaction and inquiry processing, periodic and exception reporting, and maintenance of accurate and secure files.

As indicated in Chapter 1, a data base is a structured set of related files organized so that access to the data is facilitated and redundancy is minimized. Generally, groups of files within the data base are linked by some common characteristic such as a social security number. When an MIS is implemented, several data bases are linked into an organizational data base (see Illustration 15-6). An organization may have only one organizational data base that includes all its files. However, it is more common to find several organizational data bases supporting an MIS.

Within an MIS, a single transaction can cause the updating of all related data base files at one time. For example, the recording of a credit sale may also update the accounts receivable file, the inventory stock file, the shipping order file, and the product sales file. An MIS data base should reduce the amount of data kept repetitively—that is, duplicated in two or more of these files. It should also insure that the data is current since all related files are updated whenever a transaction affecting them occurs.

To access an MIS data base effectively, a *data base management system*, or **DBMS**, is used. The data base management system is a part of system software that handles the complex tasks associated with creating, accessing, and maintaining the data base. This system software provides the instructions necessary for the computer to handle the manipulation of the data.

Comprehensive data is required as input, to make it possible for the MIS to provide the planning, control, and decision-making information needed by management as output. The characteristics and sources of this data were noted previously. In addition to being able to extract data from the data base, the MIS should be able to perform statistical and related

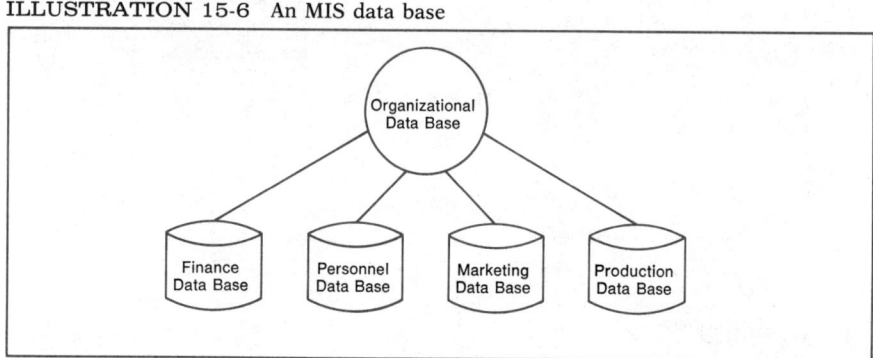

ILLUSTRATION 15-6 An MIS data base

analyses as required by managers. Management often has a need to evaluate alternative plans of action or strategies. **Simulation**, or **modeling**, allows the imitation of an event, a process, or an object that must be studied prior to the making of a management decision. Models can help reduce the uncertainty in decision making. A large number of alternatives can be tried using a computer-based model to simulate the results that could occur for each alternative. A model simulates an event, a process, or an object that would otherwise be too costly or time-consuming to create. For instance, if an organization is considering a change in employee retirement plans, it can simulate the operation of a number of plans over a number of years to determine the costs of each plan. Management considering a new plant can simulate its operation in a number of different locations in the country. This simulation may represent the operation of the plant over a number of years considering such factors as availability and cost of labor, utility rates, shipping facilities, tax rates, and climate.

○ MIS AS SEEN BY THE USER

The primary users of an MIS are identified in Illustration 15-7. The routine processing accomplished by clerical personnel is least affected by the installation of an MIS. They will collect and record essentially the same transaction data. Some additional data collection will be necessary to support the expanded functions of the MIS. Procedures for data editing and validation will be set up to increase accuracy.

ILLUSTRATION 15-7 Primary uses of an MIS by organizational employees

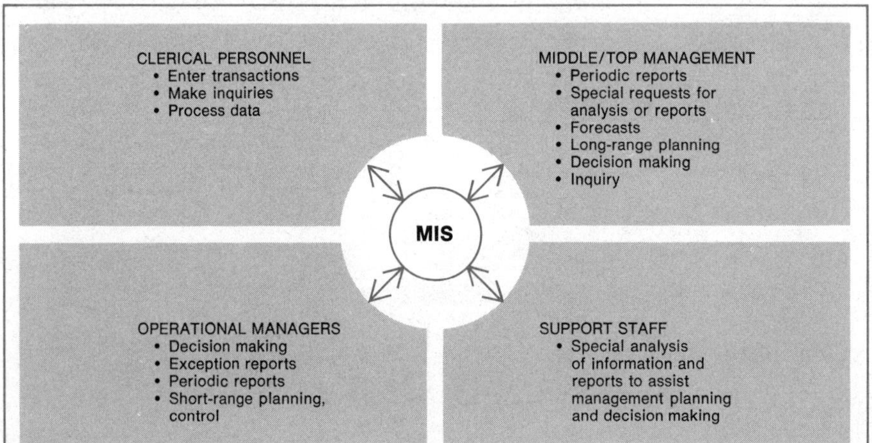

CLERICAL PERSONNEL
- Enter transactions
- Make inquiries
- Process data

MIDDLE/TOP MANAGEMENT
- Periodic reports
- Special requests for analysis or reports
- Forecasts
- Long-range planning
- Decision making
- Inquiry

OPERATIONAL MANAGERS
- Decision making
- Exception reports
- Periodic reports
- Short-range planning, control

SUPPORT STAFF
- Special analysis of information and reports to assist management planning and decision making

CHAPTER 15: MANAGEMENT INFORMATION SYSTEMS

Most levels of personnel in the organization will be required to provide more data for use in the MIS. In return, they should be able to obtain more information, including special reports. The information should be obtainable in a more accurate and timely manner. The data provided by each of the departments in the organization will no longer be considered the possession of that department. The user will have to recognize that the data belongs to the entire organization. The user should also understand that the data will be used at several levels in the organization.

Functional Subsystems

The MIS of an organization is generally viewed as a *federation of information systems*. This view has been accepted for several reasons.

First, management information systems are developed around the functions to be managed. A distinct function is often the basis for the creation of an information system (*subsystem*) to meet the information needs of the managers of the function. The managers of the function are responsible for defining and collecting the data needed in the subsystem and for insuring its accuracy as it is entered into the organizational data base.

Second, many of the information systems in use prior to the introduction of a computer-based MIS were developed primarily for the functional areas that had to be managed. Thus, in many instances, the structures of these systems (now, in effect, subsystems) are incorporated into the MIS as it is developed.

The relationship between the functional subsystems of an organization and the organizational data base(s) is shown in Illustration 15-8. Depending on the size and complexity of the organization, the subsystems may be divided further into component subsystems. For any of the subsystems, the data base management system is the link between the user and the information the user needs from the data base(s).

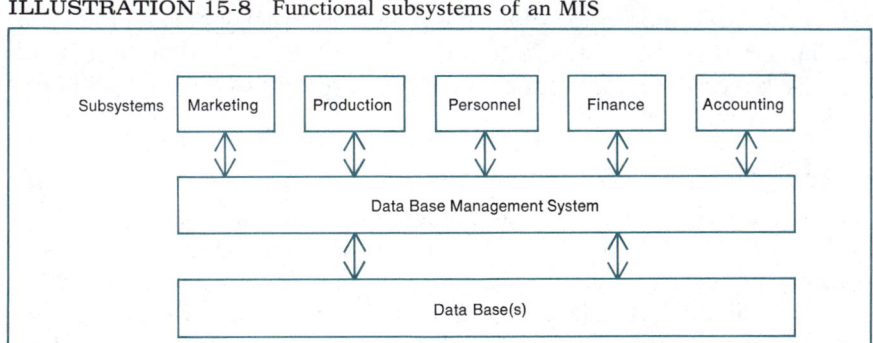

ILLUSTRATION 15-8 Functional subsystems of an MIS

Subsystems	Marketing	Production	Personnel	Finance	Accounting

Data Base Management System

Data Base(s)

DESIGN OF THE MIS

Much of what was discussed in Chapter 3 concerning system analysis and design of data processing systems can be applied in designing an MIS. Although the subject is quite complex and is often the topic of an entire book, three approaches to MIS design are identified here. There is no single, agreed-upon approach for designing an MIS; however, top-down design, bottom-up design, and a combination of these two approaches have been used extensively.

Top-Down Design Approach

The key to this approach to MIS design is top management involvement. The objectives of the organization are the basis for planning and designing the subsystems needed within the organization. Top management is deeply involved in this approach to MIS design to insure that all of the information needed to meet organizational objectives is identified and provided. Thus, the overall system information needs are considered first. Then the design of the various subsystems and data bases proceeds, to meet these needs. Subsystems are further subdivided as necessary until each individual data processing application is identified and designed. The necessary files are also designed at this time.

Bottom-Up Design Approach

In designing an MIS using this approach, the common business applications are identified and developed first. These include the applications discussed in Chapter 2, which are required for the daily operation of the organization. Identification and design of the subsystems can be started after the applications are designed. Then the interrelationship of the subsystems is established through the data base. This design process is continued until the highest-level planning and control applications are designed. A bottom-up approach allows for the orderly development and implementation of the MIS, with the first emphasis placed on basic applications that can provide the most immediate benefit to the organization.

Combination Design Approach

Although the top-down design and bottom-up design approaches are alternative methods of designing an MIS, it is possible to use a combination of these two designs. In such a situation, the top-down design approach is used to define the overall system information needs. The logic of the bottom-up design approach is used to identify and develop the common business applications that can provide the most immediate benefit to the organization. The extent of use of each design approach is based upon the organization's internal environment.

INSTALLATION OF THE MIS

The installation of the computer system to support the MIS will extend over a long period of time. Progressing from the initial planning stages of the MIS through the actual installation of the computer to support the system may take from one to two years. In most organizations, the changes in processing methods and the need for data base capability necessitate replacing an existing computer with one capable of supporting the MIS. The computer that is selected should not only be capable of supporting the MIS that is being designed but also allow for future expansion of it.

The normal procedure for selecting a computer system is to develop specifications for the processing capabilities needed by the system and some minimum equipment specifications to meet those needs. Computer vendors are then invited to submit proposals for computer systems that will meet the specifications. Often the proposed systems are tested prior to a selection's being made. These tests are called **benchmarks**. They usually include performance testing, to insure that the computer system proposed by the vendor is capable of meeting all performance requirements stated in the specifications.

After a computer has been selected, it must be installed and personnel trained to operate it. At this point, the process of computer system conversion and implementation begins. Often, processing on the old computer system is continued as usual until the new computer system has been tested thoroughly. Both computers are run in parallel, and their processing results are compared. For example, the monthly payroll may be run on both computers and the processing results checked to see if they are the same.

OPERATION AND CONTROL OF THE MIS

It has been shown above that an MIS should be designed to provide for all of the activities needed to establish and maintain files, for transaction and inquiry processing, and for periodic and exception reporting.

Files must be defined, established, and maintained so that the MIS can provide the proper information in an organized and controlled manner. When defining a file, its use and the source of the data within it should be considered. What other files, if any, will be associated with the file? Will these files be linked together by some common characteristic? The organization of the file should make the data within it easily obtainable for its expected use. The data should be retrievable in a meaningful manner.

After files have been defined and established, the processing of transactions or management requests results in data being entered into or retrieved from the files. It is important that this data be accurate. Further, access to the data should be restricted to those who have the need and the authority to use it. It has already been established that accurate data entry is an extremely important step in any data processing system. Once data has been recorded and verified, it may be used many times within an MIS. Proper control procedures should be included in an MIS to insure the accuracy of all data entered into any files and to prevent unauthorized use of the files.

It is likely that a variety of persons within the organization will access the MIS at some level. Clerks will be responsible for entering data; managers will make inquiries for decision making; and data processing personnel will maintain and operate the system. Many of these users will communicate directly with the computer through terminals located throughout the organization. A typical terminal has a keyboard similar to that of a typewriter. It usually has some type of display capability, either a screen similar to a television screen or printer type of output. (See Module A for further discussion of terminals.)

Because terminals make it easy for users to access the MIS, internal controls within the MIS must limit this access to the appropriate levels. For example, an inventory clerk should not be able to access the payroll file or the personnel file from a terminal.

Transaction and inquiry processing are generally associated with clerical personnel. An airline reservation clerk may make an inquiry to determine the availability of an airline seat. If a seat is available, the clerk may record the reservation (enter a transaction). A telephone sales clerk may record sales transactions phoned in by customers.

Management is likely to use the inquiry capability of the MIS to obtain information that is needed immediately. A sales manager interested in determining whether or not any salesperson has reached the weekly sales quota may use a terminal to request this information. Thus, it is possible for management to obtain information through inquiry processing that would otherwise require the preparation and subsequent analysis of a report. Often, a complete report is not needed by management. Rather, the answer to some specific question is wanted. The MIS should be able to provide this type of inquiry information in a usable form and within a short time period.

Periodic reporting provides management with information that is needed on a regular basis for decision-making purposes. It is the responsibility of managers to identify the reports they need and the information required on the reports. These reports must be supplied on a timely basis so that they can be used to full advantage in the decision-making process.

Exception reports have been discussed previously, so they need not be discussed again here. However, it should be noted that the MIS should be designed to provide these reports automatically—that is, whenever an exception condition needing management attention is sensed by the system.

THE BEHAVIORAL SIDE OF THE MIS

One of the major problems encountered in the design and implementation of an MIS is obtaining the acceptance and cooperation of the personnel who will interact with the system. An MIS is not installed without top management support. This may not be the case with lower levels of management and other operating personnel. Each level of personnel within the organization participates in the design and operation of the MIS and is affected in a different way by it. How each of these groups perceives its relationship to the MIS is critical. People resist change, especially if they suspect that they will be adversely affected by it. Change is necessary when an MIS is implemented. Changes usually occur in the structure of the organization and in the functions of the personnel. How disruptive these changes seem to personnel affects the degree of acceptance and support they give the MIS.

Personnel who believe their jobs may be threatened are likely to resist the implementation of the MIS. Clerical workers are least likely to feel threatened. Middle managers are most likely to feel that their jobs are jeopardized.

A positive program of educating personnel about the MIS and how it will affect them can have a tremendous impact on the support they give it. Personnel who have any direct contact with the MIS should clearly understand the purpose and characteristics of the system as it affects them. Those who are influenced by the MIS are more likely to support it if they feel that they have participated in its design.

How will personnel react if they do not support the implementation of the MIS? Few will attempt sabotage, but some cases have been reported. Clerical personnel responsible for entering data into the MIS may not do so accurately. Middle management may resist using the information provided by the MIS and rely on other sources instead. In some cases personnel will resist supporting the MIS regardless of the steps taken to encourage them to do so. These personnel should be identified and removed from positions where they can impact the performance of the MIS.

○ EVALUATION OF THE MIS

Formal evaluation of the installed MIS should continue as an ongoing project. The evaluation of the MIS can be performed in a variety of ways and at several levels within the organization. The evaluation should assess: (1) the technical performance of the hardware and software; (2) the use of the MIS by the management in the organization; (3) the effectiveness of the various subsystems in achieving the stated MIS design objectives; and (4) the cost/benefit provided. The evaluation of the MIS should be conducted either by a committee of middle and top management, or by a group of information systems personnel and management. Management representing the major MIS subsystems or functions must be involved in the evaluation. They are best able to assess whether or not the MIS is meeting their information needs. In any case, the group needs the technical support of information systems personnel. In some instances outside consultants may be used in the evaluation process.

The hardware and software supporting the MIS should be reviewed to determine whether or not they are meeting the objectives of the MIS in the most effective manner. Included in this evaluation should be an examination of the utilization levels of the hardware and software and of their reliability.

The extent that managers are using the current MIS can be determined by: the number of reports they request, the number of terminal inquiries that are made, the ratings they place on the value of information supplied, and the frequency of its use.

Managers should be asked to determine whether the MIS meets the design objectives specified for their subsystems or functions. Suggestions and recommendations for system improvements should be requested. Interviews with clerical and other support personnel should be conducted to uncover problems if it is determined that the MIS does not meet the specified design objectives. These problems may include faulty system design and personnel problems related to both system design and implementation.

The cost/benefit analysis of the proposed MIS considered expected costs of the system and anticipated savings in relation to the benefits provided by it. This same cost/benefit proposal can now be used in a comparison with the actual costs and benefits being experienced.

○ SUMMARY

1. Management needs accurate, timely, complete, concise, and relevant information. It helps them to make decisions—to be effective in

achieving the objectives of the organization. Lower-level managers typically need short-range control information to make decisions about the daily functions of the organization. Higher-level management needs summary information that indicates whether or not objectives of the organization are being met. The sources of information for low-level management are primarily within the organization. Higher-level management requires information from external sources also.

2. A management information system differs from a data processing system in that the former emphasizes the information needed for decision making, while the latter emphasizes the processing of daily transactions. An organization functions through transactions, which it must process to carry out its day-to-day activities. The payroll must be prepared; sales must be recorded; and payments on account must be recorded. These data processing activities are clerical in nature. They follow rather standard procedures. The computer is useful for these clerical data processing tasks. An MIS includes this transaction processing. It also provides information about the past, present, and future (forecasts) as each relates to the decision-making environment of the organization.

3. An MIS should provide planning and control information to support management decision making. Planning information is needed at the strategic, tactical, and operational levels. Planning information can be identified as environmental, competitive, and internal.

4. An MIS is a computer-based system that supports managerial decision making through a data base, comprehensive data analysis capabilities, and models. In its operation, it must provide for the definition of files that are accurate, secure, and maintainable; transaction and inquiry processing; and periodic and exception reports.

5. A data base is a series of integrated files containing the data needed by an organization for its operation. An organization may have one data base containing all of its files. It is more likely to have several data bases for this purpose. Often, some common characteristics of the files in the data base are used to link the files together for access purposes.

6. A data base is created, accessed, and maintained through a series of computer programs called a data base management system.

7. The MIS of an organization is often viewed as a federation of information systems. Each of these can be considered a subsystem that is a part of the MIS.

8. Several approaches have been taken in designing an MIS. The top-down, bottom-up, and combination approaches are often used. The first approach places emphasis on top management involvement in the planning process to insure the MIS reflects the objectives of the organization. The second approach emphasizes the development of the lowest-level processing applications first; it leaves the building of the higher levels of the system until later. The third approach uses an appropriate combination of the bottom-up and top-down approaches.

9. Prior to installation of an MIS, an organization should consider the effect the MIS will have on personnel, such as creating new jobs and eliminating others, and requirements for training. The installation of the computer system to support the MIS will occur several years after the MIS is first planned. Computer selection tasks include the development of specifications, evaluation of computer vendors' responses to specifications, and computer capability testing.

10. Terminals are likely to provide a major part of the access to the MIS, both to process transactions that occur and to make inquiries for management information. The MIS should provide the periodic reports needed by management and exception reports to identify problems that need management attention.

11. The success of an MIS in an organization is directly related to the support that personnel are willing to give it. Personnel will generally support the implementation of an MIS to the extent that they feel: (1) they have participated in its design as it affects them; (2) they have been clearly and honestly informed about its implementation; and (3) their jobs are not threatened by it.

12. The evaluation of an installed MIS should be a continuous process. A formal evaluation committee or group should be established. It should include representation from top management. The evaluation process should assess the technical performance of the hardware and software, the management use of the MIS, whether the MIS meets design objectives, and the cost/benefit provided.

REVIEW QUESTIONS

1. Within the concept of information processing, what is the relationship between data, information, and data base?

2. Discuss the five desired properties of management information.

CHAPTER 15: MANAGEMENT INFORMATION SYSTEMS

3. How does a data processing system differ from a management information system?
4. What are the three basic sources of information for management planning?
5. What is the importance of a data base to an organization?
6. What are the important benefits of an efficient data base management system?
7. Discuss how the four categories of primary users of an MIS use the capabilities it provides.
8. What are three approaches to designing an MIS?
9. What personnel problems may be encountered when designing and implementing an MIS?
10. Discuss the four areas that should be assessed when evaluating an MIS.

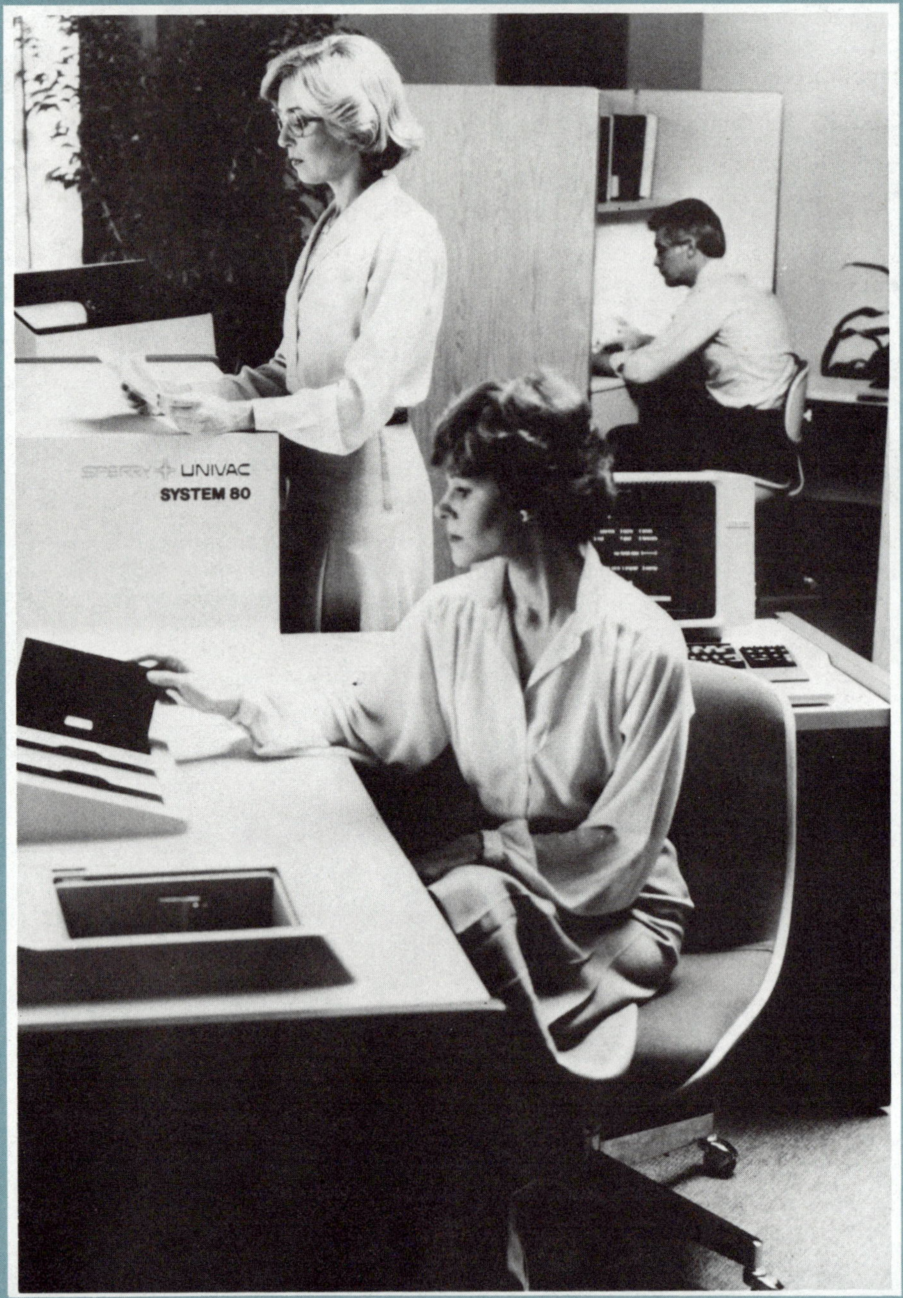
SPERRY UNIVAC
SYSTEM 80

CHAPTER 16

MANAGEMENT INFORMATION SYSTEMS APPLICATIONS

ESSENTIAL PRINCIPLES OF
INFORMATION SYSTEMS DEVELOPMENT
Background
Technical and Developmental Factors
Behavioral and Organizational Factors
Conclusion

MARKETING INFORMATION SYSTEM

AN INTEGRATED
MERCHANDISING INFORMATION SYSTEM

AN MIS IN HIGHER EDUCATION
Objectives for Design
Conceptual Design
System Outputs; Key Data Elements
Information Flow
System Software
Data Classification Scheme
Information Systems
Planning Model
Implementation Plan
MIS Implementation Considerations
Conclusion

Opposite: A management information system may use several smaller computers in a distributed system.

In the preceding chapter, the information needs of management were discussed. The use of a management information system to meet these needs was proposed. There are several hundred thousand business computer systems in operation today. The processing capabilities of these computer systems vary. Some provide only the basic transaction processing needed in day-to-day business activities (data processing). Others encompass an integrated MIS that provides both transaction processing and management information.

The objective of this chapter is twofold: (1) to present a journal article that summarizes and reinforces the material of Chapter 15 and (2) to discuss three management information systems.

The article discusses research findings and practical business experiences related to management information systems. The characteristics of management information systems are discussed first. This discussion is followed by an examination of data management, data independence, and the structure of an MIS. Finally, behavioral and organizational principles involving employee resistance to the development of an MIS, user and management involvement in MIS development activities, and the integration of an MIS into the organization are discussed. Thus, this article provides a reinforcement of the material discussed in Chapter 15 and a framework for discussing the three examples presented in this chapter. Publications referred to in the article are listed at the end of the chapter.

The first two MIS examples are relatively brief. Each serves primarily as an indicator of how an MIS can be used in a representative, current business environment. The third example is a case study. It looks in depth at the design, development, and implementation of an MIS by a large state university system.

ESSENTIAL PRINCIPLES OF INFORMATION SYSTEMS DEVELOPMENT*

The use of computer-based management information systems (MIS) to support managerial decision making has increased significantly since computers were introduced into the business community during the 1950's. The realization of a number of distinguishing characteristics of MIS has come with this increase in use and investigation of computer-based systems. These characteristics form the basis for an emerging set of very fundamental and basic principles of systems development for management information systems.

---

*This section is reprinted by permission from James A. Senn, "Essential Principles of Information Systems Development," *MIS Quarterly*, Volume 2, Number 2 (June, 1978), pp. 17–26.

This discussion presents and examines some MIS development principles and characteristics as we know them today. Many are drawn from experiences that organizations have had developing and using these systems while others are based on research findings through both field studies and laboratory experiments. While this report draws together knowledge about MIS principles, it is hoped that the basic set will be expanded substantially as the field continues to grow and mature.

Background

One of the problems in dealing with the subject of management information systems is that in the past there has been no agreement on exactly what the term means. The Society for Management Information Systems has examined this problem in depth and has developed an extensive list of the various ways the term has been defined [16, 38].

The primary emphasis of MIS is that of providing decision support to management as contrasted with mere transaction processing to replicate clerical functions. Throughout this discussion the term *MIS* will be used when referring to decision-oriented activities, and data processing or transaction processing systems will imply clerical activities. The important point to remember is that MIS is aimed at more than replication of clerical processing of data.

An information system is organized; it condenses and filters data until it becomes information for use in decision making at various levels of the organization. Ideally an MIS should provide outputs that are reliable, timely, and accurate to support making decisions. Today this frequently involves the use of computer systems. However, an information system does *not* presume computer processing. Instead, it requires a system that can deliver the necessary information for management in a timely fashion at a reasonable cost. In many instances, information may be transmitted as either an oral or written report. Some manual systems may produce information on a routine basis at fixed time intervals, perhaps monthly or quarterly, and sometimes the information may be produced on request as study results based on a special analysis.

The important point to recognize is that systems for clerical processing have quite different purposes from systems for providing information for management decision making, and that systems of either type need not involve computer processing. Despite the fact that important differences exist between the two, there is definitely a relationship. Efficient clerical systems are vital to the operation of large, highly complex organizations. Frequently these systems form the basis for organizational information systems [23]. An organization may have many clerical systems, parts of which provide inputs to a management information system.

Based on these fundamental realizations, it is logical to conceive of a management information system as

" ... an organized method of providing past, present and projection information relating to internal operations and external intelligence. It supports the planning, control, and operational functions of an organization by providing uniform information in the proper time-frame to assist the decision-making process."[25]

We can begin to assemble technical and developmental, and then behavioral and organizational factors from this common definition that should be guidelines for development and use of computer-based management information systems.

Technical and Developmental Factors

The technical and developmental factors associated with information systems focus on the structure of the components comprising the system. They also deal with the role of data and how it is managed within the system framework.

A federation of information systems. The views of the MIS model in the literature and among practitioners in industry and government have generally taken one of two forms. The early view was one of MIS as a total, global system carefully integrated into all parts of the firm. The system was monolithic in form under this philosophy, where formal information networks were interrelated by conscious design *before* implementation. The underlying assumptions were that managers' information needs could be identified and/or anticipated, as could the ways in which such information might be used. As a result, the total systems approach is based on the thought that it is appropriate to define explicitly the proper information flows to management and then to design a system that would assume the continual support of these flows.

One of the most disconcerting factors underlying the global concept was the fact that system expectations, requirements, and use change as the MIS exists over time. Hence what might be considered a total system today most likely will be only a partial system tomorrow. Similarly, it is somewhat naive to assume that it is possible for one person or one group of managers and experts to design a total or global MIS, to develop effective boundaries and interfaces with the various organizational systems, and to integrate *the* system into the management stream.

Out of dissatisfaction with the global view came a more workable framework for MIS development. This view distinguishes an MIS as being dependent on lower-level activities in the firm because it draws upon and integrates information from the several functional area information systems, such as the marketing information system and the production information system, to provide a uniform body of details and knowledge for uncertainty reduction in decision making.

Speaking directly to this issue, Terrance Hanold, Past Chairman of the Executive Committee of The Pillsbury Company and an Honorary Founder of SMIS, indicates that:

> "As distinguished from an information system, I conceive of a management information system to consist of a cluster of business information systems ... MIS is a symbol rather than a descriptive name, which designates an integrated complex of information systems of such variety and sophistication and interrelationship as experience qualified by rational assessment determines to be essential or useful to the general executive management of the business enterprise."[22]

Herbert Schwartz, while at the U.S. Atomic Energy Commission, used essentially the same framework and context for development of the MIS:

> "The management information system for an entire organization must be visualized as a supersystem of systems, as a federation of management information systems. Only the most monolithic of organizations can build and gain strength from a single total system ... The federation should be structured as a set of systems, each system tightly integrated internally, but only loosely integrated when taken together."[34]

The same view is repeatedly expressed in the literature of the field.

This approach enables specialists to collect the information that they are best trained to gather. The accountant should be concerned with the collection of accounting information, the financial specialist should focus on the collection of financial knowledge, and so forth. Each has the training in a particular area of knowledge and should be more proficient in these activities than one with background in another area of the firm. Interchange of the information can then be accomplished to insure that each functional area receives the information that it requires from other areas. We will focus on this aspect more in the following sections on management of data. But, the principle of these systems is that *a management information system is a federation of functional area information systems.*

Data as the center of MIS. The central resource in a management information system is data. Initial reaction to such a statement is often that it is an obvious fact that does not merit comment. However, past and present activities of some organizations involved with MIS seem to indicate that this principle is not always operationalized.

Data should be the central resource in an MIS since it provides the base from which processing takes place to develop the information needed for managerial decision making. Emphasis should be placed on data as opposed to hardware and software. We saw an era in which the attention of systems developers and users was focused on hardware and software during the early days of computer-based systems. The focus in many instances was on acquiring more and more computer power and larger machines. Much attention was also devoted to the development of a diversity of unique languages and software systems [32]. This was the day of the super-salesman, the glass-enclosed computer palace, and the aura of "gee whiz" systems [39]. Data almost seemed to play a secondary role as everything revolved around the hardware and software.

As applications grew in sophistication, so too did a large portion of the users. Many persons came to realize that the data that these machines processed is the key to success. The data for business applications was recognized as a resource of the firm and thus came to be controlled and managed. As more and more users came into the information systems arena, they too placed their emphasis on data rather than on hardware or software. Data became the resource and hardware and software the tools—almost a complete reversal from the early days. Requirements for an improved level of technology came with the increased emphasis on data that allowed the users to gain the support they wanted without the need for large-scale purchases of equipment or development of applications software. Thus the new view of data's place in the organization led to developments such as minicomputers, networks and distributed processing, teleprocessing methods, and data base management systems. These developments in effect de-emphasize hardware and software, even while they advanced the state of the art, and reinforce the central nature and importance of data. Manufacturers and vendors, however, do not always want us to view the world through these eyes; therefore, there are many camps that still do not pay proper respect to the role of data in computer-based information systems. We will see this more in the next section on data bases. However, there is little question for the majority of persons involved with MIS that *data is the central resource in effective management information systems.*

The data base in MIS. The data base is at the foundation of an MIS. It is the primary factor in a collection of information systems that enables integration of the various business information systems, thereby providing uniform knowledge to managers and decision makers throughout the organization. Since the basic underlying purpose of an MIS requires that the information be drawn from throughout the enterprise, it follows that the data base should cut across organizational lines. A data base, in other words, can be viewed as *more than* the ordinary collection of all data stored for one or more related computer-based application programs. It is visualized as a generalized, common, integrated collection which fulfills the data requirements of all application programs which must access it. Additionally, the data within this entity must be structured to model the natural data relationships that exist in an organization [33].

It should be pointed out, however, that the data base does not contain all the data used in an organization. Various functional areas maintain files of data that are not needed by other parts of the enterprise. A record, however, should be maintained along with the data base indicating where these "outside" files exist.

A high volume of data enters the data base from throughout the organization. Each department or division provides data and information for storage and use by other parts of the company. A large number of forms for the data typically are found in the input stream, because of the diversity of data sources. Yet if the data base truly is intended to serve to integrate and interface the various functional areas as well as to provide support to corporate-level management, a certain amount of control needs to be placed over entering data. Haphazard recording of facts will result in service to no one and to eventual degradation of the data base to the extent that it is used by few persons. Incoming data should conform to a predetermined definition of form and should be stored according to precise rules. Data that does not match the definition should not be allowed to enter the data base.

The issue of data exchange or data use is an important one in that it should be feasible through the data base to provide uniform information across functional area lines. That is, two managers requesting information on sales volume, for example, should receive the *same picture* of the state of sales, regardless of the area of the organization in which they are located. Further, although the form of the information may vary, e.g., sales in dollars versus sales in product units, the picture portrayed through the data should remain constant.

Control of the data base is an important aspect of MIS activities. An equally important factor, however, is the assurance that the data will be available when it is needed. It must be remembered that the data base will change over time due to the nature of incoming facts and because of demands which users make on it. As this resource is in existence, users' reliance will increase, assuming that it is properly designed, and they will expect more extensive support from it. Consequently, the data base itself must be adaptable to the demands made on it. This capability is referred to as *evolvability* [20].

In general, the data base plays a central role in management information systems. This is to say that *the data base is at the foundation of an MIS and makes possible integration of the business information systems. It must be controlled and used as a management resource to insure reliability, integrity, and evolvability.*

Data independence. There needs to be a certain amount of independence between the way data is stored and the way different users intend to deal with it in a certain application. Conflicts frequently can arise between storage structures (the way the data is physically stored on devices and media) and data structures (the way each user views the data he or she needs). What may be the most efficient organization of data in stored form may not be best in terms of the data structures of the individual users. Yet the system should be able to accommodate user requirements while still physically dealing with the data in the most efficient manner. In addition, one user should be able to adjust his or her requirements without causing a change in the way data is stored. In turn, it should be possible to restructure the data base when it is necessary because of new organization-wide requirements or because of improvements in computer-related technology. The restructuring efforts should not affect the users or their applications.

We do not yet have the means to accomplish all facets of this objective, but it is clear that *independence between the stored versions of the data and the requirements of each individual user should be sought whenever possible.*

Lifestream systems. First, attention in MIS development needs to be given to the basic underlying system activities in the firm, i.e., the "business of the firm." Establishment of systems to support these functions, such as sales order processing, accounting, and purchasing, is important because of the sheer volume of activities in each of these areas, implying that potential cost savings can be realized if automation leads to more effective performance levels. In addition, the high level of understanding of the tasks performed in these areas usually means minimal difficulty in including them within the overall MIS framework.

Ease of conversion is not the only reason for giving priority to development of lifestream systems. Organizations may experience cost savings and higher levels of profits or revenue by decreasing the time devoted to basic transaction-oriented systems, and coupling this with improved accuracy and increased volume [13]. However, it is also essential that transaction data from these activities be captured for inclusion in the data base. The combination of cost savings, increased volume of processing, and improved data capture lead to the conclusion that *first attention in the development of management information systems should be given to the firm's basic lifestream systems.*

Information system structure. Information system analysts and users typically have been concerned with *what information* should be provided to the user or decision maker and into which report it should be incorporated. It is, however, also necessary to focus on being able to provide information that is appropriate to the characteristics of both the decision maker and the decision task. Information system structure consists of characteristics of the person, the decision environment, and the information system, each of which has an impact on various measures of decision effectiveness [17]. Mason and Mitroff developed a similar framework which indicated a need to focus on the individual decision maker, the problem being examined, the organizational context, and a mode of presentation for the necessary information [28]. The information structure in both frameworks is believed to have an impact on various measures of performance and decision effectiveness.

A series of experiments, The Minnesota Experiments, was conducted to determine whether or not the above beliefs appear valid [9, 17, 35]. Each of the nine experiments in the series examined various aspects of the decision support problem. The evidence from these efforts strongly suggests that a relationship exists between information system structure and decision effectiveness. It appears that information requirements and related requirements may vary with changes in form or media of information, but performance levels may not necessarily be affected. The studies also appear to confirm Ackoff's previously published beliefs that more information need not lead to improved performance and that the manager may not need the information he or she wants [1, 31].

Consequently, system designers and users alike should pay close attention to the structure they adopt for management information system efforts. It appears that it is possible to improve information system efficiency without decreasing decision effectiveness: *the structure of a management information system significantly impacts managerial decision effectiveness.*

Behavioral and Organizational Factors

Too often in developing systems *the people* in the system are overlooked and an inordinate amount of attention is given to the technical factors. It is essential that systems people consider possible resistance to the system and the need for top management and user support.

Resistance to MIS. Introduction of MIS projects necessitates consideration of some of the behavioral aspects of change. A change may be ideal in both a technical and an economic sense, but this is no guarantee of its success. Unless persons want a change or the introduction of new techniques, it cannot significantly improve operating effectiveness or efficiency.

Management information systems frequently result in changes to the formal structure of an organization (e.g., adjustments in department boundaries, individual responsibilities, and communication channels), or to the informal structure (e.g., work relations, work group norms, or status). Such changes potentially affect many persons. However, the method by which they are introduced may be an overwhelming factor in determining its acceptance and its success. Also, resistance to the introduction should be anticipated and steps taken to prevent its occurrence.

When the information system specialist is faced with the problem of gaining system acceptance from operating managers and personnel, he or she is inclined to offer as evidence the same issues that were responsible for top management approval. The logic is relatively straightforward. If the project will result in reduced operating costs or increased profits, decreased decision time, job streamlining, or more accurate information on activities, it is often expected that managers will welcome such a system. The fallacy in this reasoning centers around the use of logic to change managers' attitudes about the job and the way it is performed. Attitudes may not be formed in a logical manner, as indicated repeatedly in the psychology literature, nor are they changed through the use of logic. Emotion and not logic is a key factor in attitude change [40]. The systems person is most illogical in attempting to use logic to affect attitude change. The result of improper handling of change is a form of resistance, which falls into the categories of:

Aggression. Physical or nonphysical attack on the information system in an attempt to make it either inoperative or ineffective.
Projection. A means by which persons can "energize" their resistance to the introduction of an information system (blame the system).
Avoidance. Withdrawing from or avoiding interaction with the information system, often as a result of frustration [18].

Problems such as these can easily develop if systems are not considered as major changes in various aspects of organizations. Acceptance of MIS activities cannot be based solely on the use of logic or measures of efficiency: *improved performance in organizations will not necessarily prevent resistance to the introduction of management information systems applications.*

Top management support. Successful development, implementation, and operation of an MIS require continued support of and interaction with top corporate management. The importance of top management support for such systems has been noted often in the literature [3, 4, 14, 15, 19, 24], but in many instances the importance of involvement has been overlooked in application settings. The proper organizational philosophy and attitude as seen in managerial climate, for example, are necessary to assure that a change of the magnitude of an MIS project will not be viewed unfavorably. If top management would, for example, indicate that it feels change is generally disruptive and an imposition on managers, then it is logical that MIS developments will not be favorably regarded by employees. Since change is a common phenomenon in business and government today, particularly in the area of new procedures and managerial tools, management needs to communicate this to its people.

Top management support of MIS means more than just allocation of funds, although this is certainly an important factor. It also means assistance in establishing the chain of support needed in the various parts of the enterprise. Formal and informal structures may be altered because of MIS development. If top managers are involved in such developments through the establishment of systems goals and objectives along with operating procedures, support from operating and middle management levels should be more easily obtained. After all, if top management feels that an activity is important enough to devote valuable time and effort to it, perhaps the change is an important, significant, and necessary one which all persons should support. Although the mere involvement and support of top management is not sufficient to insure system success, it is necessary. Thus, we can state that a fundamental principle of computer-based information systems is that *top management involvement, interaction, and support are necessary but not sufficient factors for successful development and introduction of systems.*

User interaction—the project team.   It is necessary also, in addition to top management involvement in the MIS, to have user interaction. The logic here is that since an individual manager or employee will be using outputs from a system to do his or her work, he should be involved in the effort to develop the supporting system. The inputs of these individuals need to be heard directly.

It has been widely held in the past that establishment of clear objectives was a significant factor in achieving success with MIS project activities. Research indicates, however, that this is not quite accurate. Powers and Dickson [29] examined this factor in a field study on correlates of success with MIS projects. The results of this study, which involved firms in manufacturing, finance, marketing, transportation, and utilities, indicate that clarity of MIS project objectives is *not* related to user satisfaction, nor to any other criterion of success. There were some projects in those studied where the initial objectives were reportedly vague. However, through a gradual process of evolution where the users worked quite closely with the information systems staff, the users defined their objectives and information/decision-making environments. As a consequence, these projects resulted in products with which the users were highly pleased.

An additional aspect to user participation is that a *lack of correlation* was found between a successful project and utilization of a project team comprised of MIS staff and user personnel. The managers who eventually used the outputs created by the MIS project activities in several cases in the study did not themselves participate on the teams. Rather, they delegated the team membership to staff personnel in their departments. Consequently, while there was user participation, the manager who later used the system and its outputs and rated it in terms of his own information requirements did *not* participate. Even though the assignment of user area staff personnel to project teams may be reasonable and effective for data processing or information systems developments where the primary requirement is for procedural expertise, this delegation by managers in an MIS environment appears detrimental in terms of the manager's satisfaction with the results of the project. Consequently, *successful management information systems efforts require the direct involvement and participation of the managers who will use the system outputs.*

Integration upon implementation. It follows that management information systems should be integrated into the decision system such that they are a *natural* part of daily activities, since they are designed to support managerial activities. These systems too often are somewhat extraneous to the managers when they are designed, and do not fit his or her normal way of operating. In other words, the systems are designed with the apparent underlying assumption that the manager will change to fit the system. Consequently, the systems are often perceived as "being in the way" and seem almost like an extra task for the manager rather than being of assistance.

When systems are developed and implemented, they should be integrated into the managerial process. However, the only way this can successfully come about is when the MIS project fills a real need or a hole in the information network. It does this either by providing information previously not readily available or by providing information already available with *less difficulty* and/or *greater reliability* than before. In either case, *an MIS project should be integrated into the organization upon its implementation. This is done by insuring that the system is designed to fill a real information need.*

Conclusion

The field of computer-based management information systems has developed dramatically since the first introduction of computers into business decision making. We can now begin the statement of principles to guide others who are becoming involved with these systems. Much more research and development, however, is needed to answer the many questions being raised by theorists and practitioners alike.

MARKETING INFORMATION SYSTEM

A major apparel manufacturer had used computers for several years to perform data processing activities. Yet the management in merchandising planning did not have access to the information needed to accurately plan and monitor fashion trends in order to react quickly in product production. A marketing information system was installed to provide this capability. The system provides sales history information from previous seasons to support merchandise planning. Included is information on product lines: sales volume, inventory classification, price, type of fabric, and so forth. Information for the current season, including sales, forecasts, production runs, and a computerized projection of sales data, is also provided. The information system allows management to identify trends. Management is better equipped to define marketing objectives and to determine whether or not the objectives are being met.

Many businesses need product planning information. They usually rely on reports that are produced on a monthly or quarterly basis to aid in planning. The unique feature of this marketing information system is that it is inquiry-based. Managers without data processing experience can use terminals connected to a central computer to make inquiries about the various phases of preseason product planning (Illustration 16-1). Because the managers are communicating directly with the computer, it is called an online inquiry. The advantage of online inquiry is that the manager does not have to wait for a report to be prepared to get an answer to a question. Inquiry usage in this system includes: (1) interpreting sales history to define marketing classifications of products, (2) the study of trends of individual product sales to assist in determining which product styles to develop, and (3) the forecasting of costs by apparel fashion groups.

Personnel in purchasing also use the system to make long-term commitments on fabric purchases. A visual display terminal can display companywide requirements for fabric for the entire season.

Manufacturing personnel use the system to determine production requirements for various apparel styles. After the production season has started, the system is used to compare planning production by apparel groups and determine whether or not any problems exist because of under- or over-forecasting. This usage continues throughout the season. It is augmented with exception reports as needed.

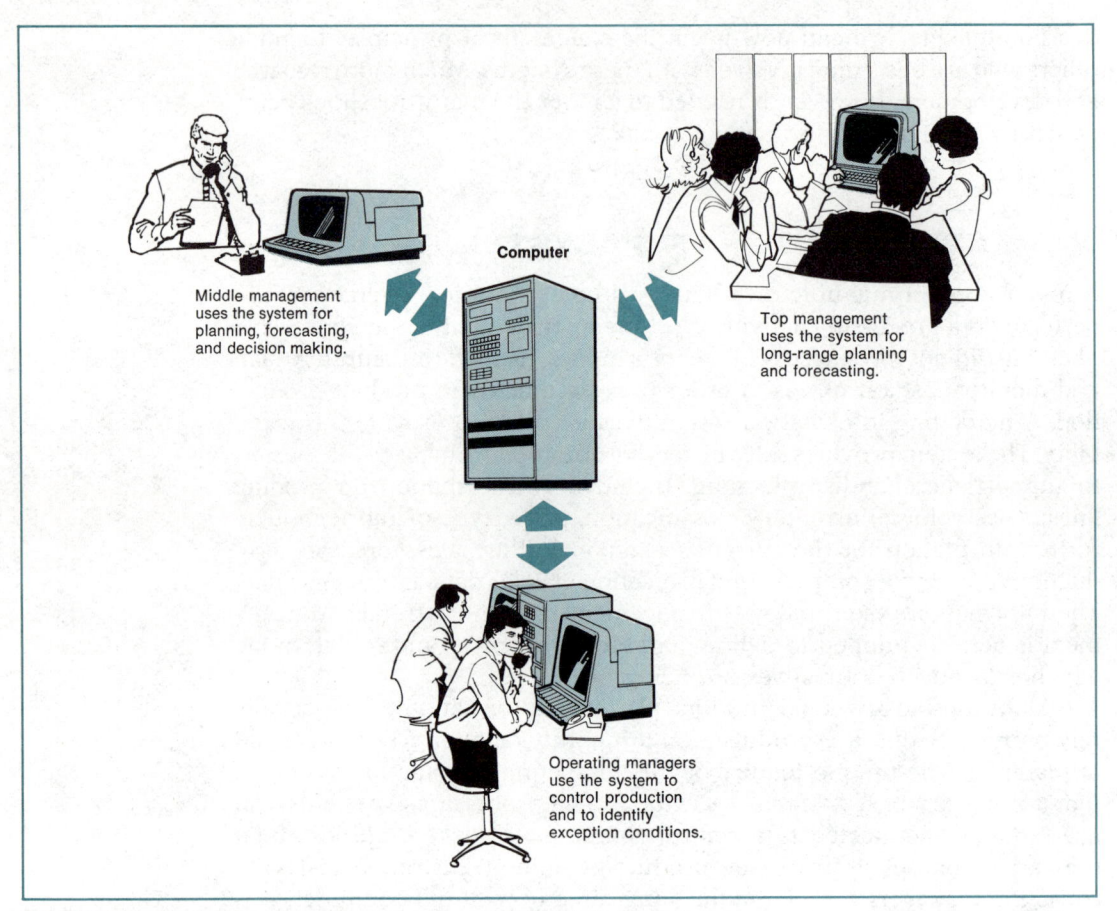

ILLUSTRATION 16-1   Inquiry system for marketing information

Thus, this marketing information system is a direct aid to both middle management and operating managers. Middle management uses the system for planning, forecasting, and decision making. The operating managers use the system to control production and to identify conditions needing immediate management attention.

AN INTEGRATED MERCHANDISING INFORMATION SYSTEM

One of the nation's largest retailers had used a computerized data processing system for over 10 years. However, in the 1960s, as business expanded and more stores were opened, top management recognized that it must make some changes in its information system in order to maintain its competitive position. As the structure of the organization expanded, it became more difficult for the existing data processing system to provide the kind of information that management needed for decision making. It was recognized by management that poor decisions due to a lack of accurate, timely, and complete information can have a major impact on profitability. The nature of the retailing business requires quick response to consumer trends and to economic conditions affecting these trends. Because of the physical separation of the territorial management from corporate headquarters, it was difficult to provide the needed information in a timely manner for decision-making purposes.

A new information system was developed and installed in two phases. First, a series of regional computer centers was established. Each one served a group of retail stores to provide merchandising and inventory information, processing of customer credit accounts, and general store accounting. Next, each store was equipped with cash-register terminals connected to a computer located within the store. (Such cash-register terminals are commonly referred to as point-of-sale terminals. They are discussed in more detail in Module A.) Thus, the second phase was the development of a merchandising information system that collected sales activity data through terminals.

Illustration 16-2 is a generalized system flowchart showing the point-of-sale portion of the merchandising information system. The sales clerk enters a sale by pressing the appropriate keys on the point-of-sale terminal. For each transaction, the following data is collected: employee identification number, merchandise division, item identification number, quantity, unit price, type of transaction, and (for credit sales) customer credit card number. The point-of-sale terminal calculates the total sale, adds any sales tax to determine a final total, and prints a customer receipt. The sales data from each terminal transaction is recorded in the store computer system as it occurs.

At the end of each day, every regional computer system communicates with the computers in all stores in its region to obtain the sales activity data for that day. In this way, the sales activity data is entered into the merchandising information system for the company.

Each store computer is also used for some local processing and reporting. This allows each store manager to obtain certain reports needed for store decisions without waiting for their preparation and distribution from a regional computer center.

At each regional center, the sales activity data from all of the stores in the region is processed to create a series of files for accounts receivable, inventory control, product-line activity, payroll, and finance. These files become part of the merchandising information system. In addition to serving the specific functions indicated, they provide information for management reports.

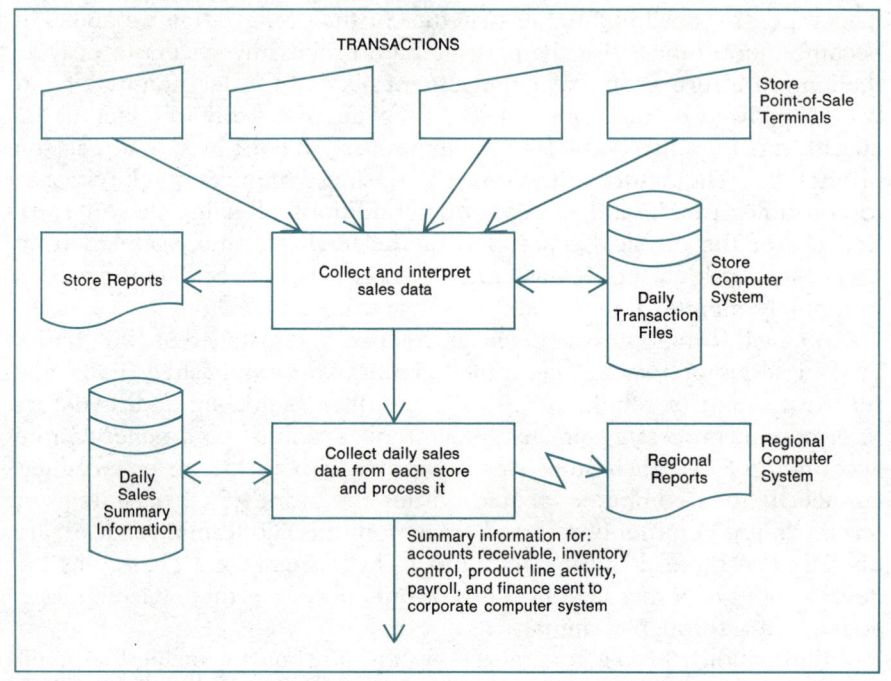

ILLUSTRATION 16-2 Point-of-sale portion of merchandising information system

The merchandising information system can provide a great deal of information for management decision making. It does so in a very timely manner. Summarization of information takes place at each level in this information system to provide the reports needed by management at the store, region, and corporate level. The information that is collected and processed by each of the regional centers is summarized and forwarded to the corporate headquarters. A computer system at the corporate headquarters utilizes the summary information provided by each of the regional computer centers to provide top management information.

○ AN MIS IN HIGHER EDUCATION*

Objectives for Design

Currently, efforts are underway to develop management information systems at a wide spectrum of colleges and universities, both public and private, as well as within groups of institutions at local and state levels.

---

*From Roger W. Comstock, "MIS in Higher Education," *Management Controls* (Sept. 1970), published by Peat, Marwick, Mitchell & Company and adapted with their permission.

Obviously, the objectives for system design vary from one organization to another, as do the objectives of the organizations themselves. Nevertheless, there is sufficient commonality to warrant discussing the objectives of a particular statewide public system, used here for purposes of illustration.

In the state in which this system was established, careful consideration was given to what the objectives of a project to develop a higher-education management information system should be. The objectives finally selected included:

The system must provide meaningful management information to the board of regents and to university administrators. This probably will necessitate the development of common but somewhat different systems at individual institutions to meet common but somewhat different needs.

Common definitions must be developed and applied at all universities in order that data supplied by the system may be comparable.

The system taken as a whole must not be oriented to any particular institution or application area.

The plan and resulting systems must be as flexible as possible to permit modification to meet changing objectives and to accommodate new educational methods and procedures. The plan must be devised to provide a firm foundation on which to base new systems development over the next several years. This will not decrease the need to identify as many of the future needs as possible early in the project.

The program for development must be structured so that it can be accomplished in distinct steps. Milestones must be charted at which project progress may be reviewed and new directions taken, if warranted. Provision must be made to review and fund discrete tasks associated with the project, and to pass on their applicability and urgency in the future. The project must also be planned so that some results are achieved at an early date. Confidence and interest tend to lag in direct proportion to the length and cost of the project.

The results of a project of this nature are only as good as the depth of commitment of key administrators and the amount of effort each is willing to devote to its development. The system incorporates many of the tools that administrators will use in seeking to satisfy institutional objectives. Hence, the reports to be provided must be fitted closely to the characteristics and requirements of the offices that will use them. For example, the methods by which faculty time utilization is classified can be critical when making decisions with regard to staffing levels, academic personnel policy, and individual advancement.

The personnel responsible for setting up this MIS project recognized that unless serious attention were paid to the project plan by key administrators, the resulting systems would fall short of the utility expected of them. University officials had to recognize this and be ready to commit a considerable portion of their time and energy to the project, despite other pressing demands on their time. A broad policy framework within which development of the system could proceed had to be established. Procedures as to how information would be controlled and disseminated had to be developed. Checks and balances had to be built into the administrative structure to insure against improper issuance or use of data. The integrity and the identity of the individual and of the institution had to be preserved.

Conceptual Design

The first step in the actual development of an MIS should be the creation of a conceptual design. Many managers do not like to bear the cost of developing such a plan (which has no immediate operational results), but it is absolutely essential to develop an overall understanding of the interrelationships of such operating functions as registration, financial aids, space allocation, staffing and course scheduling, and unit costs.

The primary elements of the conceptual plan are definitions of the management-level system outputs, the information flow, the system software and programming languages to be used, the key data elements needed, a data classification scheme, a list of required subsystems, constraints of a planning model, and a plan for implementation.

System Outputs; Key Data Elements

The system output generally consists of a set of reports designed to serve management needs at various points in the management process. These reports may be oriented to such diverse elements of university administration as program planning and budgeting, faculty evaluation, and control of the auxiliary enterprises. They should be clearly and specifically designed. Each design should include a definition of each field contained in the report, and statements of the purpose of the report, how it will be used, and the frequency and manner of distribution.

If the MIS is to provide for inquiry via terminals or specifically written programs for such jobs as student accounts and registration, the nature of the inquiries allowed and the constraints to be applied to this method of using the system must be defined.

Once the required reporting structure has been defined, data elements needed to produce the reports must be identified. These elements can then be grouped into logical file structures—a first step in the definition of the various information system master files.

Information Flow

The information flow description will consist of a set of system flowcharts and a brief narrative. Each flowchart should depict the manner in which key data elements will be handled from the time that they are originated in machine form to the point where they are incorporated into the various system outputs. To do this, it is necessary to define the major related master file update runs and the related master file structures. Once these have been defined, it will be possible to display: the manner in which data is captured by each of these systems and in which it flows from one system to the next; the basic master file structure; and the techniques by which the management reporting system of the MIS can extract the data it needs most efficiently.

The system flowchart constructed for the student records system (subsystem) is shown as an example in Illustration 16-3. It depicts clearly the inputs and outputs of the subsystem and the requirement for a student master file.

System Software

After the system outputs and system flowcharts have been designed, it should be possible for the system designer to prepare gross specifications for the operating software required in the MIS. This includes the executive system, the type of file management software to be used, the requirements for inquiry, and the basic programming language (or languages). It is advisable to include these specifications in the conceptual design.

Data Classification Scheme

A data classification scheme is needed to permit input transactions to be coded so that the individual data elements will be routed properly along the information flow path to be summarized in management reports. This scheme may include the chart of accounts, the space classification system, course designations, time utilization codes, departmental numbers, and the like. While it is impractical to completely define the scheme during the conceptual state, a basic structure for classification should be provided.

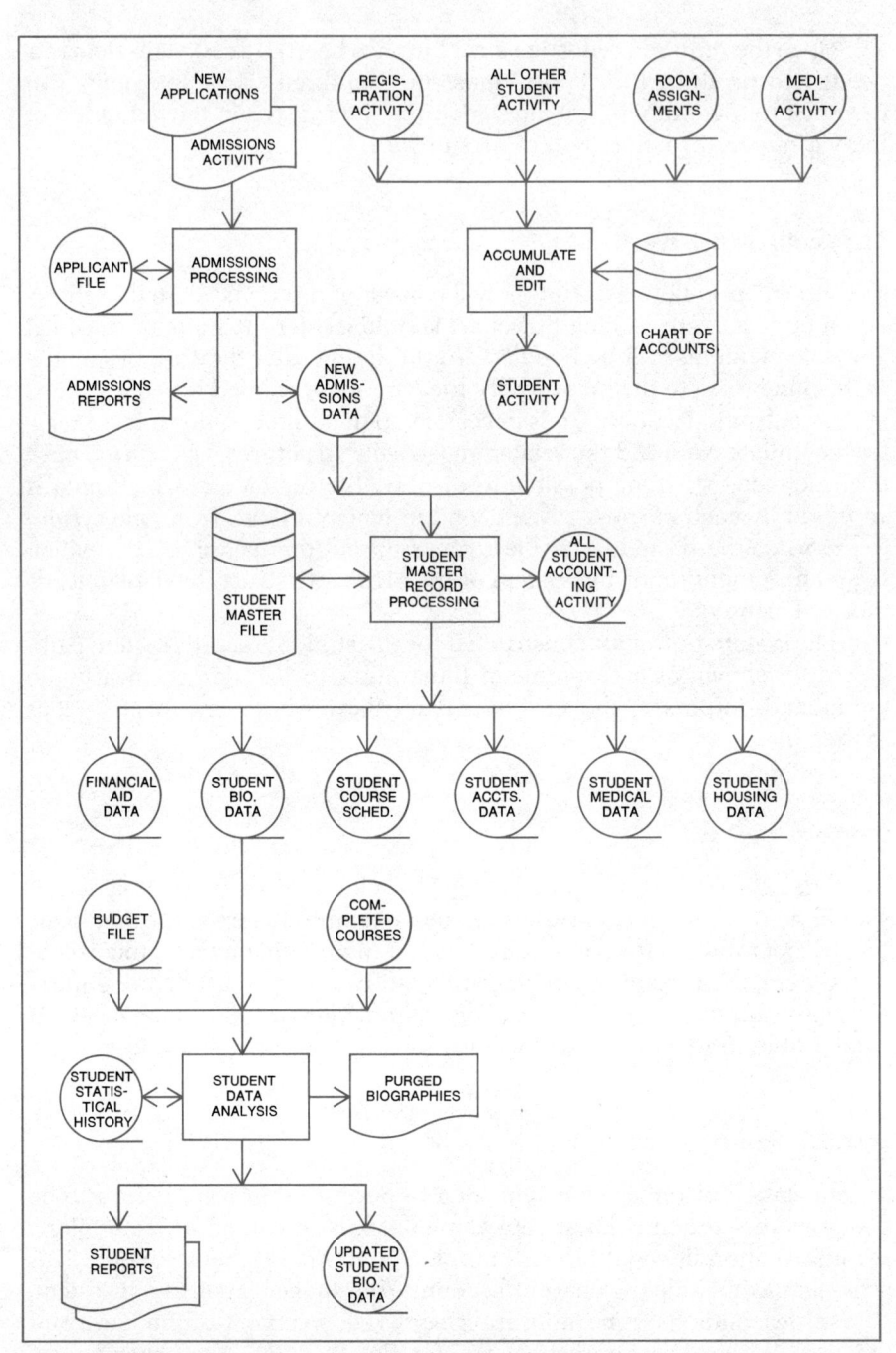

ILLUSTRATION 16-3 Student records subsystem

Information Systems

The conceptual plan should include a list of the subsystems needed to support the management reporting system of the MIS. This list should provide the facts below for each of the systems:

- Name and basic functions
- Frequency of operation
- Gross estimate of time and effort required to make it operational, if applicable
- Priority for implementation in the light of institutional needs and available resources

If the systems are not in operation currently, many of these facts will be rough estimates. However, such estimates are essential to the making of an informed evaluation of the time and resources required to implement the MIS.

Planning Model

An additional element to be considered in creating the conceptual plan is the use of a university planning model. If implemented, such a model provides an analytical description of meaningful relationships among program activity levels and resources under varying circumstances. With the aid of currently available computers, demands on each resource can be computed rapidly for a specified program of activities and policy constraints. The model functions with initial planning data to provide the administration of a college or university with projections of future enrollments, staffing and faculty requirements, facilities requirements, and the like.

A pictorial description of the basic modules or computational steps of a representative planning model is shown in Illustration 16-4. This model is perhaps most applicable to a small college or group of small colleges. Such a model can be developed in stages, consistent with the available data.

Some basic estimating relationships that can be developed from the initial planning data for use in the planning model are:

- Fixed and variable costs as a function of grade levels and programs
- Student and staff attrition
- Instructional hour demand by grade level and major program
- Student/course/classroom-lab space utilization
- Construction cost estimating

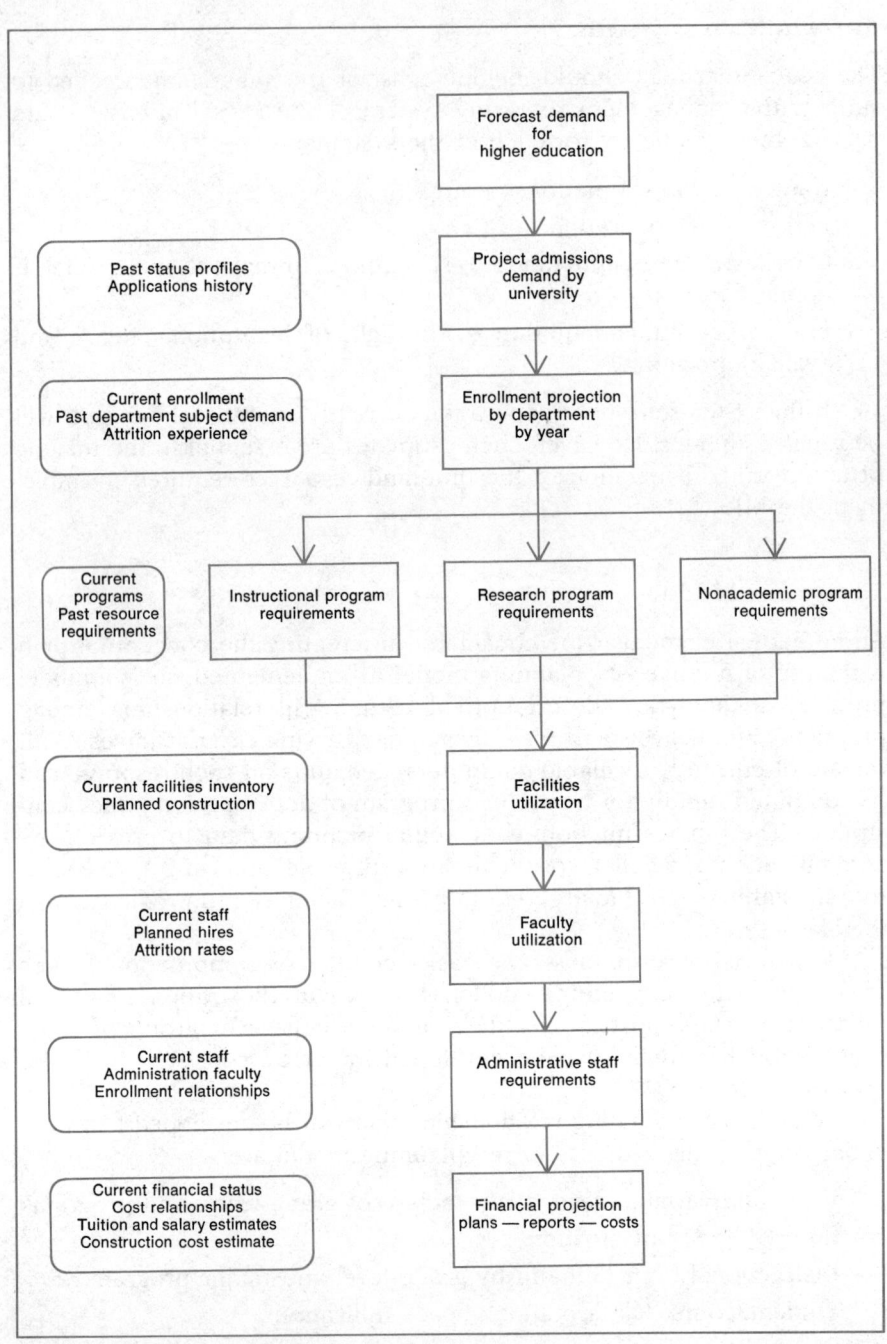

ILLUSTRATION 16-4 Planning model

Implementation Plan

Finally, using the data set forth above, together with similar estimates for the management reporting system and other software required, an implementation plan should be prepared for management approval. The plan should address the following items:

1. Overall time frame for implementation of the MIS, as well as completion dates for subsidiary elements.
2. Checkpoints for management review and approval. These should be designed in such a way that the project can be redirected or even temporarily halted without undue disruption at each checkpoint, depending upon overall conditions at that time.
3. Priority schedule for implementation of individual subsystems. Is it more important, for example, to start work now on payroll or on a library system?
4. Estimates of resources required for completion by all parties to the project. These resources include personnel, management participation, vendor assistance, and computer time for program testing.

Once the conceptual plan has been established, it is possible to proceed with the design and implementation of individual subsystems with reasonable confidence that they will fit into the MIS framework.

MIS Implementation Considerations

Though an MIS obviously can produce tangible and exciting benefits, developing it is a large undertaking. Substantial amounts of person power, money, and time are required. Problems, pitfalls, and consequences should therefore be anticipated if possible. Here are some areas that call for such special inquiry:

- *User motivation.* This is perhaps the single greatest potential pitfall for an information system. If the user of the system and the individuals responsible for supplying data to the system are not disposed to work for the success of the system, it will fail—no matter how well designed. It is a simple matter for a disgruntled employee to "permit" erroneous data to enter the system, or not to submit data at all. It is equally easy for an unhappy administrator to not use the information the system provides. Every employee involved with the system must be motivated to use it properly; conversely, the system must be designed to aid in that motivation.
- *Early results.* When senior management and funding agencies are asked to support multiple-year projects with thousands or millions of

dollars, they become anxious to see results. The system development should be organized in such a way that tangible system outputs are produced early, preferably within the first year.
- *The simple approach.* An information system is a complex undertaking. The expectations of the intended user tend to reinforce the inventiveness and enthusiasm of the system designer. Too often, this leads to a sophisticated design that is neither desirable nor attainable the first time around. As the system is being developed, managers should favor consistently the simple approach. To the extent that simplicity can be achieved, the chances of realizing a successful system increase.
- *Maximum system flexibility.* It is in the nature of management to change; else, it would not be management. As management needs change, so do management's requirements of the information system. For this reason, a flexible design is imperative. An organization should not expect to achieve the optimum system on the first go-around. The system design should be an iterative process, in which the results of experiences are built upon to improve the capabilities and responsiveness of the system.
- *Data purification.* Early in the project, it is necessary to develop standard data definitions and promulgate them to all potential sources of data for the information system. Also vital is the review of historical data to determine how it may be incorporated into the information system data base without distortion. An information system that provides reports based on nonstandard data is less than useful; it can have a negative impact on the functioning of an institution.

Conclusion

An MIS must deal with quantified data. Because of this, many administrators, particularly those dealing with academic programs, have become concerned that the system will eliminate the quality factor from consideration. Their argument is that decisions more often will be made on the basis of quantitative data selected by the system designer for presentation to the administration. They fear that quality of education will be bypassed as a factor in educational decisions. Several potential solutions exist.

The information system designer should be aware of this danger and attempt to avoid it. Management, too, must learn to use information system outputs interpretively. Rather than expect the system to provide answers, management must recognize that certain constraints exist with regard to the aggregated data supplied. For example, a summary of laboratory hours may include hours spent in chem labs, music practice sessions, and physical education courses. Each of these, in fact, may require separate treatment.

Finally, management must also learn to question the "facts" neatly presented on a computer printout; to evaluate them for reasonableness in relation to other known information; and to consider both quantitative and qualitative aspects of a question before reaching a decision.

SUMMARY

1. One example of an MIS is a marketing information system established by a major apparel manufacturer. Managers can enter online inquiries to obtain product information for planning, forecasting, and decision making. Operating managers also use the system to control production and to identify conditions needing immediate management attention.

2. A large, geographically distributed retailer obtains information for decision-making purposes by means of a three-level marketing information system:
   a. Individual retail stores collect sales activity data through point-of-sale terminals.
   b. Regional computer centers collect store data for accounts receivable, inventory control, product-line activity, payroll, and finance purposes.
   c. A computer system at corporate headquarters processes regional summary data to provide top management information.

3. The development of a higher-education MIS is a major undertaking. The conceptual design of the system must define the management-level system outputs, information flow, system software, data classification scheme and key data elements needed, information systems, subsystems, and an implementation plan. A planning model may be useful. After all of these system characteristics have been defined, the design and implementation of the individual information subsystems can proceed.

REVIEW QUESTIONS

1. What is the primary emphasis of an MIS?

2. Discuss six technical and developmental factors associated with information systems.

3. Discuss four behavior and organization factors to be considered in MIS development.

4. What problem did a major apparel manufacturer solve by replacing a data processing system with a marketing information system?

5. Discuss the two phases of integrated merchandising information system development and installation experienced by one of the nation's largest retailers.

6. Discuss the design, development, and implementation of an MIS as described in the higher education case study.

References

[1] Ackoff, R. L. "Management Misinformation Systems," *Management Science*, Vol. 14, No. 4, December 1967.

[2] Anthony, R. N. *Planning and Control Systems: A Framework for Analysis*, Division of Research, Graduate School of Business Administration, Harvard University, Boston, 1965.

[3] Argyris, C. "Management Information Systems: The Challenge to Reality and Emotionality," *Management Science*, Vol. 17, No. 6, February 1971.

[4] Argyris, C. "Resistance to Rational Management Systems," *Innovation*, Issue 10, 1969.

[5] Bedford, N., and Onsi, M. "Measuring the Value of Information—An Information Theory Approach," *Management Service*, Vol. 13, No. 4, January-February 1966.

[6] Bennis, W. G. *Organization Development: Its Nature, Origin and Prospects*, Addison-Wesley Publishing, Reading, Mass., 1969.

[7] Blumenthal, S. *Management Information Systems: A Framework for Planning and Development*, Prentice-Hall, Inc., Englewood Cliffs, N.J., 1969.

[8] Boyd, D., and Krasnow, H. "Economic Evaluation of Management Information Systems," *IBM Systems Journal*, Vol. 2, March 1968.

[9] Chervany, N. L., and Dickson, G. W. "An Experimental Evaluation of Information in a Production Environment," *Management Science*, Vol. 20, No. 10, June 1974.

[10] Chervany, N. L., and Dickson, G. W. "Economic Evaluation of Management Information Systems: An Analytical Framework," *Decision Sciences*, June-October, 1970.

[11] Churchill, N. C., Kempster, J. H., and Uretsky, M. *Computer-Based Information Systems for Management: A Survey*, National Association for Accountants, New York, 1969.

[12] Cougar, J. D., and Knapp, R. W. *Systems Analysis Techniques*, John Wiley and Sons, New York, 1974.

[13] Cougar, J. D., and Wergin, L. W. "Small Company MIS," *Infosystems*, Vol. 21, No. 10, October 1974.

[14] Dean, N. J. "The Computer Comes of Age," *Harvard Business Review*, Vol. 46, No. 1, January-February 1968.

[15] Dearden, J. "MIS Is a Mirage," *Harvard Business Review*, Vol. 50, No. 1, January-February 1972.

[16] Dickson, G. W. "Management Information Systems: Definitions, Problems, and Research," *Society for Management Information Systems Newsletter*, July 1970.

[17] Dickson, G. W., Senn, J. A., and Chervany, N. L. "Research in MIS: The Minnesota Experiments," *Management Science*, Vol. 23, No. 9, May 1977.

[18] Dickson, G. W., and Simmons, J. K. "The Behavioral Side of MIS," *Business Horizons*, Vol. 13, August 1970.

[19] Diebold, J. "Bad Decisions on Computer Use," *Harvard Business Review*, Vol. 47, No. 1, January-February 1969.

[20] Everest, G. C. "Objectives of Database Management," *Information Systems: Proceedings of the Fourth International Symposium on Computers and Information Sciences (COINS-72)*, December 1972, Plenum Press, New York, 1974.
[21] Gorry, G. A., and Scott Morton, M. S. "A Framework for Management Information Systems," *Sloan Management Review*, Vol. 13, No. 1, January 1971.
[22] Hanold, T. "The Executive View of Management Information Systems," *SMIS Special Report*, The Society for Management Information Systems, Chicago, September 1972.
[23] Head, R. V. "Management Information Systems: A Critical Appraisal," *Datamation*, Vol. 13, No. 5, May 1967.
[24] Hertz, D. B. "Unlocking the Computer's Profit Potential," McKinsey and Company, New York, 1968.
[25] Kennevan, W. "MIS Universe," *Data Management*, September 1970.
[26] Lucas, H. C., Jr. "An Empirical Study of a Framework for Information Systems," *Decision Sciences*, Vol. 5, No. 1, January 1974.
[27] Lucas, H. C., Jr. *Toward Creative Systems Design*, Columbia University Press, New York, 1974.
[28] Mason, R. O., and Mitroff, I. I. "A Program for Research on Management Information Systems," *Management Science*, Vol. 19, No. 5, January 1973.
[29] Powers, R. F., and Dickson, G. W. "MIS Project Management: Myths, Opinions, and Reality," *California Management Review*, Vol. 15, Spring 1973.
[30] Pratt, J. W., Raiffa, H., and Schlaifer, R. *Introduction to Statistical Decision Theory*, John Wiley and Sons, New York, 1966.
[31] Rappaport, A. "Management Misinformation Systems—Another Perspective," *Management Science*, December 1968.
[32] Schubert, P. F. "Directions in Data Base Management Technology," *Datamation*, Vol. 20, No. 9, September 1974.
[33] Schwartz, M. H. "MIS Planning," *Datamation*, Vol. 16, No. 17, September 1, 1970.
[34] Senn, J. A., and Dickson, G. W. "Information System Structure and Purchasing Decision Effectiveness," *Journal of Purchasing and Materials Management*, Vol. 10, No. 3, August 1974.
[35] Simon, H. A. *The New Science of Decision*, Harper Brothers Publishers, New York, 1960.
[36] Tiechrow, D., and Hershey, E. A., III. "A Computer-Aided Technique for Structured Documentation," *Data Base*, Vol. 8, No. 1, Summer 1976. pp. 7–9.
[37] *What Is a Management Information System?* Research Report Number 1. The Society for Management Information Systems, Chicago, 1970.
[38] Williams, L. K. "The Human Side of Systems Change," *Systems and Procedure Journal*, July 1964.
[39] Withington, F. G. "Five Generations of Computers," *Harvard Business Review*, Vol. 52, No. 4, July-August 1974.
[40] Wolk, S. "Resistance to EDP: An Employee-Management Dilemma," *Data Management*, Vol. 6, No. 9, September 1968.

UNIT SIX

DATA PROCESSING MANAGEMENT AND THE COMPUTER INDUSTRY

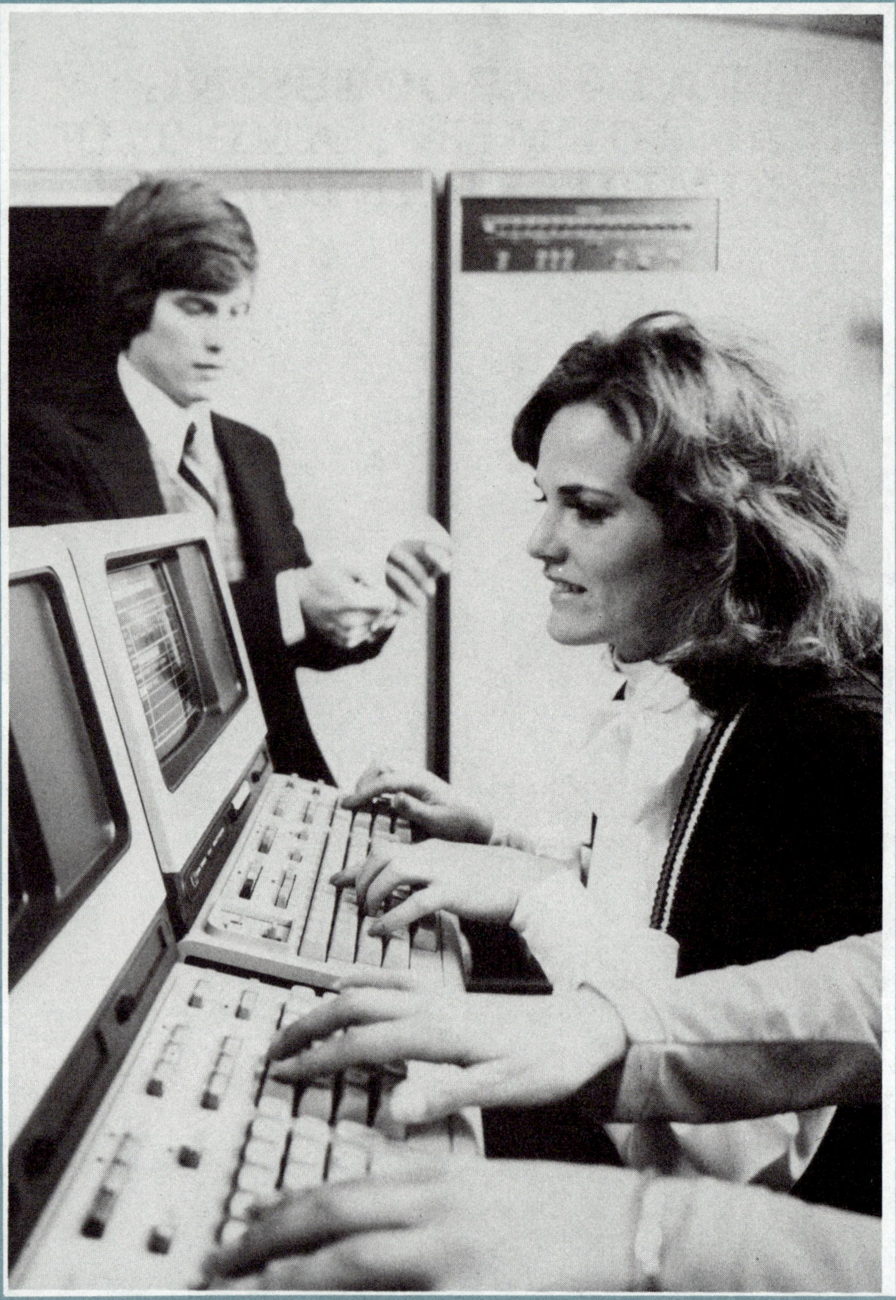

CHAPTER 17

THE ORGANIZATION AND THE DATA PROCESSING DEPARTMENT

THE APPLICATION OF COMPUTERS
IN BUSINESS ORGANIZATIONS

THE SELECTION AND INSTALLATION
OF A COMPUTER SYSTEM
The Cost of the System
The Time Required for Installation
General Practices

THE CONTROL OF A DATA PROCESSING SYSTEM
Top Management Control
Data Processing Department Management Control
Controls during the Processing of Data
The Evaluation of Error Controls

COMPUTER SYSTEM SECURITY
Fraud
Physical Security
Recovery Procedures

THE DATA PROCESSING DEPARTMENT
Job Descriptions
The Separation of Functions
The Location of the Data Processing Department
within the Organization

Opposite: The computer operator uses the console display-keyboard to communicate with the system.

The discussions thus far in this text have centered primarily around the hardware and software characteristics of data processing. An underlying assumption of these discussions has been that the hardware and software are located within the organization.

The discussion within this chapter centers around the decisions to obtain the hardware and software, where they will be located within the organization, and the qualifications that people who are going to work in the data processing department should have.

○ THE APPLICATION OF COMPUTERS IN BUSINESS ORGANIZATIONS

There are four basic ways in which computers are being used in business organizations to assist management in the accomplishment of organizational objectives. The first way is to print information required to instruct employees concerning how to perform various activities in accordance with the policies of the organization. Thus, computers alleviate a portion of the paperwork that otherwise must be done manually.

A second way in which computers are used in business organizations is to make routine management decisions. For example, a computer can be programmed to detect when the stock quantity of an inventory item is reduced via sales to a predetermined reorder level. It can be directed to print the information necessary to order a certain quantity of the particular inventory item when such a situation occurs.

A third way in which computers are used in business organizations is to provide progress reports with respect to the performance of particular activities. Up-to-date progress reports provide management with the information needed to control the performance of the particular activities.

A final way in which computers are used in business organizations is to provide information about a particular topic in response to management requests for the information. This is the most important way in which computers can be used because a manager is provided the information needed to make correct and timely decisions. This information could be stored in file cabinets, but then it would have to be updated manually. Also, a manual record of what was where would have to be maintained. If a great quantity of information had to be stored, many file cabinets and a large amount of storage space would be required.

○ THE SELECTION AND INSTALLATION OF A COMPUTER SYSTEM

The fundamental criterion for deciding whether or not to install a computer system in a business organization is whether or not the system will help to increase profits. For a not-for-profit or governmental organization, the criterion is whether or not the computer will result in either reduced operating costs and/or significantly improved ability to provide service to customers, clients, or the public.

The installation of a computer system is a major capital expenditure. It requires a substantial initial outlay of resources. It also changes the procedures for processing data. It may alter the operations and management structure of the organization. Obviously, a decision to install a computer system is an expensive and important one; such a commitment should be made only after careful analysis. Consideration of at least the factors discussed below is mandatory.

The Cost of the System

The basic cost considerations involved in acquiring a computer system can be compared to those involved in acquiring an automobile. The initial consideration is whether to purchase or lease the computer system. Most computer systems are leased because this approach provides flexibility with respect to making changes in the computer system (see "Computer Manufacturers" and "Leasing Companies" in Chapter 18).

Most leasing contracts include a provision for regular maintenance. If the computer system is purchased, its maintenance must be performed by specially trained personnel within the data processing department. Alternatively, a contract must be signed with an organization that can provide maintenance. Since maintenance on a computer system is needed only periodically, it is usually less costly to sign a maintenance contract with another organization than to hire maintenance personnel. However, an overriding consideration is how long it will take the maintenance personnel to respond to a maintenance problem. The direct and indirect costs to the organization resulting from the computer system being inoperable ("down") throughout this period of time must be evaluated.

Also, similar to an automobile, the value of a computer system depreciates over time. By leasing the system, the organization avoids assuming the risk of obsolescence. A computer usually becomes **functionally obsolete** before it becomes **operationally obsolete**. That is, since a computer has no moving parts, its "wear-and-tear" is nominal; it need not be traded because of hard use. A computer system becomes unable to perform the type or volume of data processing activity required of it before it becomes unable to actually operate as it was built to operate.

Finally, when acquiring an automobile, any options, such as air conditioning and stereo-radio, are extra-cost items. Their cost is added to the basic cost of the automobile. A similar situation is true when acquiring a computer system. Every equipment component is separately priced, and many desirable features are extra-cost options. Therefore, a basic computer system (with or without various options) can be acquired for any of several prices.

Fortunately, the cost of computer system equipment has been steadily declining since the introduction of computers. Looking at it from another perspective, there have been major improvements in the performance of computer system equipment; more computing power can be acquired without a corresponding increase in cost.

The Time Required for Installation

Complete installation of a computer system requires many months of preparation. As a rough guide, installing a batch-oriented data processing system requires from 12 to 24 months. That is, after the decision is made to investigate the feasibility of installing a computer system, from one to two years may be required to reach the point where the system is satisfactorily processing business data. In some cases, the total elapsed time can be reduced by performing some tasks simultaneously rather than one after another. Even so, a year of selection and preparation activity is probably a minimum. For an inexperienced organization, two years is more reasonable. Adequate planning and preparation time for the final selection and installation of equipment ranges from 8 to 15 months. The time needed depends on the computer installation experience of the organization, the complexity of the system, and related factors. A complex realtime system requires two to three years for the steps from initial investigation to successful operation.

General Practices

While many computer systems in current use are successfully performing data processing activities, others are fraught with problems. The problems are rarely caused by incorrectly functioning equipment. They may be caused by the failure of certain software to correctly instruct the computer. However, the problems are usually caused by the failure of responsible personnel to adhere to one or more of the following general practices during selection and installation: (1) enlist top management's participation and support, (2) develop adequate plans and controls, and (3) consider possible employee problems and take steps to prevent such problems from arising.

Top management's participation and support in the selection and installation of a computer system is a necessary condition for success. Since the installation of a computer system can be disruptive to the organization, the entire organization must understand that top management is solidly behind the new system. Lower levels of management tend to support what is clearly supported by top management.

The installation of a computer system extends over a long period of time. If the installation is not properly planned and controlled, the activities involved in installing the system will not be completed on time. Furthermore, the components of the system will not mesh correctly.

Finally, employees who have not been informed as to the objectives and purposes of installing a computer tend to oppose the computer. The computer system should be installed with due regard for its impact on people in the organization and on organizational operations. Special precautions should be taken to guard against disruptions of operations during installation of the system. The specific process of evaluating a computer system, selecting equipment, and installing the system must be tailored to fit the characteristics of the organization. It is imperative that management consider possible employee problems as a result of the installation of a computer. It is wise to develop and implement a plan of action to solve these problems before they occur.

THE CONTROL OF A DATA PROCESSING SYSTEM

The processing of data is often carried out with a higher error rate than is desirable because top management does not require that the proper level of error control be exercised. The proper level of control cannot be established or maintained without cost. The manager who understands the problems, methods, and procedures involved in achieving control is able to evaluate the expected results of maintaining it compared to its cost. While there are some control problems in computer data processing that are not found in manual data processing, there are also unique, new control methods and procedures available to the manager because of the capabilities of the computer.

Top Management Control

Within an organization there exists a hierarchy of control of a data processing system. The highest level of control is exercised by the top management of the organization. Thus, top management has the overall responsibility for the efficient and effective operation of the data processing system. This responsibility should be exercised over the activities involved in four data-processing-related areas. These are:

- *The authorization of major changes in the data processing system.* Top management is responsible for evaluating proposals concerning major changes in the data processing system in terms of costs and benefits. An improved or new data processing system is similar to a large expenditure for an addition to a plant or for equipment; any proposal for a major change should receive careful scrutiny before resources are committed to the project. The work of the data processing department affects the nature and extent to which other departments must process data. It also affects the information available to them. Top management's understanding and evaluation of any proposed change are necessary for adequate control of the data processing activity. A requirement for top management approval forces data processing management to do adequate preplanning.

- *The post-installation review of the actual cost and effectiveness of the data processing system.* There is a tendency among data processing personnel to underestimate the cost and difficulty of implementing a new or improved data processing system. Top management should follow up on proposals involving changes in the data processing system; they should evaluate the reasons for any deviations from planned cost, planned schedule, and estimated benefit. The assessment of performance resulting from the post-installation review should aid management in evaluating future requests for changes in the system.
- *The review of the organization of the data processing department and the various methods and techniques used to control the data processing activity.* Top management has the responsibility for insuring that competent, adequately trained management personnel are employed within the data processing department. The organization and control practices of the data processing activity should be subject to top management review.
- *The monitoring of the performance of the data processing activity.* Finally, top management is responsible for monitoring the performance of the data processing department and reporting any deviations from expected levels of performance. The monitoring should be guided by established performance standards and reporting procedures. Three areas of performance should be monitored: (1) the cost of data processing activities compared to their expected cost, (2) the frequency and length of delays in meeting processing schedules, and (3) the number of errors detected at various control points.

Data Processing Department Management Control

Below top management, the next level of responsibility for control of the data processing system lies with the manager of the data processing department. Specifically, the data processing manager is responsible for the day-to-day control of activities performed within the department. An in-

CHAPTER 17: THE ORGANIZATION AND THE DATA PROCESSING DEPARTMENT

adequate level of control of the data processing system is an indication of a weakness at this level of management.

Although a separation of functions is not always economically feasible in small and medium-size data processing departments, a fundamental aspect of control is to have each of the various data processing functions (duties) performed by a different person within the department. This separation acts as a guard against the possibility of individual incompetence and/or fraud.

Basically, two types of control should be provided for and exercised concerning the data processing activity: (1) internal data processing control, which is exercised by the data processing department, and (2) external data processing control, which is exercised by one or more individuals independent of the data processing department.

Internal data processing control is concerned with insuring that the processing of data is performed correctly and that no data is lost or mishandled within the department. For example, consider an accounts receivable application. At scheduled intervals, the accounts receivable transactions are processed against the current accounts receivable master file to produce an updated accounts receivable master file. The monetary sum of the transaction records and the prior balances of all master records should equal the total of the new balances of all records on the updated master file.

The external data processing control function can be exercised in several ways. For example, a department that uses the computer, such as the accounting department, can compare manually calculated totals in one or more of the accounting-related files with corresponding totals calculated by the computer.

Controls during the Processing of Data

The use of a computer system requires new controls for detecting and controlling errors that arise during the use of such a system. Examples of the types of controls required are:

1. Verification procedures to check the conversion of source data into machine-readable form
2. Control totals to detect any loss of data or failure to process data items
3. Computer programs and manual procedures to guard against the misuse of files stored on machine-readable media such as disk and tape
4. Hardware features to detect hardware malfunctions
5. Computer program checks to guard against errors by the computer operator

In a manual system, internal control relies upon such factors as human alertness and judgment, care, acceptance of responsibility, and division of duties. After the data processing activity is computerized, many controls based on such factors are no longer available. However, a computer program can be an effective substitute for many human controls. For example, in a manual system, a clerk detects an error when an item on a shipping document is not on the applicable price list. In a computer operation, the possibility of a nonmatch such as this must be provided for in the computer program. Once programmed, the nonmatch routine will be executed faithfully by the computer. In most instances, computer checks can be more extensive than those performed manually.

The Evaluation of Error Controls

There are error control procedures to prevent or detect almost any type of error. Despite the availability of these procedures, however, an error such as preparing and distributing a weekly payroll check for $1000 instead of $100 still occurs. In such instances, fundamental controls are not being exercised.

Error controls, like all other controls, require an expenditure of resources. For example, programmed error controls (programmed controls, for short) take up valuable storage positions. These controls need to be part of the data processing system, but there is an associated storage cost.

Before implementing a programmed control of a particular error, the merits of the control should be evaluated. The following questions should be asked:

1. How frequently might the error occur?
2. What are the monetary and nonmonetary consequences of not detecting the error?
3. What is the cost of detecting the error?
4. If the error is missed at this point in the data processing system, will it be detected at a later point?
5. What are the consequences of detecting the error at a later point in the data processing system?

Error controls must also be established to guard against the possibility of human errors. These controls are needed throughout the preparation of a program and the data it is to process, the processing of the data, and the distribution of the results. In fact, the necessity for, and the effectiveness of, specific controls cannot be viewed in isolation. Rather, all of the internal and external data processing controls applicable to a particular application must be considered. The organizational and management environment in which they are applied must be evaluated. All of these factors, in combination, determine the quality of the control exercised over and during the processing of data.

COMPUTER SYSTEM SECURITY

Another vital aspect of EDP system control is the establishment and enforcement of security mechanisms. Some potential areas of exposure, and actions that can be taken to reduce or eliminate them, are discussed below.

Fraud

In addition to the control procedures discussed thus far, control procedures must be established to safeguard data against *fraud*—the manipulation of data for unfair or unlawful purposes. On a regular basis, there should be an investigation of such areas as:

- Over-limit violations, such as payroll checks that exceed allowable dollar amounts
- Discrepancies between computer records and physical counts, such as a difference between the physical inventory count and the perpetual record maintained through the computer
- Values that change radically without apparent reason, such as an expense that has been fairly constant changing without apparent cause
- Items for which statistical analyses indicate changes from normal relationships; for example, the gross profit percentage in a business tends to be constant and can therefore be used as a standard for comparison with data produced by the computer

The protection of data against fraud is related to the protection of data for accuracy. Procedures can be set up with this goal in mind.

First, a duplicate copy of all data sent to the data processing department should be kept by the individual sending the data. The copy should be retained for a specified, appropriate period of time—at least, until after the data is known to have been processed successfully.

Second, any changes or errors in the data or in the program that processes the data should be reported directly to the data processing manager. In addition, for certain types of changes to data, advance approval from the data processing manager should be required.

Third, in a centralized organizational structure, the data processing department can be isolated so that it will not be directly subjected to undue pressure from a powerful or large user who wishes to make improper program runs. Any request for processing, especially one concerning funds or supplies, should be stated in writing and signed by an authorized manager. Unfortunately, small organizations cannot make effective use of this procedure.

Physical Security

The data processing department handles various types of data, some of which is vital to the survival of the organization. Control procedures against the unauthorized use or destruction of this data must be developed.

Personnel access to certain areas of the computer center should be restricted to individuals having a legitimate need to enter the areas. Access to the restricted areas can be controlled by use of a key, a badge-activated lock, and/or a security guard. Large computer centers are often protected by electronic security systems based on badge-activated locks. Such systems are controlled by a computer that checks a special code on an identification badge when the badge is placed in a slot on or near a door that is to be unlocked. If the code is valid, the door can be opened by the person wanting to enter. If the code is not valid, the door remains locked. Badge-controlled locks with different levels of access authorization can be used for the various rooms in the computer center to further limit access. For example, a programmer's identification badge may allow access to a terminal room and an output distribution area, but not to the main computer room. These electronic security systems may be combined with closed-circuit TV cameras. The cameras project images of restricted areas to a security guard. The guard can then visually determine whether or not the persons shown on the screen are authorized to enter the areas.

Additional safeguards are required to control access to computer files and/or organizational data bases by users at terminals. Security mechanisms such as a "password," which a user must enter into the terminal, and/or a catalog of authorized users, which is checked by the computer, should be established.

One way to control confidential output is to retain it on a tape or disk and to keep the tape or disk in a safe until a printout is needed. This method protects the output against fire, theft, or easy access for duplication. If necessary, similar procedures can be established for programs and data files. Access to the safe should be authorized only by the data processing manager.

To minimize accidental loss of data during processing, several control steps can be taken:

1. Files should be clearly labeled to identify their contents.
2. In the case of tape storage, the file-protect ring should be removed from the tape reel. This helps to prevent the accidental writing of data on the tape when the reel is mounted on a magnetic tape unit.

3. Duplicate (backup) copies of programs and data files should be preserved a specified period of time for reference or substitution in case original files are lost or destroyed. The handling and disposition of these backup copies should be outlined in the recovery plan for the installation.
4. Insurance against fire or loss of replaceable equipment and supplies, as well as fidelity insurance to protect the organization from employees' dishonesty, should be obtained. Although the number of losses resulting from dishonest employees is not large, the concentration of a large amount of vital data under the jurisdiction of relatively few persons makes fidelity insurance advisable.

Recovery Procedures

Today, most data processing departments have established recovery plans that provide for processing backup in case a disaster causes the computer system to fail. Among the disasters that must be allowed for are fire, flood, and equipment failure. The recovery plan should identify data files and programs critical to the operation of the business. Any one of several methods may be used to provide the processing backup required. A business may contact another organization having a computer with similar processing capability and arrange to use that computer if needed. Large businesses having computers at several geographical locations may use these computers as processing backup for one another.

A recovery plan must also include methods of re-creating data files that become lost or destroyed. If copies of the data files and related programs are kept at different locations, it is only necessary to re-create or reprocess the transactions that have affected the files since they were last copied. This task is a much simpler one than reconstructing the entire programs and data files.

THE DATA PROCESSING DEPARTMENT

The data processing department is an important department within an organization for two basic reasons: (1) the expense involved in maintaining the components of the computer system, and (2) the role of the department as a service department with respect to the receiving, processing, and storing of data, and the distribution of results to management or other individuals or groups. If this function is not performed correctly, the activities of the organization may be impaired.

A data processing department should be managed according to the same basic management principles as other departments within the organization. There are, however, several organizational features and operating procedures that are unique to the data processing department. The way

UNIT SIX: DATA PROCESSING MANAGEMENT AND THE COMPUTER INDUSTRY

the department is organized depends in part on the size and goals of the organization it serves. The data processing department of a medium-size organization may be structured as shown in Illustration 17-1.

Job Descriptions

A job description gives the title of the position being described and outlines the functions that should be performed by an individual holding that position. Such a description should be prepared for each position within the data processing department. The number and types of positions vary somewhat among data processing departments. The following general job descriptions cover the most common ones.

Data processing manager. The manager of a data processing department is responsible for the overall planning, organizing, staffing, directing, and controlling of the data processing activity. Thus, the data processing department manager should possess the same basic managerial skills as the managers of other departments within the organization.

Many persons now holding positions in data processing management have been promoted from within their departments, after having acquired the necessary background and experience. However, an increasing number of organizations are recruiting college graduates who are not presently members of their organizations for this position. Anyone who desires a career as the manager of a data processing department should complete

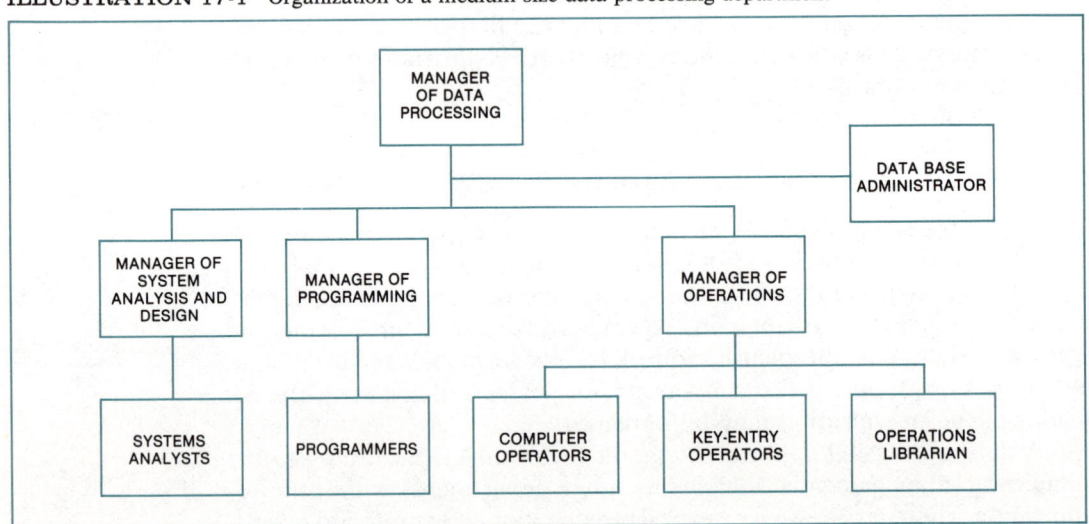

ILLUSTRATION 17-1 Organization of a medium-size data processing department

the requirements for a college degree. The type of college degree needed for this position is somewhat dependent upon the nature of the data processing performed by the department. A business administration degree with a primary concentration in data processing and some practical experience is appropriate for a manager of a business-oriented data processing department. A scientific, mathematics, or statistics degree with a minor concentration in computer science and some practical experience is appropriate for a manager of a scientific-oriented data processing department.

As the number of data processing personnel and the magnitude of the data processing activity increase, it becomes necessary for a data processing manager to have one or more assistants. Some of the more common assistant supervisory positions are:

- The manager of systems and procedures, in charge of all system analysis and the maintenance of the program library
- The manager of programming, in charge of all programming, debugging, testing, and maintenance
- The manager of operations, in charge of all activities concerned with the use of equipment and the scheduling of data processing jobs

Systems analyst. When a decision is made to computerize a business data processing function (say, the preparation of an organization's payroll), the programmer(s) responsible for coding the programs within the system must be given certain information. Providing the information is a responsibility of the systems analyst. The systems analyst evaluates the present system, determines the information required from the system, and designs data processing procedures for providing that information. Then the analyst outlines the system and prepares system specifications to guide the programmer(s) in writing the programs required.

The type of educational background that a systems analyst should possess is somewhat dependent on whether the analyst works within a business-oriented or scientific-oriented data processing department. The kinds of system studies to be performed also affect this consideration. In general, however, a college graduate with a background of management, computer science, and mathematics should find excellent opportunities for employment and advancement as a systems analyst.

Data base administrator. The data base administrator (DBA) is primarily a manager. A person in this position should have a good foundation in data processing and in the business of the organization, but the DBA need not be a computer specialist. That is, the DBA must have the technical background needed to make management decisions. Other personnel within the data processing department can be expected to have the practical experience needed to implement them.

The DBA must manage the DBA staff to insure orderly development of data base projects, to satisfy data base users, and to plan for future data base requirements. The DBA must plan and budget the staff and available data base resources. As conflicts arise, these resources must be reallocated to achieve maximum organizational benefits. Finally, the DBA is responsible to upper management for data base projects. Periodic reporting and negotiation for resources to accomplish present and planned activities are a part of this responsibility.

A college graduate with a background in management and in data processing is a potential candidate for this position. Since many organizations are just beginning to take advantage of data base technology, and the position of data base administrator is a relatively new one, there are numerous opportunities for qualified individuals.

Programmer. A programmer prepares the computer programs required in the system designed by the systems analyst. The programmer may use flowcharts, structure charts, and pseudocode when preparing the programs. The programmer codes the logic of the program in the appropriate language, debugs and tests the program, and provides any additional program documentation required. Programmers often interact with the computer system through terminals when writing, debugging, and testing programs. (See Illustration 17-2.)

Programming requires a logical mind, an attention to detail, an ability to determine the procedure required to solve a problem, and a knowledge

ILLUSTRATION 17-2 Using a terminal to write, test, and debug programs

CHAPTER 17: THE ORGANIZATION AND THE DATA PROCESSING DEPARTMENT

of the language used to code the program.

Some sophisticated, highly specialized, business-oriented or scientific-oriented applications require a formal educational background in a particular area. Generally, however, a four-year college degree is not required to obtain a good programming job. Anyone who desires to work as a programmer in a business-oriented data processing department should obtain some formal education that emphasizes appropriate business administration courses; accounting, mathematics, and statistics courses are desirable. Anyone who desires to work as a programmer in a scientific-oriented data processing department should obtain some formal education emphasizing computer science and mathematics courses. All programmers should have some college-level education, if possible, because (1) some employers use the attainment of, or failure to attain, a college degree as the major basis for considering (or not considering) programming applicants, and (2) a general educational background assists programmers in understanding the structure and activities of an organization.

Operations librarian. An operations librarian controls, stores, and issues data files, programs, and operating procedures for computer processing according to schedule or need. A person in this position also maintains records of the files stored on tape and/or disk in the library for subsequent processing or historical purposes. The librarian transfers backup files to, and retrieves them from, alternate storage site(s). Finally, the librarian is responsible for the file purging system and controls the periodic cleaning and conditioning of magnetic tapes and, as required, disk packs.

Anyone who desires to work as an operations librarian should have at least a high school diploma and be familiar with basic data processing concepts. In addition, it is desirable that the individual have high-level clerical aptitudes, particularly, in record-keeping and coding skills.

Computer operator. A computer operator operates the computer according to the general operating procedures of the department and any particular operating procedures required for successful execution of specific programs. The operator is responsible for mounting tapes and disks and changing printer paper forms. (See Illustration 17-3.) An operator may perform some preventive maintenance (cleaning and minor adjustments) on the equipment. The operator must be alert to detect any operational problems that arise during the execution of a program and take appropriate action accordingly.

A person desiring to be a computer operator should have at least a high school diploma. Formal training can be obtained through a private business or technical school, a community or junior college, or, in some instances, a high school. A basic part of any formal training should be on-the-job experience.

UNIT SIX: DATA PROCESSING MANAGEMENT AND THE COMPUTER INDUSTRY

ILLUSTRATION 17-3 A computer operator checks off completed jobs

Keypunch or key-entry device operator. A keypunch or key-entry device operator prepares data for entry into a computer by transcribing the data from source documents to either punched cards or magnetic disk or magnetic tape. Data entry requires a high level of manual dexterity, alertness, and practical thinking. Formal training can be obtained through a private business or technical school, a community or junior college, or, in some instances, a high school.

The Separation of Functions

As the job descriptions above indicate, at least seven unique job categories exist within data processing departments. A point made earlier is that the functions within these jobs should be performed by different individuals. Although a complete separation of functions is not economically feasible in many small and medium-size data processing departments, the systems analyst, programmer, and computer operator should be different persons. If all three positions cannot be held by different persons, it is especially important that at least the systems analyst and the programmer be different persons. This separation of functions has one advantage mentioned earlier: The possibilities of incorrect processing of data and/or fraud are reduced. Another advantage is that operational efficiency within the department is increased since the functions require different levels of training and skill.

The Location of the Data Processing Department within the Organization

The data processing department may be located in any of several places within the organization. The most common approach is to have the manager of the data processing department report to the chief financial or accounting officer, say, the vice president of finance, the treasurer, or the controller. (See Illustration 17-4.) There is a growing tendency to move the manager of the data processing department to a higher position in the organization. In cases where the department is a service center for many departments, the possibility of conflict over the scheduling of the computer and the design of common files requires that the data processing manager be on the same organizational level as the managers of the departments being served.

○ SUMMARY

1. There are many applications of computers in a business organization. Generally, they can be grouped into four categories. First, the computer is used to instruct employees and reduce the amount of paperwork required. Second, the computer is used to make routine management decisions. Third, it is used to produce progress reports. Finally,

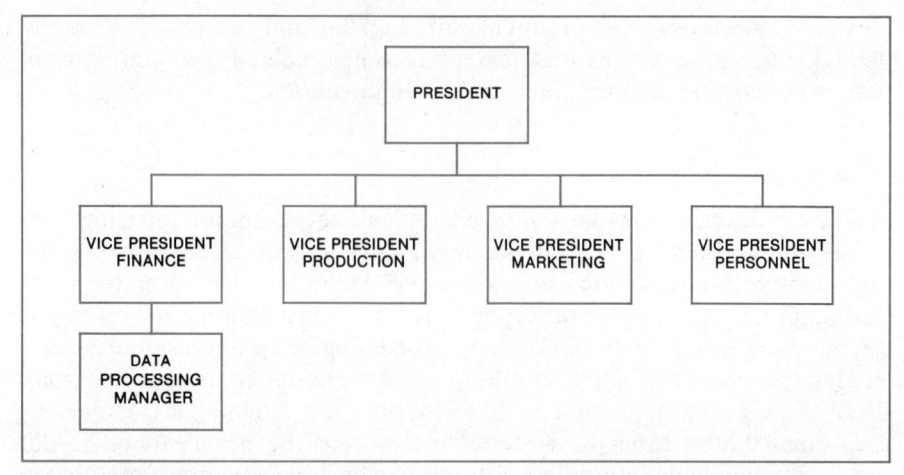

ILLUSTRATION 17-4 Location of the data processing department within an organization

    it provides information concerning a particular topic in response to management requests for the information.

2. Some of the considerations for the selection and installation of a computer system include the cost of the machine plus any options that are deemed important, the time required to install the system, and other general practices such as enlisting top management's support, developing adequate plans and controls, and anticipating possible employee problems.

3. The overall responsibility for the control of the data processing department belongs to top management. They are responsible for authorization of major changes, review of cost and effectiveness, review of the organization of the data processing department and the techniques used to control the data processing activity, and monitoring the performance of the data processing activity.

4. Control during the processing of data is an important phase of any data processing activity. This may include verification procedures to check the conversion of source data into machine-readable form, control totals to detect any loss of data or failure to process data items, computer programs and manual procedures to guard against misuse of files, hardware error detection features, and checks to guard against operator errors.

5. Some levels of error control, though possible, may not be feasible in a system. Some considerations when determining feasibility are: how frequently the error occurs, the monetary and nonmonetary consequences of not detecting the error, the cost of detecting the error, the probability of detecting the error at a later point in processing, and the consequences of detecting the error at a later point.

6. Computer system security measures should provide for protection against fraud, unauthorized access, and computer system disasters. Data processing department control procedures must be established to safeguard data against the manipulation of data for unfair or unlawful purposes. The physical security of the computer system and data must be established by developing control procedures to prevent its unauthorized use. Recovery plans should provide for processing backup and for re-creation of data files.

7. The data processing manager has responsibility for the overall control of activities within the data processing department. Other positions within the data processing department exert varying degrees of control over the functioning of the department. Some of the positions which are subordinate to the data processing manager are the systems and procedures manager, the programming manager, the operations manager, the systems analyst, the data base administrator, the programmer, the operations librarian, the computer operator, and the keypunch or key-entry device operator. Each of these individuals is concerned with a given aspect of the overall performance of the data processing department and tends to exercise control over a corresponding sphere of interest.

REVIEW QUESTIONS

1. What factors should be considered when selecting and installing a computer?
2. Discuss the hierarchy of control of a data processing system.
3. Why are controls important during the processing of data? What are some of these controls?
4. What is computer system security and what are potential sources of damage and danger?
5. Briefly discuss the job of a data processing manager.

6. What are the typical duties of a programmer?
7. Contrast the job responsibilities of the systems analyst and the programmer. Which position requires the greater educational background? Explain.
8. What is a data base administrator and what are his or her primary functions?

CAREER PROFILE

Carolyn Cammarata
Associate Systems Engineer
Computer Task Group

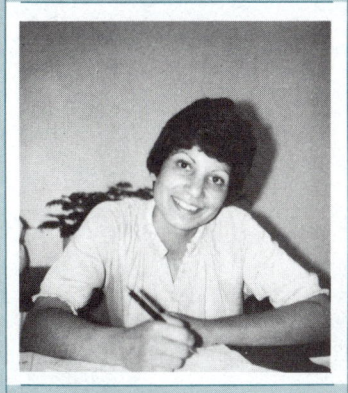

Background Experience

I graduated from Robert Morris College with a major in Accounting. My first encounter with electronic data processing was through required courses in programming languages. Because I enjoyed the courses and seemed to have a natural aptitude for programming, I took additional courses and completed a minor in Computer Science.

After graduation, I accepted a position as programmer trainee with Computer Task Group (CTG), an independent contracting company. The first five weeks on the job were spent in an intensive training program. I learned programming logic (including file maintenance, table handling, and binary searches) and structured programming techniques. I also learned about available commercial software packages, and how they relate to various business applications such as inventory control, general ledger, accounts payable, and accounts receivable. I have received additional training at CTG in various languages, applications, and system analysis and design. As a result, I have progressed from trainee to junior programmer, programmer, and associate systems engineer.

Primary Job Responsibilities

Corporations contact CTG for assistance for a variety of reasons. Sometimes, the client company lacks expertise in a particular area. Sometimes the client is understaffed or needs help in meeting a deadline. Other times we are called in to do feasibility studies and to design new or improved systems.

Just as the reasons we are called upon differ, so do other factors. I've worked at a variety of Fortune 500 corporations as well as at much smaller firms. I've been involved with very diverse hardware, ranging from very large mainframes to minicomputer systems. I've worked with almost every type of business application, with many conversational languages, and in batch, on-line, and data base environments.

Communication skills and the ability to adapt rapidly to different surroundings and applications are key requirements of this job. I must be able to talk with users to identify and analyze problems in existing systems and to work toward solutions under the pressure of time. While the diversity is a challenge, it is one of the things I like about the job. At one time I may be working on the design of new input forms or writing or modifying programs. Another time, I may be helping develop new test or production systems.

What Has Made You Successful?

Training and education are particularly important in this field of constantly changing technology. CTG has been excellent in providing this training and in expanding upon my college courses.

Human relations skills are important in a field such as this. I must put people at ease even when I'm trying to discover the causes of problems. I must be able to understand a wide variety of business environments and applications. Flexibility and adaptability are crucial to succeeding in this type of work.

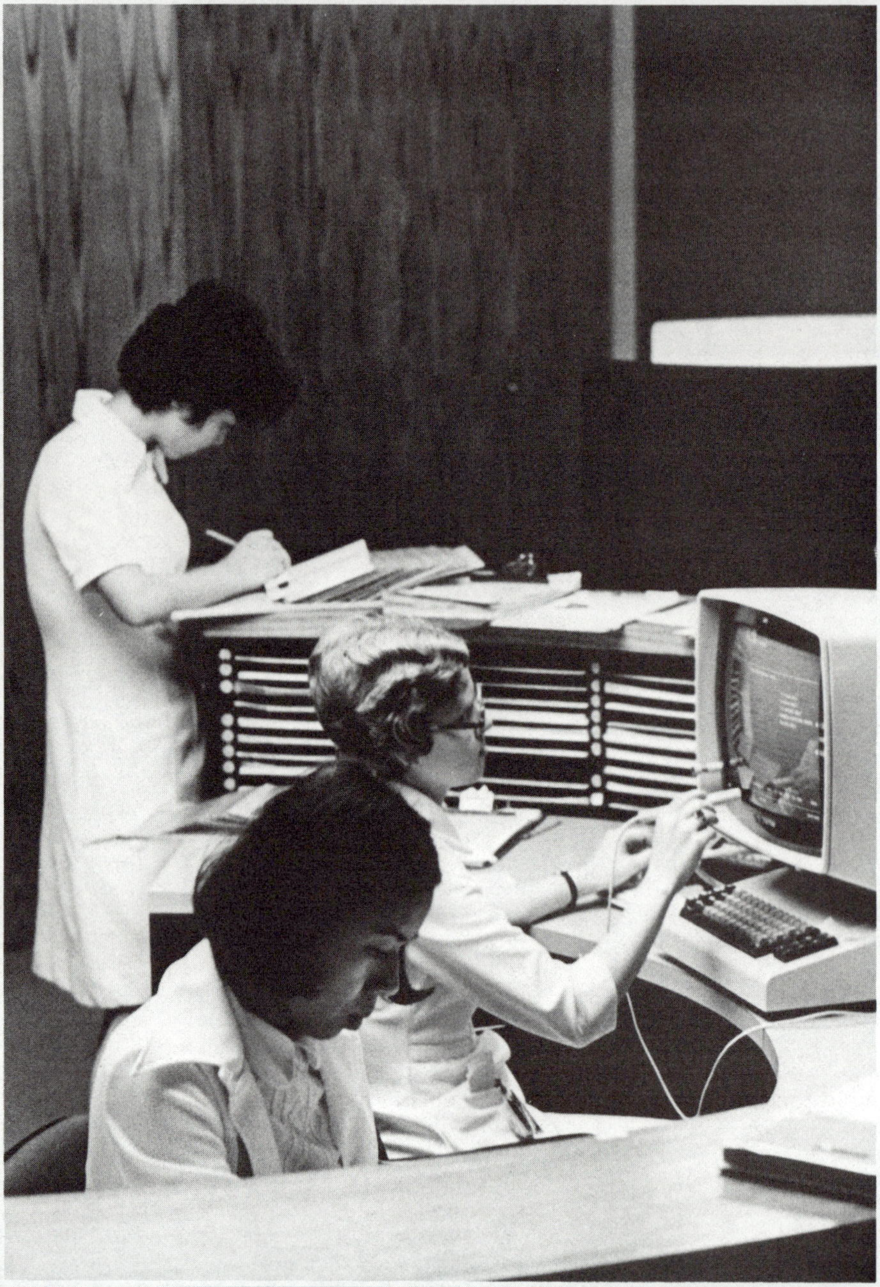

MODULE D

SOCIAL IMPLICATIONS OF THE COMPUTER

AUTOMATION

INDIVIDUALITY AND THE COMPUTER

PRIVACY AND THE COMPUTER

ELECTRONIC FUNDS TRANSFER

THE CONTROL OF COMPUTER SYSTEMS

MICROCOMPUTERS
AND PERSONAL COMPUTING

SOCIETAL IMPACT

THE FUTURE

Opposite: Terminals conveniently placed within a hospital allow nurses to make inquiries about patients.

Today we are facing a revolution—the computer revolution, fostered by the emergence of the computer as one of the most significant inventions of this century. With the Industrial Revolution, machines performed many of the functions that humans had used muscles for. In the computer revolution, the computer is performing many of the functions of the brain. The ability of the computer to store, retrieve, analyze, and make decisions about information gives it powers once thought to be uniquely human. The sheer speed of the computer makes it impossible for humans to compete with it in performing many tasks. Some tasks beyond human solution just because of the time involved in the solution can now be solved by the computer. Its potential use in society seems unlimited. New applications are being identified constantly. The effects of its use are being felt in many ways.

Just as the automobile created many problems for society, so has the computer. Because the computer is such a general-purpose tool, it has the capability to help solve many of the problems that it creates. In fact, the computer offers the potential for solution to many of the problems facing our society today. It is one of the most universal tools available.

The impact of the computer has been experienced by society in many ways. Some people have greeted it with enthusiasm; others have damned it. Many are only casually aware of its impact on their lives, even though it has affected everyone in a number of ways and will continue to do so.

In the early 1950s, the potential of the computer could not be measured, even by some of its promoters. One major computer company president predicted that the potential market for the computer in the United States would be less than 100 units. These projections were based primarily on the scientific use of the computer. By the end of the 1950s, the computer had also established itself as a business tool capable of manipulating large amounts of data.

The computer is here to stay and its potential is staggering. It has, among other things, made possible space travel, provided a solution to the information processing explosion, altered industrial processing techniques, improved health care, and been used as an instruction tool in education. It will play an important role in the progress our society makes in solving the energy problem. As energy becomes more expensive, computerized control of energy-consuming devices will become common. Everything from the home heating system to the family car will be monitored by microprocessors to insure efficient use of energy.

The power of the computer is no longer confined within the walls of the computer center. Through time sharing and microcomputers, almost any individual can now have access to a computer. Time sharing allows a number of users to access a computer through terminals connected by communication lines to a central computer. It provides access to computers to organizations or individuals who cannot afford to own or lease a large computer, yet require its processing capability. (See also "Time-Sharing Systems" in Chapter 14.)

Terminals have become a common sight to most of us. The airlines were among the first to use terminals connected to a computer. They installed them to make seat reservations. Now terminals are used in many retail stores to record sales, to reserve tickets for public events, to process customer banking transactions, and to check customer credit. Terminals are now in use in many offices. It is predicted that, in less than a decade, all desks in new office buildings will be equipped with terminals.

The widespread use of the computer is due in part to its cost. Consider that today's computer systems are about 100 times cheaper and 1000 times faster than early computers. Relative to the functions the computer performs, its cost is usually less than that of any alternative method of performing the same functions. The cost and speed of today's computers are primarily the result of the large scale integration of components on semiconductor chips. The number of components that can be placed on a chip increases each year; each increase raises the power of the computer and at the same time reduces its cost. In the past two decades, the number of components per chip has increased at the rate of about 75 percent per year. It is expected that this trend will continue through this decade.

The development of the microcomputer has brought the cost of a computer within the reach of almost anyone who desires to use it. Microcomputers at costs equal to those of color television sets are now available. The low cost of the microprocessor has led to its use in a variety of consumer products, including cars, microwave ovens, electronic games, television sets, sewing machines, and stereo equipment.

Our way of life has changed and will continue to change as a result of the computer. The computer is no longer just a tool for problem solving; it now predicts, diagnoses, and recommends solutions to problems.

A full discussion of how computers affect society is not within the scope of this text; such a discussion could easily cover several volumes. The purpose of this module is to acquaint the reader with some of the social implications of computer utilization, the control of computer systems in society, and future trends in applications and technology.

AUTOMATION

One of the issues faced by our society as a result of the computer has been that of the replacement of workers by computers. In some instances, the function performed by a person is taken over by a computer; in others, the job itself is eliminated. When human work is replaced by an automatic, computer-directed or machine-directed process, the work is said to be ***automated***. The use of machine-directed processes is called ***automation***. ***Technological unemployment***, or ***job displacement***, takes on real meaning to a person whose job is eliminated by an automated system. Automation has also contributed to "silent firing." Under this approach, employees are not fired when an automated system is installed, but jobs are allowed to go unfilled or are eliminated when employees retire or quit.

It is difficult to determine the number of workers who have been replaced by computers. Many studies have been conducted to determine the effects of automation; however, their findings are not consistent. One study estimates that as many as 40,000 workers per week are displaced by the computer. The U.S. Labor Department, in a study of 20 companies using computers for the first time, found that the impact was not as great as expected. Of a total of about 3000 employees, only 16 percent either retired or quit one year after the computer was installed. During the same period, nine employees were fired. It may be some time before the full impact of automation can be determined.

Most of the jobs eliminated by computers to date have been low-level jobs requiring a minimum of education. First to go were the accounting-related jobs where manual bookkeeping was done. With computerized accounting, fewer people were required to prepare the data for processing. In many cases a redefined job required less skill because the computer performed routines and decision making that the worker had done previously. For example, word-processing computer systems are now making an impact on office jobs. These systems allow the preparation of letters from tape or disk master files, thus eliminating most of the typing associated with letter preparation. Clerical jobs involving routine, repetitive tasks are now performed by computers in many organizations.

In some instances, technological unemployment resulting from the elimination of low-level jobs is offset by new jobs created as a result of the computer. However, if new jobs are created, they tend to require a higher level of education than the eliminated jobs did.

Automated industrial operations are common in new plants being built today. Heavy industries use computer-controlled machines to perform such functions as welding, painting, machining, and metal stamping. These machines, referred to as industrial robots, often function in environments considered hazardous to humans. They are also used to handle materials that may be radioactive, poisonous, or extremely hot or cold. An industrial robot usually consists of one or more arms or components controlled by a computer to make movements that either control a machine or perform specific tasks. Through a series of such machines an entire production line can be automated. For example, one computer manufacturer now produces semiconductor memory chips from a completely automated production process. Some work toward a robot of the future has been conducted at several universities. Machines have been built that can operate in response to voice commands and perform such functions as: stacking and counting blocks; proceeding to a specific location within a room or building; and locating different-shaped objects within a room. All of these machines are far from any of the robots depicted in current science fiction movies. Much more progress must be made in this field before such a robot can be produced.

A whole new class of jobs may be created with the introduction of the microcomputer. This low-cost computer can be used in a variety of office machines and factory equipment to perform functions that require a degree of skill and decision making. Businesses are increasingly turning to microprocessor-directed office and factory equipment to increase worker productivity and reduce costs. This will increase the productivity of some workers; it may allow one worker to do what was formerly done by several.

For the person with little education or training, job displacement poses a real problem. Many organizations are providing job retraining and education to minimize the impact of job displacement. Nevertheless, in the immediate future, finding employment opportunities for unskilled and minimally educated people will continue to be a problem. If one conclusion can be drawn from the impact of automation, it is that workers will continually need to update their education and/or retrain. In the long run, it seems that the computer will continue to create new jobs requiring varying levels of education and training.

Another challenge, as a result of automation, is what to do with an ever-expanding amount of leisure time. The work week continues to shrink (some predict that by the year 2000, the average work week will be 15 hours). What will the worker do when the work week is reduced because of automation and the computer? This question is yet to be answered. Even the definition of *leisure* is in dispute at this time. One school of thought supports the ancient Greek definition, which is essentially that leisure is freedom from the necessity of doing anything. Many sociologists define leisure as free time. In either case, the question above poses a real problem that needs to be studied. The computer itself is likely to have a major impact on how people spend their leisure time. Microprocessor-controlled electronic games are already very popular. Microcomputers are being applied in a wide variety of ways to entertain people.

Many people insist that automation and computers in general will impose conformity upon the members of society. The Industrial Revolution actually began the trend to conformity by allowing the mass production of uniform products. One expert feels that the computer can be used to reverse this trend because he sees the computer as a means of designing individualized objects at a low cost. By using a computer to design objects, it becomes possible to do a large number of different design processes for many people; anything a computer can be instructed to do (even the creation of unique designs) can be done many times.

INDIVIDUALITY AND THE COMPUTER

The impersonal aspects of computerized systems are emphasized repeatedly by those opposing computers. In one student demonstration, for example, a sign read, "Do not fold, bend, or mutilate; I am a human being." This message is one indication of a growing frustration with computerized systems. They are seen by many as a threat to our individuality. Everyone has either experienced some frustrating experience with a computer system or heard of someone else's frustrating experiences.

The latitude and power given to the computer is a problem with which one must deal. The computer is allowed in some instances to take extreme action, such as terminating a person's utility service for nonpayment or canceling credit privileges, without human intervention. Mistakes occur in any computerized system; however, the likelihood of such mistakes can be minimized by careful design.

Design strategies can be altered so that extreme actions such as the automatic termination of utility service or credit are no longer possible. Alternatively, the function can remain but steps can be taken to prevent any occasional mistakes. This may be costly. Many computerized systems are designed with minimum cost in mind. Occasional mistakes may be less costly to deal with than designing the system so that they cannot occur. When mistakes do occur, some computerized systems are designed to ignore them even if detected (again, it may be less expensive to lose a customer than to deal with the mistake).

Another aspect of computerized systems that has been attacked is the computer-analysis of information to predict the behavior of individuals and organizations. On a personal level, an individual who has one accident may lose his or her car insurance despite 15 to 20 prior years of accident-free driving because a computer statistically points the person out as a bad risk. If an organization relies on a computerized system for the selection of employees, it may behoove a prospective employee to build a good computer record to enhance the chances of obtaining employment and of future promotions or advancement. Businesses use predictive techniques to create and promote new consumer products. Politicians use similar techniques to determine which voters are important to their campaigns and what issues are likely to be vital.

MODULE D: SOCIAL IMPLICATIONS OF THE COMPUTER

○ PRIVACY AND THE COMPUTER

Those who fear that the computer will impose conformity upon society are also concerned that the computer will be used to invade individual privacy. The term *privacy* as used here refers to the rights of each individual regarding the collection, processing, storage, release, and use of data concerning the activities and characteristics of the individual.

A vast amount of data concerning most Americans has been or is being centralized in computer data banks from which it can be retrieved at the touch of a button. These **data banks** are large computer files that contain data about an individual for some purpose. They have been established by all types of private and public organizations. A major problem with data banks has been that individuals had no direct control over the personal data stored or released. Once the data was collected, it has been very difficult for individuals to determine if any of the data is false or to challenge any of the data and get it changed.

The trend toward computer data banks was started by the Federal government, which currently has a variety of data banks. The Social Security Administration, Internal Revenue Service, Secret Service, FBI, Veterans Administration, Defense Department, Department of Transportation, Department of Labor, Justice Department, and Department of Housing and Urban Development are among groups using them. (See Illustration D-1.) These federal data banks serve a number of purposes, some of which have been attacked as invading the privacy of the individual. Private data banks maintained by insurance companies, hospitals, credit rating services, banks and savings institutions, and other businesses collect data from customers as a condition of providing some specific customer service.

Many of the data banks used by the Federal government are accessed by means of social security numbers. These numbers could serve as a common key, making it easy to retrieve all of the data concerning an individual if the data banks were tied together in one large data bank. To a certain extent, this step was proposed by a government committee in its recommendation for the creation of a **National Data Center**. Its purpose would have been to consolidate data collected by over 20 federal agencies in order to allow statistical analyses by individual agencies. As proposed, it would not have included personnel data or dossiers kept by the FBI and other federal law enforcement agencies. Because of the concern expressed by the U.S. Congress and others about its potential misuse, the National Data Center was not created.

State and local governments maintain data banks for a variety of uses also. These include motor vehicle registration, tax collection, welfare programs, police information networks, and criminal justice systems.

Department of Health, Education and Welfare: 693 data systems with 1.3 billion personal records including marital, financial, health and other information on recipients of Social Security, social services, medicaid, medicare and welfare benefits.

Treasury Department: 910 data systems with 853 million records that include files on taxpayers, foreign travelers, persons deemed by the Secret Service to be potentially harmful to the President, and dealers in alcohol, firearms and explosives.

Justice Department: 175 data systems with 181 million records including information on criminals and criminal suspects, aliens, persons linked to organized crime, securities-laws violators and "individuals who relate in any manner to official FBI investigations."

Defense Department: 2219 data systems with 321 million records pertaining to service personnel and persons investigated for such things as employment, security or criminal activity.

Department of Transportation: 263 data systems with 25 million records including information on pilots, aircraft and boat owners, and all motorists whose licenses have been withdrawn, suspended or revoked by any state.

Department of Commerce: 95 data systems with 447 million records, primarily Census Bureau data, but including files on minority businessmen, merchant seamen and others.

Department of Housing and Urban Development: 58 data systems with 27.2 million records including data on applicants for housing assistance and federally guaranteed home loans.

Veterans Administration: 52 data systems with 156 million records, mostly on veterans and dependents now receiving benefits or who got them in the past.

Department of Labor: 97 data systems with 23 million records, many involving people in federally financed work and job-training programs.

Civil Service: 14 data systems with 103 million records, mostly dealing with government employees or applicants for government jobs.

ILLUSTRATION D-1 Federal data banks

MODULE D: SOCIAL IMPLICATIONS OF THE COMPUTER

○ ELECTRONIC FUNDS TRANSFER

Bankers have discussed for some time the prospect of a *cashless-checkless society*. While it is not likely that cash and checks will be eliminated, steps have been taken in that direction.

The first step was the bank credit card, which became an instant success. With the introduction of point-of-sale terminals, credit cards can be used for instant credit verification, cash advances, transfer of savings account funds to cover credit purchases, and check verification.

It is likely that the majority of transactions dealing with money will be handled electronically in the future. The electronic transfer of money is referred to as *electronic funds transfer*. Basically, it involves communication between two or more computers transferring funds from one account to another electronically. Electronic funds transfer is now used for check clearing, payments of bills through banks and savings institutions, and federal payments to individuals. Check clearing is handled through automated clearing houses used by some banks. It is anticipated that all banks will eventually use electronic funds transfer. Illustration D-2 shows how an electronic funds transfer system can be used for customer purchases at a shopping center.

The Federal government now operates over 30 automated clearing houses. They provide a system for the electronic transfer of funds between banks throughout the United States. The Federal government plans to

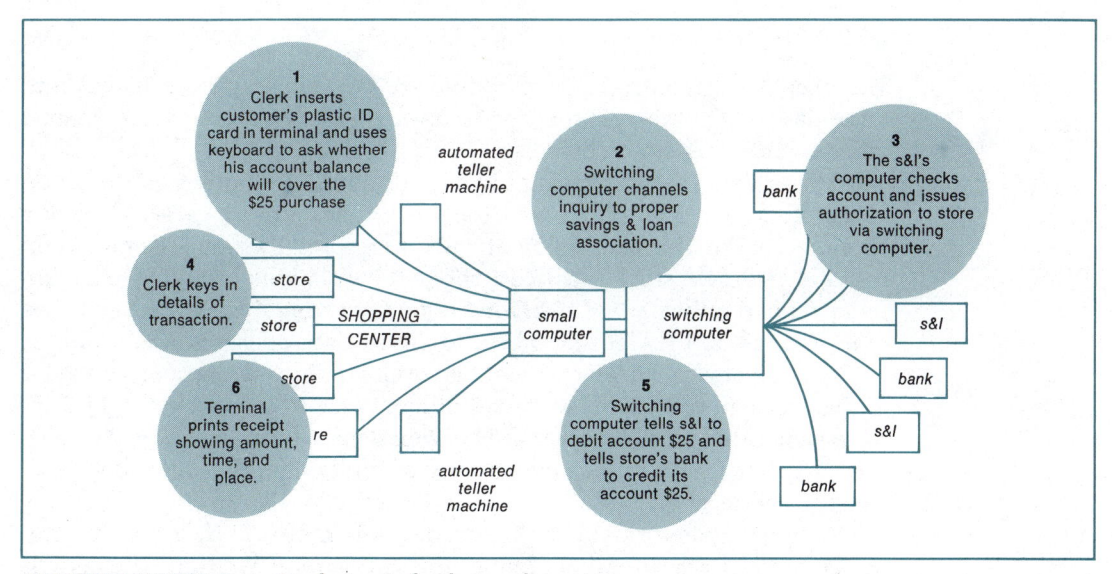

ILLUSTRATION D-2 An electronic funds transfer system

eventually make most social security payments through its electronic funds transfer program. The Treasury Department has indicated that its goal is to use electronic funds transfer for the some 43 million payments made each month by the government. Most of the financial transactions for an individual would be recorded in a data bank, keyed on some type of identifying number, in a full-scale electronic funds transfer system. Such a system could reveal much about an individual if the data bank were used improperly.

There is a growing concern that any kind of computer data bank is an invasion of privacy. But is it? The government has always collected data about citizens for one purpose or another. Individuals applying for credit agree to credit checking and to the establishment of a credit rating. Applications for bank loans and insurance policies require individuals to reveal personal information, which becomes part of data banks. The collection of data is not new, but the potential for dissemination of it is. The technology for centralization is available. The immediate access to data that was impossible before computer data banks is a reality. Now that terminals can be connected to computers, multiple users can access the same data bank. What kind of safeguards can be built into such a system to prevent unauthorized access? So great is the concern over the invasion of privacy through data banks, that a bill of rights concerning access and challenge of data bank information has been suggested.

THE CONTROL OF COMPUTER SYSTEMS

The exercise of control over computerized systems appears to fall into three basic categories: (1) passage of laws, (2) physical safeguards against misuse, and (3) system controls.

Historically, the enactment of legislation has often followed the abuse of a system. For example, it took the stock market crash of 1929 to bring about legislation that established the Securities and Exchange Commission to stop fraudulent stock practices. The first legislation pertaining to a computer-related industry was the **Fair Credit Reporting Act**. This act provides to an individual the right of access to credit data collected about him or her by a credit reporting system and an opportunity to correct errors. Prior to this legislation, an individual had little chance to see or challenge computer-generated credit reports. The **Freedom of Information Act** also provided for access to files concerning an individual that have been collected by federal agencies.

A model code for data banks was developed in 1973 by a special committee of the Department of Health, Education, and Welfare. The code is called the **Code of Fair Information Practices**. It provides guidelines for federal data banks. The code could be used as a model for all governmental and private data banks. Its basic provisions are: (1) no secret data banks containing personal data will be established; (2) the individual must have a method of determining what data is kept about him or her and how it is used; (3) a method for correcting or changing data about an individual must be provided; (4) a method must be provided to keep data collected for one purpose from being used for another purpose; and (5) an organization that creates, maintains, uses, or releases records of individuals containing personal data must insure the accuracy of the data for its defined use and must take steps to prevent its misuse.

The United States Congress enacted the first privacy law, the *Privacy Act of 1974*, with many of the features suggested in the Code of Fair Information Practices. It only applies to data banks maintained by the Federal government. Many state legislatures have similar bills pending, and some states have passed privacy bills.

Unfair information practices are subject to criminal and civil penalties under the Privacy Act of 1974. Fines of up to $5000 can be imposed on any officers or employees who violate the act or who request information under false pretenses. The act specifically exempts law enforcement agencies of the Federal government and intelligence agencies.

A Privacy Protection Study Commission was also established as a part of the Privacy Act of 1974. Its purpose was to study and recommend to the President what information practices should be applied to private groups and other organizations. As a result of the recommendations of the Privacy Protection Study Commission, Congress passed two laws in 1978 relating to privacy. The *Electronic Funds Transfer Act* directs financial institutions to disclose to customers the terms and conditions under which a particular electronic funds transfer service is to be provided. Each funds transfer transaction must be documented. The documentation must be available to the customer. Periodic statements must be provided. The law specifies that a consumer is liable for a maximum of $50 for any unauthorized transfer of funds. The consumer has a total liability of $500 under any circumstances. The *Financial Privacy Act* provides specific procedures that federal authorities must follow to obtain records concerning individuals from financial institutions.

Many businesses expect complying with privacy legislation, either state or federal, to be very costly. These costs include making computer data banks more physically secure, establishing additional computer files for reporting to data subjects, and using additional computer processing time for these activities. How much privacy is the consumer willing to pay for? This question is important because individuals must expect to pay for the costs of implementing privacy legislation in both private and governmental areas.

The implementation of electronic safeguards can insure that the unauthorized use of data files in a computer system is virtually eliminated. Computer hardware can be designed to provide a high degree of security when combined with appropriate programming. The degree of protection required in a computer system depends on the sensitivity and value of its data files. Elaborate safeguards are needed for data files that have significant financial value or contain confidential information such as medical records. Such safeguards might include coding of data as it is transmitted to or from a terminal, the use of computer-controlled security systems that limit physical access to the computer facility, and the control of computer access through the assignment of user identification codes.

A computerized system that operates without an overall set of system controls is subject to abuse. Limits and constraints must be imposed on the system to insure that it consistently achieves its stated purposes. Overall computerized system controls can be categorized as (1) those which check the accuracy of the computer hardware itself, (2) those which check the correct functioning of the programs used in the system, and (3) those which provide backup in case of system failure.

Controls that check the accuracy of the computer hardware are usually built into the computer by the manufacturer. For example, the control panel of a computer is likely to contain a series of lights that indicate abnormal hardware conditions such as overheating in the CPU, parity errors, and the failure of the various CPU components. Controls to check the correct functioning of computer programs might include: the comparison of expected program output with actual output; systematic sampling of various processing steps in a program to insure correct intermediate processing results; and the accumulation of totals, such as the number of records processed. Controls which provide backup in case of system failure include making copies of files that have been updated and providing for the use of another computer if the main computer goes down.

Adequate controls may not be applied in a system because the stated purposes or goals of the system are vague or imprecise. The goals should be redefined. The collection of data that is not necessary for the achievement of the goals should not be allowed. The data that is collected should not be retained unless it will be needed again. Although precise goals may be difficult to state in some cases, it is still possible to provide constraints on the system to avoid abuse.

MICROCOMPUTERS AND PERSONAL COMPUTING

The microcomputer has made the personal use of the computer a reality for over 200,000 Americans. This use is increasing by over 30 percent each year. Contributing to the personal use of the computer are the low cost of the microcomputer and the software aids that make it easy to use for a variety of personal computing needs. Initially, hobbyists began to build microcomputers from available components or kits. The number of hobbyists has grown tremendously. Many of them have joined computer clubs to exchange ideas and software.

At least 50 manufacturers are now producing microcomputers for a variety of users. A typical personal computer is a fully-assembled, desktop, single-user computing device. The components of a personal computer usually include a typewriterlike keyboard, a CRT, and one or more secondary storage units (typically a tape cassette unit or a floppy disk drive). A printer may be included. The software provided with these systems often includes one or more language translators and other operating-system programs. (See Illustration D-3.)

The first consumer-oriented personal computers offered by manufacturers were completely assembled and came with a limited number of programs to do such things as play games and balance checkbooks. Programs are now offered for such applications as accounting, real estate, banking, statistics, computer-assisted instruction, word processing, and mailing list processing.

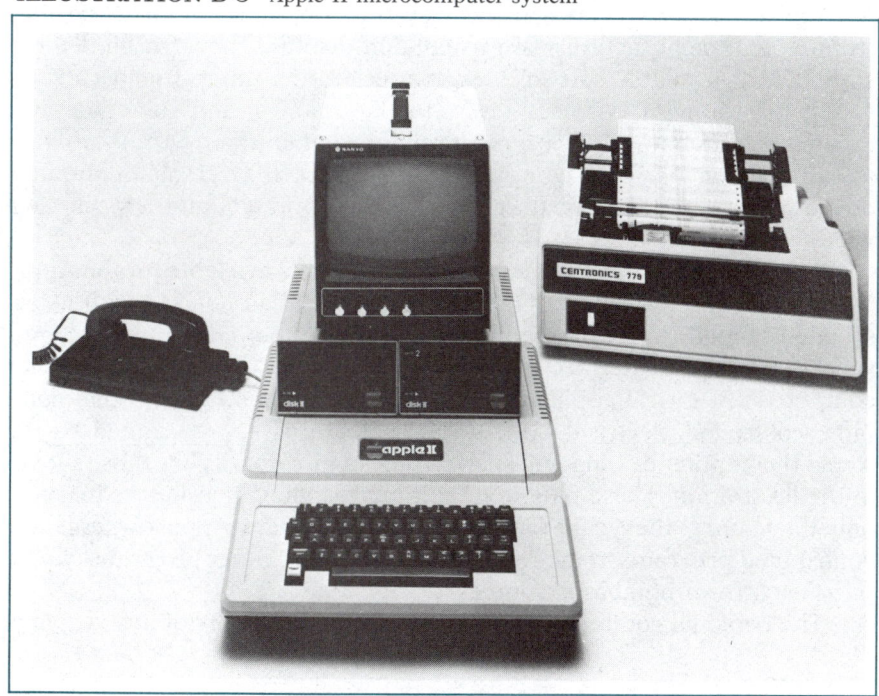

ILLUSTRATION D-3 Apple II microcomputer system

The applications for the personal computer are almost unlimited. Some purchasers may use it exclusively in the home for recreation and game playing. However, the personal computer can become an important tool for the entire family. In addition to providing entertainment, it can be used for record keeping, to control home equipment, and as a tutor. Home records for taxes, mailing and shopping lists, important family dates, and telephone numbers can be maintained with minimal effort. Most of the equipment found in the home can be controlled by a personal computer. An intruder may be detected by a security system and cause the computer to call the authorities or a neighbor, or to sound various alarms. Heating and air conditioning can be controlled to insure efficient use of energy. An electrical appliance can be started or stopped. This allows timed appliance operation for the preparation of meals, control of room lights, and timed control of home entertainment systems. As a tutor, the personal computer can instruct family members in math, physics, English, and many other subjects. Computer-assisted instruction allows each person to progress at his or her own rate and to review material until it is mastered.

A personal computer can be purchased for less than $500. Many systems cost over $5000 when additional main storage, a printer, and several floppy disk drives are included. A growing number of retail computer stores now offer assembled systems for less than $750. These retail stores are similar to stereo stores in the way they operate. Complete systems from several manufacturers are usually on display. They can be demonstrated with available software. Software is often offered to perform a variety of common business tasks, to play games, and for computer-assisted instruction. Most users purchase (rather than write) software to run on their personal computers. This use of the personal computer does not require any special knowledge of computers and appeals to a wide range of consumers.

Consider the number of features and products available for the Apple II computer in Illustration D-4. A graphics tablet can be used with its associated "pencil" to create graphic input. Voice input and output are possible. A telephone interface is available to connect the Apple II to other computers. Electrical appliances can be turned on and off through computer-controlled electrical outlets. These features can be added to the Apple II computer by plugging in electronic circuit boards like those shown in the illustration. These plug-in circuit boards allow purchasers to select only the features they want for their computers. Many Apple owners have contributed programs to the Apple Software Bank. Other programs can be purchased from numerous sources.

The personal computer has become, in the few years of its existence,

MODULE D: SOCIAL IMPLICATIONS OF THE COMPUTER

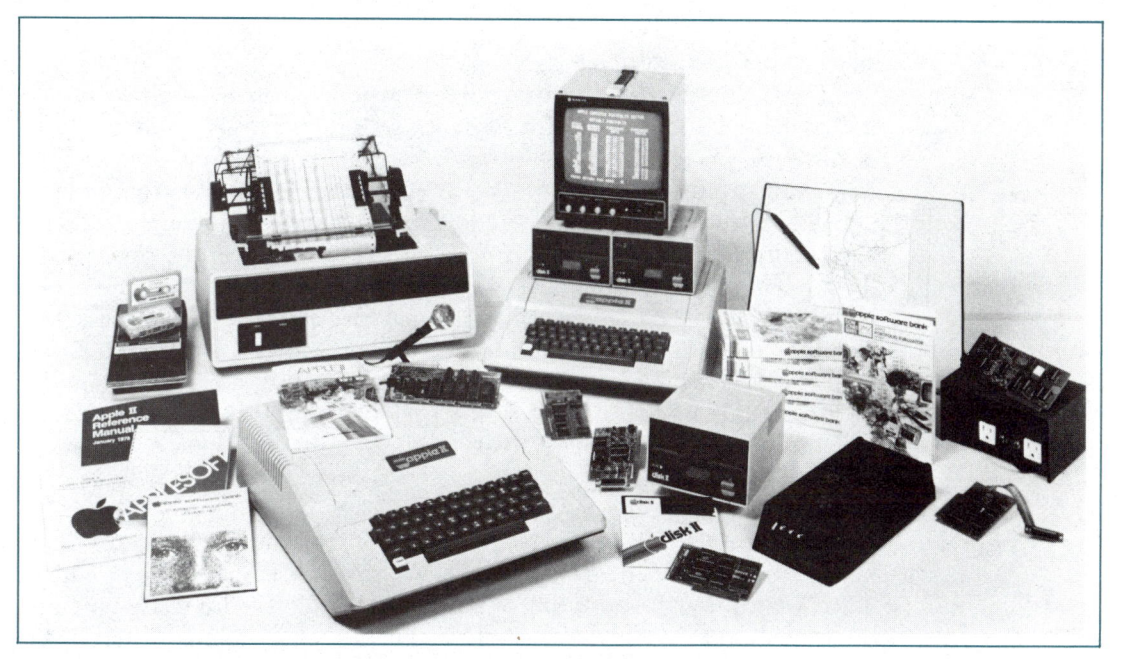

ILLUSTRATION D-4   Features available for Apple computers

the most common type of computer. The only limitations on its use are the imagination of those who use it and the rate at which easy-to-use software is made available to consumers.

SOCIETAL IMPACT

The computer is fast becoming a common sight to all of us. It is a universal tool that has influenced most of the institutions in our society. New applications for the computer are constantly surfacing. To illustrate how the computer can affect all of us, computer applications in entertainment, education, health care, and law enforcement are discussed below.

Thé computer is used in a variety of ways in the entertainment industry. Special graphic effects for television and movies are produced using computer-generated images. For example, the special effects that created the illusion of spacecraft fighting in "Star Wars" were produced with the help of a computer. The computer is also used to determine the camera angles necessary in filming. Animated cartoons can be created by drawing the desired images on a CRT screen connected to a computer. The complete cartoon can be created in color in this manner, eliminating a number of steps in producing such films.

In education, computer-assisted instruction can be used to provide individualized instruction, for review and practice, and to simulate the occurrences of certain events for demonstration purposes. Computer-assisted instruction allows students to progress at their own rate of learning and, if desired, to continue with enrichment material. Course material, class exercises, and review and practice material can all be presented to the student in this manner. The computer can be used to simulate experiments and events—a capability not otherwise present in the classroom. Through simulation, lifelike situations are presented to the student who then makes decisions about them. For example, the computer can simulate the management of a business over a period of years. The student can take advantage of this capability to try out different management methods. A physics student can use the computer to simulate a nuclear reaction or a space flight.

In hospitals, the computer helps in the treatment of patients. A patient's vital signs, such as heart beat and blood pressure, can be monitored using a computer, both during an operation and in the intensive care unit. Computers are also used to analyze patient tests, monitor prescription dosages, and assist in diagnostic procedures. In some hospitals, as a patient is admitted, his or her health history is recorded by the computer so that any special diet or drug sensitivities of the patient can be accommodated.

Law enforcement agencies at the local, state, and federal level use computers to track wanted criminals, determine if articles are stolen, check vehicle registration status, and speed up court cases. Many states have computer networks that allow both state and local police to make inquiries through terminals concerning such information as vehicle registration, outstanding traffic violations, and criminal arrest warrants. Some counties have localized police information systems for traffic violations, arrest warrants, criminal arrests, and criminal records. Many state and local information systems have access to the National Crime Information Center (NCIC), located in Washington D.C., through terminals. The NCIC maintains over six million records on stolen articles and wanted persons. Various law enforcement agencies make over a million NCIC inquiries each week, resulting in the identification of several thousand wanted persons and stolen properties. For example, a local police agency may make a terminal inquiry into a state police information system to determine if a firearm is stolen. If the state system does not indicate the firearm is stolen, the NCIC can be checked to see if it lists the firearm as stolen. Such systems can provide the public with better protection against criminals and assist in the recovery of stolen property.

MODULE D: SOCIAL IMPLICATIONS OF THE COMPUTER

THE FUTURE

To most observers, computers appear to be highly complex, sophisticated machines. However, one computer expert has commented that we are still in the horse and buggy era of the computer. Technological advancements continue to be made. What can be expected in the next 20 years?

The major hardware advance of the past decade was the development of large scale integrated (LSI) circuits. It is expected that the trend toward more circuits per chip will continue. Very large scale integration (VLSI) has led to the development of a computer on a chip, the microcomputer. It will have far-reaching effects on all of us. Mainframe computers will continue to become faster, smaller, lower in price, and easier to use. At the same time, communication with computers will be simplified as easy-to-learn conversational computer languages are developed.

New areas of computer application will be explored. The extension and refinement of present applications will continue as well. The management of most organizations will depend heavily on the development of management information systems and other decision-making tools.

Computer terminals will be a common sight in offices as distributed processing continues to develop around microcomputers and minicomputers. Offices will use computer-based electronic mail systems to send information from one point to another. Reduced costs and speed of delivery will be achieved. Small organizations not currently using computerized processing will avail themselves of its benefits as prices become lower and more software becomes available.

Automation will continue to displace jobs and create new ones as more industrial processes are automated. Industrial robots will become widespread in certain areas of usage.

Education, medicine, and law will depend more on computers to increase the effectiveness of these professions. Education is already using computer-assisted and computer-managed instruction for teaching. This trend will continue as will the development of the computer as a resource tool much like the library. Doctors will increasingly use the computer as a diagnostic and predictive tool to monitor patients' conditions. Lawyers and courts will increase their use of computers for case research and their application of computerized techniques for case investigation and analysis.

The move to a cashless-checkless society will continue as electronic funds transfer expands. The use of point-of-sale terminals will become routine for most retail businesses, thus allowing electronic funds transfer to become a widespread reality.

People will become more aware of abuses in computer usage. Legislation will be passed to protect the rights of individuals as they deal with computer systems.

Because the computer is a general-purpose tool, it is inevitable that the number of applications for which it is used will continue to grow. At the same time, it will pose new problems for our society.

○ SUMMARY

1. The computer is one of the most significant inventions of this century. It has had an impact on our way of life and will continue to do so at an increasing rate. The invention of the microcomputer will lead to universal usage of computers.

2. While the computer has served as a boon to society in solving the information-processing explosion, it has also created many problems for society. Many jobs of a routine, repetitive nature have been eliminated, and automation has allowed the replacement of many workers with computer-directed machines. Leisure time has increased and with it the problem of how to use it. Data banks contain data on most individuals. If used improperly, the privacy of these individuals may be invaded. The loss of individuality in dealing with computerized systems and the pressure to conform has led to frustrating experiences on the part of many individuals.

3. Microcomputers are now used in the home for personal computing. These computers are available through computer stores where they can be demonstrated with available software. Programs have been developed for a variety of uses—from playing games to maintaining home records. Options are offered to allow functions such as the control of electrical equipment and communication with another computer user over the telephone.

4. Some progress toward the solution of problems created by the computer is being made. Workers losing their jobs as a result of automation are being retrained or offered educational opportunities in many organizations. The Federal government has passed legislation to curb the current and potential abuses of data banks at the federal level. Many states are considering similar legislation. Computer systems are being made more secure to prevent unauthorized access to confidential information.

5. The use of computers in our society will continue to accelerate. New computers will be smaller, faster, and less expensive. The microcomputer will make computer power available to almost anyone who wants it. Electronic funds transfer will continue to develop, reducing the use of cash and checks in our society. Computer-directed products will become commonplace to most consumers and will provide a new

level of convenience to their users. Our dependence on computers will increase as our use of them continues to expand in areas such as law enforcement, health care, science, and communications.

REVIEW QUESTIONS

1. Identify two effects of automation.
2. How may users of data banks invade a person's privacy?
3. Discuss legislation that has been passed to protect a person's privacy.
4. What is an electronic funds transfer system?
5. What types of controls can be applied to computer systems?
6. What are the basic components of a home computer?
7. What are some uses of a home computer?
8. How have computers influenced entertainment, education, health care, and law enforcement?

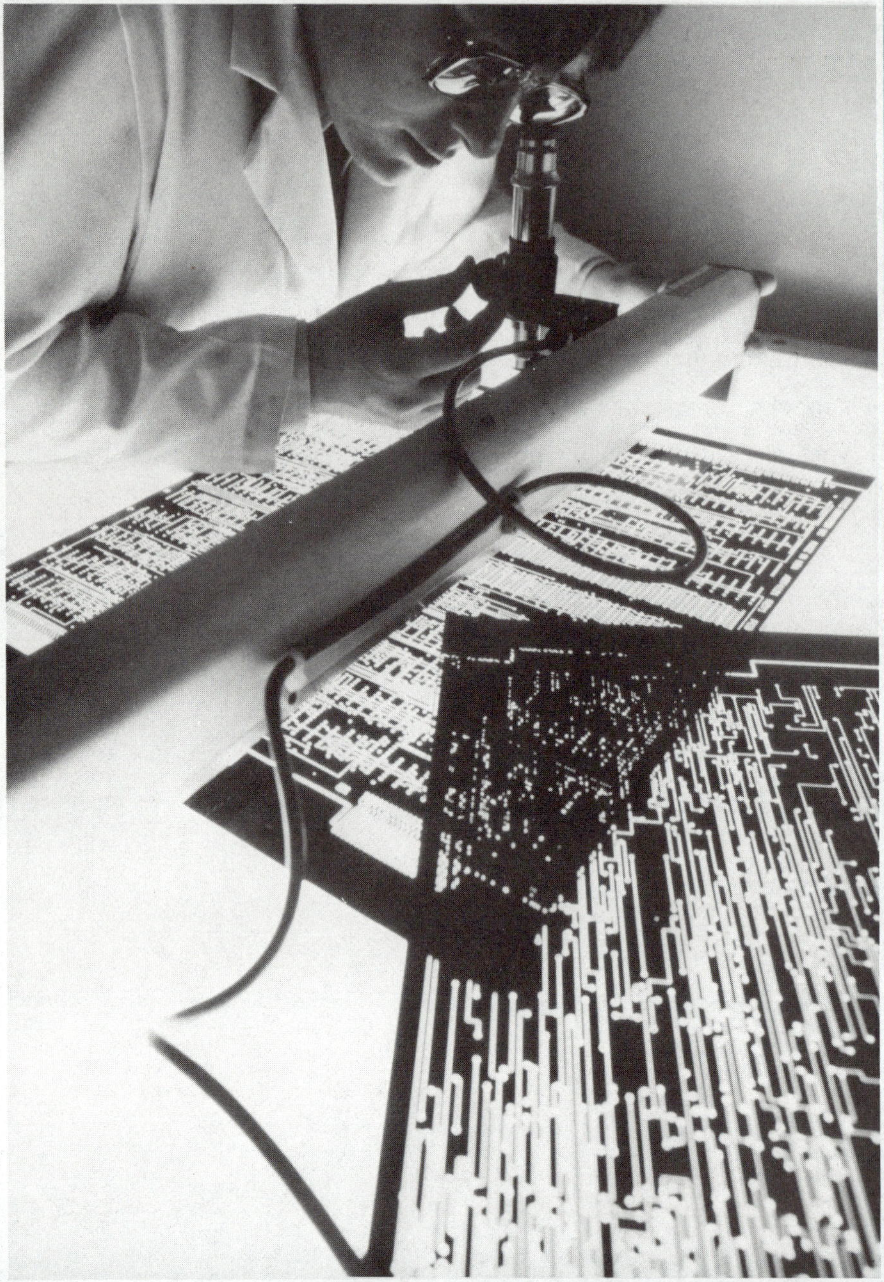

CHAPTER 18

THE COMPUTER INDUSTRY

COMPUTER MANUFACTURERS

INDEPENDENT COMPUTER PERIPHERAL
EQUIPMENT MANUFACTURERS

SOFTWARE COMPANIES

LEASING COMPANIES

COMPUTER SERVICES COMPANIES

Opposite: A technician inspects computer circuit layouts that are to be reproduced through a photographic process.

The computer industry has grown tremendously since the first commercial computer was installed in 1954. Since the late 1970s, the computer industry has been changing so rapidly that it is difficult to speak of future developments because they are being so quickly translated into current use.

The numerous applications of computers, such as payroll and inventory control, are expected to continue to expand in profit and not-for-profit organizations (especially small ones) and government. More efficient and effective computer systems will be implemented. As computer systems become more efficient and effective, applications will be developed and implemented in an increasing number of organizations. This is especially true for applications that are best accomplished by means of time sharing (such as providing information to managers for decision-making purposes).

The computer industry can be divided into five segments. These include: (1) computer manufacturers, (2) independent computer peripheral equipment manufacturers, (3) software companies, (4) leasing companies, and (5) computer services companies. Each of these computer industry segments is discussed in this chapter.

COMPUTER MANUFACTURERS

There are many computer manufacturers. They supply many kinds of computer hardware and software to the computer marketplace. As mentioned in Chapter 9, seven computer manufacturers supply most of the computer hardware and software installed in the United States.

There are two basic ways in which computer manufacturers supply hardware and software to the computer marketplace. They may sell or lease the hardware and software directly to the organization or governmental agency that is going to use it. Alternatively, they may sell the hardware and software directly to a leasing company (discussed later in this chapter), who in turn leases it to a user. As mentioned in Chapter 17, to retain flexibility with respect to making computer hardware and software changes, most hardware and software are leased. Basically, the leasing of the computer hardware and software implies that the manufacturer or leasing company retains ownership.

INDEPENDENT COMPUTER PERIPHERAL EQUIPMENT MANUFACTURERS

Because of the vast size of the leading manufacturers in the computer marketplace, they tend to overshadow the numerous companies that manufacture and provide computer hardware independently of the computer manufacturers. These companies are called *independent computer peripheral equipment manufacturers* (*ICPEMs*). Collectively, ICPEMs comprise a market force in the U.S. computer industry larger than any computer manufacturer except IBM. It is estimated that these manufacturers supply several billion dollars annually in computer hardware. Some of the relatively large ICPEMs are Telex, Memorex, Ampex, Mohawk, Calcomp, and Electronic Memories. Many of these firms place much emphasis on research and development, in addition to production and marketing activities.

The advent of the ICPEM brought more competition to an industry dominated by a few big companies. As noted for computer manufacturers, computer hardware can be either purchased or leased from an ICPEM. On the average, the cost of the hardware purchased from an ICPEM is 20 to 40 percent lower than the cost charged by the computer manufacturer. The cost of hardware leased from an ICPEM is 10 to 20 percent lower. This cost differential becomes more important as increased CPU capabilities are available at less cost. A larger percentage of the user's hardware expenditure is for peripheral equipment. In 1970, peripheral equipment was approximately 55 to 60 percent of a user's hardware cost. Today, this type of equipment is up to 80 percent of a user's hardware cost.

Quite often, ICPEM's products have exceeded the performance of the computer manufacturer's products they are designed to replace. As a result, the user has obtained a product that performs better at a lower price. The ICPEMs are often more flexible than computer manufacturers with respect to supplying hardware options and "little extras" at no additional cost. Finally, in addition to supplying functionally equivalent hardware that plugs into hardware produced by the computer manufacturers, ICPEMs have introduced their own innovative hardware especially for computer input and output. As mentioned above, there has been a large growth in their share of the computer hardware marketplace in the past several years. The computer manufacturers have been forced to take notice of these companies. They have begun to compete by lowering hardware prices, developing new hardware products, and taking an increased interest in the user's needs. As a result, the most successful ICPEMs are those that can supply hardware with uniquely practical capabilities.

SOFTWARE COMPANIES

Software companies provide system and application software and/or system analysis and programming services to organizations that elect to purchase their software and/or services. Many of the software companies can provide specialized software that is either not available from the computer manufacturer or more efficient than the software provided by the computer manufacturer. For example, system software such as operating systems, compilers, and data base management systems and application programs such as payroll, accounts receivable, and inventory control are available. Approximately 75 percent of the programs sold by software companies are application programs. The cost of a program can be up to $100,000.

Software companies provide systems analysts and/or programmers to an organization that does not employ individuals with the qualifications required to complete a particular task. They also supplement an organization's systems analysts and/or programmers during peak or overload periods created by either conversion to a new computer system or preparation of a new, complex program.

○ LEASING COMPANIES

Approximately 60 percent of computer system hardware is leased rather than purchased by users. The basic reason for this is that leasing computer system hardware, in contrast to purchasing it, provides a much more flexible approach to changing the hardware. The ability to change computer system hardware in a short period of time is especially relevant in this field because more efficient and effective hardware is continuously being introduced.

While an organization can lease or purchase computer system hardware from the computer manufacturer, the organization can also lease or purchase the hardware from a computer leasing company. Leasing companies acquire computers by purchasing them from computer manufacturers or from users who bought the computers previously. Generally, leasing companies lease their hardware for 10 to 30 percent less than the lease rate charged by computer manufacturers. Because of the risk of functional obsolescence assumed by leasing companies, the computer manufacturers do not consider them to be strong competitors. Nevertheless, the computer manufacturers have introduced price incentives primarily to encourage users to purchase rather than lease computer system hardware.

Since the leasing of computer hardware is a relatively easy business to enter, there is intense competition among leasing companies. However, the computer leasing industry accounts for only about 5 to 8 percent of the computer hardware market.

Most leasing companies depreciate their computers over a much longer period of time than computer manufacturers do. They make the following assumptions:

1. The computers that they lease have a long operational life.
2. The lease rates that they charge in order to make a reasonable profit can be maintained for several years.

3. The introduction of new computers by manufacturers will not result in a mass user movement from current computer systems to the newly introduced computer systems.

The principal risk involved in making these assumptions is the possibility that the computer hardware will become obsolete before it is fully depreciated. The assumptions proved to be correct about users of second-generation computer system hardware when third-generation computer hardware, such as the IBM System/360 series, was introduced. However, since the early 1970s, when several new series of computers were introduced, the second and third assumptions above are no longer as valid as they were. Lease rates for third-generation computer equipment introduced during the 1960s had to be reduced when a large number of System/360 users began to change to System/370 computer systems. When newer, third+-generation computer systems were introduced in the late 1970s, the same effect occurred on lease rates for most System/370 computers. Thus, leasing companies have had to give greater consideration to the fact that the purchase of older hardware increases the risk of obsolescence prior to recovery of the purchase price of the computer system and the earning of a reasonable profit.

COMPUTER SERVICES COMPANIES

A computer services company is an organization that provides computer services to organizations for a fee. Most computer services companies can provide the services periodically, on a continuous basis, or only when needed. In a majority of computer services companies, data is periodically batch-processed. An increasing number of computer services companies are providing time-sharing facilities.

Computer services companies tend to specialize with respect to the types of service they offer. Some computer services companies, especially the small ones, specialize in business-oriented applications, such as those designed for accounting functions. Other computer services companies specialize in services for a particular type of industry. For example, some banks with large data processing departments offer a complete line of data processing services to other banks in surrounding areas.

There is also considerable diversity in the amount of services offered by computer services companies. Some computer services companies provide only the processing and storing of data. Other computer services companies, especially the better established ones, provide a complete line of data processing services; they assist the customer in identifying data processing requirements, write the necessary programs, process the data, and provide the results to the customer.

An organization that considers using a computer services company is generally one that can benefit from using a computer to process one or more applications, but cannot afford to purchase or lease a computer. The service(s) that a computer services company provides can be used either in place of manual data processing or to supplement data processing performed by the organization's data processing department. Thus, a computer services company is a way for an organization to take advantage of the benefits that can be obtained from using a computer without having to assume either the problems of organizing and managing a large data processing department or the entire expense of the computer system. In either situation, an underlying consideration for an organization must be whether or not the computer services company can perform the processing at a lower cost and/or on a more timely basis than it can be performed within the organization.

The computer services industry is composed of over 3000 companies. It is diverse with respect to ownership of the companies. Most of the major computer manufacturers operate computer services companies. A large number of computer services companies are independently owned. These companies vary in size. The large ones maintain branch offices in major cities throughout the country.

Many businesses, such as banks and universities, do not need to use all of the time available on their computer systems. Thus, they enter into part-time computer service arrangements with one or more outside organizations. In some cases, the arrangements involve only the sale of blocks of time; that is, the computer services company provides only its computer hardware and software for stipulated periods of time. In such situations, the outside organizations provide their own application programs and personnel. This type of arrangement is sometimes called **block time**. In other cases, the arrangements involve the selling of a complete line of data processing services. In this type of arrangement, the organization selling the services is in competition with the computer manufacturers and independent data processing organizations.

○ SUMMARY

1. The computer industry can be divided into five segments: the computer manufacturer, the independent computer peripheral equipment manufacturer (ICPEM), the software company, the leasing company, and the computer services company. Each of these segments is tailored to a specific portion of the market once held exclusively by the computer manufacturer.

2. Computer manufacturers hold the major portion of the market for computers and computer services. They provide hardware and soft-

ware through sale or lease agreements directly to the organization or agency that is going to use it. Alternatively, they sell directly to leasing companies.

3. Facing the computer manufacturer in the computer hardware market are independent computer peripheral equipment manufacturers (ICPEMs). This group is second largest with respect to share of the computer hardware market. These companies provide computers at lower cost, and in more flexible combinations, than the computer manufacturers do.

4. Software companies provide software and/or system analysis and programming services to organizations that elect to purchase their software and/or services. They handle customers on a client basis and can often provide software services superior to those of the computer manufacturer. Software companies also provide systems analysts and/or programmers to supplement the staff of small companies or to aid companies during peak or overload periods.

5. Leasing companies purchase hardware from computer manufacturers or prior user-owners and then lease the equipment to other organizational users. The equipment is made available at a lower cost than that offered by the manufacturer. The leasing company, rather than the user, assumes the risk of functional obsolescence.

6. A computer services company works on a fee basis to provide varying degrees of hardware, software, system analysis and design, programming, and time-sharing services. These services are usually purchased by users who cannot afford a computer, but need some of the processing that a computer can perform. In this way, the computer services company specializes in an area to which the computer manufacturer is not fully committed.

REVIEW QUESTIONS

1. Explain the role of ICPEMs.
2. What is the function of a software company?
3. Discuss the three assumptions that most leasing companies use in depreciating their computers.
4. How does a computer services company operate?
5. When should an organization consider using a computer services company?
6. Is your organization's main computer purchased or leased? Why?

CAREER PROFILE

Shirley Yee
Data Base Administrator
Fireman's Fund
Insurance

Background Experience

I graduated from the University of Illinois with a degree in French. Upon graduation, I accepted a job as an assistant manager of an insurance company. My career in data processing started when I asked the insurance company to transfer me to another job because I wanted a more challenging position. The company gave me a programmer aptitude test. I qualified for their computer programmer training course. I attended classes eight hours a day for two months. Then I began programming. I worked as a programmer, programmer/analyst, and project leader prior to becoming a data base administrator. While working as a programmer, I had the opportunity to learn about a data base system by attending a computer vendors' course. This gave me the background necessary to obtain a position as a data base administrator.

Primary Job Responsibilities

My function is to provide technical assistance in the design of new data base sytems. This involves scheduling the design phase of a system—determining how long the system design will take and coordinating the effort with the programming managers responsible for implementing the system.

I also provide technical advice to programming managers on the capabilities of the computer system and the impact that their proposed systems will have on other systems being designed or currently in use. Much of my time is spent in meetings with programming managers, programmers, and systems analysts. I review proposed system designs to determine how complicated they are, whether they can be simplified, and how many programmers may be required to maintain them if they are installed.

What Has Made You Successful?

The opportunites to perform a variety of data processing jobs at different companies have given me a chance to gain a well-rounded background. This background has been valuable to me in working with data base systems at several companies. Knowing when to change jobs to advance one's career is also important. I like a job that is challenging and provides opportunities to learn about new advances that are taking place in software. Patience, tact, flexibility, and the ability to cope with stress are important because one interacts with people a great deal in the job environment.

APPENDIX A

COMPUTER SYSTEM APPLICATIONS

MANUFACTURING—CROWN AUTO TOP
MANUFACTURING COMPANY
Product Variety
Wide Coverage
A Demanding Industry: Rapid Response Is Critical
Traditional Approach Falls Short
Computerization Is the Answer
Inventory Control and Order Entry
Benefits
Upgradability in the Future

WHOLESALING—CATTO & PUTTY, INC.
Batch Mode Too Slow
Transaction Processing Mastered
A Computer Services Company
Customer Counter Service
Perpetual Inventory Control
Business Data at Fingertips

RETAILING—BIG 4 RENTS, INC.
Use of a Computer Services Company
Selection of a Computer System
Benefits
Review of Computerization Process
Future Plans

CENTRALIZE? DECENTRALIZE? DISTRIBUTE?
The Basics of the Business
Ten Big Problems
Representative Systems
Central Systems Support

APPENDIX A: COMPUTER SYSTEM APPLICATIONS

Four computer system applications are discussed in this appendix. They illustrate how businesses of various types and sizes are using computers. The applications range from basic business data processing to a comprehensive worldwide system using multiple computers. Many of the hardware and software concepts introduced in the text are reinforced here. Each application description is followed by discussion questions. The applications are:

A manufacturer reduces order processing time by computerization. This application describes how a manufacturer serving the automobile industry resolved problems experienced in servicing customer orders. The inadequacies of a manual system of order entry and inventory control are described. The benefits of converting to a computerized data processing system are pointed out. The application can be discussed after completing Chapter 9, Chapter 14, and Module A.

A wholesaler converts from batch processing to time sharing. This application describes how a wholesale equipment and parts distributor converted from a data processing system using a punched-card-oriented computer to a time-sharing computer system. The use of terminals for order entry, inventory control, application programming, customer counter service, office accounting, and top management information are outlined. This application can be discussed after completing Chapter 9, Chapter 14, and Module A.

A retailer installs a small computer system. This application describes how an equipment rental business changed from the data processing system of a computer services company to its own small computer. The benefits and problems encountered in using a computer services company, the process of selecting and installing the computer, and the lessons learned while selecting, installing, and operating the system are described. This application can be discussed after completing Chapter 9.

An information system utilizes multiple computers. This application describes how a large corporation involved in manufacturing and marketing uses a variety of computers in a comprehensive information system. The evolution of the use of computers within the corporation and the problems encountered are traced over a period of years. Centralized, decentralized, and distributed computer systems are described. A worldwide distributed computer network is outlined. The data communication and distributed data bases required are pointed out. Subsystems for marketing administration, personnel/payroll, and factory management are discussed in detail. Because of the comprehensive nature of this application, it should be discussed after completing Chapter 18.

MANUFACTURING—CROWN AUTO TOP MANUFACTURING COMPANY

"Our whole operation depends on how quickly we can process orders. You can be the best manufacturer in the world but, in our business, if you can't ship promptly to the trim shops, they'll order from other sources. Therefore, time was the biggest factor in our need to computerize. Our computer system has done everything it was supposed to ... and is reducing our order processing time by at least 50 percent." The speaker is Ronald A. Gurvis, Executive of Crown Auto Top Manufacturing Company, Inc., in Columbus, Ohio.

Product Variety

Crown Auto Top Manufacturing Company was founded in 1952 to manufacture replacement tops for convertibles. Even though automobile manufacturers no longer produce soft-top convertibles, Crown's business has continued to expand. "There are companies that take Coupe de Villes, two-doors, and hard-tops, and change them into soft-top convertibles," explains Ron Gurvis, Crown executive. "We are supplying five of the nine known companies in this business with tops. The resulting production volume for this item alone is 3500 to 4000 tops per year. We make custom tops for every type of convertible produced from 1940 on—both domestic and foreign. But servicing tops is easily our biggest operation."

In addition to convertible tops, Crown manufactures vinyl tops, automotive carpeting, grills, and customized equipment for vans. The company is also a national distributor for some 30 products. Among them are sun roofs, opera windows, chrome radiator grills, and hub caps.

Wide Coverage

As a distributor, Crown ships products throughout the United States, into Canada, and to countries as far away as New Zealand and Australia. All foreign shipments originate from the main warehouse in Columbus. Branch warehouses have been set up to provide optimal customer service in high-demand areas such as New York, Florida, North Carolina, and Georgia.

"Besides servicing our own warehouses," says Gurvis, "we supply products to many independent distributors not owned by Crown. They are located literally everywhere—for example, Chicago, California, Washington, Kansas, Texas, Iowa, Minnesota, and Wisconsin. We, indeed, service the entire country."

A large product line, combined with international distribution, imposes stringent operating constraints on any supplier within this industry.

A Demanding Industry: Rapid Response Is Critical

The lifeblood of Crown depends on satisfying a nationwide array of trim shops. "Vinyl tops are a spur-of-the-moment item," Gurvis explains. "Assume I am an automobile owner who goes to a trim shop. If the shopkeeper tells me to wait ten days for an item, I'll go to another trim shop and buy from someone else." To avoid losing sales, the pressure put on the trim shop by the end user is relayed by the trim shop directly to the manufacturer. This pressure is enormously compounded by the fact that the manufacturer deals with thousands of trim shops. The question facing Crown was how to improve order processing and inventory control.

Traditional Approach Falls Short

According to Ron Gurvis, Crown's busy season begins the first warm day in March and continues through November. That leaves about three free months during which Crown builds its inventory of 27,000 items for the following year. But that's not the entire story.

"We have a very busy office," says Gurvis. "Like most busy offices, we have plenty of headaches. Up to 800 orders per day are processed from our main warehouses—that's almost two a minute. Ninety-five percent of the orders come in by phone. They include orders for trailer-truckload shipments, not only to our various distributors, but also to our own warehouses. This creates a myriad of problems for us. We have four incoming, toll-free WATS lines for out-of-state calls, plus one for this state. We also have one outgoing WATS line. They're all constantly in use.

"Every day, about 35% of our customers call us to find out the status of their orders. They call because their customers are getting impatient."

According to Ron Gurvis, Crown was not keeping up with customer demand, servicewise. "I guess you could call it 'the old school,'" he recalls. "We did everything the hard way. Workers in the office were always on the run, taking calls and then hurrying out to the stockroom to check inventory. Each call took about 20 minutes of an office worker's time. The only mechanical devices we had were typewriters, adding machines, telephones, NCR billing machines, and ballpoint pens. We shipped 4000 items per day and worked six days per week, with significant overtime.

"Misplaced orders were a particular nuisance. Sometimes an important rush order came in. The customer demanded, and was promised, same-day shipment. However, the factory was so tied up with other orders that the special rush order never got processed. As a result, we faced a very angry customer.

"The slow handling of orders was the biggest of our many problems. We were literally running around in circles. Everything was done on paper, by hand, and then given to office 'specialists.' Each employee had his or her own little job. The whole office was in continuous turmoil. People busy at one job were not available for other jobs. We reached the point where workers taking telephone orders in the office also had to check on where the items were. We had only bare essentials for office equipment. There had to be a better way."

Computerization Is the Answer

Computerization of operations was seen as a way to reduce turnaround time and errors. "We surveyed NCR, IBM, Hewlett-Packard, and Wang," recalls Ron Gurvis. "A Wang system was chosen because it offered better performance at lower cost. We subsequently engaged a Wang-recommended local software house, Neoterics, to write the software we needed." Crown's system is comprised of a Wang VS minicomputer with one megabyte (1000K bytes) of virtual storage and 96K bytes of real storage. The peripherals include 150 megabytes of disk storage, one system console, four CRT terminals, and a matrix printer. (See Illustration A-1.)

Inventory Control and Order Entry

With the computer, Crown's daily operations have been dramatically speeded up. Major benefits are experienced in inventory control. "The system tells us what materials we have in production, what the stock numbers for items are, and what's on hand," relates Ron Gurvis. "In addition, when the quantity-on-hand for an item drops below the established minimum stock level for that item, the CRT screen flashes every time we refer to the item. Error messages appear on the screen if inconsistent data is entered. The system also provides up-to-date information on stock levels and daily transactions at each warehouse location to corporate headquarters."

A variety of stock status reports are generated. They list part number, color, material description, and stock status at the beginning and end of each week. "I can also call up on the screen any information contained in a stock status report," smiles Gurvis.

Order entry at Crown has also been transformed to a smooth function. "With the touch of a button, our office personnel can now get any order information they need, without ever leaving their desks," states Gurvis. "Before we computerized our order entry procedures, we couldn't even get the orders received on one day processed by the following day! Typically, orders received between 3 o'clock and 5 o'clock in the afternoon were not processed until noon the next day. Now, all order processing is completed within an hour or two. Our staff can apply their extra time to other jobs."

ILLUSTRATION A-1 A Wang VS minicomputer

Benefits

A great deal of phone work and leg work is now done by the computer. "Instead of having to run out and take a visual check of what's in inventory or what's in production—a task that may take ten to twenty minutes per item," Gurvis states, "we can now respond instantaneously. With the touch of a button, we can get all the information needed."

Error reduction is another major plus. "We paid an accountant to run invoices and statements on an outside computer. This procedure was error-prone," relates Gurvis. "It is now easier for us to catch errors while we are inputting data. When we turn our jobs over to outside services who are not as familiar with the details of our business as we are, they do not usually catch the errors. In-house control certainly helps."

Improved cash flow is a significant benefit enjoyed by Crown. "Money is very tight, as everyone knows," explains Gurvis. "A large number of trim shops work on a day-to-day basis. They take orders, get deposits, and call manufacturers (hopefully, us). In so doing, they depend on our ability to ship their orders as soon as possible. With our computer system, we can turn orders around quickly. Because we process more orders, and process them faster, we have improved cash flow."

Ron Gurvis expects Crown's system to be cost-justified quite rapidly. As he notes, "We believe the computer will pay for itself within five years. Furthermore, it carries out work so fast and efficiently that we have no need to expand our staff. Not having to hire additional personnel yields both direct and indirect financial benefits."

Upgradability in the Future

Crown's future plans are to upgrade its system. Two more printers and four more CRT terminals are to be installed. "We plan to put all sales and sales commissions onto the system," explains Gurvis. "There will be terminals in all warehouses. As orders are completed and shipped, the relevant information will be entered directly on the warehouse terminals. This will eliminate the three- to four-day delay we now have in receiving the confirmation of shipments by mail."

Discussion Questions

1. Discuss how the installation of a computer system helped Crown Auto Top Manufacturing Company to improve its order processing.

2. Discuss other benefits achieved by installing the computer system at Crown.

WHOLESALING—CATTO & PUTTY, INC.

Catto & Putty, Inc., a wholesale equipment and parts distributor, was founded in San Antonio, Texas, in 1939. Today it has over $2 million in annual sales. It is a showplace of efficiency, due in large part to one very productive employee—a computer time-sharing system. Bill Putty, President of Catto & Putty, says, "Access to current information and immediate processing capabilities are a must for me, our employees, and our customers. We get this and a lot more from our business computer system."

Catty & Putty sells air-cooled engines and lawnmowers. It has distributorships in Arkansas, Oklahoma, and Texas. Catto & Putty also sells parts

APPENDIX A: COMPUTER SYSTEM APPLICATIONS

and accessories—belts, chains, blades, lubricants, and tools—for these product lines. Its sales volume comprises over 12,000 inventory categories. Within these categories, it sells thousands of individual items.

The large number of transactions generated by this constantly moving inventory, along with other business functions, are handled by an in-house computer time-sharing system. Users at up to eight CRT terminals transmit and receive data in a realtime mode to and from a Datapoint 5500 business computer at corporate headquarters. The CPU has 48K of main storage. Two disk drives provide up to 50 million bytes of secondary storage. The system includes one 60 lines-per-minute printer and one 300 lines-per-minute system printer for high-volume output. (See Illustration A-2.)

ILLUSTRATION A-2 A time-sharing system for business users

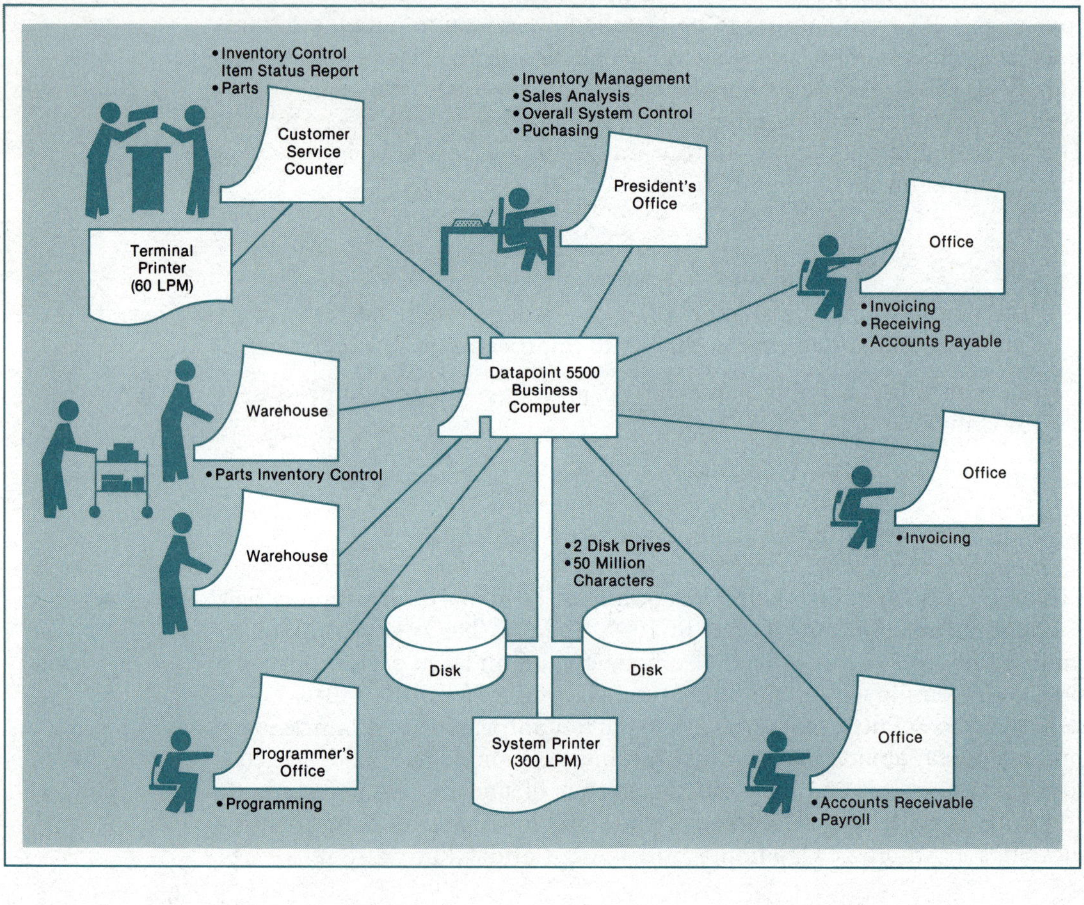

Batch Mode Too Slow

"In the early 1960s, the enormous volume of paperwork generated by our high turnover of inventory became too much for our manual data processing system to handle," says Bill Putty. "We first tried our hand at automatic data processing when we installed IBM punched-card equipment in 1962. In 1969 we converted to an IBM System/3 computer. This system was punched-card-oriented. It was designed to do batch processing. With each of these changes, we learned more about data processing and about how important it was to our business. Finally, we realized that hiring two employees to serve as full-time keypunch operators and using 'batch mode' computer operations wasn't the right approach for us. The System/3 wasn't satisfying our business requirements. It was too slow. Our inventory records were never up to date. We have always tried to operate our business on a 'realtime' basis—to serve our customers as expeditiously as possible."

Putty relates, "I never liked to be kept waiting at a counter to have an order filled, on the phone for important business information, or in a line for my turn at a computer. That's where my interest in distributed processing came from—not liking to wait. In the spring of 1975, I asked for a demonstration of some Datapoint equipment. The demonstrated system was just what we needed—a transaction-oriented computer system that provided accurate inventory status reporting."

Transaction Processing Mastered

"In order to extract maximum productivity from the system, I hired a programmer to write the programs we needed. We ran further demonstrations, signed a lease, and installed our equipment in the summer of 1975. We put CRT terminals exactly where we needed them—customer service, warehouse, receiving, and invoicing. Computer power was available to us where it was needed. We were on our way," Putty states.

Catto & Putty has mastered transaction processing by bringing computer capability to all sectors of the company. Out of 15 in-house employees, nine use the computer on a part-time basis to process their paperwork. The other six work with the system on a full-time basis. These personnel are involved in all aspects of the business. Manually generated paperwork is practically nonexistent. New employees are trained to use the system as they are trained to do their jobs. They see everything as a package. Within a month, they are "online."

"Now all of us here at Catto & Putty have full access to all our business data all the time," Putty says. "We are able to input error-free data, because the system checks the data as it is entered, when and where we need to, from source documents. This reduces our massaging of the data and virtually eliminates errors. As a result we are able to retrieve timely information, both on the CRT screens and as hard-copy printouts."

Dale Litzman works as a system programmer at Catto & Putty. This is his first job following graduation from college with a major in Management Information Systems.

"At Catto & Putty we are in our peak period of activity from August to September, in both sales and inventory," explains Litzman. "I just completed four programs that we are now using. They concern the location and deletion of nonactive inventory master items. We have just reduced our list of inventory master items from over 17,000 to around 12,000. Can you imagine how many actual shelf items and handling chores that represents?" (See Illustration A-3.)

A Computer Services Company

Catto & Putty not only handles all its day-to-day business and housekeeping tasks via computer but also acts as a computer services company to six other organizations. Their data processing needs vary. A jazz band, a fi-

ILLUSTRATION A-3 The president of Catto & Putty (seated) verifies the latest inventory master items report produced by the company's Datapoint system with a system programmer

APPENDIX A: COMPUTER SYSTEM APPLICATIONS

nance company, and a church are among Catto & Putty's clients. To meet their needs, Catto & Putty has developed an impressive array of programs. The available software includes 16 accounts receivable programs serving 700 accounts, 12 payroll files accessed by 20 programs that produce paychecks for over 100 people twice a month, 75 inventory programs, 25 general data processing programs, 21 receiving and accounts payable programs, and 34 sales analysis programs. The system generates about 20 end-of-month reports for management purposes. These reports include inventory stock status, sales reports, receipts, disbursements, trial balance, interest charges to accounts receivable, inventory on-hand catalog, suggested-order file, and others.

Customer Counter Service

Jessie Guerra, an employee of Catto & Putty for over 19 years and the representative at the customer service counter, has used all of Catto & Putty's data processing systems. Guerra reports, "I use the CRT terminal to get all the information I need for myself and our customers instantly. My inventory status is current through the last transaction, regardless of when and where it occurred within the company, or of how busy we are. When I request the inventory status of an item, I receive the item description, stock number, manufacturer, pricing structure, on-hand, on-order, on-back-order, owe-to-customer, and item warehouse location by aisle and bin number. Even after almost 20 years on the job, I'd be lost without this up-to-the-minute inventory status information. Our customer service would suffer greatly." (See Illustration A-4.)

Perpetual Inventory Control

As soon as a shipment is received at Catto & Putty, it is entered into the inventory system through a CRT terminal in receiving. The system tracks on-hand quantities of each of the firm's inventory items and monitors back-order levels. If back-orders exist for an item, a picking slip is automatically produced from the customer back-order file on an oldest-order-first-out basis. Those items are picked even before the order is stocked, thereby assuring back-order priority and that these units are not entered as active inventory.

With so many units in stock, perpetual inventory control is a must. Catto & Putty is accomplishing this on a daily basis. Periodically, a CRT terminal is placed on a mobile dolly and actually taken on inventory throughout the warehouse. Data is entered, direct from the actual counts, without the necessity of paperwork. A reorder point is established for each item. When that point is reached, the system notes it on a suggested-

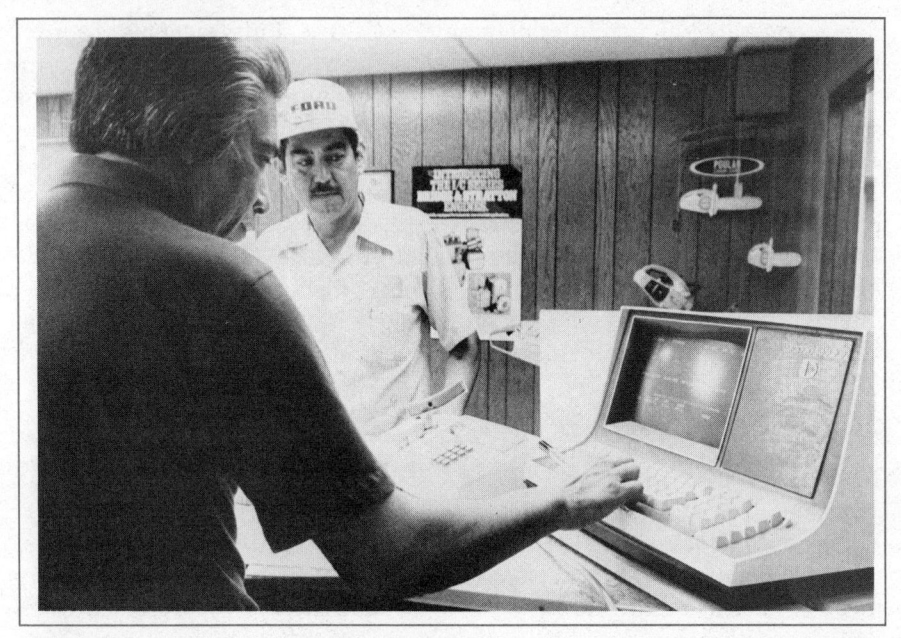

ILLUSTRATION A-4 Checking inventory status at the customer service counter

order printout. The history of each item's usage and data turnover is also noted so that purchases of the item can be made to coincide with periods of peak demand.

Business Data at Fingertips

Putty states, "I use my CRT terminal constantly. For almost every phone call and piece of correspondence that crosses my desk I consult the 'tube.' I instantly receive daily, weekly, monthly, seasonal, or annual information. It is up to date. I don't have to ask my secretary, bother the inventory manager, or check with anyone else for business data. It's all right here at my fingertips. And of course I can receive printed reports, documents, or letters with the touch of a key.

"I'm so satisfied with this 'machine' I'm terminating my lease and buying it," continues Putty. "It has certainly proven itself around here. I see no increased need within our business during the next five years that this system's technology can't handle. If a person understands his or her business, then he or she can certainly understand and use a system such as ours. It increases our awareness of any problem areas, assists with their solutions, and is invaluable in indicating and helping us to optimize opportunities."

Discussion Questions

1. Describe how Catto & Putty first used computers and the problems it encountered.

2. Discuss the benefits received by Catto & Putty as a result of installing a time-sharing computer system with respect to (1) order entry, (2) inventory control, (3) customer counter service, (4) office personnel and (5) top management information.

RETAILING—BIG 4 RENTS, INC.

In 1965 Charles Bradley purchased a rental business. In this business, small tools and garden equipment were rented from a single store in Corte Madera, California. The business had annual revenues of about $70,000. Because it was a fairly small business, Mr. Bradley ran the shop, and his wife handled most of the record keeping (data processing) using manual methods.

By 1970 it was evident that manual data processing methods were not adequate to handle the increased volume of business. The business had been expanded to include two stores offering a complete line of rental equipment including skis, party goods, heavy equipment, trucks, and tools. The most critical applications were inventory control, accounts receivable, and customer billing. These applications needed attention first.

Use of a Computer Services Company

Through the rental association that Mr. Bradley belonged to, he found out that a computer services company in Los Angeles handled the business data processing of several other rental businesses in the area. He visited two of the rental businesses using the service to determine if they were satisfied with it and to see if the available applications were suitable for his business. He retained the computer services company to provide customer billing, accounts receivable control, and a monthly rental management report showing the rental income, depreciation, and use of each piece of rental equipment. A four-digit equipment code standardized by the American Equipment Rental Association was adopted to identify all equipment listed in the monthly rental management report.

On the 25th day of each month Mr. Bradley supplied data to the computer services company. The data included the rental income for each piece of equipment, customer charges and payments, and equipment purchases or sales. This data was recorded on punched paper tape from rental contracts and other source documents and mailed to the computer services company. Customer bills were prepared from this data and mailed directly to customers. Other reports were mailed to Mr. Bradley. This processing took from five to six days each month.

In 1973, Mr. Bradley was approached by a local computer services company. The firm was interested in developing a rental industry software application package. They offered to supply the software to Mr. Bradley at no cost if he would let them use his company as a reference in promoting the software application package. The package would perform customer billing, accounts receivable processing, inventory reporting, and equipment depreciation calculations. Reports showing return on investment, aged accounts receivable, and equipment utilization would be provided.

Mr. Bradley agreed. For about the same monthly processing costs as before, additional services were provided and processing was done locally. Because the processing was done locally, the punched paper tapes were prepared and delivered to the computer services company one day and the reports were picked up the next day. The additional reports were useful for management purposes. Mr. Bradley could now determine easily which rental items were the most profitable (return on investment); how long a piece of equipment should be rented out, considering maintenance, depreciation, and repairs; and which equipment was rented the most (equipment utilization).

Mr. Bradley's monthly processing costs for these services were about $1000. Manual data processing methods were still employed for applications like payroll and accounts payable and for financial statements.

Several problems were encountered by Mr. Bradley in using the computer services companies. First, data validation was a problem. Data submitted to the computer services company was edited and an error listing produced. (See Illustration A-5.) Corrections were prepared by an employee before processing occurred. In some cases this delayed processing. When two more rental stores were opened, the additional rental volume led to an increase in the number of data errors. Customer service and profits were affected adversely.

Second, the monthly processing costs increased as the business expanded. Additional personnel were employed to maintain the manual data processing systems still in use as well. In 1978, after using computer services companies for about eight years, Mr. Bradley decided to investigate the feasibility of obtaining a computer to do all of the data processing necessary for the business.

Selection of a Computer System

Mr. Bradley and Mr. Aduna, the company controller, began the process of computer selection by visiting other rental businesses that had success-

APPENDIX A: COMPUTER SYSTEM APPLICATIONS

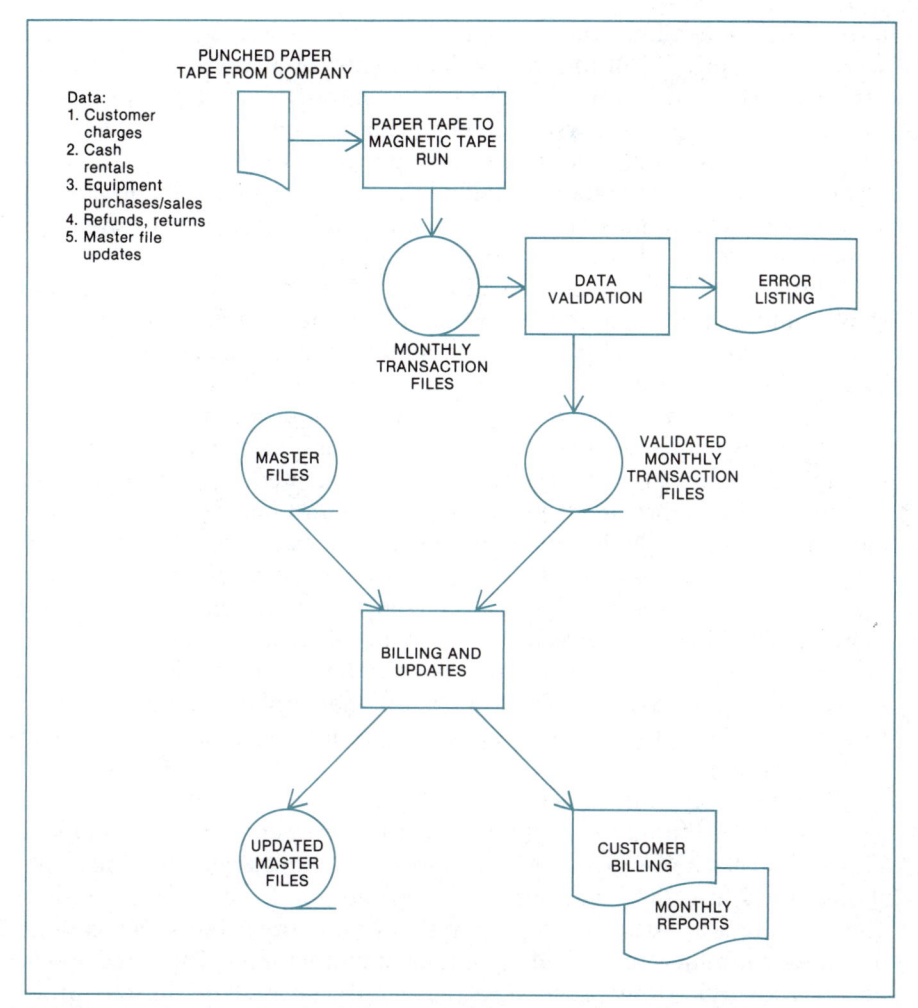

ILLUSTRATION A-5 Business data processing at the computer services company

fully installed computer systems. After these visits, they had a better idea of the potential benefits of having one's own computer. A computer consultant was retained to provide the general systems specifications and a recommendation for the computer hardware needed. The consultant was selected from among several recommended by the company's auditors.

The consultant's objective was to conduct a system study of the data processing applications in use by the business and to recommend improvements and/or changes that should be implemented with the installation of a computer. The consultant reviewed the current manual data processing applications and the applications processed by the computer services company. All of the source documents for all applications (rental contract forms, etc.) were reviewed. The outputs from all applications were also reviewed. Key personnel responsible for each of the applications were interviewed to determine processing procedures and to obtain suggestions for improvements in these applications. The current processing volume for each application was defined, and the expected growth in this volume over the next two years was estimated.

The general systems specifications developed by the consultant are shown in Illustration A-6. The consultant recommended that the computer selected should be capable of supporting terminals at each store location. The consultant felt that terminals in each store should be used for entry of rental and sales data as well as for inventory inquiries and updates.

Company management decided that the initial computer system would not include terminals. The system would be located at company headquarters and support batch processing. Company management felt that many problems might be encountered if they attempted to attach terminals at store locations to their first computer. They felt that by retaining all data processing functions at the company headquarters they could more quickly identify and respond to any problems encountered with the new computerized data processing system. The cost of implementing the system would increase because of the additional application software that would be required to provide the control needed for data validation and auditing of store transactions.

The next step was to select a computer system. The consultant suggested that the minimum configuration for the system should include a CPU with at least 48K bytes of main storage, 10 megabytes of secondary storage on disk, a 200 lines-per-minute printer, and a data-entry station. The consultant assisted in the preparation of computer bid specifications that were submitted to several computer manufacturers. These bid specifications identified the processing capabilities desired of the computer hardware as well as the application software, user training, and installation date desired. The manufacturers were asked to demonstrate their proposed system, using the application software to be provided.

It was recognized that the application software for rental management reporting and inventory control would have to be obtained from a source other than the computer manufacturer. The consultant suggested several contract software firms who could develop the software. A contract software firm was selected to provide the needed application software at a cost of about $10,000. This price included system and program design, documentation, training, and installation.

The proposals submitted by computer manufacturers were reviewed by the consultant, Mr. Bradley, and the controller. The system selected

Sales Accounting Sales order processing to include sales order entry for all transactions, cash, on-account, and documentation detail stored for master file update; credit memo entry for all sales activity; sales journal preparation with general ledger and subsidiary sales account recap and subtotals; master file update for on-account customers and rental inventory; and any error correction routines needed for these applications.

Cash Receipts of On-Account Customers and Miscellaneous Accounts Check entry with detail application to on-accounts and disbursements to miscellaneous accounts; cash receipts preparation with general and subsidiary account recap and subtotals; master file updates of on-account customers for both sales and open item records; and any error correction routines needed for these applications.

Reporting of Sales Statements prepared monthly or on demand, reflecting all account transactions such as open sales orders, current month cash receipts, credit memos, and finance charges; on-account aging of accounts receivable showing all account activity or balance-only aging.

Interactive Data Maintenance New account and item entry; existing account and item data changes.

Inventory Accounting Sales updated from the sales accounting application; data maintenance for inventory items; stock receipts for both resale and rental inventory; reporting of inventory monthly or on demand; and error correction routines for these applications.

Payables Accounting Check issuance with detailed voucher preparation; check disbursements journal preparation with general and subsidiary account recap and subtotals; vendor, supplier, general ledger, and subsidiary ledger maintenance and new account entry; payables reporting of vendor open-item on-account aging of accounts payable showing all account activity or balance-only aging both prepared monthly or on demand; purchase and expense general ledger trial balance; general and subsidiary account entry of adjustments with adjustments journal preparation; and error correction routines for these applications.

Payroll Accounting Check issuance and employee statement preparation for hourly and salaried employees paid weekly, bi-weekly, and monthly; employee earnings record update; payroll journal preparation with general and subsidiary account recap and subtotals; reporting for state and federal taxes and a quarterly employee earnings history; employee maintenance with existing employee changes and new employee entry; and error correction routines for these applications.

Rental Inventory Costing Entry Labor and materials costs of maintenance data entry; rental inventory file update; rental inventory cost entry journal preparation with recap and subtotals by general areas of cost; and error correction routines for these applications.

Financial Reporting General and subsidiary ledger maintenance and inquiry reporting to include trial balance on demand, profit and loss on demand, and balance sheet on demand.

ILLUSTRATION A-6 General systems specifications

was a Burroughs B80 with 92K bytes of main storage, a 10 megabyte cartridge disk drive, a 360 lines-per-minute printer, and a console display-keyboard for data entry and system control. (See Illustration A-7.) The system purchase price was about $40,000. Some of the additional application software needed was also purchased from Burroughs. This included accounts payable, general ledger accounting, and payroll programs. A report writer was obtained to be used by nonprogrammers to create reports and listings, and to do simple calculations. Additional charges for training and system software supplied by Burroughs brought the total system cost to over $60,000.

Company staff attended three days of user training at the Burroughs education center in San Francisco. They learned how to operate the computer system and how to use the application software. The only computer staff required were a computer operator and a data-entry operator.

For the first several months, the new system was operated in parallel with the existing data processing systems. This approach insured an orderly conversion to the new system. Processing results were verified by comparing the outputs of the systems.

Benefits

A number of benefits were provided by the new computer system. First, the system provides important management information not available through the computer services company. Mr. Bradley now receives a

ILLUSTRATION A-7 Burroughs equipment selected and installed

monthly profit and loss report for each store. The reports help to identify problems that need attention. Second, data errors have been reduced because the computer system validates all data as it is entered. This has resulted in better customer service (fewer billing errors) and improved profits. Third, the number of controller office personnel responsible for data processing has been reduced from eight to three because of the elimination of manual systems. Finally, the costs of data processing relative to the total business volume have been reduced. Further, the costs can be controlled because they do not rise directly with the increase in the number of transactions handled as they did when a computer services company was used.

Review of Computerization Process

Mr. Bradley and the controller learned a great deal in the process of selecting, installing, and operating their own computer system. Some of the things they learned are listed below.

1. Computer consultants can be valuable to a small business. They should be selected carefully. An independent consultant who is familiar with computer manufacturers' hardware should be capable of: doing system analysis and design; writing bid specifications for computer hardware and application software; reviewing bids and assisting in the selection of both computer hardware and application software; and reviewing contracts for the computer system selected and any contract programming needed.
2. Current users of systems similar to the systems under consideration should be visited. A prospective buyer should not rely only on demonstrations by computer manufacturers. Each user should be interviewed, and each system should be observed as it performs typical business data processing applications.
3. Installing a computer system requires a great deal of staff time. Key staff personnel must be prepared to work long hours when bringing in a computer system and converting from existing systems for data processing.
4. The ability to maintain processing on the computer whenever it is needed is important. Therefore, file backup, computer availability, and staffing are important. Backup is vital for all computer files. The use of the grandfather-father-son method of file retention insures that a file can be re-created if it becomes damaged, lost, or destroyed. Computer system maintenance should be readily available and under contract to minimize system downtime if a system failure occurs. Several employees should be trained in the operation of the system and be familiar with the applications so that processing of

the applications can be completed successfully, even if an employee becomes ill or leaves.

Future Plans

Mr. Bradley's rental company now operates four stores in four cities. As the processing volume increases, a larger computer will be required. An online system with several terminals at each store is being considered. Mr. Bradley recently visited a rental business in Maryland that has an online system with multiple terminals at remote locations. Because of the valuable assistance obtained from a consultant previously, a consultant will again be used to design and recommend system software and hardware. Mr. Bradley expects that, before the workload on the current system reaches or exceeds its processing capacity, an online system will be installed.

Discussion Questions

1. How did the use of the second computer services company improve data processing for Big 4 Rents?

2. What problems were encountered while using a computer services company?

3. Explain how the computer consultant assisted in the process of installing a computerized data processing system.

4. How did the installation of a computer system improve the data processing system of Big 4 Rents? What effect might the improvements have on customer service and on company profits?

5. What did the management of Big 4 Rents learn from the experience of selecting and installing a computer system?

CENTRALIZE? DECENTRALIZE? DISTRIBUTE?

Hewlett-Packard Company (HP) has been extremely successful in using both large and small computers to handle its administrative data processing in whatever environment is necessary: centralized, decentralized, or distributed. Basically, the company evolved from a purely centralized operation to its present mix by riding on the coattails of advancing technology. Its first computer experience in the late '50s and early '60s was with large stand-alone processors (and HP still has some of those). As the company grew, a central data processing facility was established at its corporate headquarters in Palo Alto, California. This facility served a number of San Francisco bay area users in a batch environment. Input and output was transferred by messenger or taxi.

In the early '70s, the center became too cumbersome to manage. It became increasingly difficult to respond adequately to the diverse needs of a large number of users. The short-term answer was to set up a remote job entry environment but still retain a centralized computing facility. Under this approach, control of the operation of application systems was transferred to the users.

During the same period, HP began to use the techniques of time sharing to meet the needs of interactive users at geographically distributed terminals. HP management envisioned a worldwide data communication network, allowing remote data entry in support of its sales and service activities. The time-sharing and remote data entry applications demonstrated the effectiveness of minicomputers. The communication network served as groundwork for what followed.

By 1973 numerous HP factories and sales offices had established their own computer systems. These systems proved to be more responsive to local management needs than the remote job entry systems were. As a result, HP began to decentralize a large portion of its previously centralized data processing.

Finally, the data communication network and decentralized computers together made it possible for HP to experiment with distributed systems. In these systems, data storage and processing functions are shared across a mix of computers and lines. Nontrivial operations are performed at multiple locations. Several of HP's major data processing application systems now operate in a distributed mode.

HP's experience with distributed processing has been positive. The company has been able to adapt to a constantly expanding geographic operation and a constantly changing organizational structure. Through distributed processing, HP organizational units meet the reporting requirements of HP management and of the governments of the various countries where HP operates, in a timely and cost-effective manner. Distributed processing has improved the accuracy of administrative data by moving a significant portion of the processing of the data to the place where it originates.

The Basics of the Business

HP has learned from experience that there is no one best way to process data. Information systems must be designed to match the organizations they support. Stated simply, a decentralized organization with strong central management requires both decentralized and centrally managed sys-

Centralized	Decentralized	Distributed
Materials services Vendor contracting Consolidated statements Legal reporting Employee benefits	General accounting Cost accounting Customer service Production Shipments Purchasing Inventorying Product assurance Payroll/personnel (15%)	Production information Customer information Orders and changes Accounts receivable Payroll/personnel (85%)

ILLUSTRATION A-8 HP's application environments

tems. (See Illustration A-8.) Understanding why this is true requires some insight into HP's business.

HP manufactures more than 4000 products for wide-ranging markets, primarily in manufacturing-related industries. The company has 38 manufacturing facilities and 172 sales and service offices around the world. It employs about 45,000 people. HP has experienced a very rapid growth of about 20% per year. Its 1979 sales were $2.3 billion.

To support this business, the company uses some 1400 computers (not including desk-top units and handheld calculators). Of these, 85% support engineering and production applications. The computers are usually dedicated to specific tasks. Many are arranged in networks. A number of them are also used in computer-aided design applications as input processors for large mainframes.

The remaining 200 computers support business applications. The largest mainframe is an Amdahl 470/V6 located in Palo Alto. (See Illustration A-9.) Nine medium-sized IBM systems are installed at other large facilities. Seventy HP Model 3000 minicomputers are used in factories and sales offices. Another 125 HP minicomputers are scattered about for data entry, data retrieval, and data communication work.

In general, the HP computers are oriented toward online applications; the large mainframes are oriented toward batch processing (although three also support online applications). The network tying all these systems together consists of 110 data communication facilities located at sales and service offices, manufacturing facilities, and corporate offices in Palo Alto and Geneva, Switzerland. (See Illustration A-10.)

Some long-standing management traditions have contributed to the successful use of all this hardware. For the past 20 years, HP has been oriented toward decentralized management responsiblity at the operating level with strong central management coordination. Local managers are

APPENDIX A: COMPUTER SYSTEM APPLICATIONS

ILLUSTRATION A-9   The Amdahl 470/V6 large computer at HP headquarters

accustomed both to making their own decisions and to reporting to management on a frequent and detailed basis.

Another important tradition has been the adoption of companywide coding standards. Universal conventions for product number, account number, part number, entity code, employee number, and other identifiers were established to meet business requirements long before computer systems were employed extensively.

But perhaps the most important systems-related management tradition has been the existence of functional advisory councils. These groups were established to resolve common local problems in such areas as order processing, materials management, cost accounting, and quality assurance. Today, these councils provide a forum in which to arrive at a consensus on data-processing-related problems and to achieve user support in building and managing complex, dispersed application systems.

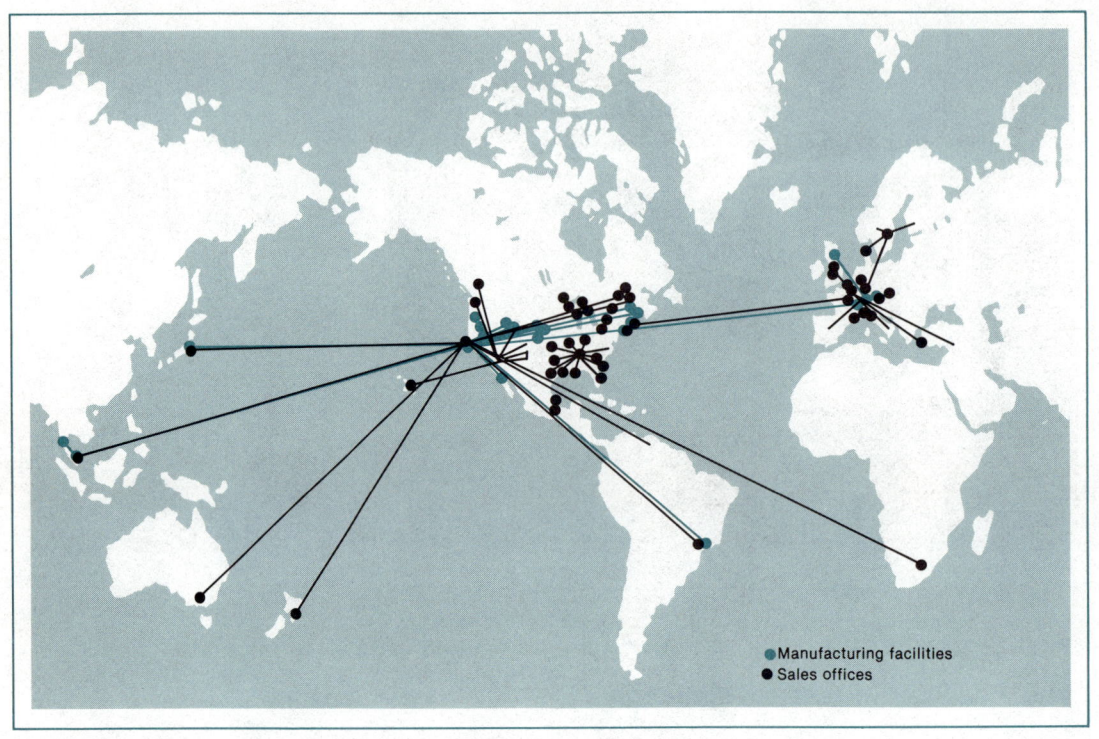

ILLUSTRATION A-10 HP's distributed processing network

Ten Big Problems

Yet progress doesn't always come easily. As its use of computers evolved, HP faced a number of challenges. Some of the most important ones are listed below:

1. Establishing a central planning and management program for companywide information systems activities so that decentralized development work could be coordinated.
2. Designing systems that could respond easily to constant geographic expansion, organizational change, and addition of new operating units.
3. Coping with ever-increasing needs for detailed, accurate information to meet management and government reporting requirements while controlling administrative costs.
4. Designing systems that could be adapted to respond to specific local needs and yet maintain companywide compatibility.
5. Getting user managers to accept responsibility for the specification and operation of their systems.

6. Convincing users in different functional areas that data is an organizational resource to be shared by all, and that individual transactions should simultaneously update the records of all functions.
7. Avoiding unnecessary duplication of effort in designing and supporting systems.
8. Developing the skills of data processing staff members to meet the needs of a growing organization, and assigning priorities to their activities.
9. Establishing, maintaining, and promoting the use of standards for hardware, software, documentation, project management, data, and auditability and control as a foundation for well-coordinated worldwide application systems.
10. Controlling security and privacy in an online, decentralized, and distributed multinational environment.

HP began to seriously address the first and most important challenge—establishing management control over companywide systems developments—about 1976. A large amount of data processing hardware had been installed in decentralized locations. Many potentially incompatible systems were being designed. Furthermore, the plans for hardware installation were not well-coordinated with the needs of systems being developed centrally. In an attempt to deal with these matters, HP established an Information Systems Planning Office. This in turn led to the creation of an Information Systems Planning Task Force (similar to the advisory councils discussed earlier). The task force was assigned responsibility for defining how HP's information systems activities should be managed.

The task force identified three organizational areas that required different approaches to system design and operation: manufacturing, sales and service, and corporate administration.

HP's fundamental organizational unit is the manufacturing division profit center. There are 38 of these. Each occupies a single plant location. Each performs a full range of business functions (including research and development, manufacturing, and marketing) as well as support functions (financial control, personnel administration, and product assurance). In many respects, each division resembles an independent company.

HP practices management by objectives and attempts to have decisions made by the people who are closest to the problems. From an organizational viewpoint, this means that the manufacturing support systems must be decentralized. There are exceptions. For example, payroll is a centrally managed distributed system.

HP's worldwide sales and service organization employs a different type of system. Customers are served by a single organization that just happens to be geographically dispersed. Sales and service activities related to specific product lines are performed by specialists. The specialists are supported by a distributed marketing administration system that ties the sales and service offices to the corporate headquarters and to the plant locations.

The third entity, corporate, provides services such as product assurance, payroll, and employee benefits. Financial and legal reporting are its responsibility. These tasks are best handled in a centralized manner.

The task force studied how existing information systems supported these various company operations. The most successful systems were those that matched the company's organization and management philosophy. This led to the conclusion that systems should be decentralized, distributed, *or* centralized, depending on management needs.

Representative Systems

The following sections describe four HP information systems or facilities and show how they match the HP organization. The first example deals with the communication system, the heart of the HP minicomputer network. The second and third examples are of two systems having distributed data bases. One has centralized master files (at two locations). The other has both centralized and distributed master files. The final example deals with decentralized systems that interface to distributed systems.

Communication network. The communication system at HP supports HP minicomputers at 110 worldwide locations. The minis perform a number of data communication functions. They handle data entry, format data for transmission, detect and correct errors, and adapt data transmission to meet the requirements of various countries. In addition, the minis support online access to local data bases.

HP started to build this network in the late 1960s. The network used paper tape I/O: it was slow, very expensive, and—even more important— extremely error-prone. In 1968, HP introduced a minicomputer oriented primarily toward scientific applications. To see whether or not the company could use the mini in business applications, HP started using it in a communication network involving intelligent terminals. The network was successful from the start. HP has continuously added to the locations served. Some years ago, CRT terminals were installed on the network. More recently, distributed data bases and an inquiry capability were introduced.

The network operates in a store and forward mode. In Europe, for instance, all data is transmitted to Geneva and concentrated there for efficient use of the overseas lines to Palo Alto. The communication system uses the standard dial-up worldwide telephone network over most routes. This helps to keep costs down, since HP pays only for the actual time used. For example, about one minute a day is needed to transmit all

HP data back and forth to New Zealand. A single dial-up call to New Zealand is clearly a lot less costly than a dedicated line. The average worldwide data volume is about 140 million characters per day. This translates into about 100,000 messages. Still the line cost runs under $50,000 per month, a very economical figure when compared with the usual communication costs of online systems handling similar data volumes.

The largest communication system applications are for marketing (60% of the traffic), accounting (15%), employee information (10%), and administrative messages (15%). HP transmits about one million orders and about three million invoices per year over the network. The network is also used extensively for file transmission.

The system is an excellent means of transmitting administrative messages (electronic mail). It is particularly effective for overseas communication, where the telephone is costly and inconvenient because of time zone differences. The cost of transmitting a letter-size message overseas is typically 30¢. This low cost, coupled with the system's speed and convenience, has resulted in a large increase in day-to-day communication between people at the operations level in U.S. and overseas offices.

As the largest user of the communication system, the marketing administration group is responsible for planning and implementing system enhancements. The enhancements are developed by a small central team of programmer/analysts. New releases are transmitted as data to the remote locations and put into operation at prearranged times. The installation of these system enhancements normally goes smoothly, but a fair amount of expertise is required at the remote locations to cope with unexpected bugs due to slight hardware differences, special local modems, and other incompatibilities.

Marketing administration system. A second application system is the distributed marketing administration system, which supports the sales and service organization. The primary objective of this system is to provide accurate and consistent information to HP customers on a worldwide basis. A centrally managed distributed system is required. Centralized, decentralized, and distributed processing occur simultaneously. (See Illustration A-11.)

Decentralized processing is used for production planning, product configuring, and shipment scheduling at the manufacturing sites. It is used for order entry and service scheduling at the sales and service offices.

Centralized processing is used for such functions as financial and legal reporting and administration of the employee benefits program at corporate headquarters.

Some forms of distributed processing are used in maintaining and accessing distributed data bases. The data for customer records originates at the sales offices, for example, and portions of the customer data base

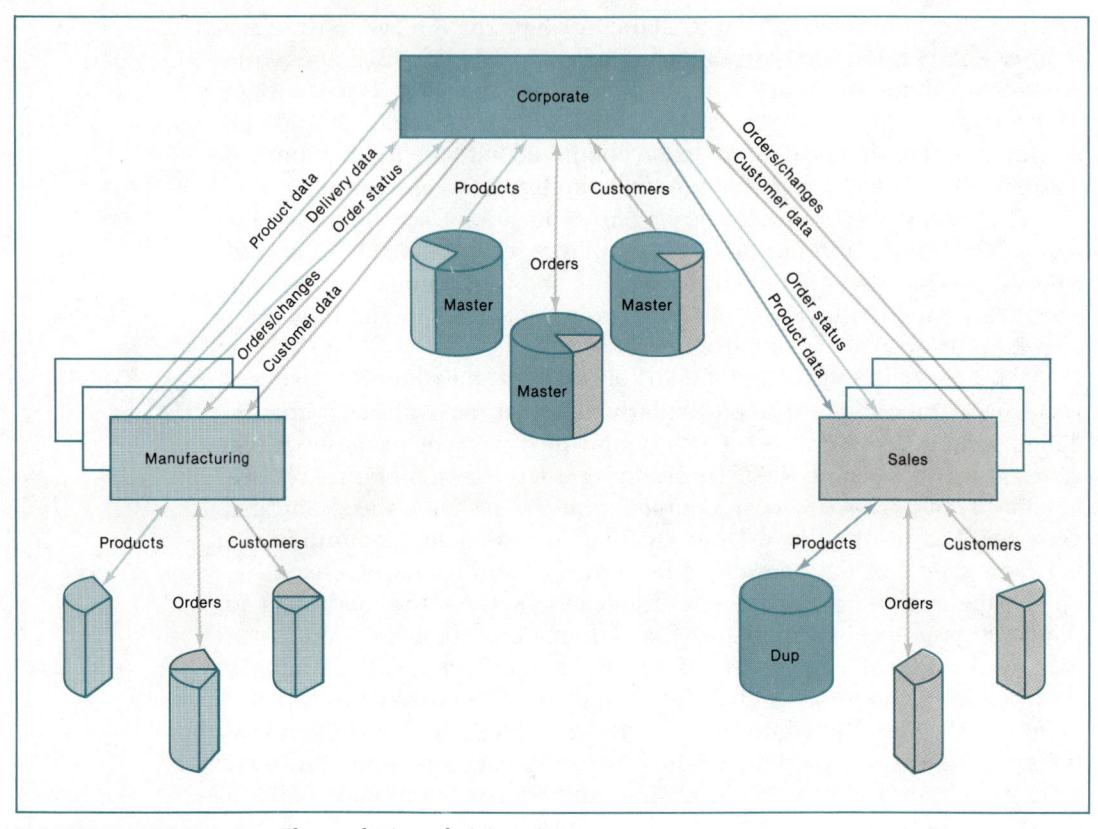

ILLUSTRATION A-11   The marketing administration system

are kept in each sales office. A complete customer data base is simultaneously maintained at corporate headquarters. Portions of the data base also exist at the manufacturing sites.

Orders and changes are entered at the sales and service offices, transmitted to headquarters where they are entered into central files, and then sent on to the factories for acceptance and delivery acknowledgement. Company order, shipment, and backlog status is maintained centrally to provide information to top management. Delivery information is transmitted from the manufacturing divisions back to the sales offices where orders are acknowledged.

Invoices are centrally processed in Palo Alto and Geneva. The credit and collection functions are decentralized to the sales offices, with central reporting of receivables status to achieve financial control.

Files of European open orders are maintained in both Geneva and Palo Alto. An order from a European sales office containing items to be supplied from a European factory and a U.S. factory is processed in Geneva. Complete detail pertaining to the U.S.-supplied items is transmitted to Palo Alto; however, only order statistics are sent to Palo Alto for the European-supplied items. Order status information is transmitted back and forth daily to keep the two files identical. A monthly audit procedure insures that nothing was overlooked in the daily updates.

Up-to-date order status change information is transmitted daily from Palo Alto to the large U.S. sales offices to provide online access for response to customer inquiries. The remote files are kept identical with the master files by computer control. That is, the update program requires each batch update to be performed in the right order. (The January 17 update cannot be performed before the January 16 update.) Local files can be re-created from the central files if recovery is necessary.

Data is collected for a period of time at remote locations and then transmitted as a batch over communication facilities. The system operates in the same manner as an online distributed system in which a significant portion of the data processing is done at more than one location. Data is batch communicated because this is the most economical method available.

In the past, HP used microfiche reports, produced once a week and mailed to the sales offices. Data retrieval was awkward and time-consuming. The reports were usually late, and printed information was transmitted daily to update them. Now, the use of CRT terminals in the sales offices to access order status information produces a labor saving of close to 20% over these former methods. Having the information directly available also cuts other costs, since fewer telephone calls to the factories for order status information are necessary.

Managing the marketing administration system is a continual challenge. Because of its wide geographic and application scope, changes must be made slowly and carefully to avoid upsetting existing features. Individual HP organizations and functions have a continuing need for enhancements and want them to be installed quickly. Functional councils, such as the Information Systems Task Force, the Order Processing Council, and the Customer Service Council, play important roles in prioritizing needs and obtaining support for overall system development plans.

Another management challenge is the coordination of international system activities. Europe, in particular, has important, unique system needs that are best developed and supported locally. The local systems must be closely coordinated with corporate systems because of the close interrelationships of transactions and files. A great deal of overseas travel, along with rotation of knowledgeable personnel, is needed to accomplish this coordination.

Important features of the marketing administration system are summarized in Illustration A-12. They can be contrasted with the features of the other HP systems discussed below.

Activity	Marketing Administration System	Personnel/Payroll System	Factory Management System
Development	Various operational units working under centrally coordinated plan	Corporate	Joint effort between divisions and corporate on modular basis
Operation	Distributed	Distributed	Decentralized (use is optional)
Data base	Centrally and locally maintained, local sales office data bases updated daily	Locally and centrally maintained, central data base updated before each payroll run	Locally maintained, serves all manufacturing facility departments
Support	Central support of basic systems, local support of alterations	Central support	Sharable systems centrally supported

ILLUSTRATION A-12 Characteristics of HP application systems

Personnel/payroll system. To comply with local laws and customs, an independent personnel/payroll system is maintained by HP in each country in which HP operates. In the United States, a distributed system pays about 25,000 employees. The payroll data is entered on CRT terminals at about 30 remote locations. Each has its own (local) daily updated disk file. The data is transmitted to Palo Alto for monthly, payroll processing. The paychecks are either transmitted back to the originating locations for printing or directly deposited in employee bank accounts.

Payroll is processed in Palo Alto rather than at the remote locations for two main reasons. First, Palo Alto has the responsibility for overall HP benefits. For example, HP has a nationwide insurance plan, a retirement program, cash profit sharing, and a stock purchase plan; all of these must be administered out of a central file.

Second, many government reports must be made on a centralized basis: retirement legislation reports, equal opportunity reports, withholding taxes, and so forth. Since the information needed for benefit administration and government reporting is produced as a by-product of the payroll system, the underlying data need only be entered into the computer system once.

The distributed data base that supports the payroll/personnel system operates in a different mode from that which is used for the sales and service system. Each division is responsible for the accuracy of the data relating to its employees. As noted above, the data is kept on local disk files and updated daily. Changes to these files are transmitted to Palo Alto several times a month where they are used to update the central file prior to payroll processing.

The audit and control procedure insures that the central and remote files are identical. After the central file is updated, all modified records are transmitted back to the originating locations for comparison. Any differences are then reported. They may arise from either of two causes. First, somewhat more strict edit routines may be applied centrally, thereby uncovering errors not detected locally. Second, certain changes to employee records may be made centrally. These are sometimes not recorded in the local files. A small but significant number of errors are detected by this audit and control procedure.

The payroll/personnel system serves a number of departments: finance, accounting, personnel, and tax. An advisory board with members from these departments reviews and approves all changes to system programs.

Eighty-five percent of HP's U.S. employees are paid by the system. The other 15% are paid by manufacturing divisions that run their payrolls locally. Personnel data for this 15% (as well as for the 85%) must be maintained in the central file to take care of the centrally administered benefit programs. Keeping this independently prepared data accurate and consistent with that prepared centrally is a significant challenge.

The remote personnel files are processed locally to produce reports on employees. In addition, they provide a timely interface to local systems such as cost accounting. The remotely used software is centrally supported, and changes to that software are released periodically.

Factory management system. The factory management system is implemented on HP 3000 minicomputers. This decentralized system supports the functions of order processing, materials management and purchasing, production planning, product assurance, service support, and accounting. It consists of a group of functional modules that access a central data base serving as an information resource for the divisions. As mentioned earlier, most systems used by the manufacturing divisions are decentralized and locally managed. Although each HP division has unique requirements that must be satisfied by its local support systems, there is a remarkable similarity in the needs of the divisions. Most HP divisions are oriented largely toward assembly operations, so the manufacturing support systems are designed around a bill of materials processor. As a general rule, 80% of the division's needs can be satisfied with the basic software. The company's return on development and support costs is maximized by the sharing of this software among the decentralized locations.

The factory management system was developed over a period of years, one system module at a time. (Examples of system modules are materials management, production planning, and cost accounting.) The work was done by joint development teams. Division personnel were responsible for the specifications and for insuring that the system modules met their functional needs. Central data processing specialists made sure that the modules operated efficiently and interfaced properly with other system modules. On completion, modules are shared by the divisions on a voluntary basis.

The factory management system is especially useful to new divisions (added at a rate of about three per year). It allows managers in these divisions to have a high level of system support capability early in their growth cycles. The system is less useful to older, established divisions with existing systems of their own. These divisions have found it difficult to justify the cost of change (especially retraining people), even though online operation and other enhancements would be helpful to them.

The factory management system architecture permits divisions to use either the complete system or individual modules that support specific functions. Many divisions have installed modules to automate activities previously handled manually. Often these modules are interfaced with existing systems implemented on IBM (or IBM-compatible) hardware.

The needs of the many divisions using the factory management system are served through a central support group. This group installs enhancements to the system on an ongoing basis, makes modifications as required to match changes in interfacing systems (such as companywide distributed systems), and helps the divisions to install individual modules. Several functional advisory boards have been established to facilitate priority setting and to keep the central support group tuned to user needs. The advisory boards must decide whether to enhance existing systems to achieve short-term benefits, or to develop new system capability to satisfy future needs.

The factory management system provides an interesting management challenge. Since one data base supports all using functions, the managers of these functions must rely on the accuracy of one another's data. Yet these managers are accustomed to individual departmental control of system resources. The payoff is consistent information and elimination of classic arguments over whose numbers are right.

To access the numbers, HP makes wide use of CRT terminals in factory applications, as well as in sales and service work. The primary advantage of these online terminals is usually thought to be that access to data, but there is an important secondary justification: paper saving. Terminal availability greatly reduces the number of printed reports required. In one study (involving another manufacturer's hardware), HP found that half the cost of installing online CRT terminals was offset by a direct reduction in the volume of printed reports required by users of those terminals.

APPENDIX A: COMPUTER SYSTEM APPLICATIONS

Central Systems Support

An important aspect of managing systems in a large worldwide company is the central systems support that ties the whole process together. At HP, four main functions are involved: (1) long-range planning, (2) "visibility and leverage," (3) personnel, and (4) standards and guidelines.

The preparation and maintenance of an overall plan for systems evolution and development is essential. Manufacturing, sales and service, and companywide personnel are involved. The manufacturing planning team is headed by the vice president of corporate services and his staff. The marketing planning team consists of staff of the vice president of marketing. Companywide planning is handled by the office of the controller. The central management job is to consolidate the results of the planning efforts of these three teams and then communicate the plans throughout the company and to upper-level management for approval or for suggested modification.

HP claims that "visibility and leverage" has played an important role in the success of its systems. A great deal of needless duplication of effort has been avoided by communicating information about information systems activities taking place throughout the company. Existing sharing opportunities have been highlighted.

Information systems personnel are very important in this effort. The growth in the number of people in this function parallels the company's dollar growth: 20% per year. Most of the hiring and development of systems personnel is decentralized, but central systems support provides an overall framework that encourages consistency. Another important responsibility of central systems support is user management education. Training programs covering the user's role in system design and operation are conducted regularly.

As mentioned earlier, HP has some well-established, companywide coding standards. Many of these arose independently of computer activities. In addition, the use of computers has helped to create and maintain standards. For example, HP's worldwide order processing system imposes a strong data standards discipline. Factories and sales offices must follow the standards in order to communicate with one another and to insure that orders are processed.

HP has put a lot of effort into standardizing documentation procedures. Documentation is of great importance as a project management tool during system design. It is also a key ingredient of HP's systems sharing program. Prospective users evaluate the utility of systems by referring to their documentation.

Most of the computers used by HP are manufactured by HP or IBM, and have compatible communication capability at the hardware level.

APPENDIX A: COMPUTER SYSTEM APPLICATIONS

Magnetic tapes can be interchanged readily. COBOL is the standard language for application programs. HP's Image data base management system is used extensively in HP 3000 minicomputer applications. There aren't an excessive number of pieces to coordinate.

In summary, HP's minicomputer systems have helped the company to find workable solutions to the ten challenges listed earlier. The systems provide consistent support for administrative activities under conditions of rapid growth and change. The sales organization is supplied the up-to-date information necessary to provide full service to customers in worldwide sales and service offices. The systems provide key information to management. They also help HP to cope with ever-increasing government reporting requirements.

HP's internal business systems are continually being improved to meet changing requirements. As this goes on, several characteristics emerge over and over again as the most significant.

Successful systems put the control of data close to the source of the data and the control of processing close to the manager responsible for the function being performed. In an organization like Hewlett-Packard, this frequently implies distributing processing. When distributed processing is called for, there are additional criteria for success. Among these are an existing set of standards and coding conventions, some mechanism whereby disagreements among users and developers can be resolved, and some facility for sharing programs and procedures among the participants.

When all of these things can be combined, as they have been at HP, user managers are satisfied, corporate managers have the data they need when they need it, and administrative productivity is increased.

Discussion Questions

1. Discuss the key differences among centralized, decentralized, and distributed computer systems.
2. Why does HP process data in three kinds of processing environments?
3. How does HP use its communication network?
4. Explain how the method of data communication used by HP saves them money.
5. Describe the types of processing used to support the marketing administration and personnel/payroll systems.
6. Discuss the four main functions of central systems support at HP.

APPENDIX B

BASIC PROGRAMMING

This appendix is provided for students who want to become familiar with the BASIC programming language. The BASIC language, as its name (Beginners' All-purpose Symbolic Instruction Code) implies, is designed to provide a simple, easily understandable means for a student to write computer programs. The design of the contents of this appendix complements the design of the BASIC language. BASIC is explained in a manner such that the student can learn it in a relatively short period of time.

All of the essential statements of the BASIC language are discussed to allow the student to write a variety of programs. Each of the BASIC statements presented is identified on the following "Contents" pages for easy reference when learning the language and writing programs.

Certain fundamental operating-system and editing commands are needed to effectively and efficiently use the BASIC language. Many of the commands required to use (1) Digital Equipment Corporation (DEC), (2) Hewlett-Packard (HP), and (3) International Business Machines (IBM) computer systems are discussed at the beginning of this appendix.

The student should refer to the *Study Guide* for questions and problems concerning the material in this appendix. Additional problems are given in Appendix C, which follows immediately.

Though an American National Standard for Minimal BASIC (X3.60-1978) was formally approved in January 1978, BASIC compilers in common use were designed and implemented prior to this standardization. Most of them contain additional features not addressed in the standard. Therefore, minor language variations exist among current BASIC implementations. These variations are pointed out by footnotes in this appendix.

CONTENTS

**TIME-SHARING OPERATING-SYSTEM
AND EDITING COMMANDS**   502
Sign-On Procedure • Language Identification • Operating-System Commands • Sign-Off Procedure

AN INTRODUCTORY PROGRAM   506

PROGRAM STATEMENT NUMBERS AND LENGTH   509
Program Statement Numbers • Program Statement Length

CONSTANTS AND VARIABLES   510
Constants • Variables

THE LET STATEMENT   513
General Considerations of the Arithmetic Assignment Statement • Arithmetic Expressions • The Multiple Arithmetic Assignment Statement • The Assignment of a Character String

THE PRINT STATEMENT   519
Printing Numbers • Printing Character Strings • PRINT Statement Rules • The TAB Function

THE END STATEMENT   524

THE READ AND DATA STATEMENTS   524
The Reading of a Character String • Examples of the READ and DATA Statements

THE RESTORE STATEMENT   529

THE INPUT STATEMENT   529

THE REM STATEMENT   531

THE STOP STATEMENT   532

CONTROL STATEMENTS — 532
The GO TO Statement • The IF-THEN Statement • The ON-GO TO Statement • The FOR-TO and NEXT Statements

EXAMPLES OF BASIC PROGRAMS — 543
Example 1. The Squaring of Numbers • Example 2. A Payroll Program • Example 3. Compound Interest • Example 4. Depreciation

ARRAYS — 550
The Naming of an Array • The DIM Statement • Array Dimensions • Subscripts and Array Elements • The Default Creation of an Array • The OPTION BASE Statement • The Storage of a Character String in an Array

AN EXAMPLE OF A BASIC PROGRAM USING ARRAYS — 557
Example 5. Adding Values in an Array

THE MAT STATEMENTS — 559
Matrix Input/Output • Matrix Arithmetic • Matrix Transposition • Initializing Matrices • Matrix Inversion

EXAMPLES OF MAT STATEMENTS — 564
Example 6. The Bubble Sort • Example 7. Bar-Chart Graphing

FUNCTIONS — 568
Predefined Functions • User-Defined Functions

THE RANDOMIZE STATEMENT — 575

SUBROUTINES — 575
The GOSUB and RETURN Statements

AN EXAMPLE OF THE GOSUB AND RETURN STATEMENTS — 578
Example 8. Finding the Mean and Median of Numbers

A SUMMARY OF THE BASIC LANGUAGE — 580

○ TIME-SHARING OPERATING-SYSTEM AND EDITING COMMANDS

The use of the BASIC language requires two types of statements. One type of statements is referred to as program statements. As discussed in Chapter 5, program statements instruct the computer in detail as to both the specific operations to perform and the order in which to perform them. This type of statement is the subject of this appendix.

Statements of the second type are called *operating-system and editing commands*. These commands, in contrast to program statements, instruct the computer as to what action to take concerning the program itself. The nature and extent of operating-system and editing commands vary. The commands required to use (1) Digital Equipment Corporation (DEC), (2) Hewlett-Packard (HP), and (3) International Business Machines (IBM) computer systems are summarized in Illustration B-1 and explained in greater detail below.

If using a time-sharing system rather than a microcomputer, the user must make sure a terminal is online before attempting to use it. Some terminals are always online; the user need only turn on the terminal and press the RETURN key. Other terminals have dial-up facilities. The user calls the computer via a telephone used for data transmission. If an appropriate telephone number is dialed, the computer will answer via a high-pitched tone transmitted over the telephone line. This signals that the computer is ready to receive input from the terminal. The user then places the telephone handset into an acoustic coupler. This links the terminal to the computer through the telephone line. The user then presses the RETURN key. This signals to the computer that the sign-on procedure is going to begin.

Sign-On Procedure

The sign-on procedure is dependent upon the particular computer system being used. On the DEC system, the user first simultaneously presses the CONTROL and C keys. The terminal prints a period. The user then enters

LOGIN

and presses the RETURN key. (All user-entered lines must be terminated by pressing the RETURN key, regardless of the computer system; this signals to the computer that the input is complete.) The terminal prints #.

On an HP system, the user may have to press the RETURN key and then the LINE FEED key. The terminal prints

PLEASE LOGIN

APPENDIX B: BASIC PROGRAMMING

	DEC	HP	IBM
Sign-On Procedure:			
User enters	CONTROL and C keys (simultaneously)	RETURN key and possibly the LINE FEED key	The sign-on procedure for an IBM system is dependent upon the system being used. The new user should ask for the specific procedure to sign on to the IBM system from the terminal.
Computer responds	.	PLEASE LOGIN	
User enters	LOGIN	HEL-D431,ABC123 or HEL-D310,	
Computer responds	#	One or more lines of preprogrammed information, such as the date and time	
User enters	1103,1571		
Computer responds	PASSWORD:	READY	
User enters	His/her password		
Computer responds	.		
Language Identification:			
User enters	R BASIC or BASIC	Depending upon the system, defaults to BASIC or user must type the word BASIC	ENTER BASIC
Computer responds	READY, FOR HELP TYPE HELP.	READY	READY
User enters	NEW		
Computer responds	NEW FILE NAME--		
User enters	PAYROL		
Computer responds	READY		
Operating-System Commands:			
To print out a program	LIST	LIST	LIST
To execute a program	RUN	RUN	RUN
To delete a line	DELETE 50	DELETE-50,50	DELETE 50
To name a program	Enter NEW during language identification	NAME-	NAME
To store a program	SAVE	SAVE	SAVE
To recall a program	Enter OLD during language identification	GET-	LOAD
Sign-Off Procedure:			
User enters	SYSTEM	BYE	OFF
Computer responds	.	0015 MINUTES OF TERMINAL TIME	One or more lines of preprogrammed information
User enters	KJOB		
Computer responds	CONFIRM		
User enters	K		

ILLUSTRATION B-1 Time-sharing operating-system and editing commands

APPENDIX B: BASIC PROGRAMMING

The initial sign-on procedure for an IBM system is dependent upon the system being used. Therefore, the user should ask for the specific procedure for the IBM system in use.

The purpose of the sign-on procedure from this point on is the same for all three manufacturers. Each system requests the user to enter his/her assigned, unique ID number and password. DEC and HP are shown below. (What the user enters is italicized.) The requirement for a unique ID number and password protects the user's data file(s) and/or program(s) from access by other users.

 #1103,1571   DEC

(The terminal responds with PASSWORD: The user then enters the password.)

 HEL-D431,ABC123   HP
  or
 HEL-D310,

The user then presses the RETURN key.

On the DEC system, the terminal does not print the password as it is entered. Thus, the password is unreadable. After receiving a valid user ID number and password, the terminal prints a period.

The HP system prints the ID number as typed by the user. It may print the password, depending upon what has been preprogrammed for that particular ID number. One or more lines of preprogrammed information, such as the date and time, and READY are printed in any case.

Language Identification

The user then specifies the BASIC language, as shown below:

 R BASIC   DEC
  or
 BASIC

 Depending upon the   HP
 system, the computer
 defaults to BASIC or the
 user must type the word
 BASIC.

 ENTER BASIC   IBM

On a DEC system, the computer responds

READY, FOR HELP TYPE HELP.

APPENDIX B: BASIC PROGRAMMING

The user who does not need help but desires to enter a new program responds by typing

NEW

The computer types

NEW FILE NAME--

The user must give the program a name, such as

PAYROL

The computer responds with the message

READY

In the IBM and HP systems, the computer either responds with READY immediately or responds with READY after the name of the language has been entered.

Operating-System Commands

The statements of the BASIC program are now entered. At the end of each line, the RETURN key is pressed. To see a listing of the partial or complete program as it exists in the computer, the user can type the system command

LIST

The computer lists the statements entered thus far, in line-number sequence.

After the complete program has been entered, it is ready to be translated into machine language and executed. To request this, the user types the system command

RUN

If there are no errors in the use of the BASIC language, the program will be executed. If there are errors, the BASIC compiler will indicate each line in error as the line is compiled. The errors must be corrected before the program can be executed.

1. To correct a line, type the line number and the correct statement. (When two lines have the same number, the last one typed is used by the computer.)
2. To delete a line on a DEC or IBM system, type the command DELETE, then the line number, and press the RETURN key. For example: DELETE 50. To delete line 50 on the HP system, type the command DELETE-50,50 and press the RETURN key. Line deletion also can be accomplished by typing the line number and then pressing the RETURN key.

APPENDIX B: BASIC PROGRAMMING

3. To insert a line, select a number between the line numbers of the lines where insertion is to occur. Use the selected number as the line number of the line to be inserted.

When all errors have been corrected, the user again types the system command

RUN

If a program is executing on an HP or IBM system, and the user wishes to stop execution, the user can press the BREAK key. On the DEC system, the user presses the CONTROL and C keys twice.

If the user wants to make changes in the program after it has been executed, the user need not retype the whole program. The lines can be changed as discussed above. When the program is ready to be executed again, the command RUN can be typed once more.

Often a user wants to store a program and data permanently so that the program and data do not have to be re-entered the next time they are needed. This is accomplished by typing the command SAVE and the program name. The DEC system requires that a program be given a name at the time it is first entered. The HP and IBM systems do not. However, a program must be assigned a name by which it can be stored and accessed. The NAME command is used to do this as shown below:

| *NAME-PAYROL* | HP |
| *NAME PAYROL* | IBM |

Once named, the program can be saved on magnetic disk or tape. The SAVE command is used as follows:

| *SAVE* | HP and DEC |
| *SAVE PAYROL* | IBM |

To recall a stored program from magnetic disk or tape, another command is used:

| *GET-PAYROL* | HP |
| *LOAD PAYROL* | IBM |

On a DEC system, the user enters OLD when the computer asks

NEW OR OLD--

The computer then responds

OLD FILE NAME--

The user enters the name of the stored program, in this case PAYROL. On all three systems, the computer responds with the message READY when the program has been recalled.

APPENDIX B: BASIC PROGRAMMING

Sign-Off Procedure

When the user is finished, a terminal sign-off command must be entered. On a DEC system, the user enters the word SYSTEM. The terminal prints a period. The user then enters

KJOB

The computer may respond with the message

CONFIRM

If it does, the user then enters

K

The computer prints two lines indicating the amount of processing time used.

The terminal sign-off procedure is less complicated on the HP and IBM systems. The HP termination command is

BYE

The computer responds

0015 MINUTES OF TERMINAL TIME

On the IBM system, the termination command is

OFF

The computer prints several lines of preprogrammed information, such as the time at which the user is signing off and the date.

AN INTRODUCTORY PROGRAM

Like the English language, BASIC must be used in accordance with certain rules and procedures. The rules and procedures that must be considered when writing a BASIC program are explained and used in illustrations throughout the appendix. For example, the BASIC program in Illustration B-2 calculates and prints the squares of certain numbers. It shows many features of the BASIC language. Illustration B-3 is a flowchart of the program.

As indicated by the flowchart, this program reads a number (READ statement). The number comes from the DATA statement. It is stored in a location called N. The program then tests to determine if the value of N is greater than 500 (IF statement). If the value of N is greater than 500, the computer will go to statement 90. Program execution will be terminated (END statement).

APPENDIX B: BASIC PROGRAMMING

```
10 REM THE READING AND SQUARING OF CERTAIN NUMBERS
20 READ N
30 DATA 50,100,150,200,250,300,350,400,450,500,550
40 IF N > 500 THEN 90
50 LET S = N↑2
60 LET A$ = "THE SQUARE OF"
70 PRINT A$;N;"IS";S
80 GO TO 20
90 END
```

ILLUSTRATION B-2   A BASIC program

If the value of N is less than or equal to 500, the computer will square the number (first LET statement). It will then print the number (i.e., the value of N) and its square (PRINT statement). The computer will then

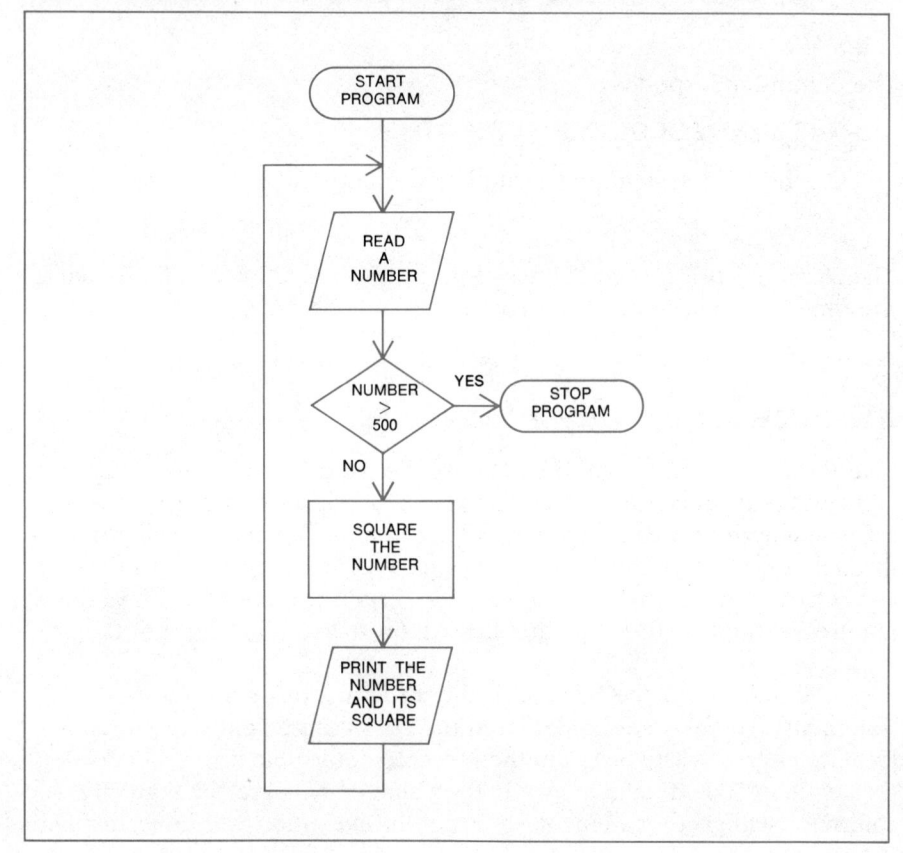

ILLUSTRATION B-3   Flowchart of the BASIC program in Illustration B-2

return to statement 20 (as directed to do by the GO TO statement) and start the process over again.

Statement 10 (REM statement) is a comment explaining what the program does, for the benefit of anyone reading the program statements. Statement 90 (END statement) tells the BASIC compiler that there are no more program statements after statement 90.

○ PROGRAM STATEMENT NUMBERS AND LENGTH

Program Statement Numbers

As shown in Illustration B-2, each statement in a BASIC program must be preceded by a statement number. (A *statement number* is sometimes referred to as a *line number*.) The number can be from 1 through 5 numerical characters in length. Successive statements do not have to be numbered sequentially. (The authors suggest that statement numbers be multiples of 10 so that up to nine additional statements can be inserted between two statements if necessary.) Embedded blanks in a statement number will be ignored by the BASIC compiler.

The magnitude of a statement number, relative to the magnitude of other statement numbers in the program, determines the order in which the program statements will be arranged in storage. The compiler arranges all of the statements into ascending order according to the magnitude of the statement numbers (regardless of the order in which they were entered into the computer). Thus, the statement assigned the smallest statement number will be the first statement in the program executed; the statement assigned the largest statement number will be the last statement in the program executed. (The authors suggest that entering statements in the order in which the computer should execute them is a good programming practice.)

If two statements in a program have the same statement number, the compiler replaces the first statement with the second statement. The advantage of this capability is that statements can be corrected while entering the program. As noted above, a previously entered statement can be deleted from the program by typing only the statement number assigned to that statement and pressing the RETURN key.

Program Statement Length

The maximum possible length of a statement is determined by the number of characters per line that the terminal will accept. A statement cannot occupy more than one print line. From the terminals in common use today, the maximum length of a statement varies from 40 to 120 characters.

The use of blanks within a statement is optional. For example, statement 80 in Illustration B-2 could have been written GOTO20. When used, blanks generally help to improve readability.

CONSTANTS AND VARIABLES

Constants

Constants are values that are fixed in a BASIC program; they cannot be changed during execution of the program. There are two types of constants: numbers and character strings.

Numbers. BASIC permits the use of three types of representations for numbers. These are:

1. *Integer numbers*—Numbers that have no decimal point and no fractional part. For example: 1, 437, and 69643.
2. *Real numbers*—Numbers that have a decimal point and may have a fractional part. For example: 1.03, 40., and 0.43992.
3. *Exponential numbers*—Numbers that are expressed in what is sometimes called scientific notation. This type of representation is most often used for very large or very small numbers. For example: 4.639412E+03, −8.47693E+04, and 3.921146E−04.

Certain rules about the use of numbers must be followed.

1. A positive number can be preceded by a plus sign.
2. If a number is negative, it must be preceded by a minus sign.
3. A number cannot contain embedded commas.
4. A number can be from 1 through 15 digits in length. The maximum number of digits is dependent upon the computer used.

The minus or plus sign, if present, is accepted by the BASIC compiler as an allowable additional character. It is not counted in determining the length of the number.

The following examples are valid integer numbers:

1
150
+16777215
0
−10
−16777215

The following examples are invalid integer numbers:

15.   (contains a decimal point)
4362−   (minus sign positioned incorrectly)
9,310   (contains an embedded comma)

The following examples are valid real numbers:

+.36
2647.19
0.
−.58
−.1478
−9327.65

The following examples are invalid real numbers:

73446   (no decimal point)
6742.12−   (minus sign positioned incorrectly)
1,983.17   (contains an embedded comma)

There are instances when a value exceeds the allowable magnitude of a real number. This problem can be handled through the use of the exponential form of representation of a number.

When the exponential form is used, a decimal exponent is attached to the real number. The exponent is composed of the character E followed by a signed or an unsigned 1- or 2-character integer number. If the 1- or 2-character integer number is unsigned, it is assumed to be positive by the BASIC compiler. The decimal exponent causes the computer to multiply the number by 10 raised to the power signified by the signed or unsigned 1- or 2-character integer number. The allowable magnitude of an exponential number varies with the computer used.

The following examples are valid exponential numbers:

5.0E0	(equivalent:	$5.0*10^0$)	= 5.0
250.34E05	(equivalent:	$250.34*10^5$)	= 25034000.
250.34E+05	(equivalent:	$250.34*10^5$)	= 25034000.
250.34E5	(equivalent:	$250.34*10^5$)	= 25034000.
−2195.63E15	(equivalent:	$-2195.63*10^{15}$)	= −2195630000000000000.
7.1E−3	(equivalent:	$7.1*10^{-3}$)	= .0071
890.75E−08	(equivalent:	$890.75*10^{-8}$)	= .0000089075
890.75E−8	(equivalent:	$890.75*10^{-8}$)	= .0000089075
−6437.19E−12	(equivalent:	$-6437.19*10^{-12}$)	= .00000000643719

The following examples are invalid exponential numbers:

7534.52E   (signed or unsigned 1- or 2-character integer number after the character E is missing)

315.2E1.4 (the 1- or 2-character number following the character E must be an integer)

Character strings. A character string is any combination of alphabetic characters (A–Z), numeric characters (0–9), and special characters (nonalphabetic and nonnumeric characters) enclosed in quotation marks.* The maximum number of characters that a character string can contain depends upon the computer being used.** There are two character strings in the program in Illustration B-2. The first is "THE SQUARE OF". The second is "IS".

Variables

A *numeric variable name* represents a number that is either (1) externally supplied to the computer prior to or during execution of the program, or (2) internally calculated by the computer during execution of the program. A *string variable name* represents a character string that is either (1) externally supplied to the computer prior to or during the execution of the program, or (2) assigned to a string variable name during execution of the program. In both instances, the name is called "variable" because the number or character string represented by the name may be changed one or more times during execution of the program. However, each numeric variable name and each string variable name can represent only one number or one character string at a time. Which numeric variable name and which string variable name will represent which numbers and strings is at the discretion of the programmer. (A numeric variable name or a string variable name is sometimes referred to as a *simple variable*.)

A variable name representing a number is composed of either a single alphabetic character or a single alphabetic character followed by a single numeric character. No special characters (e.g., +, *, &) can be used in a variable name.

The following examples are valid numeric variable names:

A
Q
B1
R7

---

*Some BASIC compilers do not require quotation marks around character strings that begin with alphabetic characters.
**When IBM's VS BASIC is used, the default length for character strings is 18. The maximum length of a character string is 255 characters.

The following examples are invalid numeric variable names:

AB   (can contain only one alphabetic character)
1A   (must begin with an alphabetic character)
Z50   (can contain a maximum of two characters)
A&   (cannot contain a special character)

A variable name representing a character string is composed of a single alphabetic character followed by a dollar sign.*

The following examples are valid string variable names:

A$
C$
Z$

The following examples are invalid string variable names:

A3   (must end with a $)
1A   (must begin with an alphabetic character)

THE LET STATEMENT

The assignment, or LET, statement is used to give (assign) a value to a variable. There are two types of assignment statements in BASIC: arithmetic and character string. The arithmetic assignment statement is concerned with arithmetic computation and the assignment of a previously determined value to a numeric variable name. The character-string assignment statement deals with the assignment of a character string to a string variable name. The BASIC keyword LET is used in both types of assignment statements.

General Considerations of the Arithmetic Assignment Statement

The general form of the LET statement as used for arithmetic assignments is shown in Illustration B-4. This assignment statement is the means by which: (1) computations involving exponentiation, multiplication, division, addition, and subtraction are performed, and (2) the final result is assigned to a variable name. It is also the means by which the value of a constant or another variable name can be assigned to a variable name.

---

*Some BASIC compilers allow a 0 or a 1 to follow the alphabetic character and precede the dollar sign in a string variable name.

APPENDIX B: BASIC PROGRAMMING

> sn LET vn = ae
>
> where:
>
> sn represents an unsigned 1 through 5 digit integer **statement** *number*.
>
> LET is a BASIC keyword that distinguishes this statement from the other kinds of statements in the program. (This keyword can be omitted when certain BASIC compilers are used.)
>
> vn represents a *variable name*.
>
> = is a special character used here as required in the BASIC language.
>
> ae represents an *arithmetic expression* that can be composed of one or more numbers, numeric variable names, functions, parentheses, and arithmetic operators.

ILLUSTRATION B-4   General form of the arithmetic assignment statement

With respect to both the general appearance and the functioning of the arithmetic operators, the arithmetic assignment statement is similar to an algebraic equation. However, two distinct factors must be considered when using an arithmetic assignment statement in a BASIC program.

1. There must be one and only one variable name on the left side of the equal sign. Thus, the following statements are incorrect. Statement 10 contains two variable names separated by a plus sign on the left of the equal sign. Statement 20 is similar. Statement 30 contains the number 5 where one variable name is required.

   ```
   10 LET A+B = X↑2+25
   20 LET I+6 = A−C+10
   30 LET 5 = J+1
   ```

2. The variable name on the left side of the equal sign is "assigned" the value of the result of the solution of the expression on the right side of the equal sign. In BASIC, the equal sign means that the value of the expression on the right side of the equal sign is assigned to the variable name on the left side of the equal sign. Thus, in the following illustrations, the number 15 is assigned to A; the sum of C and 12.5 is assigned to B; and the result of K divided by J is assigned to K. (Note that the same variable name can be used on both sides of the equal sign.)

   ```
   10 LET A = 15
   20 LET B = C+12.5
   30 LET K = K/J
   ```

APPENDIX B: BASIC PROGRAMMING

Arithmetic Expressions

An arithmetic expression can be composed of one or more operands. It usually contains one or more arithmetic operators. It may also contain one or more sets of parentheses. An operand may be either a constant or a numeric variable name. Operands must be separated by one or more arithmetic operators. An arithmetic operator is a symbol that tells the computer which arithmetic operation to perform on the two values that it separates. The following symbols are used as arithmetic operators:

Symbol*	Meaning
↑ or **	Exponentiation
*	Multiplication
/	Division
+	Addition
−	Subtraction

The result of an arithmetic expression must always be a number; that is, arithmetic operators cannot be used when dealing with character strings.

An arithmetic expression is constructed according to the following rules.

1. An arithmetic expression can be composed of a single constant or numeric variable name. Thus, the arithmetic expressions in the following arithmetic assignment statements are correct:

   ```
   10 LET M = N
   20 LET T = R
   30 LET I = 10
   40 LET X = 2.5
   ```

2. An arithmetic expression can be composed of one or more constants, one or more numeric variable names, or a mixture of constants and numeric variable names. If two constants or numeric variable names appear on the right-hand side of the equal sign, arithmetic operators must be used to separate them. Thus, the arithmetic expressions in the following arithmetic assignment statements are correct:

   ```
   10 LET M = I+N*3
   20 LET K = I/2+N
   30 LET F = T+Y
   ```

---

*Exponentiation can be represented by the arithmetic operator ↑ and/or the arithmetic operator **. The reader should refer to the BASIC manual for the computer system available to determine which arithmetic operator should be used.

3. A variable name cannot be used on the right-hand side of an arithmetic expression until it has been "defined" in the program. That is, a value must be assigned to a variable name prior to its use in an arithmetic expression. Thus, the following series of statements is correct:

    10 LET P = .25
    20 LET T = P*.05

If no value had been assigned to the variable name P, then the computer would not have known what number to multiply by the constant .05 when it got to statement 20. In the following series of statements, since no value is assigned to the variable name M, the computer will not know what value to add to K when it reaches statement 20. An error will occur.

    10 LET K = 5
    20 LET I = K+M

4. Two or more arithmetic operators cannot appear next to each other in an arithmetic expression. One or more sets of parentheses must be used to separate them. Thus, the arrangement of the division symbol and the minus sign in the following statement is incorrect:

    10 LET J = K/−5

Rather, the statement should be written as follows:

    10 LET J = K/(−5)

5. One or more sets of parentheses can be used in arithmetic expressions. The programmer has the option of enclosing in parentheses any combination of operands and operators in an arithmetic expression. When a set of parentheses is used, the operation enclosed in parentheses is performed prior to any operations not enclosed in parentheses. For example:

    10 LET A = (B*2) − (Y−T)

The operation within the set of parentheses (Y−T) will be performed prior to the multiplication operation (B*2) and the subtraction of the result of Y−T outside the parentheses.

If more than one set of parentheses is used in an arithmetic expression, the computer will perform from left to right, the operations within each set of parentheses first. It will not perform operations outside the parentheses until after all operations within the parentheses are complete. For example:

    20 LET T = 5.+(C*2.3)/(T+X)*(E↑2)

The operation within the leftmost set of parentheses (C*2.3) will be performed first; the operation within the middle set of parentheses (T+X) will be performed next; and the operation within the rightmost set of parentheses (E↑2) will be performed last. The computer will then perform the rest of the operations according to rule 6 below.

If one or more sets of parentheses are enclosed within another set of parentheses, the computer will perform the operation within each set of parentheses beginning with the innermost set of parentheses and moving to the outermost set of parentheses. For example:

30 LET K = ((7+M↑A)−(K*2))↑3

The operations within the inner leftmost set of parentheses (7+M↑A) will be performed first. The operation within the inner rightmost set of parentheses (K*2) will be performed next. The result of the inner rightmost set of parentheses will then be subtracted from the result of the inner leftmost set of parentheses (7+M↑A)−(K*2). Finally, this result will be raised to the third power.

6. The order of performance of the various operations in an arithmetic expression depends upon the types of arithmetic operations involved. The order of evaluation, subject to the order defined by any sets of parentheses, is as follows:

   a. All exponentiations (↑ and/or **) are performed first.
   b. All multiplications (*) and divisions (/) are performed next.
   c. Finally all additions (+) and subtractions (−) are performed.

If we remove all the parentheses from the previous example, we have:

30 LET K = 7+M↑A−K*2↑3

When this expression is evaluated, it will give a very different result than the original statement did. First M↑A is evaluated; then 2↑3. Then the result of 2↑3 is multiplied by K, and the result of M↑A is added to 7. Finally, the result of K*2↑3 is subtracted from the result of 7+M↑A. The major differences between the sequences of evaluation are: (1) K is multiplied by the result of (2↑3) instead of the result of (K*2) being raised to the third power; and (2) the result of K*2↑3 instead of the result of (K*2)↑3 is subtracted from the result 7+M↑A.

If the operators within an arithmetic expression are of the same level, such as two exponentiation operations, or multiplication and division, or addition and subtraction, execution of the operations is from left to right.

Consider the arithmetic assignment statement:

10 LET T = .5*C−P/S+E↑3

The operand E↑3 is evaluated first since this is the highest-priority operation. Then .5*C is evaluated. Next, the operand P/S is evaluated. (Note that since * and / are at the same level, these operations are performed left to right.) Next, the result of P/S is subtracted from the result of .5*C. Finally, the result of the subtraction is added to the result of E↑3.

A more complex arithmetic assignment statement is:

20 LET Y = ((.4*A)−2.+B)/(A+B−B↑2)

The operand within the leftmost set of parentheses (.4*A) is evaluated first. The constant 2. is subtracted from the result, and the value of B is then added to the result of these operations. Next the operations within the rightmost set of parentheses are performed. The operand B↑2 is evaluated first. Then the operand A+B is evaluated. The result of B↑2 is subtracted from the result of A+B. Finally, the overall result of the computations within the leftmost set of parentheses is divided by the overall result of the computations within the rightmost set of parentheses. The result of this division is assigned to Y.

In summary, the computer performs arithmetic operations from left to right, by the level of the operators, subject to the placement of parentheses.

The Multiple Arithmetic Assignment Statement

It is sometimes desirable to assign the same value to several variable names. This can be done by using several arithmetic assignment statements. For example, to assign the result of the arithmetic expression B + C + 10 to the numeric variable names A, X, Y, and Z, one method is to write the following statements:

```
10 LET A = B + C + 10
20 LET X = A
30 LET Y = A
40 LET Z = A
```

A more efficient programming method, however, is to use the multiple arithmetic assignment statement. Then, one statement to accomplish the above can be written as follows:

```
10 LET X = Y = Z = A = B + C + 10
```

The Assignment of a Character String

The LET statement can also be used to assign a character-string value to a string variable name. For example:

    10 LET A$ = "GROSS PROFIT"
    20 LET B$ = Z$

The character string GROSS PROFIT will be assigned to the string variable A$. The character string assigned to the string variable Z$ will be assigned to the string variable B$.

Since a character string can only be composed of characters, neither a character string nor a string variable name can be used with arithmetic operators. Thus, the following illustration makes no sense and is illegal.

    10 LET A = "5" + Z$ − B

THE PRINT STATEMENT

The results of processing accomplished during execution of a BASIC program can be printed on a user terminal by means of a PRINT statement. This statement also allows the writer of the BASIC program to determine the format (i.e., what is printed where) of a line of output. Illustration B-5 shows the general form of this statement.

A specific PRINT statement can take any of several forms, depending on the format desired for the output. For example, to skip a line on the terminal, a PRINT statement with no "list" should be used. This form is often called the *blank PRINT*.

    10 PRINT

ILLUSTRATION B-5 General form of the PRINT statement

---

                    sn PRINT list

where:
- *sn* represents an unsigned 1 through 5 digit integer *statement number*.
- PRINT is a BASIC keyword that distinguishes this statement from the other kinds of statements in the program.
- *list* represents one or more variable names, arithmetic expressions, and/or character strings separated by commas or semicolons and, if desired, one or more spaces.

To skip more than one line, the blank PRINT statement must be re-executed, or another blank PRINT statement executed, for each additional line. For example, to skip three lines, three blank PRINT statements should be written as shown below.

    10 PRINT
    20 PRINT
    30 PRINT

Printing Numbers

Another form of the PRINT statement can be used to print the numbers assigned to one or more numeric variable names. It is also possible to specify arithmetic computations in the "list" portion of a PRINT statement. Examples of both are shown in the following program. Note that the rules for performing the computations are the same as those applied in the arithmetic assignment statement with regard to the position and use of operators and parentheses.

    10 LET A = 3
    20 LET B = 18
    30 LET C = 50
    40 PRINT A
    50 PRINT
    60 PRINT B,C,6*A+100
    70 END

The number assigned to the variable name A, which is 3, will be printed on the first line. The computer will skip a line. Then the numbers assigned to the variable names B and C, which are 18 and 50 respectively, and the result of the arithmetic expression 6*A+100 will be printed on the next line.

Commas and semicolons are used to control the spacing of the values printed on a line of output.* On some terminals, the print line is divided into four standard print fields, each 18 spaces wide. Comma tabs are set by the computer every 18 spaces—at print positions 1, 19, 37, and 55. Each comma tab marks the start of a print field. After the computer prints a value in a print field, it moves to the next print field to print the next value (even if the first field was not entirely filled).

---

*The number and length of the standard print fields vary among computers. Each reader should see the BASIC manual for the available version of BASIC to determine the number and length of the standard print fields.

APPENDIX B: BASIC PROGRAMMING

```
10 LET Z = 100
20 LET B = 43.2
30 LET C = 2000.
40 LET D = -17
50 PRINT Z,B,C,D
60 END
```

In the program above, the use of commas to separate the variable names in the PRINT statement causes the number assigned to Z, which is 100, to be printed in print positions 2 through 4; the number assigned to B, which is 43.2, to be printed in print positions 20 through 23; the number assigned to C, which is 2000., to be printed in print positions 38 through 42; and the number assigned to D, which is -17, to be printed in print positions 55 through 57.

In this illustration, the printing of all of the numbers, except the one assigned to the numeric variable name D, begins in the second print position of the field. The first print position of each field is reserved for the number's arithmetic sign ($+$ or $-$). If the number is positive, the plus sign need not be printed, however. So the first print position of the field is blank. (This was the case for the numbers printed in the first, second, and third fields in the illustration.) If the number is negative, the minus sign is printed in the first print position of the field. (This was the case for the number printed in the fourth field of the illustration.)

In many situations it is desirable to print more than four numbers on a line. This can be accomplished by using semicolons rather than commas to separate the variable names in a PRINT statement. The use of a semicolon instead of a comma causes the computer to reduce the size of the print field from the standard print field length to some smaller size. The actual length of each print field depends upon the number of characters in the value being printed and the version of BASIC being used. The following table shows the spacing commonly provided when semicolons are used.

Number of Digits to Be Printed	Width of Print Field in Spaces
1 to 4	6
5 to 7	9
8 to 10	12
11 to 13	15

The computer uses the first print position of each print field for the number's arithmetic sign. If semicolons were used instead of commas to separate the variable names in the PRINT statement of the above program, the output would appear as follows. The computer would print the number

APPENDIX B: BASIC PROGRAMMING

assigned to Z, which is 100, in print positions 2 through 4; the number assigned to B, which is 43.2, in positions 8 through 11; the number assigned to C, which is 2000., in positions 14 through 18; and the number assigned to D, which is −17, in positions 22 through 24. If there are more numbers to be printed on a line than there are spaces available within the line, the computer continues printing the numbers on the next line.

Normally, the terminal carriage advances to the beginning of the next line after the execution of a PRINT statement. To continue printing on the same line later in the program, a comma or semicolon must be placed after the last item in the PRINT statement. For example:

```
40 PRINT A;B;C;D;
50 PRINT Z
60 PRINT P
```

The values of A, B, C, D, and Z will be printed on the same line, assuming that their overall length does not cause the computer to attempt to go beyond the end of the carriage of the terminal. The value of P will be printed on the next line.

Printing Character Strings

There are two situations in which a character string is printed. The first, and most common situation, is the printing of output headings. For example, the following statement will cause the character strings THE SQUARE OF and IS to be printed.

```
60 PRINT "THE SQUARE OF"; N; "IS"; A
```

If there are several headings to be printed, the use of commas to separate the headings causes the computer to use the standard print fields as it does when one or more commas are used to separate several variable names. Thus, in the following illustration, the heading ACCT NO. will be printed in positions 1 through 8; the heading DEPT will be printed in positions 19 through 22; the heading ITEM will be printed in positions 37 through 40; and the heading COST will be printed in positions 55 through 58.

```
10 PRINT "ACCT NO.", "DEPT", "ITEM", "COST"
```

On the other hand, the use of a semicolon between two character strings causes no spacing to occur between the two strings. Thus, the programmer must establish the spacing by placing the desired number of blanks within the quotation marks that enclose each character string. The following illustration shows this point.

10 PRINT "THE VALUE OF A";"   THE VALUE OF B";"   THE VALUE OF C"

In the last two character strings, there are three spaces between the first quotation mark and the letter T of the word THE. When this statement is executed, the first string will be printed, beginning in column 1. The first word (THE) of the second string will appear in column 18—only three spaces after the ending character of the first string. Semicolon tab positions do not apply.

The second type of character-string printing occurs when the character string to be printed has been assigned to a string variable name. For example:

    10 LET A$ = "NUMBER"
    20 PRINT A$

The word NUMBER will be assigned to the string variable name A$. When statement 20 is executed, the word NUMBER will be printed, beginning in column 1.

PRINT Statement Rules

The following rules should be considered when constructing a PRINT statement:

1. A comma separating two items directs the computer to follow standard print field spacing.
2. A semicolon separating two items directs the computer to follow standard print field spacing based upon the number of characters composing the items being printed.
3. Numbers are printed, beginning at the second position of the print field. The first print position is reserved for the arithmetic sign. If a number is positive, no sign is printed; the first position of the print field is blank. If a number is negative, a minus sign is printed in the first position of the print field.
4. Character strings are printed, beginning at the first position of the print field.
5. A print field is used for only one item, even if the item does not occupy all of the available print positions. Unused print positions in a field remain blank.
6. Alphabetic, numeric, and alphanumeric items are left-justified within a print field.
7. If a character string contains more characters than the maximum width of a print field, the computer will use additional print field(s) to print the character string.

8. A comma or semicolon after the last item in a PRINT statement causes the computer to continue printing on the same line if a PRINT statement is executed later in the program.

The TAB Function

One problem may occur when printing output of a BASIC program: The comma and semicolon, due to their predefined field positioning, may not provide a "pretty" printout.

The TAB function is a formatting feature available in many versions of BASIC.* It allows more exact spacing of print fields. For example:

10 PRINT A$; TAB(15); "COST"

The value assigned to the string variable name A$ will be printed. The terminal will be spaced to the print position specified within the set of parentheses immediately following the keyword TAB (print position 15). Then the word COST will be printed. The number within the parentheses is the number of the column in which the first letter of COST will be printed.

In this illustration, the string variable name A$ is followed by a semicolon. If it had been followed by a comma, the terminal would have spaced to print position 19 before detecting the TAB(15) request. The TAB function is ignored if the terminal has passed the specified print position. Therefore, it is best to use the semicolon rather than the comma in PRINT statements where the TAB function is used.

THE END STATEMENT

The END statement instructs the BASIC compiler to terminate compilation of a program. It may be used to cause program execution to terminate. Illustration B-6 shows the general form of the END statement. The END statement must be the last statement in physical sequence in the program. This means the END statement must have the largest statement number. There must be one, and only one, END statement in a BASIC program.

THE READ AND DATA STATEMENTS

In BASIC, data may be entered as an integral part of a program or from a terminal during execution of the program. The LET statement discussed above is one way in which a value to be processed can be entered as an

---

*Each reader should check the BASIC manual for the computer system in use to see if this feature is available.

APPENDIX B: BASIC PROGRAMMING

> sn END
>
> where:
>
> sn represents an unsigned 1 through 5 digit integer *statement number*.
>
> END is a BASIC keyword that distinguishes this statement from the other kinds of statements in the program.

ILLUSTRATION B-6   General form of the END statement

integral part of the program. The following program is an illustrative example. The program computes the total amount that must be paid back on a $1000 loan at 9 percent interest for 10 years.

```
10 REM THE COMPUTATION OF A 10-YEAR INVESTMENT
20 LET P = 1000
30 LET I = 9
40 LET N = 10
50 LET A = P*(1+I/100)↑N
60 PRINT A
70 END
```

The REM statement is simply a comment explaining the function of the program. The first LET statement assigns the number 1000 to the variable name P. The second LET statement assigns 9 to the variable name I. The third LET statement assigns 10 to the variable name N. The last LET statement computes the total amount of the principal and interest at the end of N (10) years and assigns the result to A. The PRINT statement prints that result. The END statement is then executed; this terminates execution of the program.

The following output is printed:

2367.36

If a large amount of data must be processed, the use of the LET statement for data entry becomes cumbersome. For example, to find the total payback amount for several amounts at several rates of interest over several periods of time, either a new program must be written for each set of values, or a LET statement must be used for each new value in the program. One way to overcome this problem is to use READ and DATA statements.

The READ statement causes the reading of data entered in one or more DATA statements as part of the program. Illustration B-7 shows the general form of this statement.

APPENDIX B: BASIC PROGRAMMING

> sn READ list
>
> where:
>
> sn represents an unsigned 1 through 5 digit integer *statement number*.
>
> READ is a BASIC keyword that distinguishes this statement from the other kinds of statements in the program.
>
> list represents one or more variable names separated by commas and, if desired, one or more spaces.

ILLUSTRATION B-7 General form of the READ statement

The following READ statement could take the place of the first three LET statements (20, 30, and 40) in the example program above.

20 READ P,I,N

This statement causes values to be assigned to the variable names P, I, and N.

The values to be assigned to the variable names listed in a READ statement are entered into the program via one or more DATA statements. Illustration B-8 shows the general form of the DATA statement.

The following DATA statement could be used to supply data to be assigned to the numeric variable names listed in the previous READ statement (P, I, and N).

30 DATA 1000,9,10

Each number, from left to right, is assigned to a corresponding variable name in the READ statement. That is, when the READ statement is executed, the number 1000 will be assigned to the variable name P; the number 9 will be assigned to the variable name I; and the number 10 will be assigned to the variable name N.

There can be as many READ and DATA statements as needed in a program. The DATA statements can be located anywhere among the other program statements. The placement of the READ statement(s), naturally, is dependent upon the logic of the program. During compilation of the program, the BASIC compiler places all of the values listed in all of the DATA statements into a combined list. The ordering of the values in the combined list is based on two rules: (1) ascending DATA statement numbers, and (2) the order, from left to right, of the values within each DATA statement. That is, the BASIC compiler takes the values in the first DATA statement and places them at the top of the combined list in order from left to right. Then the compiler goes to the second DATA statement and,

> sn DATA list
>
> where:
>
> sn represents an unsigned 1 through 5 digit integer *statement number*.
>
> DATA is a BASIC keyword that distinguishes this statement from the other kinds of statements in the program.
>
> list represents one or more numbers or character strings separated by commas and, if desired, one or more spaces.

ILLUSTRATION B-8 General form of the DATA statement

again moving from left to right, places the values in the second DATA statement in the combined list. The compiler continues this operation until all of the values in all of the DATA statements are in the combined list.

The following sequences of READ statements are equivalent:

10 READ P
30 READ I   or   10 READ P,I,N
50 READ N

Similarly, the following DATA statements are equivalent:

20 DATA 1000
40 DATA 9   or   20 DATA 1000,9,10
60 DATA 10

So that the computer can keep track of which values have been assigned to variables names, and which ones have not, the BASIC compiler uses a "pointer." This pointer is internal to the compiler. It tells the next value to be assigned when the next READ statement is executed. Initially, this pointer is "pointing" to the first value in the first DATA statement (1000, in our example). Thus, when statement 10 above is executed, the pointer is pointed at the number 1000 in the combined list and that value is assigned to P. The pointer then shifts to point at the number 9 in the combined list. When statement 30 is executed, the value 9 is assigned to I. The pointer then shifts to point at the number 10 in the combined list. When statement 50 is executed, the value 10 is assigned to N.

If the single statement form shown above is used, the computer performs essentially the same operations in assigning the values to P, I, and N. If there are more variable names in the READ statement(s) than values in the DATA statement(s), an error message is printed on the terminal and program execution is terminated. Assume the following statements are the only READ and DATA statements in a program. Execution of the READ statement would cause program termination to occur.

```
10 READ P,I,N,K
20 DATA 1000,5,10
```

The Reading of a Character String

The READ statement, in conjunction with the DATA statement, can be used to assign a character string to a string variable name. For example:

```
10 READ A$,X,B$,C$
20 DATA "NET PAY", 243.25, "1 JAN.", "1981"
```

The character string NET PAY will be assigned to the string variable name A$; the number 243.25 will be assigned to the numeric variable name X; the character string 1 JAN. will be assigned to the string variable name B$; and the character string 1981 will be assigned to the string variable name C$.

As indicated in the illustration, both string variable names and numeric variable names can be listed in a READ statement. Of course, the type of data listed in the DATA statement must match the corresponding variable name in the READ statement.

Examples of the READ and DATA Statements

The following program illustrates the use of READ and DATA statements in place of LET statements to enter values for investment computation.

```
10 REM THE COMPUTATION OF A 10-YEAR INVESTMENT
20 READ P,I,N
30 DATA 1000,9,10
40 LET A = P*(1+I/100)↑N
50 PRINT A
60 END
```

The program below reads the character strings SMITH and 6A74F and the numbers 123 and 64.3. It assigns them to the string variable names J$ and P$ and the numeric variable names F and G, respectively.

```
10 REM THIS PROGRAM READS TWO CHARACTER STRINGS
20 REM AND TWO NUMBERS AND PRINTS THEM OUT
30 READ J$,P$,F,G
40 DATA "SMITH","6A74F",123,64.3
50 PRINT J$,P$,F,G
60 END
```

The two character strings and the two numbers are printed on the terminal as follows:

```
SMITH     6A74F     123     64.3
```

THE RESTORE STATEMENT

In certain instances, it is necessary to re-read data within a program. This requirement can be accommodated via the RESTORE statement. The execution of this statement causes the pointer used by the BASIC compiler to be moved back to the beginning of the combined list of numbers and/or character strings (the first number or character string in the DATA statement with the smallest statement number), regardless of where the pointer is currently located in the combined list. The RESTORE statement is generally used when it is necessary to perform several types of calculations on the same numbers, or to reuse character strings. Illustration B-9 shows the general form of this statement.

The first READ statement below causes the computer to assign the numbers 35.2, 91, and 15 to the numeric variable names A, B, and C, respectively. Execution of the RESTORE statement causes the pointer to be moved back to the beginning of the list of values in the DATA statement. It points to the number 35.2. Thus, when the second READ statement is executed, the numbers 35.2, 91, and 15 are assigned to the numeric variable names D, E, and F, respectively.

```
10 READ A,B,C
20 DATA 35.2,91,15
30 RESTORE
40 READ D,E,F
```

THE INPUT STATEMENT

Thus far, two methods of assigning values to variable names have been discussed—the LET statement and the READ and DATA statements. A third method of assigning values to variable names is to use the INPUT statement. The distinction between the INPUT statement and the LET and READ statements is that data is entered during the execution of the program, rather than as an integral part of the program itself. Illustration B-10 shows the general form of this statement.

ILLUSTRATION B-9 General form of the RESTORE statement

>   sn RESTORE
> where:
>   sn represents an unsigned 1 through 5 digit integer *statement number*.
>   RESTORE is a BASIC keyword that distinguishes this statement from the other kinds of statements in the program.

> **sn INPUT list**
>
> where:
>
>   **sn** represents an unsigned 1 through 5 digit integer *s*tatement *n*umber.
>
>   **INPUT** is a BASIC keyword that distinguishes this statement from the other kinds of statements in the program.
>
>   **list** represents one or more variable names separated by commas and, if desired, one or more spaces.

ILLUSTRATION B-10 General form of the INPUT statement

The INPUT statement causes the computer, during execution of the program, to print a question mark on the terminal. The user at the terminal responds by typing (on the same line) the data values to be processed. The values must be separated by commas. After the values have been entered, the user presses the RETURN (or ENTER) key. The computer then assigns the entered values to the variable names listed in the INPUT statement and proceeds with the execution of the program.

As an example, consider the following program.

```
10 REM HOW THE INPUT STATEMENT WORKS
20 PRINT "ENTER X,Y,Z TO BE ADDED"
30 INPUT X,Y,Z
40 LET S = X+Y+Z
50 PRINT "THE SUM OF";X;Y;"AND";Z;"IS";S
60 END
```

When this program is executed, the computer first prints ENTER X,Y,Z TO BE ADDED. The computer then executes the INPUT statement, which causes it to print a question mark. The user at the terminal then enters, on the same line, the values to be assigned to X, Y, and Z. Assuming the values are 45.2, 25, and 15, the printing on the terminal appears as follows:

    ENTER X,Y,Z TO BE ADDED
    ? 45.2,25,15

After the user presses the RETURN (or ENTER) key, the number 45.2 is assigned to the numeric variable name X; the number 25 is assigned to the numeric variable name Y; and the number 15 is assigned to the numeric variable name Z. The computer then adds the three numbers and prints the result as follows:

    THE SUM OF 45.2   25   AND 15   IS 85.2

The following program shows how a previous example could be modified to use the INPUT statement in place of READ and DATA statements.

```
10 REM THE COMPUTATION OF A 10-YEAR INVESTMENT
20 INPUT P,I,N
30 LET A = P*(1+I/100)↑N
40 PRINT A
50 END
```

The following lines are printed on the terminal when the program is run.

```
? 1000,9,10
2367.36
```

Like the READ statement, the INPUT statement can be used to assign a character string to a string variable name. The rules that must be observed in the assignment of a character string using a READ statement must also be observed in the assignment of a character string using an INPUT statement. For example, assume the following INPUT statement is included in a program being executed:

10 INPUT A$,X,B$,C$

Further assume the input to the computer is typed as follows:

"NET PAY",243.25,"1 JAN.","1981"

The character string NET PAY will be assigned to the string variable name A$; the number 243.25 will be assigned to the numeric variable name X; the character string 1 JAN. will be assigned to the string variable name B$; and the character string 1981 will be assigned to the string variable name C$.

○ THE REM STATEMENT

The REM statement can be used to explain an overall BASIC program and/or a specific part of a program. It can also be used to describe the data represented by particular variable names. Illustration B-11 shows the general form of the REM statement.

If, because of its length, a remark, or comment, is continued on one or more additional lines, the keyword REM must be the first word of each additional line. Blanks can be included in a REM statement as desired to improve readability.

The REM statement is a nonexecutable statement; that is, it neither is processed by the BASIC compiler (translated into machine language) nor

> sn REM
>
> where:
>
> sn represents an unsigned 1 through 5 digit integer *statement number.*
>
> REM is a BASIC keyword that distinguishes this statement from the other kinds of statements in the program.

ILLUSTRATION B-11   General form of the REM statement

affects the execution of the BASIC program. Rather, it is simply printed verbatim along with other BASIC statements in the source-program listing.

THE STOP STATEMENT

The STOP statement instructs the computer to terminate execution of a program. Illustration B-12 shows the general form of this statement.

A STOP statement may be located anywhere in a program prior to the END statement. The basic consideration in deciding specifically where to place a STOP statement in a program is that it must be located at a logical end of the program. If there is more than one logical end to a program, a STOP statement should be located at each logical end. The STOP statement is not necessary if there is only one logical end to the program, but it may be used just prior to the END statement if desired.

CONTROL STATEMENTS

There are three basic groups of program control statements. One group, composed of the STOP and END statements, has been discussed. The second group is concerned with going to, or **branching** to, a specific program statement. It includes the GO TO, IF-THEN, and ON-GO TO state-

ILLUSTRATION B-12   General form of the STOP statement

> sn STOP
>
> where:
>
> sn represents an unsigned 1 through 5 digit integer *statement number.*
>
> STOP is a BASIC keyword that distinguishes this statement from the other kinds of statements in the program.

APPENDIX B: BASIC PROGRAMMING

ments. The third group of statements is concerned with executing the same program statement(s) a specified number of times, or *looping*, before continuing the normal sequence of instruction execution. The FOR-TO and NEXT statements are in this group.

The GO TO Statement

The GO TO statement is sometimes referred to as an "unconditional" or "simple" GO TO. It causes the computer to branch (go) to an executable program statement other than the statement immediately following the GO TO statement. The statement that the computer branches to may either precede or follow the GO TO statement. Illustration B-13 shows the general form of this statement.

The GO TO statement

20 GO TO 50

causes the computer to branch to statement 50.

The IF-THEN Statement

The IF-THEN statement directs the computer to make a decision regarding the truth or falseness of a relationship between two expressions. The expressions may take the form of variables (either numeric or string), constants, arithmetic expressions that must be evaluated (e.g., $B \uparrow 2$ or $(A+B)/C$), or some combination thereof. If the relationship is true, the computer will branch to a specified statement in the program. If the relationship is false, the computer will execute the statement immediately following the IF-THEN statement. Illustration B-14 shows the general form of this statement. The way the statement operates is shown in Illustration B-15.

ILLUSTRATION B-13 General form of the GO TO statement

sn GO TO sn

where:
- sn represents an unsigned 1 through 5 digit integer *statement number*.
- GO TO are BASIC keywords that distinguish this statement from the other kinds of statements in the program.
- sn represents the *statement number* of the statement to which a branch will be made.

APPENDIX B: BASIC PROGRAMMING

> sn IF e ro e THEN sn
>
> where:
>
> sn represents an unsigned 1 through 5 digit integer *statement number*.
>
> IF is a BASIC keyword that distinguishes this statement from the other kinds of statements in the program.
>
> e represents an *expression* or *value*.
>
> ro represents a *relational operator*.
>
> e represents an *expression* or *value*.
>
> THEN is a BASIC keyword that distinguishes this statement from the other kinds of statements in the program.
>
> sn represents the *statement number* of the statement to which the computer will branch if the specified relationship between the two expressions or values is *true*.

ILLUSTRATION B-14   General form of the IF-THEN statement

The relational operator is a symbol that tells what relationship between two expressions or values is being tested for. There are six relational operators. Each is shown, accompanied by its mathematical meaning, below.

Symbol*	Meaning
$>$	Greater than
$>=$ or $\geq$	Greater than or equal to
$<$	Less than
$<=$ or $\leq$	Less than or equal to
$=$	Equal to
$<>$ or $\neq$	Not equal to

The IF-THEN statement in the following illustration causes the computer to evaluate the expressions A and 50. If the value assigned to A is greater than 50, the computer will branch to statement 40. If the value of A is 50 or less, the computer will execute the statement following the IF-THEN statement (the PRINT statement).

```
20 IF A > 50 THEN 40
30 PRINT A
40 LET C = B/A
```

*Where alternatives are shown, which symbol is valid depends on the BASIC compiler used.

APPENDIX B: BASIC PROGRAMMING

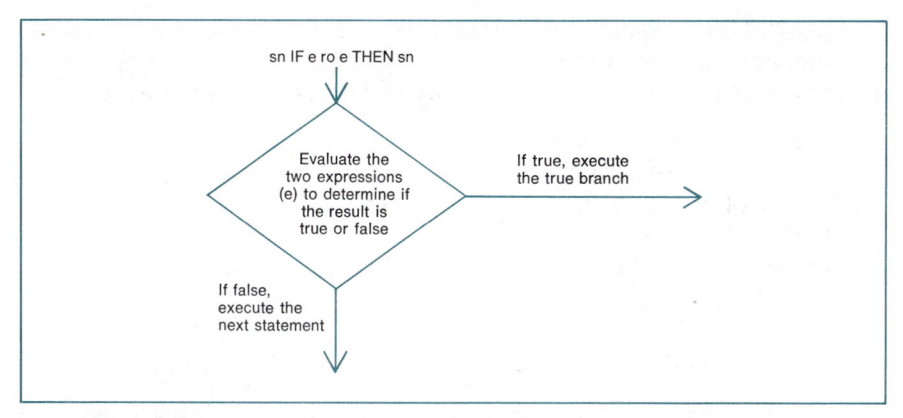

```
                    sn IF e ro e THEN sn
                            │
                            ▼
          ┌─────────────────────────┐
          │     Evaluate the        │      If true, execute
          │     two expressions     │      the true branch
          │     (e) to determine if ├────────────────────────▶
          │     the result is       │
          │     true or false       │
          └─────────────────────────┘
   If false,           │
   execute the         │
   next statement      │
                       ▼
```

ILLUSTRATION B-15   Logic of the IF-THEN statement

In the following illustration, if the result of the arithmetic expression $B\uparrow 2$ is less than the result of the arithmetic expression $X*Z$, the computer will branch to statement 70. If the result of the arithmetic expression $B\uparrow 2$ is equal to or greater than the result of the arithmetic expression $X*Z$, the computer will execute statement 20 (the LET statement).

    10 IF B↑2 < X*Z THEN 70
    20 LET B = X*Z

An IF-THEN statement also can be used to make a comparison between character strings. If a character-string constant is used, it must be enclosed in quotation marks. The comparision begins with the leftmost character of each string and moves from left to right. In general, one word is "less than" another word if it would appear prior to the other word in a dictionary. That is, BAT is "less than" CAT, and WINDOW is "greater than" HOUSE. If character strings of different lengths compare equally up to the end of the shorter of the two strings, the shorter string is "less than" the other, longer string. The BASIC compiler adds to the shorter character string the number of blanks necessary to equal the length of the longer character string, and a blank is "less than" any other character.

    10 IF A$ > X$ THEN 60
    20 IF M$ = "FRESHMAN" THEN 70

In statement 10, the character string assigned to the string variable name A$ is compared with the character string assigned to the string variable name X$. In statement 20, the character string assigned to the string variable name M$ is compared with the character string FRESHMAN.

In the following program, the numeric variable name N is assigned the value 95 in statement 10. The relationship N >= 100 in the IF is false

APPENDIX B: BASIC PROGRAMMING

so statement 30 is executed next. Then statement 40 is executed. It causes the computer to branch to statement 60. (If the relationship tested for in the IF statement had been true, statement 50 would have been executed.)

```
10 LET N = 95
20 IF N >= 100 THEN 50
30 PRINT N; "IS NOT GREATER THAN 100"
40 GO TO 60
50 PRINT N; "IS GREATER THAN OR EQUAL TO 100"
60 END
```

The ON-GO TO Statement

The ON-GO TO statement is sometimes referred to as a "computed" GO TO. It causes the computer to branch to a statement on the basis of the value of an arithmetic expression. The statement branched to may either precede or follow the ON-GO TO statement. Illustration B-16 shows the general form of this statement. On some computer systems, the format of this statement is reversed, and it it known as the GO TO-ON statement. Still other systems have neither form of the statement.*

The ON-GO TO statement is used in situations where it is desirable to branch to one of several statements in a program, based on the value of an arithmetic expression or a variable name. For example, assume that it is desired to process certain data of a large number of armed service personnel. The particular branch of service of which a serviceman is a member determines what character string is to be printed as part of the output. The number 1 indicates the serviceman is a member of the army; the

---

*Each reader should check the BASIC manual for the computer system in use concerning the use of this statement.

ILLUSTRATION B-16   General form of the ON-GO TO statement

> sn ON ae GO TO sn(s)
>
> where:
>
> sn represents an unsigned 1 through 5 digit integer *statement number*.
>
> ON is a BASIC keyword that distinguishes this statement from the other kinds of statements in the program.
>
> ae represents an *arithmetic expression*.
>
> GO TO are BASIC keywords.
>
> sn(s) represents one or more *statement numbers*.

number 2 indicates he is a member of the air force; the number 3 indicates he is a member of the marines; and the number 4 indicates he is a member of the navy. The number 5 is a "dummy"; it serves as a special end-of-file indicator.

```
10 REM READ CODES AND NAMES AND PRINT
20 REM NAME, RANK, NUMBER, AND BRANCH OF
30 REM SERVICE
40 READ A, B$, C, D$
50 ON A GO TO 60, 80, 100, 120, 200
60 PRINT "ARMY"
70 GO TO 130
80 PRINT "AIR FORCE"
90 GO TO 130
100 PRINT "NAVY"
110 GO TO 130
120 PRINT "MARINE"
130 PRINT B$, D$; C
140 PRINT
150 GO TO 40
160 DATA 2, "JAMES T. KIRK", 49031010, "CAPTAIN"
170 DATA 1, "B. NAPOLEON", 930411, "GENERAL"
180 DATA 4, "S. KING", 332110, "MAJOR"
190 DATA 5, " ", 0, " "
200 END
```

Statements 10, 20, and 30 explain the purpose of this program. Statement 40 reads data from a DATA statement. The execution of statement 50 is as follows. If the number assigned to the variable name A is 1, the computer will branch to the statement assigned statement number 60; if the number is 2, the computer will branch to statement 80; if the number is 3, the computer will branch to statement 100; if the number is 4, the computer will branch to statement 120; and if the number is 5, the computer will branch to statement 200 and stop execution.

If the value assigned to the variable name or of the arithmetic expression in an ON-GO TO statement is not an integer number, say if it is 4.3, the number will be truncated (not rounded). If the value is negative, zero, or greater than the number of statement numbers listed in the ON-GO TO statement, the ON-GO TO will be ignored.*

The statement numbers can be in any sequence; they do not have to be in either ascending or descending order. A statement number can be specified several times in one ON-GO TO statement.

---

*Some BASIC implementations treat these conditions as errors. A message is printed, and program execution is terminated.

APPENDIX B: BASIC PROGRAMMING

$$\text{sn FOR nvn} = \text{in}_1 \text{ TO in}_2 \text{ STEP in}_3$$
•
•
•
$$\text{sn NEXT vn}$$

where:

    sn represents an unsigned 1 through 5 digit integer *statement number*.

    FOR is a BASIC keyword that distinguishes this statement from the other kinds of statements in the program.

    nvn represents a *numeric variable name*. This variable name is sometimes referred to as the index variable of the FOR-TO loop.

    = is a special character used here as required in the BASIC language.

    in_1 represents an arithmetic expression, a constant, or a numeric variable name whose value is taken as the initial value of nvn when the FOR-TO statement is encountered during execution.

    TO is a BASIC keyword.

    in_2 represents an arithmetic expression, a constant, or a numeric variable name whose value is compared with the current value of nvn at the start of the loop.
If the value of nvn *exceeds* the value of in_2, the computer goes to the statement immediately following the NEXT statement.

    STEP is a BASIC keyword. It can be omitted if the value of in_3 is always 1.

    in_3 represents an arithmetic expression, a constant, or a numeric variable name whose value is either added to or subtracted from (if the value of in_3 is negative) the current value assigned to nvn after the last statement in the loop has been executed (but *before* the next comparison of nvn with in_2 at the start of the loop is made).
If STEP and in_3 are omitted, the BASIC compiler assumes that nvn is to be incremented by 1 each time the loop is executed.

•
•
•

    sn represents an unsigned 1 through 5 digit integer *statement number*.

    NEXT is a BASIC keyword that distinguishes this statement from the other kinds of statements in the program.

    nvn represents the *numeric variable name* specified in the FOR-TO statement.

ILLUSTRATION B-17 General forms of the FOR-TO and NEXT statements

The FOR-TO and NEXT Statements

The program above contains a GO TO statement that causes the computer to loop back to the beginning of the program to read the next group of data. A "dummy" set of data is included to stop the execution of the program when all the groups of data have been processed.

The FOR-TO and NEXT statements provide a simpler way to perform the loop and to stop program execution at the right time. The FOR-TO statement is considered the most powerful program statement in BASIC because of its looping capability. To tell the computer where the end of a loop is, a NEXT statement is required. The NEXT statement always appears as the last statement in a loop. Illustration B-17 shows the general forms of the FOR-TO and NEXT statements.

The way the FOR-TO and NEXT statements operate in the standard for minimal BASIC is shown in Illustration B-18. Note that this loop is a leading-decision loop—the processing steps in the loop may not be executed at all.*

A detailed explanation of representative FOR-TO and NEXT statements is given in Illustration B-19.

With respect to the FOR-TO statement, the following factors should be considered:

1. The numeric variable name, nvn, can be used in statements within the range of the FOR-TO statement. For example, the following use of I is acceptable.

    ```
    10 FOR I = 1 TO 10
    20 T = T+I
    30 NEXT I
    ```

2. The number assigned to the numeric variable name, nvn, is controlled by the computer during the execution of the statements within the FOR-TO loop. Its value cannot be changed by statements within the loop. For example, the following sequence of statements is not allowed.

    ```
    10 FOR I = 1 TO 10
         •
         •
         •
    50 I = J+K
    60 NEXT I
    ```

---

*Not all BASIC implementations follow the standard with respect to FOR-TO. In some, the loop is a trailing-decision loop; the processing steps in the loop are always executed at least once.

APPENDIX B: BASIC PROGRAMMING

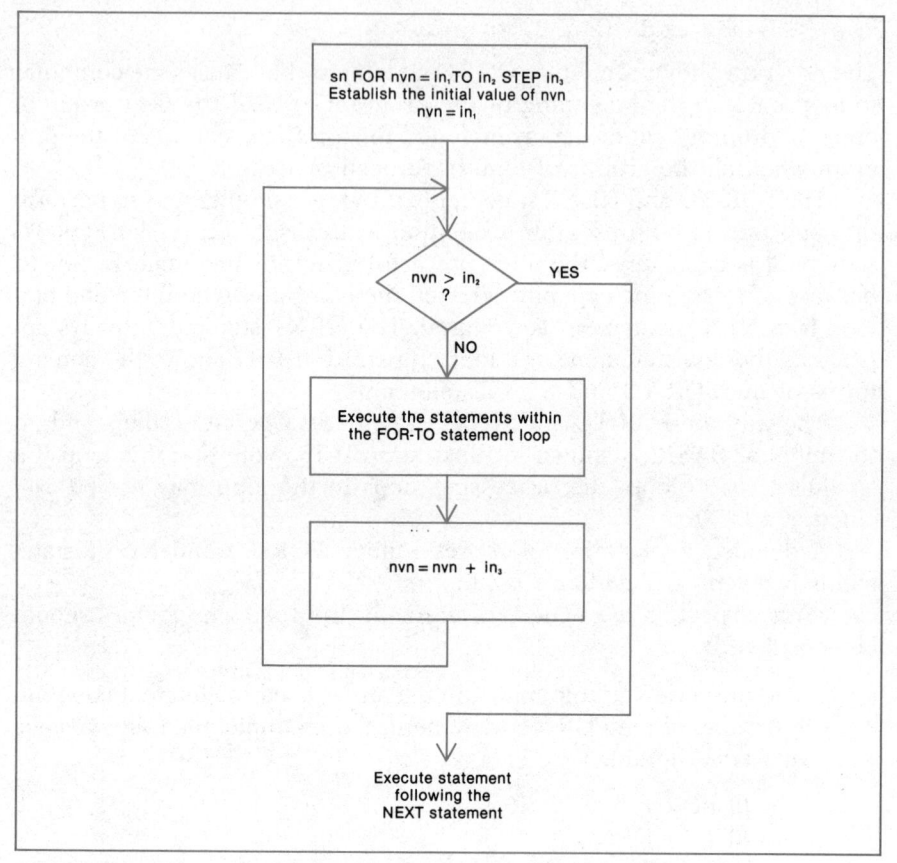

```
sn FOR nvn = in₁ TO in₂ STEP in₃
Establish the initial value of nvn
          nvn = in₁

          nvn > in₂ ?  ──YES──▶
               │
               NO
               ▼
    Execute the statements within
       the FOR-TO statement loop

          nvn = nvn + in₃

          Execute statement
             following the
           NEXT statement
```

ILLUSTRATION B-18 Logic of the FOR-TO and NEXT statements

3. If variable names are used for in_1, in_2, and/or in_3, the number assigned to each of them cannot be changed by statements within the FOR-TO loop. The following sequence of statements is incorrect because in_2 (B, in this case) is changed inside the loop.

       10 FOR I = 1 TO B STEP C
             •
             •
             •
       40 B = N
       50 NEXT I

4. The program statements within a FOR-TO loop may be located within one or more other FOR-TO loops. If the statements of a FOR-TO loop lie entirely within another FOR-TO loop, the first or "inner" FOR-TO loop is said to be "nested" within the second or "outer" FOR-TO loop.

		10 FOR I = 1 TO 25 • • • 60 NEXT I
STATEMENT KEYWORD	FOR	The keyword FOR indicates that the computer is to execute this statement and all others up to and including the NEXT statement.
NUMERIC VARIABLE NAME	I	Each FOR-TO statement has an associated numeric variable name chosen by the programmer.
INITIAL VALUE	1	The programmer indicates the FOR-TO numeric variable's initial value.
KEYWORD	TO	This is a BASIC keyword.
TEST	25	Upon each execution of the statements in the FOR-TO statement range, the value of the variable name is compared with the test value, which in this case is 25. When the value of the variable name exceeds the test value, the FOR-TO statement is considered satisfied. The value of the variable name either remains at the exceeded test value (as specified in the standard for minimal BASIC) or is reset to the last value used in the loop, depending upon the BASIC compiler being used. Control passes outside the range of the FOR-TO statement to the first statement following the NEXT statement containing the variable name in the FOR-TO statement.
INDEXING INCREMENT		The programmer specifies how much the value of the numeric variable name is to increase after each execution of the loop—in this case 1. (If no value is specified, it is understood to be 1.) The incrementation occurs before the comparison of the numeric variable name and the test value.
RANGE	• • •	The range of the FOR-TO statement is the statements within the loop; they may be executed several times or not at all.
LAST STATEMENT OF RANGE	NEXT I	The last statement must be a NEXT statement containing the same numeric variable name as the FOR-TO statement.

ILLUSTRATION B-19 A summary of the FOR-TO and NEXT statements

APPENDIX B: BASIC PROGRAMMING

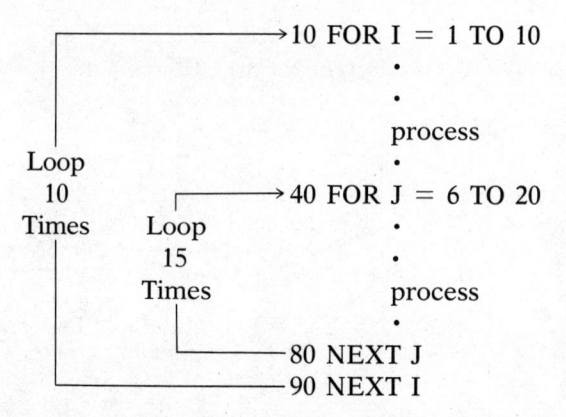

```
          ┌──────────────→ 10 FOR I = 1 TO 10
          │                         •
          │                         •
          │                      process
  Loop    │                         •
   10     │    ┌──────────→ 40 FOR J = 6 TO 20
  Times   │    │                    •
          │ Loop                    •
          │  15                     •
          │ Times                process
          │    │                    •
          │    └─────────  80 NEXT J
          └──────────────  90 NEXT I
```

The program statements within an inner or "nested" FOR-TO loop must be entirely within the next outer FOR-TO loop. For example, the following sequence is incorrect.

```
   ┌──────→ 10 FOR D = 1 TO 10
   │                •
   │                •
   │             process
   │                •
   │   ┌──→ 40 FOR E = 1 TO 5
   └───┼──  50 NEXT D
       │        •
       │        •
       │     process
       │        •
       └──  90 NEXT E
```

The NEXT statement for an inner FOR-TO loop cannot be the same statement as the NEXT statement for an outer FOR-TO loop. The following sequence will cause an error due to the attempted use of the same NEXT statement for the outer and inner loops.

```
   ┌──────→ 10 FOR I = 1 TO 10
   │                •
   │                •
   │             process
   │                •
   │   ┌──→ 40 FOR I = 3 TO 6
   │   │            •
   │   │            •
   │   │         process
   │   │            •
   └───┴──→ 80 NEXT I
```

APPENDIX B: BASIC PROGRAMMING

The computer can branch out of a FOR-TO loop at any time during the execution of the statements within the loop. However, a return to a program statement within a FOR-TO loop can be made only under the following circumstances:

1. The values of nvn, in_1, in_2, and in_3 must not have been changed.
2. If a FOR-TO loop is nested within one or more other FOR-TO loops, both the branch and the return must be made from and to the innermost FOR-TO loop.

○ EXAMPLES OF BASIC PROGRAMS

The BASIC statements introduced thus far can be used to solve a wide variety of problems. Four problem situations are presented as examples in this section. The solutions to the problems are shown in both flowchart and BASIC forms.

Example 1. The Squaring of Numbers

Write a program to read 15 integer numbers, one at a time. If a number is greater than 100, the next number should be read. However, if a number is less than or equal to 100, the number should be squared. Both the number and its squared value should be printed. Then the next number should be read.

Illustration B-20 is a flowchart of the logic required to solve this problem. The BASIC program and its output are shown in Illustration B-21.

Example 2. A Payroll Program

Write a program to compute and print the gross pay, the overtime pay, the federal and state tax, and the net pay for any number of employees.

The federal tax rate is 20 percent and the state tax rate is 7 percent. The overtime pay rate is 1.5 times the regular pay rate.

The following headings should be printed at the top of the output:

PAYROLL

| EMPLOYEE NUMBER | GROSS PAY | OVERTIME PAY | FED. AND ST. TAX | NET PAY |

Illustration B-22 is a flowchart of the logic required to solve this problem. The BASIC program and its output are shown in Illustration B-23.

544

APPENDIX B: BASIC PROGRAMMING

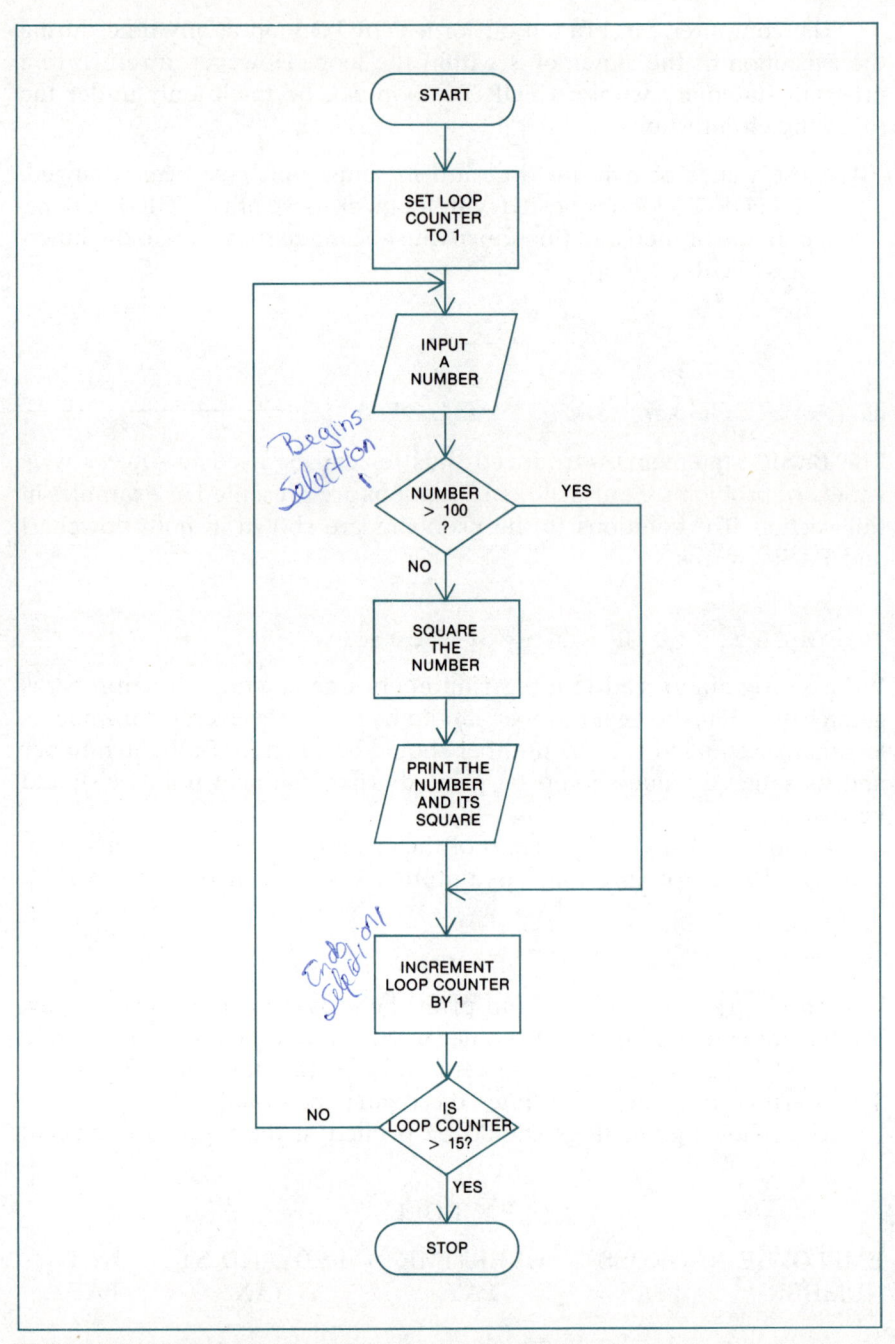

ILLUSTRATION B-20 Flowchart of a program that finds the squares of numbers

```
Example 1:
     10 REM THE SQUARING OF SEVERAL NUMBERS
     20 FOR N = 1 TO 15
     30 READ A
     40 DATA 110,90,60,85,91,16,145,98,84,114,225,180,36,75,124
     50 IF A > 100 THEN 80
     60 LET I = A↑2
     70 PRINT "THE NUMBER IS";A;"   ITS SQUARE IS";I
     80 NEXT N
     90 END
```

Output:
```
     THE NUMBER IS 90    ITS SQUARE IS 8100
     THE NUMBER IS 60    ITS SQUARE IS 3600
     THE NUMBER IS 85    ITS SQUARE IS 7225
     THE NUMBER IS 91    ITS SQUARE IS 8281
     THE NUMBER IS 16    ITS SQUARE IS 256
     THE NUMBER IS 98    ITS SQUARE IS 9604
     THE NUMBER IS 84    ITS SQUARE IS 7056
     THE NUMBER IS 36    ITS SQUARE IS 1296
     THE NUMBER IS 75    ITS SQUARE IS 5625
```

ILLUSTRATION B-21 BASIC program that finds the squares of numbers

Example 3. Compound Interest

When money is retained in a savings account, interest is credited to the account at regular intervals. Each time, the interest is added to the principal and the new total amount is used as the principal for the next interest computation. This paying of interest on interest is referred to as compound interest.

The rate of interest quoted by the savings institution is usually an annual figure. If interest is paid more often than annually, the interest rate must be divided by the number of times that interest is paid during the year.

Write a program that accepts from the terminal the name of the investor and the account number, the amount invested, the annual rate of interest, the number of years of the investment, and the number of times per year that interest is computed. The program should then compute the interest for each month and print out the old account balance, the interest paid for that date, the interest paid to date, and the new balance on a quarterly basis.

Illustration B-24 is a flowchart of the logic required to solve this problem. The BASIC program and its output are shown in Illustration B-25.

Example 4. Depreciation

There are many acceptable methods of computing depreciation. One of these is referred to as the declining balance method.

APPENDIX B: BASIC PROGRAMMING

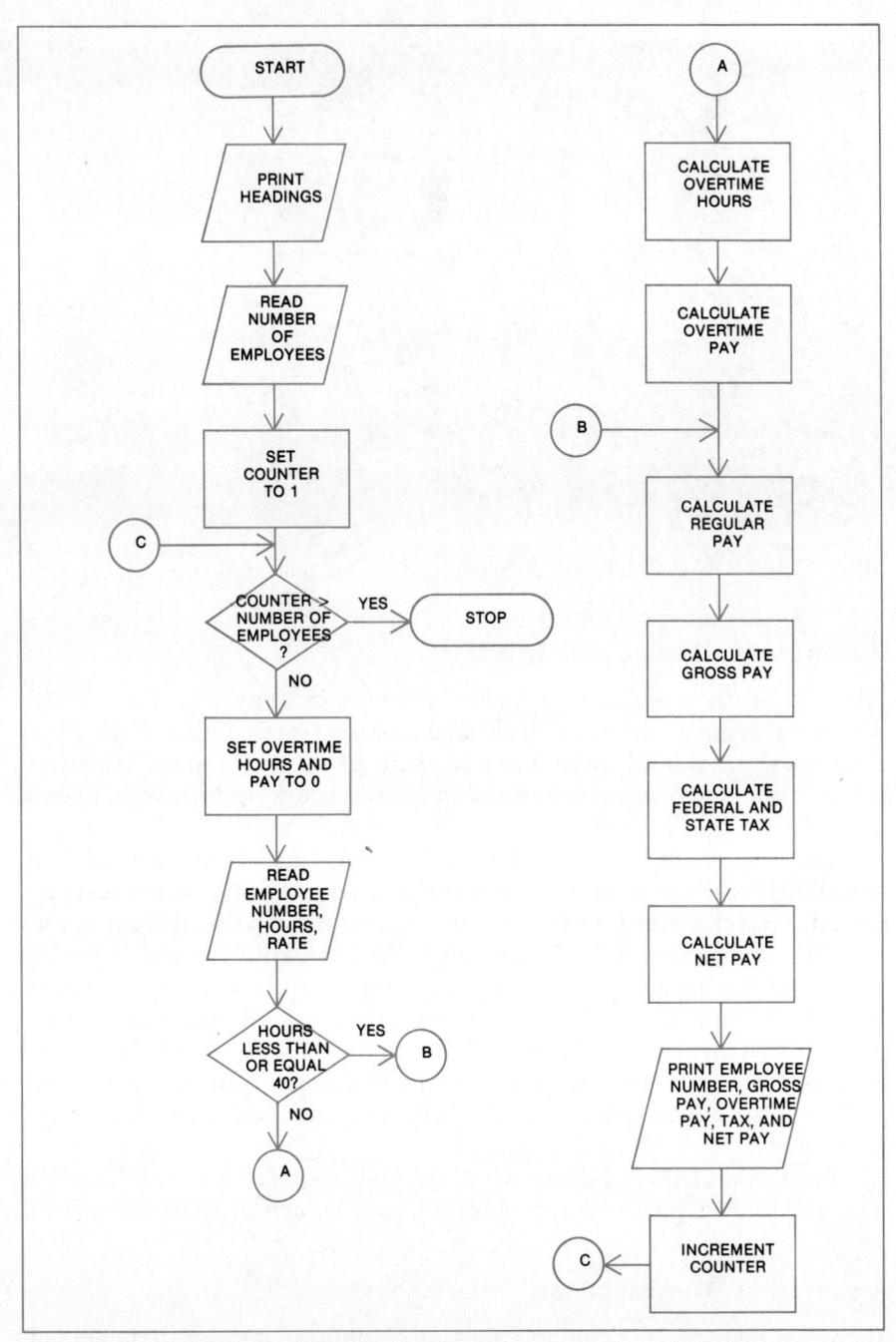

ILLUSTRATION B-22 Flowchart of a payroll program

Example 2:

```
10 REM THE COMPUTATION OF A PAYROLL
20 PRINT
30 PRINT "                    PAYROLL"
40 PRINT
50 PRINT "EMPLOYEE     GROSS     OVERTIME     FED. AND ST.     NET"
60 PRINT "NUMBER       PAY       PAY          TAX              PAY"
70 READ N
80 DATA 4
90 FOR J = 1 TO N
100 A=K=0
110 READ E,H,R
120 IF H <= 40 THEN 150
130 K = H-40
140 A = K*(R*1.5)
150 B = (H-K)*R
160 G = A+B
170 T = (G*.2)+(G*.07)
180 N = G-T
190 PRINT E,G,A,T,N
200 NEXT J
210 DATA 7456,39,1.11
220 DATA 2678,42,2.15
230 DATA 7999,40,2.05
240 DATA 2567,48,2.1
250 END
```

Output:

```
                         PAYROLL

EMPLOYEE     GROSS     OVERTIME     FED. AND ST.     NET
NUMBER       PAY       PAY          TAX              PAY
7456         43.29     0            11.6883          31.6017
2678         92.45     6.45         24.9615          67.4885
7999         82.       0            22.14            59.86
2567         109.2     25.2         29.484           79.716
```

ILLUSTRATION B-23 Payroll program

Under the declining balance method, depreciation expense is computed by applying a constant percentage to the original cost of an item less the accumulated depreciation.

The percentage is computed as follows:

$$\text{percentage} = 1 - N\sqrt{\frac{SV}{COST}}$$

where:

    N = Number of years of useful life
    SV = Salvage value at end of useful life
  COST = Original cost of item

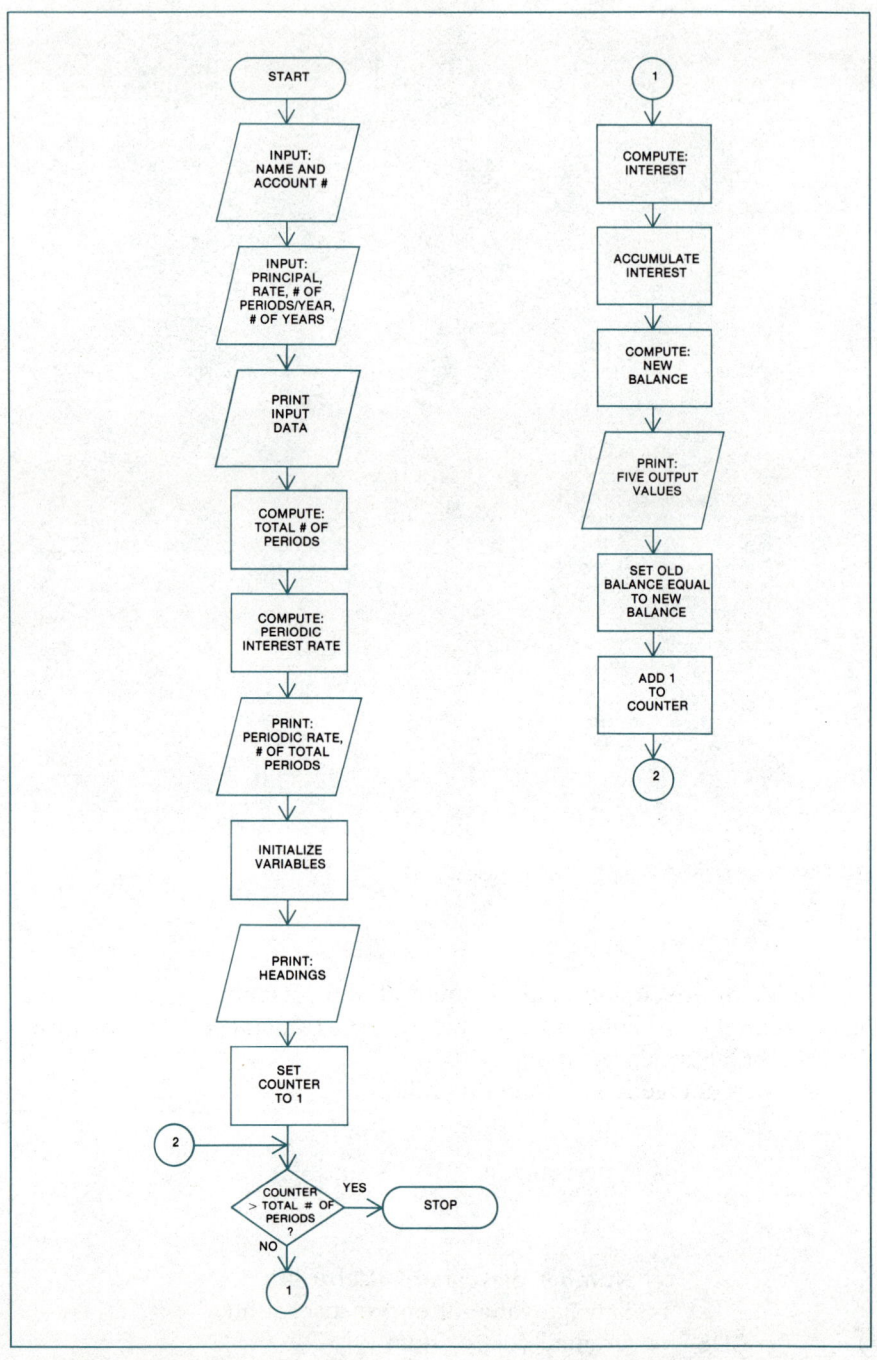

ILLUSTRATION B-24 Flowchart of a program that computes compound interest

APPENDIX B: BASIC PROGRAMMING

Example 3:
```
    10 REM A PROGRAM TO COMPUTE INTEREST PAID ON A SAVINGS ACCOUNT
    20 PRINT
    30 PRINT "TYPE YOUR NAME AND ACCOUNT NUMBER"
    40 DIM A$(25)
    50 INPUT A$
    60 PRINT "TYPE THE PRINCIPAL,THE ANNUAL INTEREST RATE,THE NUMBER OF";
    70 PRINT "INTEREST PERIODS PER YEAR,AND THE NUMBER OF YEARS"
    80 REM R = THE ANNUAL INTEREST RATE
    90 REM P = THE PRINCIPAL INVESTED
   100 REM N = THE NUMBER OF INTEREST PERIODS PER YEAR
   110 REM Y = THE NUMBER OF YEARS OF THE INVESTMENT
   120 INPUT P,R,N,Y
   130 REM N1 = THE TOTAL NUMBER OF INTEREST PERIODS
   140 REM R1 = THE RATE OF INTEREST PER INTEREST PERIOD
   150 LET N1 = Y*N
   160 LET R1 = R/N
   170 PRINT
   180 PRINT
   190 PRINT "                        ";A$
   200 PRINT "THE PRINCIPAL IS ";P;" AND THE ANNUAL RATE OF INTEREST IS ";R;"%"
   210 PRINT "THE PRINCIPAL WILL BE COMPOUNDED ";N;" TIMES PER YEAR FOR";Y;
   220 PRINT "YEARS"
   230 PRINT "THE PERIODIC RATE OF INTEREST IS";R1;"% FOR ";N1;"PERIODS"
   240 PRINT
   250 REM CHANGE THE RATE TO THE TRUE FRACTION
   260 LET R1 = R1/100
   270 REM B1 = THE OLD BALANCE OF PRINCIPAL AND PREVIOUSLY PAID INTEREST
   280 REM B2 = THE NEW BALANCE OF INTEREST TO DATE AND PRINCIPAL
   290 REM I = THE INTEREST PAID ON THAT DATE
   300 REM I1 = THE INTEREST PAID TO DATE
   310 LET B1 = P
   320 LET B2 = P
   330 LET I = 0
   340 LET I1 = 0
   350 PRINT "            OLD           CURRENT        INTEREST                    NEW"
   360 PRINT "PERIOD    BALANCE         INTEREST       TO DATE            BALANCE"
   370 PRINT "------    -------         --------       --------           -------"
   380 PRINT
   390 REM C IS THE CURRENT PERIOD NUMBER
   400 FOR C = 1 TO N1
   410 LET I = B1*R1
   420 LET I1 = I1+I
   430 LET B2 = B2+I
   440 PRINT C,B1,I,I1,B2
   450 LET B1 = B2
   460 NEXT C
   470 END
```

Output:
```
TYPE YOUR NAME AND ACCOUNT NUMBER
?
WILL B. BROKE 9-43
TYPE THE PRINCIPAL,THE ANNUAL INTEREST RATE,THE NUMBER OF INTEREST
 PERIODS PER YEAR,AND THE NUMBER OF YEARS
?
1000,9,4,2
                            WILL B. BROKE 9-43
  THE PRINCIPAL IS  1000         AND THE ANNUAL RATE OF INTEREST IS  9    %
  THE PRINCIPAL WILL BE COMPOUNDED  4      TIMES PER YEAR FOR 2      YEARS
  THE PERIODIC RATE OF INTEREST IS 1.25    % FOR  8       PERIODS

            OLD          CURRENT       INTEREST       NEW
 PERIOD    BALANCE       INTEREST      TO DATE        BALANCE
 ------    -------       --------      --------       -------

    1      1000          22.5          22.5           1022.5
    2      1022.5        23.0063       45.5063        1045.51
    3      1045.51       23.5239       69.0302        1069.03
    4      1069.03       24.0532       93.0833        1093.08
    5      1093.08       24.5944       117.678        1117.68
    6      1117.68       25.1478       142.825        1142.83
    7      1142.83       25.7136       168.539        1168.54
    8      1168.54       26.2921       194.831        1194.83
```

ILLUSTRATION B-25 Compound interest program

Write a program that accepts the original cost, salvage value, and number of years of useful life of an item. The program should then compute and print the yearly percentage, the undepreciated balance each year, and the depreciation expense each year over the item's useful life.

Note that to compute the percentage, the reciprocal of the number of years must be used as an exponent. For example, if N=2 the reciprocal is ½ or .5.

$$\text{percentage} = 1 - \left(\frac{SV}{COST}\right)^{.5}$$

A general way to write this version of the formula is:

$$\text{percentage} = 1 - \left(\frac{SV}{COST}\right)^{\frac{1}{N}}$$

Illustration B-26 is a flowchart of the logic required to solve this problem. The program and its output are shown in Illustration B-27.

ARRAYS

In many programs, values that are related in some way must be processed. For example, assume a program is to do a statistical analysis of daily sales totals for the past year. It is desirable to hold all the daily totals in computer storage at the same time in a manner which indicates the relationship in time of each total to every other total for the period.

One way to do this would be to assign each value to a unique name. This would require 365 numeric variable names just to represent the data. Since other values used in the computations will require variable names, the total number of variable names required could run easily to over 400.

The BASIC language provides a simple solution to this problem: the use of an *array*. The array is characterized by a single unique array variable name and a *subscript*.

In essence, the array is a list of locations in computer storage, and the subscript serves as a pointer to a particular location in the list. When a particular value from the array is needed for processing, the array name is specified to tell the computer which array (there can be several arrays in the program); a subscript is specified to tell the particular location in the array that holds that value. (Each location can hold one value.)

The Naming of an Array

In most versions of BASIC, an array name can be composed of only a single alphabetic character.* An array and a variable may have the same

---
*Each reader should check the BASIC manual for the computer system in use to determine how arrays are named.

APPENDIX B: BASIC PROGRAMMING

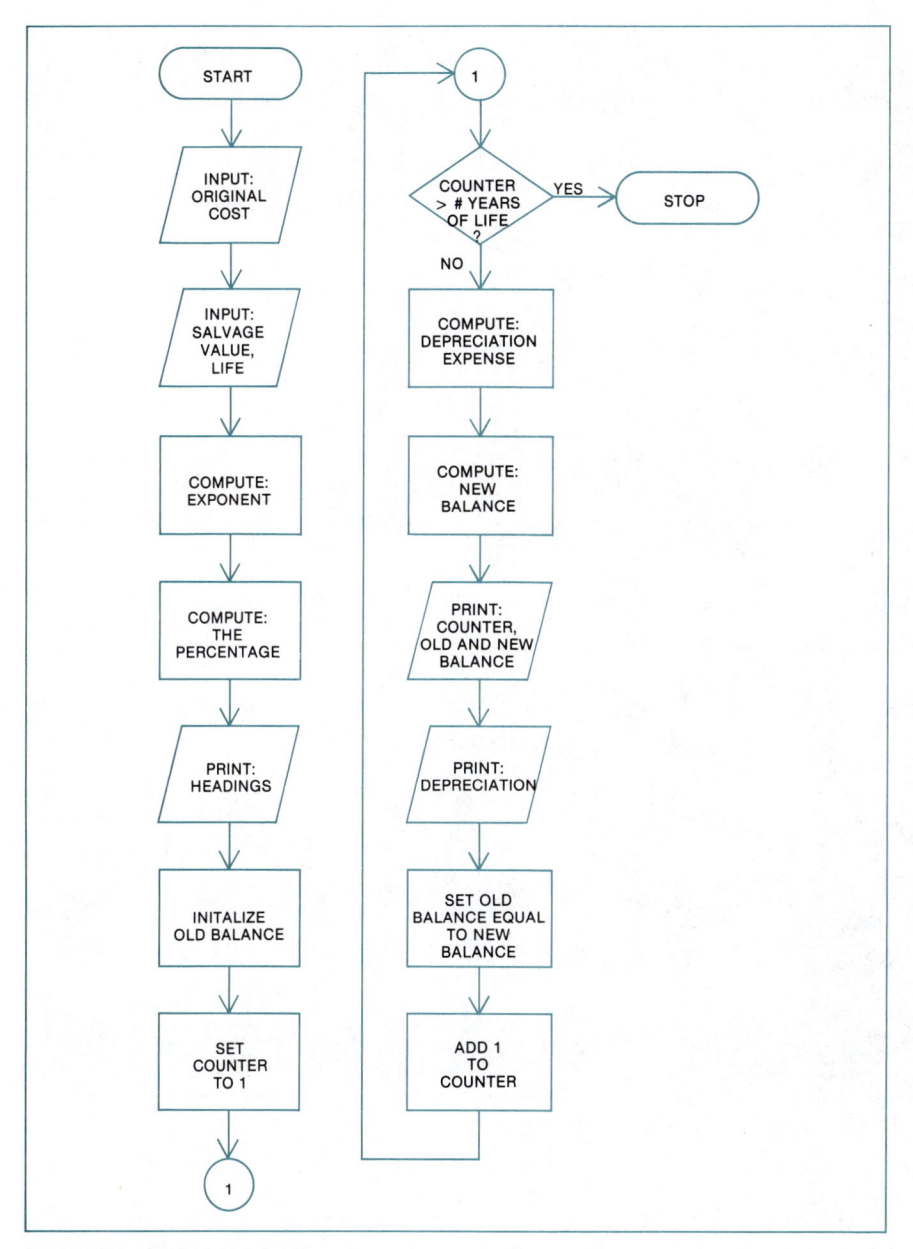

ILLUSTRATION B-26 Flowchart of a yearly depreciation program

name in the same program. However, because this can cause confusion, it should not be done. If it is necessary to have an array and a variable with the same name, a digit should be used as the second character of the variable name. For example, if arrays named A and B are used in a program,

APPENDIX B: BASIC PROGRAMMING

Example 4:

```
10 REM A PROGRAM TO COMPUTE YEARLY DEPRECIATION BY THE DECLINING
20 REM BALANCE METHOD
30 REM S = SALVAGE VALUE
40 REM N = NUMBER OF YEARS OF USEFUL LIFE
50 REM O = ORIGINAL COST
60 PRINT "TYPE THE ORIGINAL COST,SALVAGE VALUE,AND NUMBER OF YEARS OF";
70 PRINT " USEFUL LIFE"
80 INPUT O,S,N
90 REM E = THE EXPONENT FOR COMPUTING THE YEARLY PERCENTAGE
100 REM P = THE YEARLY PERCENTAGE OF DEPRECIATION
110 LET E = 1/N
120 LET P = 1-(S/O)**E
130 REM PRINT THE HEADINGS AND INFORMATION FOR THIS RUN
140 PRINT
150 PRINT
160 PRINT "THE ORIGINAL COST IS";O;"AND THE SALVAGE VALUE IS";S
170 PRINT "THE NUMBER OF YEARS OF USEFUL LIFE IS ";N
180 PRINT "THE YEARLY PERCENTAGE RATE IS ";P*100;"%"
190 PRINT "YEAR", "OLD BALANCE", "NEW BALANCE", "DEPRECIATION EXP."
200 REM B1 = THE OLD BALANCE
210 REM B2 = THE NEW BALANCE
220 REM C = THE INDEX FOR THE LOOP AND THE YEAR
230 LET B1 = O
240 FOR C = 1 TO N
250 REM D = DEPRECIATION EXPENSE
260 LET D = B1*P
270 LET B2 = B1-D
280 PRINT C,B1,B2,D
290 LET B1 = B2
300 NEXT C
310 END
```

Output:
```
TYPE THE ORIGINAL COST,SALVAGE VALUE,AND NUMBER OF YEARS OF USEFUL LIFE
?
10200,200,5

THE ORIGINAL COST IS 10200     AND THE SALVAGE VALUE IS 200
THE NUMBER OF YEARS OF USEFUL LIFE IS 5
THE YEARLY PERCENTAGE RATE IS    54.45024  %
YEAR      OLD BALANCE      NEW BALANCE      DEPRECIATION EXP.
1         10200            4646.087         5553.922
2         4646.087         2116.277         2529.801
3         2116.277         963.959          1152.318
4         963.959          439.0811         524.8779
5         439.0811         200.0003         239.0807
```

ILLUSTRATION B-27   Yearly depreciation program

and it seems necessary to use the names A and B for variables, the variable names A1 and B1 should be used instead.

The DIM Statement

A variable name is declared to be the name of an array by means of the DIM statement. Illustration B-28 shows the general form of this statement.

APPENDIX B: BASIC PROGRAMMING

> sn DIM an$_1$ (in$_1$, in$_2$) , . . . , an$_n$ (in$_1$, in$_2$)
>
> where:
>
> sn represents an unsigned 1 through 5 digit integer *statement number.*
>
> DIM is a BASIC keyword that distinguishes this statement from the other kinds of statements in the program.
>
> an$_1$, . . . , an$_n$ represent array *names.*
>
> (is a special character used here as required in the BASIC language.
>
> in$_1$, in$_2$, . . . , in$_1$, in$_2$ represent sets of one or two unsigned integer numbers which specify the number of locations to be reserved for the immediately preceding array name. If there are two integer numbers, they must be separated by a comma. If one number appears inside the parentheses, the array is a *one-dimensional* array. If two numbers appear, separated by a comma, the array is a *two-dimensional* array.
>
>) is a special character used here as required in the BASIC language.

ILLUSTRATION B-28 General form of the DIM statement

There can be several DIM statements in a program. They can be located anywhere in the program, provided that the DIM statement defining an array appears before the array name is used in processing. Each DIM statement can contain as many array names as can be accommodated on an input line.

The statement

10 DIM E(50)

causes the computer to reserve 50 locations for a one-dimensional array named E. Once the locations have been reserved for an array name, they cannot be used for anything else. Any unused locations in the array are, in effect, wasted space. The amount of computer storage needed for the program is larger than it would be otherwise.

Array Dimensions

An array may be either *one-dimensional* or *two-dimensional.* (A one-dimensional array is sometimes called a *list* or *vector.* A two-dimensional array is sometimes called a *matrix* or *table.*) Whether an array is one- or two-dimensional is determined by whether there are one or two unsigned integer numbers enclosed in parentheses immediately following the array name in a DIM statement. If there is only one number in the parentheses, the array is one-dimensional. The number indicates the number of locations or rows in the array. If there are two numbers in the parentheses, the array is two-dimensional. The first number specifies the number of rows, and the second number specifies the number of columns.

In the following statement, the one-dimensional array named P is reserved 10 rows and the two-dimensional array named T is reserved 2 rows and 3 columns.

10 DIM P(10), T(2,3)

The following list and matrix show how the arrays P and T are set up. The small numbers are the subscripts. In the two-dimensional array T, the first number indicates the row and the second number indicates the column of each location. In the one-dimensional array P, the numbers are row numbers.

$$P_1$$
$$P_2$$
$$P_3$$
$$P_4 \quad T_{1,1} \quad T_{1,2} \quad T_{1,3}$$
$$P_5 \quad T_{2,1} \quad T_{2,2} \quad T_{2,3}$$
$$P_6$$
$$P_7$$
$$P_8$$
$$P_9$$
$$P_{10}$$

The total number of locations reserved for an array can be found by multiplying the number of rows by the number of columns. (The number of columns is 1 if the array is one-dimensional.) Thus, in the preceding illustration, the first array is composed of 10 locations. The second array is composed of 6 locations.

Subscripts and Array Elements

A subscript is composed of one or two arithmetic expressions or numerical values (separated by a comma if there are two) enclosed in a set of parentheses. The subscript immediately follows the array name. The array name and its accompanying subscript refer to a particular location in the array where an array element may be stored. Similar to a variable name, an array element can be assigned a value via a LET, READ, or INPUT statement. The construction and use of a subscript are based on the following rules.

1. A subscript can be composed of numeric variable names, arithmetic expressions, and constants.
2. A subscript can take any form that an arithmetic expression can take.

APPENDIX B: BASIC PROGRAMMING

3. The hierarchy of evaluation of the operands composing a subscript is identical to the hierarchy of evaluation of operands in an arithmetic expression.
4. Depending upon the version of BASIC being used, the subscript must be zero or a number greater than zero.
5. If the evaluated result of an arithmetic expression is not an integer, if a nonstandard BASIC compiler is being used, the fractional portion and the decimal point are ignored in determining the specific storage location in an array. If an ANS BASIC compiler is being used, the evaluated result is rounded to the nearest integer.
6. An array element can be used in any program statement in which a variable name can be used.

The following statements reserve space for an array named E and then store a real number in the 10th element of the array.

10 DIM E(60)
20 READ E(10)
30 DATA 37.5

There is a distinct difference in meaning between mention of an array name and its accompanying subscript in a DIM statement, and mention of an array name and its accompanying subscript in another type of statement, such as a READ, PRINT, or LET statement. If the array name and subscript are used in the DIM statement, the computer is being told the number of locations to reserve for the array. However, if the array name and subscript are used in one of the latter types of statements, reference is being made to a specific location within that array for the processing of data.

The Default Creation of an Array

The BASIC compiler will direct the computer to reserve storage space for an array that has no more than 10 rows, or no more than 10 rows and 10 columns. Therefore, it is not necessary to write DIM statements for such arrays. A nonstandard BASIC compiler begins counting at storage location "1"; an ANS BASIC compiler begins counting at storage location "0". Thus, depending upon the BASIC compiler being used, either 10 (1 through 10) or 11 (0 through 10) storage locations for a list array, or 100 (10x10) or 121 (11x11) storage locations for a matrix array, will be reserved. The array is said to be created by default.

To create an array by default, the programmer need only use a variable name as an array, that is, use the variable name followed by a subscript in a program. The following statements cause the default creation of two arrays, A and B. Array A has 11 rows; array B has 11 rows and 11 columns.

```
10 FOR I = 0 TO 10
20 A(I) = I
30 FOR J = 0 TO 5
40 B(I,J) = I + J
50 NEXT J
60 NEXT I
```

The OPTION BASE Statement

The OPTION BASE statement allows the use of either zero or one as an array lower boundary. The general form of this statement is shown in Illustration B-29.

A program can have only one OPTION BASE statement. It must precede any DIM statement or any reference to an array element. If the program has no OPTION BASE statement, the lower boundary of an array is determined by the BASIC compiler. Whether it is one or zero depends on the compiler being used.

The Storage of a Character String in an Array

A character string can be stored in an array. The procedure described above applies to the dimensioning of an array in which character strings are to be stored except that the array name ends with $. For example:

```
10 DIM A$(25),B(15),X$(15),M(5,10)
```

The array A$ is dimensioned to store up to 25 character strings. The array X$ is dimensioned to store up to 15 character strings. As shown in this example, arrays in which character strings are to be stored can be dimensioned in the same DIM statement as arrays in which numbers are to be stored.

In the following example, a two-dimensional character-string array B$ is defined.* Since the array has 80 rows and 3 columns, it is able to hold 240 character strings. For example, the names, numbers, and major

---

*Most BASIC implementations require an array in which character strings are stored to be one-dimensional. Some, like IBM's VS BASIC compiler, also allow characters to be stored in two-dimensional arrays. The default length for a character string is 18. However, a length specification in the range from 1 through 255 can be included following the array name, if necessary. For example:

```
20 DIM B$ 12 (80,3)
```

APPENDIX B: BASIC PROGRAMMING

> sn OPTION BASE alb
>
> where:
>
> sn represents an unsigned 1 through 5 digit integer *statement number*.
>
> OPTION BASE are BASIC keywords that distinguish this statement from the other kinds of statements in the program.
>
> alb is the digit 0 or 1, to be used as the array *lower boundary*.

ILLUSTRATION B-29   General form of the OPTION BASE statement

suppliers of 80 items from a bill of materials list can be read and stored in this array.

20 DIM B$(80,3)

AN EXAMPLE OF A BASIC PROGRAM USING ARRAYS

The following problem and solution illustrate the use of arrays. There are usually several ways to successfully solve a given problem; this shows one of them.

Example 5. Adding Values in an Array

Write a program to read 15 numbers into an array named S. The program should calculate a total for each column of the array. It should then sum the column totals to give a grand total.

An application of this program logic in a business situation may be to find the total cost for each product manufactured. For example:

	Product A	Product B	Product C
Labor	_____	_____	_____
Materials	_____	_____	_____
Advertising	_____	_____	_____
Transportation	_____	_____	_____
Administrative Costs	_____	_____	_____

TOTAL FOR PRODUCT A = _____
TOTAL FOR PRODUCT B = _____
TOTAL FOR PRODUCT C = _____
GRAND TOTAL   = _____

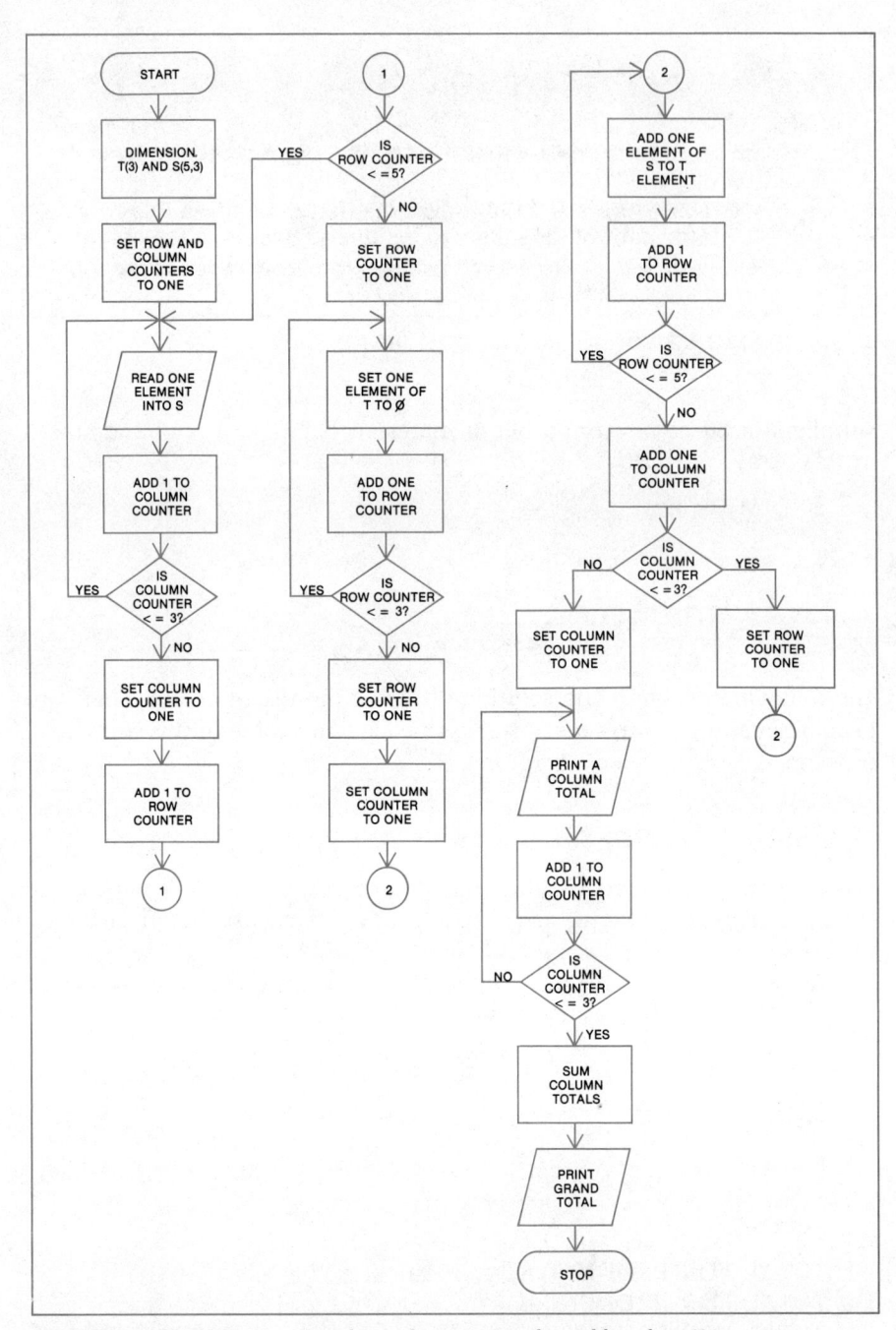

ILLUSTRATION B-30 Flowchart of a program that adds values in an array

APPENDIX B: BASIC PROGRAMMING

```
Example 5:
    10 REM CALCULATION OF THE SUM OF EACH COLUMN OF AN ARRAY
    20 REM R REFERS TO A ROW AND C REFERS TO A COLUMN
    30 DIM T(3),S(5,3)
    40 FOR R = 1 TO 5
    50 FOR C = 1 TO 3
    60 READ S(R,C)
    70 DATA 45,91,113,12,83,192,74,560,30,237,101,97,362,27,425
    80 NEXT C
    90 NEXT R
   100 FOR R = 1 TO 3
   110 LET T(R) = 0
   120 NEXT R
   130 FOR C = 1 TO 3
   140 FOR R = 1 TO 5
   150 LET T(C)=T(C)+S(R,C)
   160 NEXT R
   170 NEXT C
   180 FOR C = 1 TO 3
   190 PRINT "THE SUM OF COLUMN ";C;"OF ARRAY S IS ";
   200 PRINT T(C)
   210 NEXT C
   220 LET S=T(1)+T(2)+T(3)
   230 PRINT
   240 PRINT "THE GRAND TOTAL IS";S
   250 END

Output:
    THE SUM OF COLUMN    1    OF ARRAY S IS    730
    THE SUM OF COLUMN    2    OF ARRAY S IS    862
    THE SUM OF COLUMN    3    OF ARRAY S IS    857
    THE GRAND TOTAL IS 2449
```

ILLUSTRATION B-31 Program to add values in an array

Illustration B-30 is a flowchart of the logic required to solve this problem. The BASIC program and its output are shown in Illustration B-31.

○ THE MAT STATEMENTS

The ability to define two-dimensional arrays, or matrices, and to perform operations on the matrices, is a powerful programming tool. While operations on matrices can be programmed using the BASIC statements presented thus far, a set of 13 matrix (MAT) statements is also included in most versions of BASIC as a convenience for programmers. (See Illustration B-32.) This set allows the programmer to use fewer BASIC statements to specify a matrix operation. It makes setting up calculations a much easier task. As shown in Illustration B-32, each of the matrix statements begins with the word MAT. (In these examples, X, Y, and Z are matrices.)

APPENDIX B: BASIC PROGRAMMING

Example	Explanation
MAT READ X,Y,Z	Read data from DATA statement(s) into previously dimensioned matrices in row sequence.
MAT INPUT X,Y	Input data into previously dimensioned matrices in row sequence.
MAT PRINT X	Print the elements of matrix X.
MAT Y = X	Set the elements of matrix Y equivalent to the corresponding elements of matrix X; the elements of matrix X are not altered.
MAT Z = X+Y	Add the corresponding elements of matrices X and Y; store the sums in the corresponding elements of matrix Z.
MAT Z = X−Y	Subtract the elements of matrix Y from the corresponding elements of matrix X; store the differences in the corresponding elements of matrix Z.
MAT Z = X*Y	Multiply the elements of matrix X by the elements of matrix Y; store the products in matrix Z.
MAT Z = (V)*X	Multiply each element of matrix X by the value V (scalar multiplication) and store the product in the corresponding element of matrix Z; V can be a constant, a variable name, or an arithmetic expression. It must be enclosed in parentheses.
MAT Z = TRN(X)	Transpose matrix X; store the result in matrix Z; X is not altered.
MAT X = ZER	Store the value of zero (0) in all elements of matrix X.
MAT X = CON	Store the value of one (1) in all elements of matrix X. (CON stands for constant.)
MAT X = IDN	Establish matrix X as an "identity" matrix (diagonal elements = one; nondiagonal elements = zero).
MAT Z = INV(X)	Invert matrix X; store the inverse in matrix Z; the elements of matrix X are not altered.

ILLUSTRATION B-32 BASIC matrix (MAT) statements

Matrix Input/Output

The MAT READ, MAT INPUT, and MAT PRINT statements are used to read data into or print data from a matrix without referencing each element individually. Any number of matrices can be read or printed within the limits of the input line. When using the MAT READ statement, all of the array must be filled; if not, an error will occur.

The MAT READ statement in the following program stores six numbers in a matrix named X. The MAT PRINT statement prints these six numbers in horizontal *(row)* sequence. Row sequence means that the statement operates on all of row 1 first, then all of row 2, and so on.

```
10 DIM X(2, 3)
20 MAT READ X
30 MAT PRINT X
40 DATA 37,5,91,-27,-12,-43
50 END
```

The order in which the above program reads the data elements is as follows:

$X(1,1) = 37$
$X(1,2) = 5$
$X(1,3) = 91$
$X(2,1) = -27$
$X(2,2) = -12$
$X(2,3) = -43$

The output of the above program appears as follows:

```
 37     5     91
-27   -12    -43
```

The MAT READ and MAT INPUT statements can also be used to change the size of, or *re-dimension*, a matrix at execution time; that is, to make one or both of the previously stated (or assumed) subscripts of a matrix *smaller*. The forms are:

```
10 DIM A(25,25),B(15,7)
20 INPUT R,C
30 MAT READ A(R,C)
40 MAT INPUT B(R,C)
```

R is the new number of rows and C is the new number of columns of arrays A and B. Re-dimensioning of arrays is a technique for conserving the amount of space required for an array in a program which requires varying amounts of array space when it is run.

Matrix Arithmetic

Matrices can be made equivalent, added, subtracted, or multiplied using the five arithmetic MAT statements.

MAT Z = X	Equivalence
MAT Z = X + Y	Addition
MAT Z = X − Y	Subtraction
MAT Z = X∗Y	Multiplication
MAT Z = (V)∗X	Scalar multiplication

Certain rules must be followed in the use of these MAT statements. They are explained below.

1. For addition and subtraction, the dimensions of all matrices to the right of the equal sign must be identical. Each dimension on the left side of the equal sign must be large enough to permit the result of the operation to be stored.

    10 DIM X(5,10),Y(5,10),Z(5,100)
    .
    .
    .
    50 MAT Z = X+Y

2. For multiplication, the number of *columns* of the first matrix must be the same as the number of *rows* of the second matrix. Each dimension on the left side of the equal sign must be large enough to permit the result of the operation to be stored.

    10 DIM X(9,7),Y(7,12),Z(9,12)
    .
    .
    .
    50 MAT Z = X∗Y

3. The same matrix can appear on both sides of the equal sign in addition, subtraction, and scalar multiplication. Thus, the following statements are legal, if the matrices X and Y have the same dimensions.

    10 MAT X = X+Y
    20 MAT X = (.05)∗X
    30 MAT X = X−Y

4. Only one arithmetic operation is allowed per MAT statement. Thus, the following statement is illegal.

    10 MAT X = X+Y−Z

This illegal statement can be rewritten as shown below. Two separate MAT statements are needed to accomplish the two arithmetic operations.

```
10 MAT X = X+Y
20 MAT X = X-Z
```

Matrix Transposition

The MAT READ and MAT INPUT statements accept data in row sequence. The MAT TRN statement has the effect of resequencing a matrix into vertical (*column*) order. That is, the rows become columns and the columns become rows. The dimensions of the new matrix must be such that its column-row values equal the row-column values of the old matrix.

```
10 DIM X(5,2),Y(2,5)
   .
   .
   .
50 MAT Y = TRN(X)
```

Most versions of BASIC do not allow transposition into the original matrix. That is, the same matrix cannot appear on both sides of the equal sign when using the MAT TRN statement.

Initializing Matrices

The MAT statements ZER, CON, and IDN can be used to load specific values into the elements of a matrix without having to READ or INPUT them. All three can be used to re-dimension a matrix using the same format as the MAT READ statement.

```
MAT Z = ZER(R,C)
MAT Z = CON(R,C)
MAT Z = IDN(R,C)
```

Initializing to zero. The statement

```
MAT Z = ZER
```

stores a zero in each element of matrix Z.

Initializing to one. The statement

```
MAT W = CON
```

stores a one in each element of matrix W.

The identity matrix. The IDN statement creates an identity matrix. In this matrix, the diagonal elements are equal to one and the nondiagonal elements are equal to zero.

```
10 MAT X = IDN(3,3)
20 MAT PRINT X
30 END
 1   0   0
 0   1   0
 0   0   1
```

Note that statement 10 re-dimensions matrix X. Since there is no DIM statement defining X, it would be assumed to be 11 by 11 (or 10 by 10) if the dimensions (3,3) were not included.

The IDN statement requires that the number of rows equals the number of columns—for example, DIM X(15,15) defines a matrix that can be operated on by the IDN statement.

Matrix Inversion

The statement

MAT Z = INV(Y)

calculates the inverse of matrix Y ($1/Y$ or Y^{-1}). Matrix inversion is the most powerful of the BASIC matrix operations, accomplishing in a single statement what would be a mammoth task using regular BASIC features. Its main use is in solving simultaneous linear equations. (For a full discussion of matrix inversion and its uses, see a matrix algebra text.)

EXAMPLES OF MAT STATEMENTS

Example 6. The Bubble Sort

In business data processing, it is common to have to rearrange, or order, a list of data items. This task is referred to as *sorting*.

Write a program that illustrates the use of a *bubble sort*. This method of sorting consists of comparing adjacent elements in a list and interchanging them according to whether or not they are in order. It can be used to order the list elements into either ascending or descending sequence. In this example, the bubble sort in the program should alphabetize a list of 25 words. (The method is equally applicable to numbers.)

Illustration B-33 is a flowchart of the logic within the bubble sort method. The BASIC program and its output are shown in Illustration B-34.

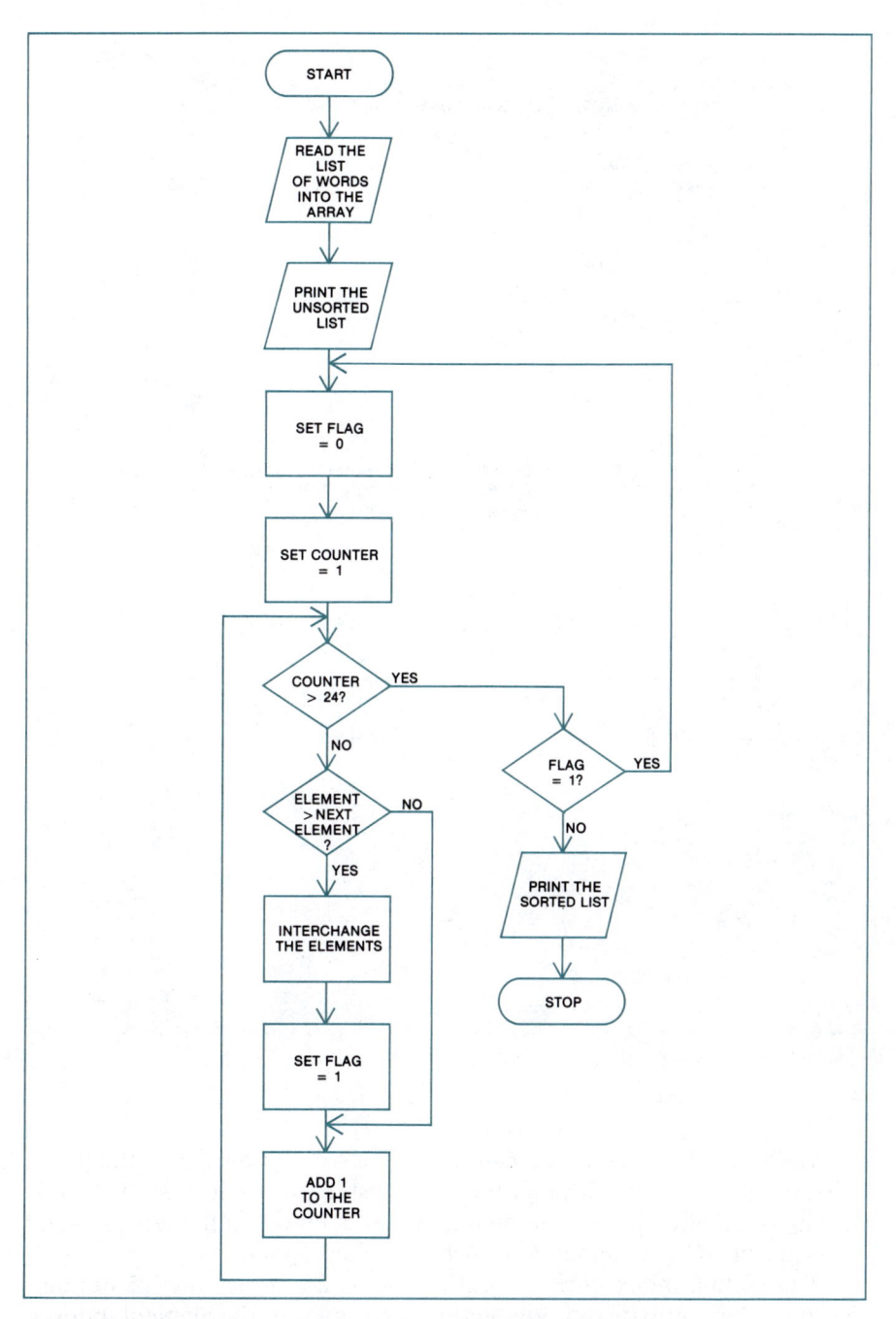

ILLUSTRATION B-33 Flowchart of a bubble sort program

Example 6:

```
10 REM A PROGRAM TO SORT 25 WORDS INTO ALPHABETICAL ORDER
20 DIM A$(25)
30 MAT READ A$
40 PRINT
50 PRINT "UNSORTED LIST"
60 MAT PRINT A$,
70 LET F = 0
80 FOR C = 1 TO 24
90 IF A$(C) <= A$(C+1) THEN 140
100 LET S$ = A$(C)
110 LET A$(C) = A$(C+1)
120 LET A$(C+1) = S$
130 LET F = 1
140 NEXT C
150 IF F = 1 THEN 70
160 PRINT
170 PRINT "SORTED LIST"
180 MAT PRINT A$,
190 DATA "BLACK","WHITE","GREEN","RED","BLUE","PURPLE","VIOLET","BROWN"
200 DATA "TAN","AQUA","GOLD","YELLOW","SILVER","GOLD","RUST","GREY"
210 DATA "ORANGE","GRAPE","MAROON","CRIMSON","COPPER","BRONZE","LIME"
220 DATA "SABLE","PINK"
230 END
```

Output:

UNSORTED LIST

BLACK	WHITE	GREEN	RED
BLUE	PURPLE	VIOLET	BROWN
TAN	AQUA	GOLD	YELLOW
SILVER	GOLD	RUST	GREY
ORANGE	GRAPE	MAROON	CRIMSON
COPPER	BRONZE	LIME	SABLE
PINK			

SORTED LIST

AQUA	BLACK	BLUE	BRONZE
BROWN	COPPER	CRIMSON	GOLD
GOLD	GRAPE	GREEN	GREY
LIME	MAROON	ORANGE	PINK
PURPLE	RED	RUST	SABLE
SILVER	TAN	VIOLET	WHITE
YELLOW			

ILLUSTRATION B-34 Bubble sort program

    The flag (F) is used to indicate when the sort is finished. If the flag is equal to 0 after a pass through the entire list, then the sort is finished. If the flag is equal to 1, then an interchange was made on the last pass and the order of the list elements must be checked again.

    The ending index number on the loop is 24 rather than 25 because the computer compares the element indexed by C to the element indexed by C + 1. If the ending index number of the loop were 25, then the computer would try to "get" element 26 of the array, which is nonesistent. An error would occur.

Example 7. Bar-Chart Graphing

It is often useful to have the computer generate the results of a program in the form of a graph. One of the easiest graphs to produce is a bar chart. The bar chart indicates—by the relative heights or lengths of bars—the relationships between values.

Write a program to print a horizontal bar chart representing sales figures for 10 years. The sales data to be processed by the program follows:

Year	Sales (in Millions)
1972	19
1973	23
1974	26
1975	31
1976	36
1977	38
1978	40
1979	41
1980	37
1981	35

The following output should be printed:

```
1972:
*******************
1973:
***********************
1974:
**************************
1975:
*******************************
1976:
************************************
1977:
**************************************
1978:
****************************************
1979:
*****************************************
1980:
*************************************
1981:
***********************************
    ----+----+----+----+----+----+----+----+----+----+----+
    1    5   10   15   20   25   30   35   40   45   50   55
```

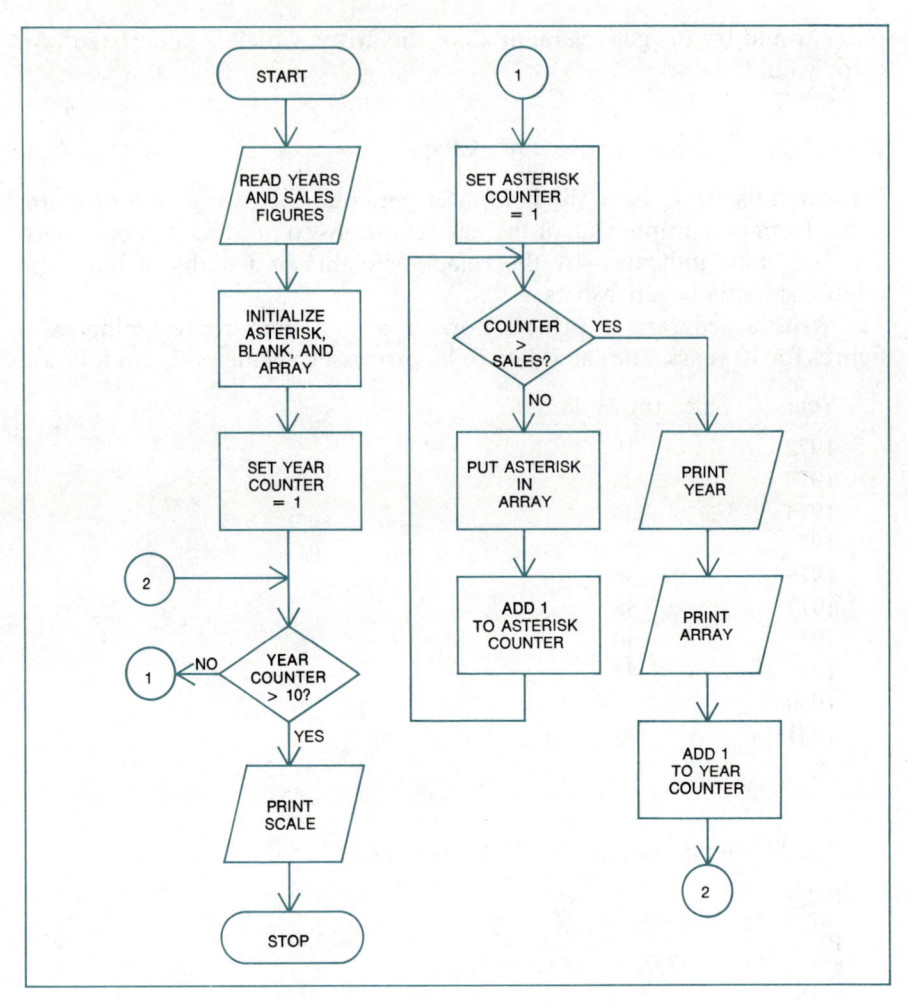

ILLUSTRATION B-35 Flowchart of a bar-chart graphing program

Illustration B-35 is a flowchart of the logic required to solve this problem. The program is shown in Illustration B-36. The program works by using the sales figures to determine how many asterisks to place in a one-dimensional array for each year. After the array has been printed for a year, it is "blanked out" (that is, filled with blanks).

FUNCTIONS

The BASIC language provides several predefined, specialized functions to solve frequently occurring mathematical problems that are relatively

```
10 REM A PROGRAM TO PRODUCE A HORIZONTAL BAR CHART
20 DIM P$(55)
30 FOR I = 1 TO 10
40 READ Y$(I)
50 READ A(I)
60 NEXT I
70 REM INITIALIZE THE VARIABLES AND THE GRAPH ARRAY
80 LET S$ = "*"
90 LET B$ = " "
100 FOR I = 1 TO 55
110 LET P$(I) = B$
120 NEXT I
130 FOR K = 1 TO 10
140 FOR I = 1 TO A(K)
150 LET P$(I) = S$
160 NEXT I
170 PRINT
180 PRINT Y$(K)
190 FOR I = 1 TO 55
200 PRINT P$(I);
210 NEXT I
220 PRINT
230 FOR I = 1 TO 55
240 LET P$(I) = B$
250 NEXT I
260 NEXT K
270 FOR I = 1 TO 55
280 LET P$(I) = "-"
290 NEXT I
300 FOR I = 5 TO 55 STEP 5
310 LET P$(I) = "+"
320 NEXT I
330 MAT PRINT P$;
340 PRINT "1    5    10   15   20   25   30   35   40   45   50   55"
350 DATA "1972:",19
360 DATA "1973:",23
370 DATA "1974:",26
380 DATA "1975:",31
390 DATA "1976:",36
400 DATA "1977:",38
410 DATA "1978:",40
420 DATA "1979:",41
430 DATA "1980:",37
444 DATA "1981:",35
450 END
```

ILLUSTRATION B-36 Bar-chart graphing program

difficult to program. Among them are square root, absolute value, sine, cosine, and logarithm. The functions common to most versions of BASIC are discussed below. (Most versions of BASIC provide several additional functions.)

The BASIC language also provides a facility that the programmer can use to define additional functions. He or she does so by means of the DEF statement. This statement is also discussed.

Predefined Functions

BASIC predefined functions can be grouped into four categories: trigonometric, exponential, arithmetic, and utility. The general form of each function is a three-letter name followed by an *argument* enclosed in parentheses. The argument—represented by X in the following illustrations—is a value passed to the function to be operated on. It is expressed as an appropriate constant, variable name, or arithmetic expression.

The trigonometric functions. There are four BASIC trigonometric functions. Their names and meanings follow:

SIN(X)   The sine of X is calculated.
COS(X)   The cosine of X is calculated.
TAN(X)   The tangent of X is calculated.
ATN(X)   The arctangent (principal value in radians) of X is calculated (angle whose tangent is X).

The BASIC trigonometric functions require the argument X to be measured in radians. (To convert a value expressed in degrees to radians, the number of degrees can be multiplied by .0174533 or divided by 57.2957795.)

In the following illustration, the sine of 20° is calculated and assigned to the variable name Z.

10 LET Z = SIN(20*.0174533)

The exponential functions. There are three BASIC exponential functions. Their names and a short explanation of each follow:

EXP(X)   The natural exponent e^X is calculated; e = 2.7182818.
LOG(X)   The natural logarithm $\log_e x$ is calculated (X must be greater than 0).
SQR(X)   The square root of X is calculated (X must have a non-negative number assigned to it).

The result obtained by using the SQR function can also be obtained by raising the argument to the one-half power—that is, .5. However, since the SQR function is incorporated in the BASIC language, execution of the function is faster than execution of a statement such as 10 LET Y = X**.5.

The arithmetic functions. There are three arithmetic functions. Their names and a short explanation of each follow:

ABS(X)   Determines the absolute value of X.

APPENDIX B: BASIC PROGRAMMING

SGN(X)   Determines the sign of X. The result is either -1, 0, or $+1$, depending upon whether X is negative, zero, or positive, respectively.

INT(X)   Calculates the largest integer less than or equal to X. X may be thought of as being located on a number scale that extends from negative infinity to positive infinity. It is used by itself to round or truncate numbers for printing or other purposes and is especially useful in conjunction with the RND function (discussed below).

Three illustrations of the ABS(X) function follow:

1. ABS(X) = 4.3   (where X = 4.3)
2. ABS(X) = 0   (where X = 0)
3. ABS(X) = 4.3   (where X = -4.3)

Three illustrations of the SGN(X) function are:

1. SGN(X) = -1 (where X = -4.2)
2. SGN(X) = 0   (where X = 0)
3. SGN(X) = 1   (where X = 54.32)

The INT function is used as shown below:

1. INT(12) = 12
2. INT(4.3) = 4
3. INT(0.5) = 0
4. INT(-7) = -7
5. INT(-4.3) = -5

To round a number to the nearest integer, the following statement can be used.

10 LET Z = INT(X+.5)

Assuming X = 6.1, then X+.5 = 6.6, then INT(X+.5) = 6, which is assigned to Z. If X = 6.7, then X+.5 = 7.2, then INT(X+.5) = 7, which is assigned to Z.

To round a number to the nearest tenth, the following statement can be used.

10 LET Z = INT(10∗X+.5)/10

Assuming X = 5.23, then 10∗X+.5 = 52.8, and INT(10∗X+.5) = 52; therefore, INT(10∗X+.5)/10 = 5.2, which is assigned to Z.

The utility functions.   The two utility functions and a short explanation of each follow:

APPENDIX B: BASIC PROGRAMMING

TAB(X)　　　Used in the PRINT statement to format output. X specifies a print position. (This function is discussed earlier in this appendix.)

RND
or
RND(X)*　　　Randomly generates a six-digit number between 0 and 1.

Several BASIC compilers allow the use of an argument as a means of controlling the starting point of random-number generation. For example, RND(50) might cause 50 iterations of the random-number generating formula to occur before a random number is calculated. If the BASIC compiler being used does not have this feature, the same random numbers will be generated every time the program is run.

The random-number generation capabilities of the BASIC compiler being used can be determined with the following programs. If the first program does not run, or if the same numbers are obtained in several runs, the second program should be run several times. The terminal user should enter various integer numbers. Some should be entered repetitively.

```
10 REM RND WITH NO ARGUMENT
20 FOR N = 1 TO 10
30 PRINT RND
40 NEXT N
50 END
```

```
10 REM RND WITH ARGUMENT
20 PRINT "ENTER AN INTEGER FOR X"
30 INPUT X
40 FOR N = 1 TO 10
50 PRINT RND(X)
60 NEXT N
70 END
```

Two illustrations of the RND function follow.

1. Assume the programmer wants to simulate a coin-tossing experiment. A 0 will represent a tail; a 1 will represent a head. On any particular toss of the coin, the probability of a 0 occurring is to be 0.5. The probability of a 1 is to be .5.

    10 LET Z = INT(RND(X)+.5)

---

*Most BASIC compilers do not require that an argument be specified for the RND function. Even some of the BASIC compilers that do require an argument, ignore it; in these cases, any constant can be used.

APPENDIX B: BASIC PROGRAMMING

The use of RND(X) will produce a value between 0 and 1. The result of RND(X)+.5 will be a number in the range from 0.5 through 1.5. The result of the evaluation of the expression INT(RND(X)+.5) will be either 0 or 1. Each has a probability of 0.5 of occurring. This result will be assigned to Z.

To simulate a biased coin, say in favor of heads occurring, for example, the programmer can add .6, .7, .8, or .9 (rather than .5) to RND(X).

2. Now assume the programmer wants to simulate the tossing of a die, where any one of the numbers from 1 through 6 can occur with equal probability on a particular toss of the die.

   10 LET Z = INT(6*RND(X)+1)

If RND(X) generates .3, then 6*RND(X) = 1.8. Then 1.8+1 = 2.8. INT(6*RND(X)+1) = INT(2.8) = 2, which is assigned to Z.

User-Defined Functions

The BASIC language facility that the user can take advantage of to define functions is the DEF statement. There may be up to 26 DEF statements in one program. Illustration B-37 shows the general form of this statement.

When a user-defined function is executed, say, in a LET or PRINT statement, the computer transfers each value assigned to each variable

ILLUSTRATION B-37 General form of the DEF statement

sn DEF FNA(X) = ae

where:

   sn represents an unsigned 1 through 5 digit integer *statement number*.

   DEF is a BASIC keyword that distinguishes this statement from the other kinds of statements in the program.

   FNA is the name of a user-defined function. The function name must consist of three alphabetic characters, the first two being FN and the third being a letter (A through Z) chosen by the user.

   (X) is an argument composed of one or more variable names. (Some versions of BASIC allow only one variable name.)

   = is a special character used here as required in the BASIC language.

   ae represents an arithmetic expression.

name or constant within the argument to its corresponding variable name in the arithmetic expression of the DEF statement. The expression is then evaluated. The result is transferred through the user-defined function name and its accompanying argument (in the DEF statement) to the original program statement. It replaces the user-defined function name and its accompanying argument in the program statement.

For example, assume it is necessary to compute the area of a circle at several places in a program. Each computation of area uses a different value for the radius. The following illustration shows one way this can be done.

    10 DEF FNA(X) = 3.1415*X↑2
    .
    .
    .
    40 LET A = FNA(7.2)
    .
    .
    .
    90 LET B = FNA(A)
    .
    .
    .
    120 LET C = FNA(A+B)

When LET statement 40, 90, or 120 is executed, the computer will replace X in the arithmetic expression of the DEF statement with 7.2, A, or A+B, respectively. The arithmetic expression will then be evaluated. The result will be assigned to A, B, or C, respectively.

A variable name can be used more than once in the arithmetic expression of a DEF statement. For example:

    10 DEF FNA(X) = (3.1415*X↑2)/X

More than one variable name can appear in the arithmetic expression. However, all variable names other than one specified in the argument must have been assigned values before the function is referenced in the program. For example:

    10 DEF FNB(X) = X**2/Y+5000
    .
    .
    .
    100 LET Y = 52
    110 LET R = FNB(A)

APPENDIX B: BASIC PROGRAMMING

The execution of statements 100 and 110 has the same effect as execution of the following statement:

100 LET R = A**2/52+5000

Another possible alternative is to include multiple variable names in the argument when defining the function (that is, in the DEF statement).* This permits multiple values to be passed to the function whenever it is used in the program. For example:

10 DEF FNC(X,Y) = X**2/Y
.
.
.
300 LET R = FNC(A,B)
.
.
.
420 LET U = FNC(K,L)

The first function reference above causes the current value of A to be squared and divided by B. The second reference causes the current value of K to be squared and divided by L.

THE RANDOMIZE STATEMENT

Most BASIC compilers cause the RND function to generate the same sequence of random (or pseudorandom) numbers each time. This is a useful feature when the function is being used to generate random numbers to test or debug a program.

If it is desired to generate different (and unpredictable) sequences of random numbers each time the program is run, the RANDOMIZE statement should be used. As Illustration B-38 shows, this statement consists simply of the keyword RANDOMIZE.

The RANDOMIZE statement generates a starting point for the list of random numbers used by the RND function. The statement must immediately precede the statement that contains the RND function.

SUBROUTINES

Some applications require that, at several different points in a program, identical sequences of operations be performed. While it is possible to

---

*Some versions of BASIC allow only one variable name to be specified in a user-defined function argument list. Each reader should check the BASIC manual for the system in use concerning the DEF statement.

APPENDIX B: BASIC PROGRAMMING

> sn RANDOMIZE
>
> where:
>
> sn represents an unsigned 1 through 5 digit integer *statement number.*
>
> RANDOMIZE is a BASIC keyword that distinguishes this statement from the other kinds of statements in the program.

ILLUSTRATION B-38   General form of the RANDOMIZE statement

write the statements describing the operations at each point where they are needed, it is more efficient to write a *subroutine*. The subroutine is composed of the necessary statements. Then, it is possible to refer to the subroutine at each point in the program where the necessary statements would otherwise have to be included. The effect is the same as if the statements were written at each point where the subroutine is referred to in the program.

A subroutine is a group of statements that solves part of an overall problem. As such, it is not used by itself; rather, it is a part of a program. The use of subroutines simplifies the writing of programs in which performance of the same computations at different points is required.

A second reason for writing subroutines is to modularize distinct functions. For example, calculating the mean, sorting numbers, and calculating the median are distinct functions. Each one can be coded within the framework of a subroutine. Each subroutine can be referred to, wherever the function it carries out is needed, in the program.

A subroutine is, either directly or indirectly, connected to a *main program* by a *calling program*. The calling program can be either the main program itself or another subroutine that is either directly or indirectly connected to the main program.

The GOSUB and RETURN Statements

The group of statements within a subroutine should follow the main program. As shown in the following illustration, a GOSUB statement is used to transfer control to a subroutine. The GOSUB statement contains the statement number assigned to the first statement in the subroutine. In this illustration, it is a REM statement. When the computer executes a GOSUB statement, it branches to the statement identified by the statement number in the GOSUB statement. There can be as many GOSUB statements as needed. They can be located anywhere in the main program and/or in subroutines.

```
 90 GOSUB 170
  .
  .
  .
160 STOP
170 REM THE STATEMENTS COMPOSING THE SUBROUTINE FOLLOW
  .
  .
  .
200 RETURN
210 END
```

After executing the statements in the subroutine, the computer does not stop. Rather, it returns to the calling program. This return occurs when the RETURN statement is encountered. The computer returns to the statement *immediately following* the GOSUB statement that caused the computer to branch to the subroutine. The computer continues execution from that point.

The general forms of the GOSUB and RETURN statements are shown in Illustration B-39.

Just as there can be as many GOSUB statements as needed, there can be as many subroutines as necessary. A RETURN statement can be located anywhere in a subroutine. The basic consideration in deciding where to place a RETURN statement is that it should be located at a *logical end* of the subroutine. If there is more than one logical end to a subroutine, multiple RETURN statements can be used.

ILLUSTRATION B-39 General forms of the GOSUB and RETURN statements

```
              sn GOSUB sn
                  .
                  .
                  .
              sn . . .
                  .
                  .
              sn RETURN
```
where:
  each sn represents an unsigned 1 through 5 digit integer statement *number*.
  GOSUB and RETURN are BASIC keywords that distinguish these statements from the other kinds of statements in the program.

AN EXAMPLE OF THE GOSUB AND RETURN STATEMENTS

The following problem and solution illustrate the use of subroutines. The functions performed by the subroutines are commonly used functions. Therefore, the subroutines may be useful not only in the program but also in other problem solutions.

Example 8. Finding the Mean and Median of Numbers

Write a program to accept a maximum of 10 numbers from a terminal user. Then it should find the mean and the median of the numbers.

The mean is the sum of all the numbers divided by the number of numbers. The median is the number in the middle of the set of numbers, after ordering.

Subroutines should be included to find the mean, sort the numbers, and find the median.

Illustration B-40 is a modular program flowchart of the logic required to solve this problem. The program is shown in Illustration B-41. The median is found by first sorting the numbers into ascending order. If the number of numbers is N, and N is odd, then the median is the number in position (N/2) + .5. If N is even, then the median is the average of the numbers in the N/2 and the (N/2) + 1 positions.

Assume that a control number of 10 (indicating that 10 numbers are to be processed) and the numbers from 1 through 10 are entered as input to the program. The interactions between the terminal user and the program will be printed out on the terminal as follows:

```
THIS PROGRAM FINDS THE MEAN AND MEDIAN FOR A MAXIMUM OF TEN NUMBERS
ENTER THE NUMBER OF NUMBERS
?10
NOW ENTER THE NUMBERS THEMSELVES ONE AT A TIME
?8
?7
?3
?2
?4
?5
?6
?10
?1
?9
THE MEAN IS = 5.5
THE MEDIAN IS = 5.5
```

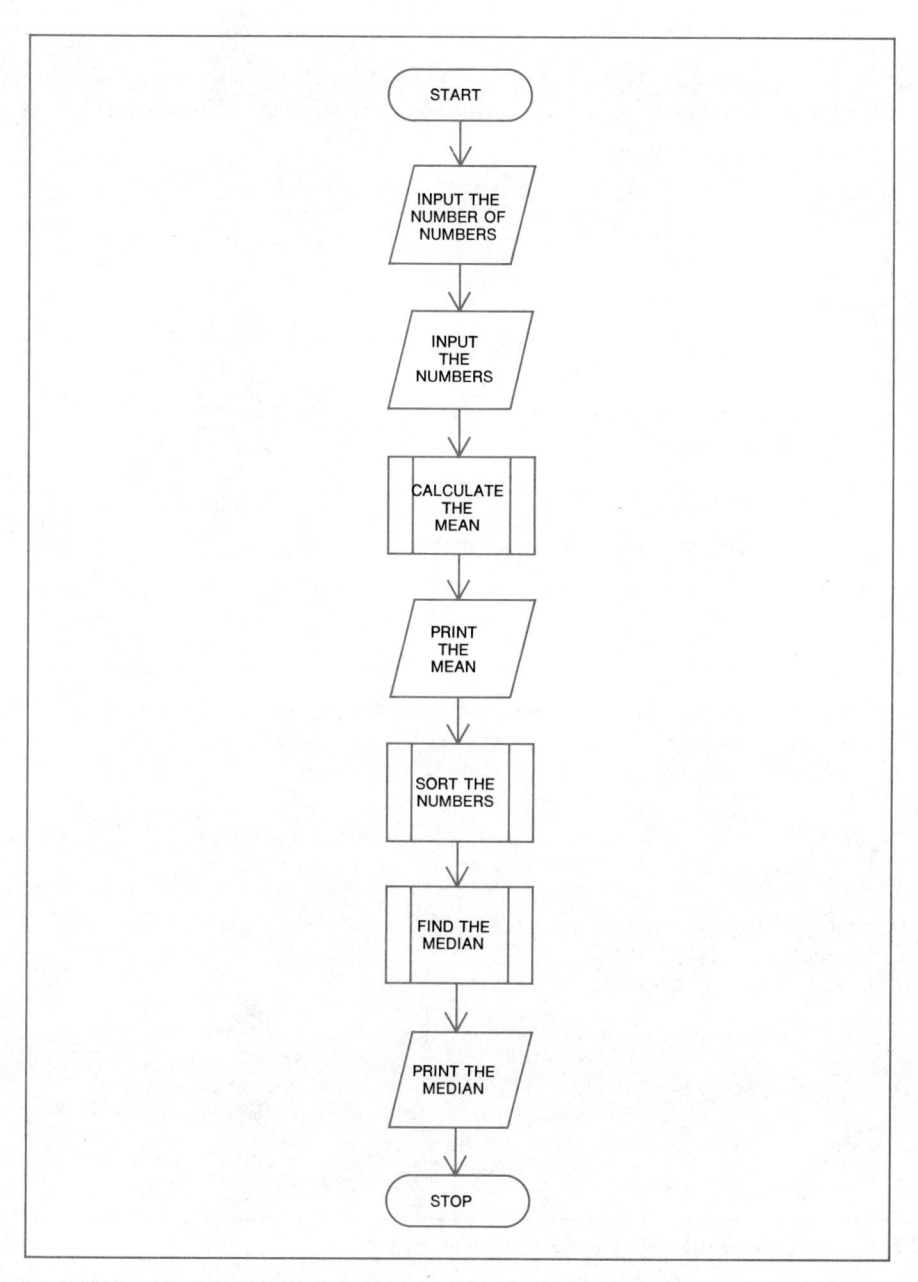

ILLUSTRATION B-40 Modular program flowchart of a program to calculate the mean and find the median of a set of numbers

```
10 DIM A(10)
20 PRINT "THIS PROGRAM FINDS THE MEAN AND MEDIAN FOR A MAXIMUM OF TEN NUMBERS"
30 PRINT
40 PRINT "ENTER THE NUMBER OF NUMBERS"
50 INPUT N
60 IF N <= 10 THEN 90
70 PRINT "NUMBER MUST BE LESS THAN OR EQUAL TO 10"
80 GO TO 40
90 PRINT "NOW ENTER THE NUMBERS THEMSELVES ONE AT A TIME"
100 REM
110 FOR I = 1 TO N
120 INPUT A(I)
130 NEXT I
140 GOSUB 240
150 PRINT "THE MEAN IS =";M
160 GOSUB 330
170 GOSUB 460
180 PRINT "THE MEDIAN IS =";M
190 STOP
200 REM
210 REM    **** THE SUBROUTINES FOLLOW ****
220 REM
230 REM    **** THIS SUBROUTINE FINDS THE MEAN ****
240 T = 0
250 FOR I = 1 TO N
260 T = T+A(I)
270 NEXT I
280 M = T/N
290 RETURN
300 REM
310 REM    **** THIS SUBROUTINE SORTS THE NUMBERS INTO ASCENDING ORDER ****
320 REM
330 F = 0
340 FOR I = 1 TO N-1
350 IF A(I) < A(I+1) THEN 400
360 S = A(I)
370 A(I) = A(I+1)
380 A(I+1) = S
390 F = 1
400 NEXT I
410 IF F = 1 THEN 330
420 RETURN
430 REM
440 REM    **** THIS SUBROUTINE FINDS THE MEDIAN ****
450 REM
460 J = INT(N/2)
470 K = N/2
480 IF J <> K THEN 510
490 M = (A(N/2)+A((N/2)+1))/2
500 RETURN
510 M = A(N/2)+.5
520 RETURN
530 END
```

ILLUSTRATION B-41 Program to calculate the mean and find the median

○ A SUMMARY OF THE BASIC LANGUAGE

The types of BASIC statements introduced in this appendix are summarized in Illustration B-42. The BASIC predefined functions introduced in

Statement	Explanation	Example	Page
DATA	Provides data.	DATA 7,4,3,27	524
DEF	Defines functions.	DEF FNA(X) = 3∗X	573
DIM	Dimensions arrays.	DIM A(50) DIM X(5,3)	552
END	Last statement of a program.	END	524
FOR-TO • • • NEXT	Begins a loop. Statements within the loop. Ends a loop.	FOR I = 1 TO 15 • • • NEXT I	539
GOSUB • • • RETURN	Branches to a subroutine. Subroutine statements. Returns control from a subroutine.	GOSUB 50 • • • RETURN	576
GO TO	Unconditional branching.	GO TO 120	533
IF-THEN	Conditional branching.	IF A > 100 THEN 30	533
INPUT	Inputs data from terminal during execution.	INPUT X,Y,Z	529
LET	Computes and assigns a value to a variable name.	LET A = C + D LET X = Y = D	513
MAT	Simplifies matrix operations.	Note: See Illustration B-32.	559
ON-GO TO	Conditional branching.	ON Z GO TO 200, 300,400	536
OPTION BASE	Sets the lower boundary of an array.	OPTION BASE 0	556
PRINT	Prints program output at terminal.	PRINT A,B,C PRINT "ACCT NO."	519
RANDOMIZE	Generates a random-number list starting point.	RANDOMIZE	575
READ	Reads data from DATA list.	READ A,B,C	524
REM	Allows comments.	REM PROBLEM 1	531
RESTORE	Allows DATA list to be re-read.	RESTORE	529
STOP	Stops execution of a program.	STOP	532

ILLUSTRATION B-42 BASIC statement types

this appendix are listed in Illustration B-43. BASIC arithmetic and relational operators are listed in Illustration B-44.

Statement	Explanation	Page
ABS(X)	Determines the absolute value of X.	570
ATN(X)	Calculates the arctangent (principal value in radians) of X (the angle whose tangent is X).	570
COS(X)	Calculates the cosine of X.	570
EXP(X)	Calculates the natural exponent of X (e^x, where e = 2.7182818).	570
INT(X)	Calculates the largest integer less than or equal to X. X may be thought of as being located on a number scale that extends from negative infinity to positive infinity. It is used by itself to round or truncate numbers for printing or other purposes and is especially useful in conjunction with the RND function.	571
LOG(X)	Calculates the natural logarithm of X ($\log_e X$).	570
RND or RND(X)	Randomly generates a number between 0 and 1.	572
SGN(X)	Determines the sign of X. The result is either −1, 0, or +1, depending upon whether X is negative, zero, or positive, respectively.	571
SIN(X)	Calculates the sine of X.	570
SQR(X)	Calculates the square root of X.	570
TAB(X)	Used in the PRINT statement to tabulate output. X specifies a print position.	524, 572
TAN(X)	Calculates the tangent of X.	570

ILLUSTRATION B-43 BASIC predefined functions

APPENDIX B: BASIC PROGRAMMING

Operator	Explanation
↑ or **	Exponentiation
*	Multiplication
/	Division
+	Addition
−	Subtraction
>	Greater than
>= or ≥	Greater than or equal to
<	Less than
<= or ≤	Less than or equal to
=	Equal to
<> or ≠	Not equal to

ILLUSTRATION B-44 BASIC arithmetic and relational operators

APPENDIX C

BASIC PROGRAMMING PROBLEMS

INPUT/OUTPUT STATEMENTS
CONTROL STATEMENTS
ARRAYS
FUNCTIONS
SUBROUTINES

APPENDIX C: BASIC PROGRAMMING PROBLEMS

This appendix contains ten programming problems. Their solutions involve the use of the BASIC language concerned with (1) input/output, (2) control, (3) array, (4) function, and (5) subroutine statements introduced in Appendix B.

INPUT/OUTPUT STATEMENTS

1. Real estate brokers are often compensated on a straight commission basis. Their total earnings are computed this way:

$$\begin{pmatrix} \text{Value of real estate} \\ \text{property sold} \end{pmatrix} \times \begin{pmatrix} \text{Commission} \\ \text{rate \%} \end{pmatrix} = \begin{pmatrix} \text{Commission} \\ \text{on sale} \end{pmatrix}$$

Assume the current commission rate is 6 percent. Write a program that computes the commissions for the following salespersons on the properties sold:

Person	Value of Property Sold
B. Smith	$40,000
	62,500
	47,500
M. Jenkins	76,250
	49,500
	57,500

2. A computer company pays its salespersons a monthly salary of $1000 plus a 1½ percent commission on equipment sold during the month. The following table shows the sales figures by person for last month:

Salesperson	Amount Sold
1	$13,500
2	21,000
3	9,600
4	24,400

Write a program to print a table containing the above information plus an additional column that shows the total salary plus commission on sales. Enter the sales, percent, and salary amounts in one DATA line.

3. The ABC Company has four divisions selling various products. Management wants to know what percent of total sales volume is generated by each division. The sales figures for the past year by division follow:

Division	Sales (in Millions)
1	2.85
2	7.62
3	3.57
4	2.81

Write a program that reads the sales data as input and generates as output a table that shows (1) the above two columns and (2) a third column headed "% OF TOTAL" that shows the percent for each division. The last column should sum to 100.

CONTROL STATEMENTS

1. Professor Jones has given three tests. He wants to talk with each student whose grade average is less than 65. Write a program to generate a list of these students and their averages, given the following data:

Student	Test 1	Test 2	Test 3
1	66	42	86
2	47	81	86
3	60	80	84
4	86	50	55
5	76	85	86
6	41	60	82
7	90	80	65
8	67	59	76
9	72	68	51
10	80	71	52

2. Most airlines have computerized reservation systems for their flights. As reservations are taken, the number of seats available begins to decline. Therefore, it is important that management be forewarned when the number of seats on a particular flight gets low, to guard against overbooking. Suppose an airline has three daily flights as follows:

Flight No.	Seats Available at This Hour
381	25
402	15
283	30

In the last four hours, the following reservations have been made for the flights:

Hour	Seats Reserved per Flight		
	381	402	283
1	5	7	0
2	7	1	2
3	5	3	3
4	5	2	5

Assume that at the end of every hour the figures for that hour are to be entered into the computer by a clerk. If, for any flight, the number of seats is 10 or less, a warning for that flight is printed out on the computer terminal. Write a program to provide, at each use, the current seating status for each flight. The program should process the above information.

3. Write a program to read 10 persons' application numbers, annual salary, rent, years employed at the same job, and years living at the same address. The computer is to print the application numbers of individuals who are eligible for a credit card. To be eligible, a person must have a salary of over $25,000 per year, or have an annual salary of over $20,000 and pay rent of less than one-quarter of a month's salary, or have an annual salary of over $15,000 and be living at the same address for more than five years, or have an annual salary of at least $10,000 and be living at the same address for at least five years and be employed at the same job for at least three years. All other applications are rejected.

Use the following data:

Application Number	Salary	Rent	Years Employed	Years Residing
605	$21,000	$560	4	5
610	18,000	500	10	14
614	35,000	750	2	10
656	11,000	280	20	19
678	15,500	400	6	2
692	8,000	200	10	11
694	32,000	850	3	3
697	12,500	375	4	6
698	40,000	950	15	8
700	20,000	395	5	5

APPENDIX C: BASIC PROGRAMMING PROBLEMS

○ ARRAYS

1. Write a program to read the following tables of numbers. The program should subtract the numbers in Table B from those in Table A and print the results.

	Table A					Table B		
4	5	0	1		4	6	1	0
5	1	3	8		3	5	1	8
0	0	2	2		0	1	2	5
3	4	6	8		7	7	5	9

2. The XYZ Company has gathered the following profit data on a monthly basis for the last two years for each of its four sales regions. Write a program to add the monthly data (Jan., Feb., Mar., etc.) of each of the years and store the sum in a matrix. The program should print the twelve monthly sums and the sales total for each of the regions.

Profits (in thousands of dollars)

Region	J	F	M	A	M	J	J	A	S	O	N	D
Year 1												
1	7	5	5	8	7	5	6	7	7	6	5	6
2	6	5	7	8	6	5	5	7	6	5	6	4
3	5	8	5	7	7	6	5	6	5	6	7	8
4	9	7	8	6	6	7	8	9	8	7	6	7
Year 2												
1	4	6	5	4	5	6	7	8	8	8	7	6
2	5	6	8	7	8	6	6	7	8	7	5	6
3	6	8	6	8	8	7	6	5	6	8	7	9
4	9	8	8	7	8	9	6	9	9	8	7	10

○ FUNCTIONS

1. Write a program to calculate $f(x) = [\exp(-bx)]/a$, where $a = 5$ $b = 2$, and x takes on integer values from 0 through 3.

○ SUBROUTINES

1. Write a program containing subroutines to find the maximum positive integer x for which the square root of x is less than 100 and to find the maximum positive integer x for which the exponent of x is less than 100.

GLOSSARY and INDEX

A

Access cycle, 96, 317–19, 352
  A computer cycle during which one access width of data is moved into or from the storage unit.
Access mechanism, 149–50, 152
  The portion of a disk drive on which read/write heads are mounted.
Access speed, 97, 317
  The time required for one access cycle.
Access time, 152, 159–60
  The speed with which a magnetic disk drive operates; the speed at which a magnetic drum functions.
Access width, 96, 317
  The number of bytes into or from which data is moved at one time during the execution of a program statement.
Accounts payable application, 29, 39, 172–74
Accounts receivable application, 29, 33–35
  Direct access system, 153–55
  Distributed system, 358
  Tape system, 133–38
Accounts receivable documents, 33–34
  Aged Accounts Receivable, 12–13, 33
  Invoice, 31–32, 39, 51–53, 133–38, 153–55
  Ledger card, 33–34
  Statement, 33
Accounts receivable, flowchart for, 49, 134, 153
Accounts receivable objectives, 33
Accuracy, 53–54, 67–68
  Card computer system, 106–07
  Disk system, 151–52
  Printer, 109–10

Tape system, 124–27, 133
Acronym, 86, 288, 294, 295
  A word formed from the first letter or letters of the words it represents; for example, FORTRAN is formed from FORmula TRANslator, and COBOL is formed from COmmon Business Oriented Language.
Address, 80
  The identification assigned to a storage location.
  See also Disk address; Storage address
Aged Accounts Receivable, 12–13, 33
  A management report containing the names of customers owing money and the period for which each amount has been owed.
Alphabetic character, 23–25, 26–27, 79
  A letter; a combination of one zone punch and one digit punch in the Hollerith code; a combination of one or more zone punches and one or more digit punches in the 96-column punched-card code.
Alphameric BCD
  See 6-bit BCD
Alphameric characters, 79
  Any combination of alphabetic, numeric, and special characters.
American National Standards Institute
  See ANSI
American Standard Code for Information Interchange (ASCII), 86, 91–93
  A 7-bit code sponsored as a standard by the American National Standards Institute.

Analog computer, 74–75
A computer that measures continuous electrical or physical magnitudes rather than operating on digits.
Analytical engine, 60
A machine developed by Charles Babbage to perform mathematical calculations on numbers in a storage unit within it.
Annotation symbol, 232–33
A flowcharting symbol used to clarify the intent of other flowcharting symbols.
ANSI (American National Standards Institute), 91–93, 175, 231, 289, 294
A government body that has promoted standardization of high-level programming languages, symbol usage on flowcharts, etc.
Applications, data processing, 17–42, 355, 416, 450–52, 465–98
See also Accounts payable application; Accounts receivable application; Billing application; Inventory-control application; Order-writing application; Payroll application; Production-control application; Sales-analysis application; Vendor-analysis application
Applications, family of, 40–41, 51–52
Applications, MIS, 385–411
Application software, 76, 81–82
A program designed to do a specific user data processing task (for example, payroll, billing, class scheduling, or mortgage loan processing).
Arithmetic/logic unit, 79
The area within the central processing unit responsible for arithmetic calculations and logical comparisons.
ASCII
See American Standard Code for Information Interchange
Assembler, 282–85
A software aid that translates an assembler-language source program into a machine-language object program.
Assembler language
See Machine-oriented assembler language
Assembler-language programming, 282–85
Assembly, 282–84

Assignment statements, 290
Program statements that cause the computer to perform computational and logical operations.
Audio-response unit, 179
A terminal that transmits output with a voice-type response.
Automatic data processing (ADP), 4
Data processing using mechanical or electromechanical machines and techniques.
Automation, 439–42, 453
The replacement of human work (person power) by an automatic, computer-directed or machine-directed process.
Auxiliary storage
See Secondary storage media
Auxiliary storage device
See Secondary storage device

B

Background program, 353
A secondary program, or the program that has command of the computer when no foreground program in a multiprogramming system is being executed.
Back-order, 32, 35, 136–37, 153–54
Backup, 140–41, 155, 425, 448
A procedure for re-creating data or records that have been lost or destroyed; duplicate copies of programs and data files preserved for security purposes.
Balancing to control totals, 421
A method of checking the accuracy of a data processing system by determining whether or not selected totals accumulated during the data processing operation balance.
Base (of tape), 120–21
The portion of magnetic tape consisting of a plastic material that provides the element of strength to the tape itself.
BASIC (Beginners' All-purpose Symbolic Instruction Code), 295, 303, 355–56, 499–588
An easy-to-learn terminal-oriented high-level programming language designed for interactive use.

GLOSSARY and INDEX

Arithmetic assignment statement
   See Assignment statement
Arithmetic expression, 515–18
Arithmetic operators, 515, 583
Array, 550–59
Assignment (LET) statement, 513–19
Blanks, use of, 510
Branching, 532–37
Character string, 512, 519, 522–23, 528, 556–57
Comma, use of, 520–23
Comments, 531–32
Constant, 510–12
DATA, 524–28
DEF, 573–75
DIM, 552–54
END, 524
Examples, 528, 543–50, 557–59, 564–68, 578–80
FOR-TO, 538–43
Functions, 568–75
GOSUB, 576–80
GO TO, 533
GO TO-ON
   See ON-GO TO
IF-THEN, 533–36
INPUT, 529–31
LET
   See Assignment statement
Line number
   See Statement number
Looping, 533, 538–43
MAT statements, 559–68
Multiple assignment statement, 518
NEXT, 538–43
Number, 510–12, 520–22
ON-GO TO, 536–37
OPTION BASE, 556–57
Parentheses, use of, 516–18
Predefined functions, 570–73, 582
PRINT, 519–24
Programming problems, 584–88
Quotation marks, use of, 512
RANDOMIZE, 575–76
READ, 524–28
Relational operators, 534, 583
REM, 531–32
RESTORE, 529
RETURN, 576–80
Semicolon, use of, 520–23
Standardization, 499
Statement length, 509–10
Statement (line) number, 509
STOP, 532
Subroutines, 575–80
Subscript, 550, 554–55
TAB function, 524
User-defined functions, 573–75
Variable, 512–13
Variable name, 512–13, 550–52
Batch processing, 205, 350, 473
   The processing of grouped data at specified intervals.
BCD
   See Binary Coded Decimal
Benchmarks, 377
   Tests of a proposed computer system, to insure that it is capable of meeting the specifications stated for it.
Billing application, 28–29, 31–33
   Direct access system, 153–55
   Tape system, 133–38
Billing documents, 31–33, 40–41
Billing, flowchart for, 51–53, 134, 153, 229–30
Billing objective, 31–33
Billing, structure chart for, 269
Binary code, 86–88
   A set of bit patterns that represent data, such as 4-bit BCD, 6-bit BCD, EBCDIC, or ASCII.
Binary Coded Decimal (BCD), 87–88, 120–22
   A bit-pattern code used to represent data (for example, 4-bit BCD or 6-bit BCD).
Binary component, 86
   A group of adjacent binary digits (bits) operated upon as a unit; a byte.
Binary digits (bits), 86
   The digits used in binary representation; 0 and 1 (off and on).
Binary representation, 82–95
   The representation of data by a two-state component such as a magnetic core.
Bits
   See Binary digits

Block diagram
See Program flowchart
Blocked records, 122–24, 130–33, 136, 139, 151, 337
One or more logical records grouped and treated as a unit (physical record, or block) for input/output processing.
Blocking factor, 130–32, 135, 337
The number of logical records grouped within one physical record, or block.
Block (on tape), 122–24, 130–33
The representation of data stored on magnetic tape in groups of characters (or bytes).
See also Physical record
Block time, 462
A period of time during which excess computing facilities exist; a block of computer processing time that may be sold to users outside of an organization.
Bottom-up design, 376
An approach to the design of an MIS that stresses first the identification and development of common business applications.
Branching (transfer of control), 74, 236–38
The alteration of sequential execution of program statements.
See also Conditional branch; Unconditional branch
Brush (brush-type) reader, 103–04, 106–07
A card reader that senses the holes in punched cards by passing the cards under metal brushes that make electrical contact with a metal roller through the holes.
Bubble memory
See Magnetic bubble storage
Buffer, 316
A storage device used to compensate for the difference in rates of flow of data from one device to another or from an input/output device to the central processing unit.
Business data processing, 4–5, 62–63, 342
See also Data processing
Business operations, 28–41
See also Applications, data processing
Byte, 80
A group of adjacent binary digits (bits) operated on as a unit.

Byte-addressable, 79–80
Having the capabilities of both word-oriented and character-oriented storage units.

C

Calculating, 6
Arithmetic manipulation of data, for example, the addition or subtraction of data items.
Calculation Specifications, 303, 306, 308
A section of an RPG program, similar in nature to the PROCEDURE DIVISION of a COBOL program, that defines the operations performed on data entering the program.
Card computer system
Accuracy, 106–07
Overlapped processing, 316–19
Speed, 102, 108
Card field
See Field, punched-card
Card hopper, 104–07
A bin or device that holds punched cards before they are manipulated by an electromechanical machine or by a machine and an operator; on a keypunch, the receptacle where cards are placed prior to punching.
Card punch, computer system, 104–07
An output device capable of punching the data held internally by the computer into punched cards.
Card reader, 102–07
An input device capable of recognizing and transmitting the characters represented by holes in punched cards.
Card read/punch, 106–07
Card stacker, 104–07
A bin or device that receives and stacks cards after they have been processed.
Card-to-tape run, 134–35, 138, 337
A data processing operation involving the conversion of data on punched cards to data on tape.
Cashless-checkless society, 445, 453
A society in which cash is replaced by a credit-card type of medium for the recording of transactions.

593

GLOSSARY and INDEX

Cathode-ray tube (CRT), 179–80
  The unit of a visual display device that receives electrical impulses and translates them into a picture on a televisionlike screen.
CC
  See Cyclic check characters
Central processing unit (CPU), 78–81, 318–19
  The machine that processes the data transferred to it by an input device and, in turn, transfers the results of the processing to an output device; the computer.
Chain printer, 113–14
  A line-at-a-time printer having a print chain that rotates horizontally across a form to position characters.
Channel, drum, 157–59
  A number of drum tracks associated with one another for the purpose of recording data (much the same as tracks are associated on a seven-track or nine-track tape).
Channel, input/output, 319–23
  A special device that controls the execution of input/output operations, thereby freeing the CPU control unit to execute other instructions of a stored program.
Character, 19
  The smallest subdivision of a file, either alphabetic, numeric, or special in type; a component of a field.
Character-at-a-time printer, 110–11
Character-oriented, 80
  Having the capability to address the storage location of a single character.
Check bit
  See Parity bit
Classifying, 6
  The grouping of like data items according to one or more common characteristics.
COBOL (COmmon Business Oriented Language), 276, 290–302
  A high-level programming language designed to handle the data processing needs of business; a programming language capable of handling masses of input and output.
CODASYL (COnference of DAta SYstems Languages, 294

CODASYL (*continued*)
  A committee composed of computer manufacturers, business and university users, and government representatives responsible for the development of COBOL.
Code of Fair Information Practices, 446–47
  A model code that provides guidelines for federal data banks.
Coding form, 257–58
  A programming and keypunching aid designed to facilitate the coding of programs in a clear, concise manner with a minimum of ambiguity.
Column (of a punched card), 22
  A vertical arrangement of punching positions on a punched card.
COM
  See Computer output microfilm
Comb printer, 113
  A line-at-a-time printer having a print bar that moves horizontally across a form to position characters.
Commands, 356, 502-07
Communication lines, 349–52
  Telephone or telegraph lines, or other lines used for communications.
Comparative Income Statement, 10–11
  A management report showing the sales and selling expenses for a past period of time, such as for a month, and the total expenditures for the year to date.
Compiler, 231, 286–87
  A software aid designed to translate high-level-language source programs into object programs; a processor that performs operations similar to those performed by an assembler on assembler-language source programs.
Compiler language
  See High-level programming languages
Computer, 74, 78
  An electronic digital computer; an electronic machine possessing internal storage capabilities, a stored program of instructions, and the capability of modifying the instructions during processing.
Analog, 74–75

Computer (*continued*)
  Digital, 60, 74–75
  General-purpose, 66, 75–76, 80
  Hybrid, 75
  Special-purpose, 75–76
Computer applications
  See Applications, data processing
Computer impact, 437–55
  On individuality, 442
  On privacy, 443–44
Computer industry, 220–22, 457–63
Computer input
  Audio-response unit, 179
  Console display-keyboard, 189, 191
  Floppy disk, 188–89, 194–96
  Machine-readable characters, 166–76
  Magnetic disk, 146–57
  Magnetic drum, 157–60
  Magnetic tape, 120–42
  Punched card, 21–28, 102–09
  Punched paper tape, 189–90
  Terminal, 177–85
  Visual display device, 179–82
Computer manufacturer, 220–22, 458
Computer operator, 429–30
  The individual who operates the computer according to the operating procedures of the department and the procedures required for successful execution of individual programs.
Computer output
  Audio-response unit, 179
  Console display-keyboard, 189, 191
  Floppy disk, 188–89, 194–96
  Magnetic disk, 146–57
  Magnetic drum, 157–60
  Magnetic tape, 120–42
  Microfilm, 192–93
  Plotter, 191–92
  Printed documents, 109–117
  Punched card, 104–09
  Punched paper tape, 189–90
  Terminal, 177–85
  Visual display device, 179–82
Computer output microfilm (COM), 192–93
  The process of photographing computer output and placing it on microfilm. Computer output is placed on magnetic tape which serves as the input to the microfilm processor that creates the microfilm.
Computer program, 228
  A series of instructions that directs a computer in performing a specific task.
  See also Stored program
Computer services company, 354, 461–62, 474–75, 477–78
  An organization that provides computer services to other organizations for a fee.
Computer storage
  See Storage, computer system
Computer system, 59–69, 201–23
  The machines; software that cause the machines to function; procedures required to prepare and process data by computer and distribute the results of processing; and people who keep the hardware, software, and procedures effectively and efficiently functioning.
  See also Card computer system; Direct access system; Tape system
  Large, 203–05, 220
  Medium, 205–07, 220
  Microcomputer, 196, 202, 215–20, 220–21, 448–51
  Minicomputer, 194–96, 202, 210–15, 220–22
  Small, 207–10, 220
Computer system, selection of, 209–10, 416–19, 478–83
Conditional branch, 237–38
  An alteration of the sequential execution of program statements, based on the results of a test for a specific condition.
Connector symbol, 232, 238–39, 245
  A program flowcharting symbol used to improve the clarity of a flowchart by reducing the number of flowlines required; a symbol used to connect an exit to or entry from another part of the flowchart on the same page.
Console, 189
  A series of switches and a panel of lights from which overall control of an executing program within a computer is exercised.
Console display-keyboard, 189, 191

A CRT and typewriterlike, special-purpose input/output device used to converse with a computer and, usually, located in close proximity to it.
Continuous forms, 109–111
A continuous paper sheet used as a recording medium.
Control, data processing system, 419–23, 446–48
Control legislation, 446–47, 453
Control programs, 330–36
Operating-system programs that initiate a job by reading job cards, loading the specified program into storage, and branching to the first instruction of that program.
Control statements, 290
Program statements that cause the computer to branch from the normal sequence of operations, make comparisons of values, perform looping operations, or stop the execution of the program.
Control total, 421
An accumulation of the values in a selected field, for example, the number of items sold, for control purposes.
Control unit, CPU, 78–79, 318–19
The area within the central processing unit that selects one program statement at a time from the storage unit, interprets the statement, and sends the appropriate electronic impulses to the arithmetic/logic and storage units to cause them to carry out the operations required; the unit responsible for directing the flow of operations and data, and maintaining order within the computer.
Conversational language
See Interactive language
Core storage, 82–84
A computer storage unit consisting of magnetic cores.
Cost
See Data processing, costs
CPU
See Central processing unit
CRT
See Cathode-ray tube
Cumulative Percent of Sales Report, 37–38
Cut forms, 109–110, 174

A paper form that has been cut to satisfy the specifications of the user; punched cards, postal cards, single paper sheets.
Cyclic check, 152
An accuracy-checking operation performed on data recorded on a magnetic disk.
Cyclic check characters (CCs), 152
Two 8-bit bytes that follow each record or block of records on disk for use in checking the accuracy of data that is written or read.
Cylinder, disk, 149–50
A number of tracks, at corresponding positions on all disks in a disk pack.
Cylinder, drum
See Drum

D

Data, 4, 40–41, 389–90
A collection of unorganized facts; a list of characters or quantities to which meaning may be given.
Data bank, 443–44, 446–47
A large collection of related data gathered for reference purposes.
Data base, 41, 205, 252, 373–75, 390–92
A structured set of related files organized in such a way that access to the data is improved and redundancy is minimized.
Data base administrator, 427–28
The individual responsible for the orderly development of data base projects.
Data base management system (DBMS), 373–75
A series of computer programs that handle the complex tasks associated with creating, accessing, and maintaining data bases.
Data cartridge, 160
Data collection, 348–50
Data communication, 176–77, 347–61
The electrical transfer of data from one point to another.
Data communication system, 347–61, 490–91
A system that reduces the time required to collect and distribute data by providing for the electrical transfer of data from one point to another.
Distributed system, 357–61, 484–96
Online realtime system, 350–53

Data communication system (*continued*)
   Online system, 349–50
   Time-sharing system, 353–57, 471–72, 502–07
Data density, 108, 129, 150
   The amount of data or the number of characters that can be stored in one record on a given input/output medium such as punched cards.
Data distribution, 348
DATA DIVISION, 295
   The division of a COBOL program that provides an in-depth description of all data to be processed by the program and the relationship between types of data.
Data independence, 392
Data processing, 3–14, 348
   Operations needed to capture and transform data into useful information and the transmission of this information to managers or other specific individuals or groups.
   Applications, 17–42, 335, 416
   Control of, 419–23, 446–48
   Costs, 53–54, 66, 202, 215–16, 220–22, 354–55, 417–18, 439, 450
   Effects on costs, 8
   Effects on customer service, 8–10, 358
   Effects on management, 10–14, 359
   Functions, 4–7
Data processing department, 420–21, 425–32
   Separation of functions, 421, 431
Data processing manager, 426–27
   The individual responsible for planning, organizing, staffing, directing, and controlling the activity of a data processing department.
Data processing personnel, 76, 82, 426–31
   The individuals who supervise and/or perform the activities involved in a data processing department or computer center.
   See also Data processing department
Data processing system, 4, 18–21, 28, 370–71
   A system used to collect, manipulate, and store data for reporting and analyzing activities and events; a network of components (people and machines) capable of accepting data, processing it according to a plan, and producing the desired information or results; a computer-based system oriented primarily to processing transactions for day-to-day operations.
Data set (modem), 177, 349–52
   A specialized device that converts data to either transmit it from its origin or receive it at its destination.
Data transfer speed, 129, 152, 155, 160
   The rate of speed (in bytes, or characters, per second) at which data can be transferred to a secondary storage device from the CPU or to the CPU from a secondary storage device.
DBMS
   See Data base management system
Debugging, 231, 259–60, 270
   The process of finding errors (bugs) and correcting them so that a program runs correctly.
Decision symbol, 232, 234–35, 255
   A program flowcharting symbol that indicates a test for a specific condition.
Declarative operation, 283
   An assembler-language operation that defines data or constants within a program.
Demand paging, 341
Demand segmentation, 341
Demodulation, 177
   The decoding of data for reception in the form of characters translated from electrical impulses.
Density (of data on magnetic tape), 129, 131–33
   The number of bytes (characters) of data recorded on one inch of tape.
Desk checking, 259
   The process of visually inspecting each line as it is keyed at a terminal or each punched card after it has been keypunched from a coding form, to eliminate errors.
Destructive read-in, 83
   The act of characters read (transferred) into a storage unit replacing any character(s) previously stored in the storage locations to which they are assigned.
Destructive write, 124
Detail file
   See Transaction file

Diagnostics, 259–60
  Descriptive error messages produced by a language translator while converting a program to binary code.
Digital computer, 60, 74–75
  A computer that operates directly on decimal digits representing either discrete data or symbols.
Digit punch, 23–24, 26–28
Digit-punching area, 23
  The 0-, 1-, 2-, 3-, 4-, 5-, 6-, 7-, 8-, and 9-rows of an 80-column punched card; the 8-, 4-, 2-, and 1-rows of a 96-column punched card.
Direct access, 146, 154–55, 157
  A method of obtaining data stored on an input/output medium directly, without referring to other records in the file. Same as random access.
Direct access devices, 145–62
  Magnetic disk, 146–57
  Magnetic drum, 157–60
  Mass storage subsystem, 160–62
Direct access system, 153–57
Direct file
  See Direct organization
Direct organization, 19, 156
  A method of file organization whereby a record can be written or retrieved by a direct access operation.
Disk, 146–52
  A circular metal platter consisting of a number of tracks on which data can be recorded as magnetized areas.
  See also Floppy disk
  Recording source data on, 150–52
Disk address, 150–51
  A reference that precedes each record on a track on disk and can be used to directly access individual records on that track.
Disk drive, 146–50, 152
  A direct access, input/output or secondary storage device that reads and writes data on a disk pack or floppy disk.
Diskette
  See Floppy disk
Disk pack, 146–50
  A medium for recording data read or written by a disk drive; a number of circular disks with surfaces on which areas can be magnetized.
  Capacity, 147, 152
Disk system, 153–55
Distributed processing, 204–05, 206, 214, 357–59
  The distribution (decentralization) of the processing and storage of data to wherever they are needed, for use wherever they are needed, according to end-user needs, with access to a central (host) computer, under either loose or tight central management control.
Distributed system (network), 204–05, 357–61, 484–96
  A data communication system in which several programs are executed concurrently by geographically dispersed or distributed computers connected in a communication network.
Distribution family of applications, 40
Division (COBOL), 295
  The highest level of the COBOL structural hierarchy, composed of sections and/or paragraphs.
Document, 30
  Any report or form used by a company.
Documentation, 261–64
  The process of describing, in detail, every phase of the programming cycle and specific facts about the program being produced.
Document symbol, 47–49
DO pattern, 272
DOUNTIL pattern, 273
DOWHILE pattern, 274–75
  See also Loop structure
Drum (cylinder), 157–59
  The permanently fixed, magnetically sensitive medium on which data is recorded in a magnetic drum.
Drum printer, 113
  A line-at-a-time printer having a cylinder with raised characters on its surface that rotates at a constant speed to position characters across a line of a form.

Dual density, 129
  The capability of a tape drive to write or read a magnetic tape in either of two densities.
Dummy module, 270
  A substitute for a module not yet coded, which is created for testing purposes.
Dump
  See Storage dump

E

EBCDIC
  See Extended Binary Coded Decimal Interchange Code
EDP
  See Electronic data processing
EDSAC, 63–64
EDVAC, 62–63, 64
Electromechanical computer, 61
  A machine (for example, Mark I) capable of performing a sequence of calculations by means of automatically controlled electromagnetic relays and mechanical arithmetic counters.
Electronic, 74
  A characteristic of a computer, dealing with the achievement of results through the movement of electronic impulses rather than the physical movement of internal parts.
Electronic data processing (EDP), 4, 67
  Data processing utilizing electronic processing methods (computer systems) rather than manual, mechanical, or electromechanical techniques.
Electronic digital computer, 61–62
  A machine capable of performing a sequence of calculations through totally electronic means by using vacuum tubes, transistors, or miniaturized circuits; a computer.
Electronic funds transfer, 445–46, 453
  A communication between two or more computers to transfer funds from one account to another electronically.
Electronic Funds Transfer Act of 1978, 447
  A federal law detailing the responsibilities of financial institutions that offer electronic funds transfer services.
Electrostatic printing, 114–15
  A printing technique in which electromagnetic impulses and heat are used to affix the composite of characters to a paper form.
Electrothermal printing, 114–15
  A printing technique that uses a special type of paper that is heat sensitive and forms characters on the paper using heat.
End-of-reel marker, 120, 122
  A metallic, reflective strip that appears on the last portion of a magnetic tape to mark its end.
ENIAC, 61–62, 64
ENVIRONMENT DIVISION, 295
  The division of a COBOL program that describes the type of computer that will compile and execute the program, and the location and type of input/output devices to be used by the program.
Error control, 94–95, 422–23
Error-handling routines
  Card system, 106–07
  Tape system, 127, 139, 337
Error message list, 259–60, 284–85
  A printed listing of diagnostics produced by a language translator.
Even parity, 94
  See also Odd parity
Exception report, 14, 36–38, 379
Extended Binary Coded Decimal Interchange Code (EBCDIC), 86, 89–92
  An 8-bit code for character representation.
E-13B type font, 167–69

F

Fair Credit Reporting Act, 446
  The first legislation pertaining to a computer-related industry; provides to an individual the right of access to credit information collected about that individual by a credit reporting system.
Family of applications, 40–41, 51–52
  Distribution, 40
Federation of information systems, 375, 388–89
  The staged, individual development, over

time, of several logically and physically integrated data bases and related applications, each of which is oriented to a particular function, such as finance, reproduction, or marketing.

Ferric oxide, 120
Microscopic metal fragments capable of being magnetized and of retaining a charge.

Field, data, 18
A portion of a record; a specific area reserved for data of a specific nature; the smallest element of a file that is processed.

Field, punched-card, 24–26
A specific number of consecutive columns reserved for one item of data on a punched card.

File, 18, 40–41
An organized group of records that relate to a particular area of business.
See also Master file; Transaction file

File access, 19
A method of referring to the records in a file.

File creation, 19
Building a file for the first time.

File Description Specifications, 258, 303–04, 308
A section of an RPG program, similar in nature to the ENVIRONMENT DIVISION of a COBOL program, that defines the files to be used by the program.

File Extension Specifications, 303, 308
A section of an RPG program that provides information concerning internal tables and disk files used during program execution.

File maintenance, 19–21, 139–40
The process of updating, adding, and deleting records in a file to reflect changes.
Flowchart for, 140
Structure chart for, 269

File-maintenance programs, 139
Special programs designed to maintain files.
See also File maintenance

File organization, 19, 155–57
See also Direct organization; Indexed sequential organization; Sequential organization

File processing, 21
The act of creating reports, resequencing files, or maintaining files.

File-protect ring, 128, 155
A plastic ring that can be placed on the back of a reel of magnetic tape or removed to protect the tape from being inadvertently written on or carelessly destroyed.

File (supply) reel, 120, 124–26
A reel on which magnetic tape is wound (similar to a motion-picture film reel).

Financial Privacy Act of 1978, 447
A federal law that specifies procedures the federal government must follow in obtaining records concerning individuals from financial institutions.

First generation, 63–66
A series of computers characterized by the use of vacuum tubes as the major design feature.

Fixed-disk, 146–48
A class of disk drives characterized by disk packs permanently attached to drives.

Fixed-word-length computer, 79–80

Floppy disk (flexible disk), 188–89, 194–96, 214, 218–19, 349
A data storage medium consisting of a single, thin flexible platter that has one or two magnetic recording surfaces; also called a diskette.

Flowcharting
Automated, 245
Program, 227–45, 255–57
System, 47–49, 228–29

Flowcharting symbols
Program, 231–43, 255–57
System, 48

Flowcharting template, 243
A flowcharting aid that contains cutout forms of the flowcharting symbols used in preparing a system or program flowchart.

Flowcharting worksheet, 243–44

Flowline, 233–34, 255–56
A line that indicates the direction of flow on a flowchart.

Font
See Type font

GLOSSARY and INDEX

Foreground program, 353
  A program that has priority over other programs in a multiprogramming environment.
Format, 252–53
  The arrangement of data.
Forms-control tape, 109
  A feature for control of the vertical skipping of printer output.
FORTRAN (FORmula TRANslator), 288–93
  A high-level programming language designed to perform numerical computations; a scientific- and mathematical-oriented language used in engineering, science, and business.
4-bit BCD, 86–88, 94, 122
Fraud, 423–24
  The manipulation of data for unfair or unlawful purposes.
Freedom of Information Act, 446
  Legislation that provides for access to files about an individual that have been collected by federal agencies.
Free-form (free-format), 308
  A characteristic of a programming language in which the coding of program statements or instructions in specific columns is not required.
Functional obsolesence, 417, 461
  The condition that exists when a computer system can no longer perform the data processing required of it due to an increased demand for computer services.

G

General-purpose computer, 66, 75–76, 80
  A computer designed to perform a variety of operations; a computer capable of accepting different programs of instruction.
Generation, computer, 63–67
  A computer-system classification based on a significant change in the design of a computer.
Generator, 286–87, 303
  A software aid that creates a computer program on the basis of specifications prepared by the programmer.

Generator language
  See High-level programming languages
GIGO (garbage-in/garbage-out), 252
  Pertaining to a computer system or program, the accuracy and relevance of output generated from incorrect or inaccurate data; the process of generating bad information from bad data.
Grandfather-father-son method, 141
  A method of backup designed to re-create files from earlier versions of the files.
Graphic display device, 181
  A visual display device that projects output in the form of graphs and line drawings and accepts input from a keyboard and/or a light pen.

H

Handwritten computer input, 174–75
Hard-copy device, 181, 182–83, 191
  Any output device that can produce printed output.
Hardware, 76–81, 453
  The machines in a computer system, including data-preparation devices, input devices, a central processing unit, secondary storage devices, and output devices.
Header label, 129, 132
  A machine-readable record at the beginning of a file that identifies the file and its contents for file-control purposes.
Head positioning, 152, 159
  Placing a read/write head over a specified track on a disk or drum.
Head switching, 152
  Activating a read/write head so that it is ready to perform its function.
Hexadecimal representation, 95–96
High-level programming languages, 280, 286–88, 309–10
  A class of programming languages that are generally machine-independent; programming languages which do not, in general, necessitate a high degree of knowledge of the machine on which programs are to be executed; compiler or generator languages,

for example, FORTRAN, COBOL, BASIC, and RPG.

Hollerith code, 23–25, 88–89
The coding scheme adopted for the 80-column punched card in which characters are represented by certain combinations of punches in 12 punching positions.

Horizontal (longitudinal) parity checking, 126–27
An operation to check the accuracy of blocks of data either read or written, by means of a longitudinal check character.

Hybrid computer, 75
A computer that combines the most desirable features of digital and analog computers; a computer capable of accepting and utilizing both discrete and continuous data.

I

IBG
See Interblock gap

ICPEM, 458–59
An independent computer peripheral equipment manufacturer; a computer hardware producer other than a computer manufacturer.

IDENTIFICATION DIVISION, 295
The division of a COBOL program that identifies the program by program name and may tell the program author, the installation at which the program was written, the date it was written, the date it was compiled, security requirements, and remarks concerning the program.

IF-THEN-ELSE pattern, 272–75
See also Selection structure

Impact printer, 111–13, 182–83
A printer that uses a mechanical printing element to strike the paper on which a character is to be printed.

Imperative operation, 283
An assembler-language operation that instructs the computer to perform a specific function; for example, addition.

Indexed sequential organization, 156
A method of file organization whereby a record can be written or retrieved by either a direct access or sequential operation.

Individuality (and the computer), 442

Information, 4, 53–54, 366–72
Data that has been captured and organized into a meaningful form; the results of data processing.

Ink-jet printer, 115
A high-speed nonimpact printer that uses a nozzle to shoot a stream of characters toward paper on which printing is to occur.

Input, 5, 76–79
The entry of data from a data source into a data processing system.
See also Computer input

Input device, 76–78, 166–76
A machine or collection of machines capable of transmitting program statements or data, recorded on an input medium or entered directly into the computer.

Input medium, 76–78
The material on which data from source documents is recorded for temporary storage until needed by the computer (for example, punched cards, paper tape, magnetic tape, or magnetic disk).

Input/output, 315–26

Input/output bound, 321–23
A characteristic of a computer system that is restricted by the speed of its input/output devices, and in which the CPU stands idle a certain percentage of the time.

Input/Output Control System
See IOCS

Input/output symbol, 232–33, 255
A flowcharting symbol that represents reading a record from some input device or writing the results of processing to an output device.

Input Specifications, 303, 305, 308
A section of an RPG program, similar to the DATA DIVISION of a COBOL program, that describes the data records to be processed by the program.

Input statements, 290
  Program statements that cause data recorded on an external medium, such as punched cards, magnetic tape, or magnetic disk, to be accepted by the computer.
Inquiry, 157, 358, 378, 397-98
  The direct access capability of searching for data recorded on a mass storage device upon command from a user.
Inquiry/response station, 181
  A terminal equipment and computer configuration that allows a search for information in response to an inquiry from an individual at a terminal functioning as both an input and output device.
Installation
  Computer system, 416-19
  MIS, 377
Instruction, 74, 282-83
Intelligent terminal, 183-85, 349-50
  A terminal with an internal processor that performs specific functions, like data editing, data conversion, and control of other terminals.
Interactive (conversational) language, 295, 356
  A terminal-oriented programming language that permits interaction between the user at a terminal and the computer during exetion of a program.
  See also BASIC
Interblock gap (IBG), 123, 129-32
  A space (containing no data) that separates two blocks of data on tape.
Internal storage, 74, 337-41
  The unit of a computer that is used to store program statements and data; memory.
  See also Core storage; Storage unit
Interpretive language, 355
  A terminal-oriented programming language characterized by its ability to check each program statement as it is entered into the system and point out any errors in the statement.
Inventory Action Report, 36-38
  A management report listing items that have fallen below their reorder points; a report showing the inventory transactions that have taken place since the last report, the current balances, and the amounts on order; a management-by-exception report.
Inventory-control application, 9-10, 28, 29, 35-38, 469, 475-76
  Direct access system, 153-55
  Distributed system, 358-59
  Online realtime system, 351-53
  Tape system, 133-38
Inventory-control documents, 9-10, 35-38
Inventory control, flowchart for, 134, 153, 237-39
Inventory-control objective, 9-10, 35-36
Invoice, 31-32, 39, 133-38, 153-55
  An output document created from the shipping order to show the number of items ordered, the price per unit for each item, and the total amount of the order; a bill.
Invoicing
  See Billing
IOCS (Input/Output Control System), 337
  Operating-system routines which provide for input and output operations, especially, operations involving magnetic tape and direct access devices.

J

Job cards, 330-36
  Control cards that govern how a program (job) is to be performed and what resources (input devices, output devices, special system programs, and amount of storage) are to be allocated to the program.
Job-control program, 331-32
  An operating-system program that processes job-card information of programs being initiated by the supervisor, and, when completed with its task, relinquishes control back to the supervisor.
Job displacement (technological unemployment), 440-42
  The replacment of routine, repetitive tasks requiring a minimum of education with a computer; the elimination of jobs due to automation, for example, performing clerical jobs by a computer rather than humans.

603

GLOSSARY and INDEX

Jobs, 330–36
Programs.

K

K, 81
   A value of 1024, in discussion of addressable storage locations (for example, 32K represents a storage unit with a capacity of 32,768 characters).
Key-entry device
   See Key-to-disk; Key-to-diskette; Key-to-tape
Key-entry device operator, 430–31
   The individual responsible for transcribing data from source documents to punched cards, magnetic tape, or magnetic disk.
   See also Keypunch operator
Keypunch
   See Card punch, punched-card system
Keypunch operator, 430–31
   The individual responsible for transcribing data from source documents to punched cards for entry into a computer.
Key-to-disk, 185–89
   A process, similar to key-to-tape, in which data is transmitted from a keyboard to magnetic disk.
Key-to-diskette, 188–89
   A process, similar to key-to-tape, in which data is transmitted from a keyboard to a floppy disk, or diskette.
Key-to-tape, 185–87
   An operation, similar to keypunching, in which data is transmitted from a keyboard to magnetic tape (without the intervening punched-card phase).

L

Label (tag), 282–83, 285
   The portion of an assembler-language instruction that represents the first storage location of the instruction and is used in branching instructions of assember-language programs.
Label checking, 129, 337
   A technique to prevent the destruction of records on magnetic tape by creating and checking a first data record (header label) containing the file name, date of creation, and date of permitted destruction.
Language translator, 259–60, 336
   A program that converts the program statements written by the programmer into the binary code of the computer; an assembler, compiler, or generator.
Large computer system, 203–05, 220
   A large computer with an internal storage capacity of millions of bytes and operating speeds of nanoseconds; a computer system that rents for $40,000 to $250,000 or more a month and has a basic purchase price of millions of dollars.
Large scale integration (LSI), 210, 215–17, 439, 453
   The process of placing thousands of electronic components and transistors on chips.
LCC
   See Longitudinal check character
Leasing company, 460–61
Ledger card, 33–34, 36–37
   An accounts receivable record of all charges and payments to a customer's account; an inventory-control record showing the issues, receipts, balance on hand, and other data for an item in inventory.
Legislation, for control purposes, 446–47, 453
Leisure, 441
   Freedom from the necessity of doing anything; free time.
Light pen, 180
Light source, 104–05
   A means of sensing the holes in a punched card or the markers on a magnetic tape.
Line-at-a-time printer, 111
Line item, 31–32, 135, 154
   A line on a shipping order or an invoice showing the number of items and the price per unit.
Loading a program, 77, 79
Load-point marker, 120, 122
   A metallic, reflective strip that appears on the first portion of a magnetic tape to mark its beginning.

Local processing, 213
  The processing of data, generally by means of a minicomputer or microcomputer, at a location remote from the central (host) computer system.
Logical record, 122–23, 139
  The data items defined by a programmer as one record.
Logic diagram
  See Program flowchart
Longitudinal check character (LCC), 126–27, 151–52
  An extra character placed at the end of every block of data to permit the accuracy of the data recorded in that block to be checked through either an even or odd parity check.
Looping, 236–38
  The repetitive execution of a series of instructions.
  See also Loop structure; Program loop
Loop structure, 271, 273–74
  A basic pattern of structured programming.
  See also Program loop
Low-level programming languages, 286
  A class of programming languages composed of machine and assembler languages; languages that are generally machine-dependent.
  See also Assembler language entries; Machine language entries
LSI
  See Large scale integration

M

Machine-dependent, 309
  A property of low-level programming languages relating to a close association with the characteristics of a particular machine (computer).
Machine-independent, 288, 309
  A property of high-level programming languages relating to the capability of being executed by different machines (computers).
Machine language, 280–82
  A programming language that is machine-dependent; a language characterized by the numerical representation of instructions.
Machine-language programming, 280–82
Machine-oriented, 282–85
  A property of an assembler language relating to the restriction of the language to one type (manufacturer) of machine (computer).
Machine-oriented assembler language, 280, 282–85, 309–10
  A programming language characterized by the use of symbolic names, or mnemonics, instead of numerical designations of machine operations.
Machine-readable characters, 166–76
  Handwritten, 174–75
  MICR, 166–69
  OCR, 169–77
  Optical bar code, 175–76
  Optical mark, 170–73
Machine (take-up) reel, 124–26
  A reel that remains on the tape drive and on which magnetic tape is wound during the processing of the tape.
Macro-instruction, 280, 285–86, 337
  An instruction that causes a series of assembler-language instructions to be inserted in an assembler-language program.
Macros (macro operation codes), 285–86
  Specific codes maintained in a macro library and referred to when specific routines, or series of instructions, are needed in a program.
Magnetic bubble storage, 86, 183–85
  An internal storage hardware medium constructed of tiny cylinder-shaped magnetic domains contained in a thin, crystalline magnetic film.
Magnetic character inscriber (MCI), 167–68
  A device used to place magnetic ink, in the form of characters, on source documents.
Magnetic character reader (MCR), 167–69
  An input device that reads special type (E-13B) inscribed on checks by an MCI.
Magnetic coating, of tape, 120–21
  A ferric oxide coating on magnetic tape, which provides the recording capability of the tape.

Magnetic core, 64, 66, 82–84
　A doughnut-shaped component of a storage unit, capable of being magnetized in either of two directions (clockwise or counterclockwise; on or off).
Magnetic disk
　See Disk entries
Magnetic-disk symbol, 153
Magnetic drum, 157–60
　A mass storage, input/output or secondary storage device that employs a permanently fixed drum, or cylinder, to record data.
　Capacity, 160
　Recording source data on, 159–60
Magnetic ink, 166–68
　A special type of ink used in recording characters on source documents to be read by magnetic character readers.
Magnetic-ink character recognition
　See MICR
Magnetic tape, 120–42, 186–87
　See also Nine-track tape; Seven-track tape; Tape entries
　Recording source data on, 120–23
Magnetic-tape symbol, 133
Mainframes, 203–10, 221
　Computers in the large, medium, and small classes.
Main storage, 353
　See also Storage unit
Management-by-exception, 14, 36, 379
　A management philosophy dealing with managing only items or situations that demonstrate significant changes from a given standard.
Management information system (MIS), 14, 41, 157, 204–05, 365–82, 385–411
　A computer-based system that provides both the routine data processing of transactions and the information required by managers to perform their managerial functions.
　Applications, 385–411
　Behavioral aspects, 379–80, 393–96
　Design, 376–77, 400–06
　Evaluation, 380
　Implementation, 377, 396, 407–08
　References, 410–11

Manipulation, of data, 5–7, 76–77
　The process of transforming data into information; the classifying, sorting, calculating, recording, and summarizing of data.
Marketing information system (example), 397–98
Mark I, 60–61, 64
Mass storage devices, 145–62
　A class of input/output or secondary storage devices capable of storing large volumes of data.
Mass storage subsystem, 160–62
　A mass storage, secondary storage device that uses data cartridges to store data.
　Capacity, 161
Master file, 19, 138–41, 153–57
　A file containing semipermanent data, for example, a payroll file.
Matrix printer, 112–13
　A character-at-a-time printer having a print matrix consisting of a 5 × 7 rectangle of pins capable of representing characters.
MCI
　See Magnetic character inscriber
MCR
　See Magnetic character reader
Medium-size computer system, 205–07, 220
　An intermediate-size computer with an internal storage capacity larger than that of a small computer and faster input/output devices; a computer system that rents for $5000 to $20,000 a month and has a basic purchase price up to one million dollars.
Megabyte, 85
　Approximately one million bytes (1024K bytes, or 1,048,576 storage locations).
Memory
　See Storage unit
Merchandising information system (example), 398–400
MICR, 166–69
Microcomputer system, 196, 202, 215–20, 220–21, 439, 448–51
　A digital computer, about the size of a typewriter, that uses a microprocessor and internal storage on a chip, and has a purchase price ranging from $500 to $10,000.

Microfilm, 181–82, 192–93
Microprocessor, 202, 215–20, 439
A miniature version of a central processing unit that is manufactured on a chip using solid-state integrated circuits.
Microprogram, 214–15
A program that is placed in a special storage area in the computer and typically performs some function that otherwise would be accomplished by a subroutine.
Millisecond, 130
One-thousandth of one second; 1/1000 second.
Minicomputer system, 194–96, 202, 210–15, 220–22
A digital computer, compact in size, with a minimum amount of internal storage, a basic rental price of $300 to $1200 a month, and a purchase of $2000 to $50,000.
MIS
See Management information system
Missing-item fault, 338–41
Mnemonics
See Symbolic names
Modeling, 374, 405–06
See also Simulation
Modem
See Data set
Modular program flowcharting, 228–30, 243–45
A technique that represents the major processing steps of a program as modules in a flowchart and uses successively more detailed flowcharts to describe each module.
Modulation, 177
The encoding of data for transmission as electrical impulses.
Module, 228, 268
A complete program or a part of a program, generally, set up to perform one function.
Monitor
See Supervisor
Multiple-Card Layout Form, 252–53
A system analysis and design aid employed to organize and design the formats of the input cards for a program.

Multiprocessing, 204
The execution of two or more instructions simultaneously in a single computer system having two or more central processing units.
Multiprogramming, 204, 205, 323–24, 333, 341–42, 352–54
The computer capability of processing more than one data processing job at one time; the capability of a computer system to execute two or more programs concurrently, thus taking advantage of CPU speed in an otherwise input/output-bound system.

N

Nanosecond, 67, 78
One-billionth of one second; 1/1,000,000,000 second.
National Data Center, 443
A proposed nationwide data bank for the collection of statistical information for government use.
Nested loop, 242–43
A programming technique by which one program loop is located within another program loop, thus permitting the inner loop to be executed one or more times whenever the outer loop is executed.
Network
See Distributed system
Nine-track tape, 120–21
A magnetic tape using eight bits to represent data and a parity bit.
Nondestructive read, 124
Nonimpact printer, 114–16, 182–83
A printer that produces an image without striking the paper with a print mechanism. Methods of printing include heat, electrostatic, ink-jet, and laser techniques.
Nonoverlapped processing, 317–18
Nonoverlapped system, 317–18
Nonvolatile, 83, 184, 216
A characteristic of a storage unit in which each character is maintained in a storage location until replaced by another character.

Numeric character, 23–24, 26–28, 79
A number; a digit punch in the Hollerith code; one or more digit punches in the 96-column punched-card code.

O

Object (machine-language) program, 280–81, 283–84, 287
A set of instructions in their lowest form; the result of an assembler, compiler, or generator operation on a source program.
OCR, 169–76
OCR-A type font, 175
Odd (even) parity, 94–95, 127
A parity-bit check to determine whether the number of on bits is odd (even) for error-detection purposes.
Offline, 77, 132–33
The condition of not being in direct communication with the computer; machines or devices that are not under the control of the central processing unit.
Offpage connector symbol, 232, 238
A flowcharting symbol used to connect an entry to or exit from another part of the flowchart on a different page of the flowchart.
Online, 77, 132
The condition of being in direct communication with the computer; machines or devices that are under direct control of the central processing unit.
Online communication system, 349–50
A data communication system in which data is transmitted directly between a terminal and a computer.
Online realtime communication system, 350–53
A data communication system in which an immediate two-way communication between a terminal and the computer is possible; the collection of data and the transmission of processed results without delay.
Op code (operation code), 280, 282–83
A machine-language or assembler-language designation of an operation to be performed.

Operand, 280, 282–83
The address(es) of data on which an operation is to be performed or of the next instruction to be executed.
Operating system, 329–42
A group of programs designed to maximize the amount of work a computer system can do; programs designed to reduce the amount of time that the computer is idle and the amount of programming required to use the computer.
Operational obsolesence, 417
The period of time (number of years) a computer will function before it suffers a complete breakdown; the number of years a computer will run or process data.
Operations librarian, 429
The individual responsible for the control, storage, and use of data files, programs, and operating procedures within an organization.
Operations manager, 427
The individual responsible for all data processing equipment and for the scheduling of data processing activities (such as keypunching and the execution of programs).
Operator's manual, 263
Program documentation designed to aid the computer operator in starting, running, and terminating the program: the meaning and response to console messages; and setup and takedown instructions for files.
Optical bar code, 175–76
A code consisting of a series of bars of varying widths that can be read by an optical light source such as a wand reader.
Optical character reader (OCR), 169–76
A specialized input device capable of reading uppercase and lowercase alphabetic, numeric, and certain special characters, and bar codes from handwritten, typed, and printed paper documents.
Optical character recognition, 170–74
Optical mark, 170–73
Optical-mark page reader, 170
An input device capable of reading and interpreting marks on special forms.

Order entry
See Order-writing entries
Order processing, 8–9, 467–71
Order-writing application, 29–31
    Direct access system, 153–55
    Distributed system, 350
    Online communication system, 349–50
    Online realtime system, 350–53
    Tape system, 133–38
Order-writing documents, 30–31, 170–72
Order writing, flowchart for, 49, 134, 153
Order-writing objectives, 30
Order writing, structure chart for, 269
Origination of data, 5
Output, 6–7, 76–77
    The dissemination and communication of the results of data processing manipulation in a usable form to the appropriate individuals or groups; usually, a printed report. *See also* Computer output
Output device, 81, 104–17
    A machine or collection of machines capable of receiving information from the computer and displaying it on an output medium.
Output medium, 81
    The material on which information is recorded for output, for example, printer forms, punched cards, or magnetic tape.
Output Specifications, 303, 307–08
    A section of an RPG program that describes the output to be produced by the program.
Output statements, 290
    Program statements that cause data stored internally to be recorded on some external medium, such as printer paper, punched cards, or magnetic tape.
Overlapped processing, 317–23
    Computer data processing involving the performance of input/output and processing operations at the same time.
Overlapped system, 315–26, 337
    A computer system capable of performing more than one operation simultaneously, thus reducing the amount of time that a system component is idle, for example, a system that can read a record, process a record read previously, and write another record at the same time.
Overlaying, 338
    The process—controlled by the programmer—of transferring segments of a large program from secondary storage into primary storage for execution, one at a time as needed, thus permitting several program segments to occupy the same storage locations at different times during program execution.

P

Packing, 90
    In EBCDIC, the representation of two numeric characters in eight bits.
Paging, 338–41
    One of two basic methods of implementing virtual-storage capability; it involves the swapping of programs or data between internal storage and a secondary storage device.
Paper tape, 189–90
    An input/output medium (similar to magnetic tape) that records and stores data in the form of punched holes along a continuous strip of paper (or other medium other than magnetic tape).
    Recording source data on, 189–90
Paper tape punch, 189–90
    An output device capable of punching holes into paper tape to represent data in a coded form.
Paper tape reader, 189
    An input device capable of reading the holes punched into paper tape.
Paragraph (COBOL), 295
    The level of the COBOL structural hierarchy composed of sentences.
Parallel method, 102–04, 106
    A method of reading (or punching) punched cards based on a row-by-row approach.
Parallel mode, 177
    The transmitting of data, one character at a time.
Parallel run, 260–61, 377
    The use of a computer program or a series

of programs simultaneously with the operation it is designed to replace to verify the correctness of the processing.

Parameter, 336
A variable factor that can be altered by the user, for example, a user-specifiable characteristic of a sort program.

Parity, 94–95, 124–27

Parity (check) bit, 94–95, 124–27, 151–52
One bit, in addition to those used to represent data, used to detect errors in circuitry.

Payroll application, 29, 39

Peripheral equipment, 102–03, 458–59
Data processing equipment that is not physically a part of the CPU but is often located in close proximity to it.

Personal computer, 218–19, 448–51
A microcomputer acquired for individual use.

Photoelectric cell, 104–05, 120, 122
A mechanism that emits an electrical impulse when activated by a light source.

Photoelectric (brushless) reader, 104–05
A card reader that senses the holes in punched cards by passing the cards under a light source that activates photoelectric cells as light passes through the holes.

Physical record, 122–23, 129–32
One or more logical records grouped for input or output purposes to reduce the time required for input/output operations and/or the amount of storage required.
See also Blocks

Physical security, 161, 423–25, 448

Plotter, 191–92
A device that produces graphic output on paper by automatic movements of a pencil or pen, or by electrostatic means.

Point-of-sale (POS) terminal, 183–84, 219–20, 445, 453
A type of terminal used in retail stores that serves the function of a cash register and at the same time collects sales data.

Portable terminal, 179, 182–83

Predefined process symbol, 232, 240–41
A program flowcharting symbol used to indicate a group of operations that are not defined on the program flowchart.

Preparation symbol, 232, 240–41
A program flowcharting symbol used to indicate a step such as setting a location to zeros or setting a binary digit position to 1 or 0 for use as a switch.

Primary storage
See Storage unit

Print area, 26–28
The area of a punched card provided for the printed representation of the characters represented by the holes punched into the card.

Print chain, 113–14
A chain of multiple sets of characters used by a chain printer.

Print Chart, 252–53
A system analysis and design aid used to design effective printed documents.

Printer, 109–117
An output device capable of printing symbols (characters) onto paper forms.

Privacy (and the computer), 443–44

Privacy Act of 1974, 447
The first privacy law passed by the United States Congress.

Problem definition, 250–55
The process of recognizing a problem and breaking it into component parts.

Problem-oriented language, 280, 288
A programming language that describes a problem and is, therefore, descriptive in nature, for example, RPG; all high-level programming languages as a class.

Problem statement, 250–51

PROCEDURE DIVISION, 276, 295
The division of a COBOL program that contains the statements that instruct the computer as to the specific operations it is to perform and the order in which to perform them.

Procedure-oriented language, 280, 288
A programming language requiring a compiler to translate a source program into an object program; a programming language consisting of a system of computational procedures designed to solve a problem, for example, FORTRAN.

Procedures, 76, 82, 255
　The guidelines that govern such data processing activities as collection, preparation, and processing of data, and distribution of results.
Process bound, 322–23
　A characteristic of a computer system that is restricted by the speed of the central processing unit, and in which input/output devices stand idle a certain percentage of the time.
Process symbol, 47–49, 133, 232–34, 255
　A program flowcharting symbol used to represent one or more operations on data, for example, a calculation or the movement of data from one location to another; a system flowcharting symbol used to represent a computer run.
Production-control application, 29, 39, 210–11
Program
　See Computer program; Stored program
Program coding, 257–59
　The process of translating the planned solution to a problem (for example, a program flowchart) into the instructions or statements of a program.
Program documentation
　See Documentation
Program-execution modification, 74
　The ability of a computer to change the course or sequence of execution of program statements because of a decision based on data in its internal storage and/or the results of one or more arithmetic or logical operations.
Program flowchart (logic diagram, block diagram), 227–45, 255–57
　A detailed, pictorial representation of the steps necessary to solve a problem.
Program library, 336
　A collection of software designed to aid the user and/or application programs.
Program loop, 236–43
　A series of instructions that is executed repeatedly.
　See also Loop structure

Programmable read-only memory (PROM), 214–15
　Internal storage similar to read-only memory, but capable of being reprogrammed by the user.
Program maintenance, 261–64, 268
　The process of revising or updating existing programs to keep them current and correct.
Programmer, 428–29
　The individual who prepares a program flowchart, codes the logic of the flowchart, debugs and tests the program, and documents it.
Programming
　Coding, 257–59, 271–74, 279
　Debugging and testing, 231, 259–61
　Defining the problem, 228, 250–55
　Planning the solution, 255–57, 268–71
Programming cycle, 249–64
　The steps through which a program must pass before it is ready for implementation; the steps of (1) recognizing and defining the problem, (2) planning the solution to the problem, (3) selecting an appropriate language, (4) program coding, (5) debugging and testing, and (6) program documentation and maintenance.
Programming languages, 279–311
　Selection of, 257, 308–10
　See also Assembler-language programming; Machine-language programming
Programming manager, 427
　The individual responsible for supervision of programming, debugging, testing, and maintenance of programs.
Program statement (statement), 95–97
　An expression that instructs the computer in detail as to the specific operation it is to perform or the order in which to perform operations.
Program-storage area, 79
　The area within the storage unit that holds program statements for access by the control unit.
PROM
　See Programmable read-only memory

611

GLOSSARY and INDEX

Pseudocode, 271, 275
An informal design language used to represent the control structures of structured programming.
Punch area, 26–27
The area of a punched card provided for the punching of combinations of holes to represent characters of data.
Punched card, 21–28, 108–09
A paper card in which holes can be punched, the combinations of which represent letters, numbers, and/or special characters.
Punched-card-deck symbol, 47–49
Punched-card equipment, 102–07
See also Card punch, computer system; Card reader; Card read/punch
Punched-card system, 21–22, 102–09, 138–39, 208
Any data processing system that employs the punched card as the basic medium for recording data.
Punched tape, 189
A tape (other than magnetic tape) on which data is recorded by punching holes along its length.
Punch station, 106–07
The position within a card punch at which holes are punched into punched cards.

Q

Quantum
See Time slice

R

Random access, 19
A method of retrieving records from a file where only records that are needed are read. Same as direct access.
Random-access memory (RAM), 216
Semiconductor storage; generally, one type of internal storage unit within a microcomputer.
Read-only memory (ROM), 214
A nonalterable storage area within the computer that is used to store microprograms.

Read station, card punch, 105–06
The position within a card punch at which a punched card is read to allow duplication or for checking purposes.
Read station, card reader, 104
The position within a card reader at which the holes in punched cards are read.
Read/write assembly, 124–27
The mechanism of a magnetic tape drive through which the magnetic tape is threaded; a mechanism containing sensors for file markers and read/write heads.
Read/write heads, 124–27, 149–50, 152, 158–60
The mechanism capable of writing data onto magnetic tape, disk, or drum by causing areas on the surface of the tape, disk, or drum to become magnetized, and of reading by sensing the magnetized areas.
Realtime, 350–51
The actual time during which a physical process takes place; the performance of a processing operation during the actual time the physical process takes place, thus permitting the results of the data manipulation to be used to direct the physical process.
Record, 18
A portion of a file containing data about a single unit in the file, for example, a customer; a collection of related data items.
Record Format, 252–54
A system analysis and design aid used to enhance the layout and design of files to promote efficient file processing.
Recording, of data, 6
Record key, 19
A field within a record that is used to organize or process the records in a file.
Remote device (terminal), 177–85, 213–14, 349–52, 378, 439, 453
A special-purpose input and/or output device located a distance from the computer.
Remote job entry, 213, 350
The placement of some of the input/output devices for a computer system at a remote location to enter data and receive processing results.

GLOSSARY and INDEX

Removable-disk, 146–48
A class of disk drives characterized by removable disk packs.
Report Program Generator
See RPG
Reproducing, 106
Duplicating the data punched into one deck of cards into another deck by using a card read/punch.
ROM
See Read-only memory
Rotational delay, 152, 159
The time required for a read/write head of a disk drive or drum to find a specified record, once head positioning has occurred; an average of one-half revolution of a disk or drum.
Routine, 285
An ordered series of instructions intended for general or frequent use.
Row (of a punched card), 22–23
A horizontal arrangement of punching positions on a punched card.
RPG (Report Program Generator), 303–08
A high-level, problem-oriented programming language designed to generate programs whose outputs are business-oriented printed reports.
Run, 47
A single execution of a computer program.

S

Sales-analysis application, 29, 39
Sales-analysis documents, 9–14, 39
Sales analysis, flowchart for, 50
Sales-analysis objective, 10–14, 39
Sales-by-Customer Report, 11–12
A management report displaying the number of items (by type) purchased by customers.
Sales-by-Item Report, 11–12
A report showing the difference between the current total sales and gross profit by item in relation to the same totals for the same time last year.
Sales-by-Salesperson Report, 12–13
A report showing the total sales and gross profit obtained by each salesperson.
Sales order, 9, 30, 40, 135, 153–55, 184
Scientific data processing, 4–5, 62
See also Data processing
"Scratch-pad" memory
See Working-storage area
Secondary storage device (auxiliary storage device), 81
An input/output device (for example, a magnetic tape unit) used either to receive temporarily stored programs or data from the control unit of the CPU or to transmit temporarily stored programs or data to it.
Secondary storage media (auxiliary storage), 81, 349–52
Input/output media (for example, magnetic tape and magnetic disk) used to store programs and data not currently being used by the computer.
Second generation, 63–66
A series of computers characterized by use of transistors as a major design feature.
Section (COBOL), 295
The level of the COBOL structural hierarchy composed of paragraphs.
Security
See Physical security
Segmentation, 338–41
One of two basic methods of implementing virtual-storage capability; it involves breaking a program into logically separable units.
Selection structure, 271–73
A basic pattern—the IF-THEN-ELSE—of structured programming.
Semiconductor, 64, 66, 83–85, 216
A very small two-state component used to form a storage unit in recent computers.
Sentence (COBOL), 294–95
The basic element of a COBOL program, analogous to a statement in FORTRAN.
Sequence structure, 271–72
A basic pattern of structured programming.
Sequential, 133, 156–57
The arrangement of one element after another, for example, as the records on a magnetic tape are ordered.

GLOSSARY and INDEX

Sequential access, 19, 146
  A method of retrieving records from a file where each record is read, beginning with the first record in the file.
Sequential file
  See Sequential organization
Sequential organization, 19, 133, 156–57
  A method of file organization whereby records are placed in a file sequence, based on a control field, and are always processed in that sequence.
Serial method, 102, 105, 106
  A method of reading (or punching) punched cards based on a column-by-column approach.
Serial mode, 177
  The transmitting of data, one bit at a time.
Seven-track tape, 121–22
  A magnetic tape using six bits to represent data and a parity bit.
Shipping order, 9, 30–32, 133–38, 153–55
  An output document resulting from the process of order writing; a document reflecting the number of items ordered and the price per unit.
Silent firing, 440
  The replacement of humans by machines (automation) in such a way that jobs are eliminated or go unfilled when employees retire or quit.
Simulation (modeling), 204–05, 374
  A process in which a model of a real situation is acted upon (by a computer), trying many alternatives in a short time so that the results of decisions can be predicted.
6-bit BCD, 88–90, 120–22
Slow-Moving Items Report, 36–38
  A management-by-exception report listing the items that have had little activity over the last 12 months.
Small business computer, 211–14
  A microcomputer or minicomputer system specifically designed for use by small businesses.
Small computer system, 207–10, 220
  A computer, small in size, with an internal storage capactiy slightly greater than that of a minicomputer; a computer that rents for approximately $1200 to $5000 per month and has a purchase price ranging from $50,000 to $250,000, for example, an IBM System/34.
Society, computer effects on, 437–55
Soft-copy device, 181
  Any output device that uses the face of a tube to display output.
Software
  See Application software; System software
Software company, 459–60
Sorting, 6, 136–38, 146, 156, 336, 564–67
  Arranging or rearranging data into some logical order to facilitate processing.
Sort program, 336, 564–67
Source-data automation, 169
  The collection of data at its source in a computer-readable form.
Source document, 5, 77
  The original paper containing business data, for example, sales orders, purchase orders, and employee time cards.
Source program, 283–84, 287
  The original instructions of a program written in either assembler language or a high-level programming language; a source deck.
Special character, 23–24, 79
  Any character that is neither alphabetic nor numeric; a combination of one, two, or three punches in the Hollerith code; a combination of zone and numeric punches in the 96-column punched-card code.
Special-purpose computer, 75–76
  A computer built for a specific purpose and generally to satisfy the needs of a particular type of problem.
Speed
  Computer system, 53–54, 67, 97, 102
  Disk system, 152, 155
  Tape system, 129–31, 132, 138
Spooling, 324–25
  The process of moving data from a slow input/output device, such as a card reader, to a higher-speed input/output device, such

Spooling (*continued*)
as a magnetic disk, prior to moving the data into the computer's primary storage unit. With respect to the movement of data from the computer, the process is reversed. The purpose of this process is to minimize the speed discrepancy between the computer and input/output devices.

Spread card, 135, 154
A punched card containing several line items, thus conserving space.

Stacked-job processing, 330–36
The processing of a stack of programs as directed by input job cards and under operating-system control.

Staging, 161–62
Retrieving a data cartridge from its cell and transferring its contents to a disk pack for computer use.

Start/stop time, 129–30
The amount of time required to stop a magnetic tape after a read/write operation has been performed; the amount of time required to start tape reels revolving at a constant speed from the stop position.

Statement, 74
The basic element in a FORTRAN program, analogous to an instruction in assembler language.
See also Program statement

Stockout, 9, 35–36
The condition that exists when an item ordered by a customer is not available in inventory.

Storage address, 80

Storage, computer system, 7, 76–77
The retention of data processing output for potential future input into the data processing system.

Storage dump, 261–62
A printout of the contents of internal storage locations for use in debugging.

Storage location, 80

Storage unit (internal storage, memory, primary storage), 79
The area within the central processing unit that receives and holds program statements and data until called for by the control unit.
See also Internal storage

Stored program, 63, 74
A series of instructions placed in internal storage and used to direct the computer.

Structure chart, 268–70
A top-down design and documentation tool used to plan the logic of a program.

Structured programming, 267–77
A method of programming that emphasizes top-down design using three basic control structures to create modules of program code that have one entry and one exit.

Subsystem, 375, 405
A system contained within a larger system. For example, a business firm (system) may be composed of three subsystems—the finance, production, and marketing departments.

Summarizing, 6
Condensing data into a meaningful, concise form such as a total or an average.

Supervisor (monitor), 331–32
An operating-system program that receives control of the computer system when a program has completed execution and prepares the system for the initiation of the next program.

Supply reel
See File reel

Symbolic language, 282–85

Symbolic names (mnemonics), 282–85
Abbreviations and acronyms used instead of numerical representations for machine operations in assembler-language instructions.

Syntax, 284
The grammatical correctness of instruction structure; rules of instruction design.

System, 46
An assembly of methods, procedures, or techniques united by regulated interaction to form an organized whole; an organized collection of people, machines, and methods required to accomplish a set of specified objectives.

GLOSSARY and INDEX

System analysis and design, 45–55, 250–55
  The process of defining the problem, acquiring data, devising input and output forms and structuring files, dividing the problem into its component parts, and establishing the basic procedures for the project.
System controls, 421–22, 448
  Controls that check the computer hardware and programs used in a system, and provide backup in case of system failure.
System flowchart, 47–49, 228–29, 399–400
  A general, overall diagram that shows the flow of data and the sequence of operations in a system.
System residence device, 332
  An online storage device, usually, having direct-access capabilities, on which programs are recorded and maintained until requested by the operating system.
Systems analyst, 46, 427
  The individual responsible for conducting system studies, determining the capabilities of systems, and preparing specifications.
Systems and procedures manager, 427
  The individual responsible for the system analysis performed within an organization and the maintenance of the program library.
System software, 76, 81, 403
  The collection of programs and operating aids associated with a computer that facilitate its programming and operation and extend its processing capabilities.
System study, 46
  An analysis of the procedures, techniques, and methods employed in the part of a data processing system under review.

T

Tag
  See Label
Take-up reel
  See Machine reel
Tape drive, 124–29
  An input/output device that reads and writes data on tape in terms of the magnetized areas that are recorded on the tape.

Tape reel, 120–21, 124–25, 128, 131–32
  Capacity, 120, 131–32
Tape system, 133–39, 146
  Overlapped processing, 317–23
Tape-to-printer program, 139, 321–22, 337
  A program that provides a representation of the contents of tapes as printer output.
Tape-to-tape program, 322–23
Technological unemployment
  See Job displacement
Teletype printer, 111–12
  A character-at-a-time printer having a teletype square containing characters.
Terminal
  See Remote devices
Terminal symbol, 231–33
  A program flowcharting symbol used to indicate the beginning or end of a program, or a pause for an error condition or operator action.
Testing, 231, 259–61, 270
  Running (executing) a program with sample input data that simulates conditions likely to be found in the real data that will be processed by the program; the process of checking the performance of a program by executing the program with test data and determining the accuracy of the results.
Third generation, 64, 66
  A series of computers characterized by the use of miniaturized circuits as the major design feature.
Third+ generation, 64, 66–67
  A series of computers characterized by the increased miniaturization of circuits and greater integration of software and hardware.
Thrashing, 341
  Excessive moving of pages or segments between virtual storage and the storage unit in a virtual-storage environment.
Tier (of a punched card), 25–26
  One of three punch areas (consisting of six rows) of a 96-column punched card.
Time sharing, 353, 438, 461, 502–07
  A technique allowing several users of an online realtime communication system to use that system on a practically simul-

Time sharing (*continued*)
    taneous basis such that one user is not aware of another user's interaction with the system.
Time-sharing system, 353–57, 471–72, 502–07
Time slice (quantum), 342, 354
    A predetermined short period of time during which one program is given control of the computer.
Top-down coding, 270
Top-down design, 376
    An approach to the design of an MIS that stresses top-management involvement.
Top-down program design, 267–71
Top-down testing, 270
Touch-tone device, 178
    A terminal that uses a keyboard (similar to touch-tone dialing) and existing telephone lines to transmit and/or receive data.
Tracing routines, 261
    Language extensions used to trace the execution of a program to determine the location of errors.
Track, 120–22, 148–50, 157–59
    One of seven or nine horizontal rows, spanning the length of a magnetic tape, on which data can be recorded; one of a series of concentric circles on the surface of a disk; one of a series of circular bands on a drum.
Trailer label, 129
    A special record following the last data record of a file that contains pertinent control information such as the number of records in the file.
Transaction (detail) file, 19, 138–41
    A file containing data of a temporary nature, for example, a file of weekly employee time cards; a file containing data of a transient nature usually processed with a master file.
Transaction-oriented system, 212–13, 350–52, 378, 473–74
    A computer system where data is entered primarily through a keyboard and processing of the data occurs in close association with the entry of it.
Transfer of control
    See Branching
Transfer rate
    The maximum number of bytes (characters) that can be read from or written to a secondary storage medium in one second; a measure of reading and writing speed.
    Disk, 152
    Drum, 160
    Tape, 129–31
Transistor, 63–66
Transport speed, 129–31
    The rate of speed (usually, in inches per second) at which magnetic tape passes through the read/write assembly of a tape drive.
True binary, 93–94
    The representation of numeric data without regard for the number of bits required.
Type font, 166–67
    A complete set of type of one size and face. *See also* E-13B type font; OCR-A type font

U

Unblocked, 130
    Having a blocking factor of one logical record per block.
Unconditional branch, 237–38
    A branch that is always taken when it is encountered.
Uninterrupted power supply, 85
Unit-record system, 21
    See also Punched-card system
UNIVAC I, 63–65
Universal Product Code, 175, 183
    An optical bar code that is placed on most of the products sold in supermarkets to identify the products and their manufacturers; a code read by an optical bar-code reader for product identification and pricing.
Upward-compatible language, 303
    A high-level programming language permitting source programs to be translated and executed on a computer system having more internal storage than the computer for which they were originally written with only minor modifications.

GLOSSARY and INDEX

User's manual, 263
   Program documentation designed to aid persons not familiar with programs in using those programs.

Utility program, 81, 336–37
   A generalized program within the operating system that performs necessary but routine jobs in a data processing system, for example, a sort routine or software to control the transfer of data from an input medium directly to an output medium.

V

Vacuum column, 124–25
   A mechanism on a tape drive that holds slack tape during tape processing; a mechanism to keep magnetic tape from breaking during starting and stopping of the file reel and the machine reel.

Vacuum tubes, 63–66

Validity checking, 106, 349–50
   A verification of the combination of holes in punched-card columns to make sure that they are valid (that is, represent data characters).

Variable-word-length computer, 79–80

Vendor-analysis application, 40

Verification
   Disk, 151–52, 188
   Tape, 124–27, 186

Vertical parity checking, 124–27
   An operation to check the accuracy of each data character written, read, or moved in storage, by means of a parity bit.
   See also Parity

Virtual storage (virtual memory), 204, 205, 337–41
   The use of a combination of secondary storage devices and paging and/or segmentation to manage the transmission of programs or data from a secondary storage device to internal storage.

Visual display device, 179–82
   A terminal capable of receiving output on a cathode-ray tube (CRT) and, with special provisions, of transmitting data through a keyboard.

Voice-response unit
   See Audio-response unit

Volatile, 85, 216
   A characteristic of a storage unit that loses its contents if the power supply is shut off.

W

Wand reader, 175–76, 183
   An optical light source used in reading source data represented in optical bar-code form.

Word, 80
   A fixed number of storage locations in a computer, treated as a unit.

Word-oriented, 80
   Having the capability to address a fixed number of storage locations as a unit, or word.

Word processing (WP), 193–95
   The input, manipulation, output, and storage of words (textual data) to produce letters, reports, and other printed documents.

Working-storage area ("scratch-pad" memory), 79
   The area within the storage unit that holds both the data being processed and the intermediate results of arithmetic/logic operations.

Z

Zone punch, 23–24, 26–28

Zone-punching area, 23
   The 12-, 11-, and 0-rows of an 80-column punched card; the B- and A-rows of a 96-column punched card.